CHRISTIAN EDUCATION

FOUNDATIONS FOR THE FUTURE

CHRISTIAN EDUCATION

FOUNDATIONS FOR THE FUTURE

EDITED BY

ROBERT E. CLARK
LIN JOHNSON
ALLYN K. SLOAT

MOODY PRESS
CHICAGO

Dedication

We, as coeditors of *Christian Education: Foundations for the Future*, dedicate this volume to two Christian educators who taught many years in the Christian education department at Moody Bible Institute in Chicago.

In memory of Dr. Doris A. Freese, who went to be with the Lord January 9, 1990. Dr. Freese exemplified the Master Teacher in her lifestyle and teaching ministry. She truly was dedicated to the biblical mission of Christian education. She touched and influenced many lives of students, faculty, and people in local church ministry through her effective modeling.

In memory of Dr. Werner C. Graendorf, who dedicated his life to Christian education and was an effective model of biblical principles in his teaching and local church ministry. Dr. Graendorf was knowledgeable and had a contagious and enthusiastic spirit. He entered the Lord's presence on May 30, 1991.

Robert E. Clark, Ed.D.
Lin Johnson, M.S.
Allyn K. Sloat, M.Ed.

Editors

Robert E. Clark (B.A., Omaha Baptist Bible College; A.B., Wheaton College; M.S., Omaha University; Ed.D., University of Denver) served for twenty-two years as professor of Christian education at Moody Bible Institute, Chicago. He is now engaged in Christian education ministry at the local church level. He is the general editor of *Childhood Education in the Church*.

Lin Johnson (B.A., Cedarville College; B.A., Moody Bible Institute; M.S., National College of Education) is a professional free-lance writer and editor and former special instructor of Christian education at Moody Bible Institute, Chicago.

Allyn K. Sloat (B.A., Trinity College; M.Ed., University of Illinois) is Pastor of Education and Adult Ministries at Winnetka Bible Church in Winnetka, Illinois.

Contents

Preface

This volume, with its focus on the future, represents two significant and deeply pervasive convictions. One is that such a ministry must find its essential heart and direction in the written Word of God.

The second conviction is that the fullest development of God's people, both as individual believers and as productive members of the Body of Christ, demands a viable Christian education ministry.

This compilation of practical guidance in contemporary Christian education is clearly viewed in biblical perspective. It is concerned with today's believer — his family and his church — and the biblical faith he seeks to build and share.

Three individuals have worked as a team of coeditors to compile, write, and edit this volume. They come from diversified backgrounds to contribute knowledge, experience, and expertise to enrich the contents of the book. Robert E. Clark served as professor of Christian education at Moody Bible Institute for more than twenty years and has served full time and as a volunteer in local church ministry. Lin Johnson is a professional free-lance writer and editor, and formerly a special instructor of Christian education. Allyn K. Sloat has ministered full time in various churches in Christian education, and is presently pastor of education and adult ministries at Winnetka Bible Church in Winnetka, Illinois.

As a symposium of forty-two writers, the book represents an invigorating cross-section, both geographically and vocationally, of a broad spectrum of evangelical Christian educators. Contributors are educators, pastors and ministers of Christian education, consultants, and those who are affiliated with Christian organizations. Each person has made a significant contribution.

This book is a biblical, introductory, and contemporary textbook on the basics of evangelical Christian education. It continues the pattern initiated in 1964 by J. Edward Hakes's volume[1] and continued in 1981 by Werner Graendorf's edition[2] on an introduction to Christian education.

The forty chapters in the present volume provide a comprehensive overview of the Christian education field. Although the primary focus of the book is on the church, the survey also includes biblical education related to the family, school, and cross-cultural setting.

The first unit of five chapters focuses on an understanding of Christian education and provides a biblical and theological basis, history, philosophy, and trends in evangelical Christian education.

The second unit, of nine chapters, considers the dynamic forces underlying the teaching-learning process, including such topics as the Christian teacher, personal Bible study, the work of the Holy Spirit, classroom management, methods, and media.

The third unit, composed of ten chapters, provides help in understanding persons from infancy through senior adulthood. Also, learning styles, the exceptional person, and cross-cultural teaching are some significant topics researched.

Unit four considers the strategy for the church and its educational ministries. Professional staff, evaluation, leadership recruitment, staff development, curriculum, small group ministries, and computers are some of the topics presented.

The fifth unit provides a perspective on concerns for a biblical basis of the family and parenting, schools, and parachurch organizations.

The chapters may be studied in units or used individually. A boxed summary outline precedes the content of each chapter. A bibliography of sources is given at the end of each chapter.

Our prayer is that this volume will strengthen individual faith and ministry, as well as deepen the vitality of Christ's work everywhere.

1. J. Edward Hakes, ed., *An Introduction to Evangelical Christian Education* (Chicago: Moody, 1964).
2. Werner C. Graendorf, ed., *An Introduction to Biblical Christian Education* (Chicago: Moody, 1981).

Part 1

The Definitive Character of Christian Education

"Christian education is not an option, it is an order; it is not a luxury, it is a life. It is not something nice to have, it is something necessary to have. It is not a part of the work of the church, it is the work of the church. It is not extraneous, it is essential. It is our obligation, not merely an option."

Dr. Howard Hendricks
Professor of Christian Education
Dallas Theological Seminary

A church bulletin board phrase "Don't just keep the faith—give it away" may well capture the essence of what Christians are commissioned to do by the Lord Jesus—in the home, in the community, in the church, and in church related organizations. We are to share the "good news" of salvation from the power and penalty of sin by faith in the redemptive work of Christ; and we are to teach the revealed truth of God's written and living Word to persons of all ages and stages of life in the process of becoming Christ's true disciples. And so as parents, pastors, and disciples of Jesus, we "teach others also"—both young and old—to know, keep, and share the faith with the generations to come.

To carry out this Great Commission responsibility, Christians must know what Christian education really is. Chapter 1 gives a clear and definitive answer to that vital question. In chapter 2 we examine the biblical basis for Christian education ministry as we build our lives, our message, our service on the teachings of the Word of God. Chapter 3 reviews our historical "roots" in the growth of Christian education. The importance of knowing "why" we do what we do in education that is Christian is addressed in the philosophical foundation of chapter 4. This helps us to keep our focus in Christian education clear and steady even as we adjust appropriately to the major trends of chapter 5, which affect our future ministry in Christian education.

Kenneth O. Gangel

1

What Christian Education Is

DEFINING BIBLICAL CHRISTIAN EDUCATION
- **Recognizes the family-centeredness of Christian nurture throughout Scripture**
- **Reaffirms the centrality of biblical revelation in the educative process**
- **Reviews the example of Jesus as teacher, mentor, and leader**
- **Rekindles the dynamic role of the Holy Spirit in the teaching-learning process**
- **Responds to the Great Commission by balancing evangelism and edification ministry**
- **Refocuses on education for spiritual growth—producing mature disciples**

Thomas Talbott once ruminated over the idea that God may have called him to be a teacher in order to show him how biblical revelation had been formed. Talbott suggests that the way teachers struggle and study to communicate truth to their classes offers a microscopic metaphor of how God revealed His truth throughout the centuries. His appropriate title simply affirms "What Teaching Can Teach Us About Scripture."[1]

1. Thomas Talbott, "What Teaching Can Teach Us About Scripture," *Reformed Journal* 36:9 (September 1986): 11.

KENNETH O. GANGEL, Ph.D., is department chairman and professor of Christian education, Dallas Theological Seminary, Dallas, Texas.

In this chapter we will strive to reverse Talbott's idea and—indeed—his title. Our concern at the beginning of this important book is to ask "What can Scripture teach us about teaching?" Or more broadly, "What can Scripture teach us about the nature and role of Christian education among evangelicals?"

> Christian education has been diversely defined over the past half century. In 1963 Randolph Crump Miller commended a simple definition by Adelaide Case: "Christian education is the effort to make available for our generation—children, young people, and adults—the accumulated treasures of Christian life and thought, in such a way that God in Christ may carry on his redemptive work in each human soul and in the common life of man.[2]

More recently, Mark Lamport observed that the primary difference between secular education and Christian education is the adjectival descriptor *Christian.* "To be *Christian,* Christian education must: have God's esteem for the human being, sense the task to be a whole-life experience of growth and maturity, and give opportunity for service through experiential action."[3]

What seems obvious from both of the above definitions (and from numerous other contributions by evangelical educators) is the absolute link between Christian education and theology. In this respect we refer to *Christian* education rather than *religious* education. The distinction falls not between New Covenant and Old Covenant truth, for evangelicals affirm the Old Testament base for Christian education. But the difference comes in articulating an education distinctly based upon theological propositions derived from the text of Scripture rather than education developed to perpetuate and propagate the tenets of a designated religious system.

To be sure, Christian education owes a great debt to the social sciences—and in the framework of a secular university, that would be its normal home. But a secular university cannot provide the natural habitat for Christian education; its absolute link to Scripture pushes the social sciences to step-child status.

Perhaps one of the best recent discussions of this linkage was prepared by Jim Wilhoit in *Christian Education and the Search for Meaning.*

> Theology is crucial to Christian education. Often Christian education has been accused of drifting far from orthodox theological teaching, particularly in regard to the Christian view of human nature and spiritual growth. This drifting is unfortunate, for Christian education is lost unless grounded in biblically based teaching. No matter how much zeal a Christian educator may have, it is of little use without an awareness of the essential theological underpinning of the faith.[4]

2. Randolph Crump Miller, *Education for Christian Living,* 2d ed. (Englewood Cliffs, N.J.: Prentice-Hall, 1963), pp. 53-54.
3. Mark A. Lamport, " 'The Hand-Me-Down' Philosophy: A Challenge to Uniqueness in Christian Education," *Christian Education Journal* 8:2 (Winter 1988): 39.
4. Jim Wilhoit, *Christian Education and the Search for Meaning* (Grand Rapids: Baker 1986), pp. 59-60.

EDUCATION IN THE PENTATEUCH

In a brilliant article published in 1987, Timothy Thomas pleads for a greater respect of the Old Testament among Christian educators, asking us to abandon our "folk canon."

> The "folk canon," which often does not include some sections of the New Testament, is content to leave out most of the Old Testament. The Old Testament "folk canon" is often comprised of Genesis, narrative materials up to the end of Esther, Psalms, the occasional Proverb, the "Christmas" sections of the prophets (courtesy of Handel), and, for those of an eschatological bent, additional sections from the prophets. Little attempt is made to see a holistic picture. Context is of low priority. Further, an undue literal emphasis on the words themselves removes from the reader and interpreter the responsibility of hearing God's Spirit speaking through the whole.[5]

In addition, Thomas suggests that "folk canon" may often be augmented by denominational publications and popularist writings. But his main complaint stems from the minimal accord afforded the Old Testament among educators.

CENTRICITY OF JEHOVAH

Education for the early Hebrews focused on learning about God. The Bible's opening statement leaves no room for flexibility regarding its main topic (Gen. 1:1). God controlled the events in the lives of His people; He initiated the covenants and law; He raised up leaders to instruct His people regarding personal and corporate righteousness. And when a generation failed to follow God's truth, turmoil inevitably followed (Ex. 1; Judg. 2:10-15).

William Barclay's classic work *Educational Ideals in the Ancient World* spells it out clearly:

> It has always to be remembered that Jewish education was entirely religious educa-tion. There was no text-book except the Scriptures; all primary education was prepa-ration for reading the Law; and all higher education was the reading and the study of it. . . . Josephus says of Moses: "He commanded to instruct children in elements of knowledge (grammata), to teach them to walk according to the laws, and to know the deeds of their forefathers."[6]

ABSOLUTE TRUTH

Long before written portions of the Scripture were circulated, God's people viewed His Word through His anointed servants as absolute. Noah proclaimed the coming Flood, and his family entered the ark (Gen. 6-7). Abraham announced his

---

5. Timothy L. Thomas, "The Old Testament 'Folk Canon' and Christian Education," *The Asbury Theological Journal* 42:2 (1987): 47.
6. William Barclay, *Educational Ideals in the Ancient World* (reprint; Grand Rapids: Baker, 1974), pp. 13-14.

vision from the Lord, and a nation came into being (Gen. 12-24). Moses thundered down from Mount Sinai and the law was given (Ex. 19-20). The Pentateuch allows no room for discussions of interpretation, no flexibility for different viewpoints. When God speaks, His people respond.

Evangelical education retains its commitment to absolute truth—namely, that truth throughout Holy Scripture is not subject to change. In a world that almost universally considers truth relative (subject to change and revision), Christian educators affirm the centrality of absolute truth.

FOCUSING ON THE FAMILY

Respected Christian educators understand the significance of the family in teaching, but rarely do we see covenant continuity more dramatically displayed than in the early books of the Old Testament. A treatment of Deuteronomy 6 will come later, but here note the dramatic text of Deuteronomy 29:29: "The secret things belong to the Lord our God, but the things revealed belong to us and to our children forever, that we may follow all the words of this law." Earlier in the chapter Moses stands before all the Israelites and reminds them one final time that the covenant of God is with the nation, but the nation is represented by its families (Deut. 29:9-15; Ps. 78:1-8; Prov. 4:3-4, 10, 20-22).

Again Barclay is helpful in emphasizing that in addition to focus on God, the center of education among the Jews was the home, "and the responsibility of teaching the child is something that the parent cannot evade, if he is to satisfy the law of God."[7]

THE TEACHING TASK

The Hebrew word for teach (*lāmad*) is translated in the Septuagint by the word *didasko*, which occurs about one hundred times. We find it most commonly in the Psalms, Deuteronomy, and Jeremiah. Old Testament usage does not primarily denote the communication of knowledge and skills but rather centers on how one's life ought to be lived (Deut. 11:19; 20:18). Deuteronomy 6:1-9 introduces a portion of Scripture dear to the hearts of many Christian educators. Moses reminded his people that "God directed me to teach you" and showed again how teaching takes place in the matrix of the family.

SERVANTHOOD

Though developed to a much greater extent in the New Covenant, the germinal idea of serving God begins early in the text of Scripture. Adam and Eve serve God by caring for His creation. The heroes of the Pentateuch are shown at their best as the servants of Jehovah. Wilhoit sees in this a call to a special kind of Christian education:

7. Ibid., p. 17.

The focus of God's concern was on action. Later in Scripture an emphasis on affections and intentions appears, but in the final analysis God requires properly motivated action, not just good intentions or a warm heart. For this reason Christian education must teach not just knowledge or skills but service of God through responsible action.[8]

EDUCATION IN THE HISTORICAL BOOKS

In the historical books little new truth surfaces regarding the teaching-learning processes of God's people. All the elements developed in the Pentateuch are retained to a greater or lesser extent, but now different kinds of teachers appear. Judges rule and prophets proclaim. Eli teaches Samuel, who in turn teaches Israel's first two kings.

Old Testament patterns begun in the Pentateuch and carried into the historical books are summarized nicely in *The New International Dictionary of New Testament Theology*:

> How then does the education of the young proceed in Israel? God commands that they obey their parents as next to him in importance. The father acts like a priest to the family. He hands on the tradition to the family; he does so in answer to the question of his children (Ex. 12:26 f.), and his answer is a confession of God's saving activity toward Israel. The children are told of this not only in words, but also by means of impressive signs in the form of monumental stones (Josh. 4:6 f., 21 ff.).[9]

By the time of Ezra and Nehemiah, scribal emphasis on education had developed to an extensive degree. We learn the secret of Ezra's success in one poignant verse: "For Ezra had devoted himself to the study and observance of the Law of the Lord, and to teaching its decrees and laws in Israel" (Ezra 7:10). Some scholars suggest that Ezra's ministry may have been a turning point in the whole pattern of Jewish education.

EDUCATION IN WISDOM LITERATURE

In the wisdom literature the moralizing and humanizing trend in education not only continues but expands. The focus changes, and a prevailing lifestyle emerges. This change is seen devotionally in Psalms and practically in Proverbs, Ecclesiastes, and Song of Solomon.

WISDOM

Educational ideals have now been developed in Israel, but the point of reference

8. Wilhoit, p. 21.
9. K. Wegenast, in "Teach, Instruct, Tradition, Education and Discipline," in *The New International Dictionary of New Testament Theology*, ed. Colin Brown (Grand Rapids: Zondervan, 1978), 3:797.

continues to be God and His revelation. Appropriately, three-fifths of the references to wisdom appear in the wisdom literature. The Greek word *sophia*, though it may denote skill in art or craft, economic shrewdness, or governmental ability, most commonly reflects the godly behavior that enables one to master life (Prov. 8:32-36). Wisdom takes on a personal connotation as the mediator of revelation (Prov. 8:1-21) who calls people to learn (Prov. 1:20; 8:32; 9:1).

INSTRUCTION

We look in vain for widespread Septuagint usage of *didaskalia* in the wisdom literature, for it appears only in Proverbs 2:17 in reference to the law considered as the will of God. *Katechesis* and *paradidōmi*, New Testament Greek words used for instruction, are not in the Old Testament. However, the Hebrew word *mûsār* rises to great importance since it appears thirty times in the book of Proverbs, usually emphasizing discipline but most commonly translated as "instruction," synonymous with wisdom throughout this portion of the Old Testament.

PHYSICAL DISCIPLINE

Of great concern to Christian educators is the role of discipline in preparing disciples. The New Testament makes a clear distinction between discipline and punishment (Heb. 12:4-13), but that distinction is less clearly defined in the Old Testament. The book of Proverbs introduces the dimension of physical correction, not earlier seen as a part of the Old Testament instructional process (Prov. 13:24; 17:10; 22:15; 29:15, 17).

EDUCATION IN THE PROPHETS

As the book of Isaiah opens, the Bible reader experiences something of a déjà vu or a first-time experience with the earlier historical books. A nation that had been taught by God and given His truth for its individual and corporate life now faced national judgment and temporary oblivion because it had rejected God's teaching. Isaiah moans, "The ox knows his master, the donkey his owner's manger, but Israel does not know, my people do not understand" (Isa. 1:3). Prophets served as the teachers in Israel both before, during, and after the Exile.

In Jeremiah 8:8 we learn of the role of the scribes, the professional class of teachers in Israel whose task it was to preserve the written and oral traditions of the nation. They became copyists, editors, and interpreters of God's truth (and man's fallible interpretation thereof). We have already noted the impact of Ezra. A. Elwood Sanner suggests that the scribes provide us with ancient historical background for varied methodology in teaching.

> The teaching methods of the scribes included public discussion, questions and answers, memorization, the exact verbal reproduction of the teacher's words, sto-

ries, oral laws, precepts, proverbs, epigrams, parables, beatitudes, and allegories.[10]

After the darkness of Exile and the strange "silence" of the intertestamental period, the stage was set for the dramatic entry of Jesus Christ into human history. God selected earth to be "the visited planet," and genuinely Christian education, as we attempt to understand and practice it today, was initiated at the coming of Jesus Christ, the incarnate Son. What Isaiah prophesied concerning Zebulun and Naphtali can be said of all those who saw His arrival: "The people living in darkness have seen a great light; on those living in the land of the shadow of death a light has dawned" (Matt. 4:16).

EDUCATION IN THE GOSPELS

The fact that Christian education must be biblical is precisely what makes it Christian. And to be entirely biblical, it must center in Christ. Students who wish to grasp firmly the theological and philosophical foundations of Christian education must master various passages in the New Testament that develop those concepts.

THE EXAMPLE OF JESUS

The presence and power of the Son of God dominate the first four books of the New Testament. Christ's incarnation, crucifixion, and resurrection are essential, of course, but His modeling/mentoring role as Master Teacher has provided Christian educators a poignant demonstration for almost two thousand years. Forty-five times the gospels call Jesus "teacher," and fourteen times they refer to Him as "rabbi." Howard Hendricks wants his readers to grasp the significance of Christ's method as well:

> No one could ever accuse Jesus of a truncated educational philosophy. He understood that all learning involves a process. He not only knew what He was to teach, but He also knew how to teach. Learning was more than listening; teaching more than telling. How did Jesus become so effective without bells and schedules, a fixed classroom, and an overhead projector or flannelgraph?[11]

THE AUTHORITY OF JESUS

How important is Matthew's brief notation at the end of his record of the Sermon on the Mount: "When Jesus had finished saying these things, the crowds were amazed at his teaching, because he taught as one who had authority, and not as their teachers of the law" (Matt. 7:28-29).

10. A. Elwood Sanner, ed., *Exploring Christian Education* (Grand Rapids: Baker, 1978), pp. 41-42.
11. Kenneth O. Gangel and Howard Hendricks, eds., *The Christian Educator's Handbook on Teaching* (Wheaton, Ill.: Victor, 1988), p. 25.

Christians argue about the significance of Matthew 16:19 and the curious phrase "keys of the kingdom." But Jews have commonly referred this to the office of teacher. Jesus called His followers to a higher righteousness and to carry through His calling as a teacher.

TEACHING OF THE DISCIPLES

In Matthew 28:20 and Mark 6:30 we see the disciples commissioned to teach; and in Luke 12:12 we learn that the Holy Spirit will be their teacher. Indeed, discipling becomes the centerpiece of teaching in the gospels, providing the link between teaching and learning. Eleanor Daniel emphasizes the significance of maturity in the discipling process:

> The purpose of Bible teaching is to bring change into the life of the learner until he has reached maturity in Christ—a life long task. This maturity is achieved when a person has a knowledge of God's Word, with understanding, that results in changed behavior: bearing fruit, growing in knowledge, becoming stronger in endurance and patience, and being thankful.[12]

The noun *disciple* (*mathētēs*) comes from the verb *manthano* meaning "to learn." Jesus' disciples followed Him nearly everywhere (Mark 6:1), and since they were learners, they stumbled and struggled as we often do (Mark 5:31; 10:24; Luke 8:9). The noun occurs 264 times in the New Testament, exclusively in the gospels and Acts. These learners epitomized the growing, developing student in the Christian education process who strives ultimately to "be like his teacher" (Luke 6:40).

ROLE OF THE HOLY SPIRIT: JOHN 16:12-15

Although we find explicit references to the Holy Spirit in the synoptic gospels, it was left to John the evangelist to detail how the third Person of the Trinity assists the teaching-learning process. Christian teachers must be intensely interested in truth, as so must their students. John promises us the Holy Spirit will guide us into truth (16:13), probably a reference to the truth about Christ, His person, and His work in the world.

Perhaps we should not limit this promise only to the immediate hearers or the first century of the Christian era. It rings true for teachers today who need the power of God's Spirit to help them comprehend spiritual truth, to allow the Spirit to glorify Christ in their lives (John 16:12-15).

Remember, too, that the Holy Spirit affects not only the teacher and the learner, but also the subject matter and the environment. His power permeates truth wherever it is found.

12. Eleanor Daniel et al., *Introduction to Christian Education* (Cincinnati: Standard, 1980) p. 93.

THE GREAT COMMISSION: MATTHEW 28:16-20

The last paragraph of Matthew offers New Testament readers a commissioning narrative much like those found in Genesis 12, Exodus 3, and Isaiah 6. Matthew alone records this mountain meeting and notes two references to it by the Lord (26:32; 28:10) and one by the resurrection angel (28:7). Mainline orthodoxy, particularly as evidenced by the twentieth-century evangelical movement, holds a traditional and somewhat normative interpretation of these five dramatic verses, namely, that this paragraph lays the foundation stone for the modern missionary movement. Yet we often fail to notice two crucial dimensions of the passage:

1. The Commission mandates both evangelism and teaching, with the latter being at least equal and quite possibly greater in emphasis.

2. The Commission has been given not only for apostles, or for missionaries alone, but to the church. The entire universal Body of Christ stands under the requirements of this great teaching commission. Jesus emphasizes here His complete lordship and authority over the church. *In its simplest and purest form, Christian education is communicating God's truth in order to make disciples*; and that process goes on in dozens of ways, structured and unstructured, throughout the life of any church that seriously heeds the commands of the New Testament.

The heart of the Commission (vv. 19-20a) contains three participles (going, baptizing, teaching) but only one command: "make disciples." Welcoming curious inquirers to the gate of the Temple at Jerusalem may have been the Old Covenant way of putting them in touch with God. But now things were to be done differently. The New Covenant has been activated by the resurrection of Jesus Christ, and the One in charge assumes His followers will be going where the needs are. Going, baptizing, and teaching are not the means of discipling, but they characterize it. The New Testament cannot conceive of a disciple who has not been baptized and instructed.

Center stage in the Commission stands the imperative—"make disciples." *How we understand the meaning of that command determines what we do with Christian education in the local church.* Many have taken it to mean sharing the gospel and thereby limit the Great Commission to evangelism at home and abroad. But genuine biblical disciples hear, understand, and obey Jesus' teaching— and that does not happen by raising a hand or coming forward in a meeting. *Jesus emphasized life change, not content transmission. He highlighted multiplication of the Body in the world, not addition of members to the roll.*

EDUCATION IN ACTS

The book of Acts opens with Christ's ascension but moves quickly to the coming of the Holy Spirit at Pentecost and the launching of the New Covenant church. Throughout its pages Luke demonstrates the dependability of Barnabas, the availability of Philip, the loyalty of Dorcas, and the consistency of Silas. To be sure, Paul dominates most of the book, but the lay leaders God gathered around him to carry out the ministry of the church played a crucial role.

CHRISTIAN EDUCATION AND THE CHURCH: ACTS 2:42-47

What is a church? The word itself (Greek *ekklēsia*) is used in the New Testament to describe a political assembly of free citizens, a Jewish assembly (as in the Old Testament), and the Body of Christ. In the third usage we see both the universal church and the local church. The universal church contains only true believers, whereas the local church may include professing Christians who have not experienced regeneration. Let us save formal definitions for the theologians and notice that in one brief paragraph at the end of Acts 2 we see the church as a devoted, sharing, and worshiping people (Acts 2:42-47).

Doctrine, fellowship, communion, and prayer occupied their days and their devotion. They spent time together and shared common goods to meet each other's needs. Verse 46 uses the word *homothumadon*, which appears eleven times in the New Testament, ten of which occur in the book of Acts. It is the key word *together* (lit., "with one mind or purpose") and describes the attitude of those early believers.

BIBLICAL PRINCIPLES OF LEARNING: ACTS 11

Acts 11 provides no treatise on learning theory, but it does demonstrate how the early church seriously committed itself to educational ministry. When Barnabas arrived at Antioch, he exercised his own spiritual gift of exhortation (encouragement), stabilizing the new believers and leading even more people to the Lord (Acts 11:19-24). But then he discovered that more was required; these new converts needed serious biblical instruction. So he went out to find the man he considered most qualified to carry out the task, and Saul of Tarsus became the first "minister of education" in a local church, assisting senior pastor Barnabas for a whole year as they "met with the church and taught great numbers of people" (vv. 25-26).

When we relate Acts 11 to chapters 2 and 4, we see a tremendous progression in the development of truth and the process of teaching in the church. But one thing does not change—*content translates to action when energized by the Spirit of God*. Without the benefit of modern learning theory those early Christians practiced what we now call "wholistic learning," which encompasses the total person—cognitive, affective, and conative dimensions.

GLOBAL TEACHING: ACTS 13

Trekking through Asia Minor for a few months was hardly "global" in terms of today's understanding, but Barnabas, Paul, and their companions set world missions in motion as they started out for Seleucia, Cyprus, and points west (Acts 13:1-5). The first missionary journey demonstrates what it really means to teach the message of Christ to other cultures. True, Paul dealt exclusively with Greek or Aramaic speaking peoples, and where possible he stayed in a synagogue setting. But the missionary business soon expanded, and on the second and third trips he began to visualize much wider boundaries for his ministry. Finally, God sent him to Rome, and there his teaching continued as "from morning till evening he explained and declared to them the kingdom of God and tried to convince them about Jesus from the Law of Moses and from the Prophets" (Acts 28:23).

ROLE OF TEACHING ELDERS: ACTS 20

Of enormous importance in understanding what church leaders do is the brief discussion with the Ephesian elders recorded in Acts 20. Here we learn that "elders" and "overseers" are used as synonymous terms (compare verses 17 and 28). Furthermore, we see that elders/overseers must function as shepherds (vv. 28-29). In Paul's own testimony he describes his ministry as preaching and teaching, testifying and proclaiming (the Greek noun *episkopē* appears in Luke 19:44; Acts 1:20; 1 Tim. 3:1; and 1 Pet. 2:12).

Though the Acts 20 passage does not specifically describe the teaching ministry of these elders, we shall see from our explorations in the pastoral epistles how much of a role Christian education plays in elder responsibility. Furthermore, the thirteen verb-form usages of *episkopos* (*episkeptomai* and *episkopeo*) show us a ministry we have come to identify with "ruling"and "ordering." The Bible describes it as a sharing, caring ministry in which elders serve God's people. Consider the texts of importance: Matthew 25:36, 43; Luke 1:68, 78; 7:16; Acts 6:3; 7:23; 15:14, 36; Hebrews 2:6; 12:15; James 1:27; 1 Peter 5:2.

EDUCATION IN THE PAULINE EPISTLES

As a premier educator, the apostle Paul offers solid emphasis for the church's instructional ministry. He seems to harmonize perfectly the roles of evangelism and edification, a balance we find difficult to maintain in the late twentieth-century church. Several specific dimensions of biblical Christian education surface, though we have opportunity to explore only a few exemplary passages.

THE ROLE OF THE BIBLE

For evangelicals the issue of biblical inerrancy and authority is foundational. Romans and Galatians develop the doctrine of salvation (among other doctrines) squarely based on the authoritative message of God's Word (Rom. 10:8-11).

Multiple quotations could be cited from current educators identifying the role of the Bible as "containing" the record of the Christian message from which the church interprets its doctrine. Evangelicals speak much more plainly about the role of Scripture in Christian education. As Gaebelein puts it,

Is there, then, a watershed, a continental divide, as it were, that separates a consistent Christian philosophy of education from all forms of eclecticism? The answer is a clear affirmative. The great divide is nothing less than the authority of the Bible and its acceptance as normative. . . . a thoroughly Christian view of education must not only be based upon Scripture; it must also stand under it.[13]

PRIMACY OF TEACHING: 1 CORINTHIANS

The letters to the troubled church at Corinth were hardly designed to identify a theology of education, but great truths about teaching flow therefrom. Paul uses *didaskō* fifteen times in his letters, two of which appear in 1 Corinthians (4:17; 11:14). Romans 2:21 uses the word in the traditional sense of teaching others; Romans 12:7 deals with the teaching office (gift) in the church; and Galatians 1:12 refers to handing on a tradition. In 1 Corinthians 4:17 Paul promises to send Timothy to remind the Corinthians of what he teaches everywhere "in every church." In the latter part of chapter 12 where Paul identifies spiritual gifts, he places teachers just behind apostles and prophets (v. 28). In chapter 14, the key idea of the entire section deals with the edification of God's people in the church (cf., 1 Cor. 11:14; Eph. 4:21; Col. 1:28; 2:7; 3:16; 2 Thess. 2:15; 1 Tim. 2:12; 4:11; 6:2; 2 Tim. 2:2; Titus 1:11).

Three of Paul's uses of *paradidōmi* (Greek "instruction") occur in 1 Corinthians (11:2, 23; 15:3). His clear intent is to describe Christian doctrine or instruction delivered at an earlier time. The Lord initiated these instructions, and Paul not only quotes existing tradition but interprets it in light of revelation he received. How different this was from the rabbis, who determined that tradition must be passed on unchanged. In other words, Paul's teaching focused on making truth applicable to people in their present needs.

EDUCATION FOR MATURITY: EPHESIANS, PHILIPPIANS, COLOSSIANS

These epistles were written to build up healthy, properly-functioning churches. Practical exhortations such as "let us live up to what we have already attained" (Phil. 3:16) and the brilliant eighth verse of the fourth chapter—"Finally, brothers, whatever is true, whatever is noble, whatever is right, whatever is pure, whatever is lovely, whatever is admirable—if anything is excellent or praiseworthy—think about such things"—show us how crucial it is to develop a maturing ministry for the preparation of disciples. Modeling methodology immediately follows in verse 9: "Whatever you have learned or received or heard from me, or seen in me—put it into practice. And the God of peace will be with you."

The rich Christology at the beginning of Colossians culminates in verse 28: "We proclaim him, admonishing and teaching everyone with all wisdom, so

---

13. Quoted in *Introduction to Biblical Christian Education*, ed. Werner Graendorf (Chicago: Moody, 1981), p. 15, and also cited in J. E. Hakes, ed., *An Introduction to Evangelical Christian Education* (Chicago: Moody, 1964), p. 41.

that we may present everyone perfect in Christ. To this end I labor, struggling with all his energy, which so powerfully works in me" (Col. 1:28-29). This marvelous model of Christian education describes what we do (warning, teaching), how we do it (personalization, thoroughness), and even why we do it (to render our students mature [complete] in Christ). Sara Little observes:

> When Christian education actually becomes the process of helping truth to be experienced and interpreted, it demonstrates the true relevance of the Christian revelation and overcomes many false dichotomies of the past in its recognition of the "organic relations" between doctrine and experience, between content and method, between truth and life.[14]

In Ephesians we find something of a high-water mark in terms of the edificational role of the church. Consider carefully one entire passage:

> It was he who gave some to be apostles, some to be prophets, some to be evangelists, and some to be pastors and teachers, to prepare God's people for works of service, so that the body of Christ may be built up until we all reach unity in the faith and in the knowledge of the Son of God and become mature, attaining to the whole measure of the fullness of Christ. Then we will no longer be infants, tossed back and forth by the waves, and blown here and there by every wind of teaching and by the cunning and craftiness of men in their deceitful scheming. Instead, speaking the truth in love, we will in all things grow up into him who is the Head, that is, Christ. From him the whole body, joined and held together by every supporting ligament, grows and builds itself up in love, as each part does its work. (Eph. 4:11-16)

There you have it. *Gifted leaders* minister to *serving people* to produce a *unified congregation* with *biblical alertness* and *spiritual growth*. Christian educators equip, enrich, and encourage God's servants so that "the whole body, joined and held together by every supporting ligament, grows and builds itself up in love, as each part does its work."

MINISTRY MODELING: 1 AND 2 THESSALONIANS

Just a quick glance at the Thessalonian epistles shows us that the church at Thessalonica profited and prospered most from the example of its educators. After describing the kind of behavior he avoided (1 Thess. 2:1-6), Paul explained his leadership style as "gentle," "caring," "loving," "sharing," "encouraging," "comforting," and "fatherly." He told them, "You are witnesses, and so is God, of how holy, righteous and blameless we were among you who believed" (v. 10). In his first letter he admonishes them to "make it your ambition to lead a quiet life, to mind your own business and to work with your hands, just as we told

---

14. Sara Little, *The Role of the Bible in Contemporary Christian Education*, rev. ed. (Richmond, Va: John Knox, 1962), p. 74.

you, so that your daily life may win the respect of outsiders and so that you will not be dependent on anybody" (4:11-12).

The Thessalonian Christians acted upon Paul's teaching sufficiently that he could write in his second epistle, "Your faith is growing more and more, and the love every one of you has for each other is increasing. Therefore, among God's churches we boast about your perseverance and faith in all the persecutions and trials you are enduring" (1:3-4).

INSTRUCTIONAL LEADERSHIP: 1 AND 2 TIMOTHY, TITUS

Finally we come to the pastoral epistles. Here we find Timothy and Titus being instructed by the apostle Paul regarding the spiritual quality of their lives and the extent of their educational ministries in Ephesus and Crete. Without minimizing the significance of the gospel, we now see that a body of doctrine must be communicated to the people of God. The word *didaskalia*, used only six times in the New Testament up to this point (Matt. 15:9; Mark 7:7; Rom. 12:7; 15:4; Eph. 4:14; Col. 2:22), occurs no fewer than fifteen times in the pastorals. Believers had developed a fixed doctrinal tradition, a corpus of truth to be perpetuated in the church. In 2 Timothy 3:16 we discover that God's inspired Scripture (lit., "God-breathed")—presumably the Old Testament—is profitable for teaching.

Words for "teaching" and "instruction" appear more than ten times in 1 Timothy alone, and one gets the impression early on that Paul purposes to instruct Timothy how to educate the believers at Ephesus. Titus 2 represents a vertical model of adult education. Eight times some form of the word *teach* appears, and we can add to those Paul's use of "train," "encourage," and "rebuke." Five educational groupings surface in the chapter: older men, older women, younger women, younger men, and slaves. Anyone who believes that Christian education is just for children needs to spend a few hours in Titus 2.

EDUCATION IN THE GENERAL EPISTLES AND REVELATION

The general epistles and Revelation continue the emphasis on teaching and the commitment to a received body of doctrine that we have found throughout the Pauline epistles, and especially in the pastorals. Peter, for example, though he does not use *didaskalia* or *paideia* ("discipline"), gives over entire paragraphs to the development of maturity in the people of God and the importance of their remembering knowledge germain to the proper practice of Christian living. In modern parlance, of course, this is nothing more nor less than Christian education (cf., 1 Pet. 1:3-9, 13-14, 22-25; 2:1-3, 11-20; 3:13-17; 4:7-19; 2 Pet. 1:5-11; 3:1-2, 14-18).

DISCIPLINE: HEBREWS

If one single word can identify the educational thrust of the book of Hebrews, it would be the word *discipline* (Greek, *paideia* [noun], *paideuō* [verb], which occurs seven times in chap. 12). A dramatic passage in Hebrews 12 emphasizes that educational process depends upon the orderliness of discipline and the requirement of punishment. The immediate context obviously deals with the heavenly Father and His earthly children; but one can quickly see a principle easily adapted to Christian parents and even classroom teachers: "No discipline seems pleasant at the time, but painful. Later on, however, it produces a harvest of righteousness and peace for those who have been trained by it" (v. 11).

The other passage of great educational consequence in Hebrews emphasizes maturity, another strategic concept in Christian education (5:11-6:3). Here the author scolds his readers, observing that they should have been teachers, but instead they need to be taught again—and not only taught, but taught the most elementary things of God's truth. In this context the word *didasko* appears in a context that reinforces its biblical emphasis—spiritual teaching aims to produce godliness and Christlike maturity.

PRACTICALITY: JAMES

What are we to say about the book of James—other than that all instructional activity by Christian teachers needs to produce some obvious behavioral effect in the lives of students. A word for "teach" (*didaskaloi*) appears only in the third chapter (3:1), which speaks to teachers without hesitation or vagueness. Here we learn that the spiritual maturity God expects in His teachers is best measured by the tongue. James issues a warning that must echo in the minds of all who adopt the mantle of instruction: "Not many of you should presume to be teachers, my brothers, because you know that we who teach will be judged more strictly" (3:1).

TEACHING AS EXHORTATION: 1 AND 2 PETER

The first epistle of Peter offers practical exhortation and comfort for believers' daily needs. Peter seems determined to link doctrine with practice. Spiritual growth through the study of God's truth appears early (2:1-3). He deals often with service and suffering (3:8–4:19), and in the last chapter of the first epistle he reminds the elders of their responsibility for modeling godly behavior before the flock.

In his second epistle Peter shows himself as both a concerned pastor and a champion of theological orthodoxy. He lists the credentials of true teachers to help his readers become discerning students of God's Word (1:12-21). False teachers are exposed, and the Lord's return is reviewed. The last verse of the Petrine epistles waves a flag commonly flown by Christian educators: "But grow in the grace and knowledge of our Lord and Savior Jesus Christ. To him be glory both now and forever! Amen" (3:18).

ASSUMPTIONS ABOUT TEACHING: 1, 2, 3 JOHN, JUDE, REVELATION

All three Johannine epistles offer exhortation important to us in the late twentieth century. In his gospel, John presents the way of salvation, challenging readers to believe. Now in the epistles he emphasizes the results of salvation in those who have already believed. The approach is personal; John avoids quotations or other scholarly distinctives. He encourages Christians to walk in the light. False doctrine can be avoided because Christians have spiritual knowledge. John claims, "I do not write to you because you do not know the truth, but because you do know it and because no lie comes from the truth" (2:21). Biblical Christian education should exhibit the characteristics of the main themes in the Johannine epistles: light, life, love, and knowledge.

The last two books of the New Testament do not add much to our understanding of educational ministry. Jude's emphasis suggests that only those who have been built up in the spiritual instruction that we have seen described in the New Testament can stand against the severe test of temptation and false teaching all around them (vv. 20-21).

The book of Revelation emphasizes again the significance of God's written revelation and its impact on local churches. Forms of the word *teach* are used only negatively (e.g., "teaching of Balaam," 2:14; "teaching of the Nicolaitans," 2:15).

So we come full circle to emphasizing the centrality of the Bible in any instructional activity that can be properly called "Christian education." Once again Sanner aids our thinking.

> The Bible is the Word of God; it is the Foundation and the final Authority for the goals and content of Christian education. In it the Christian finds his heritage from the past and his hope for the future. He discovers that he is a part of a great teaching tradition. The Hebrews used instruction effectively to perpetuate their faith and their way of life—they taught through the parents, the priest, the wise men, the prophets, the Temple and the synagogue. Jesus Himself was the Master Teacher, His disciples spread the Good News through preaching and teaching.
>
> God honors such teaching with His grace. Biblical principles of education challenge us to perform our teaching tasks with total commitment. We cannot rest content until all men come to know Jesus Christ whom to know is life eternal. To love Him, to be like Him, to serve Him, is the fulfillment of Christian education.[15]

FOR FURTHER READING

Byrne, H. W. *A Christian Approach to Education.* Grand Rapids: Baker, 1986.

Daniel, Eleanor; John W. Wade; and Charles Gresham. *Introduction to Christian Education.* Cincinnati: Standard, 1987.

Gangel, Kenneth O., and Howard Hendricks, eds. *The Christian Educator's Handbook on Teaching.* Wheaton, Ill.: Victor, 1988.

LeBar, Lois E. *Education That Is Christian.* Edited by James E. Plueddemann. Wheaton, Ill.: Victor, 1989.

15. Sanner, p. 49.

Lee, James Michael. *The Content of Religious Instruction: A Social Science Approach*. Birmingham, Ala.: Religious Education, 1985.

Pazmiño, Robert W. *Foundational Issues in Christian Education*. Grand Rapids: Baker, 1988.

Richards, Lawrence O. *Christian Education: Seeking to Become Like Jesus Christ*. Grand Rapids: Zondervan, 1988.

Sanner, A. Elwood, and A. F. Harper, eds. *Exploring Christian Education*. Grand Rapids: Baker, 1978.

Seymour, Jack L., and Donald E. Miller. *Contemporary Approaches to Christian Education*. Nashville: Abingdon, 1982.

Wilhoit, Jim. *Christian Education and the Search for Meaning*. Grand Rapids: Baker, 1986.

2

Edward L. Hayes

Establishing Biblical Foundations

RECOVER THE BIBLICAL ROOTS OF CHRISTIAN EDUCATION
- **By looking at early Hebrew and Christian approaches to education**
- **Through study of important biblical educational words**
- **For building a sound theology of educational action**
- **For revitalizing contemporary Christian education**

Christian education arises from the fertile soil of the Bible. The biblical revelation of God's dealing with His covenant people Israel and the examples of Jesus and His apostles form the seedbed for what we know today as Christian education. We look to the biblical record for both its origin and form. Its purposes, methods, and institutional expressions are rooted in the Scriptures.

All the expression "Christian education" implies in our contemporary world must somehow be subjected to the scrutiny of the explicit and implicit teachings of the Scriptures. This in no way limits the church, dictating an exact reproduction of primitive style. Rather, the biblical wellspring of principles and examples is vital to the creation, perpetuation, and renewal of Christian education endeavors.

Viewing the Bible as God's living Word can recharge Christian education at its base. Foundational to a vital church ministry is a vital and authoritative theology. Such a theology does not spring from an existential base devoid of absolutes and certainties, but from revelatory truth. Contrary to some modern thinking, such

EDWARD L. HAYES, Ph.D., is executive director, Mount Hermon Association, Inc., Mount Hermon, California.

a theology need not be viewed as wooden, lifeless, and culture-bound. The view that the Scriptures are the authoritative Word from God rather than a means of stifling the human spirit allows us to become all that God intended in His creative process. A basic presupposition for the evangelical Christian educator, then, is an authoritative Word.

The teaching function of the church flows from the Bible. It does not ignore the contemporary setting and the developmental needs of the learner, but it finds its roots in the Word of God. Sara Little wrote several decades ago that Christian education is to be "a servant and not a master of revelation."[1] That vantage point is particularly important in developing an educational stance and style. The primary focus is not on humans but on God. The human factor is by no means ignored, but it is not the point of beginning. What we think about God indicates what we do about education. When we consider any proper understanding of the biblical foundation of Christian education we must account for God. Stephen Bayne in *The Christian Idea of Education* scored this point decades ago, and it is still a guiding principle.

> The fundamental thought underlying nearly everything that we would want to say about the Christian idea of education is that God is the teacher. It is He who establishes all truth; it is He who wills that men shall know the truth; He gives us curious and reflective minds to seek the truth and grasp it and use it; He even gives us the supreme privilege of helping Him in partnership both to teach and to learn.[2]

What we think about God, however, depends on what we think about the Scriptures. To the evangelical, the Bible functions as the primary source and the only inerrant criterion of truth. This truth is one. In a sense there is no such thing as secular truth and Christian truth. God is the author of all truth. If God is the author of all truth, then we believe in a unitary wholeness and interrelationship of truth to all subject fields.

To say that the Bible contains truth on a par with scientific truth, for instance, is not quite accurate. It is also not accurate to force the Bible into making truth statements in every field of human investigation. To the degree, however, that the Bible purports to assert truths, evangelicals affirm its authority and infallibility. In other words, Christians are free to investigate all subject fields and all human wisdom, confident that God is the author of all truth. As Christians we can rest in the assurance that the Bible is our only infallible guide in judging ultimate truth. Protestant Reformer John Calvin articulated this key idea centuries ago:

> If we believe that the spirit of God is the only foundation of truth, we shall neither reject

---

1. Sara Little, *The Role of the Bible in Contemporary Christian Education* (Richmond, Va.: John Knox, 1961), p. 175. Larry Richards in *Religious Education and Theology*, ed. Norma B. Thompson (Birmingham, Ala.: Religious Education Press), p. 202, states that "the understanding of Scripture as a revelation of reality gives direction to Christian Education."
2. Stephen Bayne, "God Is the Teacher," in *The Christian Idea of Education*, ed. Edmund Fuller (New Haven, Conn.: Yale U., 1957), p. 255.

nor despise the truth wherever it shall appear. . . . They are superstitious who dare not borrow anything from profane writers. All truth is from God, and consequently, if wicked men have said anything that is true and just, we ought not reject it, for it has come from God.[3]

The crisis of the recent debate over the Scripture and its defense has tended to detract the church from its central task of actually teaching the Bible. Anyone can confess a high view of the nature of the Scripture, but ultimately the real test is whether or not it is read, taught, studied, and lived in the life and community of faith.[4] As J. I. Packer has stated so well in *Inerrancy and Common Sense:* "Scripture is the God-given record, explanation, and application of God's once-for-all redemptive words and deeds on the stage of space-time history, and that its intended function is to 'instruct' . . . for salvation through faith in Christ Jesus (2 Timothy 3:15)."[5]

The direction of our educational stance is plain. It lies in a return to a central principle of education—namely, that of going to original sources. We must teach the Bible itself. We must return to the Bible, which has made every renewal movement in Protestantism possible. Evangelicalism does well to take heed to the swinging pendulums of time, noting their correctives to imbalanced practice. But a shifting theology will correct nothing. Only the Scriptures will provide a rudder through crisis and, at the same time, chart a course to remedy the ills of society. "To lose the Bible," writes Carl Henry, "is to lose everything."[6]

JEWISH EDUCATIONAL ROOTS

The roots of Christian education run deep into the soil of Judaism. It should not seem strange that the church claims a Judaic heritage—the New Testament church was founded by Jews, the New Testament was written by Jews (with the exception of Luke), and the Bible of the early church was the Hebrew Scriptures of the Old Testament. Stuart Rosenberg calls Christians to "rediscover roots that are Semitic."[7]

Hebrew origins of Christian education have been amply chronicled by William Barclay[8] and Lewis Joseph Sherrill.[9] Certain dominant threads make up the fab-

3. John Calvin, *Commentaries on the Epistles to Timothy, Titus, and Philemon* (reprint; Grand Rapids: Eerdmans, 1959), pp. 300-301.
4. See G. C. Berkouwer, "Hearing and Doing the Word," *Christianity Today* 11 (28 October 1966):64. For a Catholic view of the role of the Bible in Christian education, see Matias Preiswerk, *Educating in the Living Word: A Theoretical Framework for Christian Education* (Maryknoll, N.Y.: Orbis, 1987). See also Susanne Johnson, *Christian Spiritual Formation in the Church and Classroom* (Nashville: Abingdon, 1989).
5. J. I. Packer, "Preaching as Bible Interpretation," in *Inerrancy and Common Sense*, ed. Roger R. Nicole and J. Ramsey Michaels (Grand Rapids: Baker, 1980), p. 187.
6. Carl F. H. Henry, "Restoring the Whole World," in *The Religious Education We Need*, ed. James Michael Lee (Mishawaka, Ind.: Religious Education Press, 1977), p. 65.
7. Stuart E. Rosenberg, *Judaism* (Glen Rock, N.J.: Paulist, 1966), p. 16.
8. William Barclay, *Educational Ideals of the Ancient World* (Grand Rapids: Baker, 1974).

ric of the rise of teaching in Hebrew history. And Hebrew history, we need not be reminded, is largely Bible history. From earliest times the Hebrews were called "the People of the Book."[10]

God, to the Hebrew, was manifest both in history and in the law. Profoundly convinced of God's leading through His covenant relationship with Israel, the Hebrews faithfully taught the young so "that they should put their confidence in God, and not forget the works of God, but keep His commandments" (Ps. 78:7). To the Hebrew the concept that God was the teacher emerged from the nature of God Himself. He was creator, covenantor, and sustainer. His will and wisdom were to be sought and cherished. Thus priest, prophet, king, sage, and scribe were all viewed as interpreters in one way or another of the grand drama of the Lord in history and in revelation.

One passage has become imbedded in Hebrew consciousness more deeply than any other. The instruction of the Shema contained in Deuteronomy 6:4-9 set the agenda for the home and the nation. So great was instruction in the eyes of God's chosen people that they equated it with life. "Take hold of instruction; do not let go. Guard her; for she is your life," wrote the sage (Prov. 4:13).

The religious rites of the Hebrew people were occasions for pedagogy. Household ritual provoked wonder, reverence, and joy—as well as questions (see Deut. 6:20). The Passover particularly kindled a reminder of the past. The Sabbath, the feast days, and the bar mitzvah were all part of a living liturgy that impressed a theology on the minds of the simple as well as the great.

Through the bitter years of Exile, Judaism survived because of an ingrained respect for education. What the Tabernacle in the wilderness and the Temple in Jerusalem were to the devout, the synagogue became to the Jew in exile. Although its exact rise is obscure, the synagogue probably emerged in Babylon. Both Josephus and Philo carry the synagogue back to the time of Moses. It developed as one of those rare educational institutions that corresponds with the nature of the faith it represents.

The principal purpose of the synagogue was teaching. Barclay writes, "It is necessary clearly to remember that the Synagogue was very much more a place of teaching than the modern Church. The object of the Synagogue Sabbath services was not public worship in the narrower sense of the term; it was not devotion; it was religious instruction."[11] It was the center where the law was explained, expounded, and applied.

Postbiblical Judaism was later to build on that Old Testament foundation. The importance of teaching in the Old Testament may also be seen in the various words used to describe the communication of God's works and word to mankind.

9. Lewis Joseph Sherrill, *The Rise of Christian Education* (New York: Macmillan, 1953).
10. For a concise treatment of the Judaic heritage and a Christian concept of learning, see Marvin R. Wilson, "The Jewish Concept of Learning: A Christian Appreciation," *Christian Scholar's Review* 5 (1976): 350-63.
11. Barclay, p. 24.

Hebrew words dealing with the concept of education, like Near Eastern thought in general, portray vivid word pictures. Selected words illustrate the emergence of an educational style.

The Hebrew word *hanak,* "to educate" or "to train," comes from a root word meaning to dedicate or consecrate. This verb is used in Proverbs 22:6: "Train up a child in the way he should go, even when he is old he will not depart from it." The education of a child from the Hebrew perspective was viewed as an act of consecration. More than worship, however, is prompted by *hanak.* It properly means "to rub the palate or gums." Here, in this simple word used to convey the notion of teaching, is a world of pictures. When a child began to be instructed in the Torah—the Hebrew law—honey and sweet cakes were used as incentive. Thus the psalmist refers to the law as sweeter than honey (Ps. 119:103), and Ezekiel the prophet, upon eating the scroll, exclaimed, "It was sweet as honey in my mouth" (Ezek. 3:3).

The most common word translated "teach" in the Old Testament is *lamath,* which means "to stimulate, to exercise in." It conjures up the idea of an animal's being placed in a yoke for learning. Another form of the same word is used to describe an ox goad. Israel is referred to by the prophet Hosea as a "trained heifer" (Hosea 10:11).

Other words richly portray teaching as separating issues and ideas, sharpening or pricking learners, and shepherding. But the richest of the words for teaching is the one from which we get the word *Torah* itself. It is derived from a word meaning "to shoot, throw, or cast." Instruction is viewed as direction from God. The law of God may be seen as that body of teaching "cast forth" by the Spirit of God. Thus, the law itself was viewed by the Hebrew people as the substance of their teaching, a light and a guide to life. Christian education does not deny the roots of its Hebrew heritage. With the dawning of a new age, the epoch of Christian tradition built firmly upon the law and the prophets. New Testament teaching did not emerge in a vacuum. Its context was the long history of a rich teaching style. It is to that new era that we now give attention.

EDUCATION IN THE NEW TESTAMENT

Christianity takes its educational cues from a cluster of sources. The example and teachings of Jesus, the apostolic preaching and writings, and the embryonic style revealed in the biblical record of early Christian worship and fellowship primarily form the base of New Testament education.

Christian teaching finds its impetus in the etymological context of pregnant Greek words that articulate the teaching function. In several dominant words that recur frequently we are able to infer a content, a style, and a context in which education is to take place.

Furthermore, the nature of the church—its mission and ministry in the world as revealed in the Scriptures—provides a framework for educational action. Such a biblical theology is too broad a subject to treat extensively in this chapter, but it must be taken into account if we are to devise a comprehensive statement on the nature of New Testament education.

JESUS THE MASTER TEACHER

Christian education had its beginning with Jesus. This is not to ignore the past, but Jesus brought unique freshness to the teaching task. He came from God, and He taught God's message as one having authority. Jesus was a teacher, and He used teaching as the chief vehicle of communication. Charles Benton Eavey has stated it well: "Teaching was His chief business. He was often a healer, sometimes a worker of miracles, frequently a preacher, but always a teacher."[12]

Chapter 6, "Christ the Master Teacher," deals with this subject in more detail, but let it be said that the educational dimension of the gospel record has provoked considerable writing. Much of the research and writing represents an attempt to view Jesus' teaching through the eyes of twentieth-century educational psychology. Even the classic work of Herman Harrell Horne,[13] first published in 1922, revealed the tone and tinting of an emerging school of religious educational thought. This assessment is not meant to discourage educational investigation into the teaching methods Jesus employed, but one must always be reminded that our categorizations, perceptions, and conclusions, in large measure, are biased by our contemporary understanding of education.

An example of that kind of attempt to make Jesus the man for all seasons is Norman Richardson's *The Christ of the Classroom*. At the peak of early twentieth-century religious education fervor he wrote, "A study of Jesus Christ's mastery, as a teacher, may be made by noting the chief characteristics of competency in teaching, as defined by the science of education."[14] Such a science of education has, or course, been defined and redefined many times over during the past six decades since Richardson wrote those words.

What serves as a caution for the study of Jesus' educational techniques must serve as a caution for educational study anywhere in the New Testament. It is both safe and profitable to pay attention to the biblical data without inferring too much by way of dogma in method. We claim dogma in faith but not dogma in methodology.

THE APOSTOLIC TRADITION

We dare not underestimate the powerful thrust of the Great Commission and its teaching directive upon the apostles. Pentecost turned timid followers into bold preacher-teachers. Those who responded to Peter's message that day continued

---

12. Charles Benton Eavey, *History of Christian Education* (Chicago: Moody, 1964), p. 78.
13. Herman Harrell Horne, *Jesus the Master Teacher* (New York: Association, 1922).
14. Norman E. Richardson, *The Christ of the Classroom: How to Teach Evangelical Christianity* (New York: Macmillan, 1931), p. 3.

steadfastly in the apostles' teaching (Acts 2:42). And it is noted that daily in the Temple and in houses the apostles kept on teaching and preaching Jesus Christ (Acts 5:42).

It is helpful to visualize the New Testament materials as forming three great emphases: to be a teacher in the New Testament sense embodies the call to faith, the explanation of the faith, and elaboration on the moral and spiritual implications of the life of faith.

Apostolic preaching formed the core of action, calling men and women to repentance. Emphasis was upon the death, resurrection, and exaltation of Jesus. Paul in his preaching developed those faith-forming themes but emphasized another dimension—Christ as preexistent agent of creation and reconciler of all things to Himself by His death on the cross.

Faith formation, faith explanation, and moral development are seen in the apostolic tradition. The ease with which the terms *preach* and *teach* are used to convey the corpus of God's truth and the curriculum of godly living attests to the fact that the teaching was no peripheral function in primitive Christianity.

EARLY CHRISTIAN WORSHIP AND TEACHING

Little is known of the primitive church style of meeting together. We usually have to rely upon the material from the postbiblical period to give insight into the corporate behavior of Christians in worship, fellowship, and learning. Several themes, however, can be developed from the New Testament data, revealing the central importance of education in the life of the early church.

In Acts we learn that the persistent behavior of Christians involved the apostles' teaching (*koinonia*), prayers, observance of the Lord's Supper, and compassionate caring—first to the saints, then toward all others. As Christianity moved outward to the larger Roman world it became necessary to emphasize family (primarily parental) responsibility in teaching. New converts from paganism could not be counted upon to know and respect the traditional Jewish roots of family education central to the Old Testament era. Furthermore, the pastoral epistles, particularly, outline ministerial duties and church responsibilities in regard to the educative task.

The Timothy letters include Pauline directives to teach the Word. Timothy is exhorted not to neglect the gift that was in him (1 Tim. 4:14) and to stir up the gift of God (2 Tim. 1:6). A strong case can be built that the gift of teaching was in Paul's mind. The tone of the two letters and the frequent reference to teaching give strong indication of the deep concern of an aging apostle for the perpetuation of the faith through a teaching ministry of the Word.

Six general themes that emphasize the importance of teaching occur in the two letters: (1) Teaching is essential for the proper handling of the inspired Word (2 Tim. 2:14-15; 3:16-17). (2) Teaching is necessary for soundness in faith (1 Tim. 4:6, 11, 16; 6:3-5; 2 Tim. 4:3). (3) Teaching is useful for the establishment of harmonious households (1 Tim. 6:1-2). (4) Teaching ability is a requirement of pastors and other spiritual leaders (1 Tim. 3:2; 2 Tim. 2:24). (5) Teaching is an essential corollary to Bible reading, exhortation, and preaching (1 Tim. 4:13; 2 Tim. 4:2). (6) Finally, teaching is vital to the perpetuation of the faith (2 Tim. 2:2).

In Titus, Paul gives similar instruction regarding teaching. Sound teaching is the retardant to error in the body of believers and the means of persuasion in the world (Titus 1:9; 2:12). Teaching is the effective vehicle of establishing order in the household (Titus 2:1-10) and is also the means of establishing the example of believers as a pattern of good works before non-Christians (Titus 2:7, 10).

The intense concern for communal sharing in primitive Christianity grew out of the Christian call to a life of discipleship. No mere recitation of creed—even one as lofty as the early affirmation of Christ's lordship—could build up the saints. It was the corporate togetherness that edified. The Word was always central. Even music was viewed as pedagogical (Col. 3:16). The life and work of the early church, as revealed in Scripture, revolved in large measure around teaching. Yet there was always a compelling missionary impetus outward from the assembly of saints to the surrounding world.

THE CHILD AND THE CHURCH

Christian education has properly emphasized the significance of childhood. Within the New Testament much is revealed about the centrality of the child in church concern. "There is no gospel picture dearer to most people," writes Barclay, "than the picture of Jesus setting the child in the midst or taking him in His arms."[15] Children's work is not to be despised. Our Lord's rebuke of the disciples, His example of setting children in the midst of them, and His comparison of the simplicity and openness of a child to receiving the kingdom of God set an agenda for church education (cf. Matt. 19:13; Mark 10:13; Luke 18:15). God is willing to care for children with guardian angels (Matt. 18:10). Christ's teaching is clear that the Christian duty to the child is absolutely binding. To receive a child is to receive none other than Jesus Himself (Mark 9:36; Luke 9:48). The child is the very pattern of the kingdom. Unless a person becomes as a child there is no entrance to God's spiritual kingdom.

Beyond the gospels, the New Testament teaching on children is meager, but it provides essential directives for church and family education. Children must obey parents (Eph. 6:1); fathers must not overdiscipline to the point of discouragement and rebellion (Eph. 6:4; Col. 3:21). Spiritual leaders must rule their own households well (1 Tim. 3:4, 12; Titus 1:6), and parents have an absolute duty to provide for their children (2 Cor. 12:14). Barclay concludes that the New Testament knows nothing about an exact curriculum of religious education in the churches for children, neither does it speak about schools. "The New Testament is certain," he writes, "that the only training which really matters is given with-

15. Barclay, p. 234.

in the home, and that there are no teachers so effective for good or evil as parents are."[16] Finally, the New Testament reveals, by example, the mature faith of Timothy whose godly mother and grandmother faithfully taught him the Word of God, which was able to make him wise unto salvation (2 Tim. 3:15).

IMPORTANT NEW TESTAMENT EDUCATION WORDS

Throughout the New Testament a variety of words are used to convey educational meanings. Ten of these are included here for study and research.

1. *Didasko*. This is the most common word in the New Testament for teaching. Roughly two-thirds of its occurrences are in the gospels and the first part of Acts. Paul, however, rarely used the word. In its noun form it is translated "doctrine" in the King James Version (Acts 2:42; 2 Tim. 3:16).

2. *Didaskolos*. This word for teacher is often used of Jesus and of other Christian teachers, including Paul (1 Tim. 2:7). An entire category of gifted Christian workers bore this title (1 Cor. 12:28; Eph. 4:11).

3. *Paideuo*. One of the richest Greek terms, this word means "to give guidance and training." The verb comes from a noun that means "little child." It is used of parental teaching (Eph. 6:4) and of the value of the inspired Word (2 Tim. 3:16).

4. *Katecheo*. This a rare word used only by Luke (Luke 1:4; Acts 18:25; 21:21) and Paul (Rom. 2:18; 1 Cor. 14:19; Gal. 6:6). We get our word *catechism* and *catechumen* ("learner") from it. The word means "to be informed, to report, to teach or instruct someone."

5. *Noutheteo*. Literally this word means "to shape the mind" and is translated "admonish" in the King James Version (1 Cor. 4:14; 10:11; Eph. 6:4; Col. 3:16).

6. *Matheteuo*. Here is the important New Testament word for "to disciple," with the noun form usually occurring most in the Bible. It occurs only in the gospels and Acts.

7. *Oikodomeo*. Used in the context of spiritual growth and maturity, this word means "to edify" or, literally, "to build up" (1 Cor. 3:9; 8:1; 1 Thess. 5:11; 1 Pet. 2:5).

8. *Paratithemi*. This words means "to set before" or "to place beside." Paul uses this word in 1 Timothy 1:18 and 2 Timothy 2:2, translated "commit" in the King James Version.

9. *Ektithemi*. Used only in Acts 11:4; 18:26; and 28:23, this word means "to explain facts in logical order" or, as it is translated, "to expound."

10. *Hodegeo*. Our final New Testament word carries with it the sense of leading, guiding, or showing the way. Judas was referred to in Acts 1:16 as a guide to those who took Jesus captive. The Holy Spirit is called a guide in John 16:13. The Ethiopian needed one to guide him into the meaning of Isaiah (Acts 8:31), the Pharisees are called blind guides to the blind (Matt. 15:14; 23:16, 24), and Christ shall one day lead saints to experience the living waters of eternal life (Rev. 7:17).

16. Ibid., p. 236.

This rich list of New Testament words needs to be explored within the various contexts. The words imply content to be taught, actions to be engaged in, and, in some cases, nuances of methodologies.

A NEW TESTAMENT THEOLOGY OF CHRISTIAN EDUCATION

The value of evangelical Christian education will rise or fall on the soundness of its theological foundations. Yet few have attempted integration of the theological disciplines with the educative process.

Where does one begin to construct a biblical theology of education? Pioneer religious educator Paul Vieth, in *The Church and Christian Education*, declared, "Christian education can find its purpose, content, and method only in the nature of Christianity."[17] Vieth was writing in a context of the new religious education endeavors that were finding their moorings in secular humanism and psychology rather than revelation. His assessment still provides a challenge for theological formulation.

Our conception of truth determines our pedagogy. It is the epistemological question that is fundamental. Here evangelicals sink their anchors deeply into revelatory truths and hold tenaciously to a literal biblicism. God is viewed as the center of education as He is viewed as the center of truth. Authority resides in God, and all truth—if it be truth—is seen as divine truth. Problems of biblical literalism are handled forthrightly. There is no plea for a wooden literalism that fails to distinguish between what is symbolic and poetical, doctrinal and practical, historical and epochal. While the human element is recognized at the same time, the Bible is accepted as infallible—that is, totally trustworthy and authoritative in all matters of faith and practice.

The authority of the Scripture, viewed as divinely revealed, in no way precludes investigation. The encounter of divine truth and human experience is cherished, although a dynamic view of revelation is rejected. The Word does not become God's Word in experience—it is already the Word of God. Objective truth stands as mentor and judge of the human experience.

Evangelical Christian education rejects the idea that theology is valuable only when it is viewed as relational. Granted, the truth must be applied to life, yet it is still divine truth quite apart from its application to living. On this point some religious educators part company with evangelical Christian education presuppositions. For instance, Randolph Crump Miller is a chief exponent of an experiential base for theology and teaching. As a spokesperson for what has come to be known as "process theology" (theology in flux without biblical norms), Miller hopes that in the future "many will see fit to work out a system of beliefs consonant with empirical and process theology."[18] Evangelicals reject this departure from

---

17. Paul H. Vieth, *The Church and Christian Education* (St. Louis: Bethany, 1947), p. 44.
18. Randolph C. Miller, "Continuity and Contrast in the Future," in *The Religious Education We Need*, ed. James Michael Lee (Mishawaka, Ind.: Religious Education Press, 1977), p. 50.

biblical roots and the adoption of current fads and moods in theology that may in some cases contradict the divine deposit of revelation in the Bible.

Evangelical rejection of theology that is captive to relativism does not negate creativity and the importance of relationships. A number of evangelical Christian education scholars have addressed those issues, all from the vantage point of orthodox faith. Lawrence O. Richards, in *A Theology of Christian Education*, uses relationship as his central motif.[19] Lois LeBar, in *Focus on People in Church Education*, emphasizes the human dimension,[20] and the Lutheran educator Allan Hart Jahsmann, in *Power Beyond Words*, investigates the nonverbal elements of our faith.[21] Another evangelical, Martha Leypoldt, in *Learning Is Change*, places heavy emphasis upon the dynamic quality of life-changing faith.[22] Each of those authors seeks to bring the correctives that Miller desires, yet on the basis of orthodox biblical theology.

Evangelical educators seek an adequate method to fit an adequate theology. God must be at the center. Authority must rest in the Scriptures. Jesus is seen as reconciler and mediator, the Holy Spirit as tutor and guide. Both teacher and learner are open for truth. Each person must internalize God's truth and be accountable for changing human character to conform to godliness. Building relationships that edify in the corporate body of Christians is valued, even essential. The church is to be engaged in vocal public witness to the gospel, and compassionate social action is not to be seen as incongruous to faith. Christian hope—based upon the reality of Christ's resurrection, ascension, and imminent return to earth—brings about a purified ethic and affects how we govern our ways and how we relate to governmental authority. Those and other motifs are building blocks for a theology of education.

Developed within the context of a biblical view of the human soul, the abject sinfulness of mankind, the necessity of divine atonement, the need for personal salvation, and the creative genius of the learner who shares, even residually, the image of God, those blocks provide a framework for evangelical educational action.

CONCLUSION

This chapter has attempted to set forth some convictions evangelicals have about the biblical basis of Christian education, its roots in both the Old and New Testaments, and its relationship to Christian theology. I agree with J. Stanley Glen, who issued a call for a recovery of the teaching ministry in our churches:

The teaching ministry is the one ministry which when taken seriously assumes the

19. Lawrence O. Richards, *A Theology of Christian Education* (Grand Rapids: Zondervan, 1975).
20. Lois E. LeBar, *Focus on People in Church Education* (Westwood, N.J.: Revell, 1968).
21. Allan H. Jahsmann, *Power Beyond Words* (St. Louis: Concordia, 1969).
22. Martha Leypoldt, *Learning Is Change* (Valley Forge, Pa.: Judson, 1971).

responsibility of communicating the truth at the human level and in human form. It insists that the substance of the Bible and of its faith, including the substance of the great confessions of the church, are essentially intelligible and must be communicated from one generation to another if the church is to be the church and men and women are to hear the word of God. This means that the teaching ministry is the guardian of what may be regarded in the best sense as the tradition of the church.[23]

Evangelicals agree that the church is a pilgrim community of memory and vision. Our contemporary task is to teach the faith in dynamic ways so that each generation will hear God speaking, see God act, and develop a credible witness to the life-changing gospel. In this holy task the Scriptures are central.

FOR FURTHER READING

Fuller, Edmund, ed. *The Christian Idea of Education.* Hambden, Conn.: Shoe String, 1975.

Gangel, Kenneth O., and Warren S. Benson. *Christian Education: Its History and Philosophy.* Chicago: Moody, 1983.

Lee, James M. *The Content of Religious Instruction: A Social Science Approach.* Birmingham, Ala: Religious Education, 1985.

LeBar, Lois E. *Education That Is Christian.* Edited by James E. Plueddemann. Wheaton, Ill.: Victor, 1989.

Pazmiño, Robert W. *Foundational Issues in Christian Education.* Grand Rapids: Baker, 1988.

Preiswerk, Matias. *Educating in the Living Word: A Theoretical Framework for Christian Education.* Maryknoll, N.Y.: Orbis, 1987.

Smart, James D. *The Teaching Ministry of the Church: An Examination of Basic Principles of Christian Education.* Philadelphia: Westminster, 1971.

Richards, Lawrence O. *Christian Education: Seeking to Become Like Jesus Christ.* Grand Rapids: Zondervan, 1988.

Wilhoit, Jim. *Christian Education and the Search for Meaning.* Grand Rapids: Baker, 1986.

---

23. J. Stanley Glen, *The Recovery of the Teaching Ministry* (Philadelphia: Westminster, 1960), pp. 25-26.

3

Wayne A. Widder

Reviewing Historical Foundations

THE FOUR LESSONS OF CHRISTIAN EDUCATION HISTORY
- Churches have always had schools of Christian education
- A church grows when Christian education is a vital part of its ministry
- Methods must vary to meet the needs of people in particular cultures
- Balance must be sought to maintain proper relationships between parents, church, and school in Christian education

---

The church is a teaching agency. From its beginning the New Testament church communicated knowledge of the God of the Bible and the principles God gave mankind to follow. Jesus told His disciples to "teach all nations"—a pattern to be continued until He returned. Over the past two thousand years education has played a significant role in the ministry of the church. The church viewed an educated person as one who was able to read and study God's Word. Believers are to search the Scripture to see if what is heard is true to biblical teaching.

The historical perspective of education in the church is vital in helping Christian educators assess the heritage of educational development. First, a historical view helps the educator evaluate—in light of sound biblical and educational principles—the purpose, curriculum, and methodology of the past. Second, history helps to understand contemporary Christian education by assisting educators in understanding the origins and reasons of the present educational

WAYNE A. WIDDER, D. Min., is professor of Christian education, Moody Bible Institute, Chicago, Illinois.

philosophies, curricula, and methodology. Third, history provides insight into the future development of Christian education. The purpose of history is to stimulate action, and as people get involved in the church's educational ministry, they are setting the direction for the future of Christian education.

Hebrew and Greek Background

The purpose of Hebrew education was to train people in the faith, the Old Testament Law and Prophets, and the traditions. The law was integrated into every area of Jewish life. Its impact is seen in relationships, the political life of the nation, and pertinent areas such as divorce and sexuality. The government of Israel was a strong supporter of education (2 Chron. 17:7-8), and Levitical priests were chosen to be the public teachers for the nation (2 Chron. 17:9). One of the reasons Levites were exempt from agricultural work and military service was so they might devote their time to study and thinking. God used the Levitical feasts to communicate truths about Himself to His people (i.e., Passover). A major function in the synagogue was teaching, which was mainly the use of questions and answers—also called the "interlocutory" method. Of course the home, under the tutelage of the father, was the central place where children were taught the law and its application to their life and society. The focus of Hebrew education was upon the one true and living God and the fact that all of life revolved around Him and emanated from Him.

The purpose of Greek education involved both the theoretical and pragmatic. The goal of the individual was to become a charming person with graceful manners, well educated in how to think for himself, with good moral character and citizenship. The schools at Athens followed this philosophy. In Sparta, however, the schools emphasized the more practical side, such as preparing to work for the state and for military service. This method of education was carried out by disciplined training and by question and answer (the catechetical approach). Greek education was established by men such as Socrates, Plato, Aristotle, and Isocrates. Even though the Greeks integrated their religion into education, their primary focus was centered on mankind. Their training was to be of one's mind through thinking and one's body through physical activity.

The concepts considered in chapter 2 provide a good basis upon which a history of Christian education may be developed.

Education in the Early Church (2d-4th centuries)

THE PURPOSE OF EDUCATION IN THE CHURCH

After the New Testament period, education in the church centered on preserving the teachings of Christ and the apostles and transmitting that information to others. Because of opposition to Christianity, the church leadership became concerned that what was taught was actually the truth presented by Christ and the apostles. They stressed the importance of establishing the New Testament canon, the creeds, and church discipline.[1] Robert Pazmiño states, "These three elements served to maintain continuity without distortion as the faith addressed a Hellenistic-Roman world marked by cultural and religious pluralism."[2]

HIGHLIGHTS OF EDUCATION IN THE CHURCH

In the early church, the home continued to be the primary place for informal teaching of biblical truths and their application to life. With the advent of the catechumenal and catechetical schools, however, parents did not feel the same pressure and responsibility for teaching their children.

The words *catechism* and *catechumen* come from the Greek word meaning "to instruct." The catechetical method follows the Socratic approach to teaching. It is a question and answer method that encourages students to think and reason. The teacher asks the questions, and the student answers. This method was common in Greek society.

The catechumenal school instructed new converts and children in the Old Testament and in the teachings of Christ and the apostles. Particularly the adult converts had little or no background in Christian truth, so this schooling was required for all those seeking fellowship into the church. C. B. Eavey states in his book *History of Christian Education*:

> The period of preparation covered two or three years. There were three grades or classes of catechumens. When first admitted, they were called *hearers*, because they were permitted to listen to the reading of the Scriptures and the sermons in the church. They received elementary instruction in the fundamental doctrines and practices of the church, and had to show by their conduct that they were worthy of promotion into a second grade or class. This second grade was that of *kneelers*, those who remained for prayer after the hearers withdrew. They received more advanced instruction and had to prove by their manner of living that they were worthy of entering upon the last stage of their probationary period. Those in this third grade were called *the chosen* and were given intensive doctrinal, liturgical, and ascetical training in preparation for baptism.[3]

The first teachers in these schools were the bishops and priests; later special teachers or able laymen were assigned the task.[4]

The catechetical schools were for the educated people of the day who tried to reconcile Christianity with philosophies in the culture. Often argumentation

1. See William Bean Kennedy, *Background Historical Understanding for Christian Education* (New York: Union Theological Seminary, 1980), p. 1.
2. Robert W. Pazmiño, *Foundational Issues in Christian Education* (Grand Rapids: Baker, 1988), p. 128.
3. C. B. Eavey, *History of Christian Education* (Chicago: Moody, 1964), p. 85.
4. Ibid., p. 85.

involved the superiority of Christianity over the philosophies, thus showing that Christianity was a viable option for life. Soon church leaders were trained at these schools. Catechetical schools were located at Alexandria, Antioch, Edessa, Caesarea, Nisibis, Jerusalem, and Carthage. Growing out of these schools came the episcopal, or cathedral, school. The most famous of the catechetical schools was located at Alexandria where Clement and Origen were leaders.

LEADERS OF EDUCATION IN THE CHURCH

Those who led in teaching Christian truth in the church were identified as church Fathers, and some were also leaders of the catechetical schools. The church Fathers' writings indicate three purposes functioning in the church: (1) the defense of Christianity, (2) fighting against false doctrine, and (3) teaching how to interpret Scripture properly.

Justin Martyr (A.D. 100-166), a student of philosophy, believed that Christianity was the truest of the philosophies. In his teachings he consciously sought to unite Christian thought with Gentile philosophy by showing the similarities between the two.

Tertullian (A.D. 150-225), considered the founder of the theology of the Western church (Augustine was the developer), held the opposite view from that of Justin Martyr and Origen. C. B. Eavey states,

> He felt that there were dangers to faith and morals in pagan poetry and philosophy; therefore the study of pagan learning by Christians should be concerned only with detecting and refuting errors. He was opposed to all attempts to combine philosophy and Christianity.[5]

Origen (A.D. 185-254) was considered by many historians as the most influential of the early writers and teachers. His impact is seen in the attempt to reconcile Christianity and pagan thought, in advocating the allegorical system of interpretation, and in his attempt to formulate a systematic theology in *De Principiis*.

Other leaders such as *Athanasius* (A.D. 295-373), *Eusebius* (A.D. 260-340), and *Chrysostom* (A.D. 345-407) were from the Eastern church. Athanasius was a brilliant student who received his theological education at the Catechetical School of Alexandria. Eusebius was the father of church history who wrote *Ecclesiastical History*, covering the period from apostolic times to A.D. 324. Chrysostom, an expositor and orator, fought for the literal approach to the Scripture. A Western Father, *Jerome* (A.D. 340-420), translated the Scriptures into a Latin version called the *Vulgate*. One final person must be mentioned: *Augustine*, who is acclaimed by some as the greatest of the church Fathers. His greatest apologetical work was the treatise *City of God (De Civitate Dei)*. He emphasized the great truth that man is a sinner and in need of salvation, which comes by God's grace

5. Ibid., p. 93.

through faith alone.[6] Augustine said, "The aim of the teacher is to cause the pupil to know, not merely to hear, the truth. To this end the teacher is to obtain from the pupil at every point all the reaction he can to the content taught."[7]

ACHIEVEMENTS OF CHRISTIAN EDUCATION

The aims of early Christian education were as follows: (1) They desired to preserve the true teachings of Christ and the apostles. (2) In the face of error and opposition, the church produced creeds and encouraged the teaching of Christianity propositionally. (3) They made the attempt (whether right or wrong) to relate Christianity to the culture and thinking of society. (4) Training classes for teaching biblical truths were started for those wanting to fellowship in the church. (5) People entering the ministry received the best higher education possible.

MEDIEVAL CHURCH EDUCATION (5TH-14TH CENTURIES)

THE PURPOSE OF EDUCATION IN THE CHURCH

During this period the main goal was to prepare those entering the clergy or monastic orders. Among the leaders there was much interest in spiritual disciplines, especially those associated with monasticism. Education for these was also in the seven liberal arts. Small groups of people separated themselves from the mainstream of the church (i.e., Brethren of Common Life and Waldenses), trained their children to read and study the Bible, and hoped to revive the pure teaching of the gospel. Education and Christian education declined during the sixth, seventh, and eighth centuries. Emperor Charlemagne sought to revive education during his reign.

HIGHLIGHTS OF EDUCATION IN THE CHURCH

The home began to make less of an impact in teaching Christian education to children. More parents were turning that task over to the church. During about five hundred years of the Middle Ages the church did a poor job of teaching. Some of the clergy were not even trained. Ignorance became widespread.

With Constantine and the acceptance of Christianity as the religion of the state, several changes occurred. Large numbers of people came into the fold of Christianity, and different methods had to be used to instruct these new members in Christian beliefs and practices. No longer was it required to attend the catechumenal school as a prerequisite for church membership. The common people received their Christian training—what little it was—through visual communication in the worship services (statues, pictures, stained glass windows, symbols of the ordinances).

6. See Earle E. Cairns, *Christianity Through the Centuries* (Grand Rapids: Zondervan, 1954), p. 161.
7. Eavey, p. 95.

Catechetical schools (which became cathedral schools) and monastic schools served to prepare persons entering the clergy or monastic orders. As bishoprics were established throughout the empire, schools were started and held in the larger churches, called cathedrals. Eavey states:

> The cathedral school was the mother of the grammar school. Grammar schools, for elementary education, first appeared in the sixth century. The meager instruction of these schools included teaching in reading, writing, music, simple calculating, religious observances, and rules of conduct. Other elementary schools were conducted by parish priests for both boys and girls and were known as parish schools.[8]

Monastic schools initially were for boys interested in entering an order. By the ninth century monastic schools were accepting all those interested in an education.

Universities began about 1200. They were started either from cathedral schools or because a great teacher was present and attracted students. Earle Cairns states, "The *universitas*, from which our word for university is derived, was a guild or corporation of students or teachers set up for purposes of common protection while the group went on with its work."[9] All students took the liberal arts course, the trivium for the bachelor's degree, and the quadrivium for the master's degree. Advanced studies could also be done in theology, law, and medicine. Memorization and logic were key skills students needed for these courses. Examinations were given orally and publicly. Two important model universities were the University of Paris and the University of Bologna.

Scholasticism rose concurrently with the rise of the universities and the introduction of Aristotle's philosophy into the educational movement in the West. Cairns states, "Scholasticism may be defined as the attempt to rationalize theology in order to buttress faith by reason."[10] Trying to determine whether or not faith was reasonable, the "scholastics" studied the Bible, the creeds, and the writings of the Fathers. Cairns elaborates,

> This intellectual speculative movement of the medieval Roman Church concerned itself with the problem of unity in man's intellectual life so that his spiritual and rational knowledge could be harmonized to give him certainty both in the realm of faith and of reason. The conflict between nominalism and realism was the great problem that the Scholastics faced in the early period of Scholasticism between 1050 and 1150. In this era the realism championed by Anselm and Bernard was victorious. During the period of High Scholasticism, between 1150 and 1300, the moderate realism championed by Aquinas won out over nominalism. But in the years after 1350, nominalism gained ground in the thinking of theological leaders of the Church.[11]

8. Ibid., p. 106.
9. Cairns, p. 261.
10. Ibid., p. 251.
11. Ibid., p. 254.

LEADERS OF EDUCATION IN THE CHURCH

Thomas Aquinas (1225-74) is a key figure in education in the church because he developed the systematic theology that was adopted by the Western church. Aquinas held that "the end of theology is God, who surpasses the comprehension of rational powers but whose existence can be established philosophically."[12] In *Christian Education*, Kenneth Gangel and Warren Benson state that educationally Thomas Aquinas "stressed that the teacher must be knowledgeable, be a skillful communicator, and view teaching as a calling by which mankind is served."[13] Joan Duvall says, "He held that the learner has the active potency to arrive at a knowledge of the unknown through discovery."[14]

Charlemagne (A.D. 742-812) sought to revive education and laid the groundwork for the revitalization of education in Western Europe. With the help of Alcuin, Charlemagne set in motion a plan for having a school in every town so that all people could receive an education.

ACHIEVEMENTS OF CHRISTIAN EDUCATION

No period of church history has been so severely criticized as this one—and with much justification. Christian training by parents was not encouraged as strongly as in the early church period. In addition, more corruption and ignorance surfaced among the church leaders. However, several good things were realized: (1) Even though the masses were illiterate, there was some movement to provide education for the general population. More schools were opened across Europe (i.e., cathedral, parish, and town schools). (2) Writings of the church Fathers were collected, copied, and circulated, thus setting a pattern for the library. (3) Scholasticism had its difficulties with an over-emphasis on the place and role of reason. C. B. Eavey states,

> On the credit side, Scholastic education dealt with content of the greatest importance—the reality of the existence of God, the attributes of God, and the relation of man to God. It gave an impetus to the study of theology and raised it to the dignity of a science. It kept alive and quickened interest in things intellectual, and it gave to many great minds a vigorous and thorough intellectual training. It led, at least in northern Europe, to the rise of the universities.[15]

12. Kenneth O. Gangel and Warren S. Benson, *Christian Education: Its History and Philosophy* (Chicago: Moody, 1983), p. 113.
13. Ibid., p. 113.
14. Joan Ellen Duvall, "Thomas Aquinas," in *A History of Religious Educators*, ed. Elmer L. Towns (Grand Rapids: Baker, 1975), p. 80.
15. Eavey, p. 113.

RENAISSANCE AND REFORMATION (15TH-16TH CENTURIES)

THE PURPOSE OF EDUCATION IN THE CHURCH

The Renaissance period did not directly promote Christian education, but it helped set the stage for the Reformation. The goal of the Renaissance was a rebirth of culture. It was the rediscovery of the Greek and Roman classics, literature, and art. The idea of going back to the originals carried over to scholars, who began studying the original Hebrew and Greek Scriptures. The goal of education in the Reformation was to teach the Scriptures, learn the catechism, and apply the principles of the Word.

HIGHLIGHTS OF EDUCATION IN THE CHURCH

The Reformers were also seen as educators in their movements. They used the universities for disseminating their teachings. The children were also schooled in the faith through catechism classes in the church and through public schools, which were usually held in church facilities. Eventually these schools would become parochial schools.

The curriculum used by the Reformers was the catechism—Lutheran Augsburg and the Reformed Heidelberg—which was a series of questions and answers on Christian beliefs. The Bible was the main source used. Although it was not the intent of the Reformers to minimize the Bible, some churches gave primary emphasis to the catechism.

The Reformers' emphasis on the "priesthood of believers" and individual responsibility meant that Christians needed to read and write if they were to study the Bible for themselves. People were encouraged to check the Scriptures to see if what was being said or done was in keeping with the truth of the Word. The Reformers proposed that the civic leaders establish schools for both boys and girls, and secondary schools, or "colleges," where humanistic and religious studies would be discussed and integrated. The Reformers also supported universal education, teaching in the vernacular, and training educated ministers.

LEADERS OF EDUCATION IN THE CHURCH

Martin Luther (1483-1546) had at the heart of his Christian education that the teaching of Christian truths was to center in the home. He supported parents' training their children in the knowledge of God. Luther believed that the teacher was only second in importance to the minister. He held that discipline (moderate but firm), memorization, repetition, and illustration were the proper methods to use. He strongly supported the idea that understanding of the material was more important than merely memorizing it. *Phillip Melanchthon* (1497-1560), who served closely with Luther, upgraded the education at the elementary and university levels.

John Calvin (1509-64) designed a plan whereby the instruction in the elementary schools of Geneva would be in the vernacular, where children would be taught the Bible, reading, grammar, writing, and arithmetic. He wrote guides and helps for the catechetical instruction of the children. His model at Geneva had far-reaching effects because it was passed along by the Dutch, Huguenots, Puritans, and John Knox.

John Knox (1515-72) established elementary schools that were controlled and supported by the church. Attendance was compulsory for boys and girls of the community for four years. Those graduating from college had to give testimony of "good character" before being allowed to enter the university.

ACHIEVEMENTS OF CHRISTIAN EDUCATION

The achievements of Christian education in the fifteenth and sixteenth centuries were as follows: (1) Teaching in the elementary schools was done in the students' own language. (2) The Scriptures were translated into the vernacular of the people. (3) All people, rich and poor, were encouraged to secure an education so they could read and study the Bible for themselves and become good citizens. (4) Men who were to become ministers of the church were well educated because they needed to be able to teach the Scriptures carefully and clearly and to be leaders in the community.

CHRISTIAN EDUCATION IN THE UNITED STATES
(16TH-20TH CENTURIES)

THE PURPOSE OF EDUCATION IN THE CHURCH

Identifying the goals of all the different groups that settled in America is difficult. Some supported Christian education for children. Others wanted only nonreligious subjects taught because they believed Christian education belonged to the parents and the church, not the schools. Still others believed in teaching only selected persons. Pazmiño states,

> Awareness of educational configurations forces the evangelical educator to consider a vast array of institutions and their interrelationships far beyond parochial concerns. For example, those primarily concerned with church education via the Sunday school cannot neglect the educational impacts of families, schools, communities, media, and the larger society in planning and implementing programs. Such influences must be considered in identifying purposes, developing strategies, implementing programs, and evaluating efforts.[16]

Although there is a great complexity, we can suggest a few of the more general purposes of education: (1) The majority of leaders agreed that education should be for all people, rich and poor. (2) It was believed by some that education was nec-

16. Pazmiño, p. 139.

essary for personal Christian growth and citizenship, whereas others believed education should only train leaders to manage the affairs of society. (3) Christian education was essential for helping people apply biblical principles to life and to develop Christian character. (4) Those supporting Christian education believed it was important to prepare people for ministry and mission.

HIGHLIGHTS OF EDUCATION IN THE CHURCH

The development of Christian education is closely associated with the general education. Much of what was happening in this post-Reformation time in Europe was also brought to America, and then affected by the freedoms of a new frontier society. Note how this worked out as a few peaks of Christian education are identified over nearly four hundred years.

American colonial education. Through the strong influence of Puritan Calvinism, early colonial America was affected by the belief that, because the Bible is an infallible book, the people must be educated so they can study and understand it. Because of this view, many people considered religious and secular education as one, saw parents as having a large role in their children's Christian training, and believed sermons should be used to instruct.

In the New England colonies a common school plan was established whereby each community provided its school building and hired its teacher. Each family was to send its children to the school and help pay the teacher's salary. The Massachusetts General Court passed an Act of 1642, which required all parents to provide an education for their children or be subject to a fine.[17] The common school held classes where children were taught reading, writing, and arithmetic. This school also became the background for the public school. There were also some "Dame" schools where girls were taught the basic skills of homemaking. The Latin grammar school also developed as a preparatory school for college. It emphasized the study of languages (Latin, Greek, Hebrew) and Christian doctrine. It served as the forerunner of today's junior and senior high schools.

The middle colonies followed a parochial plan of schooling. A greater diversity of people (Dutch, German, Mennonite, Quaker) lived here and generally established schools they had been familiar with in Europe. A parochial school was one associated with a local church for the purpose of providing Christian training for children.

Two key factors influenced the kind of school established in the southern colonies. First, the Church of England influenced the educational attitudes and design. Education was believed to be a private matter to be determined by the family and available to those who could afford it. Second, the economy was built around large plantation farms. These elements caused the forming of tutorial schools where plantation owners hired tutors to teach their own chil-

17. Gangel and Benson, p. 233.

dren and a few selected children of the community.

Postrevolutionary education developments. The formation of a new nation and the new principle of separation of church and state had significant consequences upon Christian education. First, states began developing a public school system. Second, state taxes could no longer be used for private and parochial schools. And third, Christian parents and the churches now had to find other ways of teaching their children their beliefs and practices.

During this period the Sunday school appeared. The modern Sunday school had its beginning with Robert Raikes, a journalist from Gloucester, England, who in 1780 began the first school. He saw that the poor children of his city were not receiving an education because they worked in the factories six days a week. Sunday was their only day off. Through the influence of John Wesley, who established Sunday schools at his preaching locations, and William Fox, who organized the schools into societies, the schools grew so that by 1784 there were 240,000 students. The early schools taught reading, writing, arithmetic, Bible study/catechism, and had a chapel time.

In 1785 the first Sunday school was transplanted to America and soon took on its own uniquenesses. The school became voluntary and sought to include many different religious groups. Denominational groups such as the Methodists began to adopt the Sunday school plan and promote it among its constituency. Sunday schools became more and more agencies for Christian nurturing of children, and eventually included adults. People such as Francis Asbury and Stephen Paxson established hundreds of schools in the western frontiers. The Sunday school movement held national and international conventions where curriculum plans were established and teacher training guides were developed and promoted. The uniform lesson was a plan to systematically study the Bible and to provide helps for teachers in teaching the various student age levels. The Sunday school movement in America met the void created by the state taking control of education in the school system. For a long time for many church groups the Sunday school served as the central agency for Christian education.

19th and 20th centuries. In the last half of the nineteenth century many parachurch agencies were started. The YMCA came to America in 1851, and Christian Endeavor (1881) ministered to the youth. Vacation Bible school (late 1890s), camping (about 1880), release time classes (1914), and publishing houses for Christian education materials came into existence to help the Christian community nurture its children and youth in Christian thought and character. Bible institutes and colleges were started to provide practical Christian education and practical ministry experiences. The public school was being influenced by John Dewey and at the same time liberalism came into the church's religious education programs. These two movements caused some concern about the purpose and content of religious education. The liberal element wanted to focus on the individual and his development and contribution to society. In their way of thinking, knowledge of God and His Word were secondary. Others believed strongly that a knowledge of God and His Word should have priority. Consequently, many churches and groups divided. Some of the parachurch agencies were also affected by liberal thinking. The impact slowed the growth of both Sunday school and church membership.

Currently a few things should be noted. First, during the 1950s church attendance was at its highest (48-49 percent). In many conservative churches Sunday school attendance was higher than the morning worship service. Second, during the 1960s attendance declined in both the church and Sunday school. With strong attacks on the Sunday school, a few pastors took the challenge to establish large Sunday schools. Thus came the advent of the bus ministry and other methods to increase Sunday school attendance. Third, a movement toward larger church staffs with a more focused ministry developed (i.e., pastor of visitation, pastor of teen ministry, pastor of college ministry, pastor of family ministries). Fourth, increased interest and phenomenal growth of the Christian school movement through the 1970s and early 1980s took place. This renewed interest came as a result of the discontentment with public schooling. Many saw religious and moral influences being removed from public schools and began looking for an alternate education for their children. For some this was found in the Christian school movement. Others turned to home schooling.

Leaders in Christian education. The current era of Christian education has many past and present leaders from both the liberal and evangelical camps of theology. In the past people such as Robert Raikes, William Eliot, John H. Vincent, B. F. Jacobs, D. L. Moody, and Horace Bushnell were active in Sunday school and its growth. More recently Randolph Crump Miller, James D. Smart, Lewis J. Sherrill, D. Campbell Wyckoff, John H. Westerhoff, Lois and Mary LeBar, Lawrence O. Richards, Gene Getz, Kenneth Gangel, and Warren Benson have been involved in the broader scope of Christian education.[18]

Achievements of Christian education. The achievements of recent Christian education are as follows: (1) Christian education expanded from the focus on Sunday school to include other types of children and youth ministries such as clubs, camping, vacation Bible school, and youth meetings. (2) The number and quality of teacher/leader guides expanded. The teacher/leader has also had the opportunity to attend seminars for the development of his skills. (3) The inclusion of Christian education courses in the college curriculum has helped prepare leaders and workers for educational programs in local and parachurch agencies. (4) People have been exposed to Christian teaching through the addition of these developments.

18. For a more complete listing and study of Christian educators see Elmer L. Towns, ed., *A History of Religious Educators*.

FOR FURTHER READING

Cairns, Earle E. *Christianity Through the Centuries*. Revised edition. Grand Rapids: Zondervan, 1981.

Gangel, Kenneth O., and Warren S. Benson. *Christian Education: Its History and Philosophy*. Chicago: Moody, 1983.

Latourette, Kenneth Scott. *A History of Christianity*. Revised edition. 2 vols. New York: Harper & Row, 1975.

Pazmiño, Robert W. *Foundational Issues in Christian Education*. Grand Rapids: Baker, 1988.

Rice, Edwin Wilbur. *The Sunday-School Movement, 1789-1917, and the American Sunday-School Union*. Salem, N.H.: Ayer, 1971.

Slater, Roslie J. *Teaching and Learning America's Christian History: The Principle Approach*. San Francisco: Foundation for American Christian Education, 1965.

	EARLY church	MEDIEVAL church	RENAISSANCE reformation	AMERICAN colonial	CHRISTIAN education in United States
	2nd-4th centuries	5th-14th centuries	15th + 16th centuries	17th + 18th centuries	19th + 20th centuries
Schools	Catechumenal Catechetical	Cathedral University	Parochial University	Common Parochial Tutorial University Sunday school	Parochial Christian schools Christian colleges Universities Seminaries Bible colleges Sunday schools
Writings & translations	Apostolic Creed Nicean Creed	*Summa Theologica* (T. Aquinas)	Calvin's *Institutes* Augsburg Confession	Westminster Confession	New translations and paraphrases
Influences on church	Opposition: Political Philosophical	Monasticism Islam East/West split Crusades	Rationalism Revivalism Pietism Printing Press 95 Theses	John Wesley Roger Williams Puritanism Modernism Missions	Evolution theory Communism Cults Denominationalism Billy Sunday Billy Graham C.E. agencies & publishing houses Fundamentalist-Modernist controversy
Political situation	Constantine	Charlemagne Holy Roman Empire	Charles V Henry VIII Spanish Armada	Congregationalism George Washington Thomas Jefferson	Civil War World War I World War II

4

James C. Wilhoit

Developing a Philosophy

> DEVELOPING A PHILOSOPHY OF CHRISTIAN EDUCATION
> - **Begins with the assumption that form follows function**
> - **Is more concerned with clarity than precision**
> - **Thinks of a philosophy statement as a tool to be used**
> - **Focuses on real life educational issues**

In 1886 Louis Sullivan, a Chicago architect, received a commission to design a new downtown theater and office building. The completion of the Auditorium Theater in 1888 marked a milestone in American architectural design. The exterior of the building showed what Sullivan could do with a large structure, but what caught the attention of both critics and the public alike was the magnificent theater. Its intricate decoration and wonderful acoustics won high praises. Save for some massive arches and intricate stonework the exterior of the building is quite plain and angular. It can be said that Sullivan set out to design a wonderful theater and then built the box to put it in. This rather pragmatic orientation separated him from many architects of his day who strove to build perfect edifices and then had the task of squeezing office space or theaters into them.

The recently refurbished Auditorium Theater stands today as a monument to Louis Sullivan, who believed that a building's form should grow out of its purpose or function. In his writings, this architect-philosopher called for buildings whose "form follows function." He did not believe in a stark mechanistic utility in the

JAMES C. WILHOIT, Ph.D., is associate professor of Christian education at Wheaton College, Wheaton, Illinois.

design of his buildings but an organic relationship between the form and appearance of a building and its purpose. From Sullivan's approach to architecture we can learn an important principle about designing and constructing Christian education programs: in the best Christian ministry form follows function.

FORM FOLLOWS FUNCTION

In Jesus' parable about the new wine in old wineskins we find the New Testament emphasis upon the gospel rather than the form or appearance of ministry. Jesus told this parable in response to the Pharisees' question about why His disciples did not fast publicly like John the Baptist's disciples. Jesus answered that His disciples could not fast while the bridegroom was present. He went on to tell this parable of new wine in old wineskins because He was concerned about the Pharisees' attempt to straitjacket the gospel by confining it in the religious structures (i.e., old wineskins) they knew and controlled. Jesus told the Pharisees that people do not "pour new wine into old wineskins. If they do, the skins will burst, the wine will run out and the wineskins will be ruined. No, they pour new wine into new wineskins, and both are preserved" (Matt. 9:17).

What Jesus underscored with this parable is that wine and wineskins must be distinguished. He separated something essential and primary (the gospel/wine) and something that He perceived as secondary but certainly very necessary and helpful (the ministry structures/wineskins).[1]

Jesus used this parable of the wineskins to remind us that in our ministry we always deal with two substances: the imperishable gospel and secondary human products—ministry programs. Both are absolutely necessary for effective ministry. Without the gospel the best vehicles of ministry become no more than avenues of self-improvement, and without an effective ministry structure that touches the world, the gospel is isolated and unseen.

The emphasis in the New Testament is on the purpose of the church, not on its ministry structures. The biblical writers are far more concerned with the church's doing what it should do than with its carrying out particular programs or ministries.

This emphasis on the purpose of the church requires us to step back and address the question, "Why does the church exist?" At the most basic level we must affirm that the church exists for God. God created the church, calls its members to it, sustains it, loves it, and equips it. The church exists because of God's work for His glory. Ray Ortlund provides us with a useful way of understanding the purpose of the church when he writes about its threefold calling. This threefold division allows one to find a clear home for Christian education. We can understand the purpose of the church as follows:

---

1. See Howard Snyder, *The Problem of Wineskins* (Downers Grove, Ill.: Inter-Varsity, 1975), p. 13.

UP: The church exists to glorify God. "In him we were also chosen . . . in order that we . . . might be for the praise of his glory." Ephesians 1:11-12

IN: The church is called to build up one another in love. "From Christ the whole body, joined together and held together by every supporting ligament, grows and builds itself up in love as each part does its work." Ephesians 4:16

OUT: The church is asked by Christ to reach out to the world. "You will be my witnesses in Jerusalem, and in all Judea and Samaria, and to the ends of the earth." Acts 1:8[2]

The church exists to glorify God, build up one another, and to reach out in love to the world. Christian education is an equipping ministry with the primary task of edifying Christians (an "IN" ministry) and equipping them to worship and honor God and to reach out to the world.

Notice the radical nature of this focus for Christian education. Christian education is not defined in terms of structures (e.g., Sunday school, clubs, small groups) but in terms of its purpose. The Bible gives us great latitude in how we carry out our educational mission, but it demands that we do this for the purpose of building up one another and equipping the church to worship and witness to the world.

THREE ORIENTATIONS

When we look at how the educational ministry of the church is carried out today, we find that in churches across the country there are three general approaches to conducting Christian education.

MAINTENANCE-ORIENTED PROGRAMS

The phrase "If it ain't broke, don't fix it" summarizes the planning behind a maintenance-oriented program. The people responsible for these educational programs assume they basically have good programs. Their task is to make sure the proper personnel and material are in place to keep them running smoothly and enhance their effectiveness. Maintenance orientation is one of the most common approaches to Christian education programming because program maintenance is usually the most immediate task facing lay or professional Christian education staff. Immediate maintenance problems, such as the children's church team needing a new song leader or the junior department being shorted in the curriculum order, demand attention. Although "the tyranny of the urgent" does contribute to this maintenance orientation, many leaders are also victimized by a maintenance preoccupation because of their failure to visualize how ministry could be most effective.

---

2. Raymond C. Ortlund, *Three Priorities for a Strong Church* (Waco, Tex.: Word, 1983), p. 9-11.

These maintenance practitioners listen to student feedback and comments—not with the aim of radically redesigning the program, but with the aim of fine-tuning the program in response to student needs. In this orientation it can be said that function follows form.

STRUCTURE-ORIENTED PROGRAMS

A person directing a structure-oriented Christian education program would be likely to describe an effective Christian education program by saying, "A good Christian education program has small groups at its core," or, "The best junior departments use learning centers." These educators define Christian education in terms of certain structures or programs.

For example, a structure-oriented educator might be convinced that small groups are the best way to teach adults. This person would put great resources into making sure that high-quality small groups be accessible to all the adults in the church. The assumption here is that certain methods and structures almost inevitably bring about the maturation and growth Christian education is seeking to accomplish.

There are educational costs to this structure orientation. For example, twentieth-century American educator and philosopher John Dewey argued that a structure orientation to education had led to some of the worst practices in what he despairingly called "traditional education." Dewey asserted that the common notion that a certain content (e.g., "the great books") or method (e.g., lecturing) that was inevitably educative had led to stagnation in educational innovation and a blind addiction to the status quo. Dewey passionately argued that no one method, even the favorite methods of his progressive followers, was inevitably educative.[3] In terms of the earlier discussion, then, the structure-oriented educators are another example of an orientation in which function follows form.

PURPOSE-ORIENTED PROGRAMS

"I'm trying to make these kids biblically literate. I wonder which programs will do that best?" The purpose-oriented educator is most concerned about accomplishing a goal or purpose, and he experiments with various programs and methods to see which will bring about that goal. The emphasis for this educator is on experimenting with methods and programs to see which will most effectively carry out what is seen as the ultimate purpose. With this orientation to ministry, form follows function.

Notice that in each of these three educational orientations something was held constant, something was seen as an absolute, and something was seen as relative or flexible. For example, in the structure-oriented program, the program or

3. John Dewey, *Experience and Education* (New York: Macmillan, 1938), pp. 17-23.

structure of ministry was seen as absolute (e.g., "We must have a children's church," or, "We can't be a spiritually vital church without a midweek prayer meeting"). The educator committed to having small groups or an age-graded Sunday school sees these programs as an absolute necessity. However, educational outcomes were perceived as an area where one could be far more flexible. In contrast, purpose-oriented educators find themselves committed to a particular goal (e.g., mastering new life skills, learning how to share one's faith, growing in righteousness) and see the method as an area of flexibility. The table below shows where these three orientations differ in terms of what they hold as constant (inflexible area) and where they are willing to experiment (flexible area). As evangelicals we should be wary of approaches that consider the educational goal to lie in the flexible area. Certainly, Jesus and the New Testament writers showed more concern for the goal of ministry than prescribing a *how* for ministry.

Educational Orientation	Flexible Area	Inflexible area	Emphasis
Maintenance	Goal	Status quo/program	Function follows form
Program	Goal	Methods	Function follows form
Purpose	Methods	Goal	Form follows function

Developing a philosophy of ministry does not appeal to everyone working in the area of Christian education. Too often a lack of interest in developing a philosophy is attributed to a person's unwillingness to expend the energy and discipline needed to clarify one's position. Yet many creative and disciplined educators do not take the time to develop a philosophy because they approach ministry from a maintenance orientation or a program orientation.

The person who is purpose oriented is the only one who will have an intrinsic interest in thinking philosophically about ministry. Remember, purpose for the maintenance and structure-oriented persons is quite flexible, but the purpose-oriented educator sees purpose as something given and not relative. However, the purpose-oriented educator is willing to adapt structures and ministry to fit this absolute purpose. Likewise, the purpose-oriented educator is able to give the Bible rather than tradition its proper formative role in shaping the educational ministries of the church.

WHAT A PHILOSOPHY DOES

A philosophy of ministry is a verbal and conceptual tool used to shape and evaluate a ministry. A philosophy of ministry need not be a dry and academic statement largely irrelevant to the day-to-day activities of Christian education. I find it helpful to picture a well written and well conceived philosophy statement in terms of two quite ordinary household items: a "to do" list and a tape measure. The most important thing a philosophy of ministry can do is to remind us that the main thing in ministry is to do the main thing. A "to do" list reminds us of what we want to do and helps us establish our priorities in getting them done.

A philosophy of ministry helps us focus on what Christ said are the main components for teaching and discipling in a church. As we go about teaching in a church, we begin, rightly, to wonder how well we are really doing the main thing, and that is where a philosophy can serve as a tape measure in helping us evaluate what we are about. A philosophy of ministry is not a set of abstract statements filed away to be forgotten. It is a tool designed to be used daily to guide and evaluate an educational ministry.

A PHILOSOPHY PROVIDES DIRECTION

A clear philosophy statement helps a ministry by providing a direction for the ministry as a whole as well as its various components. This direction is seen in a number of tangible ways. For example, a philosophy helps allocate scarce resources. There are many good things that can be done in a church ministry, but the main thing is to remember that we are doing the main thing—glorifying God and making disciples.

A philosophy statement helps one disperse the financial and personnel resources to the most important tasks. A clear focus also gives staff a sense of direction. Much of the perceived problem in contemporary Christian education has its origin in a lack of clear purpose at the classroom and program level. The people that are most directly involved in our educational ministries often have no clear understanding of the goals of their educational endeavors. Such a lack of purpose can devastate the personnel in these educational ministries. Purpose is vitally important for maintaining committed and motivated staff. Today, people volunteer their time in part because they want to take part in something they perceive as significant. When a program flounders and wanders with no discernable direction, people become discouraged and question the value of their efforts.

A clear orientation in a ministry helps insure a proper biblical focus. Educational ministries by their very nature come with a host of activities that must be done, and in the midst of all the flurry it is easy for a Sunday school teacher to focus on the immediate problems and lose sight of why Christ called him to a ministry of teaching and discipleship.

A PHILOSOPHY PROVIDES A MEANS OF EVALUATION

Anything worth doing is worth doing well, and to do something well requires a means of evaluation. Without a philosophy it is difficult to determine whether or not a ministry is working well, that is, accomplishing what it was intended to do. With a well-conceived philosophy in place, a ministry director can then conduct a discrepancy analysis on the program. In a discrepancy analysis one looks at what one is seeking to accomplish (i.e., the goals in one's philosophy statement) and what one is actually accomplishing. This can be done informally by talking to teachers and students, or it may be done more elaborately by external reviewers along with questionnaires and student evaluation forms.

Philosophy and evaluation go hand in hand, but this does not imply that a philosophy needs to be stated in terms of clear behavioral objectives. A useful philosophy may be written in terms that are far more impressionistic but that can be assessed by discerning believers.

WHAT A PHILOSOPHY LOOKS LIKE

In this chapter I am writing about philosophy not simply as a way of exploring and defining important concepts, but also as a tool for achieving clarity and evaluation precision in ministry. Such an applied philosophy has a number of characteristics that are not always present in more abstract philosophy.

The first characteristic of a workable philosophy is clarity. When one views philosophy as a ministry tool then one does not want that tool to be difficult to use. A philosophy that is opaque and poorly conceived does not stand a chance of becoming a significant ministry tool unless someone adds the important dimension of clarity to it. Clarity is a top priority for an applied ministry statement in a church.

A second criterion is that it must be memorable. A philosophy of ministry statement that is multiple pages long and consists of umpteen tedious points will not give the direction needed in an educational ministry. A philosophy of ministry statement needs to give sufficient detail and direction, but never at the expense of being short and memorable. Lois LeBar's book *Education That Is Christian* had a remarkable impact on the field of Christian education because of her clear and memorable statement of her philosophy—Boy, Book, Boy. Those three words summarized her belief of using both the Bible and life experience in an application-oriented Christian education.[4] (See chap. 25, p. 405 for fuller explanation.)

Two churches that have used ministry statements quite effectively have comprehensive ministry statements organized around easily remembered outlines. For example, Willow Creek Community Church in South Barrington, Illinois, summarizes its philosophy of ministry through the "four e's." These are: exaltation, edification, evangelism, and extension. Similarly, Mike Marcey, pastor of Naperville Presbyterian Church, in Naperville, Illinois, effectively summarizes his philosophy of ministry by reminding people to "tune into WFLM," meaning that people are to be involved in Worship, Fellowship, Learning, and Ministry. These four areas provide a good outline for a more comprehensive ministry statement and provide a memorable statement that people can use to guide their ministry decisions.

4. Lois LeBar, *Education That Is Christian,* ed. James E. Plueddeman (Old Tappan, N.J: Revell, 1958), p. 88.

The third criterion for an effective philosophy is that it needs to be something that sets priorities. Ministry takes place in a world of limited resources, and one is constantly finding that choices need to be made. An effective statement spells out the key priorities for a Christian education program. In a useful ministry statement, the "so what" implications of the philosophy are evident. This philosophy of ministry statement speaks about the concrete world of ministry through the abstract. It does not leave the reader simply with an abstract treatment of themes and issues in ministry but suggests how these should be accomplished.

THE ISSUES A PHILOSOPHY MUST ADDRESS

A philosophy of ministry needs to provide people with answers to the questions that frequently come up in their day-to-day work of teaching and discipling. It does little good to send people out with a map for a country they are not traveling through. A philosophy that does not address the pressing issues will be quickly set aside. In addition to the characteristics named above, it must deal with the important tensions and decision points of a ministry.

At minimum, a philosophy statement needs to deal with the four everyday tensions found in many North American Christian education ministries, and it should handle the major questions that are raised by the journalist's checklist.

FOUR TENSIONS

First, does the statement deal with the nurture versus evangelism tension? In Christian education programs for children there will be a tension between the extent to which the program should focus on nurturing children or should focus on evangelism. This tension will be felt at staff and planning meetings as teachers talk about the need to prepare the children for the future and to be discerning in regard to aspects of youth culture and media that do not support their faith. And there will be those teachers, on the other hand, who will talk about the need to have the teaching focus primarily on presenting the gospel. If the tension is allowed to go unresolved, oftentimes ministries will bounce between the two poles or will allow themselves to define Christian education exclusively in terms of either nurture or evangelism.

A second tension is often found in adult small-group ministries—the tension between instruction and fellowship. Particularly in suburban areas where adults perceive themselves under stress and in need of Christian support, there will be a pull toward allowing educational sessions to focus almost exclusively on fellowship and support. At the same time there will be people—both participants and leaders—who consider instruction to be crucially important.

The fellowship versus instruction tension can be found in many church programs. Often the either/or answer that comes down squarely favoring one side of the tension or the other does not promote the best Christian education. The felt need for support and fellowship is real, but often the best support comes from a group that is being reminded, through the ministry of teaching, about who we are as Christians.

Third, many educational programs—particularly in those aimed at youth—discover themselves caught in a bind. Should they be primarily need-oriented or content-oriented? Again, programs that are not clearly directed in this area will often find tensions between staff members and will find that the various materials they use in their ministry pull them in one direction or the other, depriving them of a lack of clear overall focus.

Fourth, one devastating problem in contemporary Christian education is the failure to be appropriately multidimensional. In other words, our Christian education often fails to educate the whole person because it only uses one channel. In part, we inherit this problem from our secular education that has become increasingly one dimensional—more focused on knowledge than on character.

The resources available for the task of human transformation are splendid. A philosophy statement should encourage teachers to take advantage of the myriad of spiritual tools available. Some Sunday school teachers resemble carpenters working on job sites with only hammers and yet who carry loaded tool boxes to work every day. Many teachers could easily enrich their teaching, but they have never learned of all the teaching tools readily at hand. A wholistic Christian education program should include three dimensions: informing, conforming, and transforming. Generally our programs are strongest at informing and weakest at transforming, but all three need to be present.

Dimension	Direction	Method	Outcome
Informing	Outside in	Teaching group and individual study, reading, ministry preparation	Knowledge
Conforming	Outside in	Modeling, accountable relationships, discipling, socialization	Practice
Transforming	Inside out	Support groups, worship and praise, spiritual disciplines, prayer, public people helping, personal reflection, counseling	Change

A philosophy statement should encourage teachers to use all the resources that God has given. The mission of human transformation cannot be accomplished when we limit our armament from the start to one-third of the available equipment.

JOURNALIST'S CHECKLIST

The writer of a philosophy statement should consider employing the so-called journalist's checklist. Ask yourself if you have covered the following areas.

1. Who? Have I defined the audience for Christian education? Who should teach? What are the characteristics of an effective teacher?
2. What? What is your method? What are the nonnegotiables in terms of teaching methods?
3. When? When does Christian education take place? Is Christian education limited only to Sunday morning programs, or is it something that should take place throughout one's life? If it takes place throughout one's life, how do you encourage that? When in a person's life cycle and/or spiritual development are certain issues best raised?
4. Where? Where does Christian education take place? Where does the Christian stand in terms of the dominant culture? Does a Christian stand in opposition to the culture?
5. Why? Have I clearly stated the ultimate purpose of Christian education?

COMPONENTS FOR A PHILOSOPHY STATEMENT

What components should be included in a philosophy statement? Though differences of opinion may exist as to what is most significant, several items should be considered. As each component is identified, some basic questions should be asked to analyze and evaluate what is being done. What terms need to be defined? Why is the component significant? What is the biblical basis for the component? How can the component be applied and/or used effectively?

1. The nature of God, that we are created in His image and we need to know Him personally
2. The state of human nature and our need for salvation
3. The nature of the church, its place in God's plan, and its functions as the Body of Christ
4. The Bible, the written Word of God and how God intended for it to be used
5. The Lord Jesus Christ, as the Living Word, the Master Teacher, and our relationship to Him personally
6. The ministry of the Holy Spirit in the lives of believers and in the teaching-learning process
7. The place of prayer in our personal lives and in the teaching-learning situation
8. The teaching-learning process and how it can be used effectively in the lives of learners
9. The nature of Christian formation; What fosters Christian maturation? The relationship of the spiritual disciplines of prayer, fasting, service and adoration to Christian maturation

10. The significance of goals and objectives in teaching and learning
11. The roles of teachers and students in teaching and learning
12. The significance of the learning environment in teaching and learning
13. The relationship between authority and creativity
14. The place of curriculum in our philosophy
15. The selection and use of methods and materials in the teaching-learning process
16. The significance of individuals and groups in the teaching-learning process
17. The place of evaluation in teaching and learning

It is imperative that the questions be researched and our philosophy thought through carefully to provide a basis for what we believe and a rationale for what we do. Several of the above items have been developed more fully in various chapters of this book. A well-written summary of significant ideas will be a rewarding experience and will provide more clear direction for ministry.

WRITING A PHILOSOPHY STATEMENT

When a good philosophy statement has been hammered out one inevitably wonders what was most valuable: the process of writing it or the end product? The process of formulating a philosophy statement gives a leadership team the opportunity to wrestle with some crucial questions and reach a consensus. The writing process takes time and will not be completed in a single planning meeting. What most matters in the development process is that the philosophy statement is owned by the ministry team. Seldom is it practical for all members to have a part in writing it, but the team members need to have the chance to study the finished statement in order to identify with it and come to value it.

A WORD OF WARNING

THE PROBLEM OF THE CODEPENDENT CHURCH

A passion that fuels this chapter is that our churches be known as healthy and God-honoring churches. Here a brief warning must be issued because a fully developed philosophy of ministry statement can be used to foster the tragic notion that skillful ministry—rather than God-derived change—could transform a person. We describe this situation using the psychological term *codependency*. In the past few years we have talked with those who were struggling with an issue they had learned to call codependency. The term is new, and the concept old, but there is a certain power in the term itself. It refers to those people who have had a significant relationship with a "dependent person" (e.g., alcoholic, drug abuser) and have adopted the codependent role of excuse-giver, rescuer, or scapegoat. As the theory goes, sometimes the codependent person actually becomes a great obstacle for the dependent person.

There are some churches driven by philosophies of ministry that become a codependent. Their philosophies of ministry emphasize empathy and compassion but do not give equal attention to accountability or "speaking the truth in love." Such churches rush too quickly to cover up pain so that people miss the message "Is change needed here?" These ministries too often offer "support" in ways that tell a person it's okay when it really isn't. These churches' unwillingness to admit the reality and persistence of human pain (which embarrasses our glib assumptions about the Christian life) and the immense cost of change often makes them an unwitting codependent.

This philosophy of ministry seems to grow out of a secret admiration for the solitary therapist who deliberately and professionally works to affect the healing of a damaged psyche. The tragedy is that under such influence, church teachers carry the image of the lone psychologist plying his trade. This is where such philosophies go astray. What do we have to offer people as teachers? Our greatest resource for healing and change is the church, the Body of Christ. It is in this fold where the healing takes place. We must be wary of allowing a philosophy of ministry statement to overly exalt the modern-day notion of the supremacy of the competent professional, rather than the biblical notion of the Body of Christ building up one another as our gifts are used for the common good.

THE DANGER OF ARROGANCE

There is the potential for arrogance that can come with the well-developed philosophy of ministry statement. I can remember a board member of a well-run suburban church being confronted by a housing activist. The activist asked why this church had done nothing to provide for the poor people of the community. The board member of the church listened politely but then said in essence: We have a well-developed philosophy of ministry. Our philosophy of ministry does not call for housing ministries. If we became involved in housing ministries, it would dilute our resources.

That board member was using the philosophy of ministry statement to do exactly what a good philosophy of ministry statement should do, but love was missing. Paul warned the Corinthians that knowledge can puff up, but love edifies. And there is a danger that a philosophy of ministry statement can give one a kind of arrogance and a sense of accomplishing more than is actually being done.

There is an old slogan prominent in the European Reformed tradition that almost always appears in Latin: *Ecclesia reformata semper reformanda*, which translates as "the church reformed and always to be reformed."[5] This was the gist of the Reformation. The church had been reformed by a renewed emphasis on the Word of God, and the church had always to be reformed by an emphasis on

5. Edward A. Dowey, "Always to Be Reformed," in *Always Being Reformed*, ed. John Purdy (Philadelphia: Geneva Press, 1985), pp. 9-10.

God's Word. A philosophy of ministry should not be an instrument that brings about "hardening of the categories." A philosophy of ministry should be an instrument that is wrought through careful study of the Word of God and is always reformed by continual study of the Word of God.

FOR FURTHER READING

Byrne, H. W. *A Christian Approach to Education*. Grand Rapid.: Baker, 1986.

Gaebelein, Frank E. *The Pattern of God's Truth*. Chicago: Moody, 1968.

Gangel, Kenneth O., and Warren S. Benson. *Christian Education: Its History and Philosophy*. Chicago: Moody, 1983.

Joy, Donald M. *Meaningful Learning in the Church*. Winona Lake, Ind.: Light and Life, 1969.

LeBar, Lois E. *Education That Is Christian*. Edited by James E. Plueddemann. Wheaton, Ill.: Victor, 1989.

Pazmiño, Robert W. *Foundational Issues in Christian Education*. Grand Rapids: Baker, 1988.

Peterson, Michael L. *Philosophy of Education: Issues and Options*. Downers Grove, Ill.: InterVarsity, 1986.

Richards, Lawrence O. *Christian Education: Seeking to Become Like Jesus Christ*. Grand Rapids: Zondervan, 1988.

Wilhoit, Jim. *Christian Education and the Search for Meaning*. Grand Rapids: Baker, 1986.

Wolterstorff, Nicholas. *Education for Responsible Action*. Grand Rapids: Eerdmans, 1980.

5

Wesley R. Willis

Trends: Waves of the Future

FUNCTIONS OF EFFECTIVE CHURCH LEADERS
- **Recognize key trends that are taking place in society**
- **Identify specific needs that should be addressed by the church**
- **Plan and implement ministries that will speak to people's needs effectively**
- **Evaluate the results of ministry using biblical standards**

One of the more difficult New Testament parables to interpret is the parable of the unjust manager. This parable is particularly difficult for evangelicals since, at first glance, it seems that Jesus commended a person for questionable business ethics.

In this parable, recorded in Luke 16:1-8, Jesus explains that a certain rich man had an employee responsible for managing his estate. (Apparently the problem of finding high quality financial advisors and managers did not originate with our generation.) The manager in Jesus' parable had not done an acceptable job, but his inadequacy seems to be more a question of judgment or strategy rather than ethics or morality. Because of the manager's failure, the rich man informed his employee that he was about to lose his position.

Naturally this concerned the manager, so he called in two major debtors and wrote down their debts. The one who owed a hundred measures of oil had his debt reduced to fifty measures. Likewise, the one who owed a hundred measures of wheat had his debt rewritten to eighty. The manager reasoned that when he lost

WESLEY R. WILLIS, Ed.D., formerly vice-president of strategic planning at Scripture Press Publications, is now dean of education at Philadelphia College of Bible, Langhorne, Pennsylvania.

his job, there would be at least two others who would feel positive toward him and perhaps take him in. Apparently the manager had sufficient authority to make such decisions because his employer did not mention the legitimacy of his actions. Indeed, the rich man commended the manager for his shrewd foresight in preparing for his uncertain future.

According to *The Bible Knowledge Commentary,*[1] Jesus' commentary, which follows the parable in the biblical text, suggests three applications. The first application is that the use of money to achieve goals is appropriate (v. 9). The second application is that being trustworthy in physical resources is a prerequisite to being entrusted with eternal resources (vv. 10-12). And the third application is that only one entity can occupy the primary position in a believer's value system (v. 13). If money is number one, then God cannot be first. Conversely, we can conclude that when God is first, then other resources can be used appropriately. These applications made by Jesus suggest a threefold approach to the future for those involved in ministry today.

First, physical resources are means to achieving our goals. Church and parachurch ministries should take Jesus' teaching to heart, and individuals would be wise to heed the admonition also. We should freely use our available resources to accomplish our goals. But this must be done wisely, not carelessly or haphazardly.

Second, if we are not faithful in the use of our physical resources, we hardly can expect to be entrusted with spiritual resources. Some church and parachurch ministries appear to be irresponsible in financial management. A church of fewer than a thousand members is often a multi-million-dollar corporation, and yet finances may well be handled by a volunteer lay person with little or no financial training. Inadequate records, no financial controls, and careless spending characterize more ministries than we might expect.

Third, money—as any other physical resource—is a servant, not the master. Ministries cannot exist primarily to build financial or physical kingdoms. Ministry scandals in the 1980s revealed some of the shameful excesses that characterized ministries where serving mammon replaced serving God as the primary objective.

It is unfortunate, but few ministries do any systematic planning with allocation of resources (both physical and human) based on clearly identified goals. Perhaps a major element in this failure is that few leaders take time to analyze carefully the needs of those to whom they have been called to minister. And this must include more than merely identifying present needs. Effective leaders must consider those needs that will be encountered in coming years, and then prepare themselves and their ministries to address those needs. If churches took time to make such analyses and then designed appropriate programs, we might see more innovative and effective ministries. But often churches seem more concerned with replicating the past than planning for the future.

1. John F. Walvoord and Roy B. Zuck, eds., *The Bible Knowledge Commentary*, 2 vols. (Wheaton, Ill.: Victor, 1983, 1985) 2: 246.

Recently an elderly church member took me aside and complained about certain programmatic elements in his church. His main contention seemed to be that these activities were different from those in the past. He concluded that the church was trying to get as close to the world as possible rather than remaining separate and pure. He could not understand that the church was targeting a specific unreached group in the community and had wisely planned activities attractive to that segment. The activities were just as biblically acceptable as those appreciated by the elderly believer. But they were different. And because they were different he rejected them. Was he wrong? Not necessarily. Perhaps church leaders had failed to bring this man and others along with them as they looked toward the future and planned programs to achieve ministry goals. But whether this believer understood and agreed with the direction or not, his church leaders had acted wisely in designing programs to meet their specific ministry objectives.

The need to understand trends and to adapt activities in light of those trends is not new. First Chronicles 11:10–12:47 records a list of those who helped David in his accession to the throne. In a sense this could be described as David's Hall of Fame. Both individuals and groups of persons are listed in this honor roll. In some cases, particular individuals or groups have been singled out and lauded for unique contributions. Among those listed, one group has been given this special recognition: "And of the sons of Issachar, men who understood the times, with knowledge of what Israel should do, their chiefs were two hundred; and all their kinsmen were at their command" (1 Chron. 12:32).

Apparently the sons of Issachar divided into two groups. One group included two hundred chiefs (or leaders) who possessed extraordinary insight. But their insight extended far beyond ordinary intelligence. Rather their fingers were on the pulse of the times. And not only were these two hundred chiefs able to discern trends, but they were able to ascertain an appropriate course of action. These leaders were tuned into reality. They recognized circumstances and trends, and they understood the implications for Israel as David and others were trying to determine an appropriate course of action.

The other group consisted of those who followed the leadership of the two hundred chiefs. The sons of Issachar included many followers who recognized insightful leaders and looked to them for guidance. Evangelical ministries—churches as well as parachurch organizations—are crying desperately for leaders who understand the times. We need leaders who have insight into conditions and trends and who possess the wisdom to give timely, appropriate direction to followers.

KEY TRENDS INFLUENCING MINISTRY

Allegedly a Chinese proverb affirms, "It is very difficult to prophesy, especially in regard to the future." Christians understand that God alone knows the future. And yet Christian leaders must plan ministries that will address the needs of people, both now and in the future. Most of us recognize the importance of planning for the future and realize just how demanding such a task is.

Rather than trying to predict specific future events, we should work at recognizing and understanding trends. As we recognize a trend, we can identify resultant needs in society and potential opportunities for ministry. Consider the following trends and see how many of them suggest potential ministry emphases for leaders looking toward the future.

GROWING AWARENESS OF SPIRITUAL NEED

For many years Americans have placed their faith in the twin gods of science and technology. Somehow we have believed we would learn all that is necessary through a systematic application of the scientific methods. And once we knew everything, we would combine that knowledge with our technical expertise to create the ideal society.

How disillusioned we have become. We finally are recognizing that lack of knowledge is a relatively minor problem. A far greater problem is the perverse human propensity to use knowledge inappropriately. Education does not change basic human character. And technology not only helps us to solve some problems, but it also creates new ones. Whether it's the side-effects of miracle drugs or environmental danger from newly discovered processes and their by-products, the problems often occur after the fact. DDT, PCBs, and chlorofluorocarbons all were received as great benefits to humanity. It was not until years later that the near extinction of eagles, the pollution of lakes, and the destruction of the ozone layer began to be understood. In spite of our education, technology, and sophistication, we have become keenly aware of inadequate answers to key problems. And churches must minister to twenty-first century persons who know so much but have few answers. Kenneth O. Gangel described this task as "ministering to *older*, more *highly educated*, increasingly *secular*, and technologically *sophisticated* congregations; who live in a society threatened by drugs, cults and violence; and in a world threatened by war, starvation and nuclear holocaust."[2]

Consequently, people are looking beyond science and technology for answers. And those answers must be spiritual in nature. Unfortunately, this does not mean that people are turning to biblical Christianity. Indeed, counterfeit spirituality is a far more commonly embraced alternative. The so-called New Age movement and other forms of counterfeit spirituality are growing at astounding rates. Regardless of the current name or specific form, the basis of counterfeit religion began in the Garden of Eden, achieved unprecedented success after the Tower of Babel and on through Babylon, and appears today in astrology, New Age, and other cults. Trends analyst John Naisbitt has documented the decline in mainline denominations but has concluded that this does not signal disinterest in spiritual concerns. His observation that 10 to 15 percent of Americans are actively involved in New

---

2. Kenneth O. Gangel, "The Church Faces the 21st Century," in *Christian Education Today* 38: 4 (Fall 1986): 8.

Age practices supports such a conclusion.[3] And this situation is not unique to the United States. The report of one Canadian study indicates that whereas only 4 percent of Canadians read the Bible daily, 13 percent read their horoscope daily. In the same study, 45 percent of Canadian young people claim to have had personal contact with the spirit world.[4]

Interest in the metaphysical, para-psychology, and the occult are clear indications of people seeking spiritual answers. Occult practices (including the worship of Satan) are presented to youth by many who exert great influence, including musicians and entertainers. And the siren calls of extrasensory insight, power, and rejection of tradition add to the appeal of counterfeit spiritual answers. Clinton Arnold states,

> From the Night Stalker slayings of Richard Ramirez to the drug-cult murders in Matamoros, Mexico, satanism is gaining increasing publicity for its frequent tie to ritual killings. Police officers throughout the country are now receiving training in identifying crimes related to the occult.[5]

Regardless of the name it goes by, counterfeit spirituality still is a lie. But unfortunately when people seek spiritual answers, a counterfeit may be more appealing than the truth.

ALTERNATIVE EMPHASES IN CHURCH PROGRAMMING

Until recent years the programs of evangelical churches shared common elements—Sunday morning worship service, Sunday school, youth fellowship meetings, Sunday evening service, and Wednesday prayer service. But times have changed. No longer do many churches view Sunday school as the primary educational agency. And there is a low level of commitment to staying with traditional programs and making them work. In fact, some church leaders give the impression that if a church has done something in the past, then that suggests a good reason to change it. Although there are many factors contributing to the change in church programming, we will consider only several here.

Changing demographics in our churches will affect both attendance and programming in the coming years. Presently a diagram reflecting the age distribution of church membership would look like an inverted pyramid. The older ages have a large representation, while the percentages decline down to children. This will not change significantly in coming years. More and more of our programming will be aimed at older attenders. As Baby Boomers face child-rearing, some of them are returning to church, recognizing their need for assistance. But until the Baby Boomlet (the increase in births as child-bearing rates of Baby Boomers

3. John Naisbitt and Patricia Aburdene, *Megatrends 2000* (New York: William Morrow, 1990), p. 280.
4. Arnell Motz, ed., *Reclaiming a Nation* (Richmond, B.C.: Church Leadership Library, 1990), p. 29.
5. Clinton E. Arnold, "Giving the Devil His Due," in *Christianity Today* 34: 11 (20 August 1990): 17.

surged) that began in the late 1980s moves through childhood and youth, we probably will not see dramatic increases in the number of children and youth attending our churches.

Another major factor in changing programs is the shift from emphasizing content to stressing relational dimensions. Small groups provide a context in which believers can share and interact with each other. Unfortunately, often such sharing/caring groups spend little time in actual study of the Word, or in seriously discussing it. Rather much of the "Bible study" consists of reading a verse and then encouraging each participant to share what it means to him or her.

Also, social value seems to have eclipsed learning in many educational programs. It's not at all uncommon for a parent to pick up a child after Sunday school and ask if that child had a good time. The question rarely is, "Did you learn something today?" or, "What was today's lesson about?" Rather the focus is on enjoying the class and having a good time.

The relational agenda in religious education is not limited to children. In one survey of adult Sunday school attenders, the adults were asked why they participated in the particular program. The most common reason given was social involvement. The relational dimension may be perceived as more valuable and significant than the content learned in class. Consequently, class activities are planned to reflect the needs and desires of class members. Perhaps these dynamics contribute to the next trend to be considered.

INCREASED SPIRITUAL ILLITERACY

In two decades, from the late sixties to the late eighties, religious education declined dramatically. Comparing statistics from the *Yearbook of American and Canadian Churches,*[6] from 1971 to 1988 reported Sunday school attendance dropped from forty million to twenty-six million. And there is no reason to believe this trend has bottomed out.

The conclusion of one survey was that in just a twenty-year period, there was a 50 percent drop in the percentage of adults who claim to have received any religious instruction as children. Consequently more and more adults are unable to articulate any meaningful religious beliefs of their own, let alone give religious instruction to their children. In congregation after congregation parents claim to be unable to instruct their children in Bible truths or to provide good answers to spiritual questions.

Such ignorance is rampant in America. Although we claim to be religious, little of our belief translates into practice. Perhaps much alleged belief is rooted in tradition or folklore rather than in knowledge of Bible truth. Indeed, most analysts of our contemporary culture conclude that we cannot even be considered a Christian nation. According to the Gallup organization, by the late 1980s 96 percent of Americans claimed to be religious, indicating that "religion is either 'very'

6. C. H. Jacquet, ed., *Yearbook of American and Canadian Churches* (Nashville: Abingdon, 1971-88).

or 'fairly important' in their lives."[7] But Gallup also estimated that fewer than 10 percent were committed, as evidenced by their practices.

George Gallup described what he called "the central weakness of Christianity in this country today: There is not a sturdiness of belief. There is a lack of knowledge of Christianity, a lack of awareness of Christian doctrines of atonement, redemption, and grace."[8] And we are not reaching out to evangelize non-Christians either. George Barna reported that since 1980 "the proportion of born-again Christians has remained constant (32 percent) despite the fact that churches and parachurch organizations have spent several billion dollars on evangelism."[9]

Although approximately 40 percent of Americans attend church, it seems to make little difference in the way they live. Gallup reported "you really don't find much difference between the churched and the unchurched in terms of cheating, tax evasion, and pilferage."[10] In contrast, he reported that some Christians live significantly different lives. "The ten percent of committed Christians wield a disproportionate influence in society because of the quality Christian lives they live."[11]

Perhaps the most sobering fact of all is that there seems to be no evidence of *improvement* among Christians. George Barna wrote, "Also be aware that levels of biblical literacy and involvement are on a slow but steady decline."[12] Many feel that the spectator mentality is increasing, with fewer and fewer attending Sunday school or any other systematic instruction. Unless something causes dramatic intervention, spiritual illiteracy shows every possibility of thriving past the turn of the century.

CHANGING ROLES AND FAMILY PATTERNS

Because the family is the foundation of society, changing patterns within the family have repercussions in society at large. Generally there is a fairly low level of commitment to family obligations. Although most people still agree that stable families are important, marriage commitment continues to be less important to many than personal satisfaction. Consequently, if a person feels unfulfilled in marriage, he often feels justified in seeking relationships outside of that marriage. Extramarital affairs, separation, abandonment, and divorce are all common. In some parts of the country the divorce rate regularly exceeds the marriage rate. A clear statement of an ethic that has rejected biblical fidelity and morality was written by Tamar Jacoby in *Lears* magazine. "Far fewer of us live in nuclear

7. George Gallup, Jr., speech given at Religion in American Life luncheon, Princeton Club, New York City, June 9, 1988.
8. Timothy K. Jones, "Tracking America's Soul" (interview with pollster George Gallup), in *Christianity Today* 33: 17 (17 November 1989): 24.
9. George Barna, *Marketing the Church* (Colorado Springs: NavPress, 1988), pp. 21-22.
10. Jones, p. 24.
11. Ibid., pp. 24-25.
12. Barna, p. 23.

families. Lots of us live with lovers we are not married to—whether of the same or opposite sex."[13]

One fallout of unstable marriages is children growing up in single-parent families or as members of multiple or blended families. The question of "Which children are mine, which are yours, and which are ours?" continues to confound family relationships. The appalling number of single-parent families who live below the poverty level continues unabated. Because of unstable or ruptured families, countless children struggle with identity problems. And many of these children somehow feel guilty because they assume they may have been the cause of such disruption. The longings and struggles of young people are reflected in a 1989 Gallup phone survey taking a cross-section of five hundred thirteen- to seventeen-year-old teens. When asked what values they considered very important, 89 percent responded that the most important value to them was "a good family life."

As one can imagine, changing roles in society add to the complexity of relational patterns. Women's roles in society continue to evolve, with significant changes taking place. In many arenas women are breaking out of the boundaries imposed by stereotypes. They are assuming increased positions of leadership in business and industry. Women often become the new entrepreneurs when they cannot find satisfactory positions in the work force. And women are moving into traditional male professions increasingly. At the same time, there is often negative reaction or backlash from those who may feel threatened by such changes or who prefer the old patterns. One of the great issues confronting the evangelical church is the role of women in leadership. The struggle to integrate biblical principles with society's agenda will accelerate in coming years.

INCREASED STRESS AND PRESSURE

Even as Americans work the shortest work week in the history of the country, and as there is a greater variety of leisure activities available, the pace of life seems to be accelerating. Someone has observed that although his leisure time allegedly has increased, other people must have it all because neither he nor his friends have any. Paradoxically, as our leisure time increases, stress, pressure, and demands on that time increase at an even faster rate.

One great contributor to stress is the two-income family. As women have moved back into the work force, they have found that the pressure of working a full day outside the home at the same time trying to maintain the homemaker role places incredible demands on one's energy. It is true that as wives have reentered the work force most husbands have increased their share of home responsibilities. But study after study indicates that women still carry the bulk of the load at home. Even where husband and wife claim to share home chores equally, the woman's "equal half" invariably is greater than the man's. Sociologist Robert Bellah quoted

13. Tamar Jacoby, "Families," in *Lears* 3: 2 (April 1990): 69.

pediatricians Benjamin Spock and T. Barry Brazelton as affirming that "for the sake of the children, the combined working hours of husband and wife should be no more than 12 hours a day. That means that if wives are also going to be at work, we need to think about how husbands can take up some of the slack and contribute more in child-care, in shopping, in all the things that make a family go."[14] The problem is compounded when we recognize that women are moving into higher-level positions, with increased responsibilities, in business and industry. And these higher-level positions ordinarily are more stressful, especially when women are competing for a limited number of management jobs.

A second significant stress-producing factor is the phenomenon of the single-parent family. In addition to all of the normal stresses and pressure that dual parents face, the single parent is called upon to handle them alone—to shoulder full responsibility for wage-earning, homemaking, and parenting with little or no assistance. Serving as both mother and father is demanding and exhausting, and it places incredible stress upon the single parent.

Another factor contributing to stress is the value system of our society. External appearances are considered very important. While we may not worry too much about what is under the surface, it is extremely important to give the right impressions. This means wearing clothing with the proper labels, driving the appropriate car, vacationing in the right places, and generally projecting the correct image. But this requires money—money that may not be readily available when there is a single wage earner. Thus both parents work to earn money so the family can look right. Bellah observed that "it is no longer possible for most families in America, in either the middle class or the working class, to make it on one salary."[15] And singles take second jobs to support the lifestyle they think others will appreciate.

And even as stress and pressure have been increasing, people have tended to isolate themselves. Extended families are less often available to give support and encouragement. Many apartment dwellers live in rigid isolation, barely greeting neighbors when they are unfortunate enough to meet each other in the hallways coming or going. Demands of career and homemaking, or the second job, further separate and isolate. As people move from rural to urban areas, or from suburban locations to cities, their ties are cut, but rarely re-formed as strongly after the move. And as people work frantically to cram recreation time into an already full schedule, those people often feel they have reached the breaking point. Stress and pressure increase and there seems to be no way out.

CONSUMERISM IN THE CHURCH

The Baby Boom generation (those born between 1946 and 1964) will be assuming increased leadership in the local church as they move into middle age. And as

14. Rodney Clapp, "Habits of the Hearth" (an interview with Robert Bellah), in *Christianity Today* 33: 2 (February 1989): 24.
15. Ibid., p. 23.

they give leadership, their values, attitudes, and lifestyles will influence ministry. James Mathisen observes,

> In the areas of values and spiritual commitment, we as religious professionals and churchpersons have felt keenly the effects of Baby Boomers. . . . Their casual approach to life was mirrored in their music, speaking, and worship styles within our churches. For many of us it was a struggle, but now we realize how profoundly the institutional church was affected.[16]

Unfortunately most churches in this country are not ministering effectively to Baby Boomers. Hans Finzel observes, "The majority of baby boomers have not been reached by any church. A poll by *People* magazine showed that baby boomers are half as likely to be in church on Sunday as the older generations."[17] But this should not be taken as an indication that this vast segment of our population is unreachable. Finzel continues, "Although many baby boomers are not attending church now, a recent Gallup poll says that fifty-four percent of the unchurched baby boomers are open to becoming involved in a church."[18]

Applying techniques of consumer marketing, selected church leaders across the country have tailored their ministries to reach the Baby Boomers. Bill Hybels, pastor of Willow Creek Community Church in South Barrington, Illinois (a leader in innovative ministry), describes his approach as, "Ask consumers what they want, then let them (as they say at Burger King) have it their way."[19] Some have criticized this approach as pop gospel and fast-food theology. But Hybels explains that his message is rock-solid biblical principles; only the medium is unorthodox.[20] In light of the trends toward lower involvement, increased biblical illiteracy, and secularization, pastors such as Bill Hybels have determined to design ministry based on the desires and needs of those to whom they are ministering—a technique that Barna describes as "Marketing the Church." After lengthy analysis Barna explained, "My contention, based on careful study of data and the activities of American churches, is that the major problem plaguing the Church is its failure to embrace a marketing orientation in what has become a marketing-driven environment."[21]

Just what are some of the characteristics of a church ministering effectively in a marketing-driven environment? It is important to recognize that church consumers want quality. And they are willing to pay for that quality. But quality must be defined as the church attenders define it. To such consumers, relevant ministries that meet their needs (as they define them) are imperative. If church

16. James A. Mathisen, "Who Are the Baby Boomers?" in *Christian Education Journal* 11: 1 (Autumn 1990): 21-22.
17. Hans Finzel, *Help! I'm a Baby Boomer* (Wheaton, Ill.: Victor, 1989), p. 28.
18. Ibid., p. 29.
19. Cindy Lafavre Yorks, "McChurch," in *USA Weekend*, April 13-15, 1990, p. 4.
20. Ibid., p. 4.
21. Barna, p. 23.

programs are perceived as irrelevant, the consumers will not "buy" these programs. And as they seek relevant ministries, there is every probability that loyalty to a specific church or denomination will decline. Rather, attenders (not members) will participate in a variety of churches depending on which ones meet their needs. Perhaps they will attend one church for worship, have their children attend age-level programs at another, belong to an eclectic small group in another context, and visit around whenever a special music program or speaker catches their fancy on a given week.

In all of this, truly biblical churches will minister effectively to the needs of those in their communities. And part of this effective ministry will include an increased emphasis on the biblical mandate to reach out to the lost and equip believers for ministry. But this is more than trick programming or novelty. According to Barna, "Perhaps the single most important marketing lesson Jesus taught was that marketing is not a one-time event, but a lifestyle. Read the synoptic gospels and marvel at His commitment to ministry."[22] Barna continues, "Paul wrote that we are to be ambassadors of Christ. In contemporary language, I interpret this to say that you and I are to be marketing agents of the church, spreading the good news through all available means and helping build the local church through our marketing efforts."[23]

CHURCH RESPONSE TO TRENDS

Leaders of evangelical ministries need not concern themselves with whether they like these trends or not. And any attempt at determining if these trends will help or hinder the growth of Christianity would have to conclude the result will be mixed. Some of the trends are positive and will facilitate ministry. Others will complicate life and make effective ministry far more difficult. But whether ministry is enhanced or becomes harder, we still have Christ's mandate to "go therefore and make disciples of all the nations" (Matt. 28:19). But how will we do this? And what are the resources at our disposal?

Perhaps the second question is easier to answer. We have the promised resource of Jesus Christ Himself. "And lo, I am with you always, even to the end of the age" (Matt. 28:20). And we have the further resource of His Holy Spirit. "And I will ask the Father, and He will give you another Helper, that He may be with you forever; that is the Spirit of truth, whom the world cannot receive, because it does not behold Him or know Him, but you know Him because He abides with you, and will be in you" (John 14:16-17).

But the fact that we have a mandate from Jesus Christ and also the spiritual resources to carry out that mandate does not absolve us from responsibility. Rather our obligation is even greater. We have received our assignment, and we have been promised resources; but the methods are up to us. And as spiritual

22. Ibid., p. 150.
23. Ibid., p. 150-51.

leaders, effective ministry may well be determined by the faithfulness with which we serve. Consider some key emphases that we should recognize in coming years.

MINISTER TO CONTEMPORARY PERSONS

The methods that were effective in one generation may not be equally effective in the next. At any point in our ministry we live in a unique cultural context. And ministry in this cultural context needs to be just as individual as the people who live in that context with their own views of life and reality. Perhaps the preponderance of older church attenders is a reflection of the church's failure to speak to people who are younger than most of our church leaders.

Hans Finzel clearly expressed the need to minister to the Baby Boom generation. We must understand what makes them tick.

> But we really only *start* there. Understanding must lead to action. We must *impact the biggest generation American has ever seen.* We will have to use different methods and different approaches—even a new language—because each generation has its own set of values and perspectives, like a new culture in a foreign land.[24]

ADDRESS REAL NEEDS

It always has been true that effective ministry speaks to the needs of persons receiving that ministry. Programs that were effective in meeting one set of needs may be ineffective when the needs change. For example, when Sunday evening was a "dead time" during the week, the Sunday evening evangelistic service may have been very effective. But that is not how most people have come to view Sunday evening. Church leaders who continue traditional Sunday evening services often find that only the hard-core committed Christians attend, with Sunday morning worship running anywhere from four to ten times the attendance of the evening. The real issue of programming has little to do with when we schedule programs and what we call them. What really matters is that leaders plan effective programs designed to meet the needs of those to whom they are called.

EMPHASIZE TEACHING BIBLE TRUTH

Biblical Christianity demands a literate constituency. Jesus Christ told His followers, "If you abide in My word, then you are truly disciples of Mine; and you shall know the truth, and the truth shall make you free" (John 8:31-32). Biblically illiterate Christians are weak Christians. And they are prone to fall prey to every whim of doctrine and false teaching that sounds good. A solid grounding in Bible and theology is the best preventative against false teaching.

But biblical knowledge must be more than propositional truth. Obviously it must begin with the facts of the Bible, but it also has to include the eternal principles of God that those facts reveal. And then those principles must be applied to

24. Finzel, pp. 10-11.

life—actualized through the daily lives of believers. If Bible facts alone are taught without including principles and application there are three possible outcomes, and two of them are negative. Instead of valid, life-related application, there may be no application at all, or the Bible may be misapplied.

EQUIP CHRISTIANS FOR MINISTRY

Christianity is not a spectator activity. Only as individual Christians discover and develop their spiritual gifts of ministry will the church become a vital force in the world. Church leaders need to help people recognize, nurture, and use their gifts of ministry to build up the Body of Christ. Such teaching and preparation also will help to solve the single greatest problem confronting church leaders— the problem of recruiting volunteer workers for ministry. The strength of a given body of believers does not depend on how strong the professional leaders are but on how strong lay persons are. When professional leaders are equipping lay persons for ministry, they are fulfilling their great calling from God.

REACH OUT TO UNBELIEVERS

The church has been accused of being afflicted with the "huddle syndrome"— Christians spending all their time focusing inward on communication with each other. And in so doing, such Christians may well neglect the vital ministry of outreach. A strong, vital church is one where Christians are living in such a way that those outside the body are attracted to Jesus Christ. Then rather than becoming weaker with each generation, the church will continue to thrive and to grow in the world—ministering effectively until Jesus Christ returns.

FOR FURTHER READING

Aeschliman, Gordon D. *Globaltrends*. Downers Grove, Ill.: InterVarsity, 1990.

Barna, George. *The Frog in the Kettle*. Ventura, Calif.: Regal, 1990.

———. *Marketing the Church*. Colorado Springs: NavPress, 1988.

Bloom, Allen. *The Closing of the American Mind*. New York: Simon & Schuster, 1987.

Brown, Marion E., and Marjorie G. Prentice. *Christian Education in the Year 2000*. Valley Forge, Pa.: Judson, 1984.

Campolo, Anthony. *Growing Up in America: A Sociology of Youth Ministry*. Grand Rapids: Zondervan, 1989.

Finzel, Hans. *Help! I'm a Baby Boomer*. Wheaton, Ill.: Victor, 1989.

McKenna, David. *Megatruth: The Church in the Age of Information*. San Bernardino, Calif.: Here's Life, 1986.

Naisbitt, John, and Patricia Aburdene. *Megatrends 2000*. New York: William Morrow, 1990.

Schaller, Lyle E. *Reflections of a Contrarian: Second Thoughts on Parish Ministry*. Nashville: Abingdon, 1989.

Part 2

The Teaching-Learning Process in Christian Education

The heart of biblical Christian education is the teaching-learning process. In order to fulfill Christ's mandate to make disciples, we need to understand how to teach effectively as well as how people learn.

Appropriately, this second unit begins with chapter 6 on Jesus Christ, the Christian educator's supreme teaching example. As He told His disciples—and us: "A pupil is not above his teacher; but everyone, after he has been fully trained, will be like his teacher" (Luke 6:40, NASB*). In order to be like the Master Teacher, we need to be acquainted with His methods as well as His character.

Next, chapter 7 defines teaching and learning from a biblical and educational perspective. The author not only outlines principles of effective teaching but also examines major learning theories.

Chapter 8 investigates the work of the Holy Spirit as "our director and resource in teaching and learning God's truth." The Spirit is another major facet of God's educational process and affects every area of that process.

One of the Holy Spirit's ministries related to education is bestowing the gift of teaching on individuals. Chapter 9 describes this gift as well as the roles and responsibilities of the Christian teacher.

Christian education focuses on teaching God's Word. So chapter 10 provides guidance for the teacher in studying the Bible in preparation for teaching. The author, an expert on the subject, explains the steps in the inductive method of Bible study.

Once the teacher understands the Bible passage, he needs to know how to communicate the truth of that passage to his students. Chapter 11 walks him through the steps of effective lesson planning: aim, hook, Book, look, and took, with adaptations for teaching younger children. This plan will help a teacher build a lesson that promotes transformation in his students' lives, which is the goal of Bible teaching.

Planning an effective lesson is not enough, however. Teachers must also manage the classroom experience so his students can and do learn. This is the subject of chapter 12.

*New American Standard Bible.

Finally, the unit concludes with two chapters (13 and 14) on methods, including one devoted to media. They describe a variety of methods and provide guidelines for selecting and using them effectively.

Warren S. Benson

6

Christ the Master Teacher

To Teach Like the Master Teacher
- **View discipling and teaching as inseparable partners**
- **Develop skills of individualized instruction as well as for large group/small group situations**
- **Teach with loving enthusiasm, humor, sensitivity, and compassion**
- **Recognize God's ability to change people**

Never one lived as Jesus did. No one ever taught like He did. Human comparisons with Christ as teacher, mentor, discipler, and even listener border on the ludicrous. He was God. Yet He remains the one Person whom all Christians are to emulate. We are commanded to follow Him as closely as our fallen humanity permits. It is a call to service and servanthood that demands that we subordinate and/or repudiate all other competing bonds.

Responding by total identification and by entrusting one's whole self to Jesus would be the height of folly and frustration except for the indwelling Spirit who enables us to achieve far greater similarity than any of us dream. The never-ending quest is to model our ministries after Christ, the supreme exemplar. He is the standard for all reflective evaluation.

WARREN S. BENSON, Ph.D., is vice-president of professional doctoral programs and professor of Christian education, Trinity Evangelical Divinity School, Deerfield, Illinois.

MASTER TEACHER/MASTER DISCIPLER

Initially it is crucial to assert that although Christ was called "teacher" or "rabbi" almost sixty times in the New Testament,[1] His ministry of teaching cannot be separated from the larger context of His life, namely that of discipling. Understanding His words without this comprehensive view robs them of some of their applicatory impact and ultimate power. Matt Friedman observes,

> Perhaps the most powerful evidence for Jesus as educator is the entourage of disciples that accompanied Him. The disciples—literally "learners"—were a community of interested persons who saw in Jesus not only a speaker of memorable ability but also a model of righteous living. As a mentor, Jesus opened up to these people not only His words, but His entire life.[2]

Lawrence Richards states,

> Jesus maintained an intimate teaching ministry with his disciples. He answered their questions about a day's events and questioned them in turn. The disciples observed Jesus' life while traveling with him, and Jesus gave them life assignments, as when he sent them out two by two. This powerful, intimate form of instruction is best understood as discipling.[3]

In teaching, Jesus Christ was always building into people's lives principles that will endure and transcend the existential moment. Those who walked with Him became a community of learners, a "collegium of lifelong followers."[4]

THE GOD-MAN

Jesus of Nazareth was the true Messiah of His people (John 1:41; Rom. 9:5) who was anointed with the Spirit and power (Acts 10:38). He was the true prophet (Mark 9:7), priest (John 17), and king (Matt. 2:2; 21:5). Orthodox Christians of every church and denomination have perennially insisted that Jesus Christ rose from the dead (1 Cor. 15) and that this doctrinal belief is a cornerstone of New Testament faith. Christianity IS Jesus Christ, who was both God and man. He is the second

1. Robert H. Stein, *The Method and Message of Jesus* (Philadelphia: Westminster, 1978), p. 1. Some might suggest that to distinguish between teaching and preaching is of some cruciality. Please see my discussion in Kenneth O. Gangel and Warren S. Benson, *Christian Education: Its History and Philosophy* (Chicago: Moody, 1983), where I state the conclusions regarding this debate found in Robert C. Worley's *Preaching and Teaching in the Earliest Church* (Philadelphia: Westminster, 1967), pp. 135, 142.
2. Matt Friedman, *The Master Plan of Teaching* (Wheaton, Ill.: Victor, 1990), p. 15.
3. Lawrence O. Richards, *Expository Dictionary of Bible Words* (Grand Rapids: Zondervan, 1985), p. 591. The reader is apprised that the essay moves back and forth freely within both concepts of teaching and discipling due to their inseparability.
4. Vernon Blackwood, "Jesus the Teacher in the Context of Education in the First Century," paper submitted in the course "History and Philosophy of Christian Education," Trinity Evangelical Divinity School (Summer 1987), p. 35.

Person of the Trinity. His death on the cross provided a perfect, sinless sacrifice for our redemption, the forgiveness of sin being available to those who by faith receive the gift of salvation.

As no other teacher, He being God (John 2:23-25) discerned men's and women's motivations as they approached Him. This is the essence of the statement that no one could ever teach as He did, in the ultimate sense of the term. However, He continues as the teacher whom we should examine and study most carefully because His teaching principles will never be outdated or become obsolete. Certainly we have learned a considerable amount regarding the teaching-learning process since Jesus' day. And although the New Testament does not purport to be a manual on this process, it is remarkably contemporary, as a cursory examination of the biblical text will demonstrate.

In discussing the master teacher concept, renowned educator Benjamin Bloom cites five criteria for identifying such persons: (1) superior knowledge of the subject, (2) skill in teaching, (3) respect from students, (4) ability to nurture students in the subject, and (5) demonstrable results.[5] Even a superficial survey uncovers a plethora of evidence of Christ's superiority as the Master Teacher. Edward Kuhlman states:

> Having submitted to the mastery of God the Father, He came not to do His own will, but the will of God, who sent Him (John 5:30). He excited the crowd's attention and earned His disciples' admiration by the personal mastery that controlled and emanated from Him; it hallmarked His ministry. Unlike the Scribes and Pharisees, He did not reduce His teaching to an insipid cookbook approach or cloud it with undecipherable esoteric jargon. He spoke with accuracy and authority.[6]

This level of authority grated on His opponents. They could not handle this forthright yet often gentle approach. While He was available for questioning and dialogue, He was in essence the Truth (John 14:6), and therefore He spoke with confidence and authority.

Jesus Christ had a complete grasp of the subject; His skill in teaching knew no limits. Even His enemies admitted that He taught with power and authority. His followers respected Jesus because in time they understood that He had come from the Father as the incarnate Son. His rigorous demands of the disciples called for the very best that was in them. He encouraged them to grow and to try out the same techniques He used in ministry. Eventually this involvement in learning caused them to stand sturdily for the truth when Christ ascended into heaven.

The Savior was the quintessential teacher. Being God in human flesh He had no weakness as a pedagogue. He modeled the truth in an ultimate sense. Christ

5. Benjamin Bloom, "The Master Teacher," in *Phi Delta Kappan* 63 (June 1982): 664-68, 715. Also see Edward Kuhlman's discussion of these concepts in *Master Teacher* (Old Tappan, N.J.: Revell, 1987), pp. 176-91.
6. Edward Kuhlman, *Master Teacher* (Old Tappan, N.J.: Revell, 1987), p. 181.

never lost touch with those He was teaching despite the loftiness of His content or the holiness of His character. He knew how to adapt to their level of understanding and used the familiar to explain the profound.

INCARNATIONAL TEACHING

David McKenna in *Power to Follow, Grace to Lead* observes:

> The incarnation of Jesus Christ is the pivot upon which our world turns. Whether to understand His life or His leadership, we must begin with the incarnation. Then, from the mystery of its paradox and the miracle of its resolution, the meaning of the "Word became flesh" unfolds before us. From His incarnate character we learn the meaning of His redemptive vision, His servant strategy and His teaching task.[7]

Christian teaching begins with the transformation of ourselves toward the likeness of Christ through the ministry of the Holy Spirit "so that the living word is once again embodied in human flesh." We need the "heart and mind of Christ in dealing with issues, but especially in working with people."[8]

Christ came to finish the work of God for the Father (John 4:34) and Christians are called to complete our service assignments with a resolute and obedient spirit. It is God through His Spirit who is the great energizer (Phil. 2:13). God provides the energy, the drive, and the motivation to get immersed in doing His will. It is His power and our availability.

THE CONTEXT AND THE CONGREGATION

Vernon Blackwood states:

> Perhaps the greatest single obstacle confronting the contemporary educator who seeks to utilize the example of Jesus to transform education can be found in appreciating the significance of his teaching-learning strategy within the existing educational environment. . . . Then . . . the meaning of any educational intervention can only be fully comprehended when the total matrix of the social, economic, political, and educational context is adequately considered. . . . The culture of Jesus' day and locus can best be portrayed as a multiplicity of layers superimposed upon one another in piecemeal fashion, having weathered the invasions of a series of empires.[9]

Blackwood further contends that Christ and the disciples were "multicultural people" who were aware of a wide spectrum of "traditions, forms, and value orientation."[10] Charles H. Nichols has developed a summary of the educational sys-

---

8. Ibid., pp. 22-23.
9. Blackwood, p. 2.
10. Ibid. See Bo Reicke, *The New Testament Era* (Philadelphia: Fortress, 1968), F. F. Bruce, *New Testament History* (Garden City, N.Y.: Doubleday, 1969), and Wayne A. Meeks, *The Moral World of the First Christians* (Philadelphia: Westminster, 1986).

tem that Jesus encountered. The Hebrew educational program was "intricately bound together with its religious system."

1. Learning and doing must be integrated. Knowledge must be applied with wisdom and understanding.
2. Education was a continual process—from the cradle to the grave.
3. General education and religious education were the same. All learning revolved around Jehovah and His writings.
4. Education was the responsibility of both parents and community. They were not only to supply it but also to demonstrate it.
5. The teacher was considered the most important factor in teaching. The rabbi was revered and respected by both the pupils and their parents.
6. Education would be carried on in any place. The environment was considered an important part of the curriculum.
7. The process of education must be gradual from the known to the unknown, from the simple to the complex, and from the immediate to the remote. When the basics were grasped more could be added.
8. Individual differences were recognized to exist in pupils. Thus different approaches were used.
9. Variety in methods were considered important. These included storytelling, sermons, readings, object lessons, demonstrations, use of humor, and questions.
10. Discipline was considered as part of the educational process. Various punishments were meted out to fit the offense.[11]

Some of these ideas were adapted from Louis Finkelstein, ed, *The Jews; Their History, Culture and Religion*, vol. 2 (New York: Harper and Brothers, 1949).

The society of that period was complex, rich, and variegated in composition throughout the Graeco-Roman-Judaeo world. In that context Jesus built a team of people who would carry on His unique mission. The training process was a most critical factor in the durability of His work.

McKenna observes:

> Jesus chose ordinary people for His Incarnational team. Their diversity of backgrounds, vocations and outlooks added to His team-building challenge. . . . Certainly, they were a far cry from the conformity that lends to cohesion in team-building. . . . Jesus took a major risk with the persons He chose to be His disciples. None of them was theologically sophisticated, trained for leadership or primed for a public image. Yet, strange as it seems, Jesus chose them for their independence, diversity, and non-conformity. But in the long run, their differences could be their strength. If they could be molded into a team that shared His vision and extended His mission, their diversity would make them effective in a variety of cultures across the world.[12]

11. Charles H. Nichols, "An Analysis of the Teaching Methodology of Jesus Christ and Its Relation to Adult Religious Education," Ph.D. diss., U. of Nebraska, 1983.
12. McKenna, pp. 124-25.

Christ taught from an educational strategy that included a ministry to the masses of people, the seventy, the twelve disciples (Mark 3:13-15), and also to His closest companions: Peter, James, and John (Mark 14:33; Luke 9:28). His peripatetic (traveling from place to place) teaching of the twelve constituted the greatest educational commune ever established. Christ recognized that the ministry He modeled with the small group and the large group would be perpetuated by the church. Unfortunately, church history is replete with instances and even eras when His methodology was forgotten or prostituted.

Jesus taught the general public, the masses, and, in particular, those of His birth and familial identification—the Jewish people. In the gospel of Mark the description of flocks of people witnessing the ministry of Jesus and hearing His words amounts to thirty-seven times as over against forty-eight instances in Matthew and thirty-eight in Luke. Mark 8:34 is one of the occasions in which both the crowd and the disciples were identified as being present together: "Then he called the crowd to him along with his disciples and said: 'If anyone would come after me, he must deny himself and take up his cross and follow me.'"

AND CHILDREN

There are few references to children in the gospels, but those mentioned are etched in our minds. Jesus was never too busy or too preoccupied to receive and interact with children. The disciples were rebuked because they failed to perceive the importance of welcoming the little ones. These were not unfeeling or insensitive men—they merely misunderstood Christ's concerns for children. This was particularly obvious on His last journey to Jerusalem. Despite the pressures and tensions of the circumstances, He made time for children (Matt. 19:13; Mark 10:13; Luke 18:15).[13]

PURPOSES PRESENT GOOD NEWS

Donald Guthrie, in discussing the message of Jesus, accurately states that Christ's message was far more important than His methods, for methods provide the medium for the message. As the Master Teacher Christ presented good news about God, Himself, His mission, the Holy Spirit, man, and fellowship.[14]

The primary mission of Jesus was to redeem us by His atoning death on the cross. His teaching, however, focused on shaping the hearers' perceptions of the kingdom of God, which dealt with the implications of one's personal relationship with the Father. His teaching had two dimensions: one present, the other future. In the parables Jesus stressed the eschatological aspects (Matt. 24; Mark 13; Luke 21).[15]

13. William Barclay, *Educational Ideals in the Ancient World* (Grand Rapids: Baker, 1974), p. 234.
14. Donald Guthrie, "Jesus," in *A History of Religious Educators*, Elmer L. Towns, ed. (Grand Rapids: Baker, 1975), pp. 26-35.
15. Ibid.

Matt Friedeman suggests that there is a "Jesus Synthesis" that adopts "three powerful objectives of God for Israel" in His teaching mission.[16] God desired a morally pure nation that would reflect the holiness of His character. It is impossible to reflect His holiness apart from the work of the Holy Spirit. Christ is the enabler.

Second, Friedeman further asserts that from character there emerges service—right action and insightful behavior. From the Old Testament understanding of priesthood comes the counterpart in the New Testament of service to our fellow man, whereby we protect the "unfortunate from oppression, strengthening moral conscience of the nation"—in essence, fulfilling the second greatest commandment, to love and serve our neighbors as ourselves.

Third, holy character and priestly service are never found without community. This concept is based in the Trinity. Friedeman states,

> [God] desires His people to reflect Him as individuals within a unified Body. God wanted His people (plural) in community (unity) because He is community—Three in One. Intimacy among God's people is a reflection of Him.[17]

We need each other for encouragement, exhortation, and accountability. Social scientists, Robert Bellah and Peter Berger assert that for group identity to remain strong, a sense of togetherness must be experienced.[18] It is through the power of transformational relationships found in the community setting of the church that Christians gain strength and discernment to engage in meaningful and significant ministries both within the Body of Christ and outside. But just how does this happen?

PRINCIPLES AND PRACTICES

D. Elton Trueblood comments on the Master's basic philosophy of ministry:

> It is no exaggeration to say that Christ's decision to select the twelve was one of the crucial decisions of the world. There is no reason to suppose that we should have ever heard the gospel apart from this carefully conceived step. Since Christ wrote no book, He depended entirely upon the faithfulness of the prepared group. Not all of them understood Him nor proved faithful yet, in the end, the method succeeded.[19]

In the local church we as leaders tend to use too many "oughts" and "shoulds" with people. Christ attacked the problem of change in theology and ministry with models as well as words. His most powerful model was His work with the

---

16. Friedeman, pp. 21-30.
17. Ibid., p. 27.
18. Robert N. Bellah, Richard Madsen, William M. Sullivan, Ann Swidler, and Steven M. Tipton, *Habits of the Heart* (Berkeley, Calif.: U. of Calif., 1985), and Peter Berger, *A Rumor of Angels* (Garden City, N.Y.: Doubleday, Anchor, 1970), pp. 18-19.
19. D. Elton Trueblood, *The Lord's Prayer* (New York: Harper & Row, 1965), p. 36.

twelve. He spent three years walking, talking, explaining, demonstrating, and assisting them in analyzing how He did ministry and how they in turn should nurture others after His ascension.

Although discipleship per se is not to be the major thrust of this chapter, this aspect must not be neglected or ignored in looking at Jesus Christ as a teacher. He did not major in methods of teaching but rather in ministry with people. When this dimension is forgotten or utilized only slightly it is a causative factor in the weakness of some evangelical churches today. Transformational relationships—that is, discipling—take more time and have less visibility, but the dividends are far greater.

We turn now to the Savior's actual teaching methodology. Lee Magness's comment builds a bridge between these two:

> One statement of Jesus, almost an understatement, may provide the clearest insight into the purposeful way Jesus taught and the objective He had in mind: "A learner is not superior to the teacher nor is a slave superior to his master. It is sufficient for the learner to become like the teacher, and the slave like his master" (Mt. 10:24-25). Learning was the means of relating to Jesus, but the goal was broader than the assimilation of facts, the adoption of a body of tradition, or even identification with a philosophical position. For the disciples, learning was living, living with and like Jesus. Perhaps, we should interpret more literally: learning was becoming, being like Jesus. Education in Christ was not even merely the mimicry of Jesus' habits; it was growth into a state of being which was Christ-like.[20]

Jesus and the apostle Paul followed no set formula and scheme. They were creative, flexible, and open to a rich variety of methods that drew people into the teaching-learning milieu. Even though both were brilliant prototypes for giving content through lectures and sermons, they also used an experiential, in-ministry model that facilitated the internalization of the material. Blackwood states that their "predominant modality was dialogue and discovery, of inquiry into the meaning of contextualization and incarnating the Word of God."[21]

On the road to Emmaus as Jesus walked with the two disciples (Luke 24:13-35), He utilized discussion (v. 14), open inquiry (v. 17), correction and clarification (vv. 25-27), role modeling (vv. 30-31), and the need for response (vv. 33-35). He was in dialogue with the disciples, engaging their minds, affections, and will with the result that they took action. Robert Pazmiño points out that Jesus' approach with the disciples often involved questions (vv. 17-19), listening and giving time for careful thought, and opening the Scriptures and exhorting. Further, Pazmiño indicates that this was Jesus' pattern even as a twelve-year-old discussing theological ideas with the premier religious thinkers in Palestine (Luke 2:41-52).[22]

---

20. Lee Magness, "Teaching and Learning in the Gospels: The Biblical Basis of Christian Education," *Religious Education* 70, no. 6 (November-December 1975): 629-35.
21. Blackwood, p. 43.
22. Robert W. Pazmiño, *Foundational Issues in Christian Education* (Grand Rapids: Baker, 1988), p. 33.

As we observe and examine the teaching of Jesus we should be reminded that the Bible is by nature an adult book. Neal F. McBride notes that it was written by adults about events happening to adults. Scripture is beamed at an adult readership and calls for the comprehension of adults. Christ ministered as an adult, chose apostles who were adults, but He occasionally illustrated adult issues through children (Matt. 19:13-15; Luke 8:49-56; 9:37-43).[23]

Further, the Master was sensitive to the ideas and themes that prevailed in that milieu. Never being anticultural, Jesus utilized the emerging culture without diminishing His own agenda and conclusions. Blackwood states,

> In comprehending Jesus's philosophy of teaching and learning, the vital place of the cultural and social context cannot be overemphasized. Congruence with cultural norms is a non-negotiable requirement of education, and they can only be abrogated sparingly and when an assortment of participants recognize the need for innovation. Thought forms, rituals, symbols, kinship patterns, meals, labor and economic systems, socialization, leisure activities, language, and much, much more provide invaluable means of operating within a culture to address it with worldview and lifestyle change, and Jesus shrunk from none of these.[24]

LUKE 4

One of the most explosive educational and theological situations presents itself by Jesus' design in Luke 4:14-30. Christ read from the Isaiah scroll (61:1-2), assumed the seated posture of a teacher, and informed the congregation that God the Father had sent Him: "The Spirit of the Lord is on me, because He has anointed me to preach good news to the poor. He has sent me to proclaim freedom for the prisoners and recovery of sight for the blind, to release the oppressed, to proclaim the year of the Lord's favor." Then He continued, "Today this scripture is fulfilled in your hearing." That was injury enough to the Jews' religious psyches, but then He told them that "only Naaman the Syrian" responded to Elisha and it was the "widow in Zarephath in the region of Sidon" to whom Elijah was sent. To these explosive words the enraged people reacted by attempting to throw Christ down the cliff, but He disappeared.

Jean Piaget would have called this passage a notable demonstration of bringing disequilibration to a society in order to force the people to make extraordinarily important decisions centered on a new data base. The claims of Christ created incredible internal dissonance that had to be reckoned with by this Jewish audience, His own hometown folk (Nazareth). Did He fit in their belief system and expectations of God's kingdom?

Jesus intentionally pried open their perceptions regarding the exclusivity of the Jewish ethos. He claimed that He had been sent by God with the answers prompt-

---

23. Neal F. McBride, "A Rationale for a Primary Focus on Adult Christian Education in the Local Church," 1979 handout.
24. Blackwood, p. 16.

ed by the ancient statement/questions of Isaiah. Here the Savior used Scripture, a stinging proverb (v. 23), the references to Elijah and Elisha, and the power of the Holy Spirit (v. 18). By asserting that He came from God and was speaking and serving in the power of the Spirit, the people, if they were to oppose Him, were defying God and His Word—the Scriptures. Christ was, according to His claims, the fulfillment of His Father's predictive words. They were opposing God Almighty.

Further, they were exhorted not to be complacent regarding the marginalized, the poor, and the oppressed—and that command continues to the present.[25] In His educational scheme Jesus addressed the whole person—body, mind, and spirit. He did not engage in mind games.

Charles H. Nichols concludes this section of the discussion on the methodology of Jesus with these summary statements:

1. Jesus selected His methods based on the ability of the student. This is seen in His teaching of Nicodemus (John 3) and the Samaritan woman (John 4).
2. Jesus selected His methods based on the attitude of the student. The methods used with the religious differed from those He used with the disciples.
3. Jesus selected His methods based on the size of the class. Compare the Sermon on the Mount (Matthew 5-7) with the discourse with the centurion (Matthew 8:5-13).
4. Jesus selected His methods based on the location of His teaching. The teaching at the Pool of Bethesda (John 5:1-47) was handled differently from the teaching in Phoenicia (Mark 7:24-30).
5. Jesus selected His methods based on the content He was trying to communicate. The methods He used in His discourses at the start of His ministry differed from those in discourses at the end of it.
6. Jesus selected His methods based on the purposes of His teaching. Compare the methods of John 5 (the feeding of the 5,000 and the lesson at sea) with John 6 (the discourse on the bread of life).
7. Jesus used a variety of methods in His teaching, however His variety was purposeful. It could be said of Him, "as a teacher he was not only a tactician with methods, but a strategist with objectives" (Horne, Herman, 1920, p. 204).
8. Jesus never let the method overshadow the purpose or the content of the lesson. Methods to Him were a means to an end, not an end.
9. Jesus based His methods on the practical, mundane lives of His students. The discourse by the sea (Matthew 13:1-35) and the discourse about riches (Matthew 19:15-20) demonstrate this concept.
10. Jesus used the methods of His day to their fullest potential. It could be said of Him, "He taught with authority" (Matthew 7:29).[26]

THE FORM OF JESUS' TEACHING

Clifford A. Wilson, Robert H. Stein, and Donald Guthrie present excellent discussions of the creative use of words that Christ used. A fine summary of these pre-

25. The poor are mentioned in the Old and New Testaments more than four hundred times. The dispossessed and the blind are readily forgotten both then and now.
26. Nichols, pp. 150-51.

sentations is developed by Vernon Blackwood.

Examples of these powerful instructional devices include: 1) overstatement and hyperbole, or exaggeration of a truth for the sake of effect (e.g., taking a log out of one's eye); 2) puns or plays on words, such as wind and spirit in John 3; 3) similes and metaphors in which comparisons between unrelated realities are made, for instance the Pharisees resembling whitewashed tombs; 4) proverbs where common occurrences are used to illustrate a higher truth, like "where your treasure is there will your heart be also" (Mt. 6:21); 5) riddles, or intentionally puzzling statements designed to stimulate thinking in new ways, for example, destroying the Temple and rebuilding it in three days (Mk. 14:58); 6) paradox or apparently contradictory sayings exemplified in the widow's coin being greater than the hefty sum donated by a rich person (Mk. 12:41-4); 7) a fortiori reasoning that argues from the greater truth, which is readily accepted, to the lesser truth which is being questioned, such as God caring for even the insignificant lilies or sparrows, and so obviously taking care of humanity; 8) irony, whereby a wryly humorous and perhaps biting contrast is made, like when Jesus accosts the religious leaders for discerning the weather but not the true religious state of Israel or themselves (Mt. 16:2-3); 9) questions, of which there are many kinds (e.g., "who do you say that I am?" or "was the baptism of John from Heaven or humankind?"); 10) symbolic actions in which a point is being made, the cursing of the fig tree, for instance; 11) poetry, including all types of Hebrew poetry, typified in "whoever would save his life will lose it/but whoever loses his life for my sake will save it" (Mk. 8:35); and 12) visual aids, such as when Jesus asked for the Roman coin to illustrate proper loyalties.[27]

PARABLES

A further word is in order regarding parables. At times Christ was intentionally opaque when talking to outsiders. In the Matthew 13 presentation of seven parables the Savior quotes Isaiah in His explanation of why He employs parables: "Though seeing, they do not see; though hearing, they do not hear or understand" (v. 13).

Robert H. Stein summarizes the reasons in three statements: (1) to conceal His teaching from those outside (Matt. 11:25-27; Mark 4:10-12); (2) to illustrate and reveal His message to His followers (Mark 4:34); (3) to disarm His listeners (Mark 12:1-11; Luke 15:1-2).[28]

Parables provide an illustration of the grace of God. Those who showed they would not hear the King were spared the revelation of further truth, for which they would have been responsible. Jesus took the disciples aside and gave them never-to-be-forgotten explanations of these stories. They were able to grasp the parables in the form He presented to them privately. Matthew 13:12 indicates that when truth is applied and obeyed more truth is given. Conversely when truth is rejected or unused it is lost.

Parables touch the hidden crevices of one's heart through the similarity between "common human experience and transcendent reality. The whole per-

27. Blackwood, p. 24.
28. Stein, pp. 41-42.

son is involved in hearing a parable, from imagination and emotion to reflection and evaluation. . . . The audience identifies with figures in the story, empathizes with the action, and vicariously experiences the impact of the lesson being taught."[29] It is educational simulation at its best.

Initially the disciples seemed slow-witted in their understanding. Further clarification through conversation brought lucidity. Having time to walk the roads and sit at lunch daily with the King of kings has to be the most enviable privilege imaginable. Yet they struggled with their limited perspective of the kingdom in which they expected Him to mount a throne before a cross.

MEANING, MEMORY, AND MOTIVATION

Stanford C. Ericksen, in *The Essence of Good Teaching,* discusses the measuring of meaning, memory, and motivation. Speaking within the school setting he contends that "the moment of instructional truth occurs when a student grasps the meaning of an important idea; all else is means to the end of understanding."[30] In contrasting the retention of meaningful and rote materials he shows their extension beyond the final examination of a course.

Retention Contrast of Meaningful and Rote Materials[31]

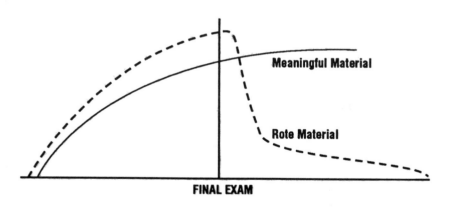

FINAL EXAM

Words, phrases, and sentences of meaningful content are retained longer than material learned by rote. The implications for teaching are clear when we observe that we should

> replace intensive coverage of factual material in the interest of helping students to comprehend a fewer number of significant ideas—concepts, generalizations, themes, laws, procedural principles, discipline—linked values, and the like. These large abstractions

30. Stanford C. Ericksen, *The Essence of Good Teaching: Helping Students Learn and Remember What They Learn* (San Francisco: Jossey-Bass, 1984), p. 6.
31. Chart from Ericksen, p. 7. Used by permission.

tie together otherwise isolated and specific pieces of information. Forgetting is countered because, as study proceeds, conceptual units become better organized and assimilated into the store of knowledge already in memory. This is the way the mind works. . . . The answer is in terms of the consecutive and cumulative effect of rehearsal (review and active participation) . . . rehearsal is the key factor for retention.[32]

Jesus elaborated, integrated, organized, and consolidated new information with their current data bases. He thus transformed the transfer of shallow meaning into a much deeper level of understanding. He did not have a storage tank philosophy of teaching. Filling notebooks or regurgitating data at exam time are not necessarily evidences of a fine course. Memorized minutiae most often have little meaning. A praxis of action and reflection, experience and content, life to truth, and practice to theory epitomizes the way Jesus taught.

THE "RAIL-FENCE" MODEL

James E. Plueddemann describes Ted W. Ward and Sam Rowen's "rail-fence model" in this manner:

The rail fence is made up of two rails held together by fence posts. The upper rail stands for truth. The bottom rail represents life. Anything that helps bring together truth and life is a fence post. The fence post may be an insight the learner discovered about the relationship of a Bible passage to a life need. Many teachers desire to build fence posts through their teaching methods. Critical reflection is another example of a fence post between truth and life. The teacher working with the Holy Spirit seeks to teach truth in such a way that it compels critical reflection between the life needs of the learner and the Word of God.[33]

Fence posts are teaching opportunities. The teacher's role is to bring the life situations and Scripture together so that God's view is accepted in the realism of life, not in the seeming abstractness of the classroom. That is why the Savior used stories and word pictures out of His hearers' lives. Certain occasions in the

32. Ibid., pp. 6-7.
33. Lois E. LeBar *Education That Is Christian,* ed. James E. Plueddemann (Wheaton, Ill.: Victor, 1989), pp. 105-6.

Master's ministry demanded the alleged artificiality of a classroom setting. However, He consistently brought reality to those contexts by using life-related stories that aroused and excited the interest and attention of the listeners. In addition, His questions penetrated their apathetic shells.

Seemingly this counters the previously made point that Christ's parables were opaque and unclear to some. However, this was by deliberate design because He did not want all to understand the mission and message that were to be perceived by the faithful alone. The others, then, were not held responsible for that which they did not understand.

QUESTIONS

No presentation of Jesus the teacher would be complete without direct reference to His magnificent use of questions. It was at the heart of His teaching. Knowing what was in the minds of His hearers gave Him a unique advantage. However, this advantage was never utilized unfairly to compel or coerce people against their wills. Neither did the power of His rhetoric demean His hearers.

Jesus delighted in asking questions that caused people to think about eternal issues. In fact, a problem-solving approach pervades the gospels. Jesus' rhetorical questions created a healthy atmosphere for considering the kingdom of God and His role in it. Although many of His Jewish listeners thrilled to the newness and freshness and vitality of His teaching, inevitably the questions would lead back to the world of reality and the Jews' treatment of others, including the hated Romans and Samaritans as well as their disregard for the poor and disadvantaged. Sometimes the people interrupted because they could not wait for Him to finish His presentation. Jesus seized these occasions as prized opportunities to counsel and guide.

Christ used questions to reprimand, test, and even silence His critics. At times He responded to their questions with one of His own to incite careful thinking and discovery learning. When they came to their own conclusions, the correct answer was more convincingly and indelibly impressed upon their minds.

Robert G. Delnay and Clifford A. Wilson suggest that Christ employed questions to open a conversation, prepare for instruction, induce reflection, pull the hearer up short, probe for motives, force an admission, provide a point of contact, and arouse interest.[34] Questions were crucial in the pedagogy of our Lord.

A Summary of Christ's Methodology

Charles Nichols gives us a helpful summation as he categorizes the teaching methods of Jesus Christ.[35]

34. Robert G. Delnay, *Teach As He Taught* (Chicago: Moody, 1987), pp. 73-83, and Clifford A. Wilson, *Jesus the Master Teacher* (Grand Rapids: Baker, 1975), pp. 117-30. See also Herman Harrell Horne, *Teaching Techniques of Jesus* (Grand Rapids: Kregel, 1971).
35. Nichols, pp. 132-33.

Visual Methods

1. Demonstration—whether cleansing the temple or washing feet, Christ taught by showing how.
2. Object Lesson—a little child or a withered tree could be used to communicate a truth.
3. Writing in the Sand—even though what He wrote was not recorded, it had the desired effect on those present.
4. Example—He was asked about prayer and love because He personified them.

Verbal Methods

1. Statements—He used a variety including direct, provocative, warning, contrasting, encouraging, and summary.
2. Questions—again He used a variety such as rhetorical, counter-question, request, and direct.
3. Proverbs and Gnomes—these "wise sayings" were often used either to start a lesson or leave an impact.
4. Quotations—He knew and used the Old Testament well, since it was a common book to His audience.
5. Parables—whether using shepherds or noblemen, these stories were a major part of His teaching.
6. A fortiori—arguing from lesser to greater seems to have been a common way for Jesus to challenge thinking.
7. Illustration—from birds to flowers, from current events or history, He used objects or events that communicated His truth.
8. Hyperbole—Jesus was a master at overstating a concept when the situation was proper, such as when dealing with the religious leaders.
9. Metaphor/Simile—Jesus could easily draw a comparison between familiar objects and the truths He wanted embedded in His student's mind.
10. Paradox/Irony—Jesus made good use of ideas that seemed contradictory, sometimes humorously and sometimes thought-provokingly.
11. Requests—He did not hesitate to make demands on His students.
12. Silence—He seemed to use this popular teaching method often to drive home a point.

Methods with Students

1. Asking Questions—He was always open to His students asking questions, even those who tried to trap Him.
2. Making Statements—He encouraged His students to interact with Him, although He did not hesitate to correct an improper statement.
3. Forcing Thinking—Jesus did not permit His students merely to listen, but He forced them to engage their thought process.
4. Forcing Involvement—He also did not permit His students to listen and do nothing, but required action.
5. Forcing Students to Face Real Issues—Jesus dealt with reality, so He put His students in life situations. He allowed inner factors to work.
6. Testing—whether on land or sea, His tests were practical.

After thirty-six years of teaching experience in elementary schools and teacher education programs at the college level and twelve years of "Scripture-combing" and meditation on His system of teaching, Regina M. Alfonso has produced her remarkable *How Jesus Taught*. Here are excerpts from the volume's conclusion:[36]

> In summary, Jesus confronted the same problems and situations that today's teacher faces. And He has the solutions, ready to share with anyone who takes the time to examine and reflect.
>
> *Teacher*
>   He could have chosen any planet
>   in any of the countless solar systems
>   he had designed
>   . . . but he chose ours
>   and he spent thirty-three years with us.
>
> He could have chosen any period
>   in our earth-history
>   as the most effective one
>   for getting his Good News spread
>   . . . but he chose a time
>   BEFORE so many great inventions
>   were even imagined
>   — before satellite communication
>   — before television
>   — even before radio
>   — before word processors
>   — before typewriters
>   — even before electricity
>   — even before printing
>   . . . but he chose a time
>   when his original team of messengers
>   could travel only on foot
>   or by ox-cart
>   or by sea-vessels powered only by men's muscles.
>
> He could have chosen any place
>   as his headquarters:
>   Rome, Corinth, Antioch, Alexandria
>   — all great cities when he came,
>   or a continent not yet discovered in the year B.C.
>   . . . but he chose to spend thirty years
>   of preparation
>   in a no-place: Nazareth,
>   and "Can anything good come out of Nazareth?"
>
> He could have spent his final three years

36. Regina M. Alfonso, *How Jesus Taught* (Staten Island, N.J.: Alba House, 1986), pp. 117-19.

— as a statesman,
   influencing governments and world powers
— as a physician,
   curing all the diseases of his time
— as a synagogue leader,
   establishing his teachings
      among educated churchmen
— as a renowned social reformer,
   founding a whole new social system
. . . but he chose to be a Teacher
      — to mold characters
      — to shape human destinies
      — to influence families
      — to affect future generations
      — to influence neighborhoods,
         cities,
            nations,
               the world
                  — to spread the Kingdom of his Father.

He closed his thirty-three years
   by directing his followers:
   "To the whole world
      and preach the Gospel
         to all mankind." Mark 16:15

And "The disciples went and preached everywhere,
   and the Lord worked with them
   and proved that their preaching was true
      by giving them the sign of power." Mark 16:20

His disciples' disciples,
   multiplied again and again and again,
   are motivated by his promise:
   "I will be with you always
      to the end of the age." Matthew 28:20

And they spend their days TEACHING
   — inspired by the life,
      the message,
         the methods,
            of JESUS, THE MASTER TEACHER.

FOR FURTHER READING

Alfonso, Regina M. *How Jesus Taught: The Methods and Techniques of the Master*. New York: Alba House, 1986.
Delnay, Robert G. *Teach As He Taught*. Chicago: Moody, 1987.

Friedeman, Matt. *The Master Plan of Teaching*. Wheaton, Ill.: Victor, 1990.

Hendricks, Howard G. "Following the Master Teacher," in *The Christian Educator's Handbook on Teaching*. Edited by Kenneth O. Gangel and Howard G. Hendricks. Wheaton, Ill.: Victor, 1988.

Horne, Herman Harrell. *Teaching Techniques of Jesus*. Grand Rapids: Kregel, 1971.

Hull, Bill. *The Disciple-Making Pastor*. Old Tappan, N.J.: Revell, 1988.

————. *Jesus Christ Disciple-Maker*. Old Tappan, N.J.: Revell, 1990.

Kuhlman, Edward. *Master Teacher*. Old Tappan, N.J.: Revell, 1987.

LeBar, Lois E. *Education That Is Christian*. Edited by James E. Plueddemann. Wheaton, Ill.: Victor, 1989.

Stein, Robert H. *The Method and Message of Jesus' Teachings*. Philadelphia: Westminster, 1978.

7

Lynn Gannett

Teaching for Learning

IN THE BIBLICAL TEACHING-LEARNING PROCESS
- **Learning involves change**
- **The student is an active participant**
- **The teacher serves as a guide**
- **The Holy Spirit plays a key role**
- **Social science research is integrated with biblical truth**
- **The dynamics of the environment either hinder or encourage learning**

TEACHING AND LEARNING

The fact that you are at this moment reading this chapter indicates that at some point in time you have sat in a classroom as a "learner" being taught by a "teacher." In fact, between formal education and church education, you have likely spent years in a classroom. Now, define *teaching*. Define *learning*. Not quite as easy as you thought? Defining teaching and learning adequately continues to be a challenge for the educational theorist.

Is teaching an art or a science? This classic question has been debated for years. Viewing teaching solely as an art or a science satisfies few educators. Most agree that both elements are involved in the teaching process. Regarding this dichotomy, Charles Silberman responds:

LYNN GANNETT, Ed.D., is a Christian education consultant, David C. Cook Publishing Company, Elgin, Illinois.

To be sure, teaching—like the practice of medicine—is very much an art, which is to say, it calls for the exercise of talent and creativity. But like medicine, it is also—or should be—a science, for it involves a repertoire of techniques, procedures, and skills that can be systematically studied and described, and therefore transmitted and improved. The great teacher, like the great doctor, is the one who adds creativity and inspiration to that basic repertoire.[1]

From the Christian perspective we must also ask, "Is teaching a *gift?*" The three major passages on spiritual gifts in the New Testament (Rom. 12:4-8; 1 Cor. 12; Eph. 4:11-13) include the gift of teaching. Roy Zuck defines this gift as

the supernatural, Spirit-endowed ability to expound (explain and apply) the truth of God. All believers in fellowship with the Lord are taught by the Holy Spirit, and all believers are responsible to teach others. All teach to some degree, but not all believers have the ability to teach others as effectively as those who have the teaching gift. It seems to be a special endowment.[2]

Teaching cannot be adequately defined without first answering the question, "What is *learning?*" Again, among educational theorists it is difficult to reach a common definition. Behaviorists exclusively emphasize changes in behavior as the outcome of learning. Cognitive theorists view the mind as the active processor of information, claiming that "*knowledge* is learned and changes in knowledge make changes in *behavior* possible."[3] Humanists see learning in light of what happens within the learner. In spite of these divergent approaches, learning has been defined generally and broadly as "a process that occurs when experience causes a relatively permanent change in an individual's knowledge or behavior."[4]

Christian educators are interested in the last phrase—"change in an individual's knowledge or behavior"—of the above definition. A commitment to the Bible as God's revelation to man cannot be content with learning that is strictly limited to Bible knowledge. Biblical learning demands a change—or transformation—in response to God's Word. Howard Hendricks simply and profoundly states: "Teaching is causing. Causing what? Causing people to learn. . . . Learning is change."[5]

Lawrence Richards identifies five levels of learning that are helpful to the Bible teacher:

1. Charles Silberman, "Technology Is Knocking at the Schoolhouse Door," in *Fortune* 74 (1966): 124; quoted in Anita E. Woolfolk, *Educational Psychology* (Englewood Cliffs, N.J.: Prentice-Hall, 1990), p. 3.
2. Roy B. Zuck, "The Role of the Holy Spirit in Christian Teaching," in *The Christian Educator's Handbook on Teaching*, ed. Kenneth O. Gangel and Howard G. Hendricks (Wheaton, Ill.: Victor, 1988), p. 38.
3. Woolfolk, p. 229.
4. Ibid., p. 159.
5. Howard G. Hendricks, *Teaching to Change Lives* (Portland, Oreg.: Multnomah, 1987), pp. 122-23

1. Rote: ability to repeat without thought or meaning.
2. Recognition: ability to recognize biblical concepts.
3. Restatement: ability to express or relate concepts to biblical system of thought.
4. Relation: ability to relate Bible truths to life and see appropriate response.
5. Realization: actualizing response: to apply biblical truths in daily life.[6]

Richards stresses that the Bible can be learned at all five levels, but at the levels of rote and recognition the facts are stressed with little meaning. The teacher's role at those levels is to provide information. At the levels of restatement, relation, and realization, learning becomes increasingly meaningful, and the teacher's role changes to that of a guide who involves students. The goal of Christian education is to move learning to the level of realization. At this level change in the learner's behavior is more likely to occur.[7]

To separate teaching and learning is only theoretically possible, for they both occur simultaneously in a process. This chapter will examine the teacher-learning process in light of biblical distinctives, summarize major learning theories, and begin to develop an integrated, biblical approach to teaching and learning. Additionally, dynamics of the learning environment and principles for effective teaching will be discussed.

DISTINCTIVES OF BIBLICAL TEACHING AND LEARNING

Roy Zuck states,

> Christian education is unique because of its *subject matter*—the Bible, God's written revelation; because of its *goal—spiritual transformation* of lives; and because of its spiritual dynamic—the work of the Holy Spirit.[8]

THE SUBJECT MATTER

In Christian education the Bible is taught. Unfortunately, the average Sunday school teacher is pleased at the end-of-the-year program when a fifth-grade class can recite the sixty-six books of the Bible and quote twelve memory verses in unison—evidence that the Bible has been taught. Many view God's Word merely as information to be acquired. The Bible is not just information about God communicated in revelation, but is God revealing Himself through information about Himself. Lawrence Richards's exegesis of Romans 1:16-32 asserts that when man is confronted with information about God, he is confronted by God. "God is known (contacted, experienced) at the point of revelation. And revelation is informational."[9] So, teaching the Bible is essential—not just to impart

6. Lawrence O. Richards, *Creative Bible Teaching* (Chicago: Moody, 1970), p. 75.
7. Ibid.
8. Zuck, p. 32.
9. Richards, p. 54.

information about God to the student, but to bring the student into contact with the living Word.

THE GOAL

Teaching the Bible is not an end in itself, but it is a means to an end. The goal of Christian education is that students know God and grow in Christlikeness. This is a transforming process. How does it happen? Students respond obediently to God's revelation. Their first response is saving faith. Further responses result in spiritual growth cultivated through an intimate knowledge of God.[10] John 14:21 reads, "He who has my commandments and keeps them, he it is who loves Me; and he who loves Me shall be loved by My Father, and I will love him, and will disclose Myself to him."

THE SPIRITUAL DYNAMIC

The task of Christian education is not merely a human endeavor—especially in the teaching-learning process. Teaching God's Word is a supernatural task in which the Holy Spirit plays a vital part. The Holy Spirit fills, guides, and gifts the teacher, illuminates the Word, opens the heart of the student to the Word, and empowers the student to respond in obedience.

In Christian education the teaching-learning process is unique. The subject matter, the goal, and the source of empowerment are supernatural. The teacher of God's Word can thrill at the privilege of being involved in such a process.

MAJOR LEARNING THEORIES

Research by educators, scientists, and psychologists has led to divergent learning theories. The purpose of this section is to provide a brief overview of the behavioristic, cognitive and humanistic learning theories focusing on their contributions and implications for biblical teaching and learning.

BEHAVIORISM

Philosophically, behaviorism has its roots in realism, positivism, and materialism. With this background it stands to reason that behavioral learning theories focus on observable behaviors rather than on internal processes such as thinking and emotions. Behaviorists view the student as part of nature—a "neutral human organism" not in relation with God. Teachers are responsible for creating an effective learning environment where behaviors will be shaped through the use of appropriate reinforcers.[11]

In the 1920s Russian physiologist Ivan Pavlov initiated a behavioristic laboratory study that examined reflex reactions. From his work, Pavlov described the process

10. Ibid., pp. 57-95.
11. Daniel Lenox Barlow, *Educational Psychology: The Teaching-Learning Process* (Chicago: Moody, 1985), pp. 149-52.

of classical conditioning (the association of automatic responses with new stimuli). Soon after, John B. Watson (1878-1958) concluded that behavior consists of conditioned reflexes and is controlled through environmental shaping. Watson clearly believed that "by controlling the child's environment, he could behaviorally engineer the child into any kind of person he chose."[12]

Behaviorism relies heavily on the work of E. L. Thorndike (1874-1949). As a result of his laboratory work with cats, Thorndike formulated three laws of learning: readiness, exercise, and effect.[13]

Thorndikes's work was the basis for the concept of operant conditioning developed by B. F. Skinner. Operant conditioning, or operant learning, is based on the theory that "a behavior (response) is expressed and is strengthened or weakened by positive reinforcement, punishment, negative reinforcement, or loss of reinforcement."[14] The principle of reinforcement has contributed to an understanding of how new behaviors (habit patterns) are learned and old, inappropriate behaviors are extinguished. Principles of behavior modification are used to help people lose weight, stop procrastinating, control spending, and even bring Bibles to church. Reinforcement techniques are frequently used to control student behavior in the classroom setting.

Social learning theory departs from traditional behaviorism in that its conclusions stem from studies on the interactions of two or more persons. Behaviorist Albert Bandura—social learning's chief proponent—not only sees individuals as products of environmental shaping but also as determinate shapers of environment.[15] One of the most significant results of Bandura's research is the theory of observational learning or modeling (learning by observing and imitating others). The focus of observational learning theory is on attention, retention, production, and motivation or reinforcement. One supporting study has indicated that both hostile behavior and moral standards are readily imitated by observers.[16] Perhaps it is true that more is *caught* than *taught*.

The weaknesses of behaviorism go beyond its denial of the inner qualities of man (spirit, conscience, sin).[17] Behaviorism does not explain why using reinforcement works with some students and not with others. In addition, its focus is on what the teacher does rather than what the student already knows, thinks, and feels. In a behavioristic classroom, the teaching-learning process can become mechanical, focusing on the proper technique rather than on the student.[18]

11. Daniel Lenox Barlow, *Educational Psychology: The Teaching-Learning Process* (Chicago: Moody, 1985), pp. 149-52.
12. Ibid., p. 136.
13. Ibid., p. 137.
14. Ibid., p. 515.
15. Ibid., pp. 144-45.
16. Woolfolk, pp. 178-79.
17. Kenneth O. Gangel and Warren S. Benson, *Christian Education: Its History and Philosophy* (Chicago: Moody, 1983), p. 333.
18. Henry Clay Lindgren, *Educational Psychology in the Classroom* (New York: John Wiley, 1972), pp. 196-97.

COGNITIVE LEARNING THEORIES

The cognitive learning theories orientation differs in many aspects from the behavioral perspective, beginning with the view of the learner. In behaviorism, the learner and his behaviors are seen as products of environmental stimuli. In contrast, cognitive learning theorists see the learner as a source "of plans, intentions, goals, ideas, memories, and emotions actively used to attend to, select, and construct meaning from stimuli and knowledge from experience."[19] The learner is an active processor of information. Cognitive learning theories focus on internal processes such as memory, abstract thinking, and problem solving.

Cognitive learning theorists have been influenced by the instrumental and pragmatic philosophy of John Dewey. Yet the heart of the cognitive learning approach stems from Gestalt psychology.[20]

Cognitive development. The work of Jean Piaget (1896-1980), a Swiss developmental psychologist, centered on devising a model that describes how individuals gather and organize information to make sense of their worlds. As a cognitive developmentalist, Piaget believed that thinking processes change dramatically from birth to maturity, although doing so gradually. Physical maturation (the biological changes that are genetically programmed), activity, and social interaction all contribute to a person's cognitive development.

Development occurs as individuals gradually pass through stages at different rates but in an orderly sequence. Piaget identified four stages of cognitive development: (1) the sensorimotor stage (birth to two years) in which the child explores the environment through motor activity and the senses; (2) the preoperational stage (two to seven years) in which the child's ability to think operationally is limited to one-way logic; (3) the concrete operational stage (seven to eleven years) in which the child can think logically about problems in concrete terms; and (4) the formal operations stage (eleven to fifteen years) in which the young person is able to solve abstract problems logically.[21]

The contribution of Piaget to the understanding of how children think can help in matching instruction to a child's developmental stage, thus avoiding overestimation or underestimation of a child's ability. In adition, this instrumental approach views knowledge as a tool to be used, and actively engages the student in the learning process.[22]

Building on the cognitive developmental work of Piaget, Lawrence Kohlberg has brought attention to the moral reasoning of children. Kohlberg views moral development as a natural process that can be nurtured, much like intellectual

---

19. M. C. Wittrock, *Educational Implications of Recent Research on Learning and Memory*. Paper presented at the annual meeting of the American Educational Research Association, New York, March 1982, pp. 1-2; quoted in Woolfolk, p. 228.
20. Iris V. Cully and Kendig Brubaker Cully, eds., *Harper's Encyclopedia of Religious Education* (San Francisco: Harper & Row, 1990), s.v. "Learning Theory," by C. R. Dykstra, p. 370.
21. Woolfolk, p. 47.
22. Ibid., p. 59.

development.[23] He "stresses that moral thinking is primarily determined by the maturation of cognitive capacities, and that the social environment provides the raw material on which cognitive processes actively operate."[24]

Through numerous studies presenting children and adults with moral dilemmas (a situation in which no choice is absolutely right), Kohlberg identifies three levels of moral reasoning. First, in the preconventional level, individuals make moral judgments based exclusively on their own perceptions and needs. In other words, "whatever is best for me must be right, I am the authority." Second, in the conventional level, individuals look to external authorities such as the law, the Bible, or society itself to determine right and wrong. Third, in the postconventional level, authority shifts as moral decisions are based on internal, personal, abstract principles, such as the Golden Rule.

For the Christian educator, two things are important to note. First, Kohlberg does not personally advocate the teaching of a particular value system. Second, according to Richards, structuralists have not demonstrated that the ability to reason at a higher level of morality has a causal relationship to behavior.[25]

Discovery learning. Jerome Bruner's discovery learning approach is based on cognitive structures (the fundamental ideas, patterns, or relationships of a subject). This approach utilizes inductive reasoning, which moves from the specific to the general. Under the teacher's guidance, students work on their own, employing intuitive thinking to discover workable solutions to problems.[26]

Information processing model. In an attempt to explain learning and memory, the information processing model compares the mind to a computer that stores and uses information. Simply stated, the ability of learners to render information as meaningful and to recall it for use is dependent on how they register and categorize input. For new information (data) to be meaningful the learner must relate the new information with what has previously been processed. Learning occurs as the information processing system and its contents grow in complexity. Significant theories based on this model include Robert Gagne's phases of learning and David Ausubel's theory of reception learning. The work of both men focuses on understanding how meaning relates to learning.[27]

HUMANISTIC THEORY

Scientific humanism came out of the Enlightenment, August Comte's positivism, and British utilitarianism. The scientific humanist "sees the scientific mind as humanity's greatest achievement and the scientific method as humanity's most powerful tool."[28] The student is viewed as basically good, curious, and

23. Gangel and Benson, p. 337.24. Barlow, p. 112.
25. Lawrence O. Richards, *A Theology of Children's Ministry* (Grand Rapids: Zondervan, 1983), pp. 154-55.
26. Woolfolk, p. 289.
27. Cully and Cully, s.v. "Learning Theory," by Dykstra, p. 370.
28. Cully and Cully, s.v. "Humanism," by D. C. Wyckoff, p. 315.

motivated to learn. The emphasis is on the "human potential" of each person rather than the mastery of information. The teacher is the facilitator of a warm, nonthreatening environment.

John Dewey. John Dewey (1859-1952) was the forerunner of progressive education. He followed in the footsteps of Jean-Jacques Rousseau, Johann H. Pestalozzi, Friedrich Froebel, and Horace Mann. As a pragmatist, Dewey was concerned with the relationship between ideas and action. Learning must be practical and usable, concentrating on problem-solving and the continuous reconstruction of experience. According to Dewey,

> The child cannot get power of judgment excepting as he is continually exercised in forming and testing judgment. He must have an opportunity to select for himself, and then to attempt to put his own selections into execution that he may submit them to the only final test, that of action. Only thus can he learn to discriminate that which promises success from that which promises failure; only thus can he form the habit of relating his otherwise isolated ideas to the conditions which determine their value.[29]

Kenneth Gangel and Warren Benson examine Dewey's objectives for education, which include: self-control, proper recognition of leisure, social efficiency, love of learning, and continuing experience. To achieve these goals, he stresses the importance of interaction, interest, activity, and the learning environment.[30]

Maslow and Rogers. Humanistic psychology is known as third-force psychology because it was developed in the 1940s in reaction to the two major forces of behaviorism and Freudian psychoanalysis. The two major contributions in education from the third-force were Abraham Maslow and Carl Rogers.

Abraham Maslow (1908-1970) is best known for his theory of motivation based on a hierarchy of needs. The essence of Maslow's theory is that individuals' deficiency needs (survival, safety, belonging, and self-esteem) must be met before they will be motivated to fulfill being needs (intellectual achievement, aesthetic experience, self-actualization, or reaching one's full potential). Maslow's focus on needs is significant but the major criticism of his theory is that individuals do not seem to respond consistently as predicted.[31]

Carl Rogers (1902-1987), a clinical psychologist, summarizes his existential-humanistic approach to education in the book *Freedom to Learn*.[32] In this work, he stresses the importance of nurturing each individual. Rogers believes that everyone has an internal motivating force that will reach its full potential in a warm, accepting environment. Therefore, the emphasis is on genuine and open

---

29. John Dewey, *Ethical Principles Underlying Education* (Chicago: U. of Chicago, 1903); quoted in Henry Clay Lindgren, *Educational Psychology in the Classroom* (New York: John Wiley, 1972), p. 202.
30. Gangel and Benson, pp. 298-300.
31. Woolfolk, pp. 314-15.
32. Carl Rogers, *Freedom to Learn* (Columbus, Ohio: Merrill, 1969), cited in Barlow, p. 190.

relationships between teachers and their students.

According to Rogers, learning involves a change in one's self-perception. Significant learning takes place when self-initiation, personal responsibility, activity, and relevance are present in the teaching-learning process. Like Maslow, Rogers's highest priority is self-actualization for each individual.[33]

Toward a Biblical Approach

An evangelical Christian reading the preceding summary of contemporary learning theories could be troubled by the underlying philosophies. Learning theorists have discovered some truth about how God created man to think, learn, grow, and change. Yet the philosophical assumptions about man, reality, values, and God are in conflict with the Bible. Our task in developing a biblical perspective on teaching and learning is to integrate properly the truth that God has revealed in His Word with the discoveries of science. Gangel and Benson write:

> Is it our conclusion that evangelical education should totally reject psychology? Absolutely not! The issue again is integration, the ability to be sufficiently eclectic while holding on to a solidly biblical theology, to apply whatever findings of psychologists—secular or religious—that may legitimately demonstrate positive correlation with biblical truths.[34]

The principle of integration is vital to the development of a biblical approach to learning. The following factors are important to consider toward accomplishing this integration.

NATURE OF THE LEARNER

The behavioristic, cognitive, and humanistic approaches all have their roots in the Darwinian theory of evolution. Scripture is clear that man is created in the image of God but as a result of the Fall has a sin nature. Redemption and transformation are possible for man through Christ's work on the cross.

The physical growth process is obvious in individuals. Scripture uses the concept of growth to describe physical maturation (Luke 2:40), knowledge of the Lord (2 Pet. 3:18), and faith (2 Cor. 10:15). The apostle Paul acknowledges a change in his cognitive ability from childhood to adulthood (1 Cor. 13:11). Christian educators cannot ignore the fact that children and adolescents are not miniature adults. Even adults represent different levels of maturity. Though questions remain to be answered in developmental research, the developmentalists have contributed much in the areas of physical, cognitive, moral, and faith development.

33. Barlow, p. 190.
34. Gangel and Benson, p. 338.

INTERNAL AND EXTERNAL FACTORS

Historically, much of education has focused on external factors (teacher, content, class members, and environment) in the educational process because they are easier to manipulate than internal factors (past experience, interests, ambitions, values, personal psychological needs, attitudes, health and comfort, self-concept, temperament, learning style, sex differences, and birth order). Skinner's emphasis on external factors has led to content-oriented education. Lois LeBar, examining the role of internal and external factors in *Education That Is Christian*, concludes, "Most Bible teachers have labored under the impression that if they taught the outer facts of the Bible, the Holy Spirit would do the inner work of regenerating the pupil."[35] This is often observed in Bible classes where the focus is on the teacher and the learner is a passive observer. In reaction to this historical preoccupation with external factors, the church has at times overreacted and adopted a humanistic orientation by focusing entirely on internal factors at the expense of God's Word. A biblical approach attempts to balance "the dynamic interdependence between the Bible and Life."[36]

> The dichotomy between teaching the Bible and teaching students is dangerous. Teaching the Bible for its own sake is idolatry. We study the Bible so that we may know God. But we worship God, not the academic discipline of the study of God. On the other hand, teaching students for their own self-actualization makes an idol out of persons, ignores the power of sin, and ignores the absolute standard of God's revealed truth.[37]

AIMS

As seen previously, the goal of Christian education is the transformation of the person. This goal is not limited to either the cognitive, the affective, or the volitional but encompasses all three—knowing, feeling, and doing.

METHODOLOGY

The goal of transformation will only take place in the arena of life. To agree with Dewey, the classroom is life—not just preparation for life. If learning is to be meaningful, it must relate to each student's own areas of need. Therefore, students must be actively involved in the discovery process. They must meet God through the Word. Again, there must be a balance between "the senses and the intellect, knowing and doing, the inner and outer, and deductive and inductive."[38]

35. Lois E. LeBar, *Education That Is Christian*, ed. James E. Plueddemann (Wheaton, Ill.: Victor, 1989), pp. 38-39.
36. Ibid., p. 58.
37. James E. Plueddemann, "Do We Teach the Bible or Do We Teach Students?" in *Christian Education Journal* 10 (Autumn 1989): 75.
38. LeBar, p. 53.

ROLE OF THE TEACHER

The teacher must be more than a teller or a facilitator. Neither alone is enough. Perhaps a more appropriate descriptor for the Bible teacher is guide. The teacher guides the students in the power of the Holy Spirit, through the process of relating God's Word to life. Modeling becomes essential to the teaching-learning process as students observe God's Word demonstrated in the life of the teacher (see chap. 9).

DYNAMICS IN THE LEARNING ENVIRONMENT

The phrase *learning environment* usually conjures up visions of brightly lit, nicely carpeted, appropriately furnished classrooms equipped with every resource a teacher would ever need to be creative. Most teachers have a vision of that picture-perfect "learning environment." Although it is important for students to be comfortable and for appropriate resources to be available, this is not the aspect of the environment that seems to have the most impact on the teaching-learning process. More important is the psychological climate—the atmosphere—that either hinders or encourages learning. An awareness of the factors that contribute to the dynamics of the learning environment will help a teacher make improvements and prevent problems.

SPIRITUAL FACTORS

As seen previously in this chapter, the Christian classroom has unique distinctives in its subject matter, goals, and spiritual dynamics. The inspired Word of God, the Bible, reveals to man the Living Word, Jesus Christ. Because the goal of Christian education is for the student and teacher to become more like Jesus Christ, He is the center of the curriculum.

Becoming more like Jesus Christ is not a natural process, but supernatural. God has provided the teacher with two supernatural helps to accomplish His goals. The first supernatural help is the Holy Spirit. In John 14:25-26 Jesus tells His disciples that the Holy Spirit "will teach you all things and will remind you of everything I have said to you" (NIV). The Holy Spirit fills, guides, and gifts the teacher, illuminates the Word, convicts, and empowers the student to respond in obedience. Second, teachers have the spiritual dynamic of prayer available to them. Through prayer hearts are prepared to receive the Word of God and the power of God is unleashed. For lives to be changed, the spiritual dynamics must be foremost in the teacher's heart and mind.

NEGATIVE EMOTIONS

Fear, anxiety, and discouragement can be major road blocks for learners. Sources of these negative emotions are numerous. They may stem from past or present experiences in the learning process, such as learning tasks, methods, or material that the student finds difficult. In addition, the impact of the family situation is extremely powerful. Many students may be in home situations where there is child or substance abuse. Emotional stress can be high as individuals adjust to divorce, single-parent homes, and blended families. Students may transfer fear, anxiety, and discouragment to the learning environment. A sensitive teacher will make feelings of security and love a priority.[39]

REJECTION

Unfortunately, not all students feel comfortable in every Bible teaching situation. Individuals may feel rejected because of their appearance, socioeconomic status, cultural background, intellectual ability, or a host of other reasons. This is especially crucial for children and adolescents who are highly affected by peer groups. Students need to feel accepted. It is important for the teacher to observe social dynamics in the learning environment and encourage students to accept one another.[40]

The preceding factors should stimulate the teacher to consider other dynamics that might be present in the learning environment. Factors such as student readiness, learning styles, and use of curriculum materials can diminish or strengthen the process of learning.

ESPRIT DE CORPS

Webster defines esprit de corps as "the common spirit existing in the members of a group and inspiring enthusiasm, devotion, and strong regard for the honor of the group." Nothing is more exciting than to be part of a group where members are devoted to each other and are enthusiastic about what is happening. Such a classroom climate will only enhance student participation as they share their lives and support each other. The teacher should provide opportunities for students to interact, play together, and work together.

CLASSROOM MANAGEMENT

The management style of the teacher (authoritarian, laissez-faire, or democratic) influences the climate of the learning environment (see chap. 12). Research studies indicate that the management style of a teacher most impacts the area of morale.[41]

TEACHER'S ATTITUDE

The saying "more is caught than taught" proves to be true because teachers' attitudes about the Lord, the Bible, themselves, and students impact learning. Most

---

39. Barlow, pp. 302-6.
40. Ibid., p. 306.
41. Barlow, p. 309.

adults have forgotten the details taught to them by their favorite teacher, but they have not forgotten the teacher. It has been said, "First the student loves the teacher, then the student loves the teacher's Lord."

PRINCIPLES FOR EFFECTIVE TEACHING AND LEARNING

It is one thing to read about learning theories, it is quite another to implement them in the teaching-learning process. As far back as 1884, there was John Milton Gregory's *The Seven Laws of Teaching*. This classic work remains contemporary, for in it Gregory details principles—or laws—which remain essential for effective teaching in today's classrooms. The laws stated are:

The Law of the Teacher. Know thoroughly and familiarly the lesson you wish to teach—teach from a full mind and a clear understanding.

The Law of the Learner. Gain and keep the attention and interest of the pupils upon the lesson. Do not try to teach without attention.

The Law of the Language. Use words understood in the same way by the pupils and yourself—language clear and vivid to both.

The Law of the Lesson. Begin with what is already well known to the pupil upon the subject and with what he himself experienced—and proceed to the new material by single, easy, and natural steps, letting the known explain the unknown.

The Law of the Teaching Process. Stimulate the pupil's own mind to action . . .

The Law of the Learning Process. Require the pupil to reproduce in thought the lesson he is learning . . .

The Law of Review and Application. Review, review, review. . . . [42]

In *Teaching to Change Lives*, Howard Hendricks builds on the work of Gregory to give further guidance to today's teacher. Hendricks stresses that first God uses the people of God, or teachers, to impact lives. Yet, there are fundamental principles, if practiced, that will give a new dynamic to teaching and will open the door for the Holy Spirit to work in the lives of students.

"*The Law of the Teacher*—Stop growing today, and you stop teaching tomorrow."[43] Teachers must permit the Word of God to transform their lives and allow their students to see God at work in them. In other words, a teacher must model the truth.

"*The Law of Education*—How people learn determines how you teach." Therefore, effective teachers provide a variety of developmentally sound methods that will keep interest high and eliminate boredom.

"*The Law of Activity*—Maximum learning is always the result of maximum involvement." Telling is not necessarily teaching. A wide variety of active meth-

42. John Milton Gregory, *The Seven Laws of Teaching*, rev. ed. (Grand Rapids: Baker, 1977), pp. 19-20.
43. Laws are from Hendricks, p. 179.

ods must be used to involve students in discovering what God is saying to them through His Word.

"The Law of Communication—To truly impart information requires building of bridges." Bridges are built outside the classroom as well as inside. By spending time with students outside the formal teaching setting, teachers get to know their students and their needs. Inside the classroom, bridges consist of arousing curiosity, gaining attention, and motivating the student before imparting information.

"The Law of the Heart—Teaching that impacts is not head to head, but heart to heart." Relationship is essential to effective teaching and learning.

"The Law of Encouragement—Teaching tends to be most effective when the learner is properly motivated." Nothing is more motivating than the awareness of a need and seeing the hope of that need being met. Effective teachers encourage learning by focusing on the relevance of truth to the student's life.

"The Law of Readiness—The teaching-learning process will be most effective when both student and teacher are adequately prepared." Student readiness involves factors such as: physical, cognitive, and spiritual development, background, experiences, and motivation. Teachers must use what they know about their students to prepare them for new truth.

A teacher's readiness is dependent on preparation. Unfortunately, the lack of adequate preparation is the source of many of the weaknesses in Christian education today. An effective teacher makes teaching a priority.

SUMMARY

Teaching and learning rarely stand alone but are intertwined in a process. Learning theorists have contributed much to the understanding of how people learn, resulting in implications for teaching. The Christian teacher, although not accepting many of secular theorists' underlying philosophies, strives to integrate sound research findings with biblical truth.

Christian educators recognize the distinctiveness of God's Word, the unique goal of transformation, and the impact of the Holy Spirit on the teaching-learning process. These factors contribute toward the development of a biblical approach to teaching and learning.

FOR FURTHER READING

Barlow, Daniel Lenox. *Educational Psychology: The Teaching-Learning Process.* Chicago: Moody, 1985.

Beechick, Ruth. *A Biblical Psychology of Learning.* Denver: Accent, 1982.

Biehler, Robert, and Jack Snowman. *Psychology Applied to Teaching*, 6th ed. Boston: Houghton Mifflin, 1990.

Ganfel, Kenneth O., and Warren S. Benson. *Christian Education: Its History and*

Philosophy. Chicago: Moody, 1983.

Gangel, Kenneth O., and Howard Hendricks, eds. *The Christian Educator's Handbook on Teaching*. Wheaton, Ill.: Victor, 1988.

Gregory, John Milton. *The Seven Laws of Teaching*. Reprint. Grand Rapids: Baker, 1954.

Hendricks, Howard G. *Teaching to Change Lives*. Portland, Oreg.: Multnomah, 1987.

LeBar, Lois E. *Education That Is Christian*. Edited by James E. Plueddemann. Wheaton, Ill.: Victor, 1989.

Pazmiño, Robert W. *Foundational Issues in Christian Education*. Grand Rapids: Baker, 1988.

Wilhoit, Jim. *Christian Education and the Search for Meaning*. Grand Rapids: Baker, 1986.

Woolfolk, Anita E. *Educational Psychology*, 4th ed. Englewood Cliffs, N.J.: Prentice-Hall, 1990.

8

C. Fred Dickason

The Holy Spirit in Education*

THE HOLY SPIRIT IN TEACHING AND LEARNING
- Recognize that His goal is personal development and maturity
- Allow His personal cultivation of teachers' lives
- Actively cooperate with His principles of teaching-learning
- Depend on Him as the only one who can make teachers effective
- Allow Him to facilitate interpersonal communication
- Seek to cultivate teacher's spiritual gifts and ministry under His supervision
- Promote reverence and response to His inspired Scripture

The often neglected person in the teaching-learning process is actually the most important. The Holy Spirit is the sovereign, most wise, and ultimate teacher of spiritual truth. He makes God's truth relevant to the persons involved and enables application that causes life and growth. Our teaching and learning efforts are in vain unless we cooperate with the Spirit.

Because the Holy Spirit was appointed by the Father, and because He is eminently qualified in His own right, we need to know Him and His role in the teaching-learning process that we may cooperate with Him in effective life and service for the Son of God.

*Editors' note: This chapter was previously published under the title "The Holy Spirit in Teaching." It appeared as chapter 8 of *Introduction to Biblical Christian Education*, edited by Werner C. Graendorf (Chicago: Moody, 1981). Minor editorial revisions have been made for use in this volume.

C. FRED DICKASON, Th.D., is chairman and professor of theology at Moody Bible Institute, Chicago, Illinois.

His Reality as a Person

What is the Holy Spirit? He is a *person* just as are the Father and the Son. Because we are made in the image of God, much of what we consider ourselves to be as persons applies to the Spirit. With the great amount of evidence and analogy available, we should have no trouble thinking of the Spirit as a genuine person.

As do all persons, divine and human, the Spirit possesses intellect (1 Cor. 2:10-11), emotions (Eph. 4:30), and will (1 Cor. 12:11). His works also affirm His personality. He is the intelligent creator (Gen. 1:2), the giver of personal life (John 3:5). He teaches (1 John 2:20), guides (Gal. 5:16-18), and speaks (Acts 10:19; 13:2). Pronouns that refer to persons are used of Him (John 15:26; 16:7, 13-15). He is the object of our personal trust, whom we may obey (Acts 10:9-21) or disobey (Isa. 63:10). And as a person, He is associated with the other Persons of the Trinity (Matt. 28:19; 2 Cor. 13:14). He meets all the definitions of a person.

The Holy Spirit is also *deity*. The Bible equates the Spirit with JHWH (Jehovah) of the Old Testament (compare Isa. 6:9-10 with Acts 28:25-27). Christ includes the Spirit in the name of deity (Matt. 28:19; note the one "name" with three personal titles). Peter says that to lie to the Spirit is to lie to God (Acts 5:3-4). The Spirit has attributes that only God possesses: omniscience (1 Cor. 2:10-11), omnipresence (Ps. 139:7-12), and omnipotence (Job 33:4). He works as God only can work. He creates and sustains life (Gen. 1:2; Ps. 104:30). He raises the dead (Rom. 8:11). He reveals God's truth (1 Cor. 2:10-11), and He creates divine life in the believer in Christ (John 3:5; Titus 3:5). He is fully God, as are the Father and the Son.

Our director and resource in teaching and learning God's truth is a genuine person and genuinely God. Without Him we could do nothing.

His Role as a Teacher

Since the Holy Spirit is a person and a member of the Godhead, He is qualified to teach as is no human. But how does He teach?

FALSE CONCEPTS

Roy B. Zuck identifies four erroneous views regarding the role of the Holy Spirit.[1] First, that He is the *total* (only) teacher. His teaching excludes human teaching, for He illumines each believer directly, and human teachers may obstruct His work. This subjective, mystical view ignores the revealed fact that the Spirit uses human teachers, as evidenced in the Great Commission (Matt. 28:19-20); the involvement of church leaders (Acts 5:42; 15:35; 18:11; 20:20; 28:31); the command to Timothy (2 Tim. 2:2); and the gift of teaching to believers (Rom. 12:6-7; 1 Cor. 12:28; Eph. 4:11). This view further limits education, either because

---

1. Roy B. Zuck, *Spiritual Power in Your Teaching*, rev. ed. (Chicago: Moody, 1972), pp. 59-65.

it is not needed, or because it excludes information or stimulation by other teachers. It can also lead to an attitude of superiority and infallibility because one's information comes directly from the Holy Spirit (fallible human understanding minimized).

A second false view sees the Spirit as a *totalitarian* teacher. He takes over the individual's responsibility for personal study or development. Human teachers need little or no training or preparation, for the results in ministry come from the Spirit. This imbalanced view results from a false view of the teacher. The teacher is more than a live book presenting truth. He is personally involved as example, expresser, and encourager for the truth (1 Tim. 4:12-16). He is personally concerned and contributing to the life and welfare of others (Acts 20:27-37; 1 Tim. 5:1-3, 17-18).

Third, some regard the Spirit as a *tandem* teacher. He adds His part after the human teacher has done his part. We give the facts, and sometime later the Spirit inserts the catalyst that activates the spiritual factor. This view fails to recognize that God works in us and through us to will and to accomplish His good plan for our lives and others (Phil. 2:12-13). As members of Christ's Body, the church, we have spiritual gifts that are to be exercised in the power of the Spirit, including teacher (Rom. 12:4-7). As Zuck points out, "When God is educating, the human teacher and the pupils are involved together in the teaching-learning process, and at the same time the Spirit is working within the teacher, on the Word of God, and within the pupils."[2]

The fourth mistaken view regards the Holy Spirit as if tethered. Bound by a humanistic philosophy of teaching, the Spirit is regarded as unnecessary to religious teaching. With the proper materials, equipment, personnel, and program, creative and well-meaning teachers can operate efficiently on natural grounds without the aid of the Spirit. This view fails to comprehend the biblical estimate of man's finiteness and fallenness, and has its only resource in sinful "flesh" (1 Cor. 2:14; 3:1-3). It elevates man's creativity and methods over God's and fails to realize that only the Spirit can accomplish the spiritual goals of Christian education.[3]

The common failure of the above erroneous views is that they fail to consider the balanced biblical revelation concerning the Spirit's role.

2. Ibid., p. 63.
3. Ibid., p. 64.

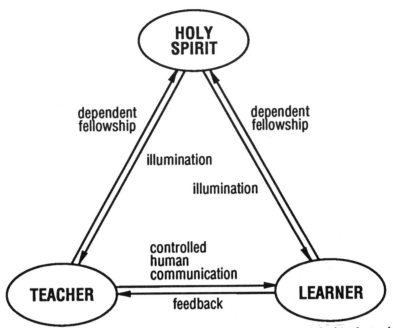

This diagram pictures the communication aspects among the persons involved in the teaching-learning process. The Spirit may teach the learner directly, or indirectly through the teacher. At any time there may be transmission and feedback along the channels indicated. A biblically informed approach to teaching-learning will take into account the dynamics suggested by the relationships involved. The Spirit illumines and enables both teacher and learner. Each, as a believer-priest, has direct communication with the Spirit. They may communicate on a human level with the Spirit controlling both of them. Teaching-learning tends to be maximized as these factory, among other pedagogical principles, are remembered and facilitated.

BIBLICAL CONCEPT

It seems clear from Scripture that there are certain principles by which the Spirit operates in the teaching role.

First, there is the principle of personal cooperation. Though salvation is totally the saving work of God by grace apart from human effort (Eph. 2:8-9), sanctification in any of its phases requires the God-assigned cooperative effort of the believer. Every command addressed to the human will is evidence of this. We are told to grow in grace (2 Pet. 3:18), to diligently add virtues (2 Pet. 1:5-8), to teach others (2 Tim. 2:2), to take pains to do the job well, not neglecting our spiritual gifts (1 Tim. 4:14-16).

"The Holy Spirit seeks to teach through human channels or instruments. Human teachers should seek to be under the full employment of the Spirit, as clean and capable instruments. . . . in the final sense, it is not they who teach, but the Holy Spirit. As instruments of the divine Teacher, they teach what the Spirit of God has revealed in His Word."[4]

4. Ibid., pp. 81-82.

This should not be understood as "letting go and letting God" in the quietistic, passive sense. The fruit of the Spirit is self-control (Gal. 5:22-23). As Ryrie puts it: "The Scripture does say very plainly that I am to do certain things that are a vital part of the process of sanctification. . . . But even in verses where the Spirit is mentioned as being involved in carrying out the exhortation, the individual is also included as a necessary part of the process."[5]

This type of cooperation is required of the teacher (1 Tim. 4:13; 2 Tim. 2:2; Titus 1:9) and of the learner (Matt. 7:24; Heb. 5:12; James 1:25). The Holy Spirit is a person who enables the person of the teacher and the person of the learner to communicate and interact with God's truth for personal and corporate growth.

Second, there is the principle of personal cultivation. The Holy Spirit revealed that we are persons made in the image of God. That means we are persons with intellect, sensibility, and will (Gen. 1:26; James 3:9). Though mankind fell and lost holiness, the image of God is retained, but is terribly marred by sin. For believers in Christ, the Holy Spirit has renewed our righteousness and holiness according to the image of Christ (Eph. 4:24). This was accomplished by His regenerating us (John 3:3, 5-6; Titus 3:5-6). He is now cultivating that new life He created within us to grow into more Christlikeness.

The teacher and learner should both recognize the great worth of the individual person made in the image of God. The Lord Jesus did. A person is of greater value than many sparrows (Matt. 6:26), than all the riches of the whole world (Matt. 16:26). In fact, the worth of man is best seen in the tremendous price of eternal death that Christ paid for each of us. Although unworthy of the least consideration because of our eternal debt and guilt, yet our worth, as made in the image of God, is indelibly written in the blood of the God-man. He did not invest His life in worthless creatures, but in unworthy sinners. That makes the job of teaching a matter of cooperating with the Holy Spirit in the cultivating of persons of extreme worth.

Cultivating is an individual responsibility. The teacher and learner have many of the same imperatives addressed to them both. Each will be evaluated for his works when Christ rewards His servants (1 Cor. 3:13; 2 Cor. 5:10; Gal. 6:4-6). The Holy Spirit cultivates both teacher and learner in a very personal way, and we must do the same.

The goal toward which we strive is personal maturity. That is one reason the Spirit gave the Word (2 Tim. 3:16-17). That is why He changes us from one stage of glory to another (2 Cor. 3:17-18). That concern must be shared by us as cooperative servants of God the Spirit.

Third, there is the principle of interpersonal communication. The Spirit operates in the individual's life, but He also operates in the corporate life, the body life of the church. The church is the Body of Christ, her risen, exalted Head (Eph. 1:20-23). Through the Spirit, Christ has supplied His Body with spiritual gifts, capac-

---

5. Charles C. Ryrie, *Balancing the Christian Life* (Chicago: Moody, 1969), pp. 64-65.

ities to serve others in various functions within the assembly (1 Cor. 12:4-7; Eph. 4:7-13). In the Body no members are without gifts. Further, no member is independent, but all members are interdependent (1 Cor. 12:14-26). In this complex of personal relationships, there is not just one teacher and not just one learner. We all in some ways are teachers and learners. All should contribute in balanced fashion, under the Spirit's control and with His gifts, to the welfare of the whole Body (1 Cor. 12:7; Eph. 4:12-16).

We must note here that the popular concept of discipling persons one by one through a particular leader is valuable to some degree, but no one person is sufficient for the complete task. Disciplers themselves must also be discipled. The whole Body must be involved in the total process.

It is also evident from Scripture that not all body life relationships occur in the formal teaching situation or even in the meetings of the assembly. Teaching-learning may be sponsored by the Spirit in any real life experience, in any personal encounter with truth, and in any interpersonal communication. The Holy Spirit can work on a personal basis before, during, and after any formal teaching-learning contact to cultivate spiritual life and maturity. However, the assembly provides the best context for total operation of spiritual gifts and overall teaching-learning (Eph. 4:11-16).[6]

"Let it be said again, the work of Christian leadership is always shown within the context of the universal church. There is no organization or institution which has any authority in Christian service apart from its connection with the church as represented by some local assembly. Everything that was done by God's people in the New Testament was church-related."[6]

To honor Christ with eternal effects and spiritual efficiency, any teaching-learning situation must apply the foregoing principles revealed by the Holy Spirit as those by which He operates.

His Responsibility in Teaching

In the administrative council of the Trinity, the Holy Spirit has been assigned by the Father and the Son the responsibility of application of the truth of God. What does He contribute to teaching?

RELATED NAMES

Certain names of the Spirit help us to grasp His contribution to teaching. The title *Spirit of Truth* indicates that He as deity is the revealer and applier of God's truth to human hearts (John 14:17; 15:26; 16:13). He makes God's objective, revealed Word of truth (John 17:17), centered in Christ who is the truth (John 14:6), to be subjectively applied truth (Eph. 1:17).

The title *Helper* (sometimes "Comforter," "Advocate") from the Greek *paracletos*, refers to one called alongside to help according to the need. This title is connected

6. Kenneth O. Gangel, *Leadership for Church Education* (Chicago: Moody, 1970), p. 185.

to the revealing and teaching ministry of the Spirit (John 14:26; 15:26). He is our helper in teaching, apart from whom we could teach nothing (Gal. 5:16-17, 25).

The title *Spirit of Wisdom and Revelation* speaks of the Spirit's work as "wising us up" by revelation. Again this points to His deity. The work involved here might have once included fresh revelation, as to the Ephesians in a day when Scripture was not yet complete and the gift of prophecy was still needed for the beginning stages of the church age. But with the completion of the whole New Testament canon, the Spirit's job is to give us wisdom concerning what has been already revealed as the complete and adequate guide for truth and practice (2 Tim. 3:16-17; Jude 3). His primary responsibility in teaching centers in the revealed truth of Scripture.

RELATED WORKS

With mention of objective truth and subjective application, we should consider the Spirit's ministries that relate to those and so to teaching.

The work of *revelation* is a disclosing of truth about God's person or will. Though God has revealed His truth in various ways,[7] His primary means were through His Son, the incarnate Word, and His Scriptures, the inscribed Word. The revelation in the Old and New Testament Scriptures was the work of the Spirit (1 Cor. 2:9-13; 2 Pet. 1:20-21). The Spirit is not now revealing new truth, hitherto undisclosed, to believers; but He is directly, or through the gift of teachers who explain the truth, applying the truth already revealed in Scripture.

The work of *inspiration* refers to that process of the Spirit when He superintended human authors so that, using their own personal powers, vocabulary, and style, they composed their contribution to the written Word of God without error in the original manuscripts.[8] Inspiration, then, gave us the inerrant record of God's choice, including revelation in propositional statements and historical events. This is the objective subject matter we are to teach (Matt. 28:19-20; 1 Tim. 4:13; 2 Tim. 4:1-4). It involves all of Scripture (2 Tim. 3:16-17) and all its teachings (Acts 20:20, 27).

Inspiration differs from *teaching* by the Spirit. Only biblical writers were involved in inspiration, whereas all believers may share in His teaching. The special superintendence upon the writers that guaranteed inerrancy in the Bible cannot be claimed under the Spirit's teaching. There is no such claim in Scripture, and teaching involves the understanding of finite and fallen minds, even though they be renewed by the Spirit. Appropriation of truth is always considered in Scripture to be subject to error.

As Zuck aptly puts it, "the Spirit's purpose in teaching is to make clear to the minds and hearts of God's children the truth which He has inspired."[9]

The work of *illumination* involves the Spirit's making clear and applying the

7. Charles C. Ryrie, *The Holy Spirit* (Chicago: Moody, 1965), pp. 34-35.
8. John F. Walvoord, *The Holy Spirit* (Grand Rapids: Zondervan, 1954), pp. 56-38.
9. Zuck, p. 34-35.

truth of Scripture. This seems to be His work with Christians that Paul mentioned in Ephesians 1:17-18. The psalmist cried for it (Ps. 119:18). Christians need illumination to discern the truth and to grow by it (1 Cor. 2:15; 2 Cor. 3:18). No new truth is revealed in the Spirit's illuminating; He is teaching on the individual level the truth that has already been revealed.

The unsaved man is unable on his own to receive the truth (1 Cor 2:14). He must first be convicted by the Spirit of the truth of the gospel and then respond to it in faith to receive the light of the gospel in the Person of Christ (John 16:7-11; 2 Cor. 4:3-6). Then, having received life and light in Christ, a person may benefit from the Spirit's illuminating the Scripture. That teaching causes growth as we receive biblical truth (1 Pet. 2:1-2). Again Zuck helpfully contributes:

> In teaching, the Holy Spirit operates on (or activates) both the written Word and pupils; one He animates and the other He illuminates. It is in this way that He communicates, or teaches, God's truth. . . . illumination is the communication of the *meaning* of the truth. . . . He guides into truth already revealed. Of course, to the believer being illumined, the truths may be new, for he has never before known them."[10]

Neo-orthodox or existential theologians hold that revelation takes place today when men respond to the witness and record of God's revelation in the Bible. To them the Bible is not the Word of God objectively. It merely contains the Word, which comes to us by revelation when we respond to it in some crisis situation of life. If we do not respond, it is not God's Word. By such doctrine they not only confuse revelation with illumination, but more disastrously they also reject any objective, revealed truth. Liberal theologians confuse inspiration with illumination. A man is inspired when he sees God's truth and responds to it with a life change. They, too, forfeit objective truth in recorded, inerrant form.

We must distinguish revelation, inspiration, and illumination used in the biblical sense. *Revelation* refers to God's objective act of disclosure in words or events. It speaks of truth's source: God. *Inspiration* refers to God's superintending men to write. It speaks of truth's inerrant record: Scripture. *Illumination* refers to God's clarifying the Scripture to believers. It speaks of truth's application: understanding.

At this point we should consider several major works of the Spirit performed for the individual. They in a large degree precede and are a prerequisite for any effective teaching ministry of the Spirit.

First, *conviction* brings the unbeliever to the place of acknowledging that the gospel is truth and that it applies to him. This work is absolutely necessary to overcome the deadness of man's sin nature and the delusion cast by Satan (John 16:7-11; 1 Cor. 2:14; 2 Cor. 4:3-6). By this the Spirit causes personal agreement with the gospel so that men may intelligently trust in Christ.

Second, *regeneration* creates a new capacity to think, feel, and perform with

10. Ibid., p. 56.

God. It renews the moral base of personality and allows both learning and teaching to be carried on through the Spirit (John 3:5-6; Eph. 4:24; 1 Pet. 1:23–2:3).

Indwelling brings the Person of the Spirit within the person of the believer. That results in a permanent personal relationship that allows the resident Spirit to work in and through the new nature implanted by regeneration (John 14:16-17). The Spirit's indwelling presence is God's gift to every Christian the moment he receives Christ (Rom. 8:9; Gal. 3:2). That is the basis of His teaching ministry in believers. However, full enjoyment of His teaching is reserved for those who are filled with the Spirit.

Fourth, *baptism* by the Spirit places the believer into Christ and into His Body, the church, upon receiving Christ (Rom. 6:1-4; 1 Cor. 12:12-13; Gal. 3:26-28). Not only does this far-reaching work place the believer into the sphere of right standing "in Christ," but it also dethrones the old sin nature through co-crucifixion with Christ (Rom. 6:6-14). This legal and moral union with Christ grants the possibility of saying no to sin and yes to God. In uniting us to Christ, the head of the church, the Spirit also places us into our own peculiar positions as members of Christ's Body. With the Spirit's gifts to us, we now may function to honor Christ and serve fellow Body members (1 Cor. 12:7, 11-13). Baptism occurs once for all at receiving Christ (Gal. 3:26-27). All Christians have it (1 Cor. 12:13). It is not to be sought since all have it, and we are never exhorted to seek it. Not all Christians, however, have the same gift; neither do all Christians have any one particular gift (1 Cor. 12:7-11, 28-30).

Fifth, the *filling* of the Spirit means the control of the person of the Spirit over the person of the believer (Eph. 5:18). Filling is the basis of all genuine and effective Christian living and service (Eph. 5:18–6:18). The Spirit keeps the old nature dethroned and under control (Rom. 6:12-14; 8:2-4; Gal. 5:16-17). This occurs only when we are given over to His will and are allowing Him to cultivate our lives and empower our service (Rom. 6:12-13; 12:1-6). His control does not eliminate our control, making us passive tools; but He operates in us and through us, in our individual personalities and abilities, to cultivate us and others through us (Gal. 5:13, 22-23; Phil. 2:12-13). Filling and baptism must not be confused. Baptism grants us position, our standing in righteousness in Christ; filling controls our practice, our expression of righteousness in the Lord. Baptism occurs once at faith, but filling occurs and continues only when we walk in obedience to God's Word (Gal. 5:16-17; Col. 3:16-17).

The teaching ministry of the Spirit is free to operate in the life of the Spirit-filled believer.

REALITY OF TEACHING

We have mentioned the Spirit's names and His works, and we come now to the reality of His teaching. We have already introduced many aspects of His ministry, but there are other factors we must consider.

Transmitting the truth. The Bible presents Christianity as objective truth from God centered in the historic God-man (John 14:6; 17:17; Col. 2:3), not merely an ethic, lifestyle, or service. The title "Spirit of Truth" refers not to truth centered in man's person or social relations, but to truth centered in God, from whom the Spirit receives the content of His message and for whom He discloses it to men (John 16:13-14; 1 Cor. 2:10-13).

So, then, the Spirit is concerned with a "given" body of objective truth concerning God, Christ, God's plan, man, salvation, and Christian life and witness. To be sure, "all truth is God's truth"[11]—even in the arts and sciences—and it should be treated in the context of Scripture and under the control of the Spirit. However, the Spirit's teaching operates primarily in the realm of *revealed truth.*[12] This seems clear from statements of Christ (John 14:26; 16:13; 17:17) and of Paul (1 Cor. 2:9-13; Eph. 1:17-18). This is the truth centered in Christ that makes us free (John 8:32).

It is that truth objectively revealed in which the Spirit would make us subjectively walk. It is called moral "light" as opposed to "darkness" of sin (John 1:5-8; 1 John 2:4-8; 2 John 1-4; 3 John 3). And it is that biblical truth that we are required to transmit under the Spirit's teaching.

We might profitably consider at this point the contribution of John 14:16; 16:13; and 1 Corinthians 2:13 to the subject. John 14:26 contains Christ's promise to the disciples of supernatural recall of His teachings. It obviously refers to teaching and remembering concerning all the things He spoke while He accompanied them on earth. The promise was to those in the upper room who had previously heard His teachings. That was necessary so that they might transmit His truth accurately in oral form. It would also enable those who would contribute to the written form of His truth in the Scriptures yet to be produced. So then it is not a promise to believers today that the Spirit will recall accurately to mind whatever we have studied in Scripture. We may extend, though, the Spirit's purpose to the preservation of the Word in manuscripts and to His participation in teaching the inspired, preserved Word. The Spirit who inspired the Word is vitally interested in teaching the Word.

John 16:13 promises, "But when He, the Spirit of truth, comes, He will guide you into all the truth." Again the "you" refers to the apostles to whom Christ had been telling many new truths connected with Himself and with the age in which He would be absent from earth and present with the Father. (Note the mystery truths, freshly revealed and not found in previous revelation, as in Matt. 13:11, 17; Eph. 3:5-6).

He had many more things to tell them, but conditions were not then ready. But after He sent the Spirit, He would continue revealing God's new truth for this age, completing God's disclosure centered in Christ so that the final product could be labeled "all the truth" (John 16:13). This is "the faith which was once for all deliv-

11. Frank E. Gaebelein, *The Pattern of God's Truth* (Chicago: Moody, 1968), p. 20.
12. Zuck, p. 44.

ered to the saints" (Jude 3), and was completed with the final "Revelation of Jesus Christ" (Rev. 1:1) in the last writing of John. Again, John 16:13 does not speak primarily of the Spirit's teaching, but of His revealing objective, normative truth for the church.[13] We may extend the principle of His purpose again, as in John 14:26. His interest in revealing new truth about Christ from God to the apostles would suggest that He would certainly be involved in the teaching of that truth.

Some consider 1 Corinthians 2:13 to refer to the Spirit's teaching ministry to all Christians. However, there are factors in the context that seem to limit the teaching to revelation and/or inspiration. The teaching falls into the sequence of communicating new truth, humanly unattainable to men such as the Corinthians and us. The order of communication is (1) truth in God's mind, (2) the Spirit's discerning God's mind, (3) revelation by the Spirit, (4) to apostles ("we" of verses 12-13), (5) in Spirit-selected words, as in Scripture, (6) to all men, who are either natural, carnal, or spiritual (as in 2:14–3:4).

Again we may say that the Spirit is interested and involved in the teaching of objective truth in His chosen words. That is evident from allusions to His lack of work in the natural man (v. 14; see also Jude 19) and from His obvious work in the spiritual man (v. 15). The "we" of 1 Corinthians 2:13 cannot be a reference to the Corinthians, who were so obviously carnal (3:1-3), for they would not be fit channels for the Spirit, neither would they qualify for infallible teaching of the Word that judges all men. Further, the "we" must be distinguished from those who are judged as spiritual through the reception of their words.

The most pointed references to the Spirit's work of teaching the believer are found in 1 John 2:20, 27. The Spirit is here named "an anointing from the Holy One," "the anointing which you received from Him [the Son]," and "His anointing." This one "abides in you," "teaches you about all things, and is true." Those are obviously references to the Holy Spirit with terms John has used before John 14-16. He is teaching all believers to apply the truth He has previously revealed and is alerting them to false doctrine. He is distinguished from the Father and the Son in the context (vv. 23, 27). The Greek word *didaskei* ("teachers") refers to an authoritative, doctrinal teaching, and the content of the teaching is connected to and based on what they had "heard from the beginning" from the apostles (v. 24). This is the central passage on the Spirit's teaching all believers the truth of the Word of God. He transmits an authoritative body of truth in His teaching ministry. He has revealed it; now He applies it.

Guarding the truth. In 1 John 2, the truth is opposed by the lie. False teachers with false teaching pervade the world, all purporting to have the truth. The

13. Zuck, pp. 36-38, holds John 14:26 and 16:13 to be valid references to the Spirit's teaching ministry today. But we must note (1) the immediate hearers were the apostles, who needed supernatural recall and revelation, (2) the context of many new truths being revealed (John 13:16, particularly 16:12), (3) the terms "teach" and "speak" may refer to revelation (John 6:63; 7:17; 12:49-50; Acts 2:16, 31; 28:25; 1 Cor. 2:13; Heb. 1:1-2), (4) references to the Spirit's receiving truth from the Father and disclosing or announcing it to the apostles (John 16:13-15), and (5) the problem with how all believers would be taught the whole truth even of Scripture.

Spirit raises the danger flag. He makes believers who know the basics about Christ and the gospel to be sensitive to false teaching. Consequently we can know all we need to know of true doctrine and discern error. This parallels the Spirit's specific teaching and warning about false doctrine of which Paul speaks (1 Tim. 4:1-6). He expects us to test all teachings and to bring them into comparison with the truth in Christ (1 John 4:1-6). He is greater than the false spirits behind the false teachers. All proposed systems and speculations must be brought captive to the obedience that Christ demands, according to His truth (2 Cor. 10:3-5). The Christian must not belong to the "cult of the open mind." He must prove all things on the basis of the Scriptures (1 Thess. 5:21-22). The Spirit will never teach or lead a believer contrary to what He has painstakingly inspired in the Bible.

Cultivating persons in the truth. We have mentioned the worth of the individual created in the image of God, and the investment of Christ's redemption of the individual. Now we need to be reminded of the personal interest the Spirit has in the individual. He jealously desires to have us fully enjoying and walking with Christ. James says, "The Spirit which He has made to dwell in us jealously desires us" (James 4:5, NASB margin). That means He is dedicated to the good of the individual and directs His activities to that end. He is doing more than producing good instruments for God; He is cultivating our persons so we may know God and love and enjoy Him forever as a person (John 17:3). Both teachers and learners are more than tools in a process. As Wayne E. Oates points out, "a *person*, however, is more than, other than, and different from the roles he perceives and enacts."[14]

We are cultivated directly by His teaching through illumination of the Word. He teaches us indirectly through godly men who have received gifts of teaching from the Spirit (1 Cor. 12:8-11, 28; Eph. 4:11). He builds us up corporately in the Body of Christ (Eph. 2:21-22; 4:12-16). He may teach in any combination: one on one, one on many, many on one, many on many. Teachers and pastor-teachers seem plural in the local assembly (1 Tim. 5:17; James 5:14), and both sexes may be involved, each teaching in his proper sphere under proper authority (Acts 18:26; 1 Tim. 2:11-15; 3:2-3; 5:17; 2 Tim. 2:2; 4:1-2; Titus 2:3-4).

We must never sacrifice the person in the process of teaching. We need lovingly to consider the person whom the Spirit highly regards, regardless of gifts, abilities, traits, position, sex, race, or station in life (1 Cor. 12:13, 22-25; Gal. 3:28; James 2:1-9).

HIS RESULTS IN LEARNERS

The Spirit's teaching is designed to produce certain basic effects in the life of the believer. First, He produces *spirituality*, which is the immediate result of the Spirit's control. Carnality characterizes those controlled by the flesh (Rom. 8:1-13; 1 Cor. 3:1-4; Gal. 5:19-21); but spirituality characterizes those controlled

14. Wayne E. Oates, *The Holy Spirit and Contemporary Man* (Grand Rapids: Baker, 1974), p. 42.

by the Spirit (Rom. 8:4, 12; 1 Cor. 2:15-16; Gal. 5:16-18, 22-23). Spirituality is that dynamic relation to the Spirit that enables growth and service (Gal. 5:25–6:10). The Spirit teaches us the Word that we may obey it (Eph. 5:18; Col. 3:16). That results in spirituality.

Second, He produces *growth*. When the believer walks according to the Word he has been taught, he may at any stage of life experience growth in grace and knowledge of Christ (2 Cor. 3:18; Eph. 1:17-19; 1 Pet. 2:1-2; 2 Pet 3:18). Growth, in turn, leads to greater comprehension, which expands ability to learn from the Spirit.

Third, He produces *maturity*. Growth with resultant maturity is a process made up of various phases, each in its own time and under the proper conditions set by the Spirit. Maturity is a condition of life in which we are grownup to some extent, properly adjusted to life's relationships, duties, and demands, with proper attitudes and development of character. Spirituality may be instant, but maturity takes time. It is the Spirit's purpose for us, and we need to plan and encourage teaching to that end.

Fourth, He produces effective *ministry*. As the Spirit has given gifts, so He encourages development of them to become more effective in various services (1 Cor. 12:7; Eph. 4:12; 1 Tim. 4:14; 2 Tim. 1:6). That involves diligent self-preparation and faithful cultivation on our part. The Spirit prompts works of edification (1 Cor. 14:12; Eph. 2:10; 4:12) and witness to the unsaved (Acts 1:8; 4:29-31). He uses His inspired Word (2 Tim. 3:16-17) and cultivates our personalities and skills. Our teaching should involve training the whole person and the proper preparation in Scripture and practical matters to evangelize and edify.

Both Zuck and Lawrence O. Richards make a pointed contribution to this subject.[15] Zuck emphasizes that Spirit-motivated learning is the highest form of intrinsic motivation.[16] The Spirit creates awareness of need, promotes desire to learn truth, and directs into relevant learning.

HIS REQUIREMENTS OF TEACHERS AND LEARNERS

There must be spiritual alignment with the supreme teacher, the Spirit of God, if any truly effective and eternal results are to be achieved. Any success must be measured by the Spirit's standards in His inspired Word (Gal. 6:7-10; 2 Tim. 3:16-17). Other standards and measurements must be checked by this (Isa. 8:20; Col. 3:16). To cooperate for successful teaching, certain conditions are mandatory, according to His Word.

There must be *a right relationship to Christ*. Without receiving Christ there is no spiritual life (John 1:12-13; 3:36). Only teachers and learners who know Christ through regeneration by the Spirit qualify for spiritual growth and service.

15. Zuck, pp. 119-23; Lawrence O. Richards, *Creative Bible Teaching* (Chicago: Moody, 1970), pp. 90-99.
16. Zuck, pp. 124-28.

There must also be *a right relationship to the Holy Spirit*. For effective service, teacher and learner should be filled with the Spirit (Eph. 5:18). Only under His control may we operate to honor Christ (John 15:1-5; Gal. 5:16-17; 5:25–6:10).

The one general condition, simply stated, for the filling of the Spirit is *obedience*, which involves heeding three basic commands. First, "Do not quench the Spirit," or do not resist Him (1 Thess. 5:19). That requires submission of the whole life and of each step of our lives to Him (Rom. 12:1-2). Our lives must be dedicated and directed by Him for effective teaching and learning (Rom. 12:4-8). Second, "do not grieve the Holy Spirit," or have no unconfessed sin (Eph. 4:30). The dedicated life can yet run into occasional sin, and it must be confessed for restored fellowship (1 John 1:9). Moment by moment cooperation with the Spirit results in enjoyment of Christ and enablement to perform His will. Third, we must "walk by the Spirit," that is, depend upon His power and His direction for the cultivation of effective life and service for Christ (Rom. 8:4; Gal. 5:16-17). We must not "be conformed to [the customs of] this world" (Rom. 12:2). Our goals, motives, and expressions should not be shaped by the world's creature-centered pleasure philosophy, but we must be transformed by the Spirit to know and do the good, acceptable, and perfect will of God.

Effective Christian teaching is enhanced by *proper gifts of the Spirit*. Not all can be as effective as some in teaching. Though all teach to some degree, the Spirit's gift of teaching gives to some the capacity to excel. Teaching is the ability from the Spirit to explain and apply the truths of God's Word, showing harmony and detail and making it personal. The Spirit teaches each Christian in the reception of the truth; however, He uses teachers to communicate that truth in digestible form. All believers should be taught by the Spirit, but not all believers communicate effectively to others what they have been taught. The gift of teaching rates first in importance after the gifts of apostles and prophets (1 Cor. 12:28; 13:8-10; Eph. 2:20; 3:5-6). We need to recognize that gift and provide opportunity and encouragement for its use.

The *gift of teaching*, as any other gift and perhaps more so, may be improved in quality by training and exercise. We must stir it up to full flame and keep it going and growing (1 Tim. 4:14; 2 Tim. 1:6). We must study the Word given by the Spirit with all diligence, privately and perhaps formally (2 Tim. 2:1-2, 15). We must also cooperate with the principles of God's pedagogy, learning to communicate effectively by all proper means, adjusting the teaching to the learners. So shall the Spirit's teaching become more effective by us to produce genuine learning. (See chap. 9 for more information.)

FOR FURTHER READING

LeBar, Lois E. *Education That Is Christian*. Edited by James E. Plueddemann. Wheaton, Ill.: Victor, 1989.

MacArthur, Jr., John F. *Whatever Happened to the Holy Spirit?* Chicago: Moody,

1989.

Pache, René. *The Person and Work of the Holy Spirit*. Chicago: Moody, 1970.

Ryrie, Charles C. *The Holy Spirit*. Chicago: Moody, 1965.

Walvoord, John F. *The Holy Spirit*. Grand Rapids: Zondervan, 1954.

Wilhoit, Jim. *Christian Education and the Search for Meaning*. Grand Rapids: Baker, 1986.

Zuck, Roy B. *The Holy Spirit in Your Teaching*, rev. and expanded. Wheaton, Ill.: Victor, 1984.

Dennis H. Dirks

9

The Teacher:
Facilitator for Change

TEACHERS WHO ARE CATALYSTS FOR CHANGE
- **Aim for change in all areas of the learner's life**
- **View learner needs as windows of opportunity**
- **Select teaching styles to match learning styles**
- **Provide for active learner involvement**
- **Guide learners toward higher levels of learning**
- **Facilitate transference of learning**
- **Nurture relationships with learners**
- **Teach for ongoing thinking**

Teachers of God's Word are unique. They are obligated to make a difference in the lives of learners. Their teaching should have impact. They can never be content with status quo. They must continually engage learners in a quest for an ever-deeper understanding of and relationship with God. Teachers of the Word are uneasy with a Christianity of ease and success, or with faith that is culturally limited or anemic. Their role is to communicate undiluted, life-transforming principles. They are not content with anything less than to challenge learner growth. To teach Scripture is to be obliged to nurture lives that are increasingly conformed to the image of Christ.

Meaningful teaching and learning take place in situations that have in common

DENNIS H. DIRKS, Ph.D., is associate dean and professor of Christian education, Talbot School of Theology/Biola University, La Mirada, California.

the Holy Spirit, a teacher, a learner, curriculum, an environment or setting, an aim, and methods that encourage learning. Of all these factors, none except the Spirit of God is more important than the teacher. The role of this human agent, the teacher, is essential. Although Scripture clearly teaches that learners have personal responsibility for change, it is also clear that God has chosen teachers to be instruments of promoting change.

Teachers whose goal is to change the direction of lives refuse to fit a stereotype. They recognize that some teaching roles—like those listed below—are ineffective in influencing people toward Christlikeness when used alone:

- telling
- convicting
- talking about God
- presenting lessons
- imparting information
- having students listen
- causing memorization
- eliciting correct answers
- packing students with facts
- filling the classroom
- building the teacher's self-image

Teaching for change involves some of these, and much more.

The root meaning of the word *educate* is to draw out rather than to fill with facts.[1] It may be compared with the role of a midwife or obstetrician. The birth attendant does not merely tell the mother all she needs to know about the birth process. The attendant helps make the birth possible. Similarly, teaching biblical content implies far more than telling. It suggests that understanding is developed and opportunities for truth to be practiced are provided. In fact the same word is used for both teaching and learning in Deuteronomy 4 and 5. God said, "The judgments which I am teaching you" (Deut. 4:1) are given so "that you may learn them" (5:1). The implication is that teaching is to cause students to learn. The biblical teacher does not think of teaching merely as things the teachers does. The teacher thinks in terms of what is to happen to the learner. The focus is on a learner orientation, not a teacher orientation. At the core of it all is a servant's heart.

GIFT OF TEACHING: PRIORITY FOR A CHANGE CATALYST

Is the spiritual gift of teaching necessary to be an effective teacher? Yes. For example, a natural talent for teaching may bring effectiveness for instructing history, yet by itself it is insufficient for teaching God's Word. A gift of teaching is essential for students' spiritual growth.

The gift of teaching is the ability to take knowledge, understanding, and wisdom of Scripture and communicate it to others in ways in which they learn and

---

1. Howard G. Hendricks, *Teaching to Change Lives* (Portland, Oreg.: Multnomah, 1987), pp. 41-43.

apply it to their lives.[2] To have the gift of teaching implies that others will learn. If students do not learn or if learning is minimal, it can be assumed that the teacher does not have the gift of teaching. This, however, does not mean that there will always be 100 percent effectiveness. Even Christ had hearers who failed to learn and to change their lives accordingly (e.g., Judas, the rich young ruler).

The focus of the gift of teaching is not so much on the teacher as on the learner. Its purpose is not merely to make teachers effective communicators, rather, it is to assist learners toward maturity. Paul indicated that the goal of teaching God's Word is to "present every man complete in Christ" (Col. 1:28). The purpose of teaching is to bring a Christian toward conformity to the image of Christ, to build up a believer to become "a mature man, to the measure of the stature which belongs to the fullness of Christ" (Eph. 4:13).

The situations in which teachers are effective vary from person to person. Some spiritually gifted teachers are most effective in one-on-one situations, others in small groups, others in small classes, whereas others are effective with large audiences.[3] Not all teachers are equally effective in all circumstances of learning. But it is equally clear that the gift of teaching, whatever the situation, requires tangible expressions of love to be effective (1 Cor. 13:1-3). It is also clear that possession and use of the gift of teaching assumes that the qualifications for spiritual leadership are met (1 Tim. 3:1-13).

The gift of teaching may be discovered by asking several questions. First, is it something to which you are drawn? Do you like doing it? Do you find enjoyment in watching someone else who does it well? Do you find yourself drawn toward ways to become more effective in teaching skills? Second, do you see yourself developing greater skill and effectiveness the more you teach? Are your fears or anxieties about teaching growing smaller, and is there a growing sense of confidence? Are the lives of learners changing? Third, do you receive confirmation from others that you have the gift of teaching? Do others sense the gift in you and recognize that learners grow as a results of your gift? If most of these questions can be answered positively, it is likely that you have the gift of teaching.[4]

GOAL OF A CATALYST: CHANGED LIVES

An effective teacher cannot be satisfied with "how well the lesson went" or "how much information I got across." Instead, to see lives changed is the most significant commitment a teacher can make. Many teachers hope for change and spiritual growth but fail to teach in such a way that it happens. Failure to accept the role of a spiritual change catalyst is to perpetuate a kind of Pharisaical learner, a condition in which the facts are well known but seldom acted upon.

To be concerned about life change is not to be unconcerned with biblical con-

---

2. Ray C. Stedman, *Body Life* (Glendale, Calif.: Regal, 1972), pp. 42-43.
3. C. Peter Wagner, *Your Spiritual Gifts Can Help Your Church Grow* (Glendale, Calif.: Regal, 1979), pp. 128-29.
4. Stedman, pp. 54-55.

tent. Rather, it is to recognize the purpose of content. The Scriptures were never intended for their own sake but were meant to bring about change. Content-centered teaching without clear concern for life change is inadequate. Throughout history, many have turned from the faith as a consequence of failure to make connections between teachings of the church and daily living. Faith's principles were relegated to isolated categories unrelated to and separated from life.

The focus of Christ's ministry was life change. Lives were clearly different as a result of contact with the Master. Christ affirmed the priority of redirected lives. Paul prioritized the role of the teacher as "admonishing every man and teaching every man with all wisdom, that we may present every man complete in Christ" (Col. 1:28). The word "complete" has the idea of maturity. It suggests that Scripture is not to be taught and mastered merely for its content. It implies dynamism, not status quo; growth, never stagnation. In fact, the purpose of God's Word is to cause change through "reproof . . . correction . . . training in righteousness; that the man of God may be adequate" (complete, mature; 2 Tim. 3:16). It is given for transformation, not mere information.

Maturity is a frequent theme in Paul's writings. The purpose of the spiritual gift of teaching, as with the other gifts, is to help believers "attain to the unity of the faith, and of the knowledge of the Son of God, to a mature man, to the measure of the stature which belongs to the fullness of Christ" (Eph. 4:13). Paul urges believers to press on to maturity (Heb. 6:1), which he elevates as a prime objective attained by having senses "trained to discern good and evil" (Heb. 5:14).

Truth is consistently linked with life change throughout the New Testament. Paul speaks of "knowledge of the truth that leads to godliness" (Titus 1:1, NIV). The teacher's role is to assist believers to "grow up in all aspects into Him" (Eph. 4:15), "to become conformed to the likeness of His son" (Rom. 8:29, NIV), and to become "transformed," a process that occurs from the inside out "by the renewing of your mind" (Rom. 12:2). It is a change that is to be so thorough and contagious that it is reproducible in the lives of others (2 Tim. 2:2). Paul points to specific changes that are the goal of teaching, such as "love from a pure heart and a good conscience and a sincere faith" (1 Tim. 1:5).

Many teachers do less to promote biblical change than to perpetuate comfortable, conventional, yet sub-biblical, lifestyles. But the teacher has an obligation to go beyond offering comfort to the contented. The purpose of teaching for life change is to accomplish the following:

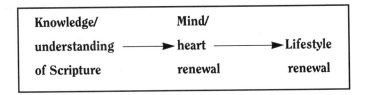

Change occurs as teachers help students meet God, not just as they learn information about Him. It is never sufficient merely to master doctrines and characteristics of God. It is possible to become so immersed in content about God that learners miss the Person of God. Such a purely intellectual or academic approach always comes up short. Students grow toward maturity when they come face to face with the living God.[5]

WHOLE PERSON CHANGE

The role of the teacher is to enable change in three major dimensions of students' lives: cognitive, affective, and behavioral. Scripture inseparably links all three. Life change does not occur as God intended unless the whole person is influenced in each domain. Cognitive change, or increase in knowledge, is essential but not sufficient in itself. Mere verbalized words or concepts are easily imitated and may not signal real change. The Pharisees fluently verbalized Old Testament law yet failed to express the principles in attitudes and lifestyle. As James indicates, to know and not to do is the same as not knowing at all (James 4:17). It is likewise easy to be stirred emotionally by biblical teaching and mistake feelings for actually doing what is commanded. No aspect of the faith is learned in the biblical sense until it is more than cognitive information or feelings. Attitudes, will, and lifestyle must also be affected.

To emphasize the importance of whole person change is not to disparage the teacher's role in communicating knowledge. As someone once said, "Burning hearts are not nourished by empty heads." Scripture consistently supports the value of knowledge as a foundation of wisdom. Whole person renewal begins with the mind (Rom. 12:2). It is in the mind that the life is shaped (Prov. 23:7).

To know in the biblical sense demands a relationship between the knower and what or who is known.[6] Contrary to common wisdom and practice, this suggests active interaction between the knower and the known, not passivity. The learner is to become actively engaged with what is to be learned. Biblical knowing also suggests two-way interaction between teacher and student. Knowing by way of one-way communication (teacher to student) is contrary to building the biblical ideal of mutual community (Rom. 12; 1 Cor. 12; Eph 4). Not only does teacher monologue not build community, it works against community building. Yet one-way communication continues to be practiced by teachers who, perhaps unconsciously, pursue power, control, and personal security.

Scripture never views knowledge in isolation from the dimensions of attitude and will. The concepts of mind and heart are irrefutably linked to such a degree that the same word is frequently used for both concepts. The heart represents intellect as well as emotions and will. Emotions are the fuel for whole person change.

---

5. Lawrence O. Richards, *Creative Bible Teaching* (Chicago: Moody, 1970), p. 19.
6. Parker J. Palmer, *To Know As We Are Known: A Spirituality of Education* (San Francisco: Harper & Row, 1983), pp. 23-29.

For example, learners must have a basic feeling of openness toward material to be learned, in order to be motivated to learn. It is the teacher's role to create a positive regard for biblical concepts. Attitudes typically progress through a series of levels that begin with a willingness to consider an idea, then move to the point of active mental engagement and deepened involvement, and finally progress so that the idea has become integrated into life. Emotions and will are closely connected with knowledge.

The concepts of knowledge and behavior are similarly inseparable. James condemns a faith that remains unexpressed in lifestyle (James 2:14-26).

NEEDS: ENTRY POINTS FOR CHANGE

Perceived or felt needs of students are windows of opportunity at which there is least resistance to change.[7] They are God-given points of entry or contact. Student felt needs generally are concerned with what is immediate or short-term. They include concerns like the following: problems to be solved, curiosity to be satisfied, knowledge that is needed, frustrations to be worked through, dilemmas requiring solution. Frequently, teachers ignore these opportunities for significant learning by focusing on their own needs. "Did I do a good job? Did I say that correctly? Do the students appreciate me?" But learner needs are the appropriate focus.

When the teaching of biblical principles is taken out of the context of daily living and placed in the unnatural environment of a classroom, the teacher's responsibility to encourage change becomes formidable. God's Word is intended to be linked with ordinary run-of-the-mill daily life. The teacher's role, then, is to bridge the gap between classroom and life. Some of the most significant connectors to life are student felt needs. The closer a teacher comes to focusing on learner needs, the greater the opportunity to influence change.

TEACHABLE MOMENTS

There are moments of opportunity when the learner is primed for change. Openness is at its peak. Motivation reaches an apex. Such instants are unpredictable points of time when both the learner's heart and mind are ready. These are strategic opportunities to reach below the surface and encourage life change. Such moments of impressionability often occur when learners experience any of the following: conflict, feelings of inadequacy, felt need, problems, goal-setting, search for meaning, difficult decision-making.

The effective teacher looks for opportunities such as these.

CHANGE INHIBITORS

Some teacher roles actually serve to inhibit student change. Teacher behaviors such as these should be avoided:

7. Hendricks, pp. 127-31.

- acting as resident expert, the answer person who must have the last word in each situation
- dispensing content exclusively, a "data dumpster"
- looking for the single "right" student answer
- focusing on a "star" student whose responses are praised over others
- rephrasing learner contributions in teacher's "better" terms
- being predictable in the classroom so that learners know exactly what to expect
- drawing lessons to "closure," leaving little stimulus for thinking outside class

Each of the preceding behaviors tends to close off significant opportunities for bringing about change.

ROLES OF A CATALYST FOR CHANGE

Even though the teacher is not solely responsible for what takes place in the learner, teachers are obligated to accept the role of catalyst for learner change. The effective teacher causes learning and change to begin. He initiates the process.

Change is sustained by repetition and reinforcement.[8] Repetition provides opportunity to examine biblical principles from a variety of perspectives. Material that is repeated also carries greater credibility for the learner. Even the disciples closest to Christ required frequent repetition.

Knowledge that is organized to progress from known to unknown builds on the learners' own knowledge and experience.[9] It is more easily remembered and acted upon when it is organized from simple to complex. Presenting arbitrary, isolated, unrelated parts encourages learners to dismiss the content. On the other hand, learners remember material longer if they find it meaningful.[10] It is also more easily transferred to life. Teachers concerned with life change will work to place biblical content in terms that have relevance to the learner.

Judgments and attitudes are more readily changed when teachers give specific illustrations and concrete examples rather than abstract information.[11] Change is likewise promoted when learners are involved in actively processing information rather than passively absorbing it.[12] Although passive learning may result in mastery of factual knowledge, it has little influence on attitudes and behavior. Active involvement has the added benefit of increasing understanding and insight. Christ referred to this characteristic of learning when He said, "He who practices the truth comes to the light" (John 3:21).

8. Jim Wilhoit, *Christian Education and the Search for Meaning* (Grand Rapids: Baker, 1986), p. 129.
9. Martin Bolt and David G. Myers, *The Human Connection: How People Change People* (Downers Grove, Ill.: InterVarsity, 1984), pp. 66-68.
10. Wilhoit, pp. 114-19.
11. Bolt and Myers, pp. 65-66.
12. Ibid., pp. 14-21.

A commitment to learner change requires that teachers be motivators.[13] As the writer of the book of Hebrews phrased it, "Stimulate one another to love and good deeds" (Heb. 10:24). Motivation is always taking place, whether positive or negative. Positive motivation is largely a product of teacher-learner relationships. It is likely to result from nurturing meaningful mutual involvement and interaction.

Teacher expectations can also cause a learner to excel or withdraw from the learning process.[14] For example, my father was told in first grade that he would never learn to read. He believed his teacher, withdrew from trying to master the skill of reading, and for many years struggled with reading. The expectations of a teacher can be powerful for good or bad. Learner motivation, however, comes not only from without but also from within. It largely results from a learner's own internal drive for competency. The effective teacher can capitalize on this drive by clearly showing the learner ways in which competence can be built as a result of what is learned.

Two biblical roles of the teacher share similar life change significance. The role of edifier is to build up and promote spiritual growth and development. It suggests encouragement of spiritual progress as a result of patient labor. The task of equipping is to fit or prepare fully. It is to equip with a goal that learners become actively engaged in the task of ministry.

A critical role of the teacher is to help learners know God, not merely know about God. To concentrate on the latter is to treat Scripture primarily as information. It results in well-informed Christians whose relationship is primarily to knowledge rather than to the living, life-changing God. It easily leads to continued spiritual immaturity and legalism. On the other hand, teaching students to know God results in believers who make responses and life adjustments based on a relationship with God. The product is learners who are motivated toward a life conformed to His teachings.

TEACHING STYLES TO PROMOTE CHANGE

One role of the teacher is to select an appropriate teaching style. Each of the four major styles is important in promoting learner transformation. No style is wrong in itself. Each is significant for certain kinds of learning, for certain learners, in certain situations.

Most teachers feel comfortable with one particular teaching style above another. Using another style requires stretching and growth and may cause discomfort. But the teacher with a servant's heart and with the learner's best interest in mind will become capable in all four styles. Clearly this requires flexibility. The effective teacher will not become exclusively bound to one style or another. To drive a stake in the tent of one style to the exclusion of others confines the teacher's

13. Hendricks, pp. 125-27.
14. Wilhoit, p. 137.

influence only to a portion of learners. Other learners who do not relate to the teacher's single style will not be reached. Instead, the effective teacher serves alternately as a transmitter of knowledge, a nurturer of the individual learner, a facilitator of cooperative learning between learners, and a guide toward learner outcomes or competencies.

1. *Informational style.* As the name implies, the informational style assists learners in the acquisition of knowledge.[15] The concern is to pass on content and to provide God's view. Knowledge clearly is a beginning of life change. Knowing God's perspective is needed before learners can change attitudes and behavior in appropriate ways.

The informational style, however, aims at more than mere information acquisition. It helps the learner categorize and organize biblical information. It assists in making sense of the world in light of Scripture. In this way it helps the learner take the first step toward wisdom, a virtue to be prized according to Proverbs and other biblical wisdom literature. This style is concerned with how the learner thinks about the subject. Identification of concerns or problems in following God's way is also an objective. Once problems are clarified, solutions to living out God's will can be developed.

2. *Personal/relational style.* The personal/relational style seeks learner growth toward wholeness and completeness through focus on the individual learner.[16] Its aim is to help the learner become all that he was meant to be in Christ. The style places emphasis on bringing to maturity inborn traits and gifts. Priority is given to developing lessons based on specific learner needs and addressing those needs in light of Scripture. Attention is directed to relationships between biblical teaching and learners' personal experiences.

The personal/relational style may at times be somewhat nondirective, giving learners opportunity to make choices and to pursue their own interests and areas of need within the limits of the scriptural aim for a given lesson. There is frequent emphasis on enhancing creative thought. Creativity promotes personal responsibility for application of knowledge to life. It encourages development of skills needed for application. Creativity also permits the learner to move beyond the boundaries of his own level of religious maturity toward greater maturity. Careful attention is given in this style to developmental perspectives. There is acknowledgment of the variety of learner characteristics that differ according to level of development. This style views issues at each level as divinely appointed, making the learner particularly vulnerable to the influence of God's Word.

3. *Interpersonal style.* The interpersonal style makes frequent use of cooperative learning.[17] Learners are involved together in understanding biblical teachings and relating them to life. This style relies on mutual learner stimulation. It

15. Bruce Joyce and Marsha Weil, *Models of Teaching*, 3d ed. (Englewood Cliffs, N.J.: Prentice-Hall, 1986), pp. 5, 23-27.
16. Ibid., pp. 7, 139-40.
17. Ibid., pp. 9, 215-17.

provides situations in which learners share insights. It provides in-class opportunity to fulfill the biblical commandment to "stimulate one another to love and good deeds" (Heb. 10:24).

The New Testament emphasis on the body of believers functioning in community with one another is likewise emphasized by the interpersonal style. Through use of learner pairs or small groups, commitment to shared responsibility is developed. Learners are encouraged to become responsible to and for each other in the Body of Christ. The style repudiates the notion that learning is only an individual process isolated from relationships. Teaching biblical content apart from learner interaction is artificial. It breeds individualism and works against the biblical ideal of life in the Body of Christ. The interpersonal style shows that spiritual development requires relationships. Spiritual maturity is not achievable outside a community of mutually committed and interactive believers.

4. *Behavioral style.* Concern with outcomes of the learning process is a primary focus on the behavioral style. Its emphasis is on learner competencies, on specific skills and behaviors that are observable.[18] A prime objective is that learners be able to do something with what is learned. Only when this occurs does the teacher consider the lesson effective.

Learners tend to imitate others for whom they have positive regard. For this reason, there is intentional effort in the behavioral style to provide for learner identification with the teacher. Identification includes a positive attitude toward, a desire to be with, and an openness to learn from the teacher. Modeling is a significant emphasis in this style. Christ affirmed the importance of modeling when He declared that "everyone, after he has been fully trained, will be like his teacher" (Luke 6:40).

Teachers who employ the behavioral style seek to make faith active. As James underscored, "faith, if it has no works, is dead" (James 2:17). The teacher who uses this style accepts a share in the responsibility to encourage learner action.

LEARNING STYLES

Learner change is facilitated as teachers adjust their teaching styles to students' learning styles[19] (see chap. 22). Failure to accommodate each learning style results in failure to connect the lesson with some learners. This may account for learner boredom, feelings that Scripture is irrelevant, or feelings of distance between learner and teacher. Principles of God's Word may seem unattainable or unrealistic. One result may even be distancing or alienation from the faith.

Differences in learning style suggest that one of the roles of the teacher is to structure teaching/learning experiences so that each learning style is provided for in each lesson. Although this takes intentional effort, it is not as daunting as it may seem. By following a "Hook, Book, Look, Took" format of lesson planning (see

18. Ibid., pp. 11, 307-16.
19. David A. Kolb, *LSI - Learning Style Inventory* (Boston: McBer, 1976).

chap. 11), there is greater likelihood that each learning style will be included.

INVOLVEMENT LEARNING

Studies indicate that most learners benefit from active engagement in the learning process.[20] Research shows that the role of the teacher is not merely to tell. If telling were all there was to learning, we would be blessed with spiritual giants. Yet the majority of Christian teaching continues to demand learner passivity. With such pervasive learner inactivity in the classroom, perhaps it is little wonder that there is little action outside class. The teacher unwittingly breeds learner passivity in other aspects of life if he primarily tells. A conventional form of Christianity, which relies on authority figures to prop up faith by providing all information and answers to problems, is also nurtured.

Involvement learning is not a matter of activity for the sake of activity. It requires meaningful activity and well-guided learning experiences. Involvement encourages learner ownership of biblical content. Where there is no ownership there is no personal investment, and there is greater likelihood of mere mental or verbal assent. The results of involvement learning are greater retention and potential for life change.

LEVELS OF LEARNING

Learning that leads to maturity in all areas of life must be challenged toward higher levels of learning. There are five recognized levels.[21] They begin with *knowledge*, an essential foundation for biblical life change. To know God's Word is undeniably a prerequisite to change in the appropriate direction. Given the paucity of biblical knowledge among Christians, many of whom have spent their lives in church, teaching for knowledge must be a priority. But to nurture learners who are able merely to repeat information hardly suggests a faith that is personally owned or acted upon. Yet teaching all too frequently stops at the knowledge level.

To know Scripture with understanding, to comprehend it, is to grasp its meaning. *Understanding*, the second learning level, goes beyond mere knowledge. It includes the ability to express biblical concepts in the learner's own words and in terms that have personal meaning. Yet even to know and comprehend are not adequate for meaningful life change. Learners must be guided toward the third level, *application*. To be able to apply is to use material in life situations that include those that may be new. It is an ability to put truth into practice. Obviously, application presupposes accurate knowledge and comprehension. The learner who is able to apply can address issues of life in ways that are consistent with Scripture.

The first two levels of learning cannot be skipped with haste to leap quickly to application. Neither can the teacher be content to consider learning complete after

20. Bolt and Myers, pp. 20-22.
21. LeRoy Ford, *Design for Teaching and Training* (Nashville: Broadman, 1978), pp. 82-84.

levels one and two, leaving the Holy Spirit to accomplish the rest. God's promise that His Word will not return to Him empty (Isa. 55:11) is no excuse for failing to consider how God's Word relates to attitudes, actions, and experiences of life.

Synthesis, the fourth level of learning, is the ability to bring biblical concepts together so that new insights are gained. For example, relating the concept of self-sacrifice to the principle of forgiveness can result in fresh understandings of the meaning of forgiveness.

The fifth learning level, *evaluation*, is the ability to determine the value of a particular decision, action, idea, or attitude in light of biblical standards. Learners may be guided, for example, to decide the validity of several potential Christian responses to social issues such as civil disobedience. To be effectively used, all levels of learning suggest the necessity of engaging learners in active involvement in the learning process.

LEARNING TRANSFERENCE

One role of the teacher is to assist learners to take what is learned in one situation and use it in another. This is known as transference of learning, a requirement for life change. There are hazards when learning is compartmentalized. Placing biblical concepts in discrete, isolated cubbyholes leads to an inability to generalize or to relate what is learned to other experiences. Segmenting what is learned results in major gaps in areas of the learner's life in which the scalpel of Scripture has not been applied. A kind of spiritual schizophrenia results. To use a biblical image, a divided mind is the product.

To listen and do what God commands (Jer. 11:4) implies transference from experience to experience and situation to situation. This was part of God's intention when He instructed the Israelites to talk to their children about His teachings in all aspects of life, as life is lived (Deut. 6). The teacher can instruct for transference by posing new situations and by drawing aspects out of past experiences that are related to the new. By beginning with what learners know and proceeding to what is unknown, the teacher utilizes the principle of learning transference.

FREEDOM TO FAIL

To teach for transference and to encourage learners to engage actively in relating Scripture to life is to risk learner mistakes and occasional failure. This, however, is a natural part of learning and is not to be avoided. Some of the best lessons of life grow out of the experience of failure. Mistakes have sometimes been described as the back door to success. They are the crucible out of which change can emerge.

Somehow teachers have the false idea that mistakes and failure are to be shunned at all cost. The underlying assumption is that failure reveals a character flaw or unacceptable inadequacy. But to teach so there is freedom to fail and to learn from failure is to recognize God's perspective. Paul reminds us that in weakness God's strength becomes evident (2 Cor. 12:9-10). It is also true that growth can occur through mistakes IF there is freedom to consider openly and reflectively those mistakes.

The world has discovered and actively used this biblical principle. Robert Townsend, former CEO of the Avis car rental corporation, was responsible for bringing Avis from the backwaters of automobile renting to become number two in the industry in just a few years. One of Townsend's guiding principles was that nothing much happens unless people are making mistakes and learning from them.[22]

The teacher's role is to provide an environment of openness. It is an atmosphere that is safe from tongue-clucking and finger-pointing. It is a surrounding in which the facade of error-free Christian experience is slowly broken down. Such an atmosphere requires the teacher to be a model of openness about personal mistakes. Not to say that the teacher should display all personal dirty laundry, but the teacher who is willing to reveal appropriate areas of personal weakness, missteps, and struggles provides freedom for learners to do so.

RELATIONSHIPS: MOTIVATORS FOR CHANGE

One of the most powerful motivational forces for changed lives is the relationship between teacher and learner.[23] This human dimension, added to the power and conviction of the Holy Spirit, provides potent fuel for the change process. The relational dimension gives flesh-and-blood reality to content. Biblical values become sought after because they are embodied in the life of a teacher for whom the student has affinity and positive regard.

A community of faith that supports and nourishes biblical ideals presumes relationships. It was true in the Old Testament and continues with heightened emphasis in the New. Christ chose twelve disciples not simply to instruct them to understand His purpose and their roles. Repeatedly, the gospels indicate that He selected the twelve that He might be with them. More than sixty times the New Testament writers remind believers to do something for, with, or to each other. Paul's own ministry to the Thessalonians was a model of relational caring.

A relational emphasis suggests that the teacher is not so engrossed in the task of structuring learning that listening and sensing learner needs are ignored. Several years ago a book was published with the title *The Geranium on the Windowsill Just Died, But Teacher You Went Right On*. Some teachers are oblivious to what goes on around them and miss opportunities to nurture relationships.

TEACHING FOR ONGOING THINKING

Once the door of the learner's mind is closed to one thing it quickly leaps to something else. To deliver a lesson that is neatly packaged to begin and end with-

---

22. Tom Peters and Robert Townsend, *Winning Management Strategies for the Real World* (Chicago: Nightingale-Conant, 1986).
23. Jere E. Brophy and Thomas L. Good, *Teacher-Student Relationships: Causes and Consequences* (New York: Holt, Rinehart and Winston, 1974), pp. 12-15.

in the class session is to restrict learner thinking to the class hour. Lesson closure is an undesirable goal, for it shuts the door to further reflection. The teacher's task is to provoke continued thought, even after the lesson is concluded. This can be done by intentionally leaving portions of the lesson open-ended. By not providing answers to every issue allows room to explore further. It leaves opportunity for seeds of thought to sprout. This is not meant to allow for sloppy teaching that is loose and totally open-ended. An effective lesson requires an idea or concept that anchors and provides solid implications. But it should likewise leave generous opportunities for wrestling with issues after the class concludes.

Christ's use of parables was a highly effective method to encourage thinking. Christ minimized teaching that was mere one-way content delivery. Instead, He used parables that employed metaphors, that raised questions and confronted people with the unexpected. The parables challenged clichés and glossed over ideas and begged the minds of hearers to probe their meaning.

DISSONANCE AND DISEQUILIBRIUM

Inertia is one of the most powerful forces working against learner change. In terms of learning theory, it is an innate drive toward equilibrium. It involves a high level of resistance to change. Yet the nature of change requires disruption of equilibrium. In fact, long-term change does not take place when learners feel comfortable. Yet much of what passes for teaching is in reality little more than reinforcement of the comfortable. Without creative tension, the change process seldom begins. Healthy discontent with "what is" in comparison with "what needs to be" can be productive.

One powerful example in Scripture is Job's friends, who suggested that a sinless life results in prosperity. After all, God blesses the upright. Their outlook flies in the face of Job's blameless, upright living, as well as his immense losses. The friends' old answers did not fit. Dissonance in the mind of the readers of Job is the result.

The role of the teacher is to create healthy dissonance or disequilibrium[24]—but not chaos. Disequilibrium occurs when there is a surprising new or different way of looking at truth. Old answers do not fit new situations. Exposure to ideas that contrast with the learner's present outlook, the unexpected, or a new facet or application of an old truth all are potential disequilibrators. The tough moments of life similarly can prompt dissonance.

LIFESPAN DEVELOPMENT

Learner development across the lifespan may be classified into categories such as intellectual, emotional, moral, physical, and social—among others. Each level of development has particular tasks and challenges that have potential for prompt-

---

24. Herbert P. Ginsburg and Sylvia Opper, *Piaget's Theory of Intellectual Development*, 3d. ed. (Englewood Cliffs, N.J.: Prentice Hall, 1988), pp. 221-33.

ing spiritual development. Each provides opportunity for application of God's Word in fresh, relevant ways. Some dimensions of development also suggest limitations to learner capacity. For example, the stages of cognitive development mean that some forms of reasoning and cognition are unavailable to the learner and must wait for a later period of development.

Christian teachers tend to approach developmental limitations in one or two ways.[25] First, they may ignore developmental stages and expect students to master material for which their development has not prepared them. In doing so, teachers run the risk of "inoculation," that is, of creating in the learner a resistance to consider the material at a later time. The learner, being unsuccessful in mastering the concepts because of developmental limitations, may avoid the possibility of future failure by avoiding the material altogether. The potential for inoculation occurs when learners are exposed to too much material and to concepts for which they are not developmentally prepared. Second, teachers may unnecessarily limit the kinds of material provided for learners. They conscientiously avoid anything that is beyond the learner's immediate grasp.

Both approaches are to be avoided. A better approach is something between the two. Clearly, overloading with content unintelligible to the learner is not productive. Yet many Christian truths that are not immediately understood can be planted like spiritual time-release capsules that open at the right moment. Rather than interfering with full understanding later, they prepare the learner for subsequent deeper meaning because of their familiarity.

NURTURING TRANSFORMATION

Teaching for life change requires roles that differ from traditional teaching. While instruction clearly is involved, instruction is most powerful when connected directly with life experiences as they occur (Deut. 6:1-9). In this regard, the classroom presents some formidable obstacles. Classroom learning tends to be formal. It holds great potential for creating distance between learner, the Word of God, and life. There is little opportunity for modeling that is connected to regular life experiences. In the classroom there is an inherent tendency to nurture the mind to the neglect of the heart. The teacher must give extra attention to minimize the inherent constraints of the classroom setting.

Importance of persons. Learners are the focal point of an effective classroom learning experience. Building community, then, becomes an essential task. It involves nurturing a feeling of belonging. Faith was never meant to be purely individual. It was meant to be worked out in the context of community. It is grown in an environment that is nonthreatening. As teachers intentionally focus on learners, they are more likely to provide an environment that is free from threats to learner security and significance. The nurturer avoids "you-judgments." There are 101 subtle and deadly ways to say "dumb idea." The classroom

25. Locke E. Bowman, Jr., *Teaching Today: The Church's First Ministry* (Philadelphia: Westminster, 1980), pp. 101-9.

cannot become a shooting gallery, either teacher to student or student to student.

Open-minded conviction. When the teacher prescribes the accepted way to think about and respond to each issue, opportunity for learner transformation is minimized. The teacher should be so assured of what he believes that there is no compulsive need to change the learner's thinking to match the teacher's own on all issues. There is openness to embrace differences.

Reflection of adversity. The difficulties of life that each learner brings to the classroom hold possibility for prompting transformation. Pain can cause gain, as James reminds us:

> When all kinds of trials and temptations crowd into your lives, my brothers, don't resent them as intruders, but welcome them as friends. Realize that they come to test your faith and to produce in you the quality of endurance. But let the process go on until that endurance is fully developed, and you will find you have become men of mature character, men of integrity with no weak spots. And if, in the process, any of you does not know how to meet any particular problem he has only to ask of God— who gives generously to all men without making them feel guilty—and he may be quite sure that the necessary wisdom will be given him. (James 1:2-5, Phillips)

But if life trials are to have the desired effect of bringing change, they require guided reflection and consideration.

Challenge conventional Christianity. Much of what passes for Christianity is little more than a kind of "cultural spirituality." It lacks spiritual dynamic, having become dry, sterile, and devoid of much meaning. It is mere rote, demands little, and is only routinely practiced. Often it is sustained by teaching that accomplishes little more than to continue complacent living. Studies indicate that the majority of believers live on the plain of conventional Christianity. The teacher has responsibility to challenge what has become the usual, commonplace, conventional habit. Growth depends on such challenge. It thrives when teachers resist a formula approach to biblical principles.

Dilemmas. Scripture is replete with dilemmas. Situations abound in which individuals were confronted with the need for decision. In some instances the dilemmas clearly involved right and wrong. In others, the choice was between good and better. But these biblical crossroads of decision making are rich with life-change potential. Guiding learners to wrestle both with biblical dilemmas and those of daily life opens the door to growth and change.

The Change Catalyst

The teacher is clearly a potential catalyst for learner change. But there is a subtle temptation to rely on old notes and long-gone experiences. It is a temptation of comfort that resists being stretched. And the results are lessons devoid of change incentive. Even if there is excitement and effective communication skills, little life-changing dynamic is present. Unless the teacher is stretching personally, there is less likelihood learners will also be stretched. Teachers have an obligation to continue to grow and intentionally to place themselves in situations where growth is encouraged.

PREPARATION

A life-changing teaching/learning situation demands careful preparation. No teacher can afford to "wing it"—not with stakes as high as in teaching to transform lives. The teacher's labor of diligence and reflective planning begins with personalizing the truth. Only when there is personal ownership of what is to be taught is there passion. A teacher's passion about what is being taught taps the emotional dimension of learning. Teacher enthusiasm and excitement, when it is genuine, not conjured or faked, is a prime ingredient in promoting life change. Only when Scripture has passed through the grid of the teacher's life is teaching with conviction possible.

Teacher preparation includes not only lesson preparation but strengthening teaching skills as well. The growing teacher, one who is increasing in effectiveness, will pursue opportunities for training. Skill-sharpening takes place through training classes, workshops, tapes, and books. The teacher who continues to be open to personal growth will also find observation of other skilled teachers beneficial.

CONGRUENCE

Effectiveness in encouraging life change in learners depends in large measure on the degree to which there is congruence in the teacher. What is taught must match what is lived. A teacher is incapable of communicating qualities or characteristics of spirituality with life impact without personal growth in those same qualities. The character of the sender in large measure determines the validity of the message for the receiver.

Congruence includes authenticity and genuineness. The authentic teacher does not deny struggles in living God's way with integrity. Neither does the teacher ignore the need for matching life with words. A measure of vulnerability is required. Far from reducing learner respect and attention to what is taught, such openness promotes trust. The teacher who has "arrived" is usually regarded with suspicion; it is always more difficult to identify with a finished product.

The importance of congruence cannot be overstated. As Christ said, "everyone, after he has been fully trained, will be like his teacher" (Luke 6:40). To model a life that does not match biblical principles is to breed learners whose lives also are not integrated.

PERCEPTIONS

To be effective catalysts for change, certain attitudes are needed. These attitudes in part carry the power of expectations. They establish patterns of teacher communication and response.

First are teacher perceptions of *self*. The teacher should feel identified with, rather than apart from, learners. A sense of identification with learners provides what is necessary for reciprocal learner identification with the teacher. A feeling of adequacy rather than inadequacy is needed. Not that there is arrogance or failure to rely on the resources of God. Instead, there is conscious recognition that when God calls to a task He provides all that is necessary to be adequate. Also necessary is to see oneself as wanted rather than unwanted. A teacher's feelings of not being wanted create anxiety in learners and interfere with learning.

Second are perceptions of *others*. To perceive others as able fosters learner hope for successful life change. Effective teachers see others generally as friendly, not unfriendly. Learners are not perceived as impeding or threatening.

A third group of perceptions have to do with *teaching itself*. Concern for freeing learners, not controlling them, is essential. The teacher needs to see teaching as self-revealing rather than self-concealing. There should be eagerness for personal involvement in helping relationships, not feelings of alienation. There is attention to furthering process, that is, helping others to search and discover, rather than always directing toward preconceived solutions.[26]

PARTNERSHIP

Teaching biblical truth is never done alone. It is always in partnership with the Holy Spirit. Responsibility for teaching cannot be given over to God. The teacher cannot say, "It's God's Word and God's learner. If God wants change He'll make it happen." To do so is to abrogate God-given responsibility. For some reason God has chosen imperfect human vessels to accomplish part of His plan for learner change. It is the teacher's role to recognize the vital partnership with the Spirit of God and cooperate with God's plan for transformation of learner's lives.

FOR FURTHER READING

Bolt, Martin and David G. Myers. *The Human Connection: How People Change People*. Downers Grove, Ill.: InterVarsity, 1984.

Coleman, Jr., Lucien E. *How to Teach the Bible*. Nashville: Broadman, 1979.

Gangel, Kenneth O., and Howard Hendricks, eds. *The Christian Educator's Handbook on Teaching*. Wheaton, Ill.: Victor, 1988.

Hall, Terry. *How to Be the Best Sunday School Teacher You Can Be*. Chicago: Moody, 1986.

Hendricks, Howard G. *Teaching to Change Lives*. Portland, Oreg.: Multnomah, 1987.

26. Jay Smith and Don-David Lusterman, *The Teacher as Learning Facilitator* (Belmont, Calif.: Wadsworth, 1979), pp. 56-63.

Richards, Lawrence O. *Teachers: Teaching with Love*. Elgin, Ill.: David C. Cook, 1988.

Wilhoit, Jim. *Christian Education and the Search for Meaning*. Grand Rapids: Baker, 1986.

Wilhoit, Jim, and Leland Ryken. *Effective Bible Teaching*. Grand Rapids: Baker, 1988.

Willis, Wesley R. *Developing the Teacher in You*. Wheaton, Ill.: Victor, 1990.

Zuck, Roy B. *The Holy Spirit in Your Teaching*. Revised and expanded. Wheaton, Ill.: Victor, 1984.

10

Biblical Feeding for Leading

PRINCIPLES OF INDUCTIVE BIBLE STUDY
- **Study the Bible text itself, before going to books about the passage**
- **Look, and look, and keep on looking**
- **Write it down**
- **Make personal application after careful study of the text**

"Your job is not to fatten geese but to train athletes." This was the charge given at graduation time to a class of rising Bible teachers. It was not long before the graduates had the opportunity to answer the challenge. Now they were the teachers. Some took the easy route and spoon-fed countless Bible facts to their classes. Others took the difficult route and chose to be athlete trainers, knowing their students would soon be on their own with open Bibles on their laps, wishing they knew how to study this great Book of God for themselves.

Training athletes—what an exciting, responsible task. The teacher is the coach, the model, and the example. And if students do not sense that a teach-

IRVING L. JENSEN, Th.D., is Bible professor emeritus, Bryan College, Dayton, Tennessee.

er's Bible is his most precious book and that his personal study of it is exciting as well as profitable, then he will lose his team. Students may come out fattened with facts (albeit eternal and true) but may miss the thrills of running the race on their own.

Teachers must ask themselves, How much do I value my own personal Bible study? Do I literally study and analyze the Bible text, or do I stay only in devotions? How enthusiastic am I? Do I pass on my enthusiasm to my classes and Bible study groups?

TEACHER AND CLASS—OUR COMMON NEED OF BIBLE STUDY

We will first consider Bible study—but not two different kinds of study, such as one by the instructor and one by the instructed. God gave the Bible to every man, so He must have intended that everyone read and study it. God "has spoken to us" (Heb. 1:2), and He had all of us in mind. The Bible's message is the same no matter who the reader is, where he lives, or even how well he can read.

TOTAL INVOLVEMENT FOR ALL

When teachers are off by themselves reading and studying the Bible, they must get totally involved with God's Word. They must keep eyes open wide, meditate long, search for answers to their questions, and open their hearts to the Word and let it probe their very being. Then they will discover things they had never seen before. And in the joy of discovery a deep desire will result: "How I wish I could get my class to taste this joy of studying God's Word!"

THE BIBLE TEACHER: TRAINER, GUIDE, AND INSPIRER

A teacher's personal Bible study should bring him closer to God. It should stir, challenge, and uplift him.

An instructor should think back over the last few times he led his class in the study of a Bible passage. He should ask himself, "When each session was over, were my students so excited over Bible study that they were already looking forward to the next session? Could they sense that the Bible was my special book? Did I leave unwritten impressions and directions about how they could experience the same joy?

To this day I have indelible memories of one of my seminary teachers. As he led us around the words and lines and paragraphs of an Old Testament passage, occasionally he would print a key word or phrase of the passage on the chalkboard to reinforce the emphases he saw in the Bible text. I could sense by his voice and the words he wrote if a climax was near. And when we reached such a destination, tingles of excitement would surge up and down my spine; I felt I was there in the middle of the Bible text. I made it one of my goals to study and teach the Bible with the same kind of enthusiasm over the Word of God Dr. Kuist had. I was convinced that Bible study was more than the fruit of labor. I saw it as an adventure, a healing surgery, and an exciting search for the eternal truths of God. And if God would ever assign me in His vineyard as a Bible teacher, I wanted to be that kind of a trainer, guide, and inspirer of my students.

AN EFFECTIVE APPROACH TO THE SCRIPTURES: INDUCTIVE BIBLE STUDY

When one considers Bible study, a natural question to ask is, "What kind of Bible study?" That is a question about method, which is simply an orderly procedure. A highly recommended method or procedure of Bible study is inductive study. The inductive method is an ideal approach in the teacher-student setting.

The inductive method of Bible study is for everyone. It does not require special abilities, only a drive to see what the Bible says. Everyone studies on his own, independent of others, but always with the help of the Spirit.

But inductive study, like all effective approaches, takes time. There are no shortcuts. The reading of God's Word alone takes time. Good teachers and good students know the value of having extended time for studying the Bible. *National Geographic* magazine tells a moving story about eighty-one-year-old Carl Sharsmith, veteran park ranger in California's Yosemite National Park, one of the world's most-loved national parks:

> Carl was back at his tent quarters after a long afternoon with tourists. His nose was flaked white and red with sunburn; his eyes were watery, partly from age but also from disappointment at hearing again an old question after a half century of summers in California's Yosemite National Park.
>
> A lady tourist had hit him with a question where it hurt: "I've only got an hour to spend at Yosemite," she declared. "What should I do? Where should I go?"
>
> The old naturalist-interpreter-ranger finally found the voice to reply:
>
> "Ah, lady. Only an hour." He repeated it slowly. "I suppose if I had only an hour to spend at Yosemite, I'd just walk over there by the river and *sit down and cry.*"[1]

We would do well to reflect on that response and apply it to our own attitude toward Bible study. All methods of Bible study demand time. And inductive study is one of them. Students who are willing to devote time to the inductive approach will come away blessed.

WHAT IS INDUCTIVE BIBLE STUDY?

Inductive Bible study is a natural, unforced approach to the Word, in which one allows the words and lines within the paragraphs to speak for themselves.

---

1. David S. Boyer, "Yosemite—Forever?" in *National Geographic* (January 1985): 55.

THE INDUCTIVE METHOD: SCIENTIFIC IN APPROACH

This procedure is aptly illustrated by the experience of a student at Harvard University, who was seeking to learn something in a special area of zoology.[2] His teacher Jean Agassiz gave him a pickled specimen of a fish, a haemulon, which was to be the sole object of his study. The student learned over a period of three long days what was involved in gaining a thorough knowledge of the fish. The advice of the professor was to the point. First, the student was to look—for how else could he master the subject? Second, he was to draw on paper what he saw, for "the pencil is one of the best eyes." Third, he was to recognize the parts of the haemulon in their orderly arrangement and relation to each other, for "facts are stupid things until brought into connection with some general law." That this method of study was fruitful is indicated by the student's later testimony: "To this day, if I attempt to draw a fish, I can draw nothing but haemulons."

When applying this "scientific" approach to the Scriptures, three stages of study are involved: observation, interpretation, and application.

1. *Observation.* The inductive method begins with the observable. We should first observe, then base our conclusions on those observations. We look for answers to questions such as: "What do I see here?" "What does the author say?" (This is content.) "How does he say it?" (This is form.) We find many important things in this "how" search. The best clues are the author's emphases of certain words and phrases and the relations between them.

Induction is the pathway of discovery, going from the specifics and arriving at the whole. We see some facts and truths for the first time, without the aid of help from others. Those discoveries are what makes the method so exciting and full of joy.

The contrasting approach is deduction, which is the route of proof. Deduction moves from the general to the specific. Deduction starts with a teaching from prior knowledge, then examines the details to see if they support the truth. An example of deductive Bible study is the Berean Christians' examination of what Paul had taught them. "They received the word with great eagerness, examining the Scriptures daily, to see whether these things were so" (Acts 17:11*b*).

2. *Interpretation.* In the inductive approach, interpretation follows observation. When we observe something in the Bible text, we ask, "What does that mean?"

The immediate context of the passage (verse, paragraph, and segment) is our best choice for learning the meaning. Marginal notes in our Bibles identify the aid of distant context, and the main concordance and dictionaries at the end of an exhaustive concordance[3] will supply any additional information we need for learning the meanings of words. For the most difficult passages we may have to seek the aid of commentaries.

2. See Irving L. Jensen, *Independent Bible Study* (Chicago: Moody, 1963), pp. 173-78.
3. For the words of the *New American Standard Bible*, use the concordance published by Holman, 1981. For the King James Version, use *Strong's Exhaustive Concordance*, published by Abingdon, 1890).

3. *Application.* Application is the goal of all Bible study. Our main concern should be not what we do to the Bible, but what it does to us. The question to ask is, "How am I involved here?" We might think of the Bible as a book about the arena of life in God's universe. The participants in that arena appearing in our passage are in this group:[4]

- God (Father, Son, Spirit) and His angels
- Satan and his hosts
- People of the world
- Myself, the reader of the passage

When we look in the Bible text for possible applications to our lives, we will find that all applications are in one or more combinations of these four areas: for example, our service for God (God), temptation to sin (Satan), our concern for a brother in Christ (people), and our growing faith (myself).

THE INDUCTIVE METHOD: ANALYTICAL IN CHARACTER

When we are face-to-face with the minute parts of Scripture—including even punctuation—and when we wrestle to know its intent in its context, we are engaging in the reading and study process known as analysis. Analysis is distinguished by its exactness and minuteness in the examination of words. Merrill Tenney made a high appraisal of the analytical method when he said, "In order to ascertain exactly what a given body of text says, one should employ the analytical method."[5]

In the analysis process the student studies the Bible itself, not words written about the Bible.

Analysis of the Bible text also involves its structure, which is how the author put the words together. The writer composed words, phrases, and sentences in a unit that appears in our Bible as a paragraph. A group of paragraphs makes up a unit we call a segment. In the Bible a segment averages twenty to twenty-five verses, which is a workable length for proceeding in the study of a book. Someone once advised: "Study the Bible the way God wrote it: segment by segment."

A segment is a unit of thought, and all the paragraphs of that segment contribute to the segment's message in their own ways. The implications of such a structure are tremendous. For instance, the second paragraph of a segment may *appear* to have no necessary relation to the first or third paragraphs, and yet because the student knows it is placed where it is for a purpose, he is challenged to find that reason. Many thrilling nuggets of gold have been discovered from such a study of relations, where "things hook and eye together."

---

4. See Irving L. Jensen, *How to Profit from Bible Reading* (Chicago: Moody, 1985), pp. 57-70.
5. Merrill C. Tenney, *The Genius of the Gospels* (Grand Rapids: Eerdmans, 1951), p. 165.

SOME PRACTICAL WAYS OF INDUCTIVE BIBLE STUDY

As suggested earlier, there are different ways of using the inductive method in Bible study. In this last section we will look at what can be done in the analysis of a segment of Scripture.

Suppose a class or Bible study group decides to study the whole book of Romans. Where do you go from there? Some selected activities of an inductive approach are described below.

PREPARATION

The first class session should be spent on background—becoming acquainted with the book's origin (for example, who wrote it and why?). The second hour should involve survey of the book. Survey is a skyscraper view. It gives you a feel of the book and identifies you with its original readers. The order of survey before analysis follows the important rule: "Image the whole, then execute the parts." A survey chart is a good help here and can save time in this opening stage of study (see survey books listed in bibliography).

IDENTIFICATION

The next step is to identify the segment and paragraph units to be studied. Most editions of the Bible show paragraph divisions, and some Bibles, such as the *New International Version*, show segment divisions such as 1:1-17; 1:18-32; 2:1-16. (Segment and paragraph division of all the books of the Bible are supplied in Moody Press's *Bible Self-Study Guides*.)

READING IS FOUNDATIONAL

Keep in mind that in these pages we are looking primarily at the observation stage of analysis. This stage begins with reading. How well you read the Bible text is a key to study of the paragraphs of a segment. (Try reading the long sentence of Romans 1:1-7 in the *New American Standard Bible*!) Your inflections, loudness, speed, pauses, and progressions show the emphases and relations that are important observations in the inductive process. Later you will record such observations on paper.

RECORDING IS A MUST

"A pencil is one of the best eyes." This counsel of Professor Agassiz applies to every field of study and communication, Bible study included. It is amazing how many doors to new observations are opened by the plain recording of one observation. The analytical character of the inductive method demands that what is observed be recorded in some way. Joseph M. Gettys cites one of many reasons for recording: "You should stress to all of your pupils the importance of working on paper, for what is written on paper releases the mind to fasten its attention on something more."[6] This applies to the stages of interpretation and application as well.

There are various ways to record our studies. I have called one of these ways the analytical chart method. The following pages will show a few things that can be done in the making of an analytical chart.

THE ANALYTICAL CHART

Most of the observation stage of analysis can be recorded on the analytical chart. One of the chart's main values is that it can register emphases and relations clearly. These are the best clues in the analysis process.

1. *The rectangle.* Draw a 4 inch by 9 inch rectangle centered on an 8 1/2 inch by 11 inch page (see accompanying chart). Then draw horizontal lines to show the paragraph division of the segment you are studying. The segment shown here is Romans 1:1-17, and the paragraphs begin at verses 1, 8, and 16. Note that inside each box you will be printing only words and phrases of the Bible text. The blank spaces of the four margins are for your own words and outlines.

2. *Talking text.* The first thing to do in the study of a Bible passage is to read the Bible text itself. One interesting and effective way to make the text come alive is to recast the words and phrases in a printed form that I call talking text.

The purpose of the talking text is to "functionalize" each word and phrase of the Bible text so that it reveals its distinctive service in the grammatical makeup of the sentence. This is not a technical exercise. As you read the lines of the paragraph, look especially for emphasized words and phrases and related facts and truths. Show these in your own way by how you print the text. This talking text is *your* project.

Read the accompanying talking text of John 4:39-42 (see chart below). Observe how various graphic devices are used to show the thought structure of the text. Those devices include underlinings, indentations, various sizes of print, capitalizations, italics, boxing, arrows, and blank spaces. As you read the talking text of John 4:39-42, see if you sense a progression leading to the climactic last two lines.

6. Joseph M. Gettys, *Teaching Pupils How to Study the Bible* (Richmond: John Knox, 1950), p. 13.

ROMANS 1:1-17

1
8
16
17

The talking text becomes the basic framework about which all your other studies are made. It is one of the best ways to become intimately acquainted with the Bible author himself.

Note that you may choose to complete only an abridged talking text, showing *main* words and phrases. This abridged form is what you will be using in the next steps of building an analytical chart.

Talking Text of John 4:39-42 (NASB)*

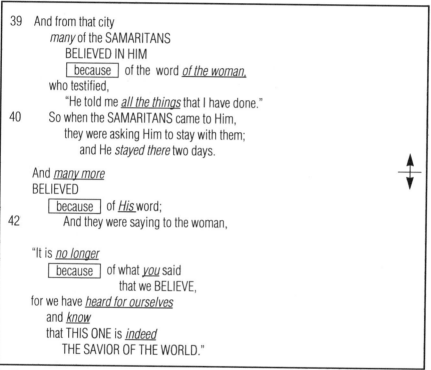

* From Irving L. Jensen's book *How to Profit from Bible Reading* (Chicago: Moody, 1985), p. 108. Used by permission.

3. *A main topical study.* A main topical study is a study of one subject of the segment—in this case Romans 1:1-17. It shows on the analytical chart as a key study, but it is not necessarily the segment's *dominant* subject. The accompanying chart is a partly completed analytical chart of Romans 1:1-17. Refer to it while you read the following procedures.

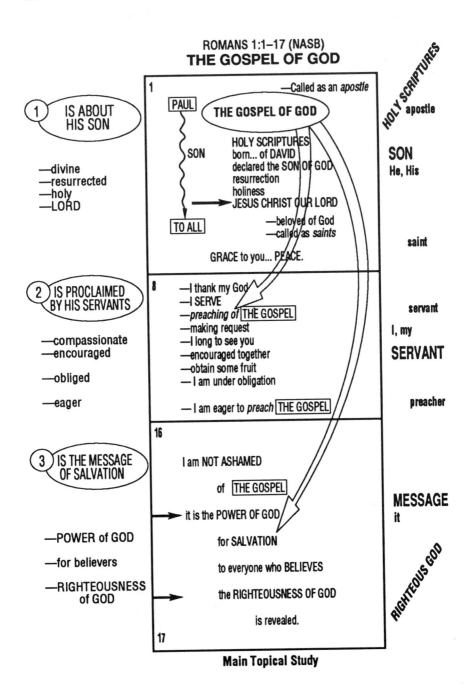

ROMANS 1:1–17 (NASB)
THE GOSPEL OF GOD

Main Topical Study

a. Record in the three paragraph boxes some key words and phrases that you observed while making your talking text. This is your starting worksheet for the remainder of your activities.

b. Look for a subject (not necessarily of the same words) that appears in each of the three paragraphs. Be thinking of developing this as a main topical study of your chart.

c. Choose a phrase in the segment that represents that subject—called key center. Circle the key center, then draw an arrow from it to a phrase in each paragraph that is related. For example, notice the following on the accompanying chart: The key center is "The Gospel of God" (v. 1). Arrows go from the key center to these related words or phrases: "Son"(first paragraph), "preaching: (second paragraph), and "for salvation" (third paragraph).

Based on those early observations, we arrive at the following main topical study, and we print it in the left margin:

> The Gospel of God
> 1. Is about His Son
> 2. Is proclaimed by His servant
> 3. Is the message of salvation

4. *Supplementary studies*. All other items, including isolated observations, outlines, and word and topical studies, make up the remainder of the analytical chart. They are printed in the margins. Note how the following are printed on the accompanying chart:

a. The first paragraph is mainly about the Son; the second, about Paul; and the third about the message. This appears to be a simple observation, but it opens the door to a number of important reflections. For example, What may have been Paul's reason for writing about the Son of God first?

b. A comparison of the segment's beginning: HOLY SCRIPTURE and ending: RIGHTEOUS GOD. How do you relate these two awesome truths?

c. Salutation that brackets the first paragraph: PAUL . . . TO ALL. Who is the subject in between?

d. Prominence of the pronoun "I" in the middle paragraph. There is much here for a study of a servant of God.

e. Notice the amplifications recorded under each of the three paragraph points: (e.g., the words *divine, resurrected, holy*, and *Lord,* under the first point).

VALUES OF THE ANALYTICAL CHART

The above studies are just a few of the many observations that may be recorded on an analytical chart. The primary value of the analytical chart is that the student has extended his analysis to the point of graphically and clearly recording his observations in black and white. The following represent some of the values related to that:

1. keener seeing
2. retention and permanence
3. seeing the whole passage simultaneously
4. integrating the various parts
5. emphasizing the primary over the subordinate
6. establishing solid foundation and motivation for the next stages of interpretation and application

VALUES TO THE TEACHER

Because of the graphic elements of the analytical chart, this method of Bible study is especially useful in teaching a group that has not already studied the Bible passage. The teacher has already become intimately involved in the passage through some form of an analytical chart beforehand. The temptation to fall back on spoon-feeding will be suppressed. Of course the teacher must adapt the presentation to the group's age and background, length of class session, size of class, and so on. It almost goes without saying that if the segment frame is sketched on a screen or chalkboard, most of the text cannot be reproduced, for want of space. Rather, key phrases are printed within the frame as the teacher proceeds in teaching the lesson. The choice of the appropriate words and phrases to be used requires wisdom in planning, but the impact of using the visual printed phrase at the right moment is tremendous. These are the truths the student will not easily forget.

The analytical chart method places high premiums on each student's Bible study, and this becomes a growing experience in his daily walk. He sees Bible study as a fascinating expedition rather than a necessary chore. What teacher would not want a part in his training?

INTERPRETATION AND APPLICATION

Earlier we saw that the three stages of inductive Bible study are observation, interpretation, and application. Much of the interpretation is done during the observation stage, which we have shown to be the key to full Bible study. And that's what application is built upon.

The application stage of Bible study is your personal search for spiritual help, food, instruction, and inspiration. The question you must keep asking is, How does this touch *me*? You identify with the persons of the Bible text, or with the original readers, or with the writer. This reference to others is not a selfish outlook. It is why God gave the Book to *you*.

Recall that earlier we said application searches the passage for what it says about the participants in the arena of life: God, Satan, people, and you. Inescapably you are in that arena. Below are listed examples arising out of those relationships. They are reminders of the kinds of applications to look for in a Bible passage. Record your applications on separate paper—there is no room on your analytical chart for many entries.

Your relationship to God:
- fellowship to enjoy
- commands to obey
- promises to claim
- prayers to echo

Your relationship to Satan:
- person to resist
- devices to recognize
- sins to avoid and confess
- armor to wear

Your relationship to others:
- in the home
- in the church
- in society
- in the world

Your own very being:
- past heritage
- present experience
- future hope

Application is the goal of all Bible study. Each passage we study is about the arena of life mentioned above. After we have observed and interpreted the text of Romans 1:1-17, recording our observations on an analytical chart, we should seek to apply its truths in ways the Spirit of God intended. Below are listed some questions that might come to us in this application stage of studying Romans 1:1-17.

ROMANS 1:1-7

How do the truths of Jesus' humanity and deity have much to do with my daily walk, such as my praying?

Paul writes that he is "set apart for the gospel of God" (1:1). Do I identify with him in any way? As a believer, am I "called" by Jesus Christ (1:7)? Do any obligations rest on my shoulders because of this? If so, what are they? I should determine in my heart to be faithful in all the obligations that I know are mine.

ROMANS 1:8-15

What do I learn from Paul's life and ministry as I study these verses: Paul said, "I am debtor" (1:14). Do I really feel indebted to lost souls? "I am ready" (1:15). Am I willing and eager to proclaim the gospel? "I am not ashamed" (1:16). Am I ever embarrassed to speak out and share the good news of salvation?

What do I learn from Paul about prayer, love, faith, and Christian service?

ROMANS 1:16-17

What do these verses reveal about God and His Son? What do the verses before them reveal? How do these truths help me spiritually?

Do I see any direct or indirect reference to the satanic world in the whole passage (1:1-17)? If so, how can I apply this to my life?

The most relaxed minutes of your Bible study should be your last ones, as you seek to apply the text. God has been speaking to you in His Word, and you have been listening and responding to it. Ask for His continued help, and thank Him for the portion of His Word that you have been studying.

FOR FURTHER READING

Braga, James. *How to Study the Bible*. Portland, Oreg.: Multnomah, 1982.

Cate, Robert L. *How to Interpret the Bible*. Nashville: Broadman, 1983.

Jensen, Irving L. *Enjoy Your Bible*. Minneapolis: World Wide, 1989.

———. *How to Profit from Bible Reading*. Chicago: Moody, 1985.

———. *Independent Bible Study*. Chicago: Moody, 1963.

McQuilkin, J. Robertson. *Understanding and Applying the Bible*. Chicago: Moody, 1983.

Wald, Oletta. *The Joy of Discovery in Bible Study*. Revised edition. Minneapolis: Augsburg, 1975.

Warren, Richard, and William A. Shell. *Dynamic Bible Study Methods*. Wheaton, Ill.: Victor, 1989.

Wilhoit, Jim, and Leland Ryken. *Effective Bible Teaching*. Grand Rapids: Baker, 1988.

11

Larry Richards with Lin Johnson

Planning for Teaching and Learning*

ELEMENTS OF AN EFFECTIVE LESSON PLAN INCLUDE
- **A specific aim that leads students to respond to biblical truth**
- **A hook that grabs attention and sets a goal**
- **A book that guides students to explore the content and meaning of the Bible passage**
- **A look that helps students relate truth to life**
- **A took that challenges student to practice biblical truth**

"Failing to prepare is preparing to fail." This old maxim contains a great deal of truth in relation to teaching. Too often a Bible teacher decides to ad lib his class time—sometimes under the guise of depending on the Holy Spirit—because preparation time was squeezed out of his week by the tyranny of the urgent. Unfortunately, the casualties become the students.

On the other hand, a prepared teacher makes his classes fresh, vital, and interesting. In return, his students are productive. Through careful planning his teaching bears fruit.

*Editors' note: Most of this chapter is adapted from *Creative Bible Teaching,* by Larry Richards (Chicago: Moody, 1970).

LARRY RICHARDS, Ph.D., is a free-lance writer living in Hudson, Florida, and is author of *Creative Bible Teaching.*

LIN JOHNSON, M.S., is a free-lance writer and editor living in Niles, Illinois; managing editor of curriculum, Lederer Messianic Ministries, Baltimore, Maryland; and coeditor of *Christian Education: Foundations for the Future.*

To grow spiritual fruit, a teacher must: (1) focus on the meaning of the Bible truth taught, (2) involve students in an active search for meaning, and (3) stimulate and guide students in the discovery process. These steps can be accomplished as one uses a framework for developing a lesson plan and for teaching students. This structure consists of a *specific aim, hook, book, look,* and *took.*

DEVELOPING A TEACHING AIM

The aim of Bible teaching is transformation. In 1 Timothy 1:5 the apostle Paul says, "The goal of our instruction is love from a pure heart and a good conscience and a sincere faith."

The trouble is, transformation is a big aim—too big. Teachers want it, but the idea of transformation or maturity does not provide helpful guidelines for constructing a specific lesson. To say, "I want this lesson to bring my students to maturity" may be commendable, but it is not meaningful. One lesson simply will not accomplish it; there are too many factors involved in spiritual maturity.

And you can see why when you break down the idea of maturity. What's involved? There is a relationship with God: prayer, Bible study, worship, meditation, praise, confession, and honesty. And then there is a relationship with our family: love, patience, guidance, discipline (both giving and receiving), and forgiveness. There is also a relationship with non-Christians and its cluster of concern: witnessing, separation from worldliness, exemplary living, consideration, suffering, and many others.

Certainly no single class, series of lessons, or even year of lessons will bring a student to maturity in Christ. So while the big aim of transformation is always there, one's teaching aim has to be more specific.

The question is, What kind of teaching aim is in harmony with the big aim of transformation? How can a teacher direct each lesson to lead students closer to that maturity?

In 1 Corinthians 2:15 Paul claims that the spiritual man "appraises all things." The Greek verb used, *anakrino,* speaks of a capacity to discern. By virtue of his salvation and relationship with God, a believer has the capacity for spiritual discernment of "all things." He can look at life the way God does. He can see the implications of God's truth for life situations and can respond in harmony with God's will. But this is only a capacity—one that is not fully developed in all believers.

The process of developing from capacity to ability is intimately related to maturity. Hebrews 5:14 says that mature men "discern good and evil." The word "discern" is from the same root (*krino*) as the word "appraises" of 1 Corinthians 2:15. It is set apart by a prefix (*dia*) that indicates that what is a capacity in all believers becomes an ability in mature believers.

Now, how do mature believers move from capacity to ability? How do they become mature? "Because of practice [they] have their senses trained to discern good and evil." These are people who have seen the implications of truth and responded appropriately. This is the educational significance of Hebrews 5:14. Growth comes by experience, by using our capacity to understand and respond.

What does this mean to the teacher whose goal is spiritual growth? Simply that his teaching aim will be to produce response. Those living responsively to God are the ones who grow and mature.

That response goal, however, needs to be tied to Scripture content. But aiming for content knowledge alone will not produce spiritual growth. So when a teacher builds a lesson, he must think in terms of the learner response he hopes to achieve and then word the aim accordingly.

BUILDING A RESPONSE AIM

Understand the passage. Understanding the passage comes first. Any response we seek to evoke must be appropriate to the true meaning of the passage. "What does this passage teach?" is the first question to ask in building a response aim. The response we aim at must be appropriate to the Word of God.

Understand implications for the learner. To guide a response aim, we need to know as much about our students' lives as possible. We can get to know them by reading about the general characteristics of their age group, through observing them, by visiting their homes, by talking with them, and by spending time with them outside of class. The better we understand their lives, the better we can tailor our lessons.

STATING THE RESPONSE AIM

When you understand the passage and see its relevance to the lives of your pupils, you are ready to state your aim. Usually several criteria are suggested for constructing aims. An aim should be:

- short enough to be remembered
- clear enough to be meaningful
- specific enough to be achieved

Be careful, however, of the temptation to become too specific. The aim should be stated flexibly—flexibly enough to permit the Holy Spirit freedom to guide each learner to the unique response He chooses for him to make.

What does a short enough, clear enough, flexible enough response aim look like? Let's construct a response aim for John 11:17-44, the biblical record of the raising of Lazarus. Note the movement of the passage.

Christ comes to Bethany and is met by Martha, who tells Him tearfully of her brother's death. In a touching expression of faith, Martha tells Jesus that she knows if He had arrived sooner, her brother would not have died. Jesus responds with a promise that her brother will rise. She agrees that Jesus is the Christ, the resurrection and the life, and believes that He will raise Lazarus on the last day.

Then Mary arrives and expresses the same confidence as her sister: "Lord, if You had been here, my brother would not have died." Then the three go to visit the tomb. There Jesus shocks everyone by ordering the stone blocking the tomb removed. Martha, full of faith a moment ago, objects: "Lord, by this time there will be a stench, for he has been dead four days." Martha was convinced that Jesus had power, even the control of eternal destiny. But she unthinkingly limited His power to act in the present.

As you read are you convicted of that same sin? How many times do you—who trust Christ as Lord and God—unthinkingly leave Him out of your life? How often have you worried and become upset? Isn't this unbelief? Christ is not limited. He can reach down into your daily life and meet every need. "Did I not say to you, if you believe, you will see the glory of God?"

Here is a passage you as a teacher want to share. So you sit down and begin to work out your aim. Your list may include the following:

- exalt Christ as a present help
- show that Christ's power is available to meet daily needs
- help my students see that Christ's power is unlimited
- show ways we unconsciously limit Christ's power
- guide my students to tap Christ's power today
- help each student discover areas in which he may be limiting Christ, and help each student begin to trust Him

There—it is not perfect, but it does express your purpose. The first two aims you wrote focus on content. The next aim focuses on content, too, but you began to think in terms of your students. The next two aims focus even more on the students. But the last one says how you hope each student will respond to the truth you are going to teach.

This last aim makes room for the fact that each student may have a different way in which he limits Christ. So the lesson will need to be structured to help the class explore various areas, so that God can pinpoint each student's need. The aim goes beyond insight. The aim is stated in terms of the response, which is actually the goal.

When you reach the point of seeing the goal of your teaching in terms of student response, you are ready to construct the lesson plan.

STRUCTURING THE LESSON

A teaching aim is developed from studying the passage. It spells out the response you are striving for. Thus it gives a clear idea of where you want to go. But getting there requires a definite structure.

HOOK

Let's say you have prepared the lesson. You have been gripped by the truth you are about to teach. You have seen it work in your life. When you come to class, you are excited about the lesson.

But your students are not. They have not had your experiences, and they are not thinking about your lesson. They have their own problems. An adult student may be worrying about his job. A teenage student may be replaying last night's game or nursing the tragedy of a rejected date. A child student may be thinking about playing outside after class. All differ, but each comes to class operating on his own wavelength. You must entice a student to leave his thoughts and share yours.

And so the hook. Fishermen use a hook to bring fish out of the lake into the boat. Teachers also use a hook to bring their students into the Word of Life.

There are several qualities of a good hook: first, it gets attention, and second, it sets a goal. Preachers call this a "need step," which is something to answer the question, "Why should I listen to this?" If this sermon or lesson is going to be about something important to me, I want to pay attention. If it is an irrelevant recounting of dusty data, I do not! When students have no reason for learning—no reason that is important to them—it is difficult to hold them. But set a goal they want to reach, and they will stay with you.

The third quality of a good hook is that it should lead naturally into the Bible study. For example, a hook may be as simple as asking a question: "When do you get scared?" It may be drawing pictures of times when students were afraid. Or it may be making bumper stickers or creating radio commercials that focus on what love is. There are a lot of options to choose from. But no matter what method you use, a hook should begin in real life and prepare students for the Bible study or story. It should not consist of Bible content.

BOOK

During the book part of the lesson, a teacher tries to clarify the meaning of the passage studied. This is when you help students to acquire—and understand—biblical information.

It is not necessary—and usually is not wise—to try to teach an entire Bible chapter or lengthy passage in sixty minutes or less. Your aim may dictate that you focus on only part of the passage—but not to the exclusion of its context.

A variety of methods are available for helping students understand biblical content. The more students are involved in discovering biblical truth for themselves, however, the more they will retain. Whatever the method, the purpose of this part of the lesson remains constant: give biblical information and help students understand it.

LOOK

When students understand what the Bible says, it is time to move on to implications. Their knowledge must be tempered with "spiritual wisdom and understanding" (Col. 1:9). So plan this part of the process to guide your class to insight into the relationship of the truth to everyday life.

The first step is to discover principles from God's Word that apply to us today. In the raising of Lazarus, for example, one principle is that Christ's power is unlimited and available to meet our needs.

The second step in relating truth to life is to explore relevant areas of applying those principles. One effective way of doing this with junior age and older students is an open class discussion. For example, you might ask, "In what areas do high school students need Christ's power today?" By focusing on the age group in general, you protect students from feeling personally threatened and like they are exposing their weaknesses and sins. Role playing and case studies are other effective methods of exploring ways to apply truth to everyday life.

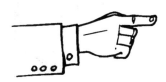

TOOK

But like a vaccination, the Word of God is of no effect until we can say it "took." Response is required. Normally response to teaching will take place outside of class, in weekday life. James 2:17 says, "Faith, if it has no works, is dead." For spiritual growth and reality in Christian experience, faith demands response in all the varied situations of human life.

Often we leave Bible classes full of good intentions. We promise to be more loving that week, more dedicated. But because the resolution is vague—because we have not gone beyond the generalization to plan how we will change—no change takes place.

The effective teacher helps students respond by leading them to see God's will and by helping them decide and plan to do it. At this point, you need to get very personal and ask everyone to choose a way to apply the truth they have just studied. For example, you might ask students to examine their lives for areas in which they are limiting Christ's power (i.e., not discussing their faith with a friend because they are afraid) and then to trust Christ to empower them in one area that week. It is helpful to distribute note cards and have everyone write down their decisions to remind them to follow through after class.

ADAPTING THE STRUCTURE FOR YOUNGER CHILDREN

Preschoolers and early elementary children are not mentally capable of studying the Bible text and wrestling with and following through on application. Therefore, the lesson structure needs to be adapted for them.

The major goal of teachers of young children is to communicate Bible truth or Bible information. For preschoolers, the information that's particularly relevant is not moral in character (what God wants believers to do). The relevant truths are those that tell who God is—truths that give children a biblical picture of the world, of themselves, and of Christ.

For primaries, teaching should relate to the children's present needs and experiences. The goal in Bible teaching is not first of all to instill ideas that students will need to know "someday." The goal is to bring pupils into vital relationship with God today. Teaching must be structured to help children make their own discoveries and respond to God on their own level.

Ideas and responses take on meaning for young children as they are associated with experiences. Thus the best way to communicate biblical ideas to children is to teach them in a context of activity and experience related to the aim.

With young children, teaching wears an unusual face. The hour is filled with activities, carried on with many shifts between active and quiet times. Yet the whole hour is carefully patterned. As students arrive, a teacher guides them into activities that help them begin to think along the line of the day's theme.

In good curricula, several activities that fit the theme are suggested for each lesson. Activities may include coloring a picture, taking a picture walk, or creating objects out of modeling clay. New words and ideas the children need in order to understand the Bible story may be introduced. Or the teacher may help children recall experiences like those of people in the Bible story or situations in which biblical truth may be applied. In any case, these activities form the lesson hook and create a readiness for the Bible story.

Instead of helping children explore Scripture for themselves during the book section, the teacher tells the Bible story with an open Bible. An effective teacher will incorporate a variety of visuals with the story to arouse and keep the children's interest and help them understand the story better.

After the Bible story, the boys and girls again engage in activities (singing, handwork, and so on) that repeat the scriptural truth of the aim. These activities help young children to work on the response aim of the lesson in class, since their ability to carry over biblical truth into the week is either nonexistent or very limited. Simple application—most often suggested by the teacher—is woven throughout the lesson, and there is no took.

SUMMARY

Using this framework of a specific aim, hook, book, look, and took simplifies lesson planning. It also helps a teacher build a lesson that promotes transformation in the students' lives. And that, after all, is the goal of Bible teaching.

FOR FURTHER READING

Coleman, Jr., Lucien E. *How to Teach the Bible*. Nashville.: Broadman, 1980.

Edge, Findley B. *Helping the Teacher*. Nashville: Broadman, 1959.

———. *Teaching for Results*. Nashville: Broadman, 1956.

Gangel, Kenneth O., and Howard Hendricks, eds. *The Christian Educator's Handbook on Teaching*. Wheaton, Ill.: Victor, 1988.

Richards, Lawrence O. *Creative Bible Teaching*. Chicago: Moody, 1970.

Sisemore, John T. *Blueprint for Teaching*. Nashville: Broadman, 1964.

Wald, Oletta. *The Joy of Teaching Discovery Bible Study*. Minneapolis: Augsburg, 1976.

Wilhoit, Jim, and Leland Ryken. *Effective Bible Teaching*. Grand Rapids: Baker, 1988.

Willis, Wesley R. *Make Your Teaching Count!* Wheaton, Ill.: Victor, 1985. Teacher training kit also available.

Michael S. Lawson

12

Managing the Classroom Experience

THE EFFECTIVE CLASSROOM TEACHER/MANAGER
- **Understands how previous classroom experiences shape student expectation**
- **Shifts the emphasis from covering material to managing time, information, and setting**
- **Appropriates the best behaviors to facilitate learning**

Jesus often had an informal and unstructured approach to education—frequently teaching on a hillside or lakeshore. The subtropical climate in Israel made Jesus' outside ministry not only possible but pleasant. So how can Jesus be a model for those of us who teach in classrooms?

Jesus' skillful teaching also flourished in the more traditional environment of the synagogue and the Temple.[1] The gospels record Jesus' presence at the Temple on many occasions. And Luke notes that Jesus attended synagogue routinely (John 18:20; Luke 4:16).

1. Matt Friedman, *The Master Plan of Teaching* (Wheaton, Ill.: Victor, 1990), p. 15.

MICHAEL S. LAWSON, Ph.D., is professor of Christian education, Dallas Theological Seminary, Dallas, Texas.

During Jesus' day, the synagogue and the Temple were formal education centers. Their services were organized and followed a predetermined format.[2] Jesus observed established traditional procedures by teaching freely in both of these formal settings without breaking protocol. No one ever accused Jesus of being out of order, even when He drove the money changers from the Temple. What they did challenge was His authority and the controversial content of His teaching.

Paul followed in Jesus' footsteps by teaching in many synagogues (Acts 13:14; 14:1; 17:1, 17; 18:4; etc.). Often Paul's ministry began in the local synagogue, then expanded to the community when he became an unwelcome guest. Both Jesus and Paul were comfortable and accustomed to both formal and informal teaching settings. They both utilized the natural gatherings of people effectively.

Today classrooms in churches and schools constitute the most common formal educational settings. In fact, most people probably view formal education as exclusively a classroom experience. In the past, classrooms were places where information was dispensed. Slowly teachers have been moving away from the information dispensing model to the classroom management model. A major report to Westminster Theological Seminary entitled "Technology and the Seminary: The 90's and Beyond" says, "Teachers will have become more managers of sophisticated learning activities than merely teachers of students in classrooms."[3]

Managing a classroom differs in significant ways from merely dispensing information. Note a few of the ways in the following list. Managing a classroom:

1. focuses on many student activities in addition to passively receiving information
2. utilizes both the time and the setting to assist in learning
3. assumes a dynamic interchange between student and teacher that promotes learning, not just listening

Classrooms by their very nature create a unique atmosphere for education. In fact, many students share some common classroom experiences. These dynamics shape students' thinking, actions, and expectations of Christian education. Students may even carry behavior patterns from previous classroom experiences into Christian education. Some of these experiences mold students in ways counterproductive to Christian education. A teacher who manages his classroom well must first account for previous counterproductive experiences.

---

2. Alfred Edersheim, *Sketches of Jewish Social Life* (Grand Rapids: Eerdmans, 1970), pp. 265-80. Alfred Edersheim, *The Temple: Its Ministry and Services* (Grand Rapids: Eerdmans, 1969), pp. 61-81.
3. "Technology and the Seminary: The 90's and Beyond," produced by The Center for the Application of Technology to Biblical and Theological Education for Westminster Theological Seminary, Philadelphia, January 1990.

COMPENSATING FOR PAST EXPERIENCES

In 1968 Philip Jackson published *Life in Classrooms*. In that book, Jackson analyzed the everyday classroom experiences of grade school children. Jackson's insights identify some of the powerful conditioning influences of classroom experiences. In the past, educators and parents viewed school as preparation for the "real world." Jackson argues that school *is* the real world. A person who attends school through college will be somewhere in his forties before he spends an equivalent amount of time anywhere else. The impact of conditioning through classroom experiences carries into adulthood and affects the classroom experiences of people at all age levels in church education.[4]

Life in Classrooms examines a wide range of invisible but significant classroom influences on students. Crowded conditions, social distraction, and the disengaging of feelings from actions stand out as counterproductive to Christian education. In addition (though not mentioned by Jackson), the presence of difficult individuals within the group and the competitive nature of modern education complicate the classroom experience of students. Successful classroom strategies must account for these unseen forces that tug at students.

CROWDED CONDITIONS

Crowded conditions exist in most school classrooms because of economic realities. Even the most aggressive teachers spend only a few minutes with each student in a given day. Because teachers must spread themselves among so many students, children understand classrooms to be places where they receive little personal attention. Even the brief attention they receive may be interrupted by another student. Questions go unasked and unanswered.

Church facilities are often as crowded as school classrooms. Moreover, students rarely discriminate between school and church classrooms. If students experience depersonalization at school, chances are they expect it at church.

But the church need not follow the public school model. The church can and should recruit enough volunteers so that students receive more attention than anywhere else—except, it is hoped, their own homes. The genius of the Sunday school structure has always been small, personal classes. The Christian classroom must never lose the personal touch of life on life as the church goes about its business of making disciples. The classroom experience may be formal, but it should never be impersonal.

Teachers of children, youth, and adults should ask:

1. Do I specifically welcome a new student?
2. Do I know an equal amount of information about each student?
3. Do I listen to and talk with each student?

4. Philip W. Jackson, *Life in Classrooms* (New York: Holt, Rinehart and Winston, 1968), p. 4.

4. Do I make and receive phone and mail contact with each student outside of class?
5. What did I learn about each student today?

SOCIAL DISTRACTION

The crowded conditions of school classrooms can create another unwelcome backlash for Christian teaching. While sitting right next to people, one is often ordered not to look at them, speak to them, or observe what they do. "Do your own work" is a common message. This social detachment must be sustained for extended periods of time.

More often than not, each student in school functions independently. Thus education is perceived largely as an individual rather than group activity. This procedure may develop a core of quiet observers. The demands of school may put a premium on sitting patiently but not thinking interactively.

On the other hand, Christian students need many opportunities to articulate their faith. People often hear their own errors while attempting to express beliefs in their own words. "Come let us reason together . . . " may need to become as much the motto for Christian teaching as "Preach the word" is for pastoral ministry.

Christian students also need time to think through how they should apply what they believe to new and rapidly changing circumstances. The information explosion that characterizes the last part of the twentieth century brings a dazzling array of difficulties to Christians. Thinking through each issue without the benefit of others is both unwise and hazardous. Listening to other Christians discuss how Scripture applies to a particular problem becomes a crucial educational exercise.

When used exclusively, highly individualistic approaches to education can work against the building of Christian community. The mood of American society promotes individual rights rather than developing the common good. However, the church is not just a collection of individuals "doing that which is right in their own eyes." The church constitutes a Body that demands cooperation and coordination. Under those conditions, requiring people to think together becomes even more critical. The educational process should promote a sense of community as people learn how to deal with different opinions while treating each other with respect.

Teachers of children, youth, and adults should ask:

1. When do my students listen to the thoughts of their peers?
2. What activities will promote both cooperative learning and a sense of community?
3. How will students express genuine concern for absent or damaged members?
4. Is there anything the class can do together to implement what was learned?

DISENGAGING FEELINGS FROM ACTIONS

Jackson describes another student behavior pattern unique to classrooms but counterproductive to Christian education.

> They must be able to disengage, at least temporarily, their feelings from their actions. It also means, of course, that they must be able to re-engage feelings and actions when conditions are appropriate. In other words, students must wait patiently for their turn to come, but when it does they must still be capable of zestful participation. They must accept the fact of not being called on during a group discussion, but they must continue to volunteer.[5]

Only the most aggressive students persist in this kind of environment. Perhaps this experience is even desirable in a market economy driven by competiton and personal ambition. A kind of sorting takes place that reflects the larger culture as students find their own place among their peers.

But this survival-of-the-fittest approach to education has limited value in Christian education, where the church must bring everyone to maturity (Col. 1:28). Bringing one person to maturity does not diminish anyone else from coming to maturity. If students carry this competitive notion into Christian classroom experiences, the result will frustrate the real objective. Some students lose their zest for learning as well as their self-confidence in a school classroom. This may happen even though the school does its best. Christian teachers must create classrooms that compensate for prior experiences. Drawing people out, listening to their opinions, challenging deeper thinking, integrating new thoughts with Scripture and other learning exercises require preplanned strategies. These methods often feel awkward and unfamiliar to students. Christian teachers may need to recondition students to these important processes.

The title of Oletta Wald's book, *The Joy of Discovery*, should become the goal of Christian education in every class hour. Christian teaching should reawaken the childhood enthusiasm for learning in every student, not just the highly motivated or aggressive. Implementing discovery learning opportunities week by week depends on good curriculum and good judgment. The crucial nature of the task warrants our best effort.

Teachers of children, youth, and adults should ask:

1. What will happen during this hour to strengthen students' confidence in their use of Scripture?
2. What will students discover for themselves from the Scriptures?
3. Will their discoveries provoke a desire to learn more?
4. Will I need to provide additional encouragement for certain students?

5. Jackson, p. 18.

DIFFICULT INDIVIDUALS

Every teacher has observed the phenomenon of one troubled student completely altering the dynamics of a classroom. Often he may require more time to instruct, keep on task, and correct, thereby robbing other students of precious moments with the teacher. When that person is absent, the classroom moves out from under the cloud and everyone heaves a sigh of relief.

Christian teachers can expect to find difficult people in every age group. The hyperactive child, the rebellious teen, and the obnoxious adult are extreme examples. Sometimes the individual may not be as problematic as these examples, but he nevertheless alters the classroom experience of others. Often difficult people are completely unaware of their impact on others. They proceed on the assumption that what seems good for them must be good for everyone else.

Sometimes the difficult person belongs to the pastor's family or the family of some other church leader. Dealing with these individuals fairly often presents delicate problems for a teacher. Favored treatment may be expected but should be avoided. Here, published policies and rules fairly enforced often provide the only answer.

At times a small pocket of dissenters feeds on each other and creates problems for teachers and other students. If vocal, dissenters can change the agenda for the silent majority. Christian teachers who adroitly manage these occasional groupings salvage the class for the other students. Otherwise the classroom experience may be so charged with tension that the goals of Christian education cannot possibly be accomplished.

Occasionally the difficult person is actually the teacher. A certain chemistry exists between students and their teacher. A perfectly capable teacher may not fit in every class. The class simply may not like him. Invariably the teacher must move, or the class will atrophy. Classrooms full of volunteer students differ from those full of students required to attend.

Christian teachers must deal directly with difficult individuals. Failure at this critical point alters the classroom experience for all the students. The uncertainty, tension, and frustration may drive even good students away.

Teachers of children should ask:

1. Is this a pattern of behavior or just a bad day?
2. What is the least I can do and still correct the problem?
   Teachers of youth should ask:
1. Is there something that needs attention, that is, behind the behavior?
2. Is there any way to resolve this without involving the parents?
   Teachers of adults should ask:
1. Can I solicit this person's help outside class in a way that will soften the disruptions inside class?
2. Can I establish some guidelines that will minimize class disruption?

In schools the primary measuring device for a student is his grades. No measurement for character qualities exists to counterbalance the powerful impact of grades. Students often generalize these academic evaluations into character qualities. How they think of themselves is based on their achievement in some specific academic arena. They gauge their ability to learn by the grades assigned in the classroom setting. Many assume that B's or C's indicate some diminished capacity. Based on these appraisals, some avoid additional formal education.

Many adults use their early classroom experiences to predict present or future classroom success. If they have negative experiences they may endure a self-fulfilling prophecy in the Christian classroom. Christian teachers need to help students overcome unfavorable comparisons and move toward an evaluation based on biblical standards. Christian teachers need to avoid experiences that put students into competitive settings. They should not follow the academic model, although they may borrow academic words to describe the learning occasion. Terms such as Sunday school, vacation Bible school, and institute of biblical studies appear frequently in church settings.

Teachers of children, youth, and adults should ask:

1. How are students evaluating their progress in the Christian life?
2. How should students evaluate their progress in the Christian life?
3. How can I help each student realize his or her unique contribution to the Body of Christ?

Teachers trying to manage classrooms need to understand what image of the classroom their students bring with them from school. Christian teachers will need to give large amounts of personal attention, engage students in a cooperative form of learning that fits the Christian community approach to life, compensate for students who have lost their zest for learning, develop an open yet disciplined atmosphere where everyone can participate, and help restore lost confidence.

PREPARING EDUCATIONAL CLASSROOM EXPERIENCES

Managing a classroom experience requires planning. Experienced teachers quickly discover that students learn more than the spoken content of the class. The teacher can plan what students will experience by thinking from their point of view. Use of class time, the setting where learning takes place, and student involvement contribute to the overall experience.

CLASS TIME

Each classroom session contains three major time components: the beginning, the middle, and the end. By thinking of class time with these three components in mind, the teacher can isolate different activities necessary to the successful completion of that portion of time. The actual time used in each segment may vary from setting to setting, but the movements remain the same.

The beginning of each class time serves several purposes. Regardless of age, people are interested in other people. If the class members are strangers, they will want to make the acquaintance of others around them. If people know each other, renewing acquaintances becomes the primary activity. People may suppress that desire, but it pulls at them. Teachers often wonder why students continue to whisper after the signal for the beginning of a class. The students simply did not have enough time or were not encouraged to greet one another. Less time is needed if the group meets on a daily basis than if it meets on a weekly or monthly basis.

The beginning of a class should include some activity that orients the student to what will be happening during the session. People do not mean to leave life behind when they walk into a classroom. Often they come in hurried or exhausted. In any case, they rarely come in with the upcoming subject fresh on their minds. This activity focuses the entire group on the main idea that will be discussed.

The middle part of the classroom session should occupy the bulk of the time. Plans for this section require decisions about how much time to devote to discovery, processing, or integrating information.

In managing the classroom effectively, the wise teacher will use a variety of methods to keep students attentive and involved personally. Methods of self-discovery such as exploring the investigating ideas, discussing, reacting, sharing, illustrating, and applying will provide meaningful involvement, encourage positive behavior, and eliminate many potential behavior problems.

Sometimes lecture is appropriate in acquiring needed information, particularly with older age groups. However, other procedures work as well as lecture when used properly. For instance, copies of articles distributed and read in class relieve the teacher from relying on note-taking capabilities and partial memories. Reading with predetermined questions or looking for specific emphases makes the reading even more pertinent. The teacher can devote the remainder of class time in discussion of the items deemed most important. Modern technology provides a formidable array of equipment with alternative methods for delivering information.

The VCR makes dramatic presentations possible sources of instruction for contrast or enrichment. Computers connected to compact disc players produce astonishing results. The random access to enormous amounts of material saves time and offers almost limitless combinations of visual, musical, and written information. The visuals include the picture quality of video cassettes without the inconvenience of linear access through a tape. As more and more information becomes accessible, many students will prefer acquiring information through this dynamic medium.

Access to information of every kind may move rapidly to an individual computer quest. But the processing of Bible information for character development and assessment will still be done interpersonally and in groups.

Having people practice discovering truth in the classroom under rigid supervision and guidelines helps them acquire both study skills and needed information. Ultimately students should approach God's Word without fear to discover for themselves what He has to say for their lives. Students must become more independent from the teacher and dependent on the Holy Spirit.

In the past, teachers have often believed that their calling was to dispense information. Students frequently bypassed the process by leaving classes with the observations and conclusions of the teacher. They were left to their own devices to rearrange the material into something that had meaning for them. Processing material helps cement information to memory. Classroom time should include opportunities for students to rework important information into meaningful packages.

If processing is not given adequate time, students will sense the information requires only short-term memory. Students perceive exactly how important something is by how much time the activity receives. Teachers who claim they value discussion but allow only a few minutes each session for questions have communicated effectively their real values. If students need to control certain information, then significant time needs to be devoted to that exercise.

The teacher may decide that the middle section should not be devoted to information acquisition but should be used to integrate information the students already know. The need for this should be obvious. Students may cite biblical passages but not comprehend their relevance for life. Or a familiar social problem and relevant biblical information may have never come together in their thinking. Under these conditions, students do not need to acquire more information, they need time to think about what they have already learned and integrate it.

Depending on available time and need, a teacher might include one or all of these three emphases in a given session. By changing the vehicle for discovering, processing, or integrating information, an almost endless array of interesting activities can be used to move the student through the main part of the classroom experience. No two class sessions need be exactly alike.

Ending a classroom session correctly is just as important as beginning and sustaining a session. The purpose for a conclusion should be to summarize and consolidate what has been accomplished during the middle portion of the lesson. Perhaps the students will even need to formulate a plan of action. Implementing what they learn enables them to practice obedience to the Word of God. Some teachers prefer to generalize applications for everyone. General applications tend to be least effective because each individual struggles with specific needs. If at all possible, the teacher should create an activity that allows students time to make the lesson personal. Students may wish to share their plan or pray for one another. This procedure provides an opportunity for opening the next session with personal conversation and follow up.

Teachers of children, youth, and adults should ask:

1. Was the time managed proportionately?
2. Did we focus on the essential information?
3. Did we consolidate the gains of the hour with adequate summary activities?
4. Were the students participants or observers in the process?

CLASS SETTING

The setting in which the class meets also affects the learning experience. Lighting, odors, temperature, noise, seating arrangements, and aesthetics affect how students learn. The more flexibility and control afforded each of these, the more the teacher will be able to manage the classroom experience. The more these are uncontrolled, the more the teacher must compensate and adjust.

Lighting. Key concerns revolve around dimming natural light and artificial light for projection purposes. The teacher must be sure that enough light is provided for the task at hand whether it be reading from a passage or viewing a film clip.

Odors. Both pleasant and unpleasant odors can detract from the classroom experience. One church building has a bakery next door. When the ovens open promptly at noon, maintaining attention becomes extremely difficult. The teacher should be sensitive to both actual and possible distractions in this area. In addition, introducing smells into a Bible lesson can create powerful memories.

Temperature. The temperature of a room is perfect when no one notices it. A too hot or too cold room creates drowsiness or the inability to concentrate. A slightly cool room heats up as more bodies arrive. Men and women seem to have different heating and cooling requirements. Age affects people's tolerance as well. Young children and older people require warmer conditions than the average adult. A teacher may need three or four room monitors to help decide the thermostat setting.

Sound. Sounds can facilitate or hinder the learning process. In an empty room with new students arriving, music may make conversation more acceptable. Silence can be threatening, and the sound of your own voice can be startling. Outside noises can also be distracting, and should be controlled where possible. Hard surface floors create considerably more noise when students move chairs around. Carpet or carpet patches soften the shuffling.

Seating. Teachers communicate a great deal about a classroom experience through seating arrangements. The room's focus may change dramatically depending on how the chairs are arranged. Lecture halls and living rooms both have their place as classrooms, but they differ radically in the purposes they serve. With each lesson's separate purpose comes a seating arrangement designed to facilitate the appropriate activities.

Aesthetics. Many modern evangelical buildings require the most space for the least cost and largely ignore aesthetics. Yet aesthetics do affect thinking. What one thinks while standing in the Sistine Chapel differs from what one observes while standing in a 15 by 25 foot concrete block classroom. Careful attention should be given to color. Some colors are cool, and some are warm. Some are exciting, and some are soothing. Each affects students differently. Their use depends on the room's primary purpose. Room decorations contribute to the learning experience. Everyone's attention wanders from time to time during a lesson. Posters, banners, and other brief visual reminders may reinforce a lesson or theme, thereby enhancing the classroom experience.

Teachers of children, youth, and adults should ask:

1. Which elements in my setting can I control?
2. Are these assisting in the learning experience?
3. What can I do to improve the classroom setting?

Implementing a Planned Experience

Ultimately the teacher must implement the plan. The best plan will not replace the teacher at this point. In every way the demeanor of the teacher welcomes the student into the learning experience. Harry Murray developed and published a "Teacher Behaviors Inventory" in *The Teaching Professor.*[6] Designed primarily for the college teacher, Murray designates eight general areas with numerous specific behaviors identified in each area.

Only the positive traits from three of the eight areas are reproduced here. Because they relate to almost any classroom teacher's behavior, test yourself to see how you are doing.

Enthusiasm: use of nonverbal behavior to solicit student attention and interest.

- speaks in a dramatic or expressive way
- moves about while lecturing
- gestures with hands or arms
- exhibits facial gestures or expressions
- walks up aisles beside students
- gestures with head and body
- tells jokes or humorous anecdotes
- smiles or laughs while teaching
- shows distracting mannerisms

Interaction: techniques used to foster students' class participation.

- encourages students' questions and comments during lectures

6. Harry Murray, "Teacher Behaviors Inventory," in *The Teaching Professor* (October 1988): 3-4.

- praises students for good ideas
- asks questions of individual students
- asks questions of class as a whole
- incorporates students' ideas into lecture
- presents challenging, thought-provoking ideas
- uses a variety of media and activities in class

Rapport: quality of interpersonal relations between teacher and student.

- addresses individual students by name
- announces availability for consultation outside of class
- offers to help students with problems
- shows tolerance of other points of view
- talks with students before or after class

Teachers personalize the plan by relating to the student in these and other ways. No plan can be more effective than the teacher who implements it.

SUMMARY

Managing a classroom experience qualifies as an art form. The teacher tries to blend all the proper ingredients into the session while compensating for prior experiences and using the time and setting in ways that facilitate students' learning. All of this presupposes that the teacher is so familiar with the material at hand that he can select what to emphasize, delete, or merely mention. Quality classroom experiences are normally the product of comprehension of the subject, good planning, and enough practice to be proficient at working with students. There are few shortcuts to excellence in teaching or managing classroom experience.

FOR FURTHER READING

Bolton, Barbara; Charles T. Smith; and Wesley Haystead. *Everything You Want to Know About Teaching Children*. Ventura, Calif.: Regal, 1987.

Christie, Les. *When You Have to Draw the Line*. Wheaton, Ill.: Victor, 1988.

Dobson, James. *Dare to Discipline*. Wheaton, Ill.: Tyndale, 1973.

Fisher, Jean. "Managing the Classroom Effectively." In *Childhood Education in the Church*, rev. ed., edited by Robert E. Clark, Joanne Brubaker, and Roy B. Zuck. Chicago: Moody, 1986.

Halbert, Barbara Lee. *Creative Discipline for Young Children*. Nashville: Broadman, 1980.

Haystead, Wesley. *Everything You Want to Know About Teaching Young Children*. Ventura, Calif.: Regal, 1989.

Long, James D., and Virginia H. Frye with Elizabeth W. Long. *Making It Till Friday: A Guide to Successful Classroom Management*, 4th ed. Princeton,

N.J.: Princeton Books, 1989.

Price, B. Max. *Understanding Today's Children*. Nashville: Convention, 1982.

Waldrop, C. Sybil. *Understanding Today's Preschoolers*. Nashville: Convention, 1982.

Wilhoit, Jim, and Leland Ryken. *Effective Bible Teaching*. Grand Rapids: Baker, 1988.

13

Robert J. Choun, Jr.

Teaching and Learning Strategies

METHODS OF TEACHING
- **Methods are communication tools**
- **Method selection is based on lesson aims and learner age-group characteristics**
- **Learning comes through involvement**
- **Methods should be used with variety**
- **A changed life is the criteria for evaluating**

IMPORTANCE OF TEACHING METHODS

Teaching methods are akin to blueprints. Long before construction begins, an architect designs a building according to the needs of its future occupants. He considers many factors: What is the purpose of the building? What adaptations must be made to accommodate special needs? What is the condition of the site? What is my budget and time schedule? Are construction materials and crews available?

Similar factors must be considered in the design of a lesson: Which teaching method will best communicate the lesson aim? Which method is most appro-

ROBERT J. CHOUN, Jr., D. Min., is associate professor of Christian education, Dallas Theological Seminary, Dallas, Texas.

priate to the needs and characteristics of the learners? Can the method be used within the limitations of time and facilities? Do the learners have the necessary skills and have access to the needed materials? Failure to consider any of these factors will bring the lesson down on the head of its designer.

WHAT IS A METHOD?

A method is a way of doing, a tool, a catalyst, and a means of access. A method is not a time-filler, an end in itself, or a purposeless activity. As an illustration, consider a Sunday school class of five year olds.

The five year olds arrive at staggered times during the first half hour. They are free to wander about the room and play with classmates while the teacher and assistants keep order and prepare lesson materials. After most of the class has arrived, the children sit in rows, sing a few songs, and listen quietly while this week's story of "Dorcas Was Kind" is read from the curriculum. After the reading, the children are quizzed on the facts of the story. With the time remaining each learner will work on a coloring page. In this example, methods have been employed but not applied.

The redesigned lesson, which applies teaching methods, maximizes the use of time, facilities, and resources.

Interest centers. As children arrive they are directed to an area where a lesson-related activity, led by an adult, is underway. At the Home Living Center, youngsters pretend to give food and clothing to others in need. In the Block Center, learners are encouraged to show kindness by sharing blocks. In another part of the classroom, students help prepare a fruit salad to be taken after church to the home of a shut-in.

Music and motion. Active songs that relate to the lesson theme of kindness are sung. The learners join in with rhythm instruments and strum the autoharp with the teacher's help.

Storytelling. A teacher tells the story to small groups of six to eight children. Interesting visuals and dramatic skill hold learners' attention. Teachers refer to the children's experiences at the interest centers.

Art. Drawings by children can be sent as cheery notes to sick classmates or elderly church members.

Drama. Children experience the feelings of the needy by role-playing modern-day situations that parallel those in the lesson.

The applied methods in the lesson's redesign can be called "learning activities." Each activity encouraged participation from the learner and promoted the aim of the lesson. In the interest centers, each child was introduced to the lesson aim and became involved in a related activity. In this way, learners had experiences on which to base an understanding of the lesson. Because learning increases with the number of senses involved in the process, music and motion were used to reinforce the concepts. The telling of the Scripture lesson provided the facts, but carefully planned questions helped learners go beyond knowledge of the lesson to feelings about it. A modern-day story helps to transfer the lesson concept to a common situation. The children's participation in its telling helps them to "rehearse" the application of what they have learned.

A teaching method is an activity that communicates knowledge, identifies feelings or attitudes, and emphasizes behavior.

GUIDELINES IN SELECTING METHODS

Just as the architect needs to know the purpose of the building, the teacher needs a clear understanding of the aim of the lesson before selecting the methods to be used in its presentation. Once satisfied that the aim of the lesson meets the teacher's goals for the learners and their needs, the teacher can begin method selection. These factors must be considered:

1. Does the teacher possess the ability and skill to use the method?
2. Do the learners have the required skill or level of understanding?
3. Is the method appropriate for the size of the group?
4. Does the method meet the needs of the learners?
5. Does the method help accomplish the lesson aim?
6. Will the method meaningfully involve the learner?
7. Is the method appropriate for the subject matter being taught?
8. Are the facilities, equipment, and supplies available?
9. Does the schedule provide enough time?
10. Does the method provide variety in the learning experience?

Some criteria of methods are subtle and difficult to describe. No method should be so overwhelming in its complexity or dramatic presentation that it overshadows the lesson aim and becomes the message itself. Like music and lyrics, message and method must work in harmony.

A good indication of a method's chance of success is the degree to which it involves the learner. Studies have shown that three days after a lesson, students will retain only 10 percent of what they heard, but 90 percent of what they were able to hear, see, and do.[1] The best way to learn is through involvement in the learning process. Involvement and participation in the lesson helps students to "own" a new concept and apply it to their lives. Teaching Bible truths without teaching their application to daily life is like teaching skin diving without water.

---

1. Ed Stewart, Neal McBride, Sherie Lindvall, and Monroe Marlowe, *How To Do Bible Learning Activities for Adults* (Ventura, Calif.: Regal. 1982), p. 5.

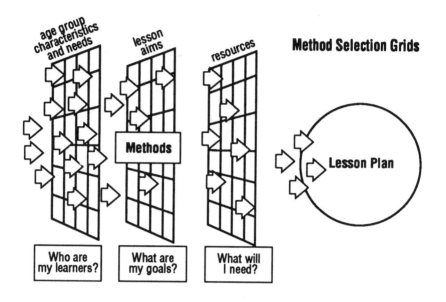

Using Methods Effectively

No architect could design homes without a thorough knowledge of stresses, foundations, and construction materials. No teacher should use a method in the classroom without first reviewing the skills and materials it requires. If the method involves learner participation (good methods usually do), the teacher must evaluate not only his own abilities but also the learners' in the light of the required skills. A group discussion method called "neighbor nudge" is useful for teens and adults but not children. A sensory experience called a "feely box" is a big hit with young children but makes adults feel silly. As learners age, they depend less on touch, scent, and taste senses and rely most heavily on vision and hearing.

Choosing and Using Creative Teaching Methods

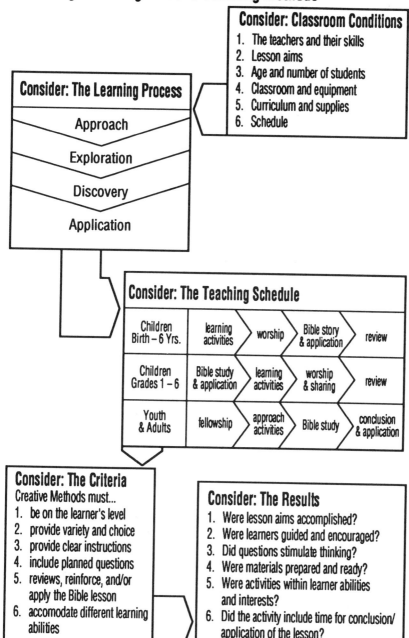

Consider: Classroom Conditions
1. The teachers and their skills
2. Lesson aims
3. Age and number of students
4. Classroom and equipment
5. Curriculum and supplies
6. Schedule

Consider: The Learning Process

Approach

Exploration

Discovery

Application

Consider: The Teaching Schedule

Children Birth – 6 Yrs.	learning activities	worship	Bible story & application	review
Children Grades 1 – 6	Bible study & application	learning activities	worship & sharing	review
Youth & Adults	fellowship	approach activities	Bible study	conclusion & application

Consider: The Criteria
Creative Methods must...
1. be on the learner's level
2. provide variety and choice
3. provide clear instructions
4. include planned questions
5. reviews, reinforce, and/or apply the Bible lesson
6. accomodate different learning abilities

Consider: The Results
1. Were lesson aims accomplished?
2. Were learners guided and encouraged?
3. Did questions stimulate thinking?
4. Were materials prepared and ready?
5. Were activities within learner abilities and interests?
6. Did the activity include time for conclusion/ application of the lesson?

Kenneth Gangel, chairman of the education department at Dallas Theological Seminary, states that "learning must start where the student is."[2] Books on human development can provide teachers with valuable information regarding what concepts learners comprehend at various stages. Children, youth, and adults process information in different ways and use different kinds of experiences to evaluate new concepts. Physical age, however, should not be used as an indicator of Bible knowledge or spiritual maturity. The best way to find out the level of a student is to establish a personal relationship. A caring teacher will find ways to accommodate a student who lags behind in academic skills but shines in artistic endeavors.

Teachers must be sensitive to the climate and mood of their classes. The interrelationships of students affect the classroom atmosphere—and these change from week to week. A teacher must take the temperature of a class before using a method that involves intimate sharing of attitudes or experiences. Adult classes will be initially resistant to creative methods, so teachers of that age group should introduce the class to low-level involvement methods until the group feels more comfortable with participation.

With the encouragement of learner participation comes the combined blessing/problem of learner input. Each contribution to the lesson must be acknowledged. Only in extreme cases should a learner's comment be considered incorrect. Even then, a tactful teacher will be able to soften the blow and allow the contributor to save face. Teachers should make frequent use of questions that require only subjective answers and can never be answered incorrectly.

Most methods that encourage learner involvement work best on a small group level. Small groups allow each learner to participate and have access to a teacher. Among older teens and adults, spiritually mature class members can serve as group guides and develop their own leadership ability.

Occasionally the setup of a classroom will inhibit creative teaching methods. Miniature pews screwed to the floor in children's classrooms are a prime example. Imaginative use of space and facilities can accommodate most activities. Messy art activities can be permitted if student clothing is protected by old shirts or plastic bags. A plastic tub filled with water can serve for water activities or a cleanup station for finger painters. Stacking chairs and tables can provide surfaces for tabletop work one week and space for movement the next. Tabletops that rest across the tops of pews can provide writing surfaces for an adult class that meets in the sanctuary. Fabric draped across tension rods wedged in a closet doorway can serve as a puppet theater. Teachers must not allow facilities to dictate programming.

One of the keys to effective use of methods is a clear set of instructions. How many instructions can be given at one time depends largely on the complexity of the steps and the age of the participants. Among older elementary children, teens, and adults, the steps to an activity can be written on the board, projected on an

2. Kenneth O. Gangel, *The Church Education Handbook* (Wheaton, Ill.: Victor, 1985), p. 105.

overhead, or printed on cards distributed to each small group. When using art activities with young learners, distribute only the materials that accompany each instruction.

All the materials needed for the activity should be on hand. Learners of any age will quickly lose interest when an activity is halted to hunt for supplies. Listeners are sure to drift off while a lecturer flips pages in search of a particular quote. If audiovisuals are to be used, be sure they have been tested. Light levels, lines of vision, and noise from next door can all be factors in the success of their use.

TYPES OF METHODS

There are a myriad of methods, some of which are more appropriate for certain ages because of the interests or abilities of the learners. Teachers should learn to use a variety of methods, since even the most stimulating activity will become boring with overuse. Listed below are some types of creative methods.

METHODS IN CHRSTIAN EDUCATION

Audiovisual methods:

Arts and crafts
Banners
Bulletin boards
Cartoons
Chalkboards
Charts
Clay
Collage
Comics
Crayon sketches
Curios
Demonstrations
Diagrams
Diorama
Displays, exhibits, and
    specimens
Drawings and doodles
Field trip
Filmstrip, record/tape
Finger painting
Finger plays
Flannelgraph
Flashcards
Flip charts
Graphs
Hook-n-loop board
Interviews
Langauge laboratories
Lecture

Magnet board
Maps and globes
Mobiles and kinetics
Models
Montage
Mosaics
Motion picture
Murals
Music
Object lesson
Opaque projection
Outlining
Overhead projection
Paintings
Pegboard
Photographs/photography
Pictures (flat)
Picture walk
Pocket chart
Posters
Printing
Puppets and marionettes
Real objects
Record player and records
Rebus
Rhythm band
Sand table
Slides: still pictures and
    write-on slides
Story reading
Storytelling
Tape recorder and cassettes

Television and closed-circuit TV
3-D viewer
Time lines
Videotape
Vinyl boards

Discussion methods:

Agree-disagree
Brainstorm
Buzz groups
Case studies
Cell groups
Circle response
Conference/committee
Debates
Forum
Guided discussion
Interest groups
Interview
Listening teams
Neighbor nudging
Panel discussion
Question box
Seminar
Speeches
Symposium
"What would you do?"
Workshops/institutes

Dramatic methods:

Charades

Dialogue
Dramatic reading
Mime
Monologue
Pantomime
Play
Role play
Silhouettes
Skit
Sociodrama
Spontaneous drama
Story play
Tableau
TV/radio show

Project methods:

Apprenticeship
Assignment/homework
Case study
Computers
Craft and handwork
Group work

Handbook/notebook
  inductive study
Interest and learning centers
Laboratory experiment
Live animals and plants
Newspaper
Newsletter
Problem solving
Programmed learning
  and instruction
Reports
Research
Sensory experiences
Supervised study
Survey
Team teaching
Textbook study
Unit of learning
Verse memorization
Workbook or manual

Self-Expression methods:

Catechism

Choral reading/speaking
Circle conversation
Creative writing
Drill
Games
Informal conversation
Memorization
Paraphrase
Practice/drill
Puzzles
Question and answer
Play time (instructive)
Reading
Review
Sharing time
Show and tell
Simulation games
Spontaneous speaking
Story writing/telling
Surveys
Testing

A teaching method that is sometimes overlooked is the classroom and its furnishings. A room that is dreary and uninteresting casts a pall over the lesson. A room that is overstimulating is the opposite—but no less harmful—extreme. The classroom should be light, airy, and cheerful. The learners' physical comfort must be considered in the selection of chairs, tables, lighting, temperature control, acoustics, ventilation, and floor covering. Chairs and tables should be movable to accommodate a variety of teaching methods. Visuals such as charts and posters should be on the learner's eye level. Learner resources should be accessible. Surfaces should be designed for easy cleanup. The typical adult class that provides each learner with a view of the back of the head of the learner seated directly in front discourages participation.

Another often overlooked teaching method is the attitude of the teacher toward the lesson and the learners. If the teacher shows little interest in the lesson, neither will the class. If the teacher displays a lack of preparedness, so will the students. If the teacher's lifestyle proves that the Bible truths taught in church have no application for daily life, that will be a more lasting lesson than the ones heard in Sunday school.

EVALUATING METHODS

The success of a method cannot be measured by the attractiveness of an art project, the volume of a music activity, or the excitement generated by a live goldfish in class. The method that created the most mess may have been the one that encouraged the greatest participation. To evaluate the usefulness of a method consider the following:

1. Did the method meet the needs of the learners?
2. Did the method accomplish the lesson aim?
3. Did the method encourage student interest and participation?
4. Did students retain information?
5. Did students display changed attitudes?
6. Did students display changed behavior?

When changed behavior indicates that the Bible truth has been communicated not only in fact but in feeling, it is time to set new goals for the class. With the new goals come new lesson aims—and a need for a greater variety of teaching methods. To assist teachers, the church should set up a resource room of supplies, stock the library with reference books, and provide regular training events.

SUMMARY

Most authors on the subject of teaching methods refer to those used by the Master Teacher. Throughout His earthly ministry, Christ employed storytelling, object lessons, questions, illustrations, and other techniques. There was no need to separate medium from message. Christ was both.

With the wide variety of media available today, there is a danger of getting absorbed in the teaching method and losing sight of the message to be taught. Teachers' goals for their students grow out of the students' needs. Goals dictate specific lesson aims based on Bible truths. Bible truths communicated through skillfully used teaching methods will make a lasting impact on the learners, resulting in life changes. The process sounds automatic, but without the catalyst of the loving care of the teacher, methods are meaningless.

Teachers will do well to remember that God could have simply sent His message of love in oral or written form. Instead, He delivered it in person.

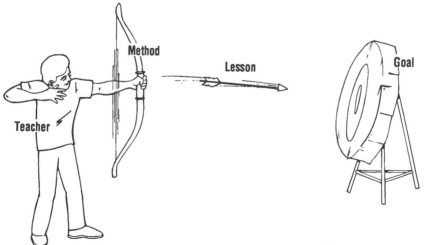

FOR FURTHER READING

Barrett, Ethel. *Storytelling—It's Easy!* Grand Rapids: Zondervan, 1960.

Bolton, Barbara J. *How to Do Bible Learning Activities, Grades 1-6,* Books 1 and 2. Ventura, Calif.: International Center for Learning, 1982, 1984.

Bundschuh, Rich, and Annette Parrish, comp. *How to Do Bible Learning Activities, Grades 7-12,* Book 2. Ventura, Calif.: International Center for Learning, 1984.

Burba, Linda. *Everybody Ought to Go to Learning Centers.* Grand Rapids: Baker, 1981.

Clark, Robert E.; Joanne Brubaker; and Roy B. Zuck, eds. *Childhood Education in the Church,* rev. ed. Chicago: Moody, 1986.

Gangel, Kenneth O. *24 Ways to Improve Your Teaching.* Wheaton, Ill.: Victor, 1974. Teacher training kit also available.

Johnson, Lin. *Bible Alive!* Cincinnati: Standard, 1988.

Klein, Karen. *How to Do Bible Learning Activities, Ages 2-5,* Book 1. Ventura, Calif.: International Center for Learning, 1982.

LeFever, Marlene D. *Creative Teaching Methods.* Elgin, Ill.: David C. Cook, 1985.

Smith, Judy Gattis. *26 Ways to Use Drama in Teaching the Bible.* Nashville: Abingdon, 1988.

Stewart, Ed, and Neal McBride. *How to Do Bible Learning Activities, Grades 7-12,* Book 1. Ventura, Calif.: International Center for Learning, 1982.

Stewart, Ed, et al. *How to Do Bible Learning Activities, Adults,* Book 1. Ventura, Calif.: International Center for Learning, 1982.

Wilbert, Warren W. *Strategies for Teaching Christian Adults.* Grand Rapids: Baker, 1984.

14

C. Keith Mee

Instructional Media and Learning

FACTORS IN LEARNING
- **Learners are responsible**
- **Learning is "in the search"**
- **Research skills are essential**
- **Leaders are assistants to learners**
- **Learning requires pertinent information**
- **Information is found in media**
- **Media must be readily available**
- **Libraries make media available**

Since the beginning of the world, no one has ever lived and experienced the number and variety of resources available through media as are available today.

Television, videos, cassettes, discs, overheads, films, filmstrips, pictures, books, objects, curios, drama, chalkboards, 3-D scenes, arts and crafts, and a multitude of other sources have flooded the market for use in and out of the classroom. Because of the proliferation of resources available, purposes for teaching must be

C. KEITH MEE, M.S., is retired from the Baptist Sunday School Board, church media department, and is currently media library director, Two Rivers Church, Nashville, Tennessee.

clearly defined to increase effectiveness in the selection and use of various kinds of media.

This chapter will answer such questions as: What is media? Why is media significant? What are some of the kinds of media? What are some guidelines for evaluating and selecting media? How can we use media effectively? What criteria should we use in evaluating media?

DEFINITION OF MEDIA

Media are the tools of education. Every job has tools specifically designed for the task. To do a job well and efficiently a person must have and know how to use the correct tools. In the case of learning and teaching these tools include all kinds of media.

Media is the plural form of *medium*. A medium, with respect to the kinds used in teaching and learning, refers to that which contains and/or is used to communicate information. "The term 'media' means devices which contain and/or transport information."[1]

A medium is that which serves the function of relaying or facilitating the transfer of items between parties. In our use of the word, the parties are recipients and originators. Recipients are viewers, listeners, readers, learners, teachers, classes, and congregations. Originators are authors, actors, photographers, theologians, and economists. In short the originators are persons with messages, ideas, entertainment, and information.

Information is the general word for the item to be transferred. Information comes in many forms: facts, definitions, descriptions, ideas, interpretations, instructions, and procedures.

SIGNIFICANCE OF MEDIA

Everything we know comes to us directly or indirectly through media. Even our own ideas and experiences are confirmed or interpreted by communications from people who have researched or experienced the same thing.

Media not only serves to confirm or interpret our own thoughts and experiences, but media also stores or preserves mankind's knowledge. Actually, in terms of longevity, we have not improved much over the ancients. Clay tablets and papyri are still in existence from thousands of years ago. Today, archival longevity is fifty years. Microfilm, a compact means of storing information, will develop "measles" in about fifty years and obliterate the information. Much of the paper we use will deteriorate in our lifetime because of acid, used in manufacturing the paper, reacting with moisture in the air. This will destroy our records, unless they are transferred to another medium. There is hope for preservation of data on

---

1. Keith Mee, *The Learning Team: the Learner, the Leader, and the Library*, rev. ed. (Nashville: Convention, 1987), p. 27.

compact discs. These discs are described as "indestructible." The problem is recoverability. Reading a disc requires electronic equipment—not at all as convenient as a book, which can be read anywhere there is light.

In spite of the difficulties in preservation of information, media enables mankind to store all information in ways that facilitate retrieving it. Problems of permanence will undoubtedly be solved.

Not only do media enable us to access the world's rapidly expanding store of knowledge, but they also enable mankind to share data. Distance and time are not barriers to learning from other persons. Television enhanced by satellites, videocassette recorders, computers, fiber optics, telescopes, and microscopes enable us to observe almost anything in the world or out of the world, whether it be as small as an atom or as large as a galaxy. Sharing data person to person, in the classroom, or with billions of people around the world, is made possible by media.

Why Use Audiovisuals

In my book *How to Use Audiovisuals*, I discuss twelve values or reasons for using audiovisuals.[2] These are:

1. *Secures attention*. Attention spans vary greatly and many people have poor listening skills. Therefore, the first task of the teacher is to gain and hold attention of the learners to stimulate increased learning.

2. *Teaches faster*. Because of limited time for teaching, the vast amount of material to be taught, and the fact that learners *hear* differently, teachers can use audiovisuals to overcome these problems.

3. *Makes learning uniform*. Students come from a wide variety of backgrounds and cultural experiences and have different vocabularies. Audiovisuals enable teachers to build uniformity through mental images.

4. *Paces the presentation*. By listing key ideas on a chart or overhead, a teacher can pace the discussion leisurely in covering the essentials without feeling rushed at certain points of the discussion.

5. *Bridges the time gap*. Audiovisuals can help teachers review the past through drama, films, and videos. The future can also be visualized through imagination, research, and skills of gifted people.

6. *Bridges the distance gap*. The world is shrinking through media. Students can increase their understanding of the conditions of people and nations, or travel anywhere on earth and beyond through effective use of audiovisuals.

7. *Provides substitute experience*. We cannot experience everything in life, nor would we want to. However, through audiovisuals we can enter experiences vicariously and develop feelings and some understanding of a variety of situations.

8. *Facilitates memory*. Symbols, drawings, diagrams, and special treatment of key words give us mental hooks on which to hang facts for later recall.

2. Keith Mee, *How to Use Audiovisuals* (Nashville: Convention, 1979), chap. 1, pp. 10-21.

9. *Multiplies participation.* When people say and do they remember more than when they only see and hear. Through meaningful participation learners can handle, present, discuss, and make things. Their ability to remember will increase greatly.

10. *Increases variety in presentations.* Variety helps hold interest and attention. With the host of available possibilities of audiovisuals, there is no reason for a teacher to get into a rut in teaching.

11. *Deepens understanding.* When persons can visualize as well as verbalize, see a process in action, have better attention, bridge time and distance gaps, and participate meaningfully, they very likely will gain much better understanding of what they are learning.

12. *Makes learning more enjoyable.* Satisfaction, self-discovery, anticipation, increased participation, and learning will all contribute in making the total experience more fun—more enjoyable.

Audiovisual media enhances communication by providing color, motion, amplified sound, and magnified images. They utilize both seeing and hearing. Words that are missed by the ear can be corrected or completed by the eye. Emphasis can be given to key words by enlargement or style of lettering. Persons, whose attention lapses, can reengage the process with the aid of visuals that show where the discussion has been and where it is currently. Things hard to describe with words are often clearly and quickly communicated with pictures, diagrams, and graphs.

Recorded sight and sound enable the originator to supply a message at a time of his or her convenience while the recipient may also receive the message at a convenient time. Individuals, on occasion, can receive information while doing other tasks such as driving or ironing. Audiocassettes and compact disks have made it possible to salvage otherwise wasted minutes.

Using a video camcorder to record our performance enables us to see ourselves in action. This can show us the flaws in speaking or singing much more accurately than practicing before a mirror or even before family or friends, who are sometimes too tactful to tell us the truth.

Through media, especially books, we can research or study any subject, question, or problem. Whatever the subject, "a book has probably been written about it. Books are windows to the world. Anyone who can read, or listen to someone else read, can 'travel' anywhere in the world through books. He can think thoughts after the most famous men and women. He can be inspired by the lives of both the living and the dead. He can be instructed by experts in any field of knowledge or endeavor. Why should men remain ignorant when knowledge is available so readily?"[3]

---

3. Mee, *The Learning Team*, p. 37.

KINDS OF MEDIA

We are blessed with an immense variety of media. For discussion's sake, we shall divide media into two general categories: print and nonprint, or printed and audiovisual.

The printed group is divided into bound and unbound. And the audiovisual category is divided into projected and nonprojected.

PRINTED MEDIA

Bound media are sometimes divided into hardback and paperback books, but this distinction is not important for our discussion because many titles come in both forms. A more useful division is to think of books in three groups: reference books, textbooks, and general books. Within reason, and with exceptions, books are our most dependable source of information. Authors and publishers put their reputations on the line with books. Their peers and their critics read the material and any "off-the-wall" statements can be embarrassing. This potential for embarrassment tends to improve accuracy. An exception is when an author writes for a specific audience. As long as his primary audience accepts the material, he may have little care about what other groups think.

A more significant value of books is that practically all knowledge is available in them. When it comes to the details of a subject, nothing tops books.

Unbound material includes newspapers, magazines, pamphlets, tracts, and other small printed pieces such as leaflets, booklets, and brochures. Because of deadlines and the compulsion to beat the competition, it is difficult to get a complete or an accurate report from newspapers. Weekly news magazines give more complete reports than daily newspapers. Religious literature, often in magazine form, is produced to support educational programs in churches. These materials help guide a systematic study of Scripture. Usually, these materials lack some details and thus need to be supplemented with information from Bible study helps and other materials. Whatever a person's interest, there is probably a magazine on the subject. The last decade has witnessed an explosive increase in the number of magazine titles.

Smaller printed pieces provide a smattering of information and generally refer the reader to other sources for additional data. Tracts provide a means of sharing bits of information on a great variety of subjects. They are designed to motivate the reader to seek further help, or to persuade him to a change of idea.

AUDIOVISUAL MEDIA

Projected audiovisuals include those that enlarge images and/or amplify sound. In recent years, dramatic new media have begun to replace some of the old dependable kinds. Three of the older kinds have been hit hard. These are motion pictures, filmstrips, and recordings. Audiocassettes, videocassettes, and compact discs are among the forms gaining rapidly in usage and displacing some of the older forms.

An abundance of audiocassette and videocassette material suitable for use by Christians and churches currently exists. A future entry that has great potential is a combination of the computer and the compact disc. (The Bible is already available in this medium.[4]) Another possibility, particularly for church media libraries, is computer software. Many church libraries are already using computers for library administration and in the place of the card catalog.

Video has become a dominant medium. The videocassette recorder (VCR) and camera (camcorder) have revolutionized this medium. Many fine religious/educational videocassettes are on the market, with new titles appearing regularly.

For teaching purposes, video has several distinct advantages over the motion picture. The simplicity of operating the VCR is one advantage. The remote control with fast forward, rapid reverse, stop action, and frame-by-frame advance enables the teacher to use color, motion, and sound to illustrate points, explain procedures, and stimulate discussion.

Camcorders and professional quality video cameras give churches the potential for producing messages for use in education, outreach, worship, and ministry. With video, churches can show visitors messages that explain the plan of salvation and describe their church's facilities, services, and activities.

Motion pictures still have a place in the teaching/learning process. Generally, motion pictures are being used with larger audiences. Size of image—that is, the ability to fill a large screen and still retain color and clarity—is the one major advantage this medium has over video.

Filmstrips are still being used in teaching though few new titles are being produced. Many churches have a collection of filmstrips and at least one projector. Some projectors have builit-in audiocassette players to provide sound while advancing the film electronically. A filmstrip may be used for previewing, providing content, or reviewing. Class members can be involved in presenting the film and/or writing their own narrative to describe the pictures.

Overhead projectors continue to be one of the most versatile teaching tools. Two advantages are: the projected image is visible in a lighted room and the teacher can face the audience while pointing out details, revealing points one at a time while still being able to see the outline through the cover paper.

The most common method to make overhead transparencies is by hand, using blank acetate sheets and water-soluble pens. The office copy machine can also be used to make transparencies. The infrared process is popular because of the variety of material that is available. Color can be added with adhesive material.

Making a point with overlays is an effective technique. Adding copy to professionally prepared transparencies is facilitated by protecting the transparency with a sheet of blank acetate. Too small lettering is the most common mistake.

4. "CD Libraries: New Power for Home PCs," in *Popular Science* (May 1990): 75.

Bold lines, five-sixteenth inch high letters, and fifteen words to a transparency is about right. A transparency of typewritten copy cannot be read past the second row of the audience. It is good to use line drawings to illustrate the words. For additional suggestions on transparencies see the bibliography.

Slides are commonly used in churches—most churches have at least one slide projector and a historical collection of slides. Some churches have equipment for making multimedia presentations that requires at least two slide projectors and a dissolve control. Presentations can be enhanced by using an audiocassette recorder that is equipped with a device to record control signals. With this equipment the narration can be prerecorded along with signals to advance the slides automatically.

Preparing a slide presentation can be an effective learning experience. Under the guidance of a leader, the individual or group is given an assignment to produce a program. The learning value is in writing an objective for the program, selecting pictures for the presentation, and in wording the narration. The experience of producing the program and presenting it to one or more groups combines to produce real learning. The subject of the presentation can be promotional, devotional, or educational. Quality programs can be processed and placed in the media library for historical purposes or for future use. For more help on producing such programs see the bibliography.

Opaque projectors are both versatile and useful. Any picture, page in a book, or object that is small enough to insert in the projector can be projected. The opaque projector is often used to enlarge copy for posters.

Disadvantages of the opaque projector are that it is heavy and must be used in semidarkness. By providing a rolling stand that is reserved for use with the opaque, some of this disadvantage can be resolved.

Audio recordings include audiocassettes, reel-to-reel recordings, compact discs, and disc recordings. At present, audiocassettes dominate the field of recorded religious materials. Not much is available in other formats. Disc recording production has almost ceased. Controversy concerning the legality and distribution of duplication and recording equipment for compact discs remains unsolved. Reel-to-reel recordings are used almost exclusively for historical material and editing purposes.

Audiocassettes provide music for worship and quiet time for preschool groups. As mentioned previously, they are used to control multimedia slide presentations and the narration for filmstrips. Many churches have a library tape service that provides copies of the church's services to radio/television audiences, to church members, and to homebound persons. Also, many media libraries have a fine collection of audiocassettes for circulation. Additional information on audiocassettes is listed in the bibliography.

Nonprojected audiovisuals include objects, flat pictures, posters, charts, maps, globes, chalkboards, cling boards, and models. Because many of these items are free, inexpensive, or can be prepared by the teacher, they are more readily available than other types of media. Although the homemade variety of visual may lack professional quality, it has the advantage of being designed to support specific lessons or points in a presentation. Well-equipped media libraries provide a special area or room set aside for media preparation. Teachers and leaders should have convenient access to equipment and supplies needed for making nonprojected visuals, promotional posters, and bulletin board displays. Even though teachers may not have access to professionally produced audiovisuals, there is no reason they cannot have some kind of visual to enhance their lesson presentation. Nonprojected audiovisuals offer endless possibilities for colorful, creative, attention-getting tools. For more information on making nonprojected visuals and for setting up a media preparation room, see the bibliography.

GUIDELINES FOR SELECTING MEDIA

Many people have different reasons for selecting media. Media library staff select media for the church's circulating collection. Teachers and leaders select media to support specific teaching or presentation objectives. Individuals choose media to share with persons who need a witness or a ministry. And people choose resources to meet personal or family needs. Some of these needs include: (1) satisfying curiosity, (2) solving problems, (3) securing data for writing or speaking assignments, (4) enriching personal or family devotions, (5) reading to young children, and (6) using in leisure time activities. There are guidelines that if followed will produce good choices in all of these situations. However, we will discuss only two—selection guidelines for media libraries and guidelines for teachers and leaders.

EQUIPPING MEDIA LIBRARIES

With the help of library staff and other leaders, the media library director has many things to keep in mind when selecting media. These include: scriptural and doctrinal accuracy, needs of the congregation, finances, and lasting value.

Scriptural and doctrinal accuracy is usually defined by a person's theological position. The Christian community classifies itself with terms such as liberal, moderate, conservative, and fundamental. Because churches differ, books and audiovisuals that are acceptable in one church may not be tolerated in another. Because this is a local church matter, the library director needs to be thoroughly knowledgeable of the church's position and be careful to select materials that support and interpret that position. A church is what it is because of the people who make up that church, who hold to common beliefs. Those beliefs are supported by the church's preachers and teachers, and the media library is part of that team.

Needs of the congregation vary from church to church, such as geographical location, age of the church, average age of the congregation, education level, and church programs and ministries. Titles should not be added to the library that have no apparent relationship to the needs and objectives of the church. Under the leadership of the library director, the library staff should seek out and secure resources that will encourage, inform, and challenge the congregation.

Finances—obviously and unfortunately—have much to do with the selection of media for the library. Money spent on the library ministry is a good investment. In many churches funds available from the church budget are supplemented by memorial gifts. Media library directors must be thoroughly knowledgeable of the church's programs in order to give priority to titles that relate to and support the work of the church.

Lasting value is an objective in selecting library materials. The ideal title is one that can meet an immediate need and still be useful for years to come. A good example of media that have lasting value are Bible study helps. When a church uses a balanced Bible study curriculum and the library consistently secures related reference books, ultimately the library will have a comprehensive collection of Bible study materials.

There are other categories of concern. The needs of families and individuals for nonprogram related material must not be neglected. The library may be the only resource in the church where some individual and family needs can be met. Titles of lasting value can be found for subjects such as doctrine, Christian life, family, parent and child relationships, and biography and fiction.

For other guidelines and suggestions for selection of media, including audiovisual equipment, see the bibliography.

MEDIA NEEDS FOR TEACHERS AND LEADERS

Teachers and leaders have at least three areas of need for media that relate to their leadership responsibilities: their home library, resources to enrich their teaching and leading, and media for use in witnessing and ministering. Much of the media that they need should be available from the church's media library. But some books, because of constant need, ought to be in their home or personal library.

Selecting media for home libraries requires much thought. Buying books on impulse results in cluttered shelves of unused volumes. Media needed at home include: basic Bible study helps and books and tapes that give guidance in the individual's various areas of responsibility. At minimum the Bible study helps should include: a one-volume commentary, a dictionary, an atlas, an unabridged concordance, and several translations of the Bible. The media library can help teachers and leaders select reference materials that have the vocabulary and format they like.

Selecting media for teaching and leading requires a knowledge of people, teaching techniques, the subject, and the value and use of media. The basic question is, What media is needed to help reach the teaching or learning goal?

Knowledge of class members and their abilities is needed to help the teacher choose books and audiovisuals that are on the learners' level. The simplest medium that will meet the need is almost always the best choice. If the item is no longer current, it may still be used if the leader is prepared to update the outdated sections.

If the church has a library, leaders should spend time getting acquainted with the collection. Knowing what is available will help the leaders think of possibilities and save time in searching for related books and audiovisuals. The teacher's guidance material for the course of study is another aid to identifying related media. Lesson writers and editors often suggest titles and procedures for using them.

As the teacher prepares the lesson, he should be alert to concepts that need further explanation, words that need to be defined, Scripture needing further interpretation, situations that need to be illustrated, and places that need to be described or located on a map. Not only should the teacher find sources for this information, but these occasions should be seen as opportunities to involve class members in searching for related media.

Teachers and leaders select media for two primary reasons: (1) to provide data for a comprehensive and in-depth study of the subject under consideration, and (2) to help communicate and clarify the concepts, meanings, principles, skills, interpretations, and applications involved in the subject.

Teachers and leaders need to become familiar with a variety of media types and titles. The more titles they know, and the more skill and experience they have, the more effective they will be in selecting media to enrich teaching and learning.

Using Media Effectively

WHAT IT INVOLVES

Using media in teaching involves securing the media, previewing the titles, planning the session, arranging the room, and practicing the presentation.

Securing the media usually involves a visit to the media library. When the teacher has determined what titles and equipment are available, he checks the materials out or reserves them for the date needed. If the titles are not in the library—and if the materials are not needed soon—the library may be able to borrow items from another library, purchase them, or contact a borrower to have them returned. Obviously, teachers who plan ahead have a better chance of securing media.

Previewing the titles is essential. Titles of media are sometimes misleading. For this reason, the teacher should carefully preview audiovisuals and examine books. Studying the material will help the teacher know which part to use when all of it is not available.

Planning the session is needed for effective use of media. Planning for the use of audiovisuals and books includes the following: how to introduce, how to make assignments to class members, when and where to pause for discussion, and whether or not to use an audiovisual for preview, content, or review. Planning for the use of materials will result in their proper use as tools. Media—especially audiovisuals—should not be used as a substitute for the teacher or for the teacher's preparation.

Arranging the room properly involves visibility and safety. If at all possible, the teacher should set up the room and test all the equipment prior to class. If several pieces of equipment are used, one or more assistants may be needed. When others help, a rehearsal session may be required.

Visibility requires attention to seating and to lighting. The diagram below shows the best viewing location. No one should be seated closer than two screen or monitor widths or further away than six widths. Although a television is smaller than a projection screen, the image usually does not include as wide an angle. This compensates, in part, for the smaller screen. Visibility is not good from the front corners of the room.

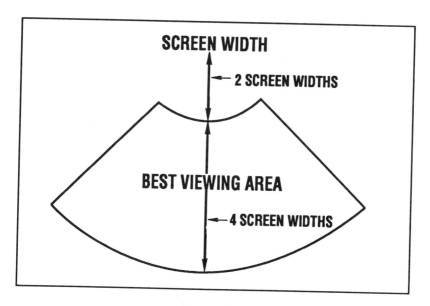

SCREEN WIDTH

← 2 SCREEN WIDTHS

BEST VIEWING AREA

← 4 SCREEN WIDTHS

In classroom settings, chairs should not be set up in front corners. In auditoriums, these corners should be roped off. Presenters should anticipate light conditions at the time of the session. Windows should be darkened when necessary.

Safety considerations involve marking exits, clearing aisles, and providing adequate electrical supply. Placing of chairs or equipment in narrow aisles should be avoided. Electrical cords that cross traffic-ways should be taped down. Electricity needs should not exceed supply, and extension cords should be large enough to accommodate electrical need. Ushers are needed to seat latecomers safely.

Practicing the presentation will avoid many pitfalls. Without a rehearsal, it is difficult to anticipate every condition. This is especially true the first time a person uses a medium. The more complicated the session and the larger the audience, the more essential it is to practice. Carelessness by leaders has given audiovisuals a reputation they do not deserve. Most of the time everything goes well, but people tend to remember the disasters. Avoidance of distractions is essential to good communication in the classroom.

THE LEARNING TEAM CONCEPT

WHAT IT INVOLVES

Every endeavor that involves two or more people requires teamwork. For teamwork to occur, several conditions must exist: a common cause, a respect for responsibility, skillful participants, and a game plan.

A common cause means that each member of the team knows and accepts the objectives of the educational endeavor. In the Christian setting, the objective is usually spiritual growth. The hoped for outcome is that each participant will grow into the likeness of Christ. We have the promise in Romans 8:28 that God works everything to the good of those who love Him and are called according to His purpose. Then in verse 29 we read, "For whom he did foreknow, he also did predestinate to be conformed to the image of his Son." Also, Philippians 2:13 assures us that "it is God which worketh in you both to will and to do of his good pleasure." God has a plan for us, is at work in us, and it is our place to cooperate with Him both personally and corporately.

In developing the learning team concept, a respect for responsibility must be evident. We need to accept responsibility for ourselves and expect others to do the same for themselves. We learn to be responsible through experience. It is necessary, therefore, to know what we are responsible for and then do it. It is also necessary for us to know what the other person is responsible for and expect him to do it. In the case of learning, there are certain actions that must be done by the learner if learning is to occur. If we do these things for him, we may think we are helping him when actually we are hindering him. Each member of the learning team has specific responsibilities.

The learner is responsible for learning. Teachers can no more learn for him than they can eat, drink, sleep, or exercise for him. The old adage, "You get out of it what you put into it," certainly applies to learning. In a real sense learning is in the search. When we search for answers ourselves, at least five values accrue to us:

1. The truth becomes our own. No longer do we have to accept it because someone else said it is so, but we have now thought it through and have accepted it for ourselves.

2. It prepares us for future searches. One of the greatest needs is for every person to learn how to learn. Each time we find an answer for ourselves, we develop learning skills that can be applied in future searches.

3. The process of searching aids recall. Everyone has difficulty maintaining 100 percent attention to a lecture, sermon, or even to a stimulating discussion. When we are searching for something, we are paying attention. If attention lapses, we go nowhere, unlike the class discussion that goes on without us when our attention is diverted. Such concentration enables us to remember the things we have considered.

4. The search provides informaton about related subjects. Even truths are not islands unto themselves. For example, justification and sanctification are tied together because there can be no sanctification prior to justification. Subject matter is better understood when related topics are involved.

5. Searching for answers makes us aware of error. When we travel through unfamiliar territory, we sometimes end up on dead-end streets. The driver will probably remember the dead-ends on the next trip through that territory, but it is unlikely that the passengers will remember. This is similar to a class where the teacher does all the research. The teacher is the driver, while class members are passengers. In order for the learner to understand something well enough for it to be useful, he must possess an adequate amount of accurate information about the subject in question. Missing information or misconstrued data can cause a person to misapply or misjudge the situation.

The leader must remember and respect the fact that learning is the learner's job. The teacher or leader can serve in several roles that are consistent with this fact. These roles are: as lead-learner, assistant to the learner, and as a counselor.

As the lead-learner, the teacher is freed from being embarrassed when he does not know the answer to a question. Pretending to be an authority can be uncomfortable. In this role, he realizes his need to learn and the class is encouraged by observing growth in their teacher.

As an assistant to the learner, the teacher is in an enabling role. He motivates, introduces subjects, asks questions, presents alternatives, gives suggestions, makes assignments, and recommends sources of data. He is careful to put responsibility on the learner when the learner is ready to accept it.

As counselor—a role the leader inherits with his position—the leader must first be available. He must be careful not to appear so busy that learners assume he does not have time for them. Second, he must be trustworthy. Learners should know he can keep a confidence. Third, he must be a good listener. Other counseling skills are also desirable, but being a listener is a good start.

The competent teacher will succeed in merging three areas: the needs of the learner, the subject being studied, and information from related resources. Assignments to learners should be designed to encourage them to give attention to aspects of the subject that relate to their needs. Usually this will involve study of related resources and recitation in class. The diagram below, taken from

The Learning Team,[5] indicates that the more the three circles overlap, the more successful the educational experience becomes.

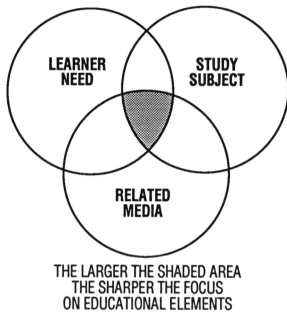

THE LARGER THE SHADED AREA
THE SHARPER THE FOCUS
ON EDUCATIONAL ELEMENTS

The media library is the third member of the team. Churches without a library are short a teammate and should take steps to remedy the deficiency. The media library should be located centrally and be easily accessible. The primary responsibility of the library is to provide media needed by learners and leaders. Availability of media is crucial to their use, and their use will be in direct proportion to availability. The easier it is to locate and secure a specific book or tape, the greater the likelihood it will be used. A well organized and strongly supported media library staff will anticipate the informational needs of church programs and individuals.

After identifying needs, the media are secured, processed, and cataloged. In addition to providing media, the library promotes the use of media. Like a business, the library needs to advertise. To complete its responsibility, the library should offer training in the use of the media. Library workers have opportunity to function as teachers and leaders when people come to the library for help. On these occasions library workers need to observe the same guidelines as other teachers. This involves letting the learner be responsible by helping him learn how to find resources for himself.

One of the more important opportunities for library workers is that of working directly with learners in extended study projects. Many people have person-

5. Mee, *The Learning Team*, p. 86.

al needs for studying a subject that may be unrelated to anything being offered in the church's educational program(s). On these occasions the library worker will suggest resources and a course of action for researching the subject.

Skillful participants means that team members have the knowledge and skills required for doing their part of the job. When there are persons who lack this ability, steps should be taken to correct the deficiency. An ongoing goal of teachers should be to help learners learn how to learn.

A game plan is essential, if there is to be teamwork. All members of the team need to know what is going on. Leadership should seek to help learners understand the learning team concept.

Church leadership would do well to develop learning teams of learners, leaders, and library workers.

Reaching learning objectives depends on the availability of teaching/learning tools, on each team member knowing his responsibility and doing it, and each team member respecting the responsibilities that belong to their teammates.

EVALUATING THE USE OF MEDIA

Our use of media should be evaluated continually as to the effectiveness of what we are doing. Several questions can serve as criteria for evaluation.[6]

1. Are the materials appropriate?
2. Will the media chosen meet the needs of the learners?
2. Will the media help reach the learning goal?
3. Are the media easily available?
4. Can the media be seen and heard comfortably?
5. Does the leader have the skill to use it effectively?
6. Are the media on the level of the learners?
7. Is sufficient time available to use it effectively?
8. Are the physical conditions suitable?
9. Does the anticipated result justify the cost?
10. Will a simpler or less expensive tool do as well?
11. Are the media accessible for ease in use?
12. Is training provided for those who use the media and equipment?

Other questions may be added to the criteria. The important thing is to be sure we are accomplishing what we intend to do efficiently and effectively. The most effective evaluation will be done on a systematic and regular basis with emphasis on improving and doing a better job than we are now doing.

---

6. Mee, *How to Use Audiovisuals*, pp. 23-30.

FOR FURTHER READING

Anderson, Jacqulyn, comp. *How to Administer and Promote a Church Media Library*. Nashville: Broadman, 1984.

Bouldin, Don. *Ears to Hear, Eyes to See: Witnessing Through Media*. Nashville: Broadman, 1987.

Darkes, Anna Sue. *How to Make and Use Overhead Transparencies*. Chicago: Moody, 1977.

Doan, Eleanor, comp. *Visual Aid Encyclopedia*. Ventura, Calif.: Gospel Light, 1967.

Ezell, Mancell. *Instructional Media for Churches*. Nashville: Convention, 1991.

Hack, John. *How to Make Audiovisuals*. Nashville: Broadman, 1979.

————. *How to Operate a Cassette Tape Ministry*. Nashville: Broadman, 1981.

Kemp, Jerrold E. *Planning, Producing and Using Instructional Media*, 6th ed. San Francisco: Harper & Row, 1989.

Mee, Keith. *How to Use Audiovisuals*. Nashville: Convention, 1979.

————. *The Learning Team: the Learner, the Leader, and the Library*. Revised edition. Nashville: Convention, 1987.

Minor, Edward O. *Handbook for Preparing Visual Media*, 2d ed. New York: McGraw-Hill, 1978.

Part 3

The Ministry Is to People

We tend to think of Christian education in terms of programs, ministries, activities, and organizations. But its primary focus should be on people. After all, Christ's mandate is to make disciples, not perpetuate programs.

This unit looks at people in education—big people, little people, people in all shapes and colors. To be effective teachers, workers, and parents, we need to understand the people with whom we work.

Appropriately, the first half of this unit is devoted to understanding various age groups—infants and preschoolers (chap. 15); elementary-age children (chap. 16); junior and senior high students (chap. 17); and young, middle, and senior adults (chaps. 18 and 19). Each chapter focuses on their characteristics and needs, how they think and learn, and how to teach and minister to them.

The next two chapters look at people from a different perspective. They focus on specific groups—single adults (chap. 20) and exceptional persons (chap. 21). Each one describes categories within these target groups, as well as characteristics and needs. The authors also offer guidelines for ministering effectively to these groups.

Another approach to looking at people is understanding their learning styles, the subject of chapter 22. Because we do not all learn the same way, this chapter is designed to help education workers and parents be aware of the different kinds of learners and implications for teaching them.

Finally, this unit looks at people from a cultural perspective. Chapter 23 introduces the concept of cross-cultural teaching and learning and provides an overview of major characteristics of cross-cultural groups. The last chapter (24) examines characteristics and needs of three major cultural groups: African Americans, Hispanics, and Asian Americans.

15

Valerie Wilson

Infants and Preschoolers

MEETING THE NEEDS OF INFANTS AND PRESCHOOLERS
- **Know the characteristics of the children with whom we work**
- **Recognize the inherent worth of each life**
- **Model the Biblical truths we seek to teach**
- **Provide opportunities for children to learn in harmony with their development**
- **Give the best in personnel, facilities, and resources to the teaching of children**

"Let the little children come to me, and do not hinder them, for the kingdom of heaven belongs to such as these" (Matt. 19:14). With those words—and His subsequent actions—the Lord Jesus elevated early childhood to a position of respect and importance. Those who are concerned about the educational ministry of the church must not develop the attitude of the disciples; namely, that ministry is only for adults. A church that wants to be New Testament in every sense of the word must care about and provide for even the youngest individuals who come through

VALERIE WILSON, M.R.E., is editor of children's materials, Regular Baptist Press, Schaumburg, Illinois.

its doors. What are little children like? What do they need from us? How do they learn? How can we minister to them? These issues are the focus of this chapter.

CHARACTERISTICS OF INFANTS AND YOUNG CHILDREN

Because the learner is central in the educational process, we need to understand the development of children from birth through five years of age. No two children are alike, and no two children develop on exactly the same timetable. But as Margaret Jacobsen has pointed out, "Children of the same age are more alike than they are different."[1] Listed below are characteristics that are generally true at each stage of development.

THE INFANT (BIRTH TO TWELVE MONTHS)

Birth through three months. The full-term newborn baby usually weighs between six and nine pounds and is normally eighteen to twenty-one inches long. Boys are usually slightly heavier and a little longer than girls. The birth weight normally doubles by the end of six months and triples by one year. The head of a newborn is about one-fourth of his total body length.

Physical needs dominate the early weeks of an infant's life. A newborn sleeps eighteen to twenty hours per day. When he is awake, he needs to be fed, changed, and cared for. The newborn cries when he awakens, and he cries when he is uncomfortable. A crying baby needs attention. Repeated studies have proved that nothing is gained by letting a baby "cry it out."

The senses of sight, taste, smell, and hearing are keen in the newborn. He is capable of feeling pain, heat, and cold. He learns through touch. He can identify various adults in his life by the way he is held. "Handling a baby is clearly one of the few effective ways of changing a baby's state from distress to comfort."[2]

By the second and third months, the infant can track moving objects with his eyes. He is attracted by hanging toys and mobiles. By the end of this period, he may begin to gurgle and coo.

Four through six months. During the second and third months of life, the infant becomes much more active. He learns to roll over and sit up. He also learns to know his family members, and he may cry when he is separated from them.

Also during this time, the baby learns to pick up an object, and he will tightly grasp anything in his hand. He learns that letting go intentionally is fun too, even though adults may become frustrated picking up objects time after time.

Seven through nine months. During some time in this age period, the first tooth appears. A teething baby is often fretful and fussy, and adult caregivers need to keep this in mind.

1. Margaret B. Jacobsen, *What Happens When Children Grow* (Wheaton, Ill.: Victor, 1977), p. 22.
2. Burton White, *The First Three Years of Life* (New York: Prentice-Hall, 1985), p. 29.

The growing infant is working on his coordination. He learns to pull himself into an upright position, and he may begin to crawl.

This age baby needs toys to stimulate his curious mind: nesting toys; small blocks; bright, wooden beads; large spools; large plastic rings; soft, cuddly toys.

Ten through twelve months. The last quarter of the first year finds the baby eating solid food and drinking from a cup. He can usually maintain a standing position without support and may even take a few steps. He needs to be protected from danger, but he also needs opportunities to explore. Before his first birthday a child is able to use his thumb and forefinger together. He shows increasing evidence of coordination.

By this age the baby responds more and more to adult attention. He enjoys games such as pat-a-cake and peek-a-boo, and objects such as simple pull-apart, put-together toys, boxes, spoons, nonclip clothespins, a ball, and blocks. Books with one word per page and simple pictures are suitable for the child as he nears his first birthday.

Needs. The needs of infants are largely physical, but it is important that these physical needs be met by a loving caregiver, whether at home or in the church. As physical needs are met in a loving, gentle way, the infant develops a sense of trust and security, and this, according to developmental theorist Erik Erickson, is the developmental task of an infant. Furthermore, "the basic foundation of a child's personality is being formed in his earliest interchanges with nurturing adults."[3]

Those who work with newborns and infants in the church nursery should view their role as service unto the Lord. They have "responsibility of helping the infant form his first and most lasting impression of the place called church. Long before he knows anything about what is *taught*, he will know how he *feels*.[4] If a child learns from his earliest days in the church that he can trust people to care for his physical needs, that child will some day be able to trust God for his spiritual needs. "Trust is essential not only for self-control and human relationships but also for faith, through which the growing child relates to God."[5]

The people who work with infants must be calm, gentle, quiet, and loving.

> Love is communicated more effectively through attitude and action than through verbalization for the young child. He feels deeply and responds to a quiet, calm, and unhurried atmosphere in which he feels secure and comfortable. Those who work with young children should be calm, collected, and secure themselves in order to transmit those same feelings to the children.[6]

3. Ibid., p. 12.
4. Valerie Wilson, "Understanding Infants and Toddlers," in *Childhood Education in the Church*, ed. Robert E. Clark et al. (Chicago: Moody, 1986), p. 89.
5. Judith Allen Shelly et al., *The Spiritual Needs of Children* (Downers Grove, Ill.: InterVarsity, 1982), p. 26.
6. Robert Clark, "The Learner: Children," in *Introduction to Biblical Christian Education*, ed. Werner C. Graendorf (Chicago: Moody, 1981), p. 132.

Some churches recruit couples to work in the church nursery, a practice with a great deal of merit. "A child's life is richer when, from the beginning, he has the benefit of both a masculine and a feminine approach to the world. . . . Children of both sexes need to feel a hairy hand, a more muscular hand, a bigger hand, a calloused hand."[7] (Considering the rise of reported cases of child molestation in various kinds of child-care facilities and considering the possibility of some parents making unfounded accusations, it may be wise for a church to allow only designated workers to change a child's diapers or accompany young chlidren to the bathroom.)

The infant not only needs loving adults to care for him; he also needs a spotlessly clean and adequately equipped church nursery. The church that wants to minister to infants and their parents "must do its utmost to provide clean, responsible, efficient, friendly, and loving service to infants and their parents."[8]

THE TODDLER (ONE YEAR OLD)

Physical characteristics. The toddler is the child from thirteen to twenty-four months. "Toddler" is a good designation, because it is during this time period that the child learns to walk. There is no great advantage in how early a child learns to walk. He learns when he is ready, on his own physiological timetable.

Another area of physical development for the one year old is his increased dexterity with his hands. "He can pull off his cap and socks, open boxes, unscrew lids, put pegs into holes, scribble, turn book pages one at a time, and build a tower with four or five blocks."[9]

His sleeping habits change. He will sleep only two or three hours during the day and eleven to twelve at night. He does tire, however, and church programs must include opportunities for rest.

By the end of the toddler year, a child is usually thirty-two to thirty-four inches long and weighs thirty-three to thirty-six pounds.

Mental characteristics. A toddler has a brief attention span and a short memory, but his language development is increasing. By his second birthday he will have a 250- to 300-word vocabulary. He is able to name objects or pictures in a book, and he begins to use words in combination.

Social characteristics. The toddler's world is egocentric: *me* and *mine*. He has little concept of others. His play is characterized as "parallel": he wants to do the same thing as another child but not with another child.

The toddler tends to treat people much as he treats things: feeling them, pushing them, trying to manipulate them. Sometimes his behavior is misunderstood by the adults around him. He is probably not misbehaving; he is exploring his world. When a child exhibits such behavior, it is best to separate him from the

---

7. James Hymes, *The Children Under Six* (Englewood Cliffs, N.J.: Prentice-Hall, 1963), p. 249.
8. Wilson, p. 89.
9. Ibid, p. 90.

other child.

Emotional characteristics. A toddler is characterized by emotional insecurity. He has difficulty adjusting. Jacobsen suggests that "simplicity and order" are important in order to help create a sense of security.[10] At church, the room arrangement, personnel, and schedule should be much the same from week to week.

The toddler's emotional reactions to his world are often based on his physical state. If he is tired, hungry, or insecure, he will be more uneasy than if he is rested, fed, and content.

Spiritual characteristics. Spiritually, the toddler has an open mind and receptive heart. He is capable of receiving basic, biblical truths such as God made me, God loves me, Jesus loves me. Simple songs and large, uncomplicated pictures of whole objects or persons can be used to introduce these truths. In regard to spiritual development, the toddler "assimilate[s] more in attitudes and actions than from understanding concepts."[11]

Needs. The developmental task of the toddler (and two year old) is autonomy versus shame and doubt. The child moves toward self-control and independence. Therefore, the toddler needs room, and he needs opportunities to explore. He does not belong in a crib nursery, neither is he ready for a two-year-old class. He needs a place, personnel, and program tailor-made for his stage of development. Those who work with toddlers should have the same characteristics as those who work with infants.

THE TWO YEAR OLD

Physical characteristics. "The two-year-old is a rather complicated, firmly established, social being."[12] He is about three feet tall. He will gain about five pounds during this year and add two or three inches to his height. He sleeps about twelve hours at night and still needs an afternoon nap. Toilet training is usually accomplished during this year, and church workers need to cooperate with parents in this.

"Action" is a key word for a two year old. The hardest thing for him to be is inactive. His developing muscles demand use.

Mental characteristics. The two year old likes to explore, and he learns by experimenting. He has about three hundred words in his vocabulary. He does not understand time and space. His memory is undependable, so repetition is important. His attention span is only two or three minutes.

Social characteristics. The two year old is similar to the toddler in that his world is egocentric. He is a loner. He does not relate well to other people, even those his own age. He is very possessive of his toys. This continues to be an age of parallel

10. Jacobsen, p. 33.
11. Clark, p. 132.
12. White, p. 110.

play. Two year olds play side-by-side, not together.

Spiritual characteristics. The two year old begins to associate God with the wonders around him. In addition to the basic truths introduced to toddlers, a two year old can learn that God takes care of me; Jesus is my friend; Jesus is God's Son; the Bible is God's Word. "A two-year-old easily senses and catches the spiritual attitudes of home and church."[13]

Needs. The expression "terrible twos" came about in part because the two year old tends to be so negative. His world is full of things he cannot do, so he asserts himself by saying no. (Remember, he is moving toward independence.) Those who work with twos can reduce these negative responses by avoiding questions that invite no for an answer. When there is in fact no choice, do not offer one.

The two year old needs adult restraints and protection. He needs a combination of freedom, reasonable restriction, and guidance.

THE THREE YEAR OLD

Physical characteristics. The three year old weighs thirty-four to forty pounds and is thirty-two to forty inches tall. His physical development has advanced to the place that he can ride a tricycle well, climb stairs, and feed himself neatly. He needs less nighttime sleep and may not need an afternoon nap. He has good bowel and bladder control, and "accidents" are infrequent. His small muscle development is advanced to the stage that he can fasten and unfasten most buttons—a skill he likes to use in the I-can-do-it-myself time of life.

Mental characteristics. The three year old is capable of imaginative, imitative play. He has a vivid imagination. He adds four hundred to six hundred words to his vocabulary. He enjoys talking and can carry on a limited conversation. In fact, the three year old seldom *chooses* to be quiet. He likes to use his developing language skills. "One of the characteristics of the well-developed three-year-old is the tendency to hold conversations with adults as if they were peers. . . . Comfortable, effective parents [and teachers] move naturally into responding to such language and into carrying on modest conversations."[14]

He is curious about the world around him, and his ability to reason is developing. He can draw distinguishable objects and print some letters. His coloring is less crude than it was at age two. He likes to make up stories, and he enjoys rhymes and nonsense verse.

Social characteristics. The three year old likes to be with other people. He plays more easily with other children and is more willing to share his toys with them. He wants to please the adults in his life, and one way he does this is by offering to be a helper.

Emotional characteristics. He is growing in self-direction and self-control, although both two and three year olds have many fears. Some of these are real-

13. Jacobsen, p. 50.
14. White, p. 177.

istic; some are not. But adult care-givers need to treat all fears as real and continue to help young children feel safe and secure in their environment.

Spiritual characterstics. This child still "catches" much of his religious training. He learns a great deal by observing the attitudes and actions of adults. For instance, a three year old may repeat a phrase in prayer that he has heard an adult use even though he has no idea what it means. His increased mental capabilities enable him to remember the details of Bible stories and to recall some Bible verses and songs.

Needs. A three year old needs adults who are willing to give simple, honest answers to the many questions he asks. When he asks about spiritual things (Where is heaven? How big is God? Where did Grandma go?), he needs simple, biblical answers.

The child's questions are an indication of the developmental task of initiative. His sense of initiative during ages three and four is "particularly prominent in [his] increasingly more proficient verbal interactions. . . . The prime vehicle for this new use of language is the question."[15]

FOUR AND FIVE YEAR OLDS

Physical characteristics. A four year old is in a period of rapid growth; thus he tires easily. He is constantly on the go. His large muscles need exercise (as much as four hours a day), and his small muscle coordination is improving. The growth rate slows some for the five year old, but he still has lots of energy. The child begins to lose his chubbiness, and he gets taller, with longer arms and legs. His eye-hand coordination improves a great deal. Girls mature more rapidly than boys.

Mental characteristics. The four year old wants a reason for everything, so "why" becomes a common word. ("Because I said so" does not satisfy the developing mind of a four year old.) He likes to experiment with words and will often make up nonsense words or silly rhymes. He can concentrate for longer periods of time, but he is easily distracted.

The four year old begins to recognize letters and may be able to print all or most of his name. The five year old is learning to print.

The five year old begins to acquire a sense of time. He is interested in the clock and *when* things will happen.

During these two years, a child will gain increased ability to use scissors, to color, and to recognize and work with shapes.

Four and five year olds have attention spans of five to seven minutes. Children will grow restless if activities are too long. But attention can be sustained if the child is interested in what he is doing.

The four year old has about 1,200 words in his vocabulary; the five year old, 1,500 to 2,000. A five year old recognizes about 75 percent of what is said to him.

15. David Elkind, *Miseducation: Preschoolers at Risk* (New York: Alfred A. Knopf, 1987), pp. 116, 119.

We cannot minimize the effect of television on the mental development of children. Little children are exposed to much more of the world than were children of previous generations. They can name people and places because they have heard and seen these on television. Programs such as "Sesame Street" have fostered early word and letter recognition and language development—even in a second language.

Social characteristics. The four year old moves into the area of "cooperative play" (as opposed to the parallel play of a two year old). He can play *with* other children.

A five year old likes to help, and he thrives on adult attention. He has a strong sense of conformity. If one child makes a statement, the other children in the group are quick to agree.

Emotional characteristics. These children have more emotional control than a two or three year old, although a four year old will alternate between aggression and calm behavior. Fours and fives usually evidence fewer fears, but they still need a secure, loving environment.

Spiritual characteristics. The four year old is developing a growing understanding of the difference between right and wrong. He can learn that wrong actions are sin in God's eyes. He can feel sorry for his sin. He needs to know, though, that God's love is unconditional. God loves him even when he does something naughty.

The four year old thinks of God in a literal way. He is willing to talk to God, and will pray about the smallest details of his life. Spontaneous worship is possible as the young child realizes the greatness or goodness of God.

Because of increased social development during these years, experiences outside the home are important to the child. "Sunday school and church can be extremely significant to preschoolers. They enjoy going (unless they have had bad experiences) and often prod their parents into attending church. Preschoolers will also insist that parents practice religious customs learned in school or in the homes of other children."[16]

Needs. A four year old and a five year old need a wide variety of experiences and opportunities to use their increasing language ability. They need opportunities to exercise choice. "The arrangement of the classroom into 'interest areas' is particularly supportive of the child's sense of initiative inasmuch as it provides opportunities for the child to choose the area he or she would like to work in."[17]

Young children need adults who model the truths they are teaching. Children are quick to sense inconsistencies. The qualities of love, kindness, and forgiveness must be evident in the lives of those who work with little children. If we want God to be real and near-at-hand to a young child, then He must, indeed, be that to us.

Occasionally a three year old (usually nearing his fourth birthday) or a four or five year old will make a decision to receive Christ as Savior. This is usually a

16. Shelly, p. 34.
17. Elkind, p. 167.

child whose parents take an active role in his spiritual training. Great care should be exercised in this regard. Little children want to please adults, and they want God to love them. The church worker must be careful that decisions are not made on this basis alone. Children "need sufficient background in spiritual teaching to respond intelligently on an individual basis. Foundations in readiness in spiritual development are extremely important."[18]

HOW YOUNG CHILDREN LEARN

The Swiss psychologist Jean Piaget did extensive research on children's cognitive development. His findings provide two general categories for the age children we are considering in this study. He called the years from birth until age two the period of sensorimotor intelligence. During this time, the child does not "think" conceptually. He learns primarily through his senses. The child from ages two to seven is in the stage of development that Piaget called preoperational thought. This period is characterized by language development and the ability to classify or categorize, but the child does not understand why or how an object could have more than one classification. Keeping these designations in mind, we can make some general statements about how young children learn and relate these statements to learning in the church.

SENSORY EXPERIENCES

A young child is dependent on physical, sensory experiences because he does not possess language development. He learns through the things he sees, hears, smells, tastes, and touches. "It is recognized that children have a need to move about and speak out. They learn by actively exploring and coordinating information received from a mutliplicity of sense modalities."[19]

The church nursery and children's classrooms need to provide a variety of sensory experiences. In addition to hearing (which is the sense to which most education is directed), the young child needs to see, taste, smell, and touch. When we tell a child, "Don't touch," we are denying him a learning experience. The learning environment in the church should invite children to touch.

REPETITION

Memory is a function of intelligence that develops as the child grows. Short-term memory is in evidence by the time a child is two. Limited memory means repetition is vital to learning: the same routine, the same stories, the same songs, the same personnel. These aspects of sameness are important to young children. It is usually the adults who work with little children who tire of the repetition.

18. Clark, p. 135.
19. Herbert Zimiles, "Psychodynamic Theory of Development," in *Handbook of Research in Early Childhood Education,* ed. Bernard Spodek (New York: Free, 1982), p. 148.

Children themselves thrive on it.

LIMITED ATTENTION SPANS

The attention span of a young child is as limited as his memory. A general rule of thumb is one minute for each year of age. This means a two year old has a two-minute attention span. What can be accomplished in that amount of time? Just "snatches" of truth. Stories for young children must be brief, but the same story can be repeated several times.

LITERAL THINKERS

As young children move from the sensorimotor to the preoperational stage of mental development, we must remember that their thinking is literal, concrete. Symbolism is inappropriate in teaching young children. "Children must learn with understanding in literal, concrete, and simple vocabulary that is on their level intellectually and spiritually."[20]

We can challenge a child more by horizontal enrichment (by elaborating on what the child already knows) than by vertical acceleration (by introducing totally new and abstract concepts)."[21]

CURIOUS NATURE

Little children are known for their curiosity. As stated earlier, *why* is the favorite word in the vocabulary of the preschooler. Often a child is seeking the *purpose* for something rather than a detailed explanation. A child who asks a very deep question rarely wants that kind of answer. Elkind points out that a young child's "verbal skills far outpace [his] conceptual knowledge." In other words, the child sounds smarter than he really is.[22]

LEARN THROUGH PLAY

"It is clear that play and learning activities are interrelated and that certain types of learning are facilitated by certain types of play."[23] If we use White's definition that play is "an activity in which a child was clearly having fun while being active," [24] we immediately realize that much of what goes on in the learning environment of young children is play: building with blocks, tending to a doll, working with clay, rolling a ball. But these activities (which are only representative of the

20. Clark, p. 140.
21. Elkind, p. 122.
22. Ibid., p. 119.
23. Coris Sponseller, "Play and Early Education," in *Handbook of Research in Early Childhood Education*, p. 231.
24. White, p. 275.

many types of "play" that occur in a church room) are all opportunities to learn spiritual truths.

LEARN BEST IN KEEPING WITH THEIR DEVELOPMENT

Perhaps as much as anyone else, Elkind has alerted us to the dangers of rushing children through childhood. In his book on preschool education, he points out that education is not a race.[25] We need to remember this in the church. There is no spiritual merit to be attained by reciting the books of the Bible in order at age three—a feat that some church educators might find desirable. Rather, we should seek to "provide young children with a rich and stimulating environment that is, at the same time, warm, loving, and supportive of the children's own learning priorities and pacing. It is within this supportive, nonpressured environment that infants and young children acquire a solid sense of security, positive self-esteem, and a long-term enthusiasm for learning."[26]

Ministering to the Young Child at Church

It is important that each child in a church's ministry be seen as God's special creation. He is like other children in some respects, but he is also unique. It is unfair (and unwise) to compare one child to another (even in the same family). Each child must be valued for the special individual he is.

Children are not little adults, and adults who work with little children should not expect adult behaviors of them. Adults must allow children to be just that: children.

The church ministers to infants and toddlers and their parents through the cradle roll department. This ministry of the church "capitalizes on going into the home, but it also makes provision at the church for the care of infants and toddlers."[27]

The church needs to carefully plan its curriculum (learning experiences, including printed materials) for young children. "Curriculum planning begins with an analysis of children's developmental characteristics, consistent with their unique needs, interests, and modes of thinking."[28]

The church's program for young children must provide variety. Active children tire easily, so the activities we provide for them must be both active and quiet. Large muscles need activity, but the program must also provide opportunities to be quiet. The younger the child, the more variety he needs. A two or three year old needs ten to twelve changes of activity per hour; a four or five year old needs six to ten changes.

25. Elkind, p. 83.
26. Ibid., p. 8.
27. Meryl Welch, *Cradle Roll Handbook* (Schaumburg, Ill.: Regular Baptist, 1979), p. 3.
28. Ellis D. Evans, "Curriculum Models and Early Childhood Education," in *Handbook of Research in Early Childhood Education*, p. 111.

Careful thought and planning should be given to support ministries for parents. Although the cradle roll department usually functions as part of the Sunday school, other ministries are also possible. Day care centers, nursery and preschools, MOPS (Mothers of Preschoolers), and other such programs are attempts to help meet the needs of today's parents. In many regards, this is a frightening day in which to rear children. A church needs to give serious consideration to ways in which it can strengthen the homes and families in its sphere of ministry.

Not to be neglected in this ministry are situations that deviate from the standard functional family. Children from single-parent homes, children of divorce, abused children, as well as "normal children," need the ministry of the church. Surely our Lord extended His invitation to come to all children.

Those who minister in Christ's stead in His church need to extend open arms to children and families. It could easily be argued that no investment a church makes has as great a dividend as that which is invested in the lives of young children and their parents. Let us heed the example of our Lord: "And he took the children in his arms, put his hands on them and blessed them" (Mark 10:16).

FOR FURTHER READING

Barbour, Mary A. *You Can Teach 2s and 3s*. Wheaton, Ill.: Victor, 1981.

Beechick, Ruth. *Teaching Kindergartners*. Denver: Accent, 1980.

———. *Teaching Preschoolers*. Denver: Accent, 1979.

Clark, Robert E.; Joanne Brubaker; and Roy B. Zuck, eds. *Childhood Education in the Church*, rev. ed. Chicago: Moody, 1986.

Elkind, David. *Miseducation: Preschoolers at Risk*. New York: Alfred A. Knopf, 1987.

Haystead, Wesley. *Everything You Want to Know About Teaching Young Children: Birth-6 Years*. Ventura, Calif.: Regal, 1989.

———. *Teaching Your Child About God*. Ventura, Calif.: Regal, 1983.

LeBar, Mary, and Betty Riley. *You Can Teach 4s and 5s*. Wheaton, Ill.: Victor, 1981.

Richards, Lawrence O. *Preschool: The Huggable Learners*. Elgin, Ill.: David C. Cook, 1988.

Waldrop, C. Sybil. *Understanding Today's Preschoolers*. Nashville: Convention, 1982.

16

Robert E. Clark

Elementary-age Children

HELPING ELEMENTARY SCHOOL-AGE CHILDREN LEARN
- **Describe what primaries and juniors are like**
- **Identify key needs in view of their total development**
- **Discover how we can meet their needs in practical ways at home and at church**
- **Apply principles in teaching effectively as we help them learn**
- **Meet their needs as persons when we teach them**

Here they come—those elementary-age children with adventurous spirits, abundant energy, expanding attention spans, and eagerness to learn. They are curious and creative, ask endless questions, and display obnoxious behavior periodically. Sometimes they do not listen carefully and have difficulty concentrating on the subject at hand. They want to be on the move and have their needs met momentarily! At times they are loud, boisterous, and unruly. But what a challenge to reach and teach them for Christ!

Children are not miniature adults, and we should not expect adult behavior from them. Childhood is a distinct period in life. In Western culture, childhood extends from birth through eleven years of age. Even before a child is born, researchers emphasize the importance of the prenatal period from conception until birth. Studies have shown that the unborn child is affected through his envi-

ROBERT E. CLARK, Ed.D., formerly professor of Christian education at Moody Bible Institute, Chicago, Illinois, is coeditor of *Christian Education: Foundations for the Future*, and currently engaged in Christian education ministry at the local church level.

ronment as he develops in his mother's womb. "Nutrition, drugs, radiation, illness and even the expectant mother's emotions may influence child development."[1]

Even though the Bible is central as our final authority and serves as our textbook in Christian teaching, the school-age child plays a prominent role in the teaching-learning process. The Bible is taught to lead the child to Christ as Savior and guide him in continued growth toward Christlikeness.

Learners are developing people. God has ordained that individuals grow through various stages in life. Each stage contributes to and lays a foundation for the stages that follow. As the individual develops, different kinds of needs are met. Each stage has its growth, characteristics, and developmental patterns that are generally typical of that stage. By better understanding the characteristics and needs of children at all levels, parents and teachers can be more effective through the developmental stages. Children come in all sizes, shapes, and behaviors!

One purpose for understanding the individual as a learner is to discover ways to meet his needs as a whole person. Many divergent activities and experiences will enable parents and teachers to meet a child's needs. Individuals grow at their own rate of development as needs are met and as new needs emerge. Evidence of growth in the lives of the students is one of the greatest rewards in teaching and learning.

This chapter is designed to help teachers and parents have a better understanding of their elementary-age children in grades one through six, and to provide practical suggestions for meeting the needs of children. During the foundational childhood years, the basic structure of personality, habits of life, and character are fairly well developed. The school-age years provide opportunity for the child to develop as a person, perfect skills, and adjust to a wider, broadening world. The patterns of life become increasingly complex and more difficult to change as a person enters adolescence and adulthood. The significance of the childhood years cannot be overemphasized in preparing children for their future.

CHARACTERISTICS AND NEEDS OF ELEMENTARY-AGE CHILDREN

Children during the school-age years have similar general characteristics. "Specific characteristics evident in this pattern of development make it possible to generally predict how a child will respond at a certain age . . . but never let these general growth and development patterns become a mold into which you expect every child to fit at a specific age."[2]

---

1. John Bergan and Ronald Henderson, *Child Development* (Columbus, Ohio: Merrill, 1979), p. 70.
2. Barbara Bolton, Charles Smith, and Wesley Haystead, *Everything You Want to Know About Teaching Children*, Grades 1-6 (Ventura, Calif.: Regal, 1987), p. 39.

PHYSICAL DEVELOPMENT

School-age children are extremely active and energetic. They are growing rapidly in every area of personality. They have periods of uneven growth and through the various stages reach plateaus in their physical development. We need to view a child's development as "a series of hills and valleys rather than a smooth, inclining plane."[3]

INTELLECTUAL DEVELOPMENT

Intellectually, school-age children are discovering the world about them, and their mental development expands tremendously from ages six to eleven. Though they are sharp intellectually, they have limitations. They are literal in their thinking and have difficulty understanding symbols, generalizations, and abstractions. They think specifically and do not readily relate ideas together.

Elementary-age children have accomplished two stages in intellectual development, according to Jean Piaget. They have already passed through the *sensorimotor* period from birth to two years of age. The infant begins to differentiate himself from objects, and relies heavily on sensory experiences as his chief source of learning.

The second stage is the *preoperational* thought, which includes the years from two through seven. In this stage a child can classify or categorize, but uses only one attribute at a time. He makes judgment on how things appear rather than on the basis of a mental operation.

Concrete operations range from about seven to ten or eleven years. The child is able to define, compare, and contrast in logical thought patterns. However, he is still concrete in his thinking.

Formal operations begins at eleven or twelve years of age. The individual can think and reason abstractly. Religious symbolism begins to have meaning.[4]

EMOTIONAL DEVELOPMENT

Emotionally, elementary children are learning self-control. Through their relationships with their families, the peer group, and other relationships, they are developing control. Usually by the time a child is eleven he has learned to control his emotions and may often repress them to conform to adult or peer pressure and behavior standards.

SOCIAL DEVELOPMENT

Socially, most school-age youngsters are friendly and have learned to relate to other people in the social context. As they start to school, they have new rules and

3. Ibid., p. 39.
4. Elsiebeth McDaniel and Lawrence O. Richards, *You and Children* (Chicago: Moody, 1973), pp. 19-21. See also Jack Smolensky, *A Guide to Child Growth and Development*, 2d ed. (Dubuque, Iowa: Kendall/Hunt, 1977), pp. 92-94.

regulations to follow. They come from diverse cultural backgrounds with varying parenting styles, rules, and regulations. When they enroll in school, they have a new set of rules imposed by administrators and teachers. Most children realize they can be happier and more secure by complying to such standards of behavior. As they learn to control themselves, they discover they can work in groups and enjoy interacting with others, particularly those in their own peer group.[5]

A primary child feels more secure when he pleases and is accepted by adults. By the time a child is a junior, he is more influenced by his peers and wants peer approval. Signs of seeking independence from parents and other adults are also more evident. Children today are likely to be more expressive and outgoing because of a permissive society, the desire to be involved actively and vocally, and the emphasis placed on personal development, self-discovery, and self-expression.

SPIRITUAL DEVELOPMENT

Spiritually, children can grasp biblical concepts and apply scriptural principles to their lives if the concepts are taught on their intellectual level and related to their everyday experiences. *How* children are taught those concepts is almost as important as *what* they are taught. Children are capable of learning new concepts, but they are often influenced more by attitudes and actions of others than by the concepts they learn. The foundation for spiritual development is laid early in life. Positive Christian examples of parents are likely to influence the child more than any other source.

The majority of children do not receive Christ as Savior until the primary or junior years. However, if children are reared in a Christian home, they may be ready for salvation much earlier. During the preschool years, basic concepts and attitudes are taught. Intellectual development provides opportunity for comprehension, spiritual readiness, and response. The plan of salvation must be presented simply and clearly so the child understands how he can trust Christ as his personal Savior.

THE PRIMARY CHILD (AGES SIX THROUGH EIGHT)

What is unique about the primary child? How is he different from younger or older children? Why is a primary child referred to as the "pleasing primary"? What is he like as a person?

PHYSICAL DEVELOPMENT

The primary child is growing rapidly and unevenly. His larger muscles have

---

5. Grace Craig, *Human Development*, 5th ed. (Englewood Cliffs, N.J.: Prentice-Hall, 1989), pp. 313-15.

developed, but he is uncoordinated in his finer muscles. Individual development is erratic, and children should not be compared solely on the basis of their sizes or skill in coordination. The child has much energy and wants to be actively involved doing things with his entire being. It is possible for him to overdo because of his excessive energy and uneven growth. As a result, he may even bring undue strain on his heart or cause damage to other parts of his body. He needs alternating periods of activity interspersed with times of quietness.

The primary does not like long, intricate projects because of a lack of finer muscles coordination. Many a good project has ended up in a wastebasket because the child lost interest in what he was doing. The project may have also been discarded because of inferior feelings or too great a stress on competition. Also, the child may have thought his project did not compare in quality with what another child produced. Comparisons between children should be minimized.

INTELLECTUAL DEVELOPMENT

The primary child is a careful observer. He likes to see how things work and shows greater interest in the process than the product. He enjoys tearing things apart but usually gives up trying to put them back together. He is beginning to reason more verbally and is developing skills in self-expression. His vocabulary is increasing rapidly with a vast difference evident between the first grader and the third grader.

He is beginning to learn the skills of reading, writing, and arithmetic. Usually the formal process of reading begins in first grade, although kindergarten lays the foundation for reading through visual symbols and perception in preparing for the more formal steps. By third grade the child has made great strides in reading and writing skills and in making the transition from manuscript to cursive writing.

The primary child is still literal and concrete in his thinking and does not make the transition from literal to symbolic, abstract meanings or generalizations. Parents and teachers need to communicate on his level without talking down to him as a little child. Primary children are developing a worldview and are beginning to relate to the past and future. However, most of their thinking and reasoning are related to the immediate present. Older primaries are beginning to think logically or chronologically, and are also beginning to contrast and compare, but need guidance and help from adults in making the transition.

Primaries like to please adults and work hard to meet adult expectations. Consequently, they may become frustrated if too much is required of them and may get discouraged if standards are set too high. The primary years are important in developing a positive self-image. Parents and teachers need to do all they can to encourage and build wholesome self-concepts.

EMOTIONAL DEVELOPMENT

The primary child is sympathetic to those his own age. He may be so moved by a story or illustration that he becomes tearful as he identifies with a child who has been injured, ill, or mistreated. He has a tender compassion and wants to express his love and concern in practical ways. What an ideal time to lay a foundation in missions and social or spiritual concern for others.

The primary is still unstable in his emotional control. He is gaining more self-control through adult or peer pressure, but reacts and expresses how he feels without thinking at times, especially when he is fatigued. Most of the time he is happy, noisy, and giggly, and may give the impression he does not have a care in the world. However, he may be troubled about something at home or school and have difficulty expressing his feelings. He needs to learn to express himself in acceptable ways so he does not become withdrawn, repressed, or vocally aggressive.

SOCIAL DEVELOPMENT

The primary child usually makes friends quickly, even with strangers. His friends tend to change often. Girls and boys have short-lived relationships. In the early primary years girls and boys play together frequently, but as they approach the third-grade level a gradual change takes place. Most boys and girls choose members of the same sex for their playmates. Different interests develop. Play activities become more selective by sex.

> Many of the differences in sex roles are due to cultural expectations of masculine and feminine behavior. Parents expect male children to be "real boys"—and females to be "real girls." Fathers particularly seem to teach specific gender roles by reinforcing femininity in daughters and masculinity in sons.
>
> The learning of sex roles begins in infancy. More rigid stereotypes develop by the time children are in the middle childhood years. Parents and others working with this age level need to be careful not to stereotype children or activities. Many activities can be used effectively with both sexes. It is more important to emphasize the development of individual personalities, interests, and skills in sex role behavior.[6]

Group work can be exciting for the primary child. He likes to join in group activities and has begun to learn how to relate and socialize with other members of the group. He can take simple leadership roles and participate actively. A cooperative rather than a competitive spirit, with an emphasis of teamwork, is possible with adult supervision and guidance. Primaries can be taught to respect authority, be aware of others and their needs, and build positive interpersonal relationships through group work.

SPIRITUAL DEVELOPMENT

The Lord Jesus Christ can be real to primary children. If the children have

---

6. Robert Barron, J. Omar Brubaker, and Robert E. Clark, *Understanding People*, 3d ed. (Wheaton, Ill.: Evangelical Training Assoc., 1989), p. 41. See also Craig, pp. 77-79.

been taught well about Him, He is their very best and wonderful Friend who can do anything. The primary child can understand literal biblical concepts that are taught on his intellectual and spiritual level. Parents and teachers can be models through their life examples in such matters as consistent attendance, participation in church activities, and in living for Christ in their daily lives.

A primary knows right from wrong and can tell the difference between fact and fantasy. Scripture needs to be applied to familiar, everyday experiences. The plan of salvation can be understood. The child may be ready to receive Christ as Savior. Home backgrounds will make a difference in ability to comprehend the plan of salvation. The analogy of the human family and God's family may be one of the most effective ways to present the gospel. In the contemporary setting with broken families, single-parent households, and fatherless children, we need to be careful how we teach about a loving heavenly Father when a child may know nothing about a loving, caring earthly father. Some children may have difficulty relating to this concept unless they grow up in a two-parent, stable Christian family with a father who models the role of a loving and caring heavenly Father.

Terminology used in teaching spiritual truth needs to be defined simply and clearly with literal and concrete explanations. The primary child may need assurance of salvation and to know what to do if he sins after becoming a child of God (1 John 1:9). With adult guidance and careful teaching, primary children can grow in Christ and witness for the Lord as they live for Him day by day.

> How should one teach primaries? In the ways they learn best—stories, questions, projects, role playing, reading, singing, and drawing. Some learning activities demand seeing and hearing; other activities demand bodily movement, creative thinking, and small muscle control. Spending an hour in one activity is never justifiable. Be ready to change activities to meet the childrens' needs and to accomplish your teaching goals.[7]

THE JUNIOR CHILD (AGES NINE THROUGH ELEVEN)

What makes juniors different from other people? Why are they sometimes called "jumping juniors"? What are they like as total personalities? Juniors are usually in grades four through six in school and are in the prime of life in many ways. The word *doer* can describe their entire personalities because they are doers in every way.

PHYSICAL DEVELOPMENT

Juniors abound with energy. Most juniors are extremely active and never seem to tire. They have excellent health and love the out-of-doors. Their lives are filled with adventurous activities. They have slower, more steady growth, and are well coordinated in larger and finer muscles. Sometimes they are untidy in their

---

7. Elsiebeth McDaniel, *You Can Teach Primaries* (Wheaton, Ill.: Victor, 1981), p. 15.

appearance and their care for personal property because they are too busy to be bothered. Toward the end of the junior years, girls' personalities tend to develop more rapidly than boys'.

INTELLECTUAL DEVELOPMENT

Juniors are exciting people to teach. They are alert, keen, and critical. The questions they ask are thought-provoking and demonstrate they can think and reason logically. They may even question authority. Their concepts of time, space, and number have increased greatly. They now have a worldview and can study maps, geography, and history. As indicated earlier in the chapter, juniors are in the period of concrete operations. Even though they can understand symbolism and abstractions more readily than primaries, do not assume they understand without careful explanations. They are capable of comparing, contrasting, organizing, classifying, and sequencing items concretely. Because they are developing intellectually, they still have some limitations in their thinking processes and are still mainly literal thinkers.[8]

Juniors are in the "golden age" of memory. Most of them can memorize quickly and easily if challenged. However, if children are slower in their ability to memorize, they may become discouraged and give up trying. Negative attitudes toward learning are developed if too much is expected of juniors, or if they feel they cannot handle the demands placed on them

> Those working with this age level, however, must be careful that these children do not compete just for the sake of competing or winning an extrinsic reward. Some children may feel left out because they do not have the intellectual abilities or skills to compete. The results can be damaging to self-esteem and do great harm to children in their total development. The best kind of motivation is that which brings personal satisfaction, progress, and achievement to the individual.[9]

EMOTIONAL DEVELOPMENT

The nine through eleven year olds have fewer fears than younger children. They like to impress people with their bravery and dislike being called "cowards" or "sissies." Sometimes they cover up their feelings because of peer pressure. Juniors enjoy telling jokes and have a strong sense of humor. Many times they are quick-tempered and react hastily in situations where they are put on the spot. Juniors can be loud, boisterous, and obnoxious, but they can control their emotions if they are taught properly. They need teachers who are stable emotionally and are not sentimental or upset easily.

SOCIAL DEVELOPMENT

Juniors are more aware of their peers, are eager to be with them, and are

8. Craig, pp. 307-9.
9. Barron, Brubaker, and Clark, p. 51.

beginning to be influenced more significantly by them. They are entering the "gang stage" with peers of the same sex. Their desire for more independence from adults is obvious. They thrive on competition because they are better coordinated, have slower and steadier growth, and are capable of practicing and strengthening their skills. In their daily living they need to assume greater responsibility for their actions and behavior.

SPIRITUAL DEVELOPMENT

What age group is more ready for salvation? Juniors are responsive to salvation and Christian growth if careful foundations have been laid earlier. They are capable investigators and can, with proper guidance, do simple inductive study to discover biblical truth for themselves. They can distinguish between right and wrong, and they have a tender conscience toward God. They may try to cover up their spiritual needs by showing off or saying they really do not care. Hero worship is typical of juniors, and they are ready to be led to Jesus Christ as the perfect example whom they should follow. Those who have accepted Christ as Savior are able to have personal devotions and dedicate themselves for service to the Lord. Many juniors have made decisions to live for and serve Christ because of their willingness and eagerness to be useful.

> Building clubhouses, playing football, experimenting with chemistry sets, wrestling with their friends—juniors enjoy them all. Juniors are active and noisy and full of life. And they do not leave their interests and liveliness at home when they come to the church for Sunday school, worship, or club meetings. Juniors bring all of themselves along, sometimes to the dismay of the adult leaders. But to know junior-age children is to love them. They have a keen sense of loyalty, and if they know adults who appreciate them, they identify with those adults, are loyal to them, and learn much from them.[10]

Juniors are great people and have much in-depth potential as they are challenged. What a privilege and opportunity it is to lead them to Christ and guide them toward Christian maturity!

How to Discover Needs of Learners

Learners have many different kinds of needs. Some needs are basic to all, such as affection, security, belonging, and success.Other needs are unique to the age group. Primaries need to develop their skills in reading, writing, and basic math concepts. Juniors need to relate to their peers but not let them dictate how they should live. Some needs are individualized. Bill needs to know Christ as his personal Savior. Maria has a need to learn patience with her younger brothers and sis-

10. Marjorie E. Soderholm, "Understanding Fifth and Sixth Graders (Juniors)," in *Childhood Education in the Church,* ed. Robert E. Clark et al. (Chicago: Moody, 1986), p. 149.

ters. Jim is struggling to choose the right kinds of friends. How can we discover these needs?

CASUAL OBSERVATION

Be alert as you observe both the group and the individual. Comments, facial expressions, gestures, or questions asked may reveal a need. Seek to observe the individual in different kinds of situations such as the home, play activities, and school setting to discover more about him as a person.

INFORMAL CONVERSATIONS

The alert parent or teacher can identify individual needs and desires as they listen to students. Teachers who arrive early for scheduled activities, such as Sunday school, can spend time with students informally and find out what has taken place in their lives during the week.

INDIVIDUAL AND SMALL GROUP COUNSELING

Individuals may express themselves in small group sharing or in a one-to-one setting. The teacher can arrange to get together informally with an individual or plan a formal counseling session.

DISCOVERING CHARACTERISTICS AND NEEDS OF AGE GROUPS

What is usually expected of primaries? What are their needs as related to those expectations? How are juniors different from primaries? Even though we may describe children generally by age group, we must never forget unique individual differences.

SOCIAL ACTIVITIES

When social activities of various types are held, they are helpful in determining needs as children display the other side of themselves, which may not be as evident in a classroom setting.

HUMAN NEED REVEALED THROUGH THE BIBLE

The Bible is one of the best sources for identifying human need. As we read and study the written Word, we discover the plan of God for man, the sinfulness of mankind, and God's remedy for sin. As human beings our juniors are described well in the Word of God, and they can relate to many of the stories, illustrations, examples, and life situations.

PRINCIPLES TO APPLY IN HELPING ELEMENTARY-AGE CHILDREN LEARN

UNDERSTAND PERSONALITY DEVELOPMENT

Personality development is significant through the school-age years. Personality is defined as "the sum and substance of what a person is." A Christian personality is "a person who knows Christ as Savior and desires to make Christ the center of his life."[11] Elementary-age children are total personalities, and we must treat them as whole persons. If a child is not feeling well physically, his mental capacities will be affected; he may be antisocial and display unacceptable behavior. He may not respond spiritually. Because he functions as a total person, we must acknowledge his need for well-being in every area of personality. Sometimes a child does not know how to respond because he does not understand himself and why he feels the way he does. As we teach children we recognize the complexity of personality development and that many factors interact to make the child what he is totally.

TREAT AS INDIVIDUALS

Even though a child may be similar in many ways to others his own age, he is a unique person, and we as teachers must respect and develop that uniqueness. A child may develop a low self-esteem if he is not accepted or treated with respect as a human being during early childhood. Parents may tend to compare the child with older or younger brothers and sisters and make negative comments or belittle the child. Many children will develop more rapidly, whereas others will develop more slowly. Some will naturally be more attractive physically and outgoing socially. Many will express immature emotional reactions and behaviors. Even with all the differences in maturation, we must treat each child as a special creation of God and work with the Lord in bringing out the best. The challenge is great, but the rewards may even be greater as the child develops uniquely as an individual.

BUILD ON FOUNDATIONS LAID EARLIER IN LIFE

Dr. Clarence Benson, a noted Christian educator, had as one of his mottoes "Begin earlier!" We cannot begin too soon to mold and guide children. Childhood specialists emphasize the importance of the prenatal period, infancy, and the preschool years. If parents have provided spiritual nourishment for their children during these crucial years, elementary teachers can build on those foundations.

Many times school-age children come to us with the same or only slightly more Bible background than that of an infant or young child. We must begin from square one with the basics. However, because of their intellectual abilities, primaries and juniors can "catch up" much more quickly. We want to give them the best learning environments possible as we build on the years of early childhood or provide the basics in spiritual nurture. We need to do all we can to prepare them for the adolescent years by laying solid biblical foundations.

KNOW INTELLECTUAL AND SPIRITUAL BACKGROUNDS

Primary and junior teachers often think little about what a child has already

11. Barron, Brubaker, and Clark, p. 9.

learned intellectually and spiritually before he comes to us. Consequently, we may begin with the basics the child already has. We need to ask ourselves some questions. From what kind of home does the child come? Has he been taught many of the basic truths, or is his knowledge very limited? How much of what has been taught has become part of life? Does the boy or girl know Jesus as Savior? Are they growing in their spiritual life?

Churches need to determine the needs of and develop objectives for their school-age children in total personality development. They also need to decide what biblical content and concepts should be taught at each level during the school-age years. A long-range plan for accomplishing the objectives should be developed so those who work with children at any level know where they are going and what they want to accomplish. We need to prepare our children for living today and also for the future.

Ruth Beechick suggests the following spiritual developmental tasks of the elementary school years:[12]

1. Receiving and acknowledging Jesus Christ as Savior and Lord.
2. Growing awareness of Christian love and responsibility in relationships with others.
3. Continuing to build concepts of basic Christian realities.
4. Learning basic Bible teaching adequate for personal faith and everyday Christian living, including teachings in these areas:
   a. prayer in daily life.
   b. the Bible in daily life.
   c. Christian friendships.
   d. group worship.
   e. responsibility for serving God.
   f. basic knowledge of God, Jesus, Holy Spirit, creation, angelic beings, heaven, hell, sin, salvation, Bible history and literature.

Gil Beers also identifies basic concepts that need to be taught to school-age children in his chapter on "Teaching Theological Concepts to Children."[13] He lists in chart format theological truths about God, Jesus, the Bible, home and parents, church and Sunday school, relationships with others, angels, and last times. His information is helpful when planning what content and concepts need to be taught at the primary and junior levels.

BE AWARE OF HOW CHILDREN THINK AND LEARN

We must be aware of how elementary-age children think and learn. In his research Piaget discovered that children are not able to think abstractly until they reach the age of eleven or perhaps not until age fourteen. They think in lit-

12. Ruth Beechick, *Teaching Juniors* (Denver: Accent, 1981), p. 24.
13. Clark, Brubaker, and Zuck, pp. 369-74.

eral, concrete, and specific terms but are beginning to relate to symbols, generalizations, and abstractions.

Many teachers and parents approach children on the adult level and teach them as though they were adults intellectually and spiritually. In the process, children learn to "parrot" and give answers they think adults want to hear. Naturally children want to please; they seek to gain recognition and acceptance by responding whether or not their answers make sense. Sometimes adults thwart children's learning opportunities because they tell them everything rather than encourage them to participate and engage in self-discovery activities.

School-age youngsters need biblical content taught with literal, concrete, and well-selected vocabulary, sensory experiences, and familiar, everyday, life-related examples with which they can identify. They need to be guided in self-discovery learning activities through which they can question, analyze, and respond. The learning environments elementary children come from, their own intellectual capacities, the age levels represented, the vocabulary they use and understand, and the abilities they have in expressing themselves are all parts of their intellectual development. Children are curious creatures, eager learners, and want to discover things for themselves.

Why is it that many children lose the desire to learn or have their curiosity dulled by the time they are nearing the completion of the elementary-school years? Have teachers and parents capitalized on children's eagerness to learn, to discover, and to be creative? If we are going to teach children effectively, we must know them as individuals, be aware of their intellectual capacities, recognize their strengths and limitations, and be alert to special areas of need.

PROVIDE A MODEL-EXAMPLE

Parents and teachers need to provide a model for school-age children to follow. There is probably nothing we can do that will have any greater effect on children than the example we live before them. What we *are* is far more significant that what we *say* or *do*. In Deuteronomy 6 we are reminded of the importance of parent-modeling in everyday life. Children are careful observers and see far more than we think they do. They sense the inconsistencies in adult lifestyles, even though they may have difficulty in "seeing the big picture." If we really love God, then we must show that love in reality with our actions as well as our words. If we say it is important to study God's Word and pray, we must be consistent in doing these things ourselves. If we say we ought to be loving, kind, and forgiving, then we must exemplify those qualities in our own lives. For children, the spiritual dimension is often caught more than taught. As adults, we have a tremendous responsibility to shape pliable and easily molded children to live now and in eternity.

TEACH WITH VARIETY IN PROCEDURE AND METHODOLOGY

Because of their shorter attention spans, stored-up energy, and need for activity, elementary children must have variety in learning experiences. Adults can sit for longer periods of time, but children need to get up and move about physically to release energy stored in growing muscles. In fact, the younger the children, the more movement and space they need. If parents and teachers do not consider the need for variety and change, they automatically encourage behavior problems. Teachers need to develop sensitivity to the need for change of activity; when children become restless and begin to squirm, they may be signaling for a change of pace.

Variety in methodology is essential as we work with children. The methods used should include physical as well as intellectual change. Primaries usually need three to four changes of physical activity per hour, while juniors may require two or three changes. They can sit for longer periods of time if the activities are intellectually stimulating and provide changes in mental activity. Preschoolers enjoy repetition of the same activities used in the same way. Primaries and juniors need repetition in a variety of ways to decrease boredom and stimulate their intellectual and spiritual curiosity.

With a wide variety of modern technological equipment and current methodology, teachers need to broaden their use of creative methods to meet the needs of elementary children. Children also need methods that encourage participation, interaction, and self-expression. Of course methods and resources should be chosen in view of the objective for the session, but the wise teacher will provide variety and involvement to build interest and enthusiasm for learning.

MAKE TEACHING MORE LEARNER-CENTERED

The teacher has traditionally been central in the teaching-learning process. She plans the sessions, presents the content, and may do most of the talking. If we are concerned about meeting the needs of the student, we must shift the learning activities from the teacher to the learner.

The role of the teacher changes from one who presents material to a guide or resource person. John Dewey said that the teacher is an advanced learner in the group. She certainly should know more than the students, but she serves as a guide and facilitator in the learning process. The child's interests and needs are paramount. The student is involved personally in the process. The session is planned to meet the child's needs and help him develop as a person.

The teacher begins the process at the child's intellectual and spiritual level, giving the child the opportunity to discover what God's Word says and helping him apply the content to his life. In the process, the teacher will begin to be more aware of individual needs and how she can meet those needs, stimulate individual students to learn and grow, and observe significant changes in attitudes and behavior.

Learning styles also need to be considered in the teaching-learning process. Marlene LeFever defines a learning style as "an individualized thinking process—

a special way in which we see or perceive things . . . and way in which we process or use what we have seen."[14] She identifies four learning styles: innovative learners, analytic learners, common sense learners, and dynamic learners (see chap. 23).

DEVELOP CREATIVITY THROUGH TEACHING

Children have great creative potential, but that potential must be developed. One reason children may not develop creativity is they are stifled by adults who have lost their own creative spirits. A parent or teacher may say, "Oh, you can't do that," or, "That is much too hard for you. You'll have to wait until you are more grown up to do that."

In his psycho-social stages of life, Erik Erikson indicates that a school-age chid is confronted with the task of *industry versus inferiority*.[15] The word *industry* is derived from a Latin term that means "to build." The emphasis is on building competencies in physical, cognitive, and social skills. During the elementary years a child can develop a spirit of industry, or competency. He learns how to do things well physically. He begins to learn how to think and develops skills in relating to his peer group. The child can also feel inadequate and inferior if he is not encouraged and recognized for his efforts. Many children at this stage start out being industrious but lose their zeal and desire to learn because they are made to feel inferior and develop low self-esteem as a result of what adults and other children say or do.

Of course, a basic step in developing creativity is for parents or teachers to set a good example of being creative themselves. Rather than limit or discourage the child, they can build positive attitudes toward being creative. They can encourage the child to try. An inquisitive spirit, a different way of doing something, or an eagerness to learn a new task may develop the creative potential waiting for release.

Opportunities for creative thinking and doing must be integrated into teaching-learning situations. Children need to venture out to make choices based on their needs, interests, and curiosity, and try new ways of doing to develop their creative skills.

The Relationship Between the Person, His Needs, and Teaching

In Christian teaching-learning we desire to bring about changes in the lives of students. We teach people, not merely content or lessons from a manual or book. Each person must be taught as a complete individual. Therefore we must have a good understanding of the individual—his characteristics, patterns of growth and development, and needs.

When we teach people we teach to meet their needs. In Christian teaching

14. Marlene LeFever, *Learning Styles: Not All Kids Learn the Same Way* (Elgin, Ill.: David C. Cook, n.d.), p. 1.
15. Craig, p. 301.

the most important needs are spiritual. In order to meet spiritual needs, however, we must consider other areas as well. For example, a person must be comfortable physically if we hope to meet his intellectual and spiritual needs.

Needs in a teaching-learning situation may be as different as the number of individuals present. Some may lack in basic pyschological areas such as love, acceptance, or recognition. Other learners may have problems with self-esteem or needs relating to their relationships with other people. Some children need Christ as Savior, whereas others are in the process of growing in Christ and need help in specific areas of Christian growth. The teacher is confronted with the task of meeting various kinds of individual and group needs. In her preparation time, the teacher may find it helpful to list key student needs that she can consciously plan to meet through the content she is teaching. Whatever the approach, the teacher must be cognizant of needs and seek to meet those needs as she teaches. One of the great satisfactions in teaching-learning is when needs are being met and individuals are growing as persons and becoming more like Jesus Christ in their total behaviors.

FOR FURTHER READING

Beechick, Ruth. *Teaching Juniors*. Denver: Accent, 1981.

———. *Teaching Primaries*. Denver: Accent, 1980.

Berk, Laura E. *Child Development*, 2d ed. Needham Heights, Mass.: Allyn & Bacon, 1990.

Bolton, Barbara J.; Charles T. Smith; and Wesley Haystead. *Everything You Want to Know About Teaching Children: Grades 1-6*. Ventura, Calif.: Regal, 1987.

Clark, Robert E.; Joanne Brubaker; and Roy B. Zuck, eds. *Childhood Education in the Church*, rev. ed. Chicago: Moody, 1986.

Elkind, David. *The Hurried Child*. Reading, Mass.: Addison-Wesley, 1981.

Gibson, Joyce, and Eleanor Hance. *You Can Teach Juniors & Middlers*. Wheaton, Ill.: Victor, 1981.

McDaniel, Elsiebeth. *You Can Teach Primaries*. Wheaton, Ill.: Victor, 1981.

Price, B. Max. *Understanding Today's Children*. Nashville: Convention, 1982.

Richards, Lawrence O. *Children: The Lively Learners*. Elgin, Ill.: David C. Cook, 1988.

17

Pamela T. and Stanton D. Campbell

Junior and Senior Highers

Ministering to Junior and Senior Highers
- **Understand teenagers' characteristics, needs, and life transitions**
- **Keep our teaching fresh and contemporary**
- **Familiarize ourselves with the world in which teenagers live**
- **Offer a personal relationship of acceptance, forgiveness, and unconditional love**
- **Develop a comfortable style of leadership and teaching that is enthusiastically accepted by your particular students**
- **Learn to teach at two levels for both churched and unchurched students**
- **Set measurable goals**
- **Be thankful for small victories**

Understanding Youth and Their World

A missionary steps out of the hand-carved canoe onto the shore of a remote tropical island. In the background she can hear strange music and rhythms. She approaches the natives cautiously. They look rather strange in their unusual

Pamela T. Campbell, M.A., is adult education editor, Victor Books, Wheaton, Illinois, and youth director, Lisle Bible Church, Lisle, Illinois.

Stanton D. Campbell, M.A., is senior editor, Life Journey Books, David C. Cook, Elgin, Illinois, and youth director, Lisle Bible Church, Lisle, Illinois.

dress (scant, at that) of leather, feathers, and other odd-looking features—make-up, hairstyles, and so forth. Yet the missionary's heart is filled with joy and wonder at this God-given opportunity to bring the gospel to these people. She is likely to be the only person who will ever talk to them about the glory of the living God and the love and forgiveness of Jesus Christ.

———

The junior high Sunday school teacher steps out of his second-hand station wagon onto the sidewalk of First Suburban Church. As he nears his classroom, he can hear that awful rock music blaring from one of the kid's portable stereos. He enters the room cautiously and is surrounded by young people with leather jackets, feather earrings, too-short skirts, outlandish hairstyles, and clothes combinations that make him wonder what is wrong with parents today. The teacher's heart is filled with dread. He did not want this assignment, but the superintendent had used the old "suffer for the Lord" tactic. OK, so the teacher is willing to spend the next hour going through the curriculum lesson he was supplied, but he knows these kids are not at all anxious to hear what he has to say. Everyone knows junior highers aren't interested in spiritual growth—only in having fun. Why should the teacher be the only person who dares to intrude on these students' otherwise purely secular lifestyles?

———

The missionary eagerly anticipates her work with the natives. She begins to learn the language and practices until she can understand it and communicate fluently. She searches for meaning behind the islanders' customs and worship habits. She talks to them about their values and priorities, and she soaks in everything she hears. Later, when the time is right, she can use some of those things as bridges to the gospel. She tries to act as a servant to her native hosts, attempting to model Christlikeness to them. She knows that her ability to communicate will be a key to the success of her ministry.

———

The Sunday school teacher eagerly awaits the end of the quarter when he can dump his job on someone else. He is befuddled by his students—their strange sayings, song lyrics, and the buttons they wear. He thinks those kids must go home and practice being weird. He is sure the kids think he is the out-of-touch one, the way they act every time he tries to teach them eternal truths like grace, forgiveness, and sanctification. He cannot help but wonder when they're going to grow up and start acting like mature Christians.

———

The youth at your church may not seem *too* savage. Kids may come to church clean and scrubbed, wearing skirts or coats and ties. Or perhaps they appear in miniskirts, jeans, or T-shirts that endorse heavy metal groups. Either way, don't we owe them the same basic courtesies we would give total strangers? Like it or not, today's youth culture is quite different from what we remember from our own youth—and it seems to be in a constant state of flux.

A missionary to a foreign culture cannot count on using traditional evangelical teaching methods. For example, if a tribe has no form of bread, how can Jesus be perceived as the Bread of Life? The missionary must use another, more relevant, analogy to get the point of Scripture across to the natives. Similarly, our youth groups may include a number of students from divorced or broken homes, so we cannot assume a traditional lesson, teaching that God is a loving Father, will sufficiently communicate His degree of love toward every student. We must come up with more applicable comparisons.

As teachers of junior and senior highers, we must learn to be sensitive to this "foreign" culture. If we are not familiar with their world, how can we make the gospel relevant to them? Just as a missionary spends time studying the language, customs, and habits of the natives on her missionary field, it is our responsibility to discover the most effective ways to reach young people. This chapter is designed to help us begin to understand better our youth and the world in which they live. Some of these characteristics and principles may not seem applicable to every group. That is why it is crucial that we build intimate relationships with the kids in our youth groups and try to value each person as an individual with specific needs. Only when we know and understand our teenagers will we be effective in ministry to them.

TAKING THE CHALLENGE

The simple question, "Would you consider teaching the junior high class for a while?" is enough to drive some people directly to the book of James for a scriptural reply: "Not many of [us] should presume to be teachers" (3:1). It is usually easier to find five volunteers for mission work in Tierra del Fuego than one person to work with junior or senior highers.

Primary? "Of course, they're such darlings!"

Junior? "Sure, why not?"

Adult? "Now you're talking!"

Junior/senior high? "No way!"

So why are people so hesitant to work with teenagers? They can usually come up with some good excuses, most of which hide the fact that they are scared silly. Granted, there are some valid reasons to approach this task with fear and trembling, but most such reasons also reveal the tremendous needs of young people. Here are a few things that make working with young people such a unique (and potentially frustrating) job.

1. *Teenagers begin to experience spiritual metamorphosis as they realize that Mom and Dad's faith must become their personal faith.*[1] Primary students

do not question why the family goes to Sunday school and church. Juniors may grumble because they must miss some TV cartoons, but they usually go without too many protests. Adults attend out of discipline, if not enthusiasm. But for the first time, junior high and senior high students want to know, "Why do I have to go to church?" If they are not receiving some personal benefits, the question is a hard one to answer. So the poor leader continually has to come up with new ways to motivate students to come to Sunday school, Bible study, and so on. Bible stories and memory verses accumulated over the years must be converted into living, breathing, personal Christianity.

2. Teenagers are more vocal and bluntly honest than ever before in their lives. If pressed a little, they will blurt out what they think about most any topic (whether or not they have given it any previous thought). Of course, they also blurt out what they think about each other, about the leader, about the boring lessons, and anything else. This trait is not all bad, but it is up to us to learn to channel all that honesty into productive discussions rather than detrimental chit-chat.

3. Junior and senior highers are seeking identity and healthy self-images.[2] This is partially why they are so brutally vocal. Inner tension rises as they begin to realize that it is not as cool to be seen going to church as to all the right parties and social occasions. Yet during this phase of life they are drawn to the people and places from which they receive affirmation. As long as church is a place where students feel accepted, it will draw them like a magnet. They may stray away for periods of time, but most are likely to return in times of need.

4. "Tried and true" teaching methods eventually begin to wear thin for teenagers. By the time a student has gone through several years of church programs, he has experienced almost every teaching style, every brand of curriculum lessons, and every "fresh" idea ever put in print. Now, they sit there with an I-dare-you-to-show-me-something-I-haven't-seen-before look on their faces. It is enough to terrify most any potential teacher.

5. Church activities face competition from teenagers' jobs, schools, and other activities. As soon as teenagers discover the potential to make money (even if it is minimum wage), they begin to think in terms of profit.[3] In other words, two hours at a youth group meeting could be converted into about $10 mowing yards or baby-sitting. Add the additional attractions of sports and other extra-curricular activities, and church functions can face some stiff competition. Again, the leader can do a lot to determine whether the students come to church activities or go elsewhere.

6. The allure of independence brings new problems and opportunities for teenagers. Junior highers and senior highers are in various stages of becoming

1. For more information on the spiritual and intellectual development of junior and senior highers, see *Called to Care,* by Doug Stevens (Grand Rapids: Zondervan, 1985), pp. 54-60, and *Junior High Ministry,* by Wayne Rice (Grand Rapids: Zondervan, 1978), pp. 107-9.
2. Merton P. Strommen and A. Irene Strommen, *Five Cries of Parents* (San Francisco: Harper & Row, 1985), p. 46.
3. Ibid., p. 53.

more and more independent from Mom and Dad. This process is difficult for even those students who have the best of relationships with their parents. And even though the transition is inevitable, it is likely to manifest itself in various problems expressed by both parent and child. "She used to be so loving. I just don't understand what has gotten into her." "My parents just don't understand me." "My son never talks to me anymore. When he's home, he just closes himself up in his room."

Many of these problems result because both parent and child realize that growth is taking place and the relationship will never be—can never be—as simple as it once was. And whether students rebel, withdraw, or take some other course of action, their dependence on parents is likely to decrease. Consequently, they may tend to become dependent on others. This is an opportunity the church cannot afford to miss. It is far better for such students to lean on the youth group and the church. Otherwise, they will find other options that are far less beneficial.

PUTTING ON THE PITH HELMET

So suppose you have accepted the responsibility of teaching a crew of unique young people. You have either been talked into the job or you love to take on impossible challenges. Where do you go after you have said yes?

It is hard enough for the kids to keep up with the latest trends, much less parents and teachers. But if you want your ministry to be effective, you must be aware of the influences your young people encounter on a daily basis.[4] Even if you don't know a thing about today's youth culture, it is not really all that hard to catch up with what is going on. The hard part is absorbing the information without being judgmental. There are two outstanding ways to find out the things you want to know: (1) play the role of a cultural anthropologist, and (2) ask your kids. They will tell you.

Put on your anthropologist's pith helmet and strike out for brave new territory. Investigate the reading, listening, and viewing habits of your teenagers. You can start by looking through a few secular magazines that are popular with young people (*Seventeen, Rolling Stone, Muscle and Fitness, Elle*, comic books, etc.). Remember, you are looking for clues that will help you understand young people. Do not be too shocked when you see the cologne ads where a group of seemingly naked men appear to be frolicking. Hurry past the crude language, but file in your mind, *So this is where some of them are hearing this kind of talk.* Pay careful attention to advice columns in regard to handling dating, sexual activity, peer pressure, self-image, friendships, commitment, and other perpetually popular teenage topics. It does not matter whether your students actually read these magazines or not. If they do not get their information from the magazines, they will hear the same advice from friends who do read them (and absorb it all as truth).

4. Stevens, p. 65.

Tune in to a top 40 radio station.[5] Listen to lyrics, then watch MTV (the cable TV channel that specializes in rock videos and youth-oriented music) and see how those songs are visually interpreted. Note the attitudes and philosophies of the musicians and disc jockeys. If you are shocked at what you hear, you should not give up in disgust. Remember that most young people—both churched and unchurched—listen regularly to rock music. Many spend significantly more hours exposed to secular music than to all sources of Christian teaching combined.

You are not likely to agree with much of what you read, hear, and see. But you will notice one consistent fact: the information young people receive through the secular media comes in an attractive package. The magazines are slick, polished, and professional. The music is vibrant and full of life. Films and music videos make sinful behavior seem appealing (and even rewarding). Keep some of those images in mind as you set to the task of teaching spiritual truth to these people. You have a lot of powerful competition. So what can we do to offset the secular influences, backed by millions of dollars, that are affecting our young people?

First of all, recognize that you are one of only a handful of people who care about the spiritual lives of your students. Some educators have the individual well-being of students as a goal, though usually in terms of academic/physical achievement. Parents care, of course, but parents are often more out of touch with their children than they realize. Junior highers and high schoolers become adept at shielding true feelings and giving answers that parents want to hear.

So call it what you like—burden, responsibility, or opportunity—but as a leader of junior highers and/or high schoolers, you have an important job. Your job is to communicate a body of truth to these people for their own good. But they are being inundated by other sources, both positive and negative. With limited time, their first instinct will be to let "church stuff" take a lower priority—unless, of course, you can think of some way to keep them interested. That is why it is important for you to keep on your cultural anthropologist's hat. You need to know their culture inside and out so you can gain their respect and initiate communication and trust.

Second, once you have a taste of what today's youth culture is like outside the church, talk to all the young people you know—both Christian and non-Christian. Ask them about favorite music groups, sports heroes, school accomplishments, hopes and dreams, and spiritual values. Again, be careful not to appear judgmental. Suppose they tell you they enjoy that great new group The Vomit Eaters. If they see you make the same face their parents make, then they are not likely to be as open with you in the future. But you will gain their eternal respect if you respond, "Oh? I just saw them on MTV. I don't care for them myself. But I have to admit that their song 'Love Is Like a Hernia' is not nearly as disgusting as 'Let's Go Kill the Teacher.' What do you think?" After you gain a

---

5. Ibid., pp. 84-87, for more information on rock music and video media.

teenager's respect, he will be much more likely to sit through some of the songs you enjoy.

This sounds somewhat facetious, but do not miss the point. As you begin to respect a young person's opinion, even if it is immature, improper, and unbelievable, the young person becomes more open to hearing what you have to say.

Finally, remember that you can offer each student something he is unable to get from MTV, from athletic heroes, from TV/movie stars, or from rock idols. You can offer a personal relationship with the young person—a relationship that entails acceptance, forgiveness, and unconditional love. Do whatever it takes to show each person that you care for him as a special individual—not just a unit in the group. Then start to build some group unity.

DEVELOPING YOUR OWN STYLE

Once you have familiarized yourself with your young people and the world in which they live, develop a style of teaching and leading that best suits you and your group. Here are a few suggestions for getting started.

1. Consider yourself the expert when it comes to your youth group. A lot of people will have a lot to say about how to run a youth program. Read all you can find. Get lots of opinions. But remember that none of those authors/speakers knows the individuals in your group. Filter what they say. For example, you might read that a good youth group leader would allow students to fail from time to time. But maybe your group has the lowest self-image that you've ever seen. Use your knowledge and control the situation. Provide the opportunity for failure, but control the extent of potential failure so that if worse comes to worst, your students can experience failure without feeling completely devastated. Your students will frequently surprise you with their ability to do things you had no idea they could do, but you know them better than anyone. Be careful not to push them too hard or too quickly.

2. Do not be afraid to try something new. When first given teaching responsibilities, the tendency is to remember all our own good experiences and try to pass along the same truths that were important to us using the same teaching methods. But as you have realized, youth culture today is quite different from years past. So look for creative new ways to communicate truth: perhaps through games, newspaper articles, music, special speakers, projects, or mission trips. Be aware of popular social trends and find ways to use them to your advantage. (If a TV quiz program such as "Wheel of Fortune" is all the rage, design a version for your Sunday school class that the students will enjoy. But more than that, you will be able to identify the names and stories with which they are not quite so familiar. Then you can plan future sessions around those topics).

If one of your ideas does not work, do not worry about it. It is likely that the young people will have forgotten about it by next week, so there is no use in your dwelling on it. But the idea might be a good one worth trying again at a later date. Every meeting you have will be a different mix of personalities, emotions, needs, energy levels, and so forth. Maybe any idea will bomb during finals week, but one week later (during the students' newfound freedom), the same concept might be a huge success.

3. Do not be afraid to try something old. Sure, youth culture changes. But teenagers today are looking for the same things teenagers throughout history have sought—a sense of purpose, assurance of salvation, a listening ear, and answers to basic questions concerning life, death, the nature of God, and other simple everyday issues. Do not lose track of the needs of young people just because they look and act as if they do not have a care in the world. They do. They just disguise those cares. It is your job to lovingly penetrate the facade and relate to them with the gospel.

4. Allow young people to fail. It is one thing to experience small failures as described previously. But other kinds of failure keep youth leaders awake at night. When the leader of the group suddenly turns his back on all things spiritual and joins the school drinking-and-drugs crowd, when jobs and extracurricular activities become more important than church activities and you cannot seem to get more than three kids together at any given time, when the quiet, timid girl secretly announces that she is pregnant, what is the youth leader to do?

During those crisis times, students need unconditional love and acceptance more than ever—whether or not they elect to receive your care. The time will come for most leaders of young people to stand in the shoes of the father of the prodigal son. In spite of all you have done, a much-loved young person will turn his back on the church to explore the allure of the sinful world. His departure is heart-wrenching. In most cases, the student will quickly learn some hard lessons and desire to return to church friends. The return to fellowship will be difficult, and any hint of "I told you so" from the leader can be devastating. Teach by example. Open your arms and your heart, and show everyone that failure, no matter how severe, can be a step toward spiritual maturity.

5. Allow yourself to fail. Ideally, working with junior and senior highers should be a call, not a reluctant commitment. Recent statistics indicate that the length of time a youth worker spends at any single church is woefully short—under two years on an average.[6] The prospective youth worker signs up to work with the youth, and at first all goes well.

After a little initial hesitation by the young people, they soon discover that this new person has some better games than the last youth leader, and he is not quite as boring as the one before that. But after a while, familiarity breeds complacency. The students get used to the leader and discover that even new games played over and over can get old quickly. The leader's energy level falls. Less enthusiasm goes into the planning and carrying out of programs. And inevitably, some mini-crisis takes place during this time that causes the leader to recon-

6. Rice, p. 120.

sider his "call" to youth ministry. The quick and easy solution is to bail out of all responsibility and let someone else take over for a while. But this is where the good youth leaders admit that perhaps they have failed to do all they could and resolve to turn things around.

Hold yourself responsible for your faithfulness, not your success rate. Nobody who works with young people will bat 1000, and no one expects them to (except perhaps the leaders themselves). The book of Ezekiel provides an analogy relevant to youth workers, reminding us where our responsibility ends and someone else's takes over. God told Ezekiel that a watchman who sees trouble coming and warns the people is not held responsible if those people choose to ignore the sound of his trumpet (Ezekiel 33:1-5). But the watchman is held accountable for any damage done if he sees trouble approaching and fails to sound the trumpet (v. 6).

Teachers are watchmen. Their years of wisdom and experience give them spiritual insight into potential trouble their students can expect. Today's young people face unprecedented levels of peer pressure, availability of drugs, relaxed attitudes toward drinking, sexual activity, and so forth. And while we must be careful not to come down too hard or take on a condemnatory attitude, we must also be careful to keep sounding the warning trumpet in regard to these problems.

6. Don't allow youth work to replace personal devotions and worship with peers. If you happen to teach Sunday school and prepare a mid-week program for youth, it may seem that you are always planning. It takes a considerable amount of time and effort to prepare yourself spiritually—not to mention putting together games, buying supplies and refreshments, and doing the other hundreds of little things that go into youth work. And it's easy to think that you're doing your part for the kingdom each week.

Yet to keep youth work in a healthy perspective, you need to maintain your personal devotionals and regular contact with Christian peers. Never forget that if your spiritual commitment begins to slide, the probability is high that your students' spiritual lives will suffer as well. Try to plan your personal time to offset what you're doing with the youth group. For example, if you're planning a lot of Bible study for them, try reading Christian biographies or devotional material on your own. If as a group you are focusing on prayer, as an individual you could use Christian music for a while to offer praise and thanksgiving. A good variety can prevent early youth worker burnout.

THE TWO-LEVEL TEACHING APPROACH

Teaching of any kind is an intense and demanding obligation, but teachers in traditional evangelical churches have an even greater challenge. To be effective, they must learn to teach on two different levels. One large segment of their students are those who have been brought up in the church. They have accumulated hundreds of hours in Sunday school, vacation Bible school, youth group, and other church functions. They have been subjected to all kinds of teachers and curricula. And frankly, by now they are beginning to think they have heard it all. You are going to have to go beyond the basic stories and applications to hold the attention of these kids.

But then there is the other segment of students—those occasional attenders, the "fringe" kids. This segment may not even know who was in the lions' den, who taught the Sermon on the Mount, or in which testament those stories are located.

Standing before these two segments is the teacher. If the leader tries to challenge the knowledgeable kids, the others feel stupid, complain that the meetings are boring, or quietly drift away. But if the leader shifts the focus to the unchurched kids, the regulars are quick to exclaim: "We already know this story!"

And again, since no two youth groups are alike, it is up to you to figure out how to make sure all your group members continue to learn. Here are a few options to supplement your own ideas.

Option 1: Provide additional programs for "advanced" students. Many churches quickly skim off most of the best students and encourage them to participate in discipleship groups, leadership training, core group development, and so on. This provides the opportunity for regular students to mature at an advanced rate while the others are encouraged to keep going to the regular meetings. If you use this option, do so with a word of caution. The danger in this structure is that it tends to dichotomize the group into the Pharisees and the publicans. It is up to the leader to prevent such an attitude.

Option 2: Create situations where the churched kids have the opportunity to teach the fringe students. People who know next to nothing about the Bible can learn just as easily from a novice as from a seasoned pro. But by taking on teaching responsibilities (even for short periods of time), your churched students will peruse the Scriptures a little more closely than normal—and will learn more. And as they begin to field questions from other students (or a mischievous leader), they will begin to see the need for study at a deeper-than-surface level.

Option 3: Mix the knowledgeable students with those who are unfamiliar with the Bible. If you know your students well you can create a balanced mix of study groups that blend the knowledgeable students with the others. As long as discussion questions are phrased the right way, both segments can participate. (For example, include a lot of opinion questions and then make clear transitions to biblical passages. Everyone has an opinion, so everyone begins on an equal basis.)

Option 4: Separate the regular students and fringe kids for study within the same group. Put one subgroup in a circle, put the other subgroup in a second circle, and give them the same list of questions or Bible passages to discuss. When groups members discover that they are among people approximately as informed as they are, most of them will feel free to open up. The insights of one group may be quite different from the other, but that is OK. The important thing is that both groups are continuing to learn.

Option 5: Play a lot of games that subtly teach biblical facts or principles. Feelings of intellectual superiority or inferiority flourish in settings that are reminiscent of school. You can alleviate much of this problem by avoiding an academic atmosphere. Utilize resources such as Youth Specialities Ideas books for simple, nonintimidating Bible games and quizzes. Do lots of role plays. Sing. Create. Your "regular" churched kids have a comfortable advantage with the "regular" methods of teaching. Balance things out a little by mixing up the teaching methods and creating an environment where everyone can learn.

Option 6: If you know your group members well enough, you can create an atmosphere where your churched, comfortably mature, regular church attenders can learn from the fringe group. This option is the most difficult yet may be the most effective. The fringe subgroup of your students is likely to be much more informed about the harsh realities of life. If you can get them to open up in a group setting, the other group members may experience quite an eye-opening revelation.

Your regular, churched kids are not exempt from the temptations to drink, experiment with drugs, or get involved in sexual activity. But for some of the others in your group, these things may be normal activities at home. If not a problem with family members, many may have stories to tell of friends who have suffered the consequences of such things—alcoholism, abuse, drug addiction, and more. One real life "horror story" from someone in the group may have a far greater effect on your "comfortable" church kids than another Bible passage to add to their repertoire. As you try to help the fringe students become more knowledgeable about the Bible, try also to help your biblically informed students become more aware of life beyond the church walls.

GOAL SETTING

As you begin to work with young people, set goals for what you hope to accomplish. Evaluate and rework your goals frequently.[7] But do not be too disappointed if you come up short of your plans. It is no disgrace to fail to meet a goal. In fact, sometimes you will need to look hard for small victories in the midst of failures. As hard as you try, some of the students you thought had the most potential are going to give up on you, the group, and the church. You may spend hours preparing and months going through a particular portion of the Bible, only to discover a few weeks down the line that the group has all but completely forgotten what you taught. In such cases, don't worry.

In spite of preset goals and personal desires, in the final analysis, any student who does not leave the church during the teenage years can be considered a victory for the leader. When you look at your youth group, you may see a lack of knowledge, the complete absence of maturity, and a multitude of other shortcomings. But when you look at your youth group, learn to see a *group*. You have a *group* of people whom you can still influence.

7. Ridge Burns and Pam Campbell, *Create in Me a Youth Ministry* (Wheaton, Ill.: Victor, 1986), pp. 169-72.

Statistics tell us that nowhere near half the young people reared in Christian homes choose to be active Christians as adults.[8] But you still have a group that you have not lost to the world—not yet, at least. Rejoice in that fact if you can find no other source of joy.

It is not unusual for teenagers to go through hot and cold cycles of spiritual maturity. If the leader is not careful, he will be more aware of the problems than the growth. But often, without anyone even realizing it, the overall spiritual temperature keeps going up. Even though your losses will be more apparent, do not lose sight of all that is going right.

It may not seem that your kids are learning much. Theological concepts may not sink in. Facts and figures may remain mixed up in their minds. But do not get frustrated, because there are still a number of lessons these young people are learning. Depending on the example the leader sets, they can learn about grace and forgiveness in a personal way. They can see firsthand what it is like to receive unconditional love (or as close to it as any human can provide). They can discover the value of trust in a leader and in each other. They can experience freedom and responsibility. Are not such lessons more important than their being able to recite the books of the Bible or name the twelve apostles? Before you know it, they may even learn to take these newly acquired values outside the church walls and begin to develop them in the context of their friends, family, and the secular world.

A BIBLICAL RATIONALE

Some leaders are likely to suggest that we should expect more from our young people than merely their attendance. Are we just to be a baby-sitting service during their teenage years? No, we should never set our sights that low. Yet there is something to be said for setting big goals but settling for meager results. In closing, let's look at both an Old Testament and New Testament example.

When the Israelites had trudged through the desert and were standing just outside of the land God had promised them, the twelve spies went in to check things out. When they got back and gave their reports, Joshua and Caleb were the only two spies who showed sufficient maturity and faith to move forward. They were quickly outvoted and almost stoned by the others. Yet when God revealed Himself to the Israelites and sentenced them to another forty years in the wilderness, He did not create an exemption for Joshua and Caleb. But instead, those two had to postpone their deserved reward voluntarily for the good of the others. (See Numbers 13-14 for the details of this account.)

A parallel theme on a New Testament level is provided by Paul in 1 Corinthians 9. He wrote, "To the weak I became weak, to win the weak" (v. 22). No, he was not referring specifically to teenagers, but the principle still holds. Sometimes, for the

8. Dennis Miller, "Christian Teenagers—They're Leaving the Flock," *Moody Monthly*, September 1982, pp. 11-13.

good of the youth group as a whole, teachers need to set aside their quest of developing teenage spiritual giants. When you take a close look at teenagers, they are not yet mature physically. They have far to go before they achieve emotional maturity. Their social relationships are still developing. So how can we expect them to be spiritually mature? The process takes time, so we do well to hold on to them during this turbulent period of their lives.

Teaching junior highers and high schoolers is difficult. It requires time, energy, and wisdom that would have taxed Solomon. It is not a job for those who need frequent affirmation or ego boosts. It is ministry in the fullest sense of the word.

Yet for those willing to serve God in such a foreign culture, the rewards are more than sufficient. (They are rarely immediate, but they are abundant.) If you do decide to take on the "wonderful horror" of reaching teenagers with spiritual truth, and if you ever come to the point where you are ready to give it all up, we close with the secret that has kept a lot of people going.

Before you quit in frustration, ask ten adults to describe the person(s) who had the most influence on their lives. Most people recall a teacher or leader who cared about them during their turbulent teenage years—someone who cared enough to establish a relationship and spend a little time with them. And they will tell stories not about what they learned, but rather what they felt. After a number of such stories, you may well return to youth work with a new sense of wonder and anticipation. Remain thankful for small victories and let God complete His perfect work in each of your students in His own timing.

The missionary weeps as her canoe takes her away for the last time. The natives can function on their own now, and she is no longer needed there. She feels both the sorrow of separation and the profound joy of knowing that God will continue to provide everything these people need. She will miss those wonderful people to whom she ministered, and she feels an unspeakable wonder at being a part of their spiritual development. Someday she will be united with them again in eternity. And in the meantime, she begins to look forward to what God has in store for her next.

The youth leader decides to . . . well, from this point, the story is up to you.

FOR FURTHER READING

Campolo, Anthony. *Growing Up in America: A Sociology of Youth Ministry.* Grand Rapids: Zondervan, 1989.

Johnson, Lin. *Teaching Junior Highers*. Denver: Accent, 1988.

Reed, Ed, and Bobbie Reed. *Creative Bible Learning for Youth: Grades 7-12.*

Ventura, Calif.: Regal, 1977.

Rice, Wayne. *Junior High Ministry*. Revised edition. Grand Rapids: Zondervan, 1987.

Richards, Lawrence O. *Teens: Giving Youth the Grow-Ahead*. Elgin, Ill.: David C. Cook, 1988.

_____. *Youth Ministry: Its Renewal in the Local Church*. Grand Rapids: Zondervan, 1985.

Stevens, Doug. *Called to Care: Youth Ministry and the Church*. Grand Rapids: Zondervan, 1985.

Strommen, Merton P. *Five Cries of Youth*. Revised edition. San Francisco: Harper & Row, 1988.

Veerman, David. *Reaching Kids Before High School: A Guide to Junior High Ministry*. Wheaton, Ill.: Victor, 1990.

Yaconelli, Mike, and Jim Burns. *High School Ministry*. Grand Rapids: Zondervan, 1986.

18

Perry G. Downs

*Adults: An Introduction**

MINISTERING TO ADULTS: AN INTRODUCTION
- **Understand that adults are growing and changing**
- **Design educational settings appropriate for adults**
- **Set your educational goals with adults in mind**
- **Teach in ways appropriate for how adults learn**
- **Relate your content to adult life needs**

It is now a well-known fact that the population of the United States is aging. The highly touted "baby boomers" are now well into adulthood, forming the largest group in our society. Christian education is becoming increasingly a matter of adult education as the populations of our churches are aging. We must take into account this new group of students, considering both what we need to teach them and how we must teach them.

Perhaps the worst mistake we could make would be to assume that adult education should be like the education of children and youth, only on a higher level. Adults as learners are unique, needing an educational approach designed for

*Editors' note: Leading authorities in adult education differ as to the age when adulthood begins. These differences will be reflected by the author of this chapter and the authors of the following chapter. The differing age ranges stated in the two chapters should not be viewed by the reader as contradictory.

PERRY G. DOWNS, PH.D., is associate professor of Christian education, Trinity Evangelical Divinity School, Deerfield, Illinois.

their own characteristics as learners. Moreover, all adults are not the same. They also need an educational program designed for the various developmental levels of adulthood. Twenty year olds are not the same as forty year olds — each have needs and interests unique to them.

This chapter will explore adults as learners, identifying their developmental stages and special characteristics as students. From these insights, objectives and strategies for Christian education may be drawn.

INTRODUCTION TO ADULTHOOD

There is no clear line of demarcation in our society indicating when a person becomes an adult. Primitive societies provide predictable initiation rites into adulthood. Complex societies allow for a more broadly defined transition out of adolescence into adulthood. In our society, when does a person become an adult? Susan Littwin has observed that there is a whole generation which has "postponed" adulthood, extending the adolescent transition into the late twenties or even early thirties.[1] This has created a whole group of people who do not fit our normal category of "adult," but neither are they considered "youth."

For the purposes of this chapter, adulthood will be thought of as beginning in the early twenties (usually with some sort of "marker event") and progressing on through the end of life. Normally we speak of "early adulthood" (ages 21-35), "middle adulthood" (ages 35-65), and "older adulthood" (ages 65+). The transitions into each stage have as much to do with life events as with chronological age.

It used to be that adulthood was considered all the same. After a person became an adult there were no more stages or patterns of development. But more recent studies of adult development made popular by Gail Sheehy[2] and Daniel Levinson[3] have helped us understand that adulthood is also shaped by some clear developmental patterns. Stubblefield has noted:

> Researchers now know that adulthood, including the late years, offers potential for growth and development. It is marked by stages, crises, challenges, disasters, and triumphs. The crises faced and the solutions discovered in adulthood often produce progress as dramatic and far-reaching as some of the advances made in the youngest years.[4]

The United States has one of the few cultures in the world that does not value aging. We tend to see youth as positive and the aging process as negative. In most other societies, aging is something to be valued because with it come increased experience and wisdom. A graying head is considered a badge of honor.

---

1. Susan Littwin, *The Postponed Generation: Why America's Kids Are Growing Up Later* (New York: Morrow, 1986).
2. Gail Sheehy, *Passages* (New York: Bantam, 1977).
3. Daniel J. Levinson, *Seasons of a Man's Life* (New York: Alfred A. Knopf, 1978).
4. Jerry M. Stubblefield, ed., *A Church Ministering to Adults* (Nashville: Broadman, 1984), p. 257.

But in the United States we want to hide or deny aging, coloring our hair, working to maintain youthful bodies, and not admitting our true age. Especially for the Christian, this is a sad denial of God's wisdom in creating people to age according to His plan. Scripture affirms in Proverbs 16:31 that living to an old age is a gift from God.

But whether we like it or not, growing older is a fact of life. God has designed us so that there are predictable patterns to development. Even in adulthood, there are developmental sequences that should not be ignored.

Along with the patterns of development, social structures also cause predictable patterns to adult life.[5] For example, the decade of the *twenties* is generally characterized by *great confidence*. People in this age group tend to believe they are invincible, able to accomplish anything they wish. They tend to be great risk-takers, believing everything will turn out well in the end.

People in their *thirties* tend to be *doubters,* questioning many of their life decisions. It is quite common to see these people change careers, or at least make a mid-life adjustment in their career. Sadly, this is also the time when most marriages break down. More people are divorced in the thirties than at any other time in life.

The *forties* tend to be characterized by a deep *sense of urgency*. These people realize that time is slipping by, and they need to make a mark. There is urgency in career and in family matters, probably hastened on by the first signs of physical aging. These people are facing the reality of their own mortality.

People in their *fifties* are characterized by *self-acceptance*. After five decades of living, they can reflect with a greater degree of assurance and meditation about life. The urgencies and energies of the forties are declining, and they tend to be more at peace with life.

After the *sixties* the potentials for wisdom and holiness are realized in greater depth. These people have tasted deeply of life and are capable of a *more mature faith* and trust than those of younger years.

These transitions in the adult years provide the gist for adult education. Gross has noted:

> Learning can precede, accompany, or follow life transitions. Some adults . . . learn to cope with change that has already taken place; others with a change still underway; and others with a change that lies ahead. . . . Learning can help an adult prepare for a future transition, deal with a current transition, or cope with life in a new status that he or she has already entered but cannot handle successfully.[6]

Adulthood normally lasts about three times as long as childhood and youth. The church and society as a whole are discovering more about this time of life and are learning how to help people through the transitions and turmoil of the adult

5. Levinson, pp. 49-63.
6. Ronald Gross, ed., *Invitation to Lifelong Learning* (Chicago: Follett, 1982), p. 162.

years. It will be the wise Christian educator who learns to understand and minister responsively to the adults of the church.

Because people continue to grow through adulthood, the need to learn and make sense out of life continues. Answers that were satisfying in adolescence or early adulthood may not satisfy in middle or later adult years. People will need to rethink their theology and biblical understanding throughout life as they work to find meaning in their experience from a Christian perspective. Jarvis observed:

> The quest remains, and few institutions provide opportunity for the seeking individual to discuss, to question, to query these questions and answers which themselves form the basis of the phenomenon of religious belief. The phenomenon is universal, people still ask questions of meaning and still seek answers, even though the churches may not be giving opportunity to everyone to join together in the process.[7]

Adulthood is not a time of static sameness. It is a period of growth and change, requiring educational sensitivity. Adults are different from children and youth, with needs and interests unique to their ages. What then should be the distinctives of adult education?

DISTINCTIVES OF ADULT EDUCATION

Consider two different adult Sunday school classes. In the first, the students (all adults in their forties and fifties) are sitting quietly in rows while the teacher lectures on the history of ancient Israel. Bibles are open in the students' laps, but the looks on their faces speak more of disinterest than excitement. The teacher is knowledgeable on the subject, referring to several maps displayed on the wall. Yet something seems to be missing.

In the other class students are in groups of five talking about how to pray to a sovereign God. This class is also made up of middle adults. They have been studying the attributes of God to understand better how to experience God more fully in their lives. The teacher has presented a study on the concept of divine sovereignty (the idea that God is ultimately in control of all things) and has now asked how prayer fits into the picture. This topic has been raised by the class on several occasions. Students are quite animated in their discussion, periodically disagreeing with each other in earnest but respectful ways. You have the feeling that this class is alive with learning.

The difference here is more than skill or teaching methods. It is a matter of approaching education from the perspective of *andragogy*, the science of teaching adults. The term was first used (as opposed to pedagogy, or teaching children) by Kapp in 1883[8] but has been most recently popularized by Malcolm

---

7. Peter Jarvis, "The Lifelong Religious Development of the Individual and the Place of Adult Religious Education," in *Lifelong Learning: The Adult Years* (May 1983): 21.

8. Robert K. West, ed., "The Effects of Andragogical Teacher Training," in *Journal of Adult Training* 2, no. 2 (Wheaton, Ill.: Evangelical Training Association, 1990), p. 17.

Knowles. Andragogy recognizes that there are distinctives to the ways adults learn, which lead to forms of teaching that are appropriate to them.

Knowles has developed four assumptions about the maturing process in adults, which serve to shape an andragogical approach to education. He asserts first that self-concept changes from being a dependent person to being *more self-directed*. As a result, education needs to be less controlled, allowing adults to direct their own learning agenda. If we make all the decisions for them, telling them what, when, and how they must learn, we fail to allow them to function as adult learners.

Second, Knowles observes that adults are accumulating a growing *reservoir of experiences* and insights that serve as a rich resource for learning. Effective adult education will respect and draw upon the life experiences of the learners as a resource for education. The teacher is to be a facilitator rather than the source of all knowledge.

Knowles also suggests that an adult's desire to learn will be oriented increasingly to the developmental tasks of *social roles*. As the social positions change, there are new expectations regarding the tasks that must be completed. For example, adults change from directly parenting their young children to more indirect guiding of older children. Or the changing relationship with their own aging parents requires the completion of new developmental tasks in caregiving to elderly parents. These changing tasks serve to set the learning agenda for adults.

Finally, Knowles believes that an adult's perspective on the use of knowledge changes from postponed application to *immediate application*. Adults want to know how information will help them solve their problems. Their orientation is now problem-centered rather than subject-centered. Effective adult education always stresses the usefulness of the content to the actual life situation of the adult.[9]

In the example of the two classes earlier, the first was not oriented toward adults as learners. Good information was being given, but it was not relevant to their lives, and they were not being included in the process. They were only passive receptors of information that would not help them live more successfully. As a result, they were polite, but politely uninvolved.

The second class used their experiences and minds as resources, involving them in the process. The subject matter (God's sovereignty) was related to their lives (How should we pray?) so that real life problems might be addressed. This class would be perceived as related to life and therefore relevant to adults. The result was active learning.

The environment for adult education should be designed for high degrees of trust and low degrees of risk. There should be a relaxed atmosphere where competition is nonexistent and cooperation is stressed. Adults tend to be insecure

9. Malcolm Knowles, ed. *The Modern Practice of Education* (Chicago: Follett, 1980), p. 44-45.

in competitive situations where they might easily "lose face." But a low risk environment, where it is acceptable not to know the answer or to have a problem, will serve to release anxieties and allow adults to learn. The attitude of the teacher will set the climate as friendly and relaxed in the adult classroom.

A critical aspect of the adult educational context is mutual diagnosis of needs and mutual goal setting for the class. Unlike children who can be told what they need to learn and how they should learn it, adults need to be involved in diagnosing their own needs and determining how they might be met.

Unfortunately, many churches create dependent learners who have no sense of personal responsibility for their own spiritual growth. By not involving adults in the process of planning their own educational programs, we create people who see no responsibility for their own spiritual health. Passive education tends to produce the "sit and soak" mentality prevalent in many adult education programs in our churches.

Whereas a pedagogical context leads more toward a transmissive approach to teaching, the adult program should be oriented toward inquiry. This does not mean the teacher is never to lecture or transmit information; rather it means that the focus is to be toward examination or exploration of topics by the students. Teaching methods in the adult class should be more expressional[10] than impressional.

Stressing the need for an interactive classroom, Stubblefield stated,

> Listening is never enough. Understanding must also occur. The former never guarantees the latter, as Isaiah 6:9-10 clearly reveals. Understanding is enhanced when adult learners ask questions; interact with the teacher and fellow learners; and engage in learning activities that stimulate analysis, evaluation, and comprehension. These dimensions of learning are encouraged when learners are encouraged to verbalize their ideas.[11]

Because adults serve as a rich resource for their own learning, teachers should use student insights in discussions. The teacher may not get to cover all his material because the class may do all the talking, but better learning may emerge as students explore issues relevant to them. Using learners as resources causes a change in the role of pedagogical context, in which much of teaching is "telling" the students what they need to know. But in the andragogical context, the teacher becomes a facilitator of learning, creating the context in which adults may explore issues for themselves.

The teacher will need to be sensitive to how new learning approaches are to be introduced.

The facts are that many adults have had limited experience with a variety of learning

10. Gilbert A. Peterson, ed., *The Christian Education of Adults* (Chicago: Moody, 1984), pp. 99-111.
11. Stubblefield, pp. 265-66.

activities and will be reluctant to participate in them. However, when teachers are willing to meet learners where they are and to introduce new teaching methods gradually and patiently, most adults not only will cooperate but also will profit from the learning experiences.[12]

Cassivi has observed:

> Adult learning is based on the principle that anyone can be a learner or a teacher at any time. The teacher is not seen as an individual who possesses a fixed stock of knowledge that is deemed useful. The teacher is a mediator between information and individuals; the role of the teacher is to organize opportunities for people to learn and to stimulate them to want to do so.[13]

Effective adult education considers how adults learn, and is organized to make the most of the interests and abilities of adults. Adult education also requires special objectives related to the needs and interests of adults. What are appropriate objectives for adult education in the church?

OBJECTIVES FOR CHRISTIAN EDUCATION OF ADULTS

Objectives are statements of the purposes of educational programs. They serve to clarify the desired outcomes of education, stating how the student should be helped by the educational activities. The purposes of adult education should be appropriate to the unique characteristics of adults as learners. Stubblefield suggests:

> The challenge confronting churches is to address the interests and life needs that motivate adults to learn, to feature learning methodology appropriate for adult learners, and to offer opportunities for adults to learn in the midst of life's complex issues and prepared schedules. Given the motivation, method, and opportunity, adults will learn.[14]

In the broadest sense, Christian education has a threefold goal. We teach so that our students will think Christianly, act in obedience to the will of God, and have hearts that love God and people. Spiritual maturity is a matter of the mind, heart, and will. Responsible Christian education on any level attempts to shape these three aspects of the child of God.

Beyond these, adult education should aim to develop self-reliant learners[15] who are able to nurture themselves from the Bible. Because adults are self-direct-

---

12. Ibid., p. 266.
13. Dennis Cassivi, "The Education of Adults: Maintaining a Legacy," in *Lifelong Learning* 12, no. 5 (1989): 8.
14. Stubblefield, pp. 262, 264.
15. Cassivi, p. 8.

ing learners, we should be working to unleash this characteristic in the church.

Jarvis suggests that our task is to "assist them in discovering or rediscovering beliefs and ideas that they regard as relevant to their questions of meaning."[16] Effective adult education will help learners reform their theology in light of their changing life experiences so they may apply the truths of Scripture to their current situation. Rather than being static truth, theology must be alive in the learners, affecting how they think, act, and feel.

Adults in the United States have been affected by our society in a particular way, which has profound implications for the church. Modern society has lost the notion of truth, so that even Christians tend to believe that everything — including Christian theology — is relative. As a result, it is difficult for them to conceive of their faith influencing all of life. If truth is relative, then persons can pick and choose how and when they may obey the Bible. Unfortunately, this is how many adults live out their Christianity.

A goal of adult education must be to help people think in terms of the absolute truth of the Word of God. This requires a direct confrontation with modern society, but is essential to the spiritual maturation of our people.

Finally, adult education that is Christian must help people respond to life transitions properly. Helping adults develop a theology of aging, parenting, and relationships will serve to assist them in living Christian lives in their adult years. Our objective should be to have all of our students growing in their capacity to understand and respond to their changing experiences as adults form a soundly biblical perspective.

How Adults Learn

In general, all people will learn in similar ways, regardless of age. But development does influence what sorts of learning will predominate. For example, children tend to be much more susceptible to outside influences, whereas adults are motivated internally. However, both of these approaches to learning are common to all people.

There are at least five characteristics of adults as learners that should influence the educational program of the church. First, *adults want to learn*. The idea that adults are not interested in learning simply is not true. Gross observed:

> Adults learn in order to cope with some change in their lives. . . . almost all adult learners interviewed point to their own changing circumstances as their reason for learning. As we have hypothesized, it is being in transition from one status in life to another that causes most adults to learn. Adults learn what they need to know in order to be successful in their new status. Adults enter a learning experience in one status and expect to leave in another. They will be disappointed if they go out exactly as they came in.[17]

16. Jarvis, p. 20.
17. Gross, pp. 161-62.

The proliferation of adult education programs in the United States demonstrates the wide interest in adult learning. In an important study in Canada, Alan Tough reported that adults he surveyed undertook at least one or two major learning projects every year, and some took on as many as fifteen to twenty![18] The changing roles of adults in society serve to motivate them to learn.

Importantly, this characteristic continues on into old age. Nancy Foltz suggests that the capacity to learn does not necessarily decline with age, but natural losses in hearing and seeing can affect the learning process. Moreover, older adults may respond more slowly than younger adults, but they will still maintain a high degree of accuracy.[19]

The implication to the church is obvious: we must be providing effective educational programs for adults. Adults want to learn, and the church must be prepared to teach them.

Second, *adults are motivated to learn* by one of three sources: pleasure or self-esteem, searching for answers, or meeting felt needs. If an adult can see how his learning will satisfy one of these interests he will be motivated to learn. Adults are extremely practical in their orientation to learning. They want to know how they can use what they learn.

Teachers must be able to show quickly the usefulness of a class. If adults can see how specific learning will bring them pleasure or raise their self-esteem, and will help them answer a question of interest to them, or help meet a need they feel in their lives, they will become involved. This means that adult studies must be cast in practical terms. Adults will not be interested in studying "The Theoretical Basis of Computers," but would be interested in "Using Your Personal Computer More Effectively." Adults will respond to "Effective Parenting" more readily than to "The Doctrine of Sin." This does not mean that we should not teach doctrine; rather, we must offer doctrine classes that are related to life. The doctrine of sin could be taught as "Overcoming Temptation," showing the practical usefulness of the study.

Third, *adults are problem oriented.* Children are satisfied with learning for the purpose of acquiring knowledge. Adults, however, are not interested in more information. They are interested in solving the real problems of their lives. Learning must be problem oriented to be interesting to adults. The problems may be either on a personal or a community level, but they must be real problems bothering adults. It is understood in adult education that "the most enduring source for motivation is the connection of the subject with life."[20]

This characteristic, along with the previous one, can cause some Christian educators to ignore teaching Bible or theology in favor of more immediate stud-

18. Reported by Malcolm Knowles, *The Adult Learner: A Neglected Species* (Houston: Gulf Publishing, 1973), p. 36.
19. Nancy T. Foltz, ed., *Handbook of Adult Religious Education* (Birmingham, Ala.: Religious Education Press, 1986), p. 46.
20. Cassivi, p. 10.

ies. As a result there will be numerous classes on "Communication in Marriage" or "Managing Your Finances," but almost none on "The Attributes of God." This will lead to shallow and weak Christians.

The answer is to teach Bible and theology in ways that show their relevancy to life. The success of teachers such as Chuck Swindoll and R. D. Sproul is that they relate their theology to the life situation of the student. Effective adult educators in the church will understand both the great doctrines of the church and the life issues of adults. They will find the linkages between doctrine and life and teach adults to solve their life problems through thinking and acting Christlike.

Fourth, *adults are self-directed*; they like to have a say in how and what they will learn. Children are more dependent on the teacher for direction, whereas adults wish to decide for themselves.

The problem in the church in this regard is that we have tended to create dependent learners in the spiritual realm. People who are highly self-directed in other areas of life have been taught to sit quietly and listen in Sunday school. Church people are willing to do this because it provides a break from the normal pressures of adult life. But this situation does not lead to spiritual maturity.

Given the opportunity, many adults will choose to become involved in their own spiritual education. This can be done by giving them opportunities for choice. Offering electives for adults is one way they can have some sense of self-directed learning. In smaller congregations, where there are not enough adults to offer several classes simultaneously, members of the class should be involved in deciding what they will study and how they will study it. However, the class needs to fit with an overall curriculum plan for adults approved by the Christian education committee or board.

Teaching techniques for adults should also take into account this characteristic. Students should be used as resources for research and application. Asking adults to help teach the class or explore issues related to the topic allows them to learn in more self-directed ways.

Finally, *adults have a fear of failure in the learning context*. Adults are very self-conscious, worried about how they will appear to others, fearing loss of "status" in the group. The risk of giving a wrong answer or not being able to find a passage makes them hesitant in learning situations.

Adult classes must be "low risk" places where fear of failure is not an issue. This climate can be established by the teacher who is vulnerable and humble. A non-threatening climate where good humor and honesty prevail can set the adult at ease. It is up to the teacher to create this kind of atmosphere. A mutually respectful context, where opinions can be offered without fear of ridicule, is essential to effective adult learning.

Learning is a lifelong process, fully active in adulthood. The old adage "You can't teach an old dog new tricks" is true, except for two facts — we are not teaching dogs, and we are not teaching tricks. We are helping the people of God continue to grow in faith and in obedience to the Lord. This requires sensitive educational approaches that communicate the timeless truths of Scripture in ways that are appropriate to adult learners at the end of the twentieth century.

Christian educators need to take seriously the responsibility of teaching and focus on the whole people of God. They need to understand especially the growing adult populations of the church and learn to teach in ways that are meaningful to them, respecting how God has designed the adult to learn.

FOR FURTHER READING

Foltz, Nancy T., ed. *Handbook of Adult Religious Education*. Birmingham, Ala.: Religious Education, 1986.

Fowler, James W. *Becoming Adult, Becoming Christian: Adult Development and Christian Faith*. San Francisco: Harper & Row, 1984.

Knowles, Malcolm. *The Adult Learner: A Neglected Species*. 4th edition. Houston: Gulf, 1990.

_____. *The Modern Practice of Adult Education*. Revised edition. Englewood Cliffs, N.J.: Cambridge, 1988.

Levinson, Daniel J. *Seasons of a Man's Life*. New York: Alfred A. Knopf, 1978.

Peterson, Gilbert A., ed. *The Christian Education of Adults*. Chicago: Moody, 1984.

Sell, Charles M. *Transitions Through Adult Life*. Grand Rapids: Zondervan, 1991.

Sheehy, Gail. *Passages*. New York: Bantam, 1977.

Stokes, Kenneth, ed. *Faith Is a Verb: The Dynamics of Adult Faith Development*. Mystic, Conn.: Twenty-Third, 1989.

Stubblefield, Jerry M., ed. *A Church Ministering to Adults*. Nashville: Broadman, 1986.

19

Brian C. Richardson, Stanley S. Olsen,
and Allyn K. Sloat

Young, Middle, and Senior Adults*

Ministering to Young Adults

by
Brian C. Richardson

KEYS TO UNDERSTANDING YOUNG ADULTS
- **Diversity of groupings**
- **Fragmentation of life cycles**
- **Developmental stages no longer "typical"**
- **Flexibility required in their teacher/leader**
- **Trends to consider**
- **Implications for ministry**

---

*Editors' Note: Leading authorities in adult education differ as to the age when adulthood begins. These differences will be reflected by the authors of this chapter and the author of the previous one. Since these transitions are both age variable and gradual in the unique developmental stages of each person, the differing age ranges stated by the writers of this chapter regarding early, middle, and later adulthood should not be viewed by the reader as contradictory.

BRIAN C. RICHARDSON, ED.D., is chairman, Biblical Studies Division, and professor of Christian education, Bryan College, Dayton, Tennessee

STANLEY S. OLSEN, M.A., is associate pastor, Hillcrest Covenant Church, Prairie Village, Kansas.

ALLYN K. SLOAT is pastor of education and adult ministries, Winnetka Bible Church, Winnetka, Illinois, and coeditor of *Christian Education: Foundations for the Future.*

Jim, minister of adults at First Church, became concerned that the number of young adults in the church was decreasing. He began a study to determine the problem. Jim first thought about some of the young adults attending First Church. Ellen and Dave come from a stable Christian home. Their parents and grandparents are Christians, do not smoke or drink, hold responsible jobs, and are leaders in the church and community. Jim felt Ellen and Dave have not had to face life as some other couples their ages (mid-twenties) have had to do.

Steve and Kimberly (late twenties) married right after high school. They had been intimate for two years prior to their marriage. Kim had recently become a Christian, but Steve was unsaved. Both came from dysfunctional families. Steve's father was an alcoholic. Kim's parents divorced when she was eight, and Kim was reared by her mother, also an alcoholic. Kim has been attending church and Sunday school with her only child, a seven-year-old daughter. Steve sees no value in religion and refuses to attend.

Cindy and John (late twenties) married about two years ago. It was the second marriage for both of them, and they have four young children, three that live with them. The two girls belong to Cindy by her first marriage. John has a boy from his first marriage (he lives with his mother but stays with them every weekend). Six months ago John and Cindy had a baby. Cindy's children stay with their father on weekends and are not part of the Sunday school.

Dennis and Jackie (early twenties) graduated from college and married the next month. The fact that they now feel they never see one another is a frustration to them. Both of them are career-oriented people who are finding their occupations demand both their time and energy.

Ken and Mary (early thirties) are a black couple with five children. The factory where Ken worked closed last year, and he is still unemployed. They have serious financial problems.

The situations mentioned above are just some of the diverse backgrounds and circumstances Jim's survey revealed about the young adults in his church. His research revealed the following categories:

- College students
- Married with children
- Married with no children
- Blended families
- Unwed couples living together

- Newlyweds
- Ethnic groups
- Single career persons
- Single parents
- Military personnel

With so many possible groupings for young adults, it is difficult for the average church to know where to start or what to do to reach and minister to them. The great diversity of backgrounds and needs and the fragmentation of life cycles make it difficult to address the needs of young adults in the traditional age-graded classes. Young adults have life cycle (developmental) needs; however, those must be met with direction from the Word of God. Thus, it is also difficult to minister to all of their needs in interest-graded classes.

DEVELOPMENTAL TASKS OF YOUNG ADULTS

One of the most useful ways to view young adults' progress toward maturity is to look at certain life needs (developmental tasks) that must be accomplished during the young adult years. Child workers study the different stages of development through which children progress in their growth toward adolescence in order to minister to their needs most effectively. In like manner, knowing the developmental tasks young adults need to accomplish will help us effectively minister to their needs.

Robert J. Havighurst defined a developmental task as "a task which arises at or about a certain period in the life of an individual, successful achievement of which leads to his happiness and to success with later tasks, while failure leads to unhappiness in the individual, disapproval by the society, and difficulty with later tasks."[1] The happiness and usefulness of a person in the later stages of life will be determined in a great degree by his successful accomplishment of developmental tasks during young adulthood.

The following developmental tasks of young adults are adopted from Havighurst: (1) completing or continuing education, (2) selecting a mate, (3) learning to live with a marriage partner, (4) starting a family, (5) rearing children, (6) managing a home, (7) getting started in an occupation, (8) taking on civic responsibility, and (9) finding a congenial social group.[2]

Developmental tasks provide useful clues by which church leaders can plan and implement learning experiences that will meet the needs of young adults. Those who fail to negotiate the tasks as they arise will experience personal frustration and disapproval from society. Church leaders who are aware of these developmental tasks can assist young adults in finding ways for them to cope.

In the late seventies Daniel J. Levinson and others concluded that the period from eighteen to twenty-two should be considered early adult transition, with young adulthood not actually beginning until age twenty-two. Levinson's conclusion was that those between the ages of eighteen and twenty-two have many of the privileges and advantages of adulthood, but they do not very often have the corresponding responsibilities.[3]

The percentage of young people enrolled in college today is the highest in history, but fewer are graduating. Those who do graduate are taking longer to do so, and they also take longer to establish careers and get married. "The age of extended adolescence has arrived. And it shows no signs of going away."[4] Youth

---

1. Robert J. Havighurst, *Human Development and Education* (New York: Longmans, Green, and Co., 1953), p. 2.
2. Ibid., pp. 257-59.
3. Daniel J. Levinson, with Charlotte N. Darrow, Edward B. Klein, Maria H. Levinson, and Braxton McKee, *The Seasons of a Man's Life* (New York: Ballantine, 1978).
4. "Young Beyond Their Years," *Newsweek,* special issue: "The 21st Century Family" (Winter/Spring, 1989), p. 55.

today are trying to postpone adulthood, a startling reversal of historical trends. They are postponing the step to adulthood because they regard it as abandoning a world of carefree pleasure for a world of commitment and taking care of others. Jerry Rubin once put it this way: "We ain't never, never gonna grow up. We're gonna be adolescents forever."[5]

Even though this author agrees with Levinson's position, in most churches eighteen year olds are still classified as adults. For the purpose of this chapter we will consider young adults to be all those between the ages of eighteen and thirty-five.

To develop an effective ministry with young adults we must first understand them and their culture. As the category list given above illustrates, our ministry to young adults must focus on specific needs if it is to get their attention and be successful.

CURRENT TRENDS AMONG YOUNG ADULTS

DECLINE IN NUMBERS

From 1980 to the year 2000 young adults will experience a decline in both actual numbers (50,154,000 to 41,997,000) and as a portion of the adult population (30.6 percent to 20.9 percent), according to the U.S. Census Bureau.[6] This shift reflects the aging of the "baby boomers" and the entrance of the "baby bust" generation into young adulthood. This latter group of young adults has had experiences that differ from all previous generations. During their growing up years they witnessed such things as: (1) different family life situations (about 40 percent spent part of their growing up years in a one parent home), fewer siblings, blended family experiences, less parental supervision, etc.; (2) strife over human rights, abortion, ecology, women's liberation; and soon (3) uncertainty about the future (rising prices, ecology problems, unemployment, an oil crisis, etc.).

The new generation of young adults seems to be less family oriented, more selfish, and more determined to succeed than previous generations. They are concerned about career, money, recreation, and family; but they are uncertain about how to balance them and still not convinced they really want to be leaving adolescence for the responsibilities of adulthood.

THE ETHNICITY OF OUR POPULATION

The population of the United States identified as white non-Hispanic will dip from 80 percent in 1980 to 74.2 percent in the year 2000.[7] One in three children will come from a minority group by 2020.[8]

5. "Growing Pains at 40," *Time*, May 19, 1986, p. 24.
6. 1987-88, U.S. Census Bureau.
7. Ibid.
8. "What Happened to the Family," *Newsweek*, special issue: "The 21st Century Family" (Winter/Spring 1989), p. 20.

CHANGING FAMILIES

The number of persons per household in America has declined from 3.14 persons in 1970 to a projected 2.48 in 2000. In 1987, a married couple with children under eighteen years of age composed only 27.5 percent of all households. What has been termed the "traditional" family (husband working, wife managing the home but not working outside the home, and children under eighteen years of age) constituted only 9 percent of the households.[9]

The age at which couples have their first child continues to increase. In 1986 mothers aged thirty years and older accounted for 26 percent of all first births.[10] With many adults being older when they enter the childrearing stage, the impact on their lifestyle will be great. This will create even more diversity among young adults.

The divorce rate that increased during the sixties and seventies has leveled off or declined slightly since 1980. Some of the declining rate is due to the increased age of first marriages (25.8 for men and 23.6 for women in 1987).[11] Nevertheless, the prediction is that the United States will remain as the country with the world's highest divorce rate. Because approximately 75-80 percent of those who divorce eventually remarry, the number of blended families or stepfamilies continues to increase rapidly. The prediction is that by the year 2000, more children will be part of a second marriage than of a first marriage. In addition, 1987 found approximately seven million single-parent families. Of this number 90 percent were mothers rearing a child alone.[12]

WOMEN IN THE LABOR FORCE

The number of women in the labor force has increased dramatically during the last thirty years. The Census Bureau reports that the participatory level for women in the twenty to forty-four year old segment was 70 percent in 1986 and will increase to approximately 80 percent by the year 2000.[13]

When women college students who intended to marry and start a family were asked if they planned to return to work at some time in the future, 97 percent said yes.[14] One factor contributing to this is the cost of rearing children today. At an annual income of $37,500, a two-parent family spends about $64,000 on the rearing of one child.[15]

9. U.S. Census Bureau
10. Ibid.
11. Ibid.
12. Ibid.
13. Ibid.
14. "Your Life," *USA Today*, November 1989, p. 8.
15. Ibid.

IMPLICATIONS FOR MINISTRY

A CHANGING PHILOSOPHY

By the year 2000 three-fourths of our population will be adult. Churches will need to give increased priority to allocation of budget, space, staff, and resources for adults. As an increasing number of adults is reached, it will mean bringing into churches a larger portion of persons who do not have a "Christian" background. Increased training in the "milk" of the Word, church polity, and principles for living a Christian life becomes essential.

This group is more inner-directed, concerned more about "What do I think about myself?" than anything else. Many will not be reached by traditional approaches. We must understand today's young adults — their needs, motivation, expectations, hurts, and so on — in order to be effective in our ministry to them.

THE VALUE OF TIME

An increasing number of families have both spouses working. The family — individually and collectively — is seeking more control over its time. Convenience will be something for which they are willing to pay. Daycare and childcare will become more important to these career-minded individuals who still want the best for their children. The home will be viewed as a place of refuge from the stress of work, school, and even the church.

APPROACHES FOR ETHNIC GROUPS

The church must develop materials, resources, and approaches for reaching all ethnic groups. This will require a large investment in money, personnel, and resources by churches, denominations, and independent publishers. It is a priority, however, if we are to reach this growing segment of our population with the gospel of Jesus Christ.

INCREASED CHURCH ATTENDANCE

Today's young adults are half as likely to be in church on Sunday as the older generation. Statistics do indicate, however, that church attendance increases with age. In particular, married couples with children are returning to the church.

The 1988 Gallup survey of unchurched Americans discovered a variety of reasons why people have dropped out of regular church involvement:

- 26 percent find other activities
- 25 percent experience increased independence
- 22 percent move to a new community
- 20 percent have specific problems with the church

• 12 percent have conflicting work schedules.[16]

As they reach their thirties, however, many people question why they are still unfulfilled in spite of all they have attained. For that reason the Gallup poll discovered that many who dropped out of church during their late teen or early adult years returned to the church.[17]

Young adults often drop out of church for personal reasons (such as wanting more personal freedom and leisure time) and not because they have a particular problem with the church. The church does not have to change its message to reach today's young adults; but it does need to change its program. The church needs to listen carefully to the needs expressed by young adults and to provide them with relevant biblical help.

FRAGMENTATION OF LIFE CYCLES

Some adults are starting their families while still in their teens; others are waiting until their late thirties. It is becoming more difficult to address life needs of adults in age-graded classes, periodicals, magazines, and so on. Writing more interest-related material for young adults should not be too difficult a task for those publishing periodicals and magazines. Interest-centered Sunday school classes, however, will create as many problems as they solve.

WOMEN IN THE CHURCH

Increased education, career opportunities, independent incomes, and so on, have enabled women to have a greater influence in society. They will seek a corresponding influence in the church. The church must neither ignore the contribution women can make to the church, nor give in to societal pressures that are unbiblical. The issue must be examined openly and biblically to discover the God-given position of church leadership for both men and women.

COMPLEX FAMILY RELATIONSHIPS

New family roles have been created in our society (remarried, absent parents, stepgrandparents, stepsiblings, half siblings, and so on). Divorced men tend to marry younger women. This means that the husband's children from his first marriage will be older than the children from his wife's first marriage. This will bring new problems to the couple in a blended family.

Because many children will be with one parent during the week and another

16. George Gallup, Jr., and Sarah Jones, *100 Questions & Answers: Religion in America* (Princeton, N.J.: Princeton Religion Research Center, 1989), p. 79.
17. For further information see Mark S. Jones, *Reclaiming Inactive Church Members* (Nashville: Broadman, 1988) and John H. Krahn, *Reaching the Inactive Member* (Lima, Ohio: CSS of Ohio, 1982).

parent on weekends, church leaders will have difficulty ministering to the entire family.

How to Attract Young Adults

Are there foundational ingredients necessary to attract young adults to the ministry of our churches? The Alban Institute visited twenty-eight congregations that were successfully attracting young adults to determine why they were exceptional. These churches were large and small, urban and rural, located in different parts of the country, and from different denominations.[18]

The study discovered each congregation had unique characteristics that could not be reproduced in other settings. It did, however, determine several basic elements that characterized congregations that were successful in attracting young adults.

DIVERSITY WITHIN A CENTRAL FOCUS

Effective ministries learned ways to incorporate differences — and minister to the kinds of diversity mentioned earlier in this chapter — without losing sight of their focus. Some churches offer two different styles of worship at the same time. All twenty-eight congregations used outside groups, resources, and programs to enhance the ministry of their congregation.

OPPORTUNITY FOR BELONGING

Erik Erikson advanced the idea that "intimacy" is the controlling theme for young adult development. Most young adults do not seek out a church as a place to identify with or belong to. But those who found churches with small groups (Sunday school groups, Bible study groups, discussion groups that meet for short durations, etc., where people knew their names) had the feeling of being valued, accepted—and eventually—loved. Young adults would return to congregations that provided for one-on-one encounters.

ENCOURAGED PARTICIPATION

Successful churches encouraged young adult involvement. Some young adults want to participate immediately. They are looking for "intimacy," for a substitute family, for a place to serve the Lord, and want to be involved in the life and ministry of the church. Others are tentative about church involvement and often take up to two years to decide about becoming a member. Churches that successfully reach this later group assume that young adults are committed, and

---

18. This section is adapted from research cited in Robert T. Gribbon's *Half the Congregation: An Overview of Congregational Ministry with 18 to 40 Year Olds* (Washington, D.C.: The Alban Institute, 1984).

seek ways for them to channel and express that commitment.

VISIBILITY IN THE COMMUNITY

Churches that effectively reach young adults are those that are visibly involved in the activities of the community. Pastors and members are seen participating in community affairs. They constantly interact with young adults in their environment. These churches are also willing to use nonthreatening environments — such as local restaurants and homes — to initiate young adult programming.

A WARM WELCOME

A key factor in young adults returning to a church was a friendly welcome. Many visited a church different from their denominational background. Some had no understanding of denominational distinctives. They frequently came from a pressure-oriented society where acceptance depended on performance and achievement. Many churches, therefore, had a member "adopt" a visitor. The member was responsible for personally introducing the visitor to other individuals in the church and "hosting" them at various group meetings. It was also the responsibility of the member to help visitors understand the theology and polity of their church.

FAITH RELATED TO LIFE

Young adults desire to relate faith to their everyday lives. They are looking for churches that will give them biblical guidance on issues they face every day (how to be a Christian in a "dog-eat-dog" business world, the Bible and divorce, etc.). Some of their growth as a Christian will only come if they are given a job to do for the Lord. Let them put their faith into practice.

MINISTRY TO YOUR CONSTITUENCY

Successful young adult ministries reach out to a particular constituency. A church in the suburbs concentrates on young families. One rural church has a 5:30 A.M. prayer breakfast for young farmers. An inner city church has a luncheon featuring an inspirational speaker each Monday.

CONCLUSION

The church of Jesus Christ must have a positive biblical message for all the diversified lifestyles of today's young adults. We need to respond redemptively to divorce, remarriage, unwed mothers, blended families, ethnic groups, and college students. Our role is to help young adults adjust to the new and different roles that they encounter. Although traditional approaches and methods will reach some, we will miss the majority unless we develop new and different approaches to reach the diversity of lifestyles found among today's young adults.

Diversity and unity within a biblical context so we are led by God's Word and not societal pressures is the challenge facing the church of Jesus Christ today. We must be claiming young adults for Christ. To do so we must understand them and their society — but we must also know God and His Word so that we never water down the gospel in our attempt to reach people for Him.

Ministering to Middle Adults

by
Stanley S. Olsen

KEYS TO UNDERSTANDING MIDDLE ADULTS
- **Experiencing life changes called seasons**
- **Sometimes confronting times of crisis**
- **Potential for satisfying life roles in marriage and family**
- **Planning seriously for the future**
- **Reconciling faith in relationship to life situations**

It comes upon you either suddenly—like a toothache—or unexpectedly like the creeping subtlety of a backache. Either way, when it happens, it seems like nothing to cheer about. But when middle adulthood comes it turns out not to be so bad after all.

Middle adulthood is a time of transition and change, a time for introspection and evaluation. It is also a time for anger and fear. It is a time for new commitments and satisfied recognition of both the good and bad experiences of life that form the foundation for the future.

Sometimes, around the age of forty, both men and women begin to make the transition from young adulthood (20-40) to middle adulthood (40-60). The "cumulative effects of decisions concerning such variables as age at marriage, years of education, number and spacing of children, career shifts, and change of residences all seem to make individual life histories increasingly unique."[1]

Nevertheless, there are some marked characteristics that shape this exciting time of life as well as several problems that need addressing. The local church must

---

1. Dale Goldhaber, *Lifespan Human Development* (New York: Harcourt, Brace Jovanovich, 1986), p. 439.

consider these factors as a program for ministering to adults is shaped. Designing curriculum to meet needs becomes profitable when these characteristics are considered and confronted. The purpose of this part of the chapter is to identify major middle-adult characteristics, specific idiosyncrasies that may relate to men and women, and suggest some ministry approaches that directly affect adults in this age bracket.

MIDDLE ADULT CHARACTERISTICS

MID-LIFE TRANSITION (40-45 YEARS OF AGE)

Daniel Levinson's book on what it means to be an adult is perhaps the most helpful collection of research available today. Levinson has carefully reflected on the derivation and images of the human life cycle. He speaks of two key elements he finds in the idea of life cycle. He writes,

> First, there is the idea of process or a journey from a starting point (birth or origin) to a termination point (death or conclusion). To speak of a general human life cycle is to propose that the journey from birth to old age follows an underlying universal pattern on which there are endless cultural and individual variations. Many influences along the way shape the nature of the journey, but as long as the journey continues, it follows the same basic sequence.
>
> Second, there is the idea of seasons: a series of periods or stages within the life cycle. The process is not a simple, continuous flow. There are qualitatively different seasons, each having its own distinctive character. Every season is different from those that precede and follow it, though it also has much in common with them.[2]

Levinson and his team of researchers see our lives divided into roughly four broad seasons of twenty years each. According to Levinson's hypothesis, each season of life has a bridge from one to another. Because of the variable differences of individuals, these bridges start and end at different times but are always present. Levinson divides middle adulthood into five bridge periods: mid-life transition (ages 38-40 to age 45), entering middle adulthood (ages 45-50), age 50 transition (age 50-55), leaving middle adulthood (ages 55-60), and late adult transition (ages 60-65).[3]

The first distinct period of this "season of life" usually occurs during the early forties. It is a time of transition between the young adult years and those of the middle years. It is during this sequence that the much-heralded mid-life crisis may take place.

As one turns forty, the symptoms of mid-life transition are somewhat like a bad case of spring fever—a feeling of stagnation, disequilibrium, and mild depres-

2. Daniel J. Levinson et al., *The Seasons of a Man's Life* (New York: Ballantine, 2978), pp. 6-7.
3. See chart in Levinson, p. 57.

sion. Life itself seems to be dull and bothersome. There is often a feeling of longing for something new, vibrant, and daring. Mid-life can be a time of great yearning mixed with regret and a longing for youthful rejuvenation.

Mid-life malaise takes on a variety of forms. The most common one is a long-lasting daydream about change in life—a desire to travel, have a new job, or achieve some other form of success. Frequently the daydreams are focused on the frustration of being trapped in a life structure that seems narrow and restrictive. Now the hopes and dreams of the twenties seem to be ebbing away—or have vanished. Internal frustration comes when there is a definite feeling of being boxed in, but it also includes the willingness to acknowledge that feeling and openly admit dreams are not being realized.

For some, this mid-life transition may be traumatic and turbulent—a time to focus on:

- a stagnant career
- a marriage in trouble
- problems with children or family
- physical difficulties
- emotional changes

Often the discontent may be focused on whatever aspect of life has not been developed. Men and women locked in jobs that seem to be lateral in movement may become critical and despondent.

Women in particular struggle with the realities of growing older. Approaching forty means the childbearing time is coming to an end. Many women experience intense periods of "baby hunger." Other women are still searching for the "right" partner. Still others are reeling from the reality that immersing themselves in a career during young adulthood now is "not all it was cracked up to be."

Men and women alike now are confronted with the effects of aging. As the man reaches middle age, his former trim physique is now bulging. Doubts are beginning to surface about his athletic and sexual prowess. In our youth-oriented culture, women may question their worth and desirability.

Also, during this time it is not uncommon for men and women to notice how many people—not much older than themselves—are succumbing to heart attacks, cancer, and other diseases. This view of the future is shocking for many.

> Two prerogatives of youth, being promising and being supported, are lost in mid-life. The person who is valued at twenty-five for having great potential is expected someday to deliver. By mid-life, being promising is not enough. And, the continuing need for emotional support may be less apparent. . . . the feelings of dependency continue as does the need for support . . . parents continue to be thought of as support bases . . . but even though parents may be alive they may not want to continue to *act* like parents.[4]

4. Michael P. Nichols, *Turning Forty in the Eighties* (New York: W. W. Norton, 1986), pp. 22-23.

Finally, the conflict with one's own children—whether preadolescents or adolescents—creates its own set of dynamics. Developmentally both the adolescent and the one in mid-life transition are similar. In his book *A New Design for Family Ministry* (Elgin, Ill.: David C. Cook, 1982) Dennis Guernsey talks of the relative sameness of characteristics being experienced by both parents of teenagers and the teenagers themselves. He says that both parents and teens are going through the turmoil of forming an identity.

The transition for the teen is in forming an adult identity; the transition for the parent in his middle adult years is forming an identity of "Who am I now?" As a result of the natural tension between parents and teens—and with additional stress being created through mid-life transition—both men and women may experience great tension and much doubt.

However, it is important to recognize that not everyone experiences mid-life crisis. Daniel Levinson clarifies that 80 percent of the men in his study had a tumultuous struggle with themselves and their environment at about age 40. That leaves 20 percent who apparently suffered no crisis. Although no definitive study has been concluded for women, it is assumed the same percentages apply. Because women's lives are more complicated with multiple role demands, the crises they experience may simply be more varied than men's.

Mid-life transition lasts only as long as a person is involved in terminating early adulthood and initiating middle adulthood. At about forty-five years of age (plus or minus a year or two), the developmental tasks change. Now men and women make peace with their past and begin to make choices for the next fifteen to twenty years, their middle adult years.

MIDDLE ADULT YEARS (45 - 60 YEARS OF AGE)

During this next period of time most adults are quite satisfied with their lives. Perhaps because of the decreasing sex-role polarization that comes with the post-parenting years, many adults report increased marital satisfaction during this time. The new joy of grandparenting evokes new levels of self-worth within one's family. During this time, however, a new kind of parenting occurs. Caring for aging parents is a responsibility that can be both emotionally draining and financially stressful.

During the fifties the need to focus on retirement becomes a priority. Planning for financial, physical, and emotional well-being demands a lion's share of time and energy for both men and women. The importance of vocation and work in the lives of the middle aged is increasingly changing in two ways. First, vocation is less and less a personal identity barometer, especially for men. Second, even though it is now less central in importance, it is seen as being more satisfying. The need to build for retirement, however, impacts itself in the continued need for economic growth and job security.

As has been outlined above, the middle adulthood years are a most interesting season of the life cycle. Dale Goldhaber says, "People enter it thinking they are still young and leave it wondering if they are yet old. It involves for most a period of reflection, which for some takes on rather traumatic proportions, and it involves for many a significant shift in the way they think of themselves."[5]

Developmentally, the following recap provides a listing of the adult years.[6]

The Context of Middle Adulthood

1. Modern times have affected this season of life because of longer life expectancy and the decrease in family size.
2. Compared with younger adults, middle aged adults are more satisfied with life and demonstrate a decrease in sex-role polarization.
3. One's social status and/or class is a determinative factor in the quality of the middle years, mostly as influenced by a person's work career, job security, and wage.

The Course of Middle Adulthood

1. For males, the major aspect of mid-life transition is occupation; for women, it more typically involves family and intimate relationships.
2. Lifestyle is a major factor in the determination of the degree of biological change during middle age.
3. A general description of one's biological decrease during middle age is a decrease in the body's ability to recover from stress and a reduced capacity for work.
4. Parents are generally pleased to see grown children leave home although this is tempered by a history of parent-child conflicts or unsatisfying marital relationships.
5. Soon after parenting their children, parenting their parents begins.
6. Grandparenting roles are viewed as a general delight.
7. A heightened awareness of one's own personal experiences and a feeling of being in control of one's own life occurs.

The Conclusions of Middle Adulthood

1. Middle adults place great emphasis on the interpersonal aspects of their activities.
2. Social class impacts the middle adult experience dramatically. Issues of social security, peer relationships, and vocational position influence the age of transition, and, when it is resolved, sources of satisfaction, future opportunities for growth and continued intellectual flexibility and mental competence.

Ministering to the middle adult demands some social objectives. On the basis of the assumptions made above, the following list of topics may create a springboard for a satisfying ministry with middle adults. But remember, all adults are in the process of change. What may work with one person or group may not meet another's needs at all. Be sure to listen actively and be patient to find out the level of your middle adults.

---

5. Goldhaber, p. 478.
6. Ibid. (Adapted from Goldhaber's work.)

MIDDLE ADULT CURRICULUM SUGGESTIONS

1. *Track one*—Spouse to spouse. Men and women deal with issues such as falling in love again, biological changes in marriage (menopause) and the adjustment sexually, and the empty nest.

2. *Track two*—Parenting, grandparenting, and parenting parents. Husbands and wives deal with issues such as helping their children to be on their own and then leaving them on their own, learning to be grandparents, and coping with aging parents.

3. *Track three*—You, your needs, and your future. The middle adult deals with issues such as his aging body, learning what causes stress and how to control it, his spiritual inventory, financial planning, and retiring wisely.

MIDDLE ADULTS AND SPIRITUAL DEVELOPMENT

As has been demonstrated above, mid-life brings with it a good deal of transition and soul-searching in the heart and mind of the individual. For both men and women, this time of life brings with it the opportunity to deepen one's spiritual foundations and faith actions. As James Fowler so eloquently says, "Forms of spirituality that embrace the polarities and paradoxes of Conjunctive faith invite us to attend in new ways to the movements of Spirit within and between us and to the movements of Truth in our Traditions."[7]

This means men or women of mid-life have emerging within themselves a need to see the integration of all they have experienced in life up to that point with what they have been taught since childhood as spiritual absolutes. Often this means that contradictions will meet and be reconciled through life's experiences. Often faith development moves beyond the absolutes of one's roots and to an openness for the traditions and symbols of others. This in no way means a lessening of the importance of one's tradition. It simply means the broadening of one's understanding based on experience and practice of faith.

Put another way, "Conjunctive faith exhibits a combination of committed belief in and through the particularities of a tradition, while insisting upon the humility that knows that the grasp on ultimate truth that any of our traditions can offer needs continual correction and challenge."[8]

Middle adults are putting practical handles on who God is and what He means to their lives. They are beginning to understand new ways in which Christ is showing forth the divine purpose of His life for theirs. They are fine-tuning their spiritual foundations and preparing to mature and grow all the more in the grace and knowledge of the Lord Jesus Christ.

---

7. James W. Fowler, *Becoming Adult, Becoming Christian* (San Francisco: Harper & Row, 1984), p. 146.
8. Ibid., p. 66.

Ministering to Senior Adults

by
Allyn K. Sloat

KEYS TO UNDERSTANDING SENIOR ADULTS
- **Present and future "age wave"**
- **Societal abuse of the elderly**
- **Their real needs**
- **Biblical perspective on aging**
- **Serving them—"servanting" them**
- **Models for ministry**

The statistics on the graying of America continue to pour in, and they have startling implications for the ministry of the church. Senior adults are a rapidly increasing portion of our population. John Naisbett, futurist and author of *Megatrends,* calls the present and future age wave "the most important trend of our time." If you have not noticed the age wave moving through the American population, consider the following:

- Since 1985, the number of persons in the United States over age sixty-five has exceeded those under eighteen, and this pattern will continue.
- Those persons over age eighty-five are the fastest growing group in the country.
- Average life expectancy in 1950 was 68.2 years; in 1985 it was 74.7 years; in 2020 it will be 78.1 years.
- Older persons constitute more than 60 percent of all single adults.
- In 1980, there were 26 million Americans who had reached or passed age sixty-five—11.3 percent of the population. In 1990, this group numbered 32 million persons—12.7 percent. By 2020, those over sixty-five will account for 51 million—17.3 percent of the population.
- By 2040, when the last of the "baby boomers" reach retirement, the over-sixty-five age group will number 80 million, which will constitute approximately one-fourth of the population. By that year, life expectancy for males will be eighty-seven and for females will be ninety-two.[1]

The "over sixty-five boom" is upon us, and it affects virtually every area of our society. For years we have looked at three categories of adulthood: young adult, middle adult, and senior adult. As current trends continue, we will need to con-

---

1. *The Win Arn Growth Report*: "The Church's Challenge and Opportunity of an Aging America," (Monrovia, Calif.) 26 (1989): 1.

sider the three categories of senior adulthood—the young old, the old old, and the oldest old (over age 85).[2] An amusing way of expressing senior adult life stages is: "go-go" senior adults (ages 55-70), "slow-go" senior adults (ages 70-85) and "no-go" senior adults (ages 85 and up). What is the church doing in response to the "age wave"? A growing number of churches are having effective ministries to senior adults, but in most churches one would have to answer "not enough." What can be done to minister effectively to three generations of senior adults in our congregations and communities?

A New Form of Prejudice

The American society has a lot of misunderstandings and apprehensions about the elderly. America has been accused of several forms of prejudice, including racism and sexism. Now one could add another form of prejudice—"ageism." Older people in America are often misunderstood. And worse, this lack of understanding seems often to be coupled with a lack of desire to understand. Our mentality may say "out of sight, out of mind," or "ignore it and it *will* go away," but the fact is, the graying of America will continue.

In the meantime, America focuses on the new, the young, and the innovative—while the old, the settled, and established are overlooked. David Moberg challenges the church for being caught up in that kind of mentality when he states:

> The elderly are demeaned when the youth oriented values of American society are subtly conveyed through sermons, educational programs and other church activities. Youth are highly prized as "the future of society" and [of] the church. That which is new, young and innovative is typically granted higher status than the old, elderly and well established; the "throw away mentality" of our society . . . has subtly spilled over to feelings that the elderly can also be discarded.[3]

In addition, abuse of the elderly is rising at an alarming rate, now second only to child abuse. Mickelsen suggests five forms of abuse the elderly are subjected to: (1) physical abuse; (2) families trying to control the assets of older adults; (3) neglect; (4) treating older adults like children; and (5) cutting older adults out of social and family activities.[4]

Sometimes even the church is involved in abuse of older adults. Moberg cites five ways the church dishonors the elderly:

1. The church usually emphasizes the youth and families with children. The single, the divorced, and the elderly with no children at home often feel out of place.

2. Matilda W. Riley and John W. Riley, Jr., "Longevity & Social Structure: The Added Years," *Daedalus* 115: 1.

3. David O. Moberg,"Is Your Church an Honest Ally or a Friendly Foe for the Aged?" *Christian Education Journal* 3:1 (1982): 51-64.

4. Alvera Mickelsen, "To Honor Your Parents: The Chance of a Lifetime," *Christianity Today* 25, no. 11 (1981): pp. 22-26.

2. Even in the church, some people equate worth with occupation—which has an adverse effect on retired people.
3. Church elections can dishonor the elderly when young people are elected or appointed to positions of leadership while retired people with more available time are pushed aside.
4. The architecture and construction of churches often works against ease of movement for the elderly.
5. Finally, a church's program schedule can work against the elderly, who may be afraid or unable to drive at night and therefore stay away from evening meetings.[5]

The Real Needs of Senior Adults

Gish identifies seven needs the elderly face. Understanding these needs can help overcome their greatest need—a lack of understanding about the influences on his life. Their concerns are:

1. *The loss of significant roles and significant others.* This occurs from death, retirement, and relocation.

2. *Developing a meaningful use of time.* Many older adults have not prepared for retirement and are uncertain of how to use their time constructively. The older adult must be encouraged to stay active, but it usually requires a change of focus.

3. *Physical downgrading.* Some loss of strength and ability occur, a natural part of getting older. The older adult must learn to accept changes and adapt to them.

4. *Adjusting to psychosocial changes.* Erikson speaks of ego-identity versus despair. Some will have ego-identity confirmed as they look back on life and see that it was good, thus deriving satisfaction from the work they accomplished. Others will despair, realizing there is not time to correct mistakes or complete tasks. If a person has learned to care and can show caring concern—and if one can use the wisdom and accummulated experiences of life—one finds those factors contribute to realistic spirituality.

5. *Adjusting to reduced income.* If an older adult has planned for a reduced income, he may not have much difficulty adjusting to economic changes. However, rising inflation and higher costs have an adverse effect on some elderly, particularly in the area of medical care. More and more of the elderly live at or below the poverty level in our affluent American society.

6. *Adjusting to living accommodations.* The older adult may have to move to a smaller dwelling because taking care of his own property may become difficult. If his spouse dies, the older adult must decide whether to keep the home.

7. *Coming to terms with death.* American society talks a lot about lifestyle. Perhaps it's time for the church to lead the way in developing a Christian "death-

---

5. David O. Moberg, "What the Greying of America Means to the Local Church," *Christianity Today* 25, no. 20 (1981): pp. 30-33.

style"—a way to prepare older adults for the transition from this world to a heavenly home.[6]

SOME BIBLICAL PERSPECTIVES ON AGING

We need a renewed emphasis on the significance the Bible places on aging. Honor and respect for the elderly are clearly taught in the Scriptures. Living to old age is a gift from God (Prov. 16:31). By following God's commandments, one prepares for long life (Prov. 3:1-2). There are rewards for the older adult who has lived a righteous life (Ps. 37:25-26). The psalmist says he never saw God forsake the righteous, in youth or older age. Long life brings understanding, which translates into wisdom (Job 12:12). The elderly are to be respected: "Rise in the presence of the aged, show respect for the elderly and revere your God" (Lev. 19:32). Notice that a reverence for God is translated into respect for people, including senior adults.

The fifth of the Ten Commandments is one with promise: "Honor your father and your mother, so that you may live long in the land the Lord your God is giving you" (Ex. 20:12). That command is repeated at least eight times in the Bible (cf. Lev. 19:3, Mark 7:10). The command is wholistic, demanding that children care for parents, support their parents, protect their parents, and show respect for their parents.

"Honor your father and mother" (Matt. 19:19) repeats the Old Testament theme of respect for one's parents. Ephesians 6 declares it is right for children to honor their parents, reminding children that this is the first commandment with a promise. Young men are to be submissive to those who are older (1 Pet. 5:5), and this applies to young women as well. Older men and women have the responsibility to help younger men and women in the faith (Titus 2:2-8). It should be noted that although not explicit, the Old Testament attitudes of honoring the elderly are apparently presupposed in the New Testament.

I encourage a more comprehensive study of Scripture leading toward a theology of senior adulthood that indicates:

- Older adults are people of worth.
- Older adults are people with resources to be utilized in ministry.
- Old age can be a time of great fruitfulness (Ps. 92:12-15).
- Older men and women are responsible for serving as examples and providing assistance to younger Christians.
- Older adults are a part of Christ's Body and should be encouraged to use their gifts so that the whole Body functions properly. Talents and gifts perfected through the years are too valuable to not be used in the church.
- All of us are interdependent parts of society; no one lives to himself and no one dies to himself (Rom. 14:7).

6. Dorothy Gish, "The Aging: Myths, Needs, Ministry," *The Asbury Seminarian* 39: 4 (1984): 30-39.

- The admonition to honor and respect parents/older adults is a concept that should be heeded in contemporary Christian circles.

Paul Tournier notes,

> The essential answer lies with a civilization based not merely on economic progress but on the value of the person. While not rejecting the benefits of our society, we must introduce a personal relationship into the very heart of our anonymous technological society. In other words, we must learn to love the old (as we have learned since Rousseau to love the young) for who they are—simply persons—not for what they can (or can't) do for us anymore.[7]

It is time that our understanding of words such as aging must be freed from a mechanistic, performance-oriented view. How old a person is has little to do with how many years a person has lived. We must realize that the opposite of old is not young; the opposite of old is new, and God is always doing a new thing in His people, in our lives, and in His church. In fact, the very nature of the gospel requires that the church must address its witness and mission to the needs, desires, and potential of senior adults. The church dare not remain neutral. It will either be an integrating force in the life of the older person or it will be a disintegrating force. We dare not see life's later passages or stages as denigrations. We must see them as growth and development potential, where maturity and wisdom are really recognized as valuable in their own right in our senior adults.

IMPLICATIONS AND RESOURCES FOR MINISTRY TO SENIOR ADULTS

Differentiating between what the church should do *for* the older adult and what the older adult can do for the church is difficult. By helping senior adults, they in turn help the church. By providing opportunities of service and usefulness, the church is helped greatly. If the above aspects were rated for importance, however, probably the more important one would be, "What can the older adult do for the church?" The very nature of Christianity is that as we minister we are ministered to. First and foremost, the older adult *is the church* just as significantly as are young people, children, and other adults. Let's look at some options concerning senior involvement in the church.

WHAT THE CHURCH CAN DO FOR THE ELDERLY

- Provide kitchen facilities for low-cost lunches.
- Organize a drop-in center for the elderly.
- Supply information (medical, social security, etc.).
- Organize "Adopt a grandparent."
- Provide cassettes of Sunday services or pipe in services on the telephone.

7. Paul Tournier, *Learning to Grow Old* (London: SCM, 1971), pp. 43, 63.

- Take communion to shut-ins.
- Plan seminars on retirement and death.
- Involve the elderly in a special monthly worship service.
- Provide "Call a car" to help meet transportation needs.
- Supply legal and financial aid.
- Elect senior adults to fill church offices.
- Supply church-owned apartments for the elderly.
- Plan cross-country and local special interest trips.

WHAT THE ELDERLY CAN DO FOR THE CHURCH

- Provide secretarial work.
- Organize a telephone ministry.
- Visit one another and shut-ins (especially those with similar skills).
- Help the pastor keep up with his reading by reading and taking notes for him.
- Help in the church nursery.
- Organize telephone prayer groups.
- Teach "lost" crafts to young people (baking, canning, etc.).
- Organize small groups around special interests and hobbies.
- Go on short-term missionary projects.
- Provide skilled tasks (plumbing, electrical work, surveying, accounting, etc.).
- Establish a core senior citizens group for political involvement.
- Write letters to church missionaries.

These are incomplete listings, but you can add to them as you evaluate the needs and abilities of senior adults in your church and community.

HELPING THE ELDERLY LEARN

Of course, sharing the gospel with senior adults is of primary importance—helping them to trust Jesus Christ alone as their Savior and to acknowledge Him as Lord in every area and stage of life.

As we teach senior adults how to grow in their walk with Christ, we must emphasize that senior adults can—and do—learn. One's capacity to learn diminishes very little over time. Learning patterns may change, and the speed of learning may be slower, but the ability to learn remains. We must be aware of some psychological factors affecting the way older adults learn.

- To develop a healthy self-concept, senior adults should be seen as independent and self-correcting.
- An older adult's readiness to learn is related to personal tasks and goals.
- Older adults have a vast reservoir of experience that they relate to new ideas.
- Their orientation to learning is the shifting of interest from subject-centered to problem-centered learning.

Thus, some practical implications for enhancing the teaching-learning process with senior adults is to:

- Set a slower pace to allow for slower responses.
- Create a warm environment for learning (emotionally warm and friendly).
- Provide the best classroom area possible in the church for senior adults (good accessibility, lighting, ventilation, with comfortable seating).
- Communicate loudly and clearly.
- Lend emotional support by being open, helpful, sensitive, and affirming.
- Address the unique needs of the older adults in the group.

Two ministry models that can help us in our task of providing a balanced ministry to senior adults are included. Figure 1[8] is "Ministry with Older Adults in the Local Church" by Beth Brown. This is an overview of the changes, needs, and implications for Christian education regarding older adults, plus a strategy for ministry. Figure 2,[9] entitled "Understanding Older Adults," by Marlin Hiett and Ellen Whitworth, is a presentation of the needs of older adults, implications for meeting those needs, and a suggested ministry plan for senior adults.

Most of all, the need exists to communicate to people in their later maturity that the church does care, that senior adults are loved, that they are appreciated and that they are an important part of the total life and ministry of the church. Dorothy Gish gives us ten commandments for behavior with and toward senior adults.[10]

Thou shalt:
- maintain regular contact
- include in celebrations
- be imaginative in gift giving
- listen thoughtfully to reminiscences
- not gloss over worries and/or complaints
- not embarrass or distress
- not undermine self-respect or assurance
- be on their side
- be sympathetic
- not forget to laugh

Remember, that "Thou too shalt one day be old"—God willing.

Yes, the accumulation of years gives senior adults great individuality, special needs, unique abilities and limitations, and a history that is "one of a kind." This individuality must be met. So the church stands challenged. Careful ministry attention to and with older adults may constitute one of its greatest opportunities and rewards. Wouldn't you like to hear an older woman in your church say,

8. Beth E. Brown. "Ministry with Older Adults in the Local Church," *Christian Education Journal* pp. 13-23. (Copyright Scripture Press Ministries. Used by permission.)

9. Marlin Hiett, and Ellen Whitworth. "Understanding Older Adults," *Christian Education Journal* 4, no. 2 (1983): pp. 13-23. (Copyright Scripture Press Ministries. Used by permission.)

10. Gish, pp. 30-39.

Ministry with Older Adults in the Local Church

GENERAL NEEDS OF OLDER ADULTS AND THEIR IMPLICATIONS FOR CHRISTIAN EDUCATION			
	CHANGES	**NEEDS**	**IMPLICATIONS FOR CHRISTIAN EDUCATION**
PHYSICAL	Some decrease in physical strength and health.	Physical fitness awareness and program; proper diet.	Education prior to and during the senior years as to the importance of regular exercise and good nutritional habits.
		Acceptance of physical limitations.	Teaching of the normal process of aging. Seeing these limitations as a normal part of living.
			Provision of transportation for those adults who are unable to drive.
			Architectural design providing for easy accessibility in the church.
MENTAL	No decline in intelligence but a slowing in speed of response.	Mental exercise and stimulation.	Opportunities for older adults to continue in leadership roles.
	Less certainty in emergency situations.	Proper motivation to learn.	Opportunities must be provided for serious Bible study. Active learner involvement in the discovery of truth.
	Possible memory lapses.		
	Possible senility.	Faithful contact by significant others.	The senile are not to be neglected. They still need visitation and an awareness of love in their lucid moments.
PSYCHO-SOCIAL	Retirement and reduced income.	Continued usefulness.	Avenues of service to others (ex. Foster Grandparents, VISTA, etc.) in families, church, and community.
		Economic security.	Economic counseling; pre-retirement planning.
	Loneliness and bereavement. Loss of spouse and close friends. New relationships with children and grandchildren. Establishment of satisfactory living arrangements.	Comfort, and acceptance of loss. Self-acceptance. Renewed purpose. Human interaction. Role adjustment. Need to be loved and socially included.	Counseling, support, visitation. Teaching human-worth as God's creation. Teaching the purposes of later life. Fellowship groups. Intergenerational learning situations. Family couseling. The teaching of family responsibility.
SPIRITUAL	Increased awareness of personal mortality; preparation for one's eternal destiny.	Personal relationship with Christ. Continuing discipleship.	Gospel presentation. Discipleship programs.
	Sense of guilt and failure.	Life inventory and evaluation. Continued need for Christian service opportunities.	Reminiscence in counseling; evaluation and acceptance of God's love, forgiveness, and plan for the present and future. Provision of service opportunities.

Figure 1

Understanding Older Adults

THREE-STAGE MINISTRY PROGRAM

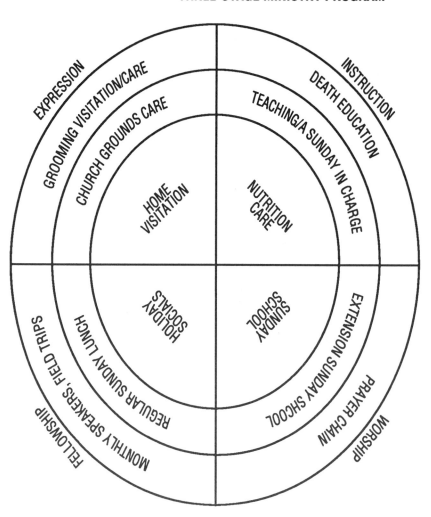

Stage 1 — Core leaders minister to the elderly.
Stage 2 — Elderly minister to each other.
Stage 3 — Elderly minister to others outside of the group.

Figure 2

"My church is the best part of my life. They put me to work for the Lord, and I'm excited." Or an older man exclaim, "When I retired, I really got busy for the Lord. Now my time is filled with useful service for Him."

Some initial steps to get started toward effective senior adult ministry are as follows:

- Determine the specific needs of senior adults in your church and community.
- Ask what activities or programs will meet their needs.
- Set realistic, attainable goals.
- Find resources in people, money, facilities, and materials necessary.

Leviticus 19:32 states, "You shall rise up before the grayheads and honor the aged, and you shall revere your God; I am the Lord" (NASB).

Let's accept the dynamic responsibility and privilege of ministry to senior adults—help them grow and serve to the glory of God.

FOR FURTHER READING*

*Also see the bibliography in chapter 18.

YOUNG ADULTS

Bellah, Mike. *Baby Boom Believers*. Wheaton, Ill.: Tyndale, 1988.

Bromley, David G., ed. *Falling from the Faith: Causes and Consequences of Religious Apostasy*. Newbury Park, Calif.: Sage, 1988.

Finzel, Hans. *Help! I'm a Baby Boomer: Battling for Christian Values Inside America's Largest Generation*. Wheaton, Ill.: Victor, 1989.

Gallup, Jr., George, and Sara Jones. *100 Questions & Answers: Religion in America*. Princeton, N.J.: Princeton Religion Research Center, 1989.

Hershey, Terry. *Young Adult Ministry*. Loveland, Colo.: Group, 1986.

MIDDLE ADULTS**

**Also see the books on baby boomers in young adults section.

Bradshaw, Charles. *You and Your Teen: A Course for Mid-Life Parents*. Elgin, Ill.: David C. Cook, 1985.

Nichols, Michael P. *Turning Forty in the Eighties: Personal Crisis, Time for Change*. New York: Simon & Schuster, 1987.

Wilson, Earl D. *Empty Nest: Life After the Kids Leave Home*. Elgin, Ill.: David C. Cook, 1986.

Wright, H. Norma. *Seasons of a Marriage*. Ventura, Calif.: Regal, 1983.

SENIOR ADULTS

Clements, William M. *Ministry with the Aging*. San Francisco: Harper & Row, 1983.

Dychtwald, Ken, and Joe Flower. *Age Wave: The Challenges and Opportunities of an Aging America*. Los Angeles: J. P. Tarcher, 1990.

Freeman, Carroll B. *The Senior Adult Years*. Nashville: Broadman, 1979.

Stafford, Tim. *As Our Years Increase*. Grand Rapids, Mich.: Zondervan, 1989.

Vogel, Linda Jane. *The Religious Education of Older Adults*. Birmingham, Ala.: Religious Education, 1984.

20

Carolyn A. Koons

Single Adults: One Is a Whole Number

Ministering to Single Adults
- **Past and present myths and realities about singleness**
- **Reasons and seasons of singleness**
- **Challenge for ministry to singles**
- **The church's goals to meet singles' needs**

For generations millions of people have expected romantic fulfillment through marriage as a God-given right. Getting married, owning a home, a recreational vehicle or maybe a vacation cabin, rearing 2.5 children, and living happily ever after became basic components of the Great American Dream. Ours was a Noah-style culture composed of couples and all the trappings of the two-by-two lifestyle. In the last three decades, however, marital patterns have changed, creating a subculture for those who go it alone. As the pendulum of marriage swings, we must recognize dramatic shifts from married to single lifestyles and deal with the resulting changes this shift is causing. As this singles subculture emerges, so do new attitudes, stereotypes, myths, and often misunderstandings.

CAROLYN A. KOONS, M.A., is dean of church relations, Azusa Pacific University, Azusa, California.

TRADITIONALLY MARRIED WORLD

Our society caters to a married lifestyle and resists attempts to change the status quo. As the singles scene takes shape, however, a contradiction of values has begun to surface. On one hand, we highly regard the values of individualism, uniqueness in thought and action, and a competitive spirit. But on the other hand we applaud conformity, group consensus, and community. For some, marriage is instrumental in fulfilling the socialization process, drawing us closer to the norm or community. Cargan and Melko, in their book *Singles: Myths and Realities*, conclude, "Thus the state of marriage is thought of as the natural order of things, and those who do not conform threaten this order; the result is that there is little room in the system for the unaccompanied person."[1] Thus the pressures and stereotypes begin.

Traditionally marriage has been viewed as a positive, "right" choice, which has subtlely created the notion that singleness is negative and a "wrong" choice. Singles often feel great pressure from society, parents, and themselves to conform to the "positive" image of marriage. Thus, the eternal search to find "the one-and-only" begins. Statements such as "I'm waiting on God for the right person" and "Marriage is God's perfect will" are proclaimed from pulpits today, heaping tremendous guilt on single individuals, affecting their self-esteem, and casting doubt on their spirituality.[2]

HISTORICAL ATTITUDES ON SINGLENESS

Single adults have been around since the beginning of mankind, but they usually constituted only 2 to 3 percent of the adult population. In the last thirty years, the percentage of singles in America has drastically risen. Since the early 1900s, society's increased awareness of singles has gradually produced a change of attitude toward unmarried people. From 1900 through the 1920s, single women—no matter what their age—were labeled "old maids," a term rarely heard today. During the 1930s and 1940s, the Depression years, single women were called "spinsters." The issue of female singleness (male singleness rarely drew this kind of interest) was attacked in several of my writings: "Does It Hurt to Be an Old Maid?", "Alarming Increase of Old Maids and Bachelors in New England," "Family Parasites: The Economic Value of the Unmarried Sister," "The Sorrowful Maiden and the Jovial Bachelor," and "There Is No Place in Heaven for Old Maids."

The 1950s and 1960s saw a turn as divorce increased in America. Articles took on more of a questioning/coaching approach: "How to Be Marriageable: Results of a Marriage Readiness Course," "A Spinster's Lot Can Be a Happy One," "When Being Single Stops Being Fun," "How to Be Human Though Single," "Study

---

1. Leonard Cargan and Matthew Milko, *Singles: Myths and Realities* (Beverly Hills, Calif.: Sage Publication, 1982).
2. Ibid.

Disputes Image of the Happy Bachelor." Lists such as "129 Ways to Get a Husband," "Six Ways of Being an Old Maid," and "Six Ways to Meet a Man" were published.

The open and oft-referred to "new morality" of the late 1960s and early 1970s unfortunately labeled singles as "swinging singles," which widened the gap between married and single adult groups further. Articles began to reflect an aggressive singles' lifestyle: "What Women Should Know About Single Men," *Bazaar's* "A to Z List on Where to Find a Man," "Humanizing the Meat Market," "Celebrate Singleness: Marriage May Be Second Best," "Movin' On—Alone," and *Newsweek's* issue "49 Million Singles Can't All Be Right."

The 1980s carried yet another image of singles. Some referred to them as the "growing" singles—hardworkers, physically active, and healthy, affluent, and introspective. The image of singles will continue to change, but it appears that singleness is here to stay. Never again will America have a 97 percent married and a 3 percent single adult population ratio.

SINGLE ADULT IDENTITY

Few men and women actually plan to be single, yet close to 65 million adults in America ascribe to the single lifestyle. For many, singleness was thrust on them by a death or divorce; they feel ostracized or branded. Others resist singleness and frantically try to alter their status. Others are teased about being single: "I can't believe you're not married yet!" And for still others, singleness is a provocative, sought-after, and flaunted lifestyle.

The American culture is a highly educated, well-informed society that understands human growth and development. Psychologists, sociologists, family therapists, and educators have been able to study human growth from conception to death. Each discipline describes growth by identifiable states, phases, and benchmarks, producing thousands of books on the topic.

Developmental theories are based on a marriage model. Traditionally in America, it has been expected that 97 percent of the population would mature, conforming for the most part to the "normal" developmental stages through high school, dating, courtship, marriage, and children. With the rise of the single phenomenon, a more than 50 percent divorce rate, and other sociological changes, these developmental patterns no longer apply to millions of never-married, divorced, or widowed adults. Stages of single adult development are not the same as developmental stages of married adults. This gap contributes to the misunderstanding, stereotypes, and myths surrounding singleness and to the growing gap between single and married adults in America.

Research on single adults and their lifestyle has not been developed in the field of family sociology, though there are a few studies dealing with divorce. Although not completely ignored by most writers on the family, singles are defined in terms of their relationship to marriage. Social psychologists are accustomed to referring to singles as "those who fail to marry" or as "those who do not make positive choices."

If singleness is discussed at all by sociologists, it is generally in terms of stereotypes and assumptions. They see singles as being hostile toward marriage or toward persons of the opposite sex; not having cut the umbilical cord from their parents; possibly being homosexual, unattractive, or having physical and psychological reasons for not finding a mate; afraid of involvement or commitment; lacking social skills for dating; having unrealistic criteria for finding a spouse; being unwilling to assume responsibility.

A divorced person is often referred to as one who failed at marriage, could not adjust, or is unable to relate. No wonder approximately 80 percent of divorced people remarry within the first two years following their first divorce.

THE NEW ADULT PHENOMENON

America is changing. We are living in a time of transition. The singles phenomenon is a large part of this change. The statistic of more than 65 million single adults is staggering and has many implications for the American culture. If the trends continue as they are, more than 50 percent of adults today will spend a significant part of their lifetime as divorced or widowed singles. One-fifth of all American families are single-parent families. There has been an increase of 80 percent in single-parent families in the past ten years. And there are more than 11 million blended families in the United States today.[3] Robert Weiss, in his book *Going It Alone,* states that "one half of all children born today can expect to spend part of their growing-up years as members of a single-parent family."[4]

Our concept of family is being redefined, reevaluated, and expanded to include singles, single parents, extended families, expanded families, and blended families. These individuals are looking for programs and ministries to assist them with the oftentime difficult journey they face.

WHY SO MANY SINGLES?

The increase in the number of single adults is a complex phenomenon, some of which is related to the individual's basic needs. Traditionally men and women have married for love, companionship, sex, mutual aid in the struggle for existence, and the desire to have children. In today's urban and industrial age, modern conveniences, career emphasis, the changing role of the family, increased divorce rate, changing lifestyles, women's rights movement, and fewer available men have made marriage less imperative as a means of providing love, aid, or children.

Though single lifestyles are often uncertain and conflicting, singles today are learning more about themselves and the world around them. As they live the single

3. *Current Population Reports,* U.S. Bureau of the Census Series (418/1988), p. 20; *U.S. News and World Report* 19 (September 1988), p. 72.
4. Robert Weiss, *Going It Alone* (New York: Harper & Row, 1981).

experience, they are able to identify three primary reasons for their current singleness: commitment to career, independence, and not having met a suitable partner.

CHALLENGES SINGLES FACE

Singleness and marriage each have rewards and disadvantages.
Advantages of single lifestyle. The first advantage of a single lifestyle is priva-
cy—being able to think and create without interruption. The second advantage
is time—having time to travel, cultivate talents, relax, entertain, be entertained.
The third advantage is freedom—being able to make independent decisions, to
form friendships, to use your time as you wish. The fourth advantage is opportunity—being able to extend borders of friendship, develop skills, and move to new
jobs and places with greater flexibility.

Advantages of married lifestyle. The first advantage of a married lifestyle is companionship—being held and loved, feeling another's presence, hearing another's voice. The second advantage is family—having children and sharing in their
care, having grandchildren as you grow older. The third advantage is help—
sharing the work, having another point of view when making decisions. The
fourth advantage is care and security—having someone to look after you, having
greater financial support.

The down side of the single lifestyle carries with it some definite struggles. These
include dealing with loneliness, a search for identity in the context of a married
society, a tendency toward or preoccupation with self, developing a pattern of
going-it-alone, and outside pressure or criticism and misunderstanding from
family and friends.

Singles list five struggles that seem to take precedence in their lives. The biggest
frustration and struggle is in being "left out" or "not included" by couples just
because a person is single. Singles want to be given leadership. They do not want
to be thrust into singles-only groups. As Britton Wood states, "Singles want to
be the church too."[5] They want to be included equally as whole, growing people.

The area of finance is difficult for some single people, especially if the single is
a parent and head of a household. Seventy-five percent of single-parent women are
on welfare in order to survive. There is no potential for two incomes. Singles
can become trapped in a "me-now" syndrome, buying and doing things for themselves. Good financial counsel is needed.[6]

Finding rewarding friendships can also be a struggle for singles. A rewarding
friendship involves sharing honesty, laughter, and crying without constant pressure to pair off in an opposite-sex relationship, or delve into questions about a
same-sex relationship. One of the biggest challenges facing the church today is to
understand the concept of community and friendship for both marrieds and singles, young and old.

5. Britton Wood, *Single Adults Want to Be the Church, Too* (Nashville: Broadman, 1977).
6. *Single Adult Ministries Journal* 4, no. 3 (January 1987): 39.

Another struggle for singles involves children, for both the custodial and non-custodial parent. Balancing work, financial pressures, and parenting—while at the same time maintaining friendships and some form of social life—is a major challenge.

Finally, singles must deal with sexual pressures and frustrations. However, so much time and energy is expended on maintaining the aforementioned areas that the sexual aspect of the singles' struggle may fall far from the top of their list. Let us remember that singles are not dead. They admit to some sexual frustration but also say that they have become "more creative and active in other ways," perhaps as a compensation for lack of sexual involvement. (It needs to be noted, however, that marriage does not preclude sexual frustrations.)

WHO ARE THE SINGLES?

It is important to understand that singles do not fall in one large group called "single adults." Today's single adult belongs to one of four different groups, each with its own subgroups, varying needs, pressure points, and social and emotional concerns.

Approximately 54 percent of today's singles are never married; 22 percent are widowed; 18 percent are divorced; and 5 percent are separated.[7] It is important to identify and understand the unique needs of each of these groups in order to minister effectively to them.

The never marrieds. Heading the list of the singles population are those who have never married: the career person, the college student, the young professional, the single missionary or priest, or the gay activist.

Stereotypes die hard. It has taken years for sociologists to reorganize the shift in the population toward singleness. These "enlightened" sociologists have at last brought an awareness of singleness into a positive light both for the professional world and to the population at large. It is true that not everyone who wants to be married will be. But it is also true that many people—more every year—are freely choosing to be part of the never-married group. This group tends to be the least understood segment of our population. Admittedly, research on the never-married individual is limited. This fact is accentuated as the Church struggles to understand and minister to this every-growing group.

Since 1970 there has been a dramatic shift in the United States' population. According to the U.S. Census Bureau, in the 1980s, women were marrying later than during any other previously recorded period of American history. The proportion of people putting off marriage in the 1980s was even greater than the increasing proportion during the 1970s. In 1985, 58.5 percent of women aged twenty to twenty-four had never married, up from 50 percent in 1980. Men have postponed marriage at least as much as women. Today individuals are postponing marriage as late as thirty-five years and older.[8]

How can we account for increase in numbers of young adults postponing mar-

7. Douglas Fagerstrom, ed., *Singles Ministry Handbook* (Wheaton, Ill.: Victor, 1988).
8. *Current Population Reports,* U.S. Bureau of the Census Series 418 (1988), p. 20.

riage and for the dramatic upward shift in the age of those who marry for the first time? Peter Stein, in his book *Single Life: Unmarried Adults in Social Context* addresses this issue by noting the following important social developments:

1. The increase in the number of women enrolled in colleges and in graduate and professional schools.
2. Expanding employment and career opportunities for women.
3. The impact of the women's movement.
4. The excess of young women at the currently "most marriageable" age, resulting in a marriage squeeze.
5. A shift in attitudes about the desirability of marriage among both college and non-college youth.
6. The increasing divorce rate, which has led many people to question the traditional appeal of marriage and family life.
7. The increasing availability and acceptability of birth control methods.

In addition, some researchers suggest that people today are moving away from marriage and family norms as these norms conflict with their potential for development and personal growth.

There are many causes behind the growing trend to never marry, and there are many individuals living within this often misunderstood segment of our society. In addition to the young singles waiting for later marriage, there are those for whom marriage is not desirable or possible. These include older singles who will never marry—either because they have not found an eligible partner or because they are satisfied with singlehood and/or are opposed to marriage. There are priests and nuns whose career choices preclude marriage. Some men and women prefer homosexual relationships to traditional marriage. And other individuals may have physical or psychological impairments that keep them from finding a mate.

Divorced singles—the formerly married. Divorce affects people of all ages, including those in their mid-to-late teens through old age, with various backgrounds, vocations, incomes, values, and religious persuasion. The intensity of their commitment to religious beliefs determines to a large extent their ability to cope with loss. The more commitment, the more resources available; hence, the more effective the coping. They are people who are "single by decree." They have been before a judge or affected by a court's decision. Lawyers and judges have been involved in their lives. These professionals usually see and treat marriage as an economic partnership rather than one motivated and controlled by love and commitment. Formerly married people, separated from once-loving relationships, are at different stages of their adjustment to loss. Those stages range anywhere between the time of divorce to time of recovery, however long the process takes. Some of these individuals are rearing children and teenagers in single-parent homes as custodial parent, and some from a distance as the noncustodial parent. This causes constant stress for some because of the continual contact with the former spouse as they comply with visitation rights.

Some individuals have been married and divorced more than once. As a result, there may be children involved from several relationships. This poses unique and challenging problems for half brothers and half sisters.

Perhaps the most important factor many formerly married people face in transition is that they wander—for the most part—in a no-man's-land without direction, searching for support, guidelines, and wisdom.

Divorce transcends all social and economic classes. It also affects people without regard to race, age, vocation, or religious persuasion. In other words, divorce can strike almost anyone. There are no proved means for predicting those who will end their marriage in a divorce settlement. A review of the divorce statistics for a number of years, however, shows us clearly that certain types of people are more likely to get a divorce than others. The results of such a survey reveals the following:

Those most likely to get divorced are: (1) those who marry young; (2) those who have more than one sexual partner prior to marriage; (3) those with less than a high school education or two or more years of graduate school (least likely to divorce are four-year college graduates); (4) women who earn $50,000 or more a year; (5) childless couples; (6) couples who have only daughters; (7) those who have been married before (50 percent divorce, 80 percent remarry, 50 percent divorce second marriage); (8) those whose parents were divorced; (9) those who lived together before getting married.[9]

The widowed. The death of a spouse is one of the most serious life crises a person faces. The immediate emotional crisis of bereavement is a critical time and must be worked through fully and carefully. During this time the church has the opportunity to minister to the many emotional and physical needs of the widowed.

Grief. The first and most obvious characteristic is grief. The grieving time can vary in length, but is a period marked by vulnerability, repressed feelings, and stress. Individuals doubt their ability to survive alone and often isolate themselves socially. There is a great need for at least one sensitive and caring friend. Each grieving person must be treated as special, unique, and respected in his or her present pain.

Fears. Fears grow and develop after the loss of a mate. Fear of the unknown, financial anxieties, and fear of being unable to cope top the list of many fears. Often with the loss of a mate is the loss of friendships they shared with other couples. This loss is accompanied by a fear of detachment, rejection, and isolation. Other fears include: the fear of meeting the opposite sex, fear of violence at home or on the street, fear of making decisions.

Sex and intimacy needs. While sex and intimacy needs face widowed people, they also have a strong need for a listening friend, someone who understands them and

9. Carolyn Koons and Michael Anthony, *Single Adult Passages: Uncharted Territories* (Grand Rapids: Baker, 1991).

will provide comfort. After a period of time, they may become sexually vulnerable and quick to remarry. Most who marry within eighteen months of their spouse's death later divorce.

Self-pity. The recovery period for widowed persons often involves a season of self-pity. This is seeing one's self as deprived or less fortunate than others. This characteristic plays into the person's memory reconstruction. They forget the good and recall the bad, often blaming others for not understanding them. The antidote for self-pity is to share self with someone else in need.

Depression. To some degree, depression is to be expected and is part of the mourning process (and can be a normal part of the recovery process). If boredom and a lack of growth stimuli become part of the widow/er's lifestyle, depression can become debilitating. There must be a plan for compensation during the "down times."

Anger and hostility. Although anger and hostility are normal for the recovering widow/er, these feelings can become harmful. As the widow/er views the deceased as having "escaped," he may develop great resentment. He may also resent God for "snatching" the loved one away. These feelings of resentment engender defensive stances that affect many areas of widowed persons' lives as they face new responsibilities and situations.

Money. Most people think of money in terms of net worth, but it may also be a significant factor in a person's self-worth. The formerly married often have difficulty with finances. Income changes and so do expenses. Care needs to be exercised in spending habits and the use of credit. Provision of income must be determined. Insurance needs and budgets must be reevaluated. There is a great necessity for objective financial counsel.

Loneliness. With the right strategy, loneliness can be used to advantage. First the widow/er needs to separate loneliness from worthiness. Next, he needs to begin the journey back to self-acceptance, self-responsibility, and self-assertiveness. In a society that honors achievement and confidence, the widow/er may sense that he has been shunned or sidestepped. This contributes further to feelings of worthlessness and isolation during the slow, quiet months of mourning.

The separated single. Separated people find identity particularly difficult. Some view them as married, whereas others view them as single. The truth is that the separated person is married but must now function as a single. It is because of this that separated people often seek the company of other singles and find their way into singles groups.

It is important that we know what the separated person is experiencing. For him, the feeling of loss is an every-moment experience. The person feels guilty about his part in the separation and is angry with himself, the spouse, or both. He is frustrated about what to do as well as how to cope with the added practical responsibilities that have come.

Along with the need to blame someone for their situation, separated people fear the future because of changes and uncertainties. They worry that finances will become a major problem. If children are involved the parent must explain the situation to them, then deal with the parent/child relationship in new and different ways.

We also need to know how other people are treating the separated person. Parents of separated persons often lack understanding and can further devastate their children. Friends may be incapable of coping with the separated person and his problems and therefore end up rejecting the person. Co-workers or colleagues frequently lack sensitivity and are unable to be supportive. All this results in the separated person feeling even more alone and alienated, opening still further the need for him to be under a caring ministry.

Anxiety and fear prevent people from being open to God's plan for them. Therefore, an atmosphere of acceptance where love and forgiveness can be experienced is much needed.

Separated people also need the opportunity to express their feelings honestly. This can be provided by personal counsel and/or in small groups where a nonthreatening atmosphere is evident.

The separated person needs godly, objective counsel without manipulation or control. Counsel that is carefully and prayerfully given can bring excellent results. Practical counsel on marriage, finances, child care, job placement, housing, relationships, and more is needed.

THE CHURCH'S MINISTRY TO SINGLE ADULTS

Fulfilling the Great Commission through ministry to single adults is a task every church in America can address.

Jim Smoke has addressed singles ministries across America since the early 1980s. Even though the overall singles ministry in the local church is being accepted and even maturing in most ministries, Smoke sees a number of things that need to take place.[10]

1. The ministry to single adults must receive total church recognition to the point of being "as important as" any other ministry in the church. It is no longer an experiment. It is a full blown ministry in much the same way as youth ministry.

2. Singles ministry must be born out of the needs of its people. As the needs change and the problems compound, the ministry must explore new ways of meeting those needs.

3. To exist as a recognized ministry in the church, both facilities and budgeted monies must be invested. This can no longer be a "broom closet" ministry. Real ministries cost real money.

4. The church at large must be educated about the singles culture. They are no longer a minority group. In many churches they far outnumber the nonsingles. Setting aside old images and developing a new understanding of single adults takes time.

10. Ibid.

5. The church of the 1990s will have to wrestle with new understanding on how it presents Scriptural teaching on divorce and remarriage. Archaic rules from another era will have to undergo change if the church is to minister to changing structure.

6. The ministry of divorce recovery must be expanded wherever it is taught. It must also include programs of recovery for all children. Children of single adults cannot be put on a shelf while their parents are involved in adult programs and events. A well-balanced single adult program includes children. Recovery from divorce, for both parents and children, is a two-year process. Programs, workshops, counseling must extend over that period of time.

7. An extended arm of any singles ministry is preparing its people for remarriage and helping them to re-form community with other remarrieds. The blended family is on the increase in our culture. It is no longer enough to just heal the hurts of a past marriage. Single people must also be educated and equipped for any new marriage.

8. The religious press must start reporting the growth, complexities, struggles, and success of the single adult person. It is sad that single stereotypes are still alive and well in religious publications.

9. The ministry to single adults will always be a different ministry in the church because it is a ministry born of people in transition. It could easily and often be described as a "group of men and women in transition looking for stabilization." Some church ministries can be set in cement for they seldom change. This will never be true of a singles ministry. It is always more difficult to work with people processing changes in their life.

10. A single adult ministry that takes itself seriously will help its people wrestle with the problems confronting the single parent's household: lack of funds, low paying jobs, insufficient child care structures, fatigue, lack of quality parenting times, and lack of affordable housing.

11. A quality singles ministry in the future will offer full education courses each year that will help their people acquire the knowledge that will improve their lives. A half-day seminar once or twice a year will not get the job done.

12. A singles ministry is not a church-provided baby sitting service for a group of adults while they stagger through singleness. It is a ministry that says, "Tell us your needs and show us how we can help you be a better and growing person."

13. Single adults in the 90s must be allowed to integrate more effectively into all aspects of church life. Two examples are: single women in leadership, and singles for church board position. The "get married and then you can serve" mentality must be abandoned.

14. Singles ministries of the 90s must incorporate the three stages of caring ministry: emergency room, extended care, and return to leadership what you have received.

15. Singles ministries in the 90s in metro areas must find ways to minister to the homosexual single adult.

16. If the church does not effectively minister to singles in the next decade, the ministry might well become a parachurch ministry.

17. The greatest field for evangelism in the 90s will be the single adult ministry.

Any maturing ministry must stay ahead of itself. This is done by looking down the road and reading both needs and trends. If half of our population today is composed of single adults, we can no longer treat them as if they were only 10 percent of the population.

For many years, single adult ministry has been hidden in the shadows of the church. Today the needs, concerns, and demands of the single adult community are in plain view.

SINGLE ADULT NEEDS

Although each church must determine the unique needs of its own single adults, there are some basic needs that all singles face. These basic needs can form a foundation for ministry design but should not be the only basis for programming since your church may have critical needs in addition to these. You will need to know what kind of single adults you have in your church since each of the four categories of single adults (i.e., never married, divorced, separated, and widowed) will have different needs. Obviously, the needs of the single never married are very different from divorced single parents. Designing a ministry to single adults at your church must start with a survey to determine what kinds of singles are involved. The following chart may help illustrate the process:

The biblical model for designing a ministry is always to identify the needs first and then plan a strategy to meet those needs through the resources that are available. No church can do it all, because the needs of single adults are as diverse as the different types of singles that make up the group. Some churches are smaller with limited resources, unable to meet all the needs of diverse groups represented in the church today. But for those churches who have identified a group of single adults to whom they want to minister, then every effort should be taken to ensure quality programming by leadership that is trained to share the responsibilities of the ministry with the single adults themselves.

SPECIAL NEEDS OF THE DIVORCED ADULT

Bill Flanagan, in his book *The Ministry of Divorce Recovery,* identifies some of the special needs of the divorced person.[11] He writes that "people going through this difficult process feel a tremendous sense of alienation, a loss of self-esteem and a monumental sense of guilt, failure and rejection." They also are accustomed to feelings of burnout as they assume added responsibilities in the area of their personal finances, children, and other household responsibilities. Separated and divorced people most often feel an overwhelming sense of loneliness, as if they were the only person going through this crisis. They tend to think that no one understands what has happened or how they feel.

Jim Smoke, in his book *Growing Through Divorce,* offers helpful insight into the recovery process.[12] These keys to divorce recovery have been beneficial to single adults across the nation.

11. Ibid.
12. Jim Smoke, *Growing Through Divorce* (Eugene, Oreg.: Harvest House, 1976).

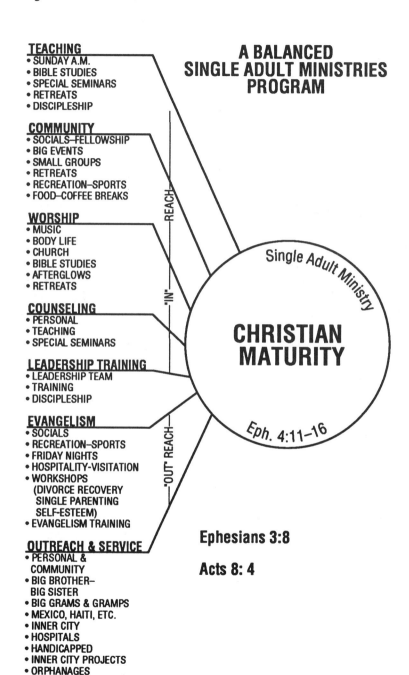

A BALANCED SINGLE ADULT MINISTRIES PROGRAM

TEACHING
- SUNDAY A.M.
- BIBLE STUDIES
- SPECIAL SEMINARS
- RETREATS
- DISCIPLESHIP

COMMUNITY
- SOCIALS–FELLOWSHIP
- BIG EVENTS
- SMALL GROUPS
- RETREATS
- RECREATION–SPORTS
- FOOD–COFFEE BREAKS

WORSHIP
- MUSIC
- BODY LIFE
- CHURCH
- BIBLE STUDIES
- AFTERGLOWS
- RETREATS

COUNSELING
- PERSONAL
- TEACHING
- SPECIAL SEMINARS

LEADERSHIP TRAINING
- LEADERSHIP TEAM
- TRAINING
- DISCIPLESHIP

EVANGELISM
- SOCIALS
- RECREATION–SPORTS
- FRIDAY NIGHTS
- HOSPITALITY-VISITATION
- WORKSHOPS
  (DIVORCE RECOVERY
  SINGLE PARENTING
  SELF-ESTEEM)
- EVANGELISM TRAINING

OUTREACH & SERVICE
- PERSONAL &
  COMMUNITY
- BIG BROTHER–
  BIG SISTER
- BIG GRAMS & GRAMPS
- MEXICO, HAITI, ETC.
- INNER CITY
- HOSPITALS
- HANDICAPPED
- INNER CITY PROJECTS
- ORPHANAGES

"REACH"

"IN"

Single Adult Ministry

CHRISTIAN MATURITY

Eph. 4:11–16

"OUT REACH"

Ephesians 3:8

Acts 8: 4

1. Finding and experiencing forgiveness
2. Letting go
3. Getting the ex-spouse in focus
4. Assuming responsibilities for myself
5. Assuming responsibilities for my children
6. Assuming responsibilities for my future

BALANCED PROGRAMMING

Once the church has identified the unique needs of single adults and has come to a realization of the issues involved in such a ministry, it is imperative to think through the philosophy of the ministry design. No successful ministry just happens. It requires forethought and preparation. The following chart helps illustrate the components of a balanced single adult ministry and the various program activities for each component.

The balanced program for a healthy single adult ministry requires both "outreach" and "inreach" elements that include: evangelism, outreach activities, teaching, building community, worship, counseling, and leadership training. It is not expected that every church will be equipped to fulfill all of these program elements, but they are presented to help churches develop a vision for what their ministries can include.

A balanced program is the goal. Outreach activities will help the single adults keep a focus on their calling to be lights in the world. The inreach activities will help fulfill the mandate of Ephesians 4:11-16 to build up and equip the members of the Body of Christ for ministry. Both must be done to have a healthy ministry to single adults.

CONCLUSION

The challenge for singles themselves and all the Body of Christ is to understand the unique journey of the single adult and the impact and importance of the contribution of singles to the marketplace, home, and church. Though we have a long way to go in the understanding of the single adult and single adult ministry, we have come a long way since its beginning in the 1970s, and today it is one of the fastest growing ministries in the church.

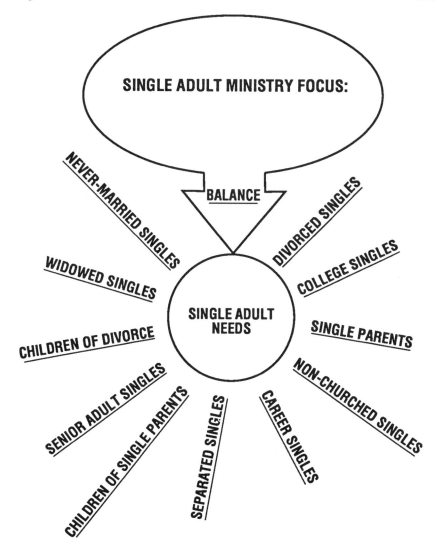

FOR FURTHER READING

GENERAL

Fagerstrom, Douglas L., ed. *Singles Ministry Handbook*. Wheaton, Ill.: Victor, 1988.
Hershey, Terry. *Young Adult Ministry*. Loveland, Colo.: Group, 1986.
Welsh, Krista Swan, ed. *Successful Single Adult Ministry: It Can Happen in Your Church*. Cincinnati: Standard, 1987.

NEVER MARRIED

Smith, Harold Ivan. *Positively Single*. Wheaton, Ill.: Victor, 1986.
Smith, M. Blaine. *Should I Get Married?* Downers Grove, Ill.: InterVarsity, 1990.
Swindoll, Luci. *Wide My World, Narrow My Bed*. Portland, Oreg.: Multnomah, 1982.

DIVORCED

Bustanoby, Andre. *But I Didn't Want a Divorce*. Grand Rapids: Zondervan, 1978.
Hershey, Terry. *Beginning Again: Life After a Relationship Ends*. Nashville: Thomas Nelson, 1986.
Morgan, Richard Lyon. *Is There Life After Divorce in the Church?* Atlanta: John Knox, 1985.
Richards, Sue Poorman, and Stanley Hagemeyer. *Ministry to the Divorced*. Grand Rapids: Zondervan, 1986.
Small, Dwight Hervey. *Remarriage and God's Renewing Grace: A Positive Biblical Ethic for Divorced Christians*. Grand Rapids: Baker, 1986.
Smoke, Jim. *Growing Through Divorce*. Eugene, Oreg.: Harvest House, 1976.

WIDOWED

Kubler-Ross, Elizabeth. *On Death and Dying*. New York: Macmillan, 1970.
Manning, Doug. *Don't Take My Grief Away*. San Francisco: Harper & Row, 1984.
Marshall, Catherine. *Beyond Ourselves*. Lincoln, Va.: Chosen, 1984.

SINGLE PARENTING

Bustanoby, Andre. *Being a Single Parent.* Grand Rapids: Zondervan, 1985.
Smith, Virginia Watts. *The Single Parent.* Revised edition. Old Tappan, N.J.: Revell, 1983.
Weiss, Robert S. *Going It Alone.* New York: Harper & Row, 1981.

21

Julie A. Hight

Exceptional Persons

TEACHING THE EXCEPTIONAL PERSON
- **All persons, regardless of exceptionality, have the same basic spiritual needs**
- **Churches have a responsibility to minister to exceptional persons**
- **Build self esteem in these individuals by providing opportunities for success**
- **Understand the abilities and limitations of the various areas of exceptionality**
- **Recognize that a person's mental age (or functioning level) may not correspond to chronological age**
- **Allow the disabled and the gifted to utilize their God-given spiritual gifts to help complete the Body of Christ**

In recent years, an awareness of the needs of exceptional persons has grown. As a result, churches have become more accessible—not only in structure but also in attitude. In addition to welcoming exceptional persons into the church, Christian educators are realizing the need to provide these individuals with appropriate and meaningful biblical instruction. When planning for the instruction of exceptional persons, educators are faced with the task of preparing a program that will meet the needs of those who are academically gifted as well as

JULIE A. HIGHT, B.A., is a free-lance writer and special education consultant living in Carmel, Indiana.

the needs of individuals who have disabling conditions, which may range from minimal to severe.

This chapter will examine the two diverse segments of exceptional persons—the disabled and the gifted. Although it may appear that the disabled and the gifted are a contradiction in terms, the concept of preparing an appropriate Christian education program for exceptional persons—regardless of the exceptionality—has similar characteristics. The various areas of exceptionality include persons who are recognized to be mentally impaired, physically disabled, sensory impaired, learning disabled, behaviorally or emotionally impaired, and academically gifted. These groups represent a large percentage of the population referred to as exceptional; however, additional disabling conditions and other types of giftedness exist. In the field of education, "a child is considered educationally exceptional if his deviation is of such kind and degree that it interferes with his development under ordinary classroom procedures and necessitates special education, either in conjunction with the regular class or in a special class or school, for his maximum development."[1] Churches today are faced with the opportunity and the responsibility of providing a Christian education to this diverse group of people.

NEEDS OF EXCEPTIONAL PERSONS

In an examination of exceptional learners, it is important to focus on the needs of these individuals rather than on the labels that often limit them. The following needs are common to everyone, not just exceptional persons: (1) the need to be loved and accepted; (2) the need to be challenged and successful; (3) the opportunity to know Christ as Savior; (4) the opportunity to grow spiritually in a consistent, loving church atmosphere; (5) the need to be needed. Everyone desires to have a purpose in life, knowing that they can make a contribution. What better place to fulfill these needs than in the church?

DEFINITIONS AND CHARACTERISTICS OF EXCEPTIONAL PERSONS

Although many needs of exceptional persons are similar, the various areas of exceptionality can be understood only when carefully defined and examined. The following definitions and characteristics are divided into two groups: disabling conditions and academic giftedness.

These areas of exceptionality focus on individuals whose functioning levels either mentally, physically, or emotionally fall below the "norm." They are often referred to as disabled, handicapped, impaired, or challenged. Specifically, "'Disability" means that one or more things that most people can do, a disabled person can't do as easily, or sometimes, at all. It's important to remember that a

---

1. Samuel A. Kirk, *Educating Exceptional Children*, 2d ed. (Boston: Houghton Mifflin, 1972), p. 5.

disability is almost never 'total' and usually affects a surprisingly narrow range of activity."[2]

DEFINING THE DISABILITIES

MENTAL IMPAIRMENT/HANDICAP/RETARDATION

According to the American Association on Mental Deficiency, "Mental retardation refers to significant subaverage general intellectual functioning existing concurrently with deficits in adaptive behavior and manifested during the developmental period." In more simple terms, the ability to learn and the capacity for putting learning to use is limited. Mentally impaired individuals have not stopped learning and growing—they are only slowed in their development.

General characteristics. Although mentally handicapped individuals are unique, several characteristics are common: deficits in memory and attention spans, additional physical or sensory handicaps, and delays in language and other areas of development. In addition, low tolerance to frustration, poor motor control, possible epileptic seizures, and interests that correspond to their mental age—not chronological age—often accompany this disability. More specifically, mental impairments can be divided into three functioning levels: educable mentally handicapped; trainable mentally handicapped; and severe or custodial mentally handicapped. These levels relate directly to the degree of retardation and corresponding abilities. Within each of these levels a wide range of abilities occur.

Educable (mildly) mentally handicapped. Educable mentally handicapped individuals constitute the largest percentage of the mentally impaired population— 84 percent. Academically, ability levels range from approximately second to sixth grade; however, specific functioning levels differ according to the individual. Socially, the needs of mildly mentally handicapped persons reflect those of their "able-bodied" peers. As adults, they live and work in the community, and are not easily identified as retarded. Spiritual needs of the mildly impaired population are similar to those of other individuals; however, the ability to grasp spiritual concepts is dependent on mental age or functioning level. For all persons, the Holy Spirit can minister and teach far beyond what statistics may dictate. Churches can provide an atmosphere of love and acceptance, guiding these individuals into a personal relationship with the Lord.

Trainable (moderately) mentally handicapped. Trainable mentally handicapped individuals constitute 13 percent of the mentally impaired population, and generally demonstrate more noticeable and severe characteristics. Academically, the expected achievement level ranges from kindergarten to second grade. Again, this estimated functioning level is based on numerous factors that can increase or decrease actual learning ability. In general, the focus of learning for moderately

2. Stephen Monjar, "What Do You Say After You See They're Disabled?" (The Rehabilitation Institute of Chicago, July 1983).

impaired persons is on functional skills: social, self-help, communication, and academic survival. Socially, behavior management is a priority. In many situations, these persons' behavior and interests correspond with their mental age or functioning level rather than their chronological age. But because behavior that is appropriate from a five to seven year old is not acceptable from an adult, often moderately handicapped persons demonstrate inappropriate social behaviors and must be consistently reinforced with socially acceptable ones. As adults, the functional skills learned will have a direct influence on the independence of lifestyle. Many of these individuals will be able to perform semiskilled work under supervised conditions in a sheltered workshop. Others may achieve competitive employment outside of the workshop environment. Spiritually, they need exposure to Sunday school and church programs. These individuals have the capacity to understand and can be taught right from wrong. Spiritual truths must be taught on a concrete level and at the correct mental age.

Severe or custodial (profoundly) mentally handicapped. Severe or custodial mentally handicapped individuals constitute 3 percent of the mentally impaired population, and are the most severely disabled. Physical handicaps and seizures are prevalent. Academic skills are minimal, and training focuses on language and motor development. Socially, a variety of maladaptive behaviors have to be consistently managed and redirected. Some individuals can learn basic skills and handle minimal self-help care. These persons often live in an institutional or group home setting and require continual care and supervision. Regardless of severity of impairment, the Holy Spirit can minister and teach these individuals. Although the spiritual understanding of persons who are profoundly mentally handicapped may not be known, the Holy Spirit can reveal to them the love of Christ through persons who love and care for them.

PHYSICAL DISABILITIES

> A physically handicapped individual is one who has a physical disability resulting from a neurological impairment (such as cerebral palsy or epilepsy), an orthopedic impairment (such as brittle bones or arthritis), or other health impairments (such as heart disease or asthma). The degree of involvement ranges from minimal afflictions to severe, crippling afflictions that force an individual to be totally sedentary.[3]

General characteristics. As with all persons, no two physically challenged individuals are alike. The various handicapping conditions are as diverse as the degree of severity accompanying them. Most physical impairments are visible, identified by special equipment necessary for mobility, such as wheelchairs, braces, or artificial limbs, or by an awkward manner of movement.

Academically, the physically disabled should not be confused with the mentally handicapped. The functioning of the body does not determine the ability of the

3. Joni and Friends, *All God's Children* (Woodland Hills, Calif.: Joni and Friends, 1981).

mind. Do not assume that persons who are physically challenged are mentally retarded. However, some physical handicaps are accompanied by a degree of retardation. Unless informed otherwise, presume that the mental abilities of these persons are not affected. An understanding of abilities and limitations is critical when preparing any Bible teaching or classroom activity.

Socially, persons with physical challenges need reassurance and stability—not overprotection. Awareness and acceptance of their needs and abilities is a priority. Often those with physical disabilities have been excluded from full participation in many facets of life. Churches offer a wonderful opportunity for growth when they are accessible to individuals who are physically challenged.

Spiritual needs are similar to those of their "able-bodied" peers. God sees past the outside packaging to the spiritual needs of the heart; therefore, churches have a responsibility to share the gospel with the disabled and provide opportunities for their spiritual growth. In addition, worship and fellowship are critical for all believers, including those with disabilities. Another area often overlooked by the "able-bodied" is that of ministry. Regardless of physically limiting conditions, all believers are given a spiritual gift or gifts for the completion of the Body of Christ. Unless physically handicapped persons are allowed to use their spiritual gift(s), the Body is incomplete. Not only do churches need to reach out and minister to the physically challenged, but the disabled need to utilize their talents and gifts to minister within the Body of Christ.

SENSORY IMPAIRMENTS

When one or more of the modalities by which stimulation and learning occur have been damaged, a partial deficiency or complete inability to receive data through that sense avenue results. These include: visual (sense of seeing), auditory (sense of hearing), kinesthetic (sense of feeling emotions), tactile (sense of touch), olfactory (sense of smell), and gustatorial (sense of taste) modalities. This section will focus on the two primary modes of learning—auditory and visual.

Deaf. Those in whom the sense of hearing is nonfunctional for the ordinary purposes of life are considered deaf. This general group is made up of two distinct classes determined by the time the loss of hearing occurred. These include: the congenitally deaf—those who were born deaf—and the adventitiously deaf—those who were born with normal hearing but in whom the sense of hearing became nonfunctional later in life through illness or accident.

Hard of hearing. Those in whom the sense of hearing—although defective—is functional with or without a hearing aid are considered hard of hearing.[4] Hearing impairments can affect one or both ears. The degree of impairment ranges from minimal to severe loss. Outwardly no obvious markers, such as a

4. Committee on Nomenclature, Conference of Executives of American Schools for the Deaf, 1938, *American Annals of the Deaf*, p. 83.

wheelchair or braces, exist that indicate the presence of a disabling condition. Frequently hearing impaired individuals are lonely and frustrated because of the tremendous isolation and barriers created by their disability. Helen Keller once stated, "Blindness separates an individual from things, but deafness separates an individual from people."

Academic learning is affected by several factors. Primarily, the onset of the hearing loss is a major concern. The time in life the hearing loss occurred indicates whether the hearing impaired persons had an opportunity to develop any language or speech skills. Understandably, the earlier the age of onset, the more difficult the education process. Churches contemplating a class or program for hearing impaired persons must realize that participation is only possible through situations that minimize the barriers: an interpreter for worship services, studies, and other special events, and curricular materials appropriate for the deaf.

As previously stated, hearing impaired persons often feel isolated and lonely. They are frequently misunderstood and appear to be unfriendly. The communication barrier results in feelings of rejection and frustration. Hearing impaired persons are the silent majority. Various studies indicate that only 5 to 8 percent of the hearing population can communicate proficiently with the deaf and hard of hearing. This figure is indicative of the degree of isolation that must be experienced by persons with hearing disabilities. In addition, not all hearing impaired persons can speech read (read lips), which makes communication more difficult. Only through education and understanding will many of the bridges separating the hearing population and the hearing impaired be overcome.

According to *Webster's New Collegiate Dictionary*, "to communicate means to impart, to convey knowledge of or information about; make known." It is the responsibility of our churches to communicate the love of Jesus Christ regardless of the method or the type of language used.[5]

Blind. Those individuals who cannot read print but who need instruction in braille are considered blind.

Visually impaired. Those persons who have lost some vision but can still learn to read print are considered visually impaired.[6] An estimated 6.4 million persons in the United States have some kind of visual impairment—that is, have trouble seeing even with corrective lenses. Of these, 1.7 million are severely impaired, which means that they are either "legally blind" or that they function as if they were "legally blind" even though their vision does not fall into that definition.[7]

Persons who are blind or visually impaired are inconvenienced, but not incapable. These individuals can participate in most activities when necessary minor adaptations have been made.

Education relies heavily on the sense of sight. Individuals who are blind or

5. Robert E. Clark, Joanne Brubaker, and Roy B. Zuck, eds., *Childhood Education in the Church*, rev. ed. (Chicago: Moody, 1986), p. 169.
6. Kirk, p. 293.
7. Joni and Friends, *All God's Children*, p. 64.

visually impaired lack the learning experiences that depend on that sense. Unless there are multiple handicaps involved, however, these individuals should participate in the full range of education programs within the church.

Socially, the blind or visually impaired may appear to be aloof or uninterested. Without the sense of sight, they cannot react to others' facial expressions. They also may have a tendency to hold their heads down or tilted forward. This behavior is a result of their disability, not a barometer of interest in an activity or program.

Visually handicapped persons need to experience the love and acceptance of Jesus Christ. Christian educators can provide an opportunity for growth and enrichment through biblical instruction. These individuals can apply the spiritual truths acquired and minister to others. Many possibilities for ministry require only spiritual insight—not physical sight.

LEARNING DISABILITIES

Children with special learning disabilities exhibit a disorder in one or more of the basic psychological processes involved in using spoken or written language. These may be manifested in disorders of listening, thinking, talking, reading, writing, spelling, or arithmetic. Learning disabilities do not include problems that are due primarily to visual, hearing, or motor handicaps, to mental retardation, emotional disturbance, or to environmental disadvantage.[8]

General characteristics. Children and adults with learning disabilities vary in their intellectual level. Some may be labeled as gifted in intelligence, whereas others may be considered below average. It is difficult to ascribe a group of characteristics to these individuals because the difference in functioning levels and abilities are so diverse. It is not uncommon for persons to be disabled in the area of reading or math yet be extremely gifted in a nonacademic area of functioning.

Research, which is going on all over the world, indicates that from 5 to 20 percent of the school population may have undetected disabilities serious enough to affect learning. Studies also show that more than 70 percent of juvenile delinquents have reading and related problems, and a large number of referrals to mental health clinics had troubles that started with failure in school.[9]

Low self-esteem is a common problem for learning in disabled children and adults. When children realize they've failed to meet their parents' and teachers' expectations, they feel inferior. As adults they may have adapted to their specific learning problems, yet past failures in school may cause a continual feeling of low self-worth. Many learning disabled adults view their school years as a time of

8. National Advisory Committee on Handicapped Children, *Special Education for Handicapped Children: First Annual Report* (Washington, D.C.: U.S. Department of Health, Education, and Welfare, January 31, 1968), p. 4.
9. Ruth D. Rowan, *Helping Children with Learning Disabilities* (Nashville: Abingdon, 1977), p. 13.

frustration and anguish. The emotional scars of living with the idea of being slow or stupid are difficult to overcome.

Christian educators can be instrumental in expressing the love and acceptance of Christ to the learning disabled. By demonstration, these individuals can realize that God made no mistake in His creation of them. Despite the difficulties, learning problems should not keep persons from ministering or participating in church programs. The only requirement necessary is that the atmosphere of our churches be one that fosters self-worth and acceptance because of God's great love for all of His children.

BEHAVIORAL / EMOTIONAL DISORDERS

A deviation from age-appropriate behavior that significantly interferes with the child's own growth and development and/or the lives of others is considered a behavioral/emotional disorder.[10]

General characteristics. Individuals who have been identified as having a behavioral or emotional disorder are regarded with apprehension, and are not easily welcomed into our churches. Lack of understanding and acceptance is the significant cause of this attitude. Failure to educate church leaders and congregations on the causes of these disorders results in fear and rejection. Among the causes of behavioral and emotional problems are physical and sexual abuse, broken homes, and extreme criticism. In addition, studies have shown that parental inconsistencies in discipline or their rejection of or hostility toward their children are positively correlated with conduct disorders.

Children with behavioral or emotional disorders often grow up to be adults with similar disorders, only to a greater degree. For those persons who exhibit severely unacceptable behaviors or criminal tendencies, confinement to residential institutions, juvenile detention facilities, or prison may be necessary. Churches need to minister to this group of individuals who so desperately yearn to experience God's unconditional love and acceptance with understanding and love.

DEFINING GIFTEDNESS

Educators have various opinions as to what identifies gifted individuals. There is also discussion as to what specific abilities—in addition to strict academic giftedness—should be included in the identification of the gifted population. The degree of proficiency in the areas of art, music, mechanics, and many others are frequently used in determining the gifted population.

10. Kirk, p. 389.

GIFTEDNESS

One who shows consistently remarkable performance in any worthwhile line of endeavor is gifted. Thus, this definition includes not only the intellectually gifted but also those who show promise in music, the graphic arts, creative writing, dramatics, mechanical skills, and social leadership.[11]

According to Herbert B. Neff, the gifted person is "one whose performance, or potential to perform, in worthwhile human endeavors requiring a comparatively high degree of intellectual abstraction and/or creative imagination is consistently remarkable."[12]

GENERAL CHARACTERISTICS

No two gifted individuals are alike; however, certain characteristics distinguish them from other persons. As children, they learn basic skills faster and require less practice. Concentration and attention spans are maintained for longer periods of time. Reading begins earlier, accompanied by greater comprehension skills. Many additional characteristics evidence themselves in gifted children, particularly relating to social and emotional development.

Academically, gifted individuals need to be challenged on the appropriate functioning level. Nothing contributes to dissatisfaction in Sunday school classes as rapidly as lessons that do not adequately meet the students' functioning level. When gifted children are placed in a classroom with age level peers, it may be necessary to supplement their program with more challenging projects. Teacher awareness and cooperation is essential to the success of these students.

Spiritually these individuals tend to understand abstract theological concepts at a much younger age. They are sensitive to and can translate their spiritual awareness into appropriate conduct.

It is the local church's responsibility to make adequate provisions for the Christian education of gifted children. In the average-size church, the number of gifted children will be small, and, as a result, they may constitute an overlooked minority.[13]

The God-given abilities and talents of this exceptional group must be conserved and developed through special Christian education.[14]

---

11. *Education for the Gifted: Fifty-Seventh Yearbook of the National Society for the Study of Education* (Chicago: U. of Chicago, 1958), 2:19.
12. Herbert B. Neff, *Meaning Religious Experiences for the Bright or Gifted Child* (New York: Association, 1968), p. 29.
13. Clark, Brubaker, and Zuck, p. 220.
14. Ibid., p. 221.

METHODS FOR TEACHING EXCEPTIONAL PERSONS

Although special training is not necessary to teach exceptional persons, the following guidelines are helpful for instructing these individuals. The following helps are divided into two categories: the disabled and the gifted.

HELPS FOR TEACHING CHALLENGED PERSONS

1. *Success.* Structure classroom situations and programs to provide successful experiences.
2. *Simplify.* Teach concepts at a concrete level. Abstract concepts confuse and frustrate.
3. *Repetition.* Truths are likely to be retained when students are required to repeat them often.
4. *Example.* Teach students by example, relating concepts to their lives and needs.
5. *Senses.* Employ as many senses as possible when teaching—sight, hearing, feeling, touch, smell, and taste. Remember, when one modality is impaired, the intact senses must be used to teach and reinforce a concept.
6. *Expectations.* Always let students know what is expected of them. This decreases the amount of behavior problems and increases opportunities for success.
7. *Consistency.* Only through consistent love and discipline can these individuals realize the unconditional love God has for them.

In addition, many special learners are easily distracted; therefore, prepare a classroom with minimal distractions. To minimize inappropriate behaviors or behavior problems, teachers should be consistent in attendance. Frequent changes in staff and classroom routine become disruptions that lead to feelings of instability and insecurity.

HELPS FOR TEACHING ACADEMICALLY GIFTED PERSONS

Traditional methods are not adequate when teaching gifted students. These individuals learn through exploration and an opportunity for "hands on" participation. The following ten categories of creative methods may serve as avenues of learning for gifted persons:

> (1) art (painting, clay modeling, etc.); (2) writing; (3) drama (pantomime, role playing, picture posing); (4) group vocals; (5) interviewing (Biblical and contemporary persons); (6) music; (7) map study; (8) construction (tabernacle, Palestinian home, etc.); (9) learning games and puzzles; and (10) research (field trips, using resource books and visual aids).[15]

15. Ibid., p. 217.

A variety of teaching methods and activities provide an optimal learning environment for the gifted; however, teachers are the key figures in the Christian education of gifted students. "The best teacher for gifted children will not necessarily be the most learned and educated, but the one who has the ability to stimulate the gifted student to maximum achievement."[16]

PLANNING FOR SPECIAL EDUCATION MINISTRIES IN THE CHURCH

Christian special education is an area of ministry that is increasing within local churches. As a result of widespread public awareness, churches are realizing the need to open their doors to the disabled. In similar manner, the educational needs of academically gifted children are beginning to be more frequently addressed in Sunday school programs. Regardless of the exceptionality that prompts the need for a particular ministry, preparation is a major factor in developing any special program. The following points are basic guidelines in the planning and implementation of a special education ministry.

DETERMINE THE NEED

The initial step of determining the need is critical to the success of a ministry. Initiating a program may be a direct result of an immediate need within the church; however, church-wide surveys are used to identify areas of concern that could ultimately lead to the development of a special ministry. A program cannot exist if no persons are available to fill the classrooms.

OBTAIN SUPPORT FROM CHURCH LEADERS

Supportive leadership is essential to the success of any ministry. Without church leadership support, a new ministry will have difficulty finding acceptance from church members. Please note that leadership support does not include planning and implementing the new program. Pastors and other church leaders are often overloaded with responsibilities and cannot be expected to participate actively in the actual development and implementation of a program of this nature. Yet their support and encouragement is a fundamental element in the overall success of a ministry to exceptional persons.

DEVELOP A PLAN OF ACTION

A plan of action is dependent on the results of the congregational survey and the nature and extent of the ministry to be developed. After the leadership gives its support to the program, various steps are necessary to begin implementation. These include: (1) informing and educating the congregation about the new ministry and requesting prayer support in all aspects of its development;

16. Ibid., p. 219.

(2) prayerfully seeking persons who are gifted teachers to assume teaching and classroom responsibilities; (3) taking initial steps to secure the proper building facilities and equipment necessary for successfully implementing the program; and (4) informing local social service agencies, schools, and group homes that a special ministry is beginning.

In providing a program for exceptional persons, we also create an opportunity for ministry to the families of those individuals. Often families are excluded from worship and fellowship because churches are not adequately prepared to meet the spiritual, education, physical, and emotional needs of challenged persons. As a result, they may experience feelings of isolation and loneliness. Churches who provide for the needs of the disabled open the door for the entire family to participate in the life of the Body of Christ.

SUMMARY

Establishing a special education ministry is not a simple, one-step process; it requires planning and perseverance. This kind of program is not for those who easily become weary or lack commitment. On the contrary, ministry to exceptional persons requires an enthusiasm and stamina that only the Holy Spirit can provide. Flexibility and a sense of humor are key ingredients in the making of a special ministries program. Prayer and preparation, commitment and stamina, and flexibility and humor are manifested in the lives of the individuals touched through a special Christian education ministry. God uses willing hands and tender hearts to present His love to challenged children and adults.

FOR FURTHER READING

Cherne, Jacqolyn. *The Learning Disabled Child in Your Church School*. St. Louis: Concordia, 1983.

Cooper, John A. *Working with Deaf Persons in Sunday School*. Nashville: Convention, 1982.

Newman, Gene, and Joni Eareckson Tada. *All God's Children: Ministry to the Disabled*. Grand Rapids: Zondervan, 1987.

Paul, James L., ed. *The Exceptional Child: A Guidebook for Churches and Community Agencies*. New York: Syracuse U., 1983.

Perske, Robert. *Hope for the Families: New Directions for Parents of Persons with Retardation or Other Disabilities*. Nashville: Abingdon, 1981.

Pierson, Jim, and Bob Korth, eds. *Reaching Out to Special People: A Resource for Ministry with Persons Who Have Disabilities*. Cincinnati: Standard, 1989.

Riekehof, Lottie L. *The Joy of Signing*, 2d edition. Springfield, Mo.: Gospel, 1987.

Sampley, DeAnn. *A Guide to Deaf Ministry*. Grand Rapids: Zondervan, 1990.

Wilke, Harold H. *Creating the Caring Congregation: Guidelines for Ministering with the Handicapped*. Nashville: Abingdon, 1980

Wood, Andrew H. *Unto the Least of These: Special Education in the Church*. Schaumburg, Ill.: Regular Baptist, 1984.

22

Understanding Learning Styles

LEARNING STYLES
- **Adapt classroom environment and procedures to how students learn**
- **Structure teaching situations to capture students' auditory, visual, and tactile/kinesthetic strengths**
- **Vary methodology so each student has opportunity to reach his or her fullest potential**

Sarah learns by listening. She enjoys her Sunday school teacher's stories and mini-lectures. She's good at class discussion and almost always volunteers to participate in role play. At the end of the forty to fifty minute class period, Sarah will remember about 75 percent of everything she heard and said. She is an auditory learner.

Jack learns by seeing. He remembers information on overheads that illustrate what the teacher is saying. He often takes notes and decorates them with swirls and geometric shapes. He enjoys reading the Bible and his Sunday school material. Jack can remember about 75 percent of what he has seen during the Sunday school hour. He is a visual learner.

MARLENE LEFEVER, M.A., is manager of educational services, David C. Cook Publishing Company, Elgin, Illinois.

Mike learns by doing. He needs to move in order to learn. Simulations, games, and projects help him process information and respond personally to it. Mike is a tactile/kinesthetic learner. Students like Mike are often at risk when they are taught in any other way.

Sarah, Jack, and Mike are equally smart, but they all have different learning styles. When their teachers teach with methods that use their primary strengths backed up with methods that use their secondary strengths, they learn more, faster, and they enjoy the learning process. Teachers capture students' strengths.

According to learning style researcher Rita Dunn,[1] a learning style is the way people concentrate when they have something difficult to learn. People use their learning styles to trigger their concentration and capture their learning strengths. Everyone has a learning style, regardless of IQ, achievement levels, or socioeconomic status.

Researcher Bernice McCarthy offers this definition: A learning style is the way a student perceives things best and the way he or she processes or uses what has been presented.[2]

A learning style is like a fingerprint—different, individualized for each student. Students of equal intelligence learn in dissimilar ways. If we are to become successful teachers we must adapt our teaching to the ways our students learn. We should not expect them to adapt to our preference.

> Learning style is in itself neutral, therefore students of various learning styles should have an equal opportunity to do well in school. However, some studies have shown that students who do not learn in the structured, analytic and linear ways expected in schools are not as successful as students whose styles "fit" better with the typical approach of most classrooms, even when the students are of equivalent intelligence.[3]

A good teacher does not need to be literate in learning-style language to be an effective teacher. Rather, learning-style language can help equip teachers to do deliberately what many have often done intuitively. It is not unusual for a student to respond positively to a part of the class that the teacher thought unimportant. Learning styles can help explain those experiences and—when

1. Dr. Rita Dunn is professor of the Division of Administrative and Instructional Leadership and director of the Center for Study of Learning and Teaching Styles at St. John's University, New York. As of spring 1990, her learning styles model, "21 Elements of Learning," was being taught in forty universities in the United States. Her students have received fifteen major educational awards for research, two of them international.
2. Dr. Bernice McCarthy has developed the 4MAT System, a learning styles model that encourages teachers to work with right and left brain techniques (see bibliography).
3. Pat Guild, "A Study of the Learning Styles of Low Achievers in Seattle Public Schools," in *The Clearing House Bulletin*, "Learning/Teaching Styles and Brain Behavior," 4, no. 2 (Winter 1990): 3. To order write: The Clearinghouse on Learning/Teaching Styles and Brain Behavior, Dr. Lois LaShell, Graduate Education Program, Antioch University, 2607 Second Ave., Seattle, WA 98121.

the teacher is aware—increase them.

Teachers who have not learned to "read" students may teach only the students who process information most like they do, or students who learn best with the traditional Sunday school model. Approximately half of the million children categorized in United States schools as learning disabled have been incorrectly identified.[4] They are "learning different." Many are visual and tactile/kinesthetic learners who are being taught primarily with auditory methods. Christian educators can reclaim this mislabeled group before they decide that God did not make their minds right, and either leave the church or never reach their full kingdom potential.

A year with a Sunday school teacher who never provides for a student's learning styles strengths can negatively affect that student's feelings about Sunday school—and perhaps God—forever. The opposite is also true. Christian educators should adapt the mind-set reflected in the old Yiddish proverb, "All our kids are prodigies," and form their curriculum in ways that allow the adage to become for the most part true.

KEY ELEMENTS OF LEARNING

Twenty-one different elements of learning, elements that determine how students learn best, are suggested in the Learning Styles Model designed by Rita Dunn and Kenneth Dunn.[5]

With professional testing[6] yielding 80 percent accuracy[7] it takes from thirty to forty-five minutes to identify the learning style of a student.[8] Testing will tell what methods will work best for which students. For example, if a youth leader discovers that half the youth group is tactile/kinesthetic, and he learns and teaches best using verbal, interactive methods, he knows he must either write off 50 per-

4. Marie Carbo, "Research Results from Five Pilot School Districts," in *Educational Leadership* (October 1987): 60.

5. Learning Styles Institute, Primary presenter: Rita Dunn, March 1988, Boston, Massachusetts, in cooperation with the Association of Supervision and Curriculum Development. For additional information see: Marie Carbo, Rita Dunn, and Kenneth Dunn, *Teaching Students to Read Through Individual Learning Styles* (Englewood Cliffs, N.J.: Prentice: Hall, 1986).

6. *Learning Style Inventory and Productivity Environmental Preference Survey*, by Rita Dunn, Kenneth Dunn, and Gary E. Price (primary version available for kindergarten through second grade) ©1987. LSI is an inventory for the identification of how individuals in grades 3 through 12 prefer to learn. Productivity Environmental Preference Survey is an inventory to identify individual adult preferences of conditions in a working and/or learning environment. ©1982.

7. Price Systems, Inc., Box 1818, Lawrence, KS 66044.

8. For clues to how a child learns, think about how that child would react if you were reading a story to her about a rabbit that went hop, hop, hop, or a boy who had a little toy drum that made rat-a-tat-tat and rum-y-tum-tum noises. Would the child "(1) Come up close, perhaps insisting on being in your lap, to see the pictures? This is a sign of a visual learner. (2) Mimic the words of the refrain or interrupt to talk about the story? This is a sign of an auditory learner. (3) Move around and do what the refrain says—hop and jump? This is a sign of a kinesthetic learner." Clues to learning styles suggested by Cheri Health Fuller, "Discovering Your Child's Learning Style," *Focus on the Family*, September 1988, p. 13.

cent of the class or rethink his teaching strategies.[9]

In testing more than 175,000 children in grades 3 through 12, researchers found that children could give valuable clues about their own learning style preferences. Interestingly, they also had little trouble identifying their teachers' styles.[10]

Each of the following elements will not affect every student. Most students are affected by from six to fourteen of them. But in the almost 900,000 people tested through 1987, no one has evidenced fewer than four.[11]

According to Rita Dunn, on an average one percent of the population cannot learn unless an element is present or absent. For example, consider the element of noise. One percent of our students absolutely needs noise in order to learn. (This percentage will rise during adolescence, then return to normal in young adulthood.) One percent needs total quiet.

On average an additional 10 percent will have a strong preference for each element, and another 10 percent will have a strong preference for or against one of the elements. The remaining 78 percent of our students will be captured by their interest in the subject, how they feel about the teacher, and the relevance they place in what is being presented. What makes learning styles so individualistic is that a different 22 percent will be affected by each element.

ELEMENTS BY DUNN AND DUNN (SUMMARIZED)

Sound. Most underachievers work better with sound, perhaps because it helps them focus on what they need to do. Without sound, they hear "non-noises" that distract them.

Light. Light affects more people than sound. Fluorescent lights bother many students, often giving them low-grade headaches. They may not feel pain, but they are uncomfortable in a room. This may translate in a Christian education context to their not liking Sunday school.

Temperature. Whenever possible provide a classroom that has warm and cool areas. Allow students to sit where they are most comfortable.

Design. Some students work best at desks, but a surprising number of students learn best when they are spread out on the rug or couches. The need for informal design increases with adolescence. It can be a very Christian response to add the costs of beanbag chairs to the Christian education budget.

Consider how many Sunday school teachers study their lessons. They find a comfortable, soft chair or perhaps even prop themselves up in bed, and sip coffee while they prepare. The casual setting makes studying easier, more enjoyable. In

9. For a clever introduction to these twenty-one elements and how they work in the classroom, see "Elephant Style" by Stephanie Santora and Janet Perrin. This photocopied booklet was designed for use with elementary children, but it is also an effective way to introduce Sunday school teachers to the concept of learning styles. To order write the School of Education and Human Services, St. John's University, Grand Central and Utopia Parkways, Jamaica, NY 11439.
10. Rita Dunn, "Can Students Identify Their Own Learning Styles?" in *Educational Leadership* (February 1983): 60-63.
11. According to Price Systems.

the same way, many students also learn best in a casual setting.

It is helpful to look at room design in terms of what needs to be accomplished by the people in that setting rather than in terms of what learning spaces have traditionally looked like. To illustrate this attitude, consider how Grandpa feeds Kjersten.

> The other day I was feeding Kjersten, the world's most perfect grandchild. She had climbed up on a small bar we have between the kitchen and dining-room. She would stand up, lie down, put her head between her knees, lie on her back and stand on her head. Wherever her mouth was, I would put the food. But if she had been my child, I would have had her sit up straight and clean up her plate, and not squirm—and both of us would have had a miserable time.[12]

When students who need informal design have their needs met, they test 20 percent higher than when they are in a formal setting.[13]

Motivation. Motivated students should be told when they are to learn, what they are to use as resources, and how they can tell when they have reached the learning objective. Unmotivated students need short assignments, few objectives, frequent feedback, supervision, and genuine praise.

Persistence. The higher the IQ the more persistent the student. This element does not change with time. Other elements may change over years, but only with strong personal motivation. Persistent students will stick with a subject until it is done, even if they do not see immediate use for the information. Students low in persistence live for the present, dislike being organized, and push the rules, often very creatively.

Responsibility. Responsible students will do what they are told. Nonresponsible students need to know why they are doing something and what makes it important to both the teacher and themselves.

Structure. Externally structured students need to know exactly what must be done. Internally structured people want to do things their own way. Externally structured students are the ones who always have their term papers done a week early. Internally structured students may be finishing minutes before the paper is due. Both groups get the work done, but they follow different "mind schedules."

Sociological elements identify what kind of group setting works best for the student. Groupings include learning by self (most gifted learners prefer this), learning in pairs, learning with peers (children in grades 3 through 8 usually learn best in small organized groups), learning on a team, learning with an

---

12. Chuck and Barb Snyder, *Incompatibility: Grounds for a Great Marriage* (Phoenix: Questar, 1988), p. 219.
13. Tom Shea, "An Investigation of the Relationship Among Preferences for the Learning Style Element of Design, Selected Instruction Environments, and Readers' Achievement with Ninth Grade Students to Improve Administrative Determination Concerning Effective Educational Facilities" (Ph.D., St. John's U. diss., 1983).

adult (often the teacher), or learning using varied methods.

Perceptual. When students are taught first in their preferred strength (auditory, visual, tactile/kinesthetic) and reinforced through their second preference, learning increases. This chapter will concentrate on the perceptual aspects of learning. We shall look at how to teach students like Sarah, Jack, and Mike as they learn using sounds, words, objects, pictures, and motion.

Intake. If a teacher munches while he studies, why is it so difficult to realize that many students will get more from Bible study if they are allowed to eat healthy food while the Bible learning activities are in progress?

Time. Many students are not morning alert, but for most churches, this is the time serious Christian education takes place. For example, 28 percent of elementary students are early morning people. The rest come to life after 10:00 A.M., and most are at high energy levels between 10:00 A.M. and 2:00 P.M.[14] In a study by J. Virostko,[15] 286 elementary children were taught math in the morning and reading in the afternoon. When the subject was taught at the students' preferred time, they improved twenty-eight points on test scores. There is only one chance in a thousand that it was not the time of day that made the difference. The next year the researcher taught the same children, and another subject was put into the preferred slot. High grades were correlated with time of day and not with subject. This study won the Kappa Delta Pi International Award for the best educational research in 1983.

Mobility. Boys tend to require more mobility than girls. When they are encouraged to be passive in Sunday school, they may become discipline problems. The less interested children are in what they are learning, the more they need to move.

Global/Analytic. Some students learn best globally. They obtain meaning from broad concepts and then focus on details. They often learn best with music, low light, and an informal classroom. Analytic learners appear to learn successively, in small steps leading to understanding. They prefer conventional, formal classrooms and structured teaching.[16] The school system—and often the Christian education system that is patterned after the secular school system—prefers the analytic student and neglects the global student.

Hemisphericity. Right brain students are global. Left brain students are analytic.[17] (The research for right and left brain if far from conclusive. There is usually a dominance, but what we know about right and left brian is open to continued

14. "How Schools Are Using Brain Research and Getting Results," Association for Supervision and Curriculum Development, 1989 panel moderated by Leslie Hart. Tape number: 2306. Statistic stated by panel member Dr. Rita Dunn.
15. J. Virostko, "An Analysis of the Relationships Among Academic Achievement in Math and Reading, Assigned Instructional Schedules, and the Learning Styles Time Preferences of 3rd, 4th, 5th and 6th Grade Students," Ph.D. diss., St. John's U. 1983.
16. Guild: An analysis of preliminary findings in one of her studies showed that predominantly the nonwhite sample was more global than analytic.
17. David Loye, "Hemispheric Consensus Prediction: Evaluation of Right or Left Brain Preference," *Sphinx and the Rainbow* (Shambhala, Boulder, and London: New Science Library, 1983), p. 176. Appendix A is an excellent prediction indicating preference and the strength of that preference.

study. Research by Jerre Levy,[18] biopsychologist at the University of Chicago, reports that the two hemispheres are so similar that when they are disconnected, they function remarkably well, although quite imperfectly. Each hemisphere makes a contrasting contribution to whatever the thinker is doing in all cognitive activities. However, the terms are helpful in that they highlight our neglect of the right-brain thinker.)

Impulsive/Reflective. The impulsive student finds it difficult to think through an answer or process before talking about it or acting upon it. Children who want to please the teacher may try to act reflectively if they like the teacher and know that reflective patterns are valued by him, but that behavior will be exhibited only when adults are watching. When they are not, the impulsive children revert to what is natural to them.

Perceptual Learning

The remainder of this chapter shall concentrate on perceptual learning, one of the twenty-one elements mentioned above. Seventy percent of all our students will show a preference for either auditory, visual, or tactical/kinesthetic learning. These preferences develop in sequence with maturation.

Almost all children are tactile/kinesthetic up through their primary years. Tactile suggests learning with hands through manipulation of resources. Writing, however, is not tactile enough for children below the fourth grade. They can write, of course, but they are concentrating on the writing skill rather than additional information that can be learned through the writing's content. The visual preference comes to the fore in some students in second grade. The auditory preference is the last to develop, usually not until the end of elementary school when the child is ten or eleven years old.

By the time they are in sixth grade, children will have a perceptual preference that will usually remain consistent for the rest of their lives. For example, in an average class of ten sixth grade students, it would be normal to find two auditory, four visual, and four tactical/kinesthetic learners. Unfortunately for eight out of ten students, 90 percent of all teaching is auditory. The teaching processes most often used by teachers are lecture, storytelling, questions and answer, and discussion.

Learning styles show remarkable resistance to change. Cinda Gorman, pastor to children and families at Fletcher Hills Presbyterian Church, El Cajon, California, points out that in her doctor of ministry program at Fuller Seminary, the students' preference for auditory, visual, or tactile/kinesthetic learning was still predominant and matched their behavior in class.

The visual learners took copious notes and drew charts and diagrams. The auditory learners placed tape recorders on their desks and listened to the tapes as

18. Jerre Levy, "Research Synthesis on Right and Left Hemisphere: We Think with Both Sides of the Brain," *Educational Leadership* (January 1983): 71.

they drove home.

One of the kinesthetic learners had amazed me for days. Rarely had he taken a note, but he contributed thoughtfully to the class discussion. While he had appeared not to be participating, he'd absorbed a great deal of material. He'd also completed a rather complicated needlepoint project! Obviously, his fingers were helping him learn.[19]

Take the following self checklist to identify your perceptual strength—visual, auditory, or tactile-kinesthetic.

Find Your Perceptual Strength—Visual, Auditory, or Tactile/Kinesthetic

©Zaner-Bloser, Inc., Columbus, Ohio. Used by permission.[20]

Directions: Complete the sentence by marking the letter on the right of the statement that is most typical of you. Then count the number of checks in each column. This will give you a rough idea of your relative strength in each area.

	(A)	(B)	(C)
1. My emotions can often be interpreted from my (A) Facial expressions (B) Voice quality (C) General body tone	—	—	—
2. I keep up with current events by (A) Reading the newspaper (B) Listening to the radio (C) Quickly reading the paper or spending a few minutes watching TV news	—	—	—
3. If I have business to conduct with another person, I prefer: (A) Face-to-face meetings or writing letters (B) The telephone; it saves time (C) Conversing while walking, jogging, or doing something physical	—	—	—
4. When I'm angry, I usually: (A) Clam up and give others the silent treatment			

---

19. Cinda Gorman, "Preaching for the Senses" *Leadership* 11, no. 2 (Spring 1990): 112-13.
20. "Find Your Perceptual Strength—Visual, Auditory, or Tactual-Kinesthetic," from *Modality*, Instructor (January 1980). From Zaner-Bloser, Inc., Columbus, Ohio (1980).

      (B) Am quick to let others know why I am
          angry   —   —   —
      (C) Clench my fists or storm off

5. When driving, I:
      (A) Frequently check the rear view mirror
          and watch the road carefully
      (B) Turn on the radio as soon as I enter
          the car
      (C) Can't get comfortable and continually
          shift position

6. I consider myself:
      (A) A neat dresser
      (B) A sensible dresser   —   —   —
      (C) A comfortable dresser

7. At a meeting, I:
      (A) Come prepared with notes and displays
      (B) Enjoy discussing issues   —   —   —
      (C) Would rather be somewhere else

8. In my spare time, I would rather:
      (A) Watch TV, go to a movie, attend
          the theater or read
      (B) Listen to the radio or stereo, attend a
          concert or play an instrument —   —   —
      (C) Engage in a physical activity of some kind

9. The best approach to discipline is to:
      (A) Isolate the student from the peer group
      (B) Reason with the student   —   —   —
      (C) Use acceptable forms of punishment

10. The most effective way of rewarding students is:
      (A) Positive written notes or awards others
          can see
      (B) Oral praise to the student in front of
          peers   —   —   —
      (C) A pat of the back, hug

Total the lines you checked in each column:

First Line: Visual

Middle Line: Auditory

Third Line: Tactile-Kinesthetic

We tend to teach in our preferred learning style. When we are motivated to push out of our comfort zone to learn to teach in other styles we achieve greater effectiveness.

TEACHING THE AUDITORY LEARNER

Wes Willis, vice president of Scripture Press, Wheaton, Illinois, shared the story of an adult teacher who suddenly started talking very, very fast. He was composed and at ease with teaching, so nervousness was not the problem. Finally someone asked him why he had begun to sound a little like an auctioneer. "Well," the teacher explained, "I learned that some students only remember about ten percent of what they hear, so I decided to talk faster. If more is said students will remember more."[21]

Not necessarily so—unless, perhaps, like Sarah in our introduction, the student is an auditory learner. More girls than boys are auditory.

Some auditory learners cannot take notes. They are so in tune with sounds that they need to pay total attention to what the teacher is saying in order to learn. Sounds will often distract them. They will not learn if on a warm Sunday the teacher moves the class out-of-doors. Often when they read, they move their lips. They are usually very good at Bible memorization.

Auditory learners often learn very well in groups. They may benefit more than other learners from "cooperative learning,"[22] a term coined by researchers David and Roger Johnson, especially if the group's activities revolve around verbal communication. In cooperative learning, as contrasted with competitive or independent learning, children work together to reach a goal. For example, small groups of four students each might work together to memorize Psalm 23. Each member of the group would help the other. "We memorized a Bible chapter," would become the rallying cry, instead of, "I memorized it first, so I'm smarter than you are." The results of their studies with first through ninth graders may indicate that cooperative learning is a tool for teaching Christian values. In twenty-five studies of first through ninth graders in which some of the children were

21. Wes Willis, "Editorial Perspective," *Christian Education Journal* (Spring 1989): 6.
22. "Cooperative Learning," *Educational Leadership* 47, no. 4 (December 1989/January 1990): 4-66.

handicapped and some were of different ethnic background, the researchers found that prejudice declined, ridicule practically disappeared, children continued to socialize during free time, students had a higher regard for school (what they were studying and their teachers), students developed more confidence in themselves, and they were intrinsically motivated.[23] They wanted to learn.

TEACHING THE VISUAL LEARNER

Jack is a visual learner. He will get from 20 to 25 percent less on tests when he is taught any other way. He needs to see words and pictures in order to learn.

He will often stop and stare into space, his mind visualizing what only he can see. Albert Einstein, for example, was a visual learner. He had a marked disability with auditory learning and the use of language. Yet he had an extraordinary ability to construct complex card houses, use building blocks, and manipulate geometrical diagrams that suggested that he had a specialized mental ability for visual-spatial perception, visual reasoning, and visual memory.[24] If he were evaluated in the traditional way, he would be learning disabled. A child with Einstein's learning style would never win the Bible quizzes or enjoy a free trip to camp for memorizing fifty Bible verses. But he may have an extraordinary visual ability that allows him to construct complex pictures and models in his mind. Perhaps this is the child who will visualize ways to reach the next generation for Christ or will discover a process that will make world hunger a thing of the past.

The visual learner needs to write things in order to remember them. Einstein, it has been said, never bothered to memorize his phone number. Why waste the energy when it could so easily be looked up?

The visual learner is usually unaware of sounds, but he can be distracted by visual stimuli. This student's face is often easy to read. Some visual learners deal with emotions that are very close to the surface. For example, many cry easily—at what is beautiful, as well as what is sad. Visual learners are our most picture-literate students.

Research on the perceptual learning styles of adults over fifty indicates that visual learning is their first choice, followed by interactive and aural (auditory), and haptic (tactile/kinesthetic). The haptic learner learns best when he can feel and touch objects. This learner needs to use hands when approaching learning. "Since learning styles impact on the amount of information processed and retained," explains researchers Michael Galbraith and Waynne James, "knowledge and utilization of an older learner's most effective learning style will enhance learning."[25]

Pictures are becoming increasingly important to the learning process for visual learners, as well as those who have visual learning as their second strength. Our

23. Alfie Kohn, "It's Hard to Get Left Out of a Pair," *Psychology Today* (October 1987): 56, 58.
24. Bernard M. Patten, "Visually Mediated Thinking: A Report of the Case of Albert Einstein," *Journal of Learning Disabilities* 6, no. 7 (August-September 1973).
25. Michael Galbraith and Waynne James, "Assessment of Dominant Perceptual Learning Styles of Older Adults," *Educational Gerontology* 10, no. 6 (1984).

students, conditioned by television, are visually literate. In fifty-five secular experiments[26] using pictures and performed by different educators, test results showed that when picture and text went together learning was higher and what was learned was remembered longer.

In one study sixth grade children were shown drawings that reinforced the main ideas of a story they had read. The control group just read the story. When tested, children who had seen the words and pictures did 24 percent better than those who had seen only words. Pictures will increase learning for most students. The visual learners understand more with them, and other students who have visual learning as their second preferred modality will also benefit.

Poor readers make even greater use of pictures than average and good readers. Poor readers in the fifth grade were tested with pictures and did 35 percent better than poor readers who did not have pictures. When tested for recall, poor readers did 133 percent better than their picture-less peers. Poor or nonreaders represent 60 million Americans, one-third of the adult population. Forty-five percent of all adults do not read even the daily newspaper—10 percent by choice, the rest cannot.[27]

There is overwhelming evidence that we should be using pictures with every lesson we teach. In no test was text without pictures better in terms of the grades students got or what they remembered.

Pictures also increase learning when the lesson is presented verbally. When talk is combined with pictures, those seeing pictures experience two-thirds more retained learning than those who did not see pictures.[28]

One reason for these results is simple repetition. The picture with words, written or spoken, forces students to use a different semantic or sensory level. So the teacher presents concepts once in words and a second time through pictures. This is superior to presenting the concept twice in words or twice in pictures.

TEACHING THE TACTILE/KINESTHETIC LEARNER

Mike's preferred learning style puts him at risk in many school and Sunday school classes. He needs movement in order to learn. Students in this group may have low visual and auditory skills. Many of them will fail if they are taught in any other way.

Often this learner cannot sit still, especially if he is engaged in an activity that does not include manipulating materials. (Writing does not constitute an active

26. W. Howard Levie and Richard Lentz, "Effects of Text Illustrations: A Review of Research" *Educational Communication and Technology: A Journal of Theory, Research, and Development*, pp. 198-232.

27. Roger Palms, "Illiteracy—A Major EPA Problem in the 1990s," *Evangelical Press Association Liaison* (January-February 1990): 1.

28. For an excellent resource on the effects of pictures with children, college students, and adults, see *Picture Books for Gifted Programs*, by Nancy Polette (Metuchen, N.J., and London: Scarecrow, 1981).

process for tactile/kinesthetic learners. They need movement, things they can touch, feel, and manipulate.) If this student is not actively involved in what is going on, the teacher has lost him. This student is not usually attentive to visual or auditory sections of the lesson. When students' learning styles and the instructional methods used are mismatched, children can become tense and even physically ill. "Frustration and stress often lead to unacceptable conduct," says Marie Carbo, director of research and staff development, Learning Research Associates. "Psychologists explain that many students prefer to be regarded as 'behavior problems' rather than as stupid."[29]

As an indication of how this child is feeling, the teacher should look beyond facial expression to the general body posture. The whole body is an index of emotion.

More boys than girls remain tactile/kinesthetic learners. As mentioned earlier, girls are more auditory. This may provide a partial answer to the questions: Why aren't more boys excited about Sunday school? Why do so many of them leave when parents no longer require them to attend? Much teaching leaves the tactile/kinesthetic students without a successful outlet for demonstrating their learning powers. All too often in the school system, they are given negative labels:

> "Red bird reading group"—Every single student knows this is the slow group. "Sit down and sit still!"—The child knows that somehow his need for movement is wrong, inappropriate.
> "F"—Testing is rarely done in a way that captures this child's strength, and he or she may begin to believe that he or she is a failure, useless, not smart.[30]

If we will be successful Christian educators, we must be about the business of removing negative, hurtful, and wrong labels our schools and Sunday schools have stuck on children. We need to remember Rita Dunn's label-removing caution: "Many children we have labelled learning disabled are really 'learning different.'"[31]

METHODS: WORKING WITH ALL LEARNERS[32]

Christian educators must look for ways to involve the strengths of all learners in every class period or learning experience. Evaluate every lesson. Is there an opportunity for the auditory learner to shine? You will probably have twice as

29. Marie Carbo, "Matching Reading Styles: Correcting Ineffective Instruction," *Educational Leadership* (October 1987): 57.
30. A helpful secular guide for teaching students effectively is Rita Dunn and Kenneth Dunn, *Teaching Students Through Their Individual Learning Styles: A Practical Approach* (Reston, Va.: Reston Publishing: 1978.) Other resources available from the School of Education and Human Services, St. John's University, Grand Central and Utopia Parkways, Jamaica, NY 11439: *How to Do Homework Through Your Own Perceptual Strength* (grade 4 through adult); annotated bibliography.
31. Dunn, *Learning Styles Seminar*, Boston, Massachusetts, 1988.
32. Marlene LeFever, *Creative Teaching Methods* (Elgin, Ill.: David C. Cook, 1985).

many visual learners and tactile/kinesthetic learners as auditory learners. Does your methodology reflect this? If not, activities must be added or adjusted—each aimed at accomplishing learning objective, each allowing students to reach that objective through their learning strengths.

Use the following list to help generate ideas for involving all learners in what happens in the classroom.

A=Auditory V=Visual TK=Tactile/Kinesthetic.

BIBLE STUDY

A—Question and answer, lecture, video curriculum, choral reading, drama, tape recordings

---

Lesson Example:

Aim: That teens will get involved in cleaning up God's world.

1. Catching teens' interest in the subject
   - Three minute video on people's destruction of our planet and discussion of what was seen and heard (auditory; visual)
   - Agree/ disagree. For each statement about our world students place themselves on a line stretched across the room to show how strongly they agree or disagree (tactile/kinesthetic)

2. What the Bible says
   - As leader reads creation story, students close eyes and visualize God's original, perfect world (vIsual; auditory)
   - Students use selected Scripture verses to (1) study inductively what God asks of His people (visual; auditory); (2) plan a scriptural choral reading with movement to share God's "earth day" message with adults in the church (auditory; visual; tactile/kinesthetic)

3. What I will do about what the Bible says
   - Choose a class project to improve the part of the earth on which this class lives (auditory; visual; tactile/kinesthetic)

Sample: Bible Picture Watching

Train students to learn from pictures by studying them. Then lead them from the picture into the Bible.
- Where does your eye go first when you look at this picture? Why do you think the artist chose this point of view?
- If you had only this picture of Jesus to look at, what things would you know or suspect are true about Jesus?
- How does this picture make you feel?
- Look at the children in the picture. Which child is most like you in t he way you feel about Jesus right now.

V—Bible picture watching (see sample), video curriculum, drawing the lesson, Bible reading

TK—Acting out the Bible story, building models of Bible scenes, relief maps, symbolic drawing (i.e., the manipulation of a tangram or pipe cleaner as a way of explaining the meaning of a Scripture passage)

BIBLE MEMORIZATION

A—Auditory repetition, verse set to music, partner coaching

V—Combine picture with Bible verse, write verse rather than speak verse to demonstrate completed section, puzzles

TK—Set verse to body movement or action chorus, computer-assisted gaming and repetition, tracing large words on chalkboard, tactile cards

GENERAL CLASSROOM METHODOLOGIES

A—Reader's theater, role play, discussion, storytelling, simulation, debate, interview, case study, listening to music, word games, small groups, buzz groups

V—Worksheets, art projects, creative writing (such as constructing contemporary parables or poetry following a biblical form), slide or video production, paper games, diagrams, show and tell

TK—Mime, liturgical movement, active simulations, graffiti wall, playing music, paper clip or wire sculpture, computer and video projects, active games, manipulating flannelgraph

PERSONAL RESPONSE TO BIBLE STUDY

A—Talk about what was learned and what response will be, role play

V—Write or draw response, create a symbolic reminder of response

TK—Mime, create clay reminder, chancel drama, making personal, meaningful symbol [33]

CHRISTIAN SERVICE PROJECTS

A—Visiting elderly and sick, making phone calls to raise support

V—Reading Scripture in worship service, writing for newspaper or to missionaries, doing bulletin boards, making banners

TK—Participate in missions projects, do nursery duty, handle church maintenance

---

33. David R. Mains, director of Chapel of the Air, has been a leader in adding tactile/kinesthetic aspects to worship. "When I preached about the woman taken in adultery, each person was handed a rock. Suddenly holding those rocks, people felt the story come alive," said Mains. "One Easter we gave everyone a six-inch nail as he or she entered the service. People were instructed to hold the nail as the choir sang. When the choir sang about Christ being wounded for our transgressions, the nails, through the sense of touch, helped people realize the love of Christ." David R. Mains, "Sensory Worship Experience," *Innovations for the Church Leader* (Fall 1984): 9-11.

In 1 John, the apostle is so excited about his discovery of who Jesus is that he cannot wait to share his joy with others, so that their joy may be as complete as his. Notice how he makes provision for all types of learners (1 John 1:1-4):

That which was from the beginning,
which we have heard [auditory], which we have seen with our eyes, which we have looked at [visual]
and our hands have touched—[tactile/kinesthetic]
this we proclaim concerning the Word of life.
The life appeared;
we have seen it [visual]
and testify to it, and we proclaim to you the eternal life, which was with the Father [auditory]
and has appeared to us [visual].
We proclaim to you what we have seen and heard,
so that you also may have fellowship with us.
And our fellowship is with the Father
and with his Son, Jesus Christ. We write this to make our joy complete.

I was in a small, western ranch community leading a workshop on learning styles. At the end of the session, an elderly man in a cowboy hat and string tie came up to me. His skin was weathered from decades in the sun, and his blue eyes were filled with tears. "Lady," he said to me, "iffen someone had told me when I was a kid that God made my mind right, I woulda done something for my Jesus."

We in Christian education need to make certain that our teaching is varied enough to catch and reward each different type of learner, each special mind.

FOR FURTHER READING

Barbe, Walter B., and Raymond H. Swassing. *Teaching Through Modality Strengths: Concepts and Practices*. Columbus: Zaner-Bloser, 1979.

Cornett, Claudia E. *What You Should Know About Teaching and Learning Styles*. Bloomington, Ind.: Phi Delta Kappa, 1983.

Dunn, Kenneth J., and Rita Dunn. *Teaching Students Through Their Individual Learning Styles: A Practical Approach*. Reston, Va.: Prentice-Hall, 1978.

Gartner, Alan, and Frank Riessman. *How to Individualize Learning*. Bloomington, Ind.: Phi Delta Kappa, 1977.

Lawrence, Gordon. *People Types and Tiger Stripes, A Practical Guide to Learning Styles*, 2d ed. Gainesville, Fla.: Center for Applications of Psychological Type, 1982.

McCarthy, Bernice. *The 4MAT System: Teaching to Learning Styles with Right-Left Mode Techniques*. Revised edition. Barrington, Ill.: Excel, 1987.

Zacharias, Raye. *Styles and Profiles*. Raye Zacharias, 1988. Available from the author, 1217 Whispering Lane, Southlake, Tex. 76092.

RESOURCE GROUPS

The following organizations offer a variety of learning styles resources, including inventories for assessing individual styles.

Center for the Study of Learning and Teaching Styles
St. John's University
Grand Central and Utopia Parkways
Jamaica, NY 11439.

McBER & Co.
137 Newbury St.
Boston, MA 02116

Price Systems, Inc.
Box 1818
Lawrence, KS 66044-1818

Hanson Silver Strong & Associates
10 W Main St.
Moorestown, NJ 08051

23

James E. Plueddemann

World Christian Education

INTRODUCTION TO CROSS-CULTURAL TEACHING-LEARNING
- **The world is facing a crisis of a lack of Bible teaching**
- **Culture influences how people think and learn**
- **People can learn to adapt teaching to high and/or low context cultures**
- **Cross-cultural Christian educators can build "fence posts" of understanding between the Bible and the cultural context**

The world is becoming a global village. All ministry is increasingly becoming cross-cultural, whether at home or abroad. We are bombarded with unprecedented opportunities for teaching all nations to obey Jesus' commands.

Yet the person who desires to obey Jesus' command to teach all nations faces unexpected challenges. The first challenge stems from growing national and racial tensions. While communication technology, speed of travel, and immigration trends pull the world closer together, racial tensions tear people apart. The second challenge is that people from various cultures think and learn differently. Many assumptions about how people think are below the level of our cultur-

JAMES E. PLUEDDEMANN, Ph.D., is chairman and professor in the Department of Educational Ministries, Wheaton College, Wheaton, Illinois.

al awareness, so that much cross-cultural teaching is ineffective.

The normal human tendency for people from every culture is to think of themselves as "insiders" and everyone else as "outsiders." The more one learns about the world, the more one learns how small his own "inside" group really is. One college sophomore walked out of a modern history course exclaiming, "The world is crawling with foreigners!" It is natural for people from every culture to feel that they are the center of the universe and never think of themselves as foreigners. Such ethnocentrism is often innocent and natural, but it cools the passion for obeying Jesus' command to teach all nations.

The United States is one of the most racially mixed nations on earth. Nowadays people talk about the United States as a "tossed salad" rather than a "melting pot." Many nationalities are mixed together, but each culture maintains its own flavor. Urban specialist Ray Bakke writes,

> The United States really is becoming a third-world country. For years the U.S. has been the largest Jewish nation. For years it has been the largest Irish nation. It is the second largest black nation in the world. (Only Nigeria of all the 53 countries of Africa has more black people than the United States.) Currently, only Mexico and Spain, maybe Argentina, have more Spanish people than the U.S. By the year 2000, Hispanics in the U.S. will outnumber Anglos. Very soon Hispanics will out-number blacks.[1]

Time magazine recently featured a cover story about America's changing colors, predicting that whites will soon be a minority. In San Jose, California, "bearers of the Vietnamese surname Nguyn outnumber the Joneses in the telephone directory 14 columns to eight."[2] These are wonderful statistics for people who have a passion for making disciples of all nations.

But many people see internationalization as a threat rather than an opportunity. Ethnocentric tensions go beyond America and are sweeping the whole world. Tribal, racial, and ethnic tensions in Africa, Asia, Europe, the South Pacific, and South America make it difficult to waken the church around the world to the growing opportunities for teaching all nations. In order for the church around the world to fulfill Jesus' command, a revival must take place. The greatest hindrance to fulfilling the Great Commission is not lack of money, personnel, or cross-cultural skills, but lukewarm churches with a dulled passion for the glory of God. We need a renewed vision of the glory of the Lord.

THE GREAT COMMISSION OF PSALM 67

Psalm 67 challenges us to have God's perspective of the world. Only when we have a passion in our hearts for the glory of the Lord will we be truly motivated for cross-cultural teaching.

---

1. Raymond J. Bakke, "The World of the 1990's: What Will Our Students Face?" *F.Y.I.* (Summer 1989): 1.
2. William A. Henry III, "Beyond the Melting Pot," *Time* (9 April 1990): 29.

Verse one is the heart-cry of Aaron's prayer: "May God be gracious to us and bless us and make his face shine upon us." We are all hungry for the blessing of the Lord on our lives. But a major reason God blesses His people is so they can be a blessing to the nations. God promised to bless Abraham and make him a great nation so that all peoples on earth would be blessed through him. God did not bless Abraham so that he could be proud and comfortable, but so he could be a blessing to the nations.

The longing of the psalmist is for the nations to praise God. "May the peoples praise you, O God; may all the peoples praise you" (v. 3). Then, and only then, will the nations be glad and sing for joy. Anyone who is aware of what is going on in the world realizes that the world is not praising God, the nations are not glad, and they are not singing for joy. The nations are wrestling with economic, political, and racial problems. The Lord God Almighty has the only solution—the good news we are commanded to teach. God's name is not being praised by all the peoples of the earth, and such a condition should motivate us for cross-cultural teaching. If we are hungry for the blessing of God in our lives, we must rekindle a passion for teaching the nations to obey all that Jesus commanded.

There are three great motivations that should stir our passion for teaching all nations: (1) God wants to bless us so that we can be a blessing to the nations. (2) The nations are in serious trouble, and we have the only good news. (3) God's name is not being glorified in all the earth. If we love the Lord, we must be deeply bothered by this fact.

THE NEEDS OF THE CHURCH AROUND THE WORLD

Almost four billion people in the world today make no claim to new life in Christ. Most of them have never clearly heard the good news. The more we can learn about the influences of culture on thinking and learning, the more likely it is that the gospel will be understood by all nations. The task of world evangelization will be enhanced if basic principles of cross-cultural teaching can be better understood.

About a billion people in the world are at least nominally Christian. One of the most urgent needs of the rapidly growing churches around the world is for culturally sensitive Bible teaching. Byang Kato warned about the dangerous lack of Bible teaching in Africa.

> Biblical Christianity in Africa is being threatened by syncretism, universalism, and Christo-paganism. The spiritual battle for Africa during this decade will be fought, therefore, largely on theological grounds. But the church is generally unprepared for the challenge because of its theological and biblical ignorance. . . . The church in Africa is suffering from theological anemia. . . .[3]

3. Byang H. Kato, *Biblical Christianity in Africa* (Accra: African Christian, 1985.), p. 11.

Luis Palau says that the church in much of the world is exploding. He points out that there are at least 50 million Christians in mainland China with very few Bibles. Regarding Africa, he comments, "It's not difficult to win Africans to Christ today. The challenge is seeing them discipled."[4] Palau says that revival in Latin America is beyond his wildest dreams. The church desperately needs people who know how to teach the Bible in multicultural situations.

Culture, Thinking, and Learning

A second obstacle to cross-cultural teaching is that there are puzzling differences in the way people from different cultures think and learn. Every human being is a thinker, but not all people think in the same way. Rules for processing information are influenced by culture, but cultural differences are variations on a common theme.

Some early studies of culture and thinking mistakenly designated non-Western thinking as "pre-logical, mystical and entwined with emotional life."[5] Even recent descriptions by some missiologists have labeled people of different continents as being either intuitive or logical. To categorize all nonindustrial societies as "pre-logical but relational beings" and high-tech societies as "logical but non-relational individualists" is a dangerous oversimplification. All people from every culture are created in the image of God with tremendous potential to think and feel. Every culture has ways for forming categories, systems for planning action, and a means for quantifying objects, people, and time.[6]

Not only are there important similarities within all cultures, there are also important differences within each culture. The amount of schooling people have can predict wide variations in thinking patterns even within the same culture. People from anywhere in the world who have several years of formal schooling use similar thought patterns. Those without formal schooling use somewhat different thought patterns even though they live in the same cultural setting. In one study, differences were observed between schooled and illiterate Tangale males of Nigeria. Even though the men lived within a few miles of each other and were of the same tribe, they displayed significant variations in the way they made categories, based on whether or not they had formal schooling.[7]

The basic patterns of thinking and human development seem to be the same in all cultures. An important study of Nigerian Bible school students found that ability to perform higher level thinking tasks increased the longer a student was in school.[8] The development of moral reasoning follows a similar pattern in many

4. Louis Palau, "Understanding Scriptures for an Exploding Church," *Front Line* 3 (1987): 8.
5. L. Levy-Bruhl, *Primitive Mentality* (London: Allen and Unwin, 1926), p. 43.
6. Marshall H. Segall, *Cross-Cultural Psychology: Human Behavior in Global Perspective* (Monterey, Calif.: Brooks/Cole, 1979), p. 97.
7. James E. Plueddemann, "The Effects of Schooling on Thinking in Nigeria with Implications for Christian Education," *Journal of Psychology and Theology* 18 (Spring 1990).
8. Mark Larson, "Cognitive Skills of Adult Nigerian Bible Training School Students" (Master's thesis, Wheaton College, Ill., 1986).

cultures but the rate and end point of development seem to be influenced by culture.[9] Studies in cross-cultural faith development show similar variations on the common theme.[10] All these studies show that cultural differences in thinking are based on fundamental cognitive structures.

AWARENESS OF CONTEXT AND CULTURE

Probably the most fundamental influence on culture and thinking is the degree of people's sensitivity to their context. Some people have a high sensitivity to the concrete context around them. Other people seem to be more interested in ideas and issues that are broader and more abstract than the immediate context. Edward T. Hall gives a helpful explanation of "high context" and "low context" people.[11] Both kinds of people can be highly intelligent and the two thinking styles both demand complex cognitive functions.

High-context people pay special attention to the concrete world around them. Everything in the immediate physical context communicates something subtle but significant: the atmosphere of the room, sounds, smells, expressions on people's faces, and body language. High-context people tend to be person-oriented. They remember people's names and details about personal events. The subtle cues in a real-life setting intuitively but intentionally communicate important information. High-context teachers tend to be more sensitive to the feelings of other people.

Low-context people, on the other hand, pay special attention to words, ideas, and abstract concepts. They may remember a conversation about an important topic but not remember the names of the people in the conversation. The specific, explicit words and ideas communicate more clearly than the implicit tone of voice. Low-context learners enjoy analyzing and comparing abstract ideas. A low-context manager will insist on a signed legal contract, whereas a high-context, person-oriented manager would put more confidence in a friendly hand-shake. A signed legal contract might seem like an insult and a sign of mistrust for a high-context leader. Low-context teachers and learners would enjoy integrating one theory or philosophy with another.

High-context people may be exceptionally able to remember events from their past experiences, whereas low-context people are more competent at recalling impersonal facts they learned in the past. For example, my mother can remember details of a lunch with a stranger in a foreign country twenty years ago. She can remember particulars about their children, their work, and what they ate together. My dad is the opposite. He was with my mother at the same lunch, but

9. James E. Plueddemann, "Moral Reasoning and Pedagogical Preferences in Kenyan and American College Students," *Religious Education* 84 (Fall 1989): 506-20.

10. Randall Y. Furushima, "Faith Development in a Cross-Cultural Perspective," *Religious Education* 80 (Summer 1985): 414-20.

11. Edward T. Hall, *Beyond Culture* (Garden City N.Y.: Doubleday/Anchor Books, 1977), p. 91.

he cannot remember anything about the event. My dad, however, is a brilliant research chemist and can imagine molecular structures for tomorrow's experiments while he sits in an easy chair in the evening working on a crossword puzzle. Although most people are adept at remembering both personal events and impersonal facts, some people may tend to be better at one or the other. High-context people more easily remember personal events, whereas low-context people more easily recall impersonal information. Preliminary research suggests that people may retrieve different kinds of information from different parts of the brain. The frontal lobe is more active in some people when they are remembering personal knowledge about past events in their lives. Impersonal knowledge of facts seems to be retrieved from the medial temporal lobe of the brain.[12] Insights about remembering and recalling information have significant implications for cross-cultural educators.

ARE THERE WESTERN THINKING STYLES?

A popular misconception is that Western values are dominated by the low-context thinking patterns of ancient Greece that encouraged people to concentrate on ideas instead of events. Thus Western educators might be adept at seeing broad patterns in a philosophy of education but be less sensitive to the needs of students.[13] But a generalization that suggests North Americans are low-context and Africans are high-context is deceptive and even dangerous. Some Africans tend toward being high-context and others low-context, which is also true of North Americans.

Recent research suggests that cultural differences are not the primary explanation for differences between the so-called Greek-oriented Western world and the non-Western world, but stem from factors such as rural-urban, industrial-agricultural, or the amount of formal schooling. For example, the teaching-learning process in rural societies anywhere in the world is often guided by consensus, conformity, and cooperation. Other studies suggest that urban and rural groups may operate with different dynamics. People anywhere in the world who live in rural subcultures tend to be more high-context and cooperate more willingly than people in urban subcultures. Teaching and learning in a low-context, high-tech society on any continent may emphasize personal convictions, individual initiative, and competition.[14]

Culture has an important influence on preferences for leadership styles. Low-

---

12. Endel Tulving, "Remembering and Knowing the Past," *American Scientist* 77 (1989): 367.
13. For a fascinating discussion of inductive Bible study in another culture, see Peter S. C. Chang, "Steak, Potatoes, Peas and Chopsuey—Linear and Non-linear Thinking," in *Missions & Theological Education in World Perspective*, ed. Harvie M. Conn and Samuel F. Rowen (Box 457, Farmington, MI 48024: Associates of Urbanus, 1984), pp. 113-23.
14. Leon Mann, "Cross-Cultural Studies of Small Groups," in *Handbook of Cross-Cultural Social Psychology*, vol 5, ed. Harry C. Triandis and Richard W. Brislin (Boston: Allyn & Bacon, 1980), pp. 167, 184.

context cultures value individual effort and personal freedom. Leadership that encourages individual participation in decision making is important. High-context societies tend to prefer leaders with powerful personalities or even autocratic and centralized styles of leadership. A charismatic personality is more important in a high-context society than the ability to generate abstract, and low-context, five-year plans.

Another research survey showed that women in many cultures around the world have similar cognitive styles.[15] In some cultures women tend to be more high-context than low-context. But again generalizations are dangerous.

Orientations toward the personal or abstract ways of thinking are good to understand for the person involved in cross-cultural teaching. A well-educated business executive in Singapore or Accra might have a learning style similar to that of an executive from Buenos Aires or Brussels.

CONTEXT AND LEARNING

No person is totally low-context, focusing only on ideas, or totally high-context, focusing only the the present context. Teaching and learning preferences fall along a continuum between very high-context and very low-context orientations. Learners who enjoy wrestling with ideas might be classified as low-context. Learners who prefer to think about the world and people around them would be more high-context. Academic schedules are rather abstract concepts divorced from the unfolding present situation. Training schools that emphasize course schedules, tight syllabi, and the amount of time to be spent on each subject would tend toward the low-context end of the continuum. Teachers that emphasize authority and relationship-building without particular attention to schedule or agenda would tend toward the high-context end of the continuum.

High -
Context

Low -
Context

The following chart may be helpful in summarizing some of the potential teaching-learning differences between high-context and low-context teaching and learning.[16] The ideas are "informed hunches" and worthy of further investigation. The two columns are not distinct categories but may be likened to extremes of a continuum. Few if any individuals are examples of extremes. In every culture there will be people who tend toward one side of the continuum or the other.

---

15. Mary S. Van Leeuwen, "A Cross-Cultural Examination of Psychological Differentiation in Males and Females," *International Journal of Psychology* 13 (1978): 441-77.

16. Many of the ideas in this chart come from the book by James E. Plueddemann and Carol E. Plueddemann, *Pilgrims in Progress* (Wheaton, Ill.: Harold Shaw, 1990).

	High-Context Teaching & Learning	Low-Context Teaching & Learning
Possible Cultural Factors	Rural Agricultural Non-formal schooling	Urban Professional Formal schooling
Culture and Thinking		
Cognitive Style	Field Dependent	Field Independent
Cognitive Function	Concrete Operational	Formal Operational
Moral Reasoning	Conventional	Principled
Faith Development	Synthetic-Conventional	Individuative-Reflective
Culture and Learning		
Time	Polychronic Many things can happen at the same time. It may be difficult to begin and end on time, or to isolate one topic at a time.	Monochronic The class will begin and end on time. Subjects can be scheduled in an orderly sequence. People will want to stick to the topic.
Communication Style	Communication will be indirect, with emphasis on nonverbal messages. Tone of voice, posture, and facial features will have group meaning. The whole context communicates.	Communication will be direct, either spoken or written. The concept being discussed will be more important than the feelings of the person making a statement. The ideas communicate.
Authority[17]	Prestige is given by the group and becomes almost permanent. Others will be expected to respect rank. Formal credentials are important and need to be evident.Leadership is	Authority is earned by individual and personal effort. It is temporary and dependent on continued performance. Formal credentials are not as important as performance.

Leadership Style	usually highly controlling in order to maintain group harmony and conformity. Leader often has "charismatic" personality. Leaders reward loyalty to the group.	Leaders will allow each person to have significant input into decision making. Group members are more likely to question the ideas and decisions of the leader. Leaders respect individual initiative from group members.
Conflict Resolution Style	Indirect resolution is sought through mutual friends. Displeasure is shown through nonverbal, subtle communication. Conflict resolution may be avoided for as long as possible.	Resolution is sought through direct confrontation. People will meet face to face and explain the difficulty verbally. Speaking the truth will be emphasized.
Teaching Goals	The purpose of the teaching will be to build interpersonal relationships. Group will be people-oriented.	The teaching will be task-oriented. Group will want to cover a specified number of verses or finish particular projects.
Preferred Bible Passages	Bible stories and history will be preferred. The Psalms and passages that encourage the imagination will also hold interest.	Bible doctrine from different parts of the Bible will be emphasized along with the didactic passages of the Epistles.
Interaction Style	High group cooperation and a tendency to conform to decisions of others will characterize style. Group harmony will be important.	Interaction will be personalized with an emphasis on individual "ownership" of ideas. Conformity will be de-emphasized.
Religious Emphasis	The Holy Spirit and the gifts of the Spirit will have special emphasis. Emotional commitment and a feeling of belonging is important.	A solid umderstanding of the Word of God and correct doctrinal belief is stressed. Expository sermons will be appreciated.

Major Focus	Testimonies and sharing of needs are emphasized. Application of biblical passages is important.	Bible study is the focus, with an emphasis on understanding and interpreting the major ideas of the passage.
Missiology Focus	Spiritual signs and wonders are important. Prayer is emphasized.	Strategizing long-range plans such as "The world by 2000" are important. Statistical church growth is emphasized.
Difficulty	Students have problems relating life needs to the objective truth of the Bible. Can lead to hearsay and syncretism.	Students have difficulty relating the objective truth of the Bible to the problems of life. Can lead to dead orthodoxy.
Strengths	Builds empathetic relationships. Christian commitment is fervent and caring.	Builds a solid understanding of God's truth. Places a healthy emphasis on personal ownership and responsibility.

INTEGRATING HIGH-CONTEXT AND LOW-CONTEXT THINKING

Both high-context and low-context learners have healthy strengths and dangerous weaknesses. Is there any way that students and teachers can have the benefits of both high-context and low-context ways of thinking? Are there ways that the weaknesses of both extremes can be overcome? Merely to aim for the middle of a continuum may not be the ideal way to emphasize strengths and de-emphasize weaknesses. Perhaps the strengths can be fused together so that learners can have the strengths of each thinking-learning style. Can Christian education work to develop people who are both caring and interactive as well as people with reflective personal convictions? Neither kind of thinking by itself is ideal. Teaching methods need to take into account both the *preferred* thinking style and also the *ideal* thinking style. Teaching should aim to build the strengths of both the person and abstract orientations, and should work to overcome the weaknesses of both orientations. The following chart illustrates the strengths and weaknesses.

17. For a fascinating discussion of cultural authority and basic values see Marvin K. Mayers, *Christianity Confronts Culture* (Grand Rapids: Zondervan, 1974), pp. 147-70. See also, Sherwood G. Lingenfelter and Marvin K. Mayers, *Ministering Cross-Culturally* (Grand Rapids: Baker, 1986).

Low-Context

	Weaknesses	Strengths
High-Context — Strengths	Independent Theoretical	Caring Personal Convictions Reflective Thinker
High-Context — Weaknesses	Dependent Unreflective	Sociable Experienced

IMPLICATIONS FOR TEACHING AND LEARNING

Learning in all cultures has much in common. But merely describing cultural preferences in learning does not necessarily tell how we should teach. Good teaching does more than merely discover cultural learning styles and adapt teaching to these styles. Some cultures are so used to oppressive teaching methods that these methods may be the preferred learning style. For example, some religions teach students to memorize a holy book in an unknown language. New Christians from that culture may prefer to memorize the Bible in the original Greek and Hebrew without understanding the meaning of the words. Empirical research may find that meaningless rote memory is the preferred learning style. An unreflective legalism based on the dictates of a charismatic leader seems to be the preferred learning style in some cultures. But it is doubtful that such learning will develop reflective, biblical Christians.

In some cultures, the educational systems are focused on passing external exams. Such a system may seem quite credible. On the other hand, the exam system can promote the "diploma disease." After a while students begin to prefer the kind of teaching that will cram meaningless facts into their heads to help them pass exams. Passing the exam to earn formal credentials rather than learning how to be a growing Christian can dominate the preferred learning style.

Thus to *describe* a culturally preferred learning style is not to *prescribe* a good teaching style. How culture affects thinking is crucial, but does not determine how one *ought* to teach. Good teaching methods will tie together the strengths of each thinking style.

PRINCIPLES FOR CROSS-CULTURAL TEACHING

Low-context learners and teachers bring many strengths to the learning situation. They are good at thinking creatively for themselves, are able to understand broad theoretical relationships, and reflectively see low-context relationships between important ideas. But they also have weaknesses to overcome. Low-context teachers and learners will not automatically be able to relate theoretical insights to personal growth in grace.

High-context learners and teachers also bring valuable strengths to Christian education. Students and teachers are willing to cooperate, will have a desire to be practical, and will want to test theories in the "real world." But high-context learners also have weaknesses to overcome. Students and teachers may be so tied to the practical that they will not be able to understand why something works. Without understanding theory, they will not be able to generalize insights into other settings.

The kind of teaching that will help students integrate personal convictions with social concern, theory with practice, the active with the reflective, and the concrete with the abstract will intentionally tie together both preferences for context. The teaching model might look like a rail fence.[18] The rail fence training model can integrate the strengths of both high- and low-context learners.

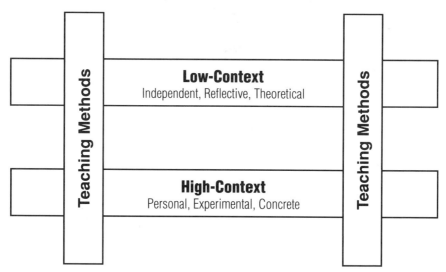

Low-Context
Independent, Reflective, Theoretical

High-Context
Personal, Experimental, Concrete

Teaching Methods

CHRISTIAN EDUCATION FOR LOW-CONTEXT CULTURES

Low-context or abstract-oriented students will prefer the kind of teaching that integrates ideas. They will prefer teachers who do not force their ideas on students or demand meaningless rote memory. They will not be impressed with the teacher's

18. For further reading on the rail fence concept, see Lois E. LeBar, *Education That Is Christian* ed. James E. Plueddemann (Wheaton, Ill.: Victor, 1989), pp. 105-11. See also, James E. Plueddemann and Carol E. Plueddemann, *Pilgrims in Progress* (Wheaton, Ill.: Harold Shaw, 1990) pp. 51-61.

formal credentials or experience if the teacher is not able to challenge them to think. They will feel free to disagree with the teacher and with other students. They may not appreciate assignments where students need to work together. Low-context students will be upset if textbooks have not arrived on time or if the course seems disorganized. They will feel free to confront their teacher directly about disagreements in assignments, grades, or theoretical consistency. They will most likely prefer academic courses such as theology or philosophy of education and try to avoid practical internships.

Classes with low-context students are rarely dull. Discussion will be free and even electric. Assignments will produce many creative and original ideas, and students will leave the course with genuine personal convictions. When these students confront teachers and other students they are not trying to be rude but are trying honestly to get to deeper issues.

There are things teachers can do to help students grow beyond the limitations of low-context thinking. Give assignments that challenge students to integrate theory with practice. When teaching a section on philosophy of education, assign students to interview or observe experienced educators to discover how their philosophy affects their practice of teaching. While being sensitive to the strength of individual effort, give some assignments that require students to cooperate and work together. Assignments can challenge students to integrate theory with practice. Ask questions that stimulate students to describe the implications of theory or theology for a practical problem in the church.

CHRISTIAN EDUCATION FOR HIGH-CONTEXT CULTURES

High-context, or person-oriented students respect the formal credentials of the teacher and will be interested in receiving formal credit for a course. They will be concerned with the practical and personal implications of the information learned. They will be willing to work together and will never forget the friendships made while in training. Students will be interested in discussing experience.

High-context students are respectful of the teacher and cooperative with each other. They are interested in the practical and personal benefits the course will have for them. They probably will not be too bothered if the textbooks do not arrive on time or if the teacher does not teach the subject matter in the order listed on the syllabus.

There are things that can be done to help high-context students move beyond the immediate context and to benefit from the power of good theory. Christian education must prepare students to solve problems, and there is nothing as practical as good theory for solving unanticipated problems. Give assignments that build on the strengths of high-context students. Since they are good at understanding the present situation, challenge them also to reflect critically on the context. For example, a teacher could give assignments to interview older Christians and generate hypotheses as to *why* they became Christians. Challenge students to contrast the actual "folk" theology of the average person in their city or village with what they know about evangelical theology. When training high-context students, begin teaching with experience and challenge students intellectually to reflect on the implications of that experience for Christian education

GENERAL PRINCIPLES

Good Christian education in any culture will challenge students to bring together practice and theory. High-context students may prefer to learn practical "how-to-do-it" techniques. But if high-context students merely learn a "bag of tricks" for ministry, they will not be able to solve complicated problems. Low-context students may prefer to study theoretical knowledge. If low-context students only learn theoretical "book knowledge" about missions, they will have difficulty knowing how to put their knowledge into practice. Teaching methods need to stimulate integration.

Good Christian education does not try to segregate students into homogeneous groups of people who have similar thinking styles. The ideal is to mix high- and low-context students together. This diversity helps to emphasize the strengths of each thinking style. Low-context theory without practice leads to hollow intellectualism, and high-context practice without theory leads to shallow pragmatism. Intentionally mixing high- and low-context students in the same class will stimulate both to see problems in the church from each other's perspectives. Encourage class discussion where both kinds of students talk with each other and broaden each other's thinking.

A good focus for Christian education is to teach problem-solving. Problems in the Christian life grow out of practical difficulties but require theoretical insights for solutions. While high-context and low-context students approach problems differently, problem-solving is a relevant activity for both. If Bible teaching merely imparts bodies of knowledge, students will not be able to use the information to solve problems. On the other hand, if Christian education teaches only behavioral skills, people will not know how to adapt those skills to different situations. Actual case studies challenge students both to think and to act, and are appropriate for either low-context or high-context students.

The learning setting should encourage students not only to learn information, but to practice what they have learned. People do not always learn from experience, neither do they always learn from books. It is the interaction between thinking and doing that produces the best learning. Neither *thinking* nor *doing* alone is adequate unless the student can be challenged to integrate the two. Christians can learn from their experience, from each other, and from the broader insights of the teacher. Teachers need to have relevant experience in the Christian life as well as theological insights for understanding that experience.

Christian education that integrates theory and practice will foster biblical growth in grace in people from any culture. It is a task with eternal significance.

FOR FURTHER READING

Claerbaut, David. *Urban Ministry*. Grand Rapids: Zondervan, 1983.

Hall, Edward T. *Beyond Culture*. New York: Doubleday, 1977.

Hesselgrave, David J. *Communicating Christ Cross-Culturally*. 2d edition. Grand Rapids, Mich.: Zondervan, 1991.

LeBar, Lois E. *Education That Is Christian*. Edited by James E. Plueddemann. Wheaton, Ill.: Victor, 1989.

Lingenfelter, Sherwood G., and Marvin K. Mayers. *Ministering Cross-Culturally*. Grand Rapids: Baker, 1986.

Mayers, Marvin K. *Christianity Confronts Culture*. Revised Edition. Grand Rapids, Mich.: Zondervan, 1987.

Plueddemann, James E., and Carol Plueddemann. *Pilgrims in Progress*. Wheaton, Ill.: Harold Shaw, 1990.

Rogers, Donald B. *Urban Church Education*. Birmingham, Ala.: Religious Education, 1989.

Segall, Marshall H., et al. *Human Behavior in Global Perspective: An Introduction to Cross-Cultural Psychology*. Elmsford, N.Y.: Pergamon, 1990.

24

*Colleen Birchett, Marta Alvarado,
and Johng Ook Lee*

Ministering to Major Cultural Groups

CHARACTERISTICS AND NEEDS OF MAJOR CULTURAL GROUPS
- **Recognize that these populations are too large to be ignored**
- **Learn about the diversity within these populations**
- **Learn to recognize the ethnic distinctives of these populations**
- **Realize that these predominantly urban groups must overcome the problems of the city**
- **Understand the needs of these major cultural groups**
- **Develop creative ways to teach these groups**

Since its beginning in Acts 2, the church has been composed of a wide variety of cultural groups. In the United States, this diversity often becomes a barrier to effective Christian education. But an understanding of the characteristics and needs of major cultural groups can help to break down this barrier. This chapter presents background information about three major groups—African Americans, Hispanics, and Asian Americans—and implications for Christian education with them.

COLLEEN BIRCHETT, Ph.D., is development editor, Urban Ministries, Inc., Chicago, Illinois.

MARTA ALVARADO, M.A., is assistant professor of Christian education, Moody Bible Institute, Chicago, Illinois.

JOHNG OOK LEE, Ed.D., is visiting scholar at the Graduate School of Education, University of California, Berkeley, California.

African Americans

by
Colleen Birchett

The agenda to be developed for African American Christian education would be used by several different groups involved: (1) African Americans themselves, (2) people who minister within the black community but who are not African Americans, (3) designers of curriculum (perhaps at the denominational level), and (4) classroom teachers.

It is being assumed that the body of information presented here can be used by any one of the groups mentioned above. However, accepting the information that follows and implementing the related suggestions may require a major shift in perspective and orientation. It may require a re-education process in which the Christian educator rejects much of the information received from the traditional media sources of this world and listens to the Lord.

Christian educators from all groups must realize that they are likely victims of miseducation about African Americans. Therefore, in order to develop educational programs within the African American community and church, one must first acquire the truth about the people for whom educational programs are being developed. Then this information must be integrated into the Christian education curriculum at the general curriculum and at the classroom level.

Of course the material must be adapted for the various age levels being taught. However, at this juncture of African American church history, there is just as great a need to focus on the content of the curriculum itself as on the methodology by which the curriculum is taught. One without the other is ineffective.

This first section of the chapter presents information that is often ignored by traditional media sources and illustrates how this overlooked information can become a part of a Christian education program. It also provides broad guidelines for teaching the content at the classroom level.

Christian education programs must develop agendas for the 1990s and the twenty-first century that continue the tradition of seeking to liberate black people and helping African Americans receive spiritual empowerment. Such programs must create an awareness among African Americans of the struggles of other oppressed people of the world, particularly of other black people throughout the world and in Africa.

CURRICULUM CONTENT AND BLACK CHURCH HISTORY

It is important for African Americans to know that the God who created them loves them. This is difficult for them to see if they are misinformed about the beauty of who they are. Part of understanding who they are is gaining the truth about what they have contributed to the world, as evidence that they are intelligent beings (not animals, as slavery once taught them). Therefore, the curriculum must stress who African Americans are and what their history is.

In emphasizing the history, however, it is important for the Christian educator to outline God's interventions in that history, how He made Himself known to black people, and how He continues to make Himself known today. History in Christian education should be taught from this perspective.

THE HISTORICAL MISSION OF THE BLACK CHURCH

Directors of Christian education and classroom teachers must understand the importance of explaining the historic and current mission of the black church. Students need to know that they are not studying in a vacuum, and that as students they are part of a historical trend in the black church. This helps them to establish identity and a sense of mission as African American Christians.

Students need to know that the term *church* is being used to refer to a body of people who believe that Jesus Christ is the Son of God and that He died for their sins, was buried, and rose again from the dead. Although some theological differences exist between some bodies of believers, the term *church* refers to any group that supports the lordship of Jesus Christ.

When the term *African American church* is used, it refers to a body of African American believers. It must be underscored, however, that this church has a history that dates back to Africa. In fact, according to recent scholarship and scientific research, the African American church has roots that can be traced at least as far back as Galilee, during the ministry of Jesus on earth.

This church was born in the midst of oppression, and throughout its history developed Christian education programs to deal creatively with the effects of oppression. Although oppression was not the sole factor responsible for the birth of the African church—or of its Christian education programs—the oppression contributed to its enhancement and development.

Students need to know that from its very beginnings, the agenda for black Christian education has always been directly related to the historical mission of the church, to the historical context in which it found itself, to its peculiar place in the kingdom of God, and to its prospects for survival in the future. That mission has been to teach the gospel (Matt. 28:18-20; John 3:16) and to empower African people to cope with the effects of oppression (John 1:12).

THE PRESENCE OF BLACK BELIEVERS IN SCRIPTURE

Jesus announced His earthly mission by standing in a synagogue of Nazareth and reading a passage from Isaiah:

> The Spirit of the Lord is upon me, because he hath anointed me to preach the gospel to the poor; he hath sent me to heal the brokenhearted, to preach deliverance to the

captives, and recovering of sight to the blind, to set at liberty them that are bruised, to preach the acceptable year of the Lord. (Luke 4:18-19)

Christian teachers who teach black students should make them aware that there are biblical scholars who support the notion that the people to whom Jesus spoke fit the American definition of blackness. Support for this notion is also evidenced by recent sophisticated archeological, linguistic, and genetic research.[1]

Although what Jesus said in the Temple was meant for all people of all nations, regardless of race, it is especially applicable to African Americans, in particular, that He chose to stand in the midst of people who had different colors of skin to make this proclamation. It is noteworthy that Jesus did not remain in the synagogue but went out to the hillsides and countryside where hurting people were and taught them. As people learned and exercised faith in Him they were healed.

Students need to consider that Jesus' ministry among people of different skin colors led to the formation of the black church in its embryonic form. Jesus' example provides the basis for a powerful argument for relating Christian education programs to wholistic ministries in the black church. Of course, students need to know that this relationship has, in the main, always existed in the African American church.

BLACKS WHO DIED FOR JESUS

Students need to know about God's interventions in the lives of early black Christians who were persecuted by the Roman government. They need to know that black people are among those who died, spreading the gospel throughout the world and establishing the Christian church (Acts 8:27; Matt. 27:32; Acts 2:1-11). Roman soldiers plundered Northern Africa, killing thousands of African Christians. They also killed many black Roman soldiers who refused to execute other Christians.[2]

In spite of Roman terrorism, however, the tradition of educating and healing continued and through effective Christian education programs the African churches thrived and the gospel was carried into African centers as far away as Nubia and Mauretania. These centers became Christian intellectual centers where some of the leading theologians of the early church emerged.[3] This all happened hundreds of years before the first black slave ever reached America.

These facts are often ignored by traditional church histories. This leaves black children feeling that the only people who were champions for Jesus were Caucasian. This is misinformation and incomplete teaching. Correction of it fos-

1. Walter McCray, *The Black Presence in the Bible* (Chicago: Black Light Fellowship, 1989), p. 34. Ivan Van Sertima, *Blacks in Antiquity* (Cambridge: Belknap Press, 1970), p. 32. Cain Felder, *Troubling Biblical Waters* (Maryknoll, N.Y.: 1989), p. 24.
2. Mark Hyman, *Blacks Who Died for Jesus* (Philadelphia: Corrective Black History Books, 1983), p. 24.
3. Ibid., p. 10.

ters a more positive identity for the black Christian student.

THE BLACK CHURCH DURING RECONSTRUCTION

The Christian education curriculum should contain information about God's interventions in the lives of His people during specific periods of pain and struggle. One of these was the period immediately following slavery in America. Students need to study the Scriptures as they apply to what happened during this time in African American history.

After the Civil War ended and slavery was made illegal throughout the United States, ex-slaves had to rebuild their lives literally from the ground up. It was extremely difficult for them to relate to an evil world system that had very recently considered them only three-fifths persons.

Many did not even have names suitable for freed persons. Most had no understanding of the institution of marriage. They had been denied family life as chattel slaves. Just being physically free and being able to go wherever one wanted to go was a new and sometimes frightening experience. They had no property, no homes, no land, no farm animals, no implements—and in some instances, they did not even have clothes that were suitable for walking among free men.

Politics had been a world closed to slaves, and about 96 percent would have been considered illiterate. To add to all of this, during the decades following the Civil War, African Americans became victims of hate groups such as the Ku Klux Klan. In spite of this oppression, however, the African American church flourished.

Church growth during this time mushroomed. By 1890, the United States census showed 24,000 black churches—with one black church per sixty black families. Church members raised 26 million dollars annually.[4] In addition to forming social service ministries (such as burial societies, benevolent societies, hospitals, employment ministries, political groups, orphanages, and retirement centers for seniors), the African American church developed Christian education programs that helped deal creatively with the effects of slavery and with new forms of oppression. By 1906, 4,779 black Sunday schools were established. Tutorial programs, voter registration classes, and classes teaching basic reading, writing, and mathematics were also offered.

During this period most of the black theological seminaries and universities (such as Wilberforce, Payne, Turner, Morehouse, Virginia Union, Bishop, Shaw, and Tuskegee) were formed.[5]

By pointing out this survival pattern of black American Christians at various points in African American history and the role that God played in it, African American Christians of today can look with hope rather than despair at their surroundings and can be prepared to develop the same enthusiasm for survival that

4. Charles Sims, *The Religious Education of Southern Negroes* (Louisville: Scripture Press Foundation, Christian Education Research Division, 1926), p. 97.
5. Ibid., p. 107.

their ancestors had. They can study the Scriptures as they apply to this struggle and use the Scriptures as examples of how Christians in the past organized in Jesus' name and built major institutions.

THE CONTEXT OF THE AFRICAN AMERICAN CHURCH TODAY

Christian educators need to broaden the perspectives of black students. Many are extremely parochial, in that their exposure is limited primarily to their neighborhoods and schools. Many are totally unaware of social trends taking place that affect the future of the black church, the community, and the black family. This kind of information needs to be integrated into the curriculum, and students need to be shown how it relates to the Great Commission that Jesus has given us in Matthew 28. They need to know how they can prepare professionally and spiritually to play their role in the struggle for survival in the black community.

Following are a few statistics that need to be discussed under the umbrella of Christian education and related to a scriptural foundation. Then programs need to be developed to turn the trends around with the power of Jesus. According to recent statistics provided by the National Urban League, murder is the second leading cause of death for black males between the ages of fifteen to twenty-four, and it is the leading cause of death for black males between the ages of twenty-five and forty-four.[6]

It appears that African Americans are killing other African Americans out of frustration. The deaths and the resulting shortage of black males in the black community is a source of emotional and physical pain for many black families. The risk of being the victim of a homicide for blacks of all ages is six times higher than for that of the white population.

Also, a disproportionate number of blacks suffer from the AIDS virus and are dying earlier from it than those in the white community. The total number of such deaths has increased 34 percent since 1987. Of these people 27 percent were African Americans, even though African Americans constitute only 12 percent of the population. However, for African Americans, the transmission of AIDS has been directly associated with drug use. The reality of the AIDS epidemic has added immeasurable emotional pain both to the victims and to their families.

Space does not permit an analysis of the losses of black men due to drugs and gang violence. In Los Angeles alone since 1985, an estimated two hundred gang members killed an estimated three hundred people. In that city more that twelve thousand people belong to gangs, with most participants being teenagers and older children.[7] Vital statistics of the United States reflect that whereas the life expectancy for black Americans is now at 69.4 years (with the life expectancy of

---

6. Robert Hill, *The State of Black America* (Washington, D.C.: The National Urban League, 1989), p. 10.
7. Walter Shapiro, "The Ghetto: From Bad to Worse," *Time*, August 24, 1987, pp. 18-19.

black men at 65.2), the life expectancy for white Americans has risen from 74.6 to 75.6.

Statistics such as the above need to be discussed in Christian education classrooms—particularly in black churches—throughout America. Christians need to begin thinking about what these statistics mean in terms of the Great Commission (Matt. 28:18-20), and how they can prepare themselves to perform their role in the struggle. They also need to discuss the responsibilities of government agencies and how to get those agencies and elected officials to respond to what African American families need. All of this is Christian education.

CONCEPTS FOR AFRICAN AMERICAN CHRISTIAN EDUCATION

Certain basic concepts should continue to be focused on and should be taught in all African American Christian education programs, and they should be used to develop the structures through which spiritual principles are taught and through which empowerment becomes realized.

CONCEPT 1: SALVATION (JOHN 3:16)

At the core of all black Christian experience is salvation through Jesus Christ. Christians everywhere have in common that they love the Lord Jesus Christ because He heard their cry. Common to all is that they came away from their encounter with Jesus Christ as changed human beings. A Christian education program is not a Christian education program if it does not give opportunities for its students to have this experience.

CONCEPT 2: HEALING (2 CHRON. 7:13-14)

Salvation involves more than just feeling good. Salvation involves allowing oneself to be healed by God from the effects of oppression.

CONCEPT 3: TALENT AND GIFT DEVELOPMENT (MATT. 25:14-30; 1 COR. 12:4-11)

The New Testament church, which contained an abundance of members of African descent, is shown in 1 Corinthians as a center where Christians could develop their gifts and talents and then use them to strengthen the institution of the church and the community. All church-based Christian education programs should build within them the opportunity for Christians to have their talents developed, to practice using their gifts, and to acquire skills needed to implement the mission of the church.

CONCEPT 4: DELIVERANCE (JOSH. 6:1-4, 15-21; EPH. 6:10-18)

Satan's goal is to destroy humankind. Throughout the Old and New Testaments, however, God is seen mobilizing His people to break out of spiritual and physical oppression. In both the Old and New Testaments, preparation, education, organization, and talent usually precede the deliverance event.

CONCEPT 5: MISSION (MATT. 28:18-20)

To be delivered and to be used of God to deliver others, a church (or community of faith) needs a sense of mission or purpose. One way of examining the concept of mission is to see it in terms of global objectives (or goals) and the specific objectives that must be met in order for the ultimate goal or mission to be accomplished.

CONCEPT 6: CULTURE

For the African American church, African American culture is the context in which Christian education takes place. The African American culture must reclaim that part of its African heritage that embodies the Nguzo Szaba principles, articulated by Maulana Karenga.

Nguzo Szaba African concepts are:

a) Imani: Faith (Heb. 11). To believe with all of our hearts in God, in our people, and in the righteousness and victory of our struggle.

b) Umoja: Unity (Eph. 4:16). To strive and maintain unity in the family, nation, community, and race.

c) Kujichagulia: Self-determination (Josh. 6:1-4, 15-21; Eph. 6:10-18). To define, name, create, and speak for ourselves.

d) Ujamaa: Cooperative economics (Ex. 35; Acts 4). To build and maintain our own stores, shops, and other businesses, and to profit from them together.

e) Kuumba: Creativity (Gen. 1:1-4, 26-28). To do always, as much as we can, in order to leave our community more beautiful and beneficial than when we inherited it.

f) Ujima: Collective work and responsibility (Acts 2:42-27). To build and maintain our community together, to make our brothers' and sisters' problems our problems, and to solve them together.

g) Nia: Purpose (Ex. 19:3-6; Titus 2:14; 1 Pet. 2:5,9). To make as our collective vocation the building and development of our community in order to restore our people to our traditional greatness.

TEACHING PRINCIPLES AND METHODS

CULTURAL DISTINCTIVES

Teachers of African Americans need to be aware of the importance of attitudes in regard to race and color. They must be convinced that in the plan of God, everyone is created equal as persons regardless of skin color or from what cultural or ethnic background the individual comes.

Teachers need to have a genuine appreciation of the African American culture and recognize the high esteem blacks have of their own cultural background. They need to be aware of the injustices in human relationships. Studies of the history of African Americans in regard to slavery and intolerable suffering needs to be understood and appreciated. African Americans want to be accepted as persons and treated fairly. They appreciate teachers who are open, fair, and unbiased. They are hungry for genuine Christian love as emphasized in John 13:35, "By this shall all men know that ye are my disciples, if you have love one to another."

Some areas that may help teachers to appreciate African American culture are: folklore, music, funerals, child-rearing practices, cooperation, and sharing.

Academically, many African Americans feel like failures because they have not had the same educational opportunities as whites. They should not be regarded as persons with low IQs or who are ignorant, but they need to feel accepted and successful and be given opportunities for constructive learning. Because of inequities in distribution of resources in public school systems, many blacks lack in basic knowledge concerning things that whites often take for granted.

Janice Hale-Benson identifies some important factors about African Americans that may help teachers be more effective in teaching them. They tend to respond to the whole picture instead of its parts. African Americans also tend to prefer focus on people and their activities rather than on things.[8]

The teacher must realize that television, radio, and video play a more significant role in the students' lives than such media may have played in the teacher's life. The older the teacher, the more this is the case. Media has had an impact on the degree to which students can concentrate on the lecture method. Students are accustomed to entertainment that is scientifically designed to take advantage of everything known about the age level of the student being entertained.

The teacher must also be aware that research has shown that African American students respond best to visual stimuli and learn best when they work cooperatively on projects. Cooperation rather than competition should be fostered, along with visual stimulation and art projects.

SPECIAL NEEDS OF STUDENTS

During the course of the classroom session the teacher should also seek ways to remediate skills that students may lack. This would include specific problem solving skills as well as reading, writing, and mathematics skills. Reading readiness skills taught in conjunction with Bible study and black history lessons are especially helpful for giving students additional practice with skills they need.

Differences also exist in backgrounds in Bible and theology. Most African Americans have no problem accepting the inspiration of the Scriptures. They believe the preacher is "God's man." In some situations, biblical background

---

8. Janice E. Hale-Benson, *Black Children: Their Roots, Culture, and Learning Styles* (Baltimore: Johns Hopkins U., 1986).

may be lacking, and the teacher may need to teach basic truth on which students can build. African Americans are interested in how Bible knowledge relates to their personal lives. As they study the Bible, the relationship of Scripture to their experience is more important than rote memorization of biblical passages. Teachers need to teach the truth and show how to apply it to life. The students may ask, "What can I take back to the black community? How can I help my brothers and sisters?"

Economic situations in which blacks are reared may be very different from the dominant American cultures. Many African Americans live in metropolitan areas and come from poor family backgrounds or poverty. The lack of financial security and means may affect other areas of life.

Also, many blacks come from broken families or single-parent homes. The rate of divorce is higher in black families. Some of these homes are run by young women who are undereducated or unskilled. Some children are physically and sexually abuse, and may distrust adults, expect failure in school, seem to have a don't-care attitude, or be hostile. They may perceive school environments as potentially threatening or hostile. They may attempt to solve their problems through physical retaliation, alcohol, or drugs.

CONCLUSION

African American culture must be understood from a biblical, historical, and contemporary perspective. Teachers need to relate the content in black history and the Bible to the students' intellectual levels, needs, and life experiences. Effective teaching principles and methods should be selected that will motivate students to want to learn and grow as individuals and reach others with the gospel.

Hispanics

by
Marta Alvarado

The Hispanic population in the United States is a heterogeneous group, composed of people from many different countries, each with its own culture, ethnic values, and history. A 1987 census report indicates that the current U.S. Hispanic population numbers 18,790,000—nearly 8 percent of the total U.S. population.[1] According to the 1980 census, two-thirds of the Hispanic population lives in

1. *Statistical Abstract of the United States: 1989, 109th Edition*, U.S. Bureau of the Census (Washington, D.C.: U.S. Government Printing Office, 1989), pp. 1-15.

three states: California (31 percent), Texas (20 percent), and New York (11 percent). Mexicans constitute approximately 61 percent of the Hispanic population, Puerto Ricans 15 percent, Cubans 7 percent, and all other groups 17 percent.[2] Eleven percent of the total Hispanic population is under five years of age, and 21 percent is between the ages of five and fourteen.[3] The size of the population and its density in a small number of states stresses the need for ministry.

DIVERSITY WITHIN THE HISPANIC POPULATION

In order to minister to the Hispanics, one must first understand the socio-historical differences within the population. Mexican-Americans, those who have immigrated from Mexico and those who were born in the United States but who are of Mexican descent, are a mixture of varying degrees of European (primarily Spanish) and Indian blood.[4] Some groups of Mexicans were inhabitants of the Southwest while it was a Spanish colony and became United States citizens by default upon the signing of the Treaty of Guadalupe Hidalgo in 1848, which ceded the southwest to the United States.[5] Others have migrated to the United States from Mexico, whereas still others were born in the United States. The immigrants came to the United States for various reasons, but most wanted to improve their economic conditions. Many were from the rural areas and were often poorly educated. They came to work in the farmlands, the vineyards, the railroads, the steel mills, or wherever they could find work. Most had intentions of one day returning to Mexico.

Puerto Rico was a Spanish territory from 1500 until 1898. The Indians on the island were virtually eliminated during the early years of the Spanish conquest, and the Spanish brought African slaves to work on the island. The African slaves, the Spanish, and the few remaining Indians intermarried. It is this mixture that characterizes the Puerto Rican population. In 1917, Puerto Rico was declared a U.S. territory, and U.S. citizenship was conferred on all its citizens. Mass migration from Puerto Rico to the U.S. mainland began in the mid-1940s. Like the Mexican, the Puerto Rican immigrant came largely from rural areas and was uneducated.[6]

Cuba was also a Spanish colony from 1492 until 1898, when it was given to the United States following the Spanish-American War. American military rule lasted until 1902, when Cuba ratified a constitution and began self-government. When Fidel Castro became dictator of Cuba in 1959, a mass Cuban exodus began to the United States. The immigrants—considered political refugees—were from

---

2. *1980 Census of Population-General Population Characteristics*, May 1983, U.S. Bureau of the Census (Washington, D.C.: Government Printing Office, 1983), pp. 1-14.
3. *Statistical Abstract*, pp. 1-15.
4. Clifton L. Holland, *The Religious Dimension in Hispanic Los Angeles: A Protestant Case Study* (South Pasadena, Calif.: William Carey Library, 1974), p. 32.
5. Ibid., p. 38.
6. Diego Castellanos, *The Best of Two Worlds: Bilingual-Bicultural Education in the U.S.* (Trenton: New Jersey Department of Education, 1983), p. 51

the middle and upper middle classes, and were mostly professionals. Like the Puerto Ricans, the Cuban population was a mixture of the African slave, the European, and the few remaining Indians. However, the Cubans arriving on American shores did not seem to be as racially mixed as were the Puerto Ricans.[7] The Cuban refugees tended to be those who were of largely European extraction.[8] Their higher socioeconomic status and their European makeup made it easier for them to assimilate into American society.

In addition to the differences arising from different socio-historical backgrounds, the Hispanic population also experiences intra-group differences. These differences are based on the length of residence in the United States, the degree of acculturation, and the extent of ethnic identity.

RECOGNIZE THE ETHNIC DISTINCTIVES

James A. Banks identifies variables within a multidimensional concept of ethnicity that can be used to determine ethnic distinctives. These are: language and dialect, ethnic values, perspectives and worldviews, behavioral styles and nuances, nonverbal communication, cultural elements, methods of reasoning and validating knowledge, and ethnic identification.[9] Each of these variables will be discussed in reference to the Hispanic population. It is important to remember that the ethnic characteristics discussed are generalizations and that the degree to which they pertain to an individual or a particular group varies.

Language. Spanish is the language spoken by most Hispanics. For the immigrant it is the primary—and in some cases the only—language of communication. The inability to function in English creates a language barrier and hinders many Hispanics from entering fully into the American economic, social, and political structure. For the Hispanic child, Spanish is often the primary language. Bilingual education programs have enabled the Hispanic child to retain the primary language while gaining skill in the English language. The result is that children from Hispanic homes will come to the church with varying degrees of English and Spanish language proficiency.

Values. The strongest value among Hispanics is the importance of the family; the individual is secondary to the needs of the family. Individual accomplishment is important in light of the honor it brings to the family. Within the family structure, the father is the center of authority, and the mother is submissive to the father. Children are taught to respect and obey their parents without question. Lines of responsibility are carefully delineated, and "older siblings are encouraged to develop a sense of responsibility toward younger children in the family."[10]

---

7. Ibid., p. 62.
8. Ibid., p. 63.
9. James A. Banks, "The Multiethnic Curriculum: Goals and Characteristics," in *Education in the 80's: Multiethnic Education*, ed. James A. Bank (Washington, D.C.: National Education Association of the U.S., 1981), pp. 109-10.
10. Charles B. Brussell, "Social Characteristics and Problems of the Spanish-speaking Atomistic

Males are expected to protect the females of the family. Sexual roles are clearly defined. Very often several generations of the family live within the same household.

Relationships outside of the family are governed by kinship ties and respect. The concept of the family is extended by means of the *compadrazgo.* "The institution of 'compadrazgo' or coparenthood extends the range of kinship beyond genetic links."[11] *Compadres* are usually baptismal godparents, confirmation sponsors, or wedding sponsors. Individuals are taught to respect the dignity of others. To question the beliefs, the accomplishments, or successes of another is to belittle the other person.[12]

Hispanics also value their religion, which is predominantly the Roman Catholic faith. The *Chicago Tribune* reports that an estimated 80 to 90 percent of Mexico's 85 million citizens are Catholic.[13] The same is true of every other Hispanic country. Frank W. Patterson reports that the evangelical work in Mexico did not begin until the 1820s, and that the first such church was established in 1864.[14] The evangelical Protestant church is a young church, and it has yet to gain large segments of the Hispanic population. New converts enter the evangelical church with little or no formal religious instruction. Baptists, Presbyterians, and Methodists began Hispanic works in the early 1900s, and these denominations tend to contain the larger of the Hispanic churches. However, there is a strong Hispanic Pentecostal movement as well, especially among the Puerto Ricans.

Ties to the Roman Catholic church are strong, with its roots in the first arrival of the Spanish to the New World. The slogan among many Hispanics is that "they were born Catholic and they will die Catholic." Church attendance is high among women and children. Important life events must be celebrated within the church in order to give them legitimacy. A marriage ceremony officiated by a justice of the peace is not considered binding unless a ceremony within the church follows.

Christianity in the form of Catholicism was early coupled with the native religious beliefs and practices. In their drive to Christianize the Indian, priests and conquerors often forced acceptance of Catholicism on the natives by the threat of the sword.[15] There was little instruction in Catholic belief and doctrine, and blind faith was the norm. In the history of many Hispanic countries, the church was used to keep the populace under control. It is therefore not surprising that faith in God and faith in natural forces became linked.

In Mexico, the Indian plays an integral part in the development of Mexican

Society," in *Teaching Multicultural Populations: Five Heritages,* ed. James C. Stone and Donald P. DeNevi (New York: D. Van Nostrand, 1971), p. 171.
11. Ibid., p. 173.
12. Ibid., p. 174.
13. "Pope Urges Compassion for Mexican Slum Dwellers" *Chicago Tribune* (May 8, 1990) sec. 1, p. 17.
14. Frank W. Patterson, *A Century of Baptist Work in Mexico* (El Paso Tex.: Baptist Spanish Publishing House, 1979), pp. 23-24.
15. Holland, p. 33.

Catholicism. The two are united in the story of the first appearance of the Virgin of Guadalupe, the patron saint of Mexico. It is told that the Virgin Mary made several appearances to a Mexican Indian named Juan Diego. She instructed him to tell the local bishop that a church be built to her on the site of her appearances. This was followed by a miraculous sign—the image of the Virgin imprinted on Juan Diego's white poncho. During Pope John Paul II's visit to Mexico in May 1990, Juan Diego was canonized.

The Indian and African influences in Hispanic religious practices is evident in the Hispanic's faith in folk medicines. *Curanderos* and spiritualists practice their native healings while seeking the blessings of a patron saint. Diseases and medical disorders are sometimes seen as being caused by imbalances of the natural order, or the results of evil spiritual powers such as in the complaint called *mal ojo*, or the evil eye.[16]

Perspective of the world. The Hispanic perspective of the world has often been described as fatalistic and present-time oriented. However, Charles Brussell points out that "the Mexican American is dedicated to living the moment to its fullest extent in the roles he finds assigned to him by God."[17] Therefore, it is not fatalism, but rather faith in the knowledge that life and an individual's accomplishments are in God's hands. It is the ability to adapt oneself to any situation and to make the best of all circumstances.

Behavioral style. Hispanic behavioral styles are greatly influenced by the values held and the perspective of the world. If all events are in God's hand, then there is no need to maintain a frantic pace, since God's will ultimately will be achieved. Respect for and submission to those in authority characterize personal and business relationships. Respect for the dignity of the individual translates into concern for upholding the conventions of gracious hospitality—of making each guest feel *en casa* or "at home."

Nonverbal communication. Genda Gay states that nonverbal communication, such as "proxemics, touch, body movements, gestures, differentiation in response-time patterns, use and quality of voice, eye behavior, and usage of objects,"[18] should be analyzed in terms of their cultural foundations. Some of the nonverbal communication used by Hispanics is often misunderstood or misinterpreted by people of other cultural groups. One example in particular is that of eye aversion. Out of respect for authority and as a sign of submission to that authority, Hispanic children are taught to bow their head and lower their eyes when speaking to an adult. However, this gesture has often been misinterpreted as a sign of guilt or willful disobedience. Even gestures used to indicate height and length are different for the Hispanic. To indicate the height of a person the index

16. Brussell, pp. 183-85.
17. Ibid., p. 181.
18. Genda Gay, "Interactions in Culturally Pluralistic Classrooms," in *Education in the 80's: Multiethnic Education*, ed. James A. Bank (Washington, D.C.: National Education Association of the U.S., 1981), pp. 50-51.

finger points out, and the palm is turned toward the speaker. To indicate the height of an animal the hand is opened and the palm is held horizontal to the ground. "Come" is indicated by opening the hand, placing the palm horizontal to the ground, and opening and closing the fingers.

Cultural elements. Aspects of Hispanic culture are familiar in varying degrees to most people in the United States. What is important to remember is that each ethnic group falling within the definition of "Hispanic" has distinctive and unique food, music, art, and literature. Ethnic cultures have been strongly influenced by the peoples who have ruled and inhabited the countries of origin—the Spanish, the African, the American, and the Indian. One can hear both the drums of the African in the rhythms peculiar to some ethnic cultures, as well as the more gentle, lilting rhythm of the Spanish guitar. Songs and hymns are both more energetic and fiery than those found in the typical Anglo-American church, as well as more mournful. The food ranges from the hot and spicy to the tasteful blends of plantains and meat. Art is influenced by Afro-Cuban forms and Indian design. Within the Hispanic population there has been a great emphasis on poetry, public recitation, and the oral transmission of culture through legends.

Cognitive Styles. Recent research regarding cognitive styles has brought insight into the differing methods of reasoning and validating knowledge by the Hispanic individual. Most of the research has focused on field independence and field dependence, or what is often referred to as field sensitivity. Though it is unclear whether an individual shows a preference for a particular learning style because of differing socialization practices, or whether it is a matter of varying degrees of right and left hemisphere functioning,[19] research seems to indicate that the Hispanic child is more field sensitive than the Anglo child. Field sensitivity is characterized by effectiveness "in tasks or situations that involve relevant social cues,"[20] responsiveness to human interest, mastery over visuo-spatial tasks, and responsiveness to group tasks. Although the Hispanic child in general appears to be more field sensitive than the Anglo child, such a generalization should never be used to stereotype the Hispanic child or to use it as an excuse for ineffective teaching.

Ethnic identification. Ethnic identification refers to the extent to which the individual chooses to identify with the ethnic group—its values, culture, language, behavior, religious beliefs, and problems. Ethnic identity is influenced by the individual's proximity to the country of origin, the extent of family pressure, length of residence in the United States, frequency of travel to the country or origin of ancestry, place of residence, and the political force of the ethnic group in the community.

In the 1960s and 1970s, ethnic pride played an important role in Hispanic communities. Groups sometimes influenced by Marxist philosophy began an era

19. Manuel Ramirez III and Alfredo Castaneda, *Cultural Democracy, Bicognitive Development, and Education* (New York: Academic Press, 1974), p. 70.
20. Ibid., p. 70.

of minority group consciousness. There was increased interest in retaining the language, retaining or learning about one's cultural heritage, and the development of Hispano-American art forms. There was also increased political activity. In some cases, revolutionary activities were used to bring about social change. In other cases, the Hispanic intelligentsia became more politically astute and began to take an active role in the political affairs of the nation. The increased awareness of the political clout of the Hispanic minority enabled bilingual education to be instituted nationwide.

THE HISPANIC MUST OVERCOME THE PROBLEMS OF THE CITY

In addition to the characteristics and needs of the Hispanic based on ethnic distinctives, there are also the characteristics and needs of the Hispanic based on his socioeconomic position in the United States. The majority of the Hispanic population lives in urban areas. In 1980, New York's population was 20 percent Hispanic, Los Angeles 28 percent, Miami 56 percent, and Chicago 14 percent Hispanic. Twenty-six percent of all cities in the United States with a population of 100,000 inhabitants or more have more than a 20 percent Hispanic population.[21] In some urban areas, the school population is comprised of a majority of the minority population.

The urban Hispanic experiences not only the problems associated with any minority group, but also the problems associated with urban areas, most often the inner city. Among these are: the pressure to acculturate, prejudice, segregation, little political or economic power, little opportunity for upward mobility, alienation, disruption of the family, a breakdown of traditional values, changing roles, disillusionment, poor education, crime, drugs, gang activity, and health risks associated with poverty and drugs. These problems, along with the associated psychological problems they engender, make the work among the Hispanic demanding.

TEACH TO THE NEEDS OF THE POPULATION AND USE ITS STRENGTHS

What are the implications for Christian education? Christian educators must first become familiar with the culture of the ethnic group with which they are working. They must learn to recognize different behavior patterns, to understand and interpret nonverbal communication, to accept perspectives different from their own,[22] and to esteem the values of that culture.

In the classroom, the teacher must be firm and yet show concern for the child.[23] Interactive styles of instruction should be used. Because of the emphasis placed on

21. *Statistical Abstract*, pp. 33-35.
22. Barbara Bowman, "Educating Language-Minority Children: Challenges and Opportunities," *Phi Delta Kappan* 71 (October 1989): 3: 119.
23. Alfredo Castaneda, "The Educational Needs of Mexican-Americans," in *The Education Needs of Minority Groups*, ed. Alfredo Castaneda, Richard L. James, and Webster Robbins (Lincoln, Neb.: Professional Educators Publications, 1974), p. 23.

responsibility of older siblings and respect to persons older than the individual, cross-age teaching will be especially effective. Children from Hispanic families will be "more likely to be motivated by those forms of reward that offer personalized support, recognition, or acceptance."[24] Topics should be made relevant to the cultural, socioeconomic, and psychological needs of the Hispanic child.

The family, especially the father, should be encouraged to participate in the religious instruction of the child. Family members should be invited to attend church functions. The Christian educator should refrain from criticism of the beliefs and practices of the family. Learning will occur best where the values of the church and the values of the family are the same.[25]

The language of instruction should be based on the language needs of the Hispanic child whether this necessitates the use of a Spanish language curriculum, an English language curriculum, or a bilingual curriculum. Currently three U.S. publishing companies produce or distribute Spanish language Sunday school curricula: Gospel Publishing House, the Sunday School Board of the Southern Baptist Convention, and Scripture Press.[26] Gospel Publishing House's curriculum is entitled *Vida Radiante* and includes materials from age two through adulthood. It is a Spanish translation and adaptation of their *Radiant Life* curriculum. The same Scripture passages constitute the basis of the lesson for both the English and Spanish language curricula.

The children's curriculum developed by the Sunday School Board of the Southern Baptist Convention is divided into two levels: *Historias Biblicas* for preschoolers and *Estudios Biblicos* for children six to eleven years of age. Young people and adults use *El Interprete*. The children's curriculum is an adaptation and translation of the English language curriculum. Both publishing companies make every effort to reflect Hispanic culture and to address the needs of the American Hispanic by way of an exclusive Spanish language curriculum.

Scripture Press distributes curricula for children and youth published by Ediciones las Americas from Mexico. The material is adapted and translated from curricula produced by Scripture Press and Gospel Light.

Finally, Christian educators must be cognizant of the limitations of resources within many Hispanic churches. They are often small churches in urban areas. Financial resources are limited, therefore the Christian educator must be especially creative in the use of limited material resources. Hispanic churches tend to be small churches, which may limit the available human resources. Efforts must be made to train and equip new converts for ministry within the church and more specifically within the Sunday school. In spite of these limitations, the Christian educator will be stimulated by the youth and vitality of the Hispanic church.

24. Ramirez, p. 72.
25. Bowman, p. 120.
26. Addresses for these publishers are: Gospel Publishing House, 1445 Boonville Ave., Springfield, MO 65802; Sunday School Board of the Southern Baptist Convention, 127 Ninth Ave. N., Nashville, TN 37324; Scripture Press, 1825 College Ave., Wheaton, IL 60187.

Asian Americans

by
Johng Ook Lee

Of the many ethnic minorities that have made America the symbolic pluralistic society of immigrants, Asian Americans are one of the physically recognizable groups with an experience and history unique in the American scene. The term *Asian American* actually encompasses several ethnic groups with distinct cultures and historical backgrounds. The major Asian American groups include the Chinese, Filipinos, Guamanians, Japanese, Koreans, Samoans, and Vietnamese, with other Pacific and Southeast Asian people making up the remainder.[1]

According to the statistics from the 1990 U.S. Census, the number of persons categorized as "Asian and Pacific Islander" increased by a startling 107.8 percent, rising from 1.5 million in 1980 to more than 2.9 million in 1990. During the same period, the black population increased 13.2 percent, the Hispanic by 63 percent, and the native American by 37.9 percent, whereas the total population of the United States increased only 9.8 percent.[2] Thus, the rate of growth of the Asian American population was almost double that of the next fastest growing minority group and more than ten times that of the United States as a whole. Partially because of this phenomenal growth in population, Asian Americans are now being perceived as a minority group that will play an increasingly significant role in American society and will warrant much more attention than it has had in the past.

For many people, Asian American minority groups evoke thoughts of elegant cuisine and mysterious communities filled with exotic curio shops, or perhaps politically tinged reactions based upon the improvement in foreign relations with the People's Republic of China or upon the threat of Japanese economic competition. Yet informed individuals are more likely to have a definite and positive image of these groups. They are perceived as once-oppressed racial minorities that have attained some degree of success and now are assimilating into the American middle class largely through their intelligence, patience, and hard work. They are likely to be admired for achieving upward mobility through their own efforts and through adherence to values most Americans find admirable. This favorable image has received a great deal of attention in newspapers and magazines, which depict Asian Americans as "model minorities."[3]

1. Florence Yoshiwara, "Success Through Education: The Asian American Myth," *Church and Society* 64:3 (January - February 1974): 24-31.
2. U.S. Department of Commerce, Bureau of the Census, *Race of the Population by States: 1990. 1990 Census of Population* (Washington, D.C.: U.S. Government Printing Office, March 1991), CB 91-100.
3. "Success Story: Outwhiting the Whites," *Newsweek* (June 21, 1971) pp. 24-25; and "Korean-Americans: Pursuing Economic Success," *Washington Post*, July 13, 1978, p. 1.

Minority people have been forced to resolve conflicts with the majority society in their own unique ways. In order to survive in a rather hostile society, it was necessary to develop their own myth of how they have overcome their problems. For the Asian Americans—as it was for many other people—the road to success in American society was through the means of education. Education was defined as the key to social mobility and financial success, and they made every effort to pave the road to success. The Asian American myth of success through education is still embraced by many Asian Americans, as well as non-Asian Americans.

However, this image of success has come under criticism, for it contains implied "lessons" to other minority groups on how progress should be made in American society. Furthermore, it ignores the high price that has been paid through the past sufferings and economic losses, the decline of traditional cultures and communities, uncritical acceptance of American values and beliefs.

> The success image overlooks existing community problems, such as mental illness, crime and delinquency, housing, health care, unemployment, welfare, the poverty of the aged, concerns of new immigrants, confusion over cultural identity, and continuing economic and social discrimination.[4]

Perhaps most important, it ignores substantial segments of the population that experience extreme deprivation.

CHARACTERISTICS OF ASIAN AMERICANS

As a consequence of living within a socially pluralistic society in America, sharp conflicts, greater assimilation, and acculturation have resulted for the Asian Americans. Where internal and external conflicts have not been adequately addressed, social pluralism has become a secularizing force and a nominalizing factor for the Asian Americans. The following table illustrates some contrasting differences between traditional Asian Americans and Western social attitudinal traits.

FAMILY NEEDS AND PROBLEM AREAS

In general, Asian Americans have displayed qualities of hard work, adaptability, and faith in the American dream of unlimited opportunity for all. This is not to say that Asian Americans are without problems. Following are some of the social needs and problem areas of the Asian American family.[5]

4. Russell Endo, "Asian Americans and Higher Education," *Phylon* 41:4 (Winter 1980): 367.
5. Bok-lim C. Kim, "The Future of Korean-American Children and Youth," *The Education of Asian and Pacific Americans* (Phoenix, Ariz.: Oryx, 1983), pp. 55-56.

CONTRASTING DIFFERENCES OF SOCIAL AND ATTITUDINAL TRAITS*

INDIVIDUALISM (WESTERN)	GROUP IDENTITY (TRADITIONAL)
INDIVIDUALISM – Autonomy – Achievement of individual goals – Trained to be individuals	COLLECTIVITY – Group identity – Achievement of goals set by others – Obligations to the group
RIGHTS AND PRIVILEGES – Responsible to self – Personal rights – Motivation based on feelings	DUTY AND OBLIGATION – Relational responsibility – Duty to others, basis of motivation
EQUALITY – Dislikes rules and control – Questions authority – Plays down superior / inferior categories	HIERARCHY – Submissive to authority, emphasis on positions in relationships – Accepts propriety
SELF-ASSERTION – Aggressive and expressive – Assertive – Open and accessible	DEFERENCE – Passive and yielding – Adherence to social politeness – Self-effacing
PERSONAL GROWTH – Social maturity – Personal development – Children taught to be personally adjusted more than academically	ACHIEVEMENT – Hard work – Financial success – Academic excellence and hard work taught at home

* Compiled from Wing Ning Pang, *The Chinese and the Chinese Church in America* (Pasadena, Calif.: Chinese World Mission Center, 1985), p. 39, and Sam Moy, "Cultural Differences Between Chinese and Americans," *About Face* [Fellowship of American Chinese Evangelicals] 6 (November 1984): 4.

1. *Unemployment and loss of sense of worth.* The frustration and loss may lead to parenting problems, since many parents feel inadequate in the role of breadwinner and model for the children.

2. *Parent-child conflicts of communication.* Children are expanding their knowledge and use of English much faster than their parents. As a result, children become impatient with the parents, and the parents feel they have lost control in communication with their children.

3. *Breakdown of traditional family structure.* No longer can the clearly defined roles and expectations in the traditional family be counted on as a source of strength in difficult and stressful times. The elderly feel lost and useless, for parents no longer feel in a position of authority and sense that they are ineffective as role models.

4. *Desire for biculturality.* In an age of cultural pluralism, biculturalism is a new area for both the minority and majority cultures to explore, but there is no real sense of how to achieve it or what problems it entails.

5. *Unrealistic expectations for children.* The desire to preserve aspects of one's own culture often puts pressure on children to behave in ways that are dysfunctional, especially if children are to satisfy other parental pressures toward academic success and economic mainstreaming.

6. *Shifting of role confusion within family.* In an economic situation where both parents must work and where there is increasing pressure from the children to communicate in English, family roles may shift rapidly and in ways that puzzle and frustrate the participants.

7. *Domestic violence.* Domestic violence is symptomatic both of the frustration and loss of direction arising from the breakdown of the traditional family structure and a shift in role expectations.

Compounded by all the usual stresses suffered by a visible minority immigrant group attempting to adapt to life in a new and radically different cultural setting, these problems also affect the educational adjustment and achievement of Asian American children in the American public school.

RELIGIOUS EDUCATION AND ASIAN AMERICAN CHURCHES

Generally speaking, the Asian American Christian communities are not much different from those in their homelands. This is particularly true among the first generation congregations. Moreover,

> the goal and practices of religious education in the Asian American churches are not much different from those in American Christian denominations. The reason is simply that the formation and development of Christian communities in Asia have been very much influenced by American churches since the turn of the century.[6]

At least two phenomena occur peculiar to Asian American religious education.[7] The first is a legacy of the nineteenth-century American Protestant churches: understanding of Christian education as a means of evangelism. The Sunday school is the strategic focal point of evangelistic endeavor. Church leaders concentrate their efforts on establishing high-quality educational programs from

6. C. Kim, "Asian Americans," *Harper's Encyclopedia of Religious Education* (New York: Harper & Row, 1990), p. 13.
7. Ibid., p. 13.

the beginning of a new congregation. Influenced by Confucian virtue of high admiration for learning, Asian Americans are eager to give their children the best available education, religious or secular. Consequently, good educational programs in a local church can draw many concerned parents to the congregation.

The second is the integration of religious education with language instruction. Some churches sponsor a separate language school alongside the existing Sunday school.

Whatever arrangement they may have, religious education in the Asian American churches has a strong cultural component in its design and intention.

Teaching Principles and Methods

Because Asians come from many parts of the world and are a diverse group of people, it is not an easy task to make suggestions that will fit all cultural backgrounds. But the following information should provide general guidelines.

Most Asians come from extended families in which many relatives live together in one household or at least in close proximity. Reverence and respect for older people are considered significant in Asian culture.

Many Asians have been reared under the British-American system of education. The teacher is an authority, and what he says is important. Therefore, lecture is a popular method of instruction. Students also have great respect for teachers and are sometimes fearful of them. To show their respect, students may rise when the teacher enters the room.

A problem in teaching Asian American students is the apparent lack of oral and writing ability. They tend to fear and avoid verbal classroom participation and to be hesitant and nervous about asking questions or apprehensive when called upon to speak. If a teacher takes time to build relationships, students will be more apt to respond and interact. Written work is often weak, disorganized, and unimaginative. These characteristics perpetuate a stereotype of Asian American students as quiet, unexpressive, and foreign in the sense that they do not appear to have mastered the English language. Part of the problem is a deficiency in language skills that in turn is attributable to many sources. The traditional Asian values that stressed obedience to authority, subordination and sensitivity to the wishes of others, and conformity and fatalistic acquiescence to outside forces did not allow or reward the quality of discussion and interaction that would develop language skills. Consequently, students often perform poorly in classroom discussions and have trouble with written work. Therefore, directions need to be stated simply and clearly. Difficult words, new vocabulary, names of people, and words spelled the same but with different meanings should be written on the chalkboard or overhead for clarification.

A second problem is the stress resulting from the pressures of high levels of school achievement exerted by families and community. From an early age, children are subject to strong family admonitions to do well in school. They are constantly reminded of the value of a good education in a competitive world, and of the sacrifices their parents make for their education especially at the college level. Asian American communities back this concern for education by prominently publicizing the names of students who win high honors or achieve outstanding grades. This heightens the sense of competitiveness among students and makes such achievements an important source of individual and family status in the community.

Many Asians are second-generation students. Their parents probably are not fluent in speaking and writing English. The children learn the language rapidly in school, but their parents prefer they speak their native language. Consequently, it is difficult for teachers to communicate with parents; but it is important for parents to understand what is being done and what progress the children are making. Therefore, teachers—like parents—need to be encouraging and motivating.

Asians may be slow in building personal relationships. They want to avoid conflicts and prefer to develop a "community spirit." They have a love and concern for others. Feelings play a significant role in their relationships. Sometimes students may be slow in expressing appreciation, but they are sincere when they do so.

CONCLUSION

The large number of immigrants from Asian countries since 1965 has led to a drastic increase in the Asian American population. This trend will continue if the United States immigration policy does not revert to one favoring European immigration.[8] The linguistic and cultural backgrounds of Asian American students have influenced their knowledge, concepts, and methods of learning. In addition, immigrant students have been influenced by the curricula, teaching methods, and other pedagogical practices of their native countries. These facts have to be examined and identified by researchers before appropriate curricula and pedagogy can be designed to meet the needs of Asian American students. Support from educational organizations, governmental agencies, and private foundations is needed to encourage research on educational issues concerning Asian American students. Such research findings will guide and direct the practitioners toward how to serve best the increasing number of Asian American students.

FOR FURTHER READING

AFRICAN AMERICANS

Foster, Charles R., and Grant Shockley, eds. *Working with Black Youth: Opportunities for Christian Ministry*. Nashville: Abingdon, 1989.

8. Sau-lim Tsang, "Asian-American Education," *Encyclopedia of Educational Research* (London: Free Press, 1982), pp. 171-73.

June, Lee N., ed. *The Black Family: Past, Present, and Future*. Grand Rapids: Zondervan, 1991.

Karenga, M. Ron. *Kwanzaa: Origin, Concepts, Practice*. Inglewood, Calif.: Kawaida, 1977.

Leland, Thomas Elgon. *Developing a Model of Religious Education for Black Southern Baptist Churches*. Louisville, Ky.: Southern Baptist Theological Seminary, 1981.

McCall, Emmanuel L. *Black Church Life-Styles*. Nashville: Broadman, 1986.

McCray, Walter A. *The Black Presence in the Bible*. Chicago: Black Light Fellowship, 1990.

———. *Discipling the Children of Black America*. Chicago: Black Light Fellowship, 1979.

Smith, Wallace C. *The Church in the Life of the Black Family*. Valley Forge, Pa.: Judson, 1985.

HISPANICS

Cordasco, Francesco, and Eugene Bucchioni, eds. *The Puerto Rican Community and Its Children on the Mainland: A Source Book for Teachers, Social Workers, and Other Professionals*. Metuchen, N.J.: Scarecrow, 1982.

Grossman, Herbert. *Educating Hispanic Students: Cultural Implications for Instruction, Classroom Management, Counseling, and Assessment*. Springfield, Ill.: C. C. Thomas, 1984.

Keefe, Susan F., and Amado M. Padilla. *Chicano Ethnicity*. Albuquerque, N. Mex.: U. of New Mexico, 1987.

Montoya, Alex D. *Hispanic Ministry in North America*. Grand Rapids, Mich.: Zondervan, 1987.

Pedraza-Bailey, Silvia. *Political and Economic Migrants in America: Cubans and Mexicans*. Austin, Tex.: U. of Texas, 1985.

Portes, Alejandro, and Robert L. Bach. *Latin Journey: Cuban and Mexican Immigrants in the United States*. Berkeley, Calif.: U. of California, 1985.

Ramirez III, Manuel, and Alfredo Castaneda. *Cultural Democracy, Bicognitive Development, and Education*. New York: Academic, 1974.

ASIAN AMERICANS

Ho, David Yau-Fai, ed. *Chinese Patterns of Behavior: A Sourcebook of Psychological and Psychiatric Studies*. Westport, Conn.: Praeger, 1989.

Magiafico, Luciano. *Contemporary American Immigrants: Patterns of Filipino, Korean, and Chinese Settlement in the United States*. Westport, Conn.: Praeger, 1988.

Man-Keug, Ho. *Family Therapy with Ethnic Minorities*. Newbury Park, Calif.: Sage, 1987.

Ng, Donald, ed. *Asian Pacific American Youth Ministry*. Valley Forge, Pa.: Judson,

1988.

Yanagisako, Sylvia J. *Transforming the Past: Tradition and Kinship Among Japanese Americans*. Stanford, Calif.: Stanford U., 1985.

Part 4

The Church's Strategies for Christian Education

The church that Jesus Christ is building in this world is still His primary means of reaching the world with His "good news." At the same time, people, resources, and programs must be properly organized and coordinated for the church to carry out effectively its educational mission of guiding persons to maturity in Jesus Christ (Eph. 4:13). This section gives us an understanding of the major areas for strategic thinking and planning in seeing quality growth take place in the church's educational ministry, regardless of the size of the church. Chapter 25 begins with an overview of the total church program. The pastor (in chap. 26) is then considered in his key role as "equipper," in which he not only preaches and teaches the Word of God but ultimately supervises that total church program. Chapter 27 discusses the multiple staff-team concept in the church and the need for professional staff persons in specialized areas of church education.

The oversight, coordination, and development of educational ministries in the church is the responsibility of the board (or committee) of Christian education, as described in chapter 28. The ongoing work of evaluation that must precede long-range planning is the topic of chapter 29, while chapters 30 and 31 deal with the heartbeat of healthy educational ministry—the recruiting, equipping, and training of lay leadership.

Principles in the proper use of curriculum materials is the focus of chapter 32; the important phenomenon of small group ministries is presented in chapter 33. This section closes with chapter 34, which addresses the computer resources available to support educational ministries, and the importance of wise planning in the management of educational facilities and equipment in the growing church (chap. 35).

25

Doris A. Freese with J. Omar Brubaker

The Church's Educational Ministry

THE CHURCH AND ITS EDUCATIONAL MINISTRY
- **Begins with Jesus Christ Himself as the Master Teacher**
- **Focuses on evangelizing, edifying, and equipping**
- **Accomplishes its mission by carrying out biblical imperatives and objectives**
- **Meets the needs of people through varied ministries**
- **Functions more as family and demonstrates interdependence under God**

Today's church seeks to meet the biblical imperatives of evangelism and edification (Matt. 28:19-20) through its total program. Although both evangelism and edification occur in all aspects of that program, edification frequently takes form in a more systematic way through the ministries or agency programs that constitute the church's educational ministry. An accurate assessment of the extent of edification and the effectiveness of educational programs or ministries may be made when certain questions are asked: What biblical principles underlie the

Doris A. Freese, Ph.D., was professor of Christian education, Moody Bible Institute, Chicago, Illinois. She is now deceased.

J. Omar Brubaker, M.A., is professor of Christian education, Moody Bible Institute, Chicago, Illinois.

church's educational ministry? How does the total church program seek to carry out such principles? What process can be used as a guide in determining and implementing ministries or programs? What educational ministries currently exist in our churches as a means of evangelizing and edifying? How can the educational program function more in/like the context of family?

BIBLICAL PRINCIPLES

General agreement exists in today's Christian society about the role and importance of the home in teaching (see chaps. 36-38). Old Testament passages command and identify the educational primacy of the family in the transmission of faith from one generation to another. Likewise, the New Testament describes the place of nurture and training in the home. Gene Getz cautions in his book *The Measure of a Family* that although functions are clearly identified in the New Testament, little is said regarding what actual form or pattern the home teaching should take.[1]

The Scriptures also describe the function of teaching as it relates to a body larger than the family, gathered specifically for instruction. In the Old Testament, Israel gathered together to hear the reading of the law. The Deuteronomy 6:6-9 passage, which outlines the teaching responsibility of the family, occurs within a body of instruction given to Israel by Moses. In other words, the gathered body was taught how to teach and live in their families. The great history of Israel was frequently rehearsed verbally by the leaders to the entire congregation (Josh. 24). Duties of Old Testament priests included teaching the law along with the sacramental duties of Tabernacle and Temple worship (Lev. 10:11; Deut. 31:10-13; Mal. 2:7). Ezra, identified as priest and scribe (Ezra 7:10-11; Neh. 8:1-4), assumed a key role in teaching the law to the exiles who returned to Israel from Babylon.

New Testament pictures of teaching begin with Jesus Christ Himself as the Master Teacher, who taught gatherings varying in size from one (Nicodemus; the Samaritan woman) to several persons (small groups of disciples) to huge crowds (five thousand sitting on a hillside). With the inception of the church as recorded in the book of Acts, teaching emerged as an essential means of instruction in doctrine and Christian lifestyle as the infant church grew under the teaching of the apostles (Acts 2:42). Paul's ministry included not only evangelizing the unsaved but also teaching new converts and strengthening them in the faith (Acts 14:21-22). Among the gifted persons in the church were those who served as pastor-teachers (Eph. 4:11) and those who taught (Rom. 12:7; I Cor. 12:28). Paul encouraged Timothy to observe the principle of multiplication in his ministry— to commit God's truth to men who would be able to teach others also (2 Tim. 2:2).

Getz's caution regarding function versus form also applies to the educational ministry of the church. Although the function of teaching is clearly indicated,

---

1.   Gene A. Getz, *The Measure of a Family* (Glendale, Calif.: Regal, 1976), p. 7.

the form, pattern, or design it should take is indistinct. The local church, therefore, is free under the guidance of the Holy Spirit to design ways to teach within certain guidelines.

THE TOTAL CHURCH PROGRAM

Both function and form are reflected in what a local church does. Whatever program a church plans and implements, it must carry out the ultimate purpose for which the church, the Body of Christ, exists. That purpose is to make disciples as summed up in the Great Commission: "Go [or more accurately, "Going," or, "As you go"] therefore and make disciples of all the nations, baptizing them in the name of the Father and the Son and the Holy Spirit, teaching them to observe all that I commanded you" (Matt. 28:19-20). The responsibility includes both evangelizing, to bring persons to Jesus Christ, and teaching them in His commandments and in the doctrines of the Word. Implied in the Great Commission is the aspect of training and equipping. How can one "go" unless he has been equipped in some way to do so (compare with Eph. 4:12-13)?

In its efforts to carry out the Great Commission, the church must marshal its entire program in the direction of that purpose. The total church program, therefore, can be defined as the entire, complete program that a local church carries on to bring persons to Christ as Savior and Lord, to guide them in growth toward Christlikeness, and to equip them for effective service in the will of God. All ministries of a local church, such as pastoral, teaching, music, evangelism, extension, and preaching, will focus on the three major areas of evangelizing, edifying, and equipping. Christian education is the work of the church.

Every age level will receive a proper and balanced emphasis in salvation, Christian growth, and service. Children, youth, and adults will be confronted with the claims of Christ for salvation. Christian children, youth, and adults will be taught biblical truths at their level of comprehension and will be encouraged to walk and grow in Jesus Christ. Christians of all ages will be trained—simply or more complexly—to share their faith in Christ and to participate in the growth process of one another through service and expression.

In the development of its program, the church will seek to allow for involvement of and ministry to the total person. Each person possesses intellect, attitudes, feelings, will, and capacity to relate to God and to others. In order to meet the needs of the whole person, the program should include four major elements: instruction, worship, fellowship, and expression-service. (Training and equipping are a part of instruction and expression.)

Those four elements are reflected in the early church as described in Acts 2:42-47. Note that the new believers devoted themselves "to the apostles' teaching" (instruction), devoted "themselves to fellowship, to the breaking of bread and to prayer" (fellowship), continued "in the temple praising God" (worship), and shared possessions with those in need (expression-service). Furthermore, they had favor with all people throughout the city, and God added "to their number day by day those who were being saved" (evangelism).

INSTRUCTION

Instruction, through preaching and teaching, relates primarily to the intellect and involves the transmission of biblical information, doctrines, and truths. It also includes training, such as the development of teaching or leadership skills. Since teaching and preaching seek to go far beyond mere intellectual exercise and expansion, instruction lays the foundation (which includes teaching the good news for salvation) for movement toward maturity in Christ as persons grow in the knowledge of Him and His Word.

WORSHIP

Worship serves as a means of expressing our thoughts about God to God. From the old English word *worthship*, it denotes the worthiness of the individual receiving reverence and honor. A right attitude that acknowledges who God is and His right to receive our praise and adoration is essential in worship. Although worship or heart expression involves the person primarily at the feeling level, it should be a result of what he knows about God. Lois E. LeBar states, "Worship is adoring God for Himself, thanking Him for all His goodness to us, and in His presence adjusting our will to His will. While instruction informs the mind, worship challenges the will and emotions. On the basis of Scriptural truth, our attitudes are shaped and conformed to His likeness."[2]

FELLOWSHIP

A third element that should be an essential part of the total church program is *fellowship*. Not only does the believer seek fellowship with his Savior and Lord, but he seeks mutual edification within the church, the Body of Christ (Eph. 4:15-16; 1 John 1:3). True fellowship goes beyond mere social or recreational activities—which may be used as a means of gathering people together and helping them feel comfortable within a group—to the building up of one another through expressions of concern, prayer and shared time, utilization of gifts and abilities, and development of warm Christian friendship. Such fellowship can take place at any age level. Even children can develop a sense of community through activities that promote cooperation rather than competition. In the context of adult ministries, LeBar says, "The depth of their fellowship with the Lord and with each other conditions the quality of the worship and evangelism of the church."[3]

EXPRESSION-SERVICE

The fourth element, *expression-service*, focuses on the need for each individ-

2. Lois E. LeBar, *Focus on People in Church Education* (Westwood, N.J.: Revell, 1968), p. 39.
3. Ibid., p. 183.

ual believer to act upon his knowledge and faith. It can take a variety of forms—believers can speak of their faith, teach, visit, serve as deacons or deaconesses, assist in the administration of the local church, train others, demonstrate hospitality, care for the sick in the congregation, pray, or lead a Bible study. Not only are possibilities for service numerous within any local body of believers, but also all ages—children, youth, and adults—can be involved.

EVANGELISM

Evangelism, the presentation of the gospel, is a major aim of Christian education as well as a biblical imperative. It is not considered one of the major elements, but it permeates all four. Instruction, worship, fellowship, and expression-service can all be used in the evangelization efforts of the church to win others to Jesus Christ. For example, at camp (which includes all four elements) a senior high student may find Christ as Savior through one of several activities. He may hear and respond in a Bible hour (instruction), he may make a decision at an evening campfire (worship), or he may be led to Christ by some fellow campers in his cabin (fellowship, expression-service). The local church should ask, Do the persons involved in our various programs and ministries clearly present the claims of Christ for salvation so that the unsaved can and will respond? Is there an emphasis on salvation as well as on Christian growth and service?

A careful examination of programs for a particular age level may reveal either an overemphasis or lack among the four elements. Each department does well to chart all the programs planned for any given year (Sunday school, Sunday evening program, camp, vacation Bible school, weekday club), and indicate the elements that receive primary emphasis in each specific program. Once a department has developed its chart, the following questions may be asked: On which elements is the most emphasis currently being placed? What elements are either missing or have an inadequate emphasis?

THE EDUCATIONAL PROCESS

One must view the church program of Christian education as composed of various parts or ministries that are educational in nature, that seek to meet the needs of the whole person, and that carry out biblical imperatives. All too frequently a program or ministry is launched on the basis of its attractive curriculum materials, its success in some other church, or its emphasis on a current issue or problem. Likewise, a program in existence may be continued for a variety of reasons, ranging from tradition and entrenchment to fear of trying something new. Rather than developing or continuing programs on such bases, the local church can plan and implement ministries following a sequential order or process—the educational process.

THE EDUCATIONAL PROCESS*

Biblical Imperatives and Objectives

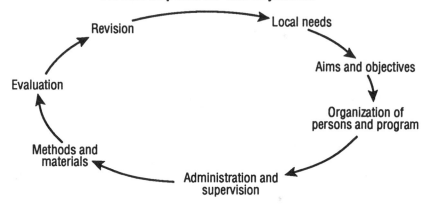

* Diagram adapted from materials suggested by LeBar, Gangel, and Getz.

BIBLICAL IMPERATIVES

The educational process begins with the biblical imperatives of evangelism and edification as seen in Matthew 28:19-20 and the related objectives determined by the local church as it views its mission in carrying out those imperatives. The following illustrates the first step in the educational process:

> Biblical imperative: Edification—"teaching them to observe whatsoever I have commanded you" (Matt. 28:20).

> Biblical objective: The local church will provide the means for effective edification whereby believers of all ages can develop into spiritually mature and effective Christians.[4]

NEEDS

When clear objectives have been written, the next step is to determine the more specific needs of the local church as they relate to the objectives. It may be well to look at particular age groups as well as at the larger fellowship of believers.

A representative body composed of teachers, leaders, and parents might meet to discuss and identify the needs of youth, for example. Both general and spe-

4. Gene A. Getz, *Sharpening the Focus of the Church* (Chicago: Moody, 1974), p. 265.

cific needs should be identified. Some needs will be common to all ages; others will apply specifically to one age group. Needs relate to various aspects of the whole person (physical, mental, emotional, social, and spiritual) as well as to organizational, administrative, and supervisory areas. For example, the following represent several kinds of needs:

Need	*Area*
A need for a plan that provides fellowship for senior citizens	Organizational
A need for the juniors (grades 4, 5, 6) to learn to do simple Bible study	Departmental
A need for a quality library for our teachers' use	Organizational
A need for trained teachers for our Sunday school	Supervisory
A need for Steve and Diane to receive Christ as Savior	Personal

AIMS

The next step in the process is to write aims or objectives that arise out of the identification of needs. An aim or objective is simply a statement of what the group or individual plans to accomplish. It gives direction to planning and implementation and serves as a checkpoint as progress of the plan is assessed. Aims will be both immediate and long-range. For example, leaders of an educational agency such as Sunday school can ask the questions: By the end of the year, what enrollment increase can we achieve? How will teachers receive training for improvement? What visitation programs will be included in the Sunday school? A teacher who is also determining aims will ask questions such as: By the end of the year, what will my pupils know about God, Jesus Christ, the Bible, the Christian life? How will their attitudes grow and change? What new or additional steps will they take in their Christian walk?

Aims may be general or specific. General aims tend to express in broad terms what is to happen within a group or individual, whereas specific aims can be linked with particular needs. However, aims of any kind—immediate or long-range, general or specific—should be written with the following characteristics, and these characteristics should be evident whether the aim is for a person, program, administration, supervision, or lesson:

- Brief enough to be remembered
- Clear enough to be written down
- Concise enough to be kept in focus
- Specific enough to be accomplished
- Accomplishable within a designated time period

Educators refer to four kinds of aims or objectives: cognitive (having to do with the mind), affective (having to do with feelings and attitudes), skill (having to do with motor development), and behavioral (having to do with conduct). A similar way of looking at aims is to identify them as *know, feel, skill*, and *do* or *conduct* aims.

The Christian worker senses the importance of communicating knowledge, but he is aware that the purpose of teaching goes far beyond the accumulation of information and facts. He therefore writes aims that not only will help persons to study and discover God's truth but will also guide them in finding ways to apply the truth to their lives. The leader—concerned with his students' overall Christian growth—writes aims to guide in that direction. He may write a single *feel* or *do* aim, or he may write a series of aims (*know* ➤ *feel* ➤ *do*), but he is ever concerned with immediate and long-range changes in the lives of persons. Jesus reminded His disciples of this in John 13:17.

ORGANIZATION OF PERSONS AND PROGRAM

The church exists as an organism or a living body that transcends time and space. Only God Himself can see the Body of Christ in its entirety at one time, and the church will continue to grow until the return of Christ. The local church body is but a small part of a much larger whole. It exists as an organization or a local gathering of believers with some structure or form that is both visible and definable. Even local fellowships that hold to a minimum of organization have some identifiable form.

When needs of the local body have been identified and aims have been written, the next step is to organize the educational ministries program to carry out the aims, which in turn meet the needs. Organization, or the framework underlying the plan, has to do with the grouping and arranging of the persons and programs. It puts wheels under the program to move it forward.

Organization is *person-related*, with job descriptions used to explain relationship and responsibilities of people to the work. It is also *program-related*. It defines the relationships of each agency or ministry to the total church program. Statements of policy and procedure help identify the task and operating plan of each agency. Organization should evidence several characteristics.

1. Organization should be *unified*. Whatever is done in the name of program should contribute to and be an integral part of the total ministry. It helps to carry out the overarching biblical objectives of the church.

2. Organization should be *simple*. It should allow the persons involved to minister freely within a minimum of necessary boundary lines. It helps facilitate rather than impede ministry.

3. Organization should be *flexible* in order to change when change is required— if or when a plan or program must be altered, supplemented, strengthened, or even discarded.

4. Organization should be *cooperative* with a sense of God's authority.[5] All persons involved in a local church ministry should be willing to follow the simple lines of authority set forth in God's Word: God, Christ, man, woman.

5. Organization should be *correlated* in that persons within a particular ministry or agency in the church education program understand its relation to other ministries. Such relationship will be evidenced in curriculum, programming, and departmentalization. Correlation of each ministry within the church education program avoids overlapping and gapping.

6. Organization should be *participative* so that members within various ministries are involved in setting goals, determining programs, and evaluating progress. The Christian worker acknowledges the picture presented by Paul in Ephesians 4:16 of the body with its many members, which in proper working order "causes the growth of the body for the building up of itself in love."

Kenneth O. Gangel reminds those involved in leadership, "In the process of departmentalization, unification, correlation, construction of organization charts and all the rest, we dare not lose sight of the fact that in the final analysis we are dealing with an *organism* and therefore must allow the church's spiritual aspects to constantly permeate the organizational process."[6]

ADMINISTRATION AND SUPERVISION

Organization of the program leads to administration (the people side of organization) and supervision. *Administration* has to do with guiding and directing the persons toward desired goals within the structure, or framework, of organization. It is the organization fleshed out in people who by common agreement now move forward to accomplish their task.

Administration is covered in chapter 28. For this discussion the functions of administration will be summarized under two major headings: delegation and coordination. Remember that ad*minister* is mostly "minister"—and that is to serve.

Delegation seeks to distribute responsibility among those involved in ministry. It involves selecting the right person for the task and holding him accountable as he fulfills his responsibility.

Coordination provides the thread that weaves through all that takes place in the educational ministry of the church. The administrator leads his workers in understanding and implementing the purposes and goals of the total church program.

---

5. LeBar in *Focus on People in Church Education*, p. 72, uses the expression "democratic under God's authority." True unity and cooperation among believers takes place only as those believers follow and function with the authority structure laid down by God in His Word.
6. Kenneth O. Gangel, *Leadership for Christian Education* (Chicago: Moody, 1970), p. 60.

Supervision relates to improving the quality of both leadership and program. It involves overseeing, motivating, maintaining proper relationships, and evaluating performance and product.

A good supervisor will guide his workers in setting and maintaining standards. He will be aware of his workers' strengths and areas that need improvement. He will seek to train them, helping them do a better job.

The following chart illustrates organization, administration, and supervision as they relate to one another.

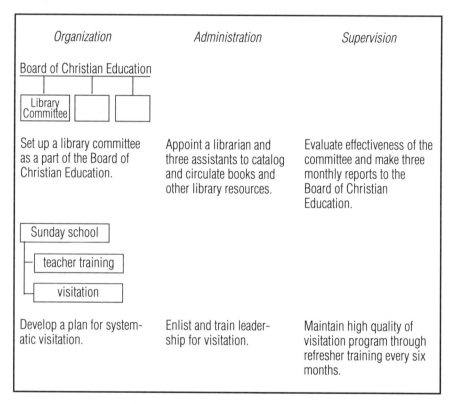

Organization	Administration	Supervision
Board of Christian Education ├─ Library Committee ☐ ☐		
Set up a library committee as a part of the Board of Christian Education.	Appoint a librarian and three assistants to catalog and circulate books and other library resources.	Evaluate effectiveness of the committee and make three monthly reports to the Board of Christian Education.
Sunday school ├─ teacher training └─ visitation		
Develop a plan for systematic visitation.	Enlist and train leadership for visitation.	Maintain high quality of visitation program through refresher training every six months.

METHODS AND MATERIALS

The educational process to this point has concentrated on the persons involved and the programs or tasks to be implemented. Persons, of course, will utilize methods and materials to carry out the tasks. Byrne defines method as an "orderly, systematic procedure employed to carry out some purpose or to gain some preconceived goal."[7] Method is simply a way of doing the task, whereas materials are the tools or aids used in any given method. Byrne places methods into two cat-

7. H. W. Byrne, *A Christian Approach to Education,* 2d ed. (Milford, Mich.: Mott Media, 1977), p. 185.

egories—administrative and instructional.

The "how" or method of the educational ministry of the church builds on an understanding of both content (curriculum) and educational process (teaching-learning). (Those aspects are discussed in detail in chapters 7 and 32). LeBar stresses the importance of the Scripture method that she refers to as person-Book-person. In it the teacher serves as a guide to help pupils "discern their own real needs, discover the answer in Scripture, and practice the truth."[8] A variation of her diagram of person-Book-person shows the relationship of pupils' needs, the Word of God, the teacher, and the Holy Spirit.

When emphasis is placed on guiding pupils to discover answers and to respond, the teaching methods take a specific approach. Rather than concentrating on delivery of a large amount of content, the teacher carefully selects methods that involve pupils in active Bible study and discovery. Interaction methods, such as question and answer, discussion, Bible search, buzz groups, and role play, will be used along with teacher focus methods, such as lecture and storytelling. Curriculum materials will be selected not only for the quality of content—that is, how clearly and accurately the Word of God is taught—but also for the process or method that is used to guide pupils in learning.

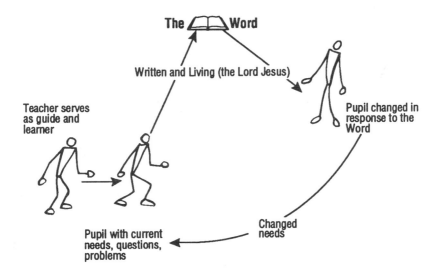

Holy Spirit

The 📖 Word

Written and Living (the Lord Jesus)

Teacher serves as guide and learner

Pupil changed in response to the Word

Changed needs

Pupil with current needs, questions, problems

EVALUATION

The final step in the educational process, evaluation, is in no sense a termination point. Continual evaluation occurs as key aspects of the total educa-

8. LeBar, p. 50.

tional ministry are examined. Evaluation looks at the program, the pupil, the process, the progress, and the product. Each aspect is examined and evaluated by asking questions such as: To what extent are persons' needs being met? To what extent are aims being accomplished? What spiritual results are evident? How can results be conserved?

More specific questions can be asked that relate to a particular program for curriculum or to individual pupils within a class. In each instance evaluation seeks to measure progress and to determine what has been accomplished. The evaluative process then results in a reassessment of needs, which may be different as a result of the accomplishment of earlier goals. New aims are written, and the educational process continues.

MEETING NEEDS OF PEOPLE THROUGH VARIED MINISTRIES

What are some forms that might be utilized to carry out the church's Christian education program? As stated before, although function is described in the Scriptures, little is said about exact form, pattern, or design. Since a church cannot have function without form, examination of a particular form or ministry should include an assessment of its function. Does it emphasize teaching (instruction) or worship? Does the ministry allow for edification of believers through fellowship? To what extent does the program encourage expression and service?

Three major time frames serve as a backdrop for examination of Christian education ministries: Sunday, weekday, and seasonal. Some teaching ministries, such as Sunday school, occur every Sunday during the year, whereas some ministries may coincide with the public school year, such as children's church or training time.

Weekdays provide opportunity for a variety of ministries, not only in form but also in duration. Such ministries may take the form of weekday clubs, fellowship organizations, Bible classes, prayer and share meetings, and training sessions. Time frames vary from short-term, such as several weeks for a training series in a particular department, to long-term, such as clubs that keep pace with the school year.

A third time frame recognizes the growing interest in and use of summer months and vacation periods such as Christmas and spring breaks. Vacation Bible school, camp, and retreat programs take advantage of such blocks of time that allow for in-depth ministry to a particular age level or group of people in the church.

SUNDAY SCHOOL

Although in some cases Sundays or weekends tend to see an evacuation of people from the home area, Sunday still remains the day on which most people choose to worship the Lord and seek instruction in His Word. For more than two hundred years the Sunday school has served the purpose of instruction—originally to teach lower class children to read and write and later to teach the Word of God to both the unchurched and the churched. Today the Sunday school has been identified as the church at study, involving people in the Word of God and training them to study it together.

What characterizes the Sunday school of today? First, it is a school that meets on *Sunday*. Sunday is still freer than other days of the week for many people and offers opportunity for the church to gather together for the purpose of instruction in the Word as well as for worship. Even churches with innovative approaches to worship and program structure provide some Sunday educational experience for children, and often for youth and adults, prior to or following the morning worship time.

Second, the Sunday school is a *school*. Its main purpose has been instruction, and it has committed itself to a systematic teaching of the Bible. In no other education ministry of the church do so many age levels receive such a systematic approach to the Scriptures. The Sunday school can teach not only biblical truths and general doctrine but can also stress the distinctive doctrines of each church. It is committed to the Great Commission, both in evangelizing and in edifying or "teaching them to observe all that I commanded you" (Matt. 28:20).

As a school, the Sunday school can departmentalize in order to teach persons on their individual levels. Although some Sunday schools use an intergenerational pattern (grouping persons across a variety of age levels—see last section of chapter), the advantage of teaching persons at their comprehension level remains strong. Children who think literally and concretely need to be taught Bible truths in that way, whereas youth and adults, who can deal with more abstract concepts, can study the same Bible truths at a more mature level.

Third, the Sunday school has been and is essentially a *lay movement*. Both in England and in the United States the Sunday school began as a movement launched and taught by lay persons rather than by clergy. In fact, it was not until the early 1800s that the church began to recognize the Sunday school as a viable and legitimate teaching agency of the church.

The spirit of 2 Timothy 2:2 is exemplified in the lay emphasis of the Sunday school. Leaders teach persons who in turn teach others. The pastor of a local body of believers can capitalize on the lay aspect of the Sunday school as he seeks to put into operation the pattern of Ephesians 4:11-12: "He gave some as pastors and teachers, for the equipping of the saints for the work of service, to the building up of the body of Christ." The pastor serves as the equipper or facilitator, teaching and training believers to do the work of the ministry—specifically, teaching in the Sunday school. The Sunday school has further served as a training ground for church leadership. Because teachers of all ages are needed to teach all ages, the Sunday school has proved to be both a recruitment and training center for current and future leadership.

Fourth, the Sunday school is *evangelistic* in its ministry. Boys and girls, youth and adults throughout the history of the Sunday school have found Jesus Christ as Savior through the ministry of faithful teachers. Though the Sunday school seeks to reach entire families for Christ and to teach all members of the family, it also provides opportunity for evangelism and teaching of children whose parents do not attend church or Sunday school. Busing of children to Sunday school is often done because parents are not opposed to letting their children attend. Every effort should be made, however, to reach the parents at the same time the children are being taught.

CHILDREN'S CHURCH

Whereas Sunday school serves a teaching function, the children's church provides opportunity for children to worship at their level of understanding and ability and to participate actively in worship. Churchtime for children is not intended to be either a second Sunday school or a substitute for Sunday school (that is, a place to leave children while parents attend only the morning worship service). Rather, children's church builds on the Sunday school experience and capitalizes on the additional time for Christian education. It provides opportunity both to train children in worship and reverence and to train them in leadership and service. Most curriculum materials for children's church provide for age-level groupings and for child participation. For best results, the children's church leadership will be selected with the same care taken in selecting Sunday school teachers. Continuity of leadership is desirable for the sake of the children and their continued growth in biblical truth and spiritual walk. Some intergenerational emphasis should also be included in the worship experience. Pastors can also show some interest in the children when they are in the regular worship services whenever they are conducted.

EQUIPPING AND TRAINING MINISTRY

Another educational ministry that can utilize Sundays is a training/equipping time that can be geared for all ages. Its major purpose has been primarily instruction and expression with a view toward developing leadership qualities in children, youth, and adults.

In some churches the time slot on Sunday evening is used for youth meetings, with an emphasis on Bible study, singing, and fellowship. Where adults are involved, the training period may take the form of instruction in elective studies such as Bible books, doctrine, teacher training, current issues, missions, family life, and leadership training.

WEEKDAY CLUBS AND BIBLE STUDIES

Weekdays also provide time for various kinds of ministry. Groups of children may meet in the afternoon or in the evening in clubs such as Awana, Pioneer clubs, and Christian Service Brigade, where there is a strong emphasis on fellowship, expression, activity, and achievement.

Home Bible classes for children, such as Child Evangelism Fellowship clubs, BCM International clubs, and Joy Clubs, tend to an evangelistic approach.

Young people may meet in the early morning before school, in the evening, or on Saturdays for Bible study or a variety of social and recreational activities. Adults utilize a variety of times in a wide range of ministries: early morning Bible study and prayer for working men, morning Bible studies for women, and evening Bible study and/or fellowship times. Often the club or home Bible class may serve as a means of evangelism.

SEASONAL MINISTRIES

Summer months and vacation periods as well as weekends have the advantage of offering blocks of time when groups can engage in in-depth experiences such as camps, retreats, vacation Bible schools, and seminars. Such experiences usually include all four program elements: instruction, worship, fellowship, and expression-service. The exception is seminars, which often focus on a particular topic such as teacher and leadership training and therefore reach a special group. Seasonal ministries may be intergenerational as well as age-graded. Family camp, family retreat, and family vacation Bible school allow all ages to learn from and fellowship with one another. Even intensified study, such as that at a family life retreat or seminar, appears informal because of the relaxed setting and atmosphere of fellowship.

INTERGENERATIONAL LEARNING

In his book *Intergenerational Religious Education*, James W. White defines intergenerational learning: "Intergenerational religious education is two or more different age groups of people in a religious community together learning/growing/living in faith through in-common-experiences, parallel-learning, contributive-occasions, and interactive sharing." He diagrams it as:

Inter	= two or more
Generational	= different age groups of people
Religious	= in a religious community together
Education	= learning/growing/living in faith through
	In-Common Experience
	Parallel-Learning
	Contributive-Occasions and
	Interactive-Sharing[9]

Various models White mentions are: family group, weekly class, workshop or event, worship service, worship-education program, and all-congregation camp.

Christian educators have recognized that young and old can and have learned

9. James W. White, *Intergenerational Religious Education* (Birmingham, Ala.: Religious Education Press, 1988), pp. 18, 33.

effectively together in life experiences. The church's educational ministry can accept the challenge that we need to improve upon learning with and from each other in various ways through its program. Insights abound in Scripture with the emphasis on education in the home, family, and community. The numerous religious rites and festivals were occasions for learning in an intergenerational context. Hebrew Christian (messianic) congregations build on this rich heritage. Teachers and leaders in the church should develop this valid option and concern.

Grouping persons across a variety of age levels—more family style—helps break the pattern of excessive age-group and departmental divisions. As noted earlier, it can be considered in the ministries of instruction and worship, as well as the seasonal ministries and fellowship opportunities. The latter provide the relaxed, information atmosphere of the less structured, longer time frame that allows for a kind of learning to take place that more closely resembles that which occurs in the home. The local church functions to bring people together. The church family must function more as family and demonstrate interdependence under God.

SUMMARY

Church educational ministries may and do take a variety of forms, as history and current practice indicate. The basic function of teaching, however, must continue to be evident. The church must continue to serve both as reinforcer of the educational ministry of the home and as educator, equipping saints and causing the growth of the church body for the building up of itself in love (Eph. 4:12, 16).

FOR FURTHER READING*

* See also the bibliographies for chapters 26-33.

Benson, Warren S., and Mark H. Senter III. *The Complete Book of Youth Ministry*. Chicago: Moody, 1987.

Byrne, H. W. *A Christian Approach to Education*. Grand Rapids: Baker, 1986.

Church Educational Ministries. Wheaton, Ill.: Evangelical Training Association, 1986.

Daniel, Eleanor. *The ABC's of VBS*. Cincinnati: Standard, 1984.

Freese, Doris A. *Children's Church: A Comprehensive How-To*. Chicago: Moody, 1982.

Getz, Gene A. *Sharpening the Focus of the Church*. Wheaton, Ill.: Victor, 1984.

LeBar, Lois E. *Education That Is Christian*. Edited by James E. Plueddemann. Wheaton, Ill.: Victor, 1989.

Miles, M. Scott. *Families Growing Together: Church Programs for Family Learning*. Wheaton, Ill.: Victor, 1990.

Raus, Bob. *Ministry Through Camping*. Nashville: Convention, 1990.

Understanding Sunday School. Wheaton, Ill.: Evangelical Training Association, 1981.

26

Donald M. Geiger

The Pastor's Educational Ministry

THE PASTOR'S MINISTRY IN CHRISTIAN EDUCATION
- **Knowing the times**
- **Focusing the vision of the church**
- **Modeling excellence**
- **Developing leadership**
- **Delegating responsibility**
- **Affirming and supporting**

Christian education that communicates, relates, convinces, and changes lives has never been a greater challenge, or more urgently important in our churches than in this decade of rapid change. And in the majority of our churches, the pastor is the key to developing Christian education ministries that genuinely reach our own people and effectively penetrate our increasingly secular society with the gospel. Even in churches large enough to have a pastor (or director) of Christian education, the leadership and support of the senior pastor is essential if Christian education is to enjoy the prominence it deserves. This has always been true, but never more so than now.

DONALD M. GEIGER, Th.M., is senior pastor of Castleview Baptist Church, Indianapolis, Indiana.

THE PASTOR'S ROLE AS VISIONARY AND OBSERVER OF SOCIETY

Like many organizations, churches are often resistant to change within their walls and oblivious to change in the culture. Today, however, change is the characterizing word in our society; prognosticators are telling us there will be more change in the next ten years than in the past thirty. In the church the pastor must be the leader in recognizing and interpreting what is happening.

Carolyn Corbin's comments were written for the business world but are equally valid for the church:

> Society is changing so rapidly that we are being called upon to navigate uncharted waters. The future is rushing into the present at such an alarming pace that we are being forced to apply new rules even before we have learned them well. . . . In fact, change is occurring so rapidly that most of us must run to keep up with the status quo. . . . The rapidity of change will become exponential. . . . However, those people who understand how to deal with change . . . will hold an edge over those who do not possess the knowledge to challenge these changes when they occur.[1]

The pastor must lead the way in understanding the times, in interpreting them to the congregation, and leading the leadership in applying God's timeless truth in ways that communicate, convince, and change lives. He must be like the men of Issachar, "who understood the times and knew what Israel should do" (1 Chron. 12:32).

Some of the crucial change agents and areas of change that will directly impact our approach to modern Christian education in the coming years include the following:

- the breakdown of the American family
- the rising number of single-parent families
- the rapid pace of life and decreasing amount of leisure time
- increasing number of two-breadwinner families
- the graying of America
- a secularized, valueless society
- the growing influence of the New Age Movement
- the changing role of women
- urbanization
- the increasing gap between the rich and poor
- drugs
- AIDS
- the increasing cultural and spiritual illiteracy
- the explosion of knowledge
- the use of high-tech in educating the young
- the change from a muscle to a mental society

---

1. Carolyn Corbin, *Strategies 2000* (Austin, Tex.: Eakin Press), pp. 5-6.

- the ever-increasing influence of television
- the baby boomer generation
- the environmental crisis
- the collapse of communism
- genetic engineering

These and many other areas of change directly and powerfully impact our people—how they live, how they learn, how they think, and the problems, temptations, and issues with which they must grapple from day to day. They certainly impact the people we are targeting to reach with the gospel.

"Business as usual" in the few hours we have them, using methods and applications that were effective thirty years ago, will not equip our people to live in the present. The pastor's first responsibility is to understand and interpret the times. In addition to newspapers and periodicals, some current books to help the busy pastor understand and interpret the times are listed at the conclusion of this chapter.

THE PASTOR'S ROLE AS VISIONARY AND GOAL-SETTER

Just as the choices in every other area of our society are multiplying, so in our churches the choices of ministries we may choose to emphasize are continually increasing, along with pressure from special interest groups within our churches to create more ministries than we can ever staff or manage. In this day of diversity, however, no church can be all things to all people.

The pastor must lead in establishing a clear, biblical, focused mission statement from which the church's objectives and goals derive.

> Leadership begins when a vision emerges. Proverbs 29:18 says, "Where there is no vision, the people perish" (KJV). The true meaning of these words is "Without a vision, the people cast off restraint." When a group is under the direction of a person who has no vision, the result is confusion, disorder, rebellion, uncontrolled license, and—at worst—anarchy.

> The principle of vision is the key to understanding leadership. With a clear-cut vision to which he is wholeheartedly committed, a person has taken the first step toward leadership. Without such a commitment to a vision, a person cannot be a leader but will be an imitation, playing at what he wishes he could be.[2]

John Haggai's *Lead On!* (Waco, Tex.: Word, 1986) and Kenneth Gangel's *Feeding and Leading* (Wheaton, Ill.: Victor, 1989) are excellent resources for learning and teaching principles of vision, goal-setting, and leadership.

The indispensable key to survival as pastor is the development of leadership in

---

2. John Haggai, *Lead On!* (Waco, Tex.: Word, 1986), p. 12.

the congregation and of genuine delegation of responsibility to them. His goal must be to discover and do well those few things that only he can do, and to delegate everything else to others. Vision-casting and goal-setting are among those few things with which he must have continuing, vital involvement.

The pastor must be a student of the culture and a visionary, however large or small the church, or whatever the size of the pastoral staff. Of course his direct involvement in Christian education ministries will vary with the size and maturity of the church. In more than 80 percent of the churches in America, the pastor is the only vocationally trained full-time person on the staff. In most of these churches he has direct leadership responsibilities in the Christian education ministries. Even in churches with a Christian education pastor or director, his active, appropriate role is indispensable.

E. Y. Mullins, former president of Southern Baptist Theological Seminary in Louisville, Kentucky, commented: "A hostile pastor equals a dead Sunday school; an indifferent pastor equals an inefficient Sunday school; an officious pastor equals a chaotic Sunday school; but a cooperating and sympathetic pastor equals an efficient Sunday school."[3]

THE PASTOR AS PREACHER AND TEACHER

The pastor is the primary educator in the church, and preaching is his most effective single education opportunity. Few of the Christian education ministries in our churches are directly mandated by Scripture, but preaching and teaching are: "Until I come, devote yourself to the public reading of Scripture, to preaching and to teaching (1 Tim. 4:13). Preach the Word; be prepared in season and out of season; correct, rebuke and encourage—with great patience and careful instruction" (2 Tim. 4:2).

Preaching provides a unique opportunity to teach. But to be effective it must be biblical, clear, interesting, organized, applicable, convincing, convicting, and encouraging. In such preaching and teaching, the pastor not only teaches the Word, he also demonstrates how to do it.

The education-oriented pastor will in his messages regularly stress the importance of Christian education, publicize the education ministries in the church, recruit, honor, and affirm its workers.

H. W. Byrne suggests ten "Pulpit Possibilities" for the promotion of Christian education in the church:

1. Stress the importance of Christian education.
2. Inform the people, promote and advertise the program.
3. Preach to meet the needs of the people.
4. Demonstrate the proper use of the Bible and correct interpretation.
5. Promote Christian family life.

---

3. H. W. Byrne, *Christian Education for the Local Church* (Grand Rapids,: Zondervan, 1977), p. 70.

6. Stress the importance of prayer and strong devotional life.
7. Preach great doctrines.
8. Apply the principles of the gospel to everyday life.
9. Train the people in the art of worship.
10. Cultivate strong financial support.[4]

Lyle Schaller strongly recommends that pastors regularly teach a Sunday school class designed to be an easy-entry class for newcomers, a haven for introverted people, for those who want to become better acquainted with the senior pastor, and for people who have not yet decided to join a "permanent" class. He suggests the room be easy to find, filled with a variety of comfortable chairs offering a wide range of choices in an informal seating arrangement, and that the class be preceded by refreshments and informal fellowship.[5]

In small churches it is often the pastor's responsibility and opportunity to offer teacher-training courses. In addition to other resources available, many of the video tape series on the market are highly effective if adequately introduced and followed up with discussion and application.

As the church grows and the staff increases, the pastor tends to become increasingly isolated from the members. The wise pastor will make sure he stays in touch, especially with the children and young people, occasionally teaching and enjoying informal fellowship times with them. A few days at their camp or retreat with them can create strong and lasting bonds of friendship that yield dividends far in excess of the investment.

If the pastor has led the church in accurately and thoroughly assessing the times and the culture and in establishing the mission, direction, and goals of the church, then his preaching and teaching ministries provide him with unexcelled opportunities to lead the church into effective and life-changing Christian education ministries.

The Pastor's Role in Helping the Church Develop a Philosophy of Christian Education

A clearly articulated philosophy of Christian education will go a long way toward ensuring that Christian education ministries are biblical and comprehensive in scope, balanced in emphasis, life-changing in results, and integrated so as to avoid omissions and duplication.

Michael S. Lawson comments in his excellent chapter, "Biblical Foundation for a Philosophy of Teaching":

A Christian philosophy of teaching begins in the Bible and forms part of the larger con-

4. Ibid., p. 97.
5. Lyle E. Schaller, *The Senior Minister* (Nashville: Abingdon, 1988), p. 146.

cept of Christian education. The Word of God offers more than the content of Christian teaching; it provides the essential philosophical framework as well. Fundamental questions, such as "Why should we teach?" "What results should we expect?" "Who mediates Christian teaching?" "How should we teach?" and "Who should we teach?" find provocative answers in the Bible. A clearly defined mandate and goal mesh precisely with the Bible's remarkable insights into the teacher, student, and God to form a stable superstructure.[6]

An adequate philosophy of Christian education must be rooted in the mission of the church. Therefore, the first step toward a philosophy of Christian education is a mission statement for the church. From that, a mission statement for the Christian education ministries can be developed. For instance, the mission statements for Castleview Baptist Church of Indianapolis are as follows:

> The Mission of Castleview Baptist Church is to glorify God, build up its members in love, and reach out to unbelievers to win them to Christ.
>
> We will seek to accomplish this Mission through worship, Bible study, prayer, fellowship, obedience to Scripture, and by sharing Christ individually and unitedly in our own community and to the world.
>
> The Mission of Christian education at Castleview Baptist Church is to provide training in the knowledge and application of the Word of God, the opportunity for believers to fellowship together as members of Christ's Body and to promote personal and corporate evangelism to reach our community with the gospel message. It is the purpose of Christian education programs to provide the broadest possible variety of opportunities for bringing men, women, and children as individuals and as families to the truth of Christ Jesus and to maturity in faith.[7]

In addition to the broad philosophical principles addressed in mission statements, a complete philosophical statement will specify that the program will be:

- comprehensive, including all the people of the church in its ministries
- unified, so the various programs complement each other, avoiding duplication and omissions
- graded, so the material and methods are appropriate for each age group
- life-changing, so people trust Christ as Savior and experience ongoing transformation by the renewing of their minds and hearts
- specific, so truth is actually learned and retained, not merely studied

The Reinhardt Bible Church of Dallas, Texas, developed a "Body of Truth" (basic Bible and doctrinal truth) for grades one through six to be thoroughly memorized at each grade level. Teachers elicited the cooperation of parents, sending home on study cards the truths to be learned that year. During the

6. Cited in Kenneth O. Gangel, *The Church Education Handbook* (Wheaton, Ill.: Victor, 1985), p. 61.
7. Constitution of Castleview Baptist Church, Indianapolis, Indiana.

spring quarter of their sixth grade, students reviewed the material for the six years along with a complementary catechism. Successful mastery of the material was celebrated with a special trip.

Keys to success, in addition to a special reward, include:

- keeping the material to be learned well within the ability of the average student
- making sure it is understandable and appropriate for each age
- enlisting the cooperation of the parents
- learning and reviewing as a class throughout the year

It is time we recognize that too many of our people attend our classes for years without ever thoroughly and permanently learning the basics. If philosophically we agree that our students should emerge from our ministries with a solid mastery of biblical truth, it is time we state it in our philosophy, prioritize it in our goals, decide exactly what it is we want them to learn, and integrate that truth into our curricula in a way that will produce results.

THE PASTOR'S ROLE AS EQUIPPER

Preparing God's people for service is one of the few things pastors are biblically mandated to do. Ephesians 4:11-12 clearly states that Christ gave pastors to the church specifically to "prepare God's people for works of service, so that the body of Christ may be built up until we all reach unity in the faith and in the knowledge of the Son of God and become mature, attaining to the whole measure of the fullness of Christ."

From this passage equipping God's people for service is clearly the key to Christ's great goal for the church, expressed here as "attaining to the whole measure of the fullness of Christ" (v. 13).

Equally clear is the fact that in the local church the pastor is the key person in the equipping process. Exactly how he will be involved will vary with the size of the church and the availability of others who can train leaders. The pastor's goal must always be to train others, who in turn can train others (2 Timothy 2:2)—in Dawson Trotman's now-famous expression "Reproduce reproducers."

TRAINING MEMBERS FOR LEADERSHIP

The first step to an equipped membership is for the pastor to become convinced that training for every member is biblical and essential and that he is the key to a successful training program. Further, he must be prepared to reprioritize his time and persistently overcome the numerous obstacles to an effective training ministry. According to Lowell Brown, the major obstacles are these: lack of vision, lack of pertinent training, lack of available time, lack of materials, lack of finances, and lack of unified philosophy.[8]

> Successful training for the laity needs the complete support of the pastor. If the pastor personally leads such experiences, concentrated effort is required for research, planning and implementation. Unquestionably, this pastoral leadership will demand a reordering of priorities.[9]

Here are seven considerations for developing a successful teacher/leadership training ministry:

1. Be a model of excellence, blameless in Christian character, thorough and imaginative in preparation, warm and convincing in presentation.
2. Offer regular teacher and leadership training courses. Lowell Brown emphasizes that these courses, to be effective, must contain five crucial characteristics:
   a. related to the age-level taught
   b. practical
   c. related to the curriculum taught
   d. experiential
   e. regular and systematic[10]

In addition, they should be offered at a time most convenient for the trainees. As the pace of life quickens and discretionary time diminishes, the Sunday school hour increasingly is becoming the favored hour.

3. Take advantage of the many excellent videos, films, film-strips, tapes, and slide programs now available from publishing houses, leadership training centers, and parachurch organizations.
4. Send and take leaders to seminars, workshops, and conventions now regularly offered throughout the country. These can be highly motivational as well as instructional.
5. Encourage teachers and leaders to visit other churches to observe counterparts who are doing an unusually good job.
6. Develop a leadership resource center and stock it with books, and especially with tapes. Listen to them yourself and describe each briefly in an annotated bibliography; recommend specific tapes to appropriate individuals. Especially encourage the men of the church to listen to good tapes in their cars. As Howard Hendricks often reminds us, it is much easier to get a busy man to listen to tapes in his car than it is to get him to read good books in his den. Remind him that a good tape should be listened to several times for maximum benefit.
7. Bring in experts for special training sessions.

8. Gangel, p. 246.
9. Ibid., p. 249.
10. Ibid., p. 246.

As the church grows, the pastor will increasingly focus on developing teachers of teachers. When the church employs a pastor or director of Christian education, many of the training responsibilities will be delegated to him or her. However, the pastor should always be vitally involved and an active collaborator in the never-ending equipping process.

THE PASTOR'S ROLE AS SUPERVISOR OF THE TOTAL CHURCH PROGRAM

Peter Drucker once told a group of pastors and other Christian leaders that he believed the four most difficult leadership positions were: (1) the president of the United States, (2) the president of a large university, (3) the administrator of a large hospital, (4) the pastor of a church of any size. Of these four, Drucker said, the most difficult was pastor.

Like it or not, the vast majority of pastors find themselves ultimately responsible for the oversight and management of the total church program. Even small churches over the years tend to multiply programs and ministries far in excess of their need or ability to staff and support. Peter Townsend, author of *Up the Organization*, wryly observed that it is about ten times as easy to begin an activity as it is to terminate one. He suggested that for over-programmed organizations the rule be that "for the next ten years, for every program begun, two be terminated."[11]

> The starry-eyed young pastor who reports to his first church expecting to do little else than study and preach the Word is in for a rude surprise when he finds out how many administrative duties confront him. Whether he likes it or not, the program of the church will not "just happen," nor can he ignore those duties and hope lay people will take care of them. In many churches lay people have not been trained sufficiently to carry out such duties, and they are looking to him to provide the necessary direction.[12]

Only that pastor who develops skills and disciplines in the areas of goal-setting and prioritizing, time management, leadership development, and delegation can hope to avoid the very real hazard of burnout, find the time and energy to do well what only he can do, and still find time for his family and himself. The place for each pastor to begin is to decide just what his priorities are and what are those things only he can do. This list will vary from pastor to pastor, but should include the following: (1) preach and teach the Word of God, (2) see that the membership is pastored, (3) lead in vision-casting and goal-setting, (4) lead in leadership development, (5) supervise the church staff, (6) work closely with the key lay leaders, and (7) become a skilled delegator.

11. Robert Townsend, *Up the Organization* (New York: Knopf, 1970), p. 93.
12. Robert C. Anderson, *The Effective Pastor: A Practical Guide to the Ministry* (Chicago: Moody, 1985), p. 277.

SETTING PRIORITIES AND MANAGING TIME

The essential key to accomplishing the sometimes overwhelming responsibilities thrust on the pastor lies in the prioritization and mastery of his time. Investment in learning the discipline of time management is not only time well spent but a life-saving necessity for every pastor.

Fortunately, numerous helpful books and seminars are available. A recent and excellent contribution to the literature is Steven Covey's *The Seven Habits of Effective People*. (See the list at the end of this chapter.)

Every pastor should master the following keys to managing his time:

1. Discovery—find out where your time actually goes.
2. Determination—pre-decide your priorities and schedule them in prime time.
3. Elimination—abandon time wasters and low-priority activities.
4. Delegation—delegate to others as much work as possible.
5. Consolidation—designate large blocks of time to important, creative tasks such as sermon preparation. "All that one can think and do in a short time is to think what one already knows and do as one has already done,"[13] wrote Peter Drucker.
6. Prioritization—put first things first and second things not at all.
7. Compression—set realistic but challenging deadlines.
8. Compromise—allow time for people, interruptions, and for the fact that most things take longer than planned.
9. Creativity—"We must take time to think, pray, talk, and do nothing" (William Barclay). Plan regular days away to pray, think, meditate, and plan.

DELEGATING RESPONSIBILITY

A second essential to self-preservation in the pastorate is delegation. Delegation is the transfer of work, authority, and responsibility for a task while retaining accountability. Unfortunately, few creative leaders are natural delegators; it is a learned skill. "I can do it better and quicker myself" is a common but fatal trap for many pastors and other leaders. However, "God seems to do nothing of himself which he can possibly delegate to his creatures. He commands us to do slowly and blunderingly what he could do perfectly and in the twinkling of an eye."[14]

Delegation is the heart of good management and the answer to the pastor's frustration. In a word, it is passing work on to others while maintaining a management check. Like time management, delegation is a skill the pastor must master.

What to delegate:

1. routine details, minor decisions
2. activities and ministries in which you are not qualified
3. activities and ministries outside your area of unique contribution
4. activities and ministries others are or could become capable of

13. Peter Drucker, *The Effective Executive* (Harper & Row, 1966), p. 34.
14. C. S. Lewis, *The World's Last Night* (New York: Harcourt, Brace Jovanovich, 1973), p. 7.

The sympathetic and understanding pastor is often reluctant to delegate to others what to him is uninspiring busywork. The happy reality is that his bane is others' blessing; his boredom may be their challenge. By our lack of delegation let us not rob others of the joy of serving and at the same time rob ourselves of valuable time and energy to do what only we can do, our primary responsibilities.

What not to delegate:
1. goal setting
2. building teamwork
3. coaching and developing subordinates
4. serious disciplinary matters
5. your primary responsibilities

Pastoring is an inexact science, and the conscientious pastor often lives with the tension of deciding when to assert strong leadership and when to back away and delegate. Norman Shawchuck's *How to Be a More Effective Church Leader* and William J. Reddin's *Managerial Effectiveness* are two excellent resources for discovering one's primary management style and for learning how to develop and when to use other styles of management. (See the reading list at chapter's end.)

How to delegate:
1. Select the responsibility to be delegated and prepare it for delegation.
2. Select the proper person for the responsibility.
3. Prepare and motivate him for his responsibility.
4. Hand over the work, making sure it is fully understood.
5. Encourage independence.
6. Maintain adequate supervisory control.

For the novice, delegation is a tightrope walk with danger on both sides—to hover too closely to the frustration of the delegatee, or ignore him completely till the project has failed or strayed irretrievably. In the early stages of delegation, gradualism is the wise course. Begin with an assignment, which although is not true delegation, is a step in that direction and allows for legitimate involvement in the details of the project. Then move to true delegation with generous supervision, reducing it as successful experience begets confidence.

Again, Kenneth Gangel's *Leading and Feeding* and Steven Covey's *Seven Habits of Highly Effective People* have excellent chapters on the subject.

THE PASTOR'S WIFE AND HER ROLE IN CHRISTIAN EDUCATION

The role of the pastor's wife is in some ways the most difficult of anyone in the ministry. In a *Leadership* article, pastor's wife Mary LaGrand Bouma wrote,

> The women who are married to ministers are usually among the walking wounded. Some are nursing serious injuries; others have received only minor cuts and scrapes

which seem to have healed easily without leaving any scars. Few escape completely unscathed.

Pastors' wives, like their husbands, suffer from discouragement. For one thing, they and their children, like their husbands, are right up there in the public eye—on display. They are almost always introduced to others as pastors' wives. One wife reminded me that no one says, "This is Janie, our plumber's wife," or "our schoolteacher's wife." But the pastor's wife is invariably presented as "our Minister's wife." I had always accepted this as a compliment, knowing that my friends who introduce me this way love my husband and are proud of me. But when I thought about it I realized that it has, on occasion, put me in an uncomfortable position. No one knows quite what to say after that kind of introduction, so there is an awkward silence.[15]

A survey by *Leadership* revealed the chief struggles pastors' wives face to be loneliness, members' many expectations, being considered "the pastor's wife," the lack of freedom to express themselves, their husband's busy schedule, and the fishbowl life.[16] However, the same survey indicated that 90 percent enjoyed being a pastor's wife; they reported that the most rewarding aspect was seeing people grow in Christ.

THE PASTOR'S ROLE IN SUPPORTING HIS WIFE

Consideration of her role as an individual, as her husband's wife, and her children's mother must precede any consideration of her role in Christian education in the church her husband pastors. Fortunately, churches and pastors are beginning to realize this important truth. As students of the Bible, pastors must lead the way in freeing and protecting their wives. To that end, pastors must:

1. Be as aggressive in promoting her interests and encouraging her to discover and develop her gifts as she is in yours. In some instances this will take her in directions not directly related to the church. Be your wife's advocate.
2. Protect her from unreasonable expectations.
3. Let her be herself.
4. Encourage her continued mental as well as spiritual growth.
5. Guard the family life, including your active involvement in it.
6. Include her in what you are doing, thinking, and feeling.
7. Appreciate her.

With that as a necessary background, the pastor's wife has the possibilities of important roles in Christian education, chief of which is that of a role model. Like it or not, the pastor, his wife, and his family are watched and imitated. One woman came to her pastor and said, "We like your sermons and all you do for us, but what the women of this church appreciate most about you is the way you

---

15. Mary LaGrand Bouma, "Ministers' Wives: The Walking Wounded," *Leadership* 1, no. 1 (1980): 63.
16. Pat Valeriano, "A Survey of Ministers' Wives," *Leadership* 2, no. 4 (1981): 65.

treat your wife. Our husbands are catching on!"

In an interview with *Leadership*, Jill Briscoe, wife of Pastor Stuart Briscoe, said, "A pastor's family is a model whether you want it to be or not. We're not models of perfection, but we ought to be models of growth. How do you do that? By falling down at times in front of the congregation. When they see you struggling, they identify."[17]

Unrealistic expectations aside, the role of the pastor's wife is qualitatively different from that of any other profession. It is a rare situation where a pastor can hope to succeed without the active involvement and support of his wife.

"Whether we like it or not, when a church calls a pastor, it does not merely hire one person. It calls a team. Even if the wife works far in the background and is not especially visible in the kind of ministry she performs, her sound and firm backing of the pastoral office is necessary if the pastorate of her husband is to flourish."[18]

Exactly how she is involved or whether she is directly involved in specific ministry at all depends on many considerations, including the following:

1. The demands of her family on her time and energy
2. The remaining time and energy she has available for ministry
3. Her gifts, training, and experience
4. God's leading
5. Her natural preferences
6. The needs of the church

These considerations will free some wives to limit their active participation to church attendance. Others will find rich and varied opportunities to minister and develop their gifts in a wide variety of ways. The most important thing is that she know herself, be herself, and find the ministry God has given her. Another important thing is that her husband vigorously support his wife in this.

PREPARING PASTORS FOR CHRISTIAN EDUCATION MINISTRY

The young pastor who leaves seminary dreaming of spending his days exegeting Greek and Hebrew texts and preaching to appreciative members is usually in for a rude awakening, and it will probably come in large measure from the Christian education ministry of his church.

As he arrives at church early Sunday morning, he may be met with a sign a frazzled teacher has posted on the junior boys' classroom: "This class is closed for the summer unless someone volunteers to teach—today!"

He may discover untrained teachers, drab, ill-equipped rooms, inappropri-

17. Interview with Jill Briscoe, *Leadership* 5, no. 3 (1984): 130.
18. Anderson, p. 71.

ate teaching materials—or perhaps none at all, nurseries without running water. And the list goes on.

Most beginning young pastors will not enjoy the luxury of a colleague trained in Christian education but will find themselves the Christian education expert of the church no matter how little they know about the subject or how disinclined they are to fulfill that function.

So here is an urgent word to pastors-to-be who are still in school:

1. Take all the Christian education and church management courses you can. Learn all you can about young children, how to care for and teach them.

2. Serve in the young children's departments in your present church. Too many college and seminary students make the mistake of teaching and leading only teens and adults. Charles C. Ryrie, master at making difficult truths simple, used to encourage his students to learn to teach young children, telling them that if they could make a six year old understand, they could probably get it across to adults.

3. When serving as an intern or as an associate on a pastoral team, try to gain practical experience at every level, even if it means extra duty. Learn from the gifted lay leaders, many of whom are superb teachers and models.

As a senior pastor:

1. Continue to read the current literature in the Christian education field and see that the insights you gain filter down to the various ministries in your church.

2. Encourage your Christian education leaders to attend training seminars and conferences, and use your influence to see that the costs are at least partially paid by the church. When you can, attend with them.

3. As you mature in the ministry, make your contribution to the next generation by training gifted young men and women as interns and associates. And when they are ready, encourage them to take off!

As the Christian education ministry in your church matures, make it your goal increasingly to delegate leadership either to the Christian education pastor or competent lay leaders. When you can limit your involvement to that of encouragement, support, enlistment of volunteers, promotion, and occasional direct involvement mutually agreeable to you and the leaders, congratulations are in order for a job well done.

FOR FURTHER READING

GENERAL

Anderson, Robert C. *The Effective Pastor: A Practical Guide to the Ministry.* Chicago: Moody, 1985.

Cionca, John R. *The Troubleshooting Guide to Christian Education.* Denver: Accent, 1986.

Gangel, Kenneth O. *Feeding and Leading.* Wheaton, Ill.: Victor, 1989.

Hull, Bill. *The Disciple-Making Pastor.* Old Tappan, N.J.: Revell, 1988.

McDonough, Reginald M. *Working with Volunteer Leaders in the Church.* Nashville: Broadman, 1976.

Miller, C. John. *Outgrowing the Ingrown Church.* Grand Rapids: Zondervan, 1986.

Schaller, Lyle E. *The Senior Minister.* Nashville: Abingdon, 1988.

Steinbron, Melvin J. *Can the Pastor Do It Alone?* Ventura, Calif.: Regal, 1987.

Stevens, R. Paul. *Liberating the Laity: Equipping All the Saints for Ministry.* Downers Grove, Ill.: InterVarsity, 1985.

Tillapaugh, Frank R. *Unleashing the Church.* Ventura, Calif.: Regal, 1985.

UNDERSTANDING THE TIMES

Anderson, J. Kerby, ed. *Living Ethically in the '90s.* Dallas: Dallas Seminary, 1990.

Blamires, Harry. *Recovering the Christian Mind: Meeting the Challenge of Secularism.* Downers Grove, Ill.: InterVarsity, 1988.

Bloom, Allan. *The Closing of the American Mind.* New York: Simon & Schuster, 1987.

Colson, Charles. *Against the Night: Living in the New Dark Ages.* Ann Arbor, Mich.: Servant, 1989.

———. *Kingdoms in Conflict.* Grand Rapids: Zondervan, 1989.

Corbin, Carolyn. *Strategies 2000.* Austin, Tex.: Eakin, 1986.

Gill, David W. *The Opening of the Christian Mind.* Downers Grove, Ill.: InterVarsity, 1989.

McCullough, Donald W. *Waking from the American Dream: What to Do When Success Fails.* Downers Grove, Ill: InterVarsity, 1988.

Naisbitt, John, and Patricia Aburdene. *Megatrends 2000.* New York: William Morrow, 1990.

27

Ray Syrstad

Professional Church Leadership

PROFESSIONAL CHURCH LEADERSHIP
- **Recognize that there is a new approach today to staffing in many local churches**
- **Understand that many dramatic changes are impacting ministry in the local church**
- **Understand the dynamics of good multiple-staff relationships**
- **Recognize the basic differences in how men and women see multiple ministries**
- **Be motivated by a servant-leadership style of ministry**
- **Understand the role of an associate minister**

"We stand at the dawn of a new era." So begins the introduction to the 1990 book *Megatrends 2000*. The introduction goes on to say, "Before us is the most important decade in the history of civilization."[1] What an opportunity and challenge for the Christian education professional serving in the local church.

1. John Naisbitt and Patricia Aburdene, *Megatrends 2000* (New York: William Morrow, 1990), p. 11.

RAY SYRSTAD, B.A., is pastor of adult ministries at Lake Avenue Congregational Church, Pasadena, California.

A new era. What will be its impact on leadership in the local church? In 1974 Douglas Stave predicted that paraministry would be the main occupational growth area in the church.[2] He was right. A major movement to bring lay para-professionals who serve part-time to church staffs has occurred. These people may be unpaid volunteers (such as the woman who serves on our staff as director of women's ministries) and may very well be females. These individuals are generally recruited from the congregation because they have demonstrated interest and ability in a certain area of ministry and possess good people skills.

Another type of paraprofessional whom many large churches are recruiting are men and women from the congregation who feel a calling to ministry as a Christian vocation. Rather than guiding these people into a seminary for training, the pastors on staff provide the training both on-the-job as well as more formal classroom training. The senior pastors in such situations note a number of advantages to this practice: (1) these people will be better prepared to address the needs of their particular congregation; (2) it is generally more economical than hiring a full-time seminary trained minister; (3) staff supervision is generally easier; (4) they are more likely to remain on the church staff for a longer period of time. Lyle Schaller says that there is a trend today in large, multiple-staff congregations to reduce the number of ordained male clergy, many of whom are generalists, and to replace them with lay program specialists.[3] Seminaries have no doubt contributed to this trend by no longer staffing their faculties with ministers who have spent fifteen or twenty years as local church pastors. The demand in seminaries has turned to scholarship, not parish experience.[4]

A new approach exists today for staffing many local churches. Performance is usually recognized as more important than credentials in hiring people. Increasingly the cry is, "People skills are more significant than technical skills."[5] Churches are realizing more and more that if a person does not possess the necessary abilities to motivate, guide, and encourage people in ministry, it matters little what degrees hang on his office wall. I have seen well-qualified, well-trained Christian education people fail in the local church ministry because they did not know how to work with people.

Some churches feel that it is a distinct advantage to have people on staff who feel called to a particular ministry as a Christian vocation. I felt a specific call to the ministry of Christian education rather than the preaching ministry, so the churches in which I have served have never had to fear that in time I would leave to pastor my own church. For me the experience was not the next step on the career ladder. Whether we see the local church ministry as Christian vocation or a profession, the opportunities for nondegree educational and training experience for the paraprofessional have multiplied at least tenfold in thirty-five years.[6]

2. Douglas Stave, "Coming Boom: Paraministry," *Christianity Today* (March 15, 1974), 40-42.
3. Lyle E. Schaller, *It's A Different World* (Nashville: Abingdon, 1987), p. 201.
4. Lyle E. Schaller, *Reflections of a Contrarian* (Nashville: Abingdon, 1989), p. 179.
5. Schaller, *It's A Different World*, p. 205.

This fact is reflected in the increased number of titles of church staff personnel. In 1989 the National Association of Directors of Christian Education changed its name to Professional Association of Christian Educators because a decreasing number of individuals in ministry were carrying the title of director of Christian education. At the church that I serve, Lake Avenue Congregational Church in Pasadena, California, that position is entitled administrative pastor of Christian education. That pastor gives administrative leadership to the early childhood director, director of children's ministry, junior high pastor, senior high pastor, college pastor, and pastor of single adults. Currently we have fifteen pastors serving a congregation of approximately 4,500. Though this seems like a large staff, we are understaffed according to the church-growth experts. They say that a typical congregation should have one pastor for every 150 parishioners.[7] Because that is often economically unfeasible as a church grows larger, many churches employ interns or staff assistants to help a pastor. This enables the pastor to spread the work load as well as give valuable experience to the assistant. To be of greatest benefit to the assistant, however, the staff pastor must be willing to share himself and his ministry with the assistant and not simply assign to that person the less desirable tasks.

As churches grow and add more ministries in an attempt to respond to the expressed needs of people, often a debate results as to what staff to add. When I entered the field of Christian education thirty-five years ago, the choice would most likely have been between a youth director or a director of Christian education specializing in children's ministries. Today the choices are quite different, depending on the needs being expressed to the church leadership. Many will believe the next pastor added should be one trained in the specialty of counseling.

The average pastor is being asked to spend an increasing amount of time in personal counseling. To address this need one pastor said that he requires that people seeking counseling from him first be willing to come to some worship services and sit under his preaching of the Word of God. In this way the Holy Spirit has an opportunity to speak directly to them about their need through the Scriptures. As the size of a church grows, some think a pastor who responds to the care of the congregation should be the next one added. Others cite the growing number of seniors in the congregation and the need for a pastor to respond to their needs. Many churches today are finding that music is one of the best ways to attract new people, so they may vote for replacing the part-time music director with a full-time minister of music who will develop a graded choir program and expand the church's outreach through music. Others may cast their votes for adding a minister to families, an activities director, or a business manager.

The position titles for a variety of potential professional church ministry staff persons in the local church that have been mentioned in previous paragraphs is certainly not inclusive of all possibilities. Every local church senior pastor, offi-

6. Ibid., p. 208.
7. Leith Anderson, "Leaning into the Future," *Leadership* 11, no. 1 (Winter 1990): 121.

cial board, and congregation must determine the primary need within the church's scope of ministry that could be best addressed through adding an additional staff person both trained and gifted to meet that ministry need. Here are some basic questions to be asked when thinking about additional church staff members:

1. Do we understand how this added staff person will positively assist us in carrying out our mission as a church?
2. Is the senior pastor ready to accept a new staff person and the supervisory and relational responsibilities required?
3. Is the official board and congregation willing to afford the required salary, housing, and benefit compensation for a new ministry staff person?
4. Do official (and unofficial but influential) leaders clearly understand the qualifications, working relationships, ministry responsibilities, and general policies for such a staff position?

The above points are the necessary components in a working job description for any church staff ministry position. Note the accompanying sample job description for the position of Youth Pastor that can serve as a model for other staff positions as well. Some additional questions to consider:

5. Is the right person for this ministry position already here in our congregational family?
6. If not, where do we look for such a staff person? Contact sources include denominational offices, other pastors and churches, Bible schools, Bible colleges, and seminaries, particularly the alumni placement offices of these schools, and professional associations such as the Professional Association of Christian Educators (PACE).[8]

JOB DESCRIPTION FOR
PASTOR OF STUDENT MINISTRIES (ORDAINED MAN) OR
DIRECTOR OF STUDENT MINISTRIES (UNORDAINED MAN)

I. Personal Qualifications

   A. Demonstrates personal maturity and godliness as biblically outlined in the fruit of the Spirit (Gal. 5) and the qualifications of an elder in the church (1 Tim. 3; Titus 1).

   B. Theologically in agreement with the church's statement of faith.

   C. In agreement with the ministry philosophy of the church.

---

8. Information about P.A.C.E. may be obtained by writing to: P.A.C.E., 8405 N. Rockwell, 5 Plaza Square—Suite 222, Oklahoma City, OK 73162.

D. If married, that marriage relationship should model God's design for marriage.

E. Has a vision to disciple and train both adults and young people for leadership responsibility in ministry to youth.

F. Has a personable and approachable personality.

G. A positive and compatible member of our pastoral team.

H. Has sufficient education and field experience to qualify for this position.

II. Working Relationships

A. Directly responsible (accountable) to the pastor of Christian education and adult ministries and the board of deacons (i.e., official governing board of the church). Indirectly responsible to the senior pastor and the Christian education committee.

B. Ex-officio member of the board of deacons.

C. Active member of the Christian education committee.

D. Close association with the pastoral staff, meeting weekly for spiritual encouragement and sharing, reporting, and both short and long-range planning.

E. Meets regularly with the pastor of Christian education and adult ministries to coordinate the total C. E. ministry.

F. Meets monthly with the high school committee to establish policy and determine the direction of the high school ministry.

III. Ministry Responsibilities

As pastor (director) of student ministries, he shall have general oversight of the church's ministry to junior high, high school, and college age students. He shall be directly involved in one area of youth ministry as a leader/model.

A. Formulates and communicates philosophy and goals of the student ministry, as well as policies and procedures for the student ministry to young people, parents, church leaders, and congregation.

B. Coordinates, at the junior high, senior, high, and college age levels, the following activities: Sunday school, mid-week outreach meeting, leadership training, Bible studies, discipleship, evangelism, campus ministries, counseling, camping and retreats, etc.

C. Provides guidance as a resource person on the Christian education committee for selection of youth curriculum materials, teacher and leadership training, and annual Christian education budgeting.

D. Supervises, with the pastor of Christian education and adult ministries, all Christian education budget expenditures for student ministry.

E. Disciples and trains both adults and young people to be equipped for leadership responsibilities in the church's student ministry.

F. Works with the missions committee in developing student missions projects that seek to develop a "Christian worldview" in the lives of our young people.

G. Keeps up-to-date in youth ministry trends through reading, seminars, conferences, and contact with other churches.

H. Works cooperatively with outside student ministries when not in conflict with church ministry (i.e., Young Life, other area ministries, etc.)

I. Oversees the church internship program as related to youth ministry in cooperation with the pastoral team.

IV. General Policies

A. The pastor (director) of student ministries shall be encouraged to attend at least one conference or seminar each year to build competence in his field. His expenses will be paid by the church as budgeted and as approved by the pastor of Christian education and adult ministries and the board of deacons.

B. The pastor (director) of student ministries shall participate in public services under the direction of the senior pastor.

C. Salary level for this position shall be established by the board of deacons with proper consideration given to educational training, years of experience, family and ministry responsibilities. He shall be subject to periodic cost-of-living and ministry proficiency increases as regularly reviewed by the board of deacons.

D. The pastor (director) of student ministries shall have four weeks of vacation each year.

E. The job description for the pastor (director) of student ministries shall be reviewed annually by the board of deacons.

Church growth, with the accompanying need to provide space for that growth, can have a negative effect on the ministry staff needed to support the added ministries. Today the costs of construction are so sizeable that churches often find it necessary to curtail the ministry budget and/or the size of the staff. In the case of two major building programs in churches where I served, once the buildings were completed and occupied, the program budgets had to be cut and staff positions go unfilled because of the cost of servicing the debt on the new construction.

As difficult as this is for present staff members, future generations will give thanks for the vision of the leadership and the people who provided these essential facilities so that the church could continue to grow. The costs of construction never decrease. Under normal circumstances in large congregations approximately 15 percent of the budget should be allocated for maintenance and capital improvements.[9]

OTHER CHANGES IN THE NEW ERA

Having served in the local church ministry of Christian education for the past thirty-four years (in five churches), I am sometimes asked if it is more difficult to serve today's congregations than it was thirty years ago. I am sure that every generation of leadership feels that in many ways their generation has been the most challenging in which to serve. We are told by Naisbitt and Aburdene that religious belief is intensifying worldwide under the gravitational pull of the year 2000, the millennium. Polls seem to suggest that Americans are more "spiritual" or "religious," but there is evidence that they are not finding it in the organized church.[10] George Barna agrees that people have a declining degree of confidence in the church, yet he predicts that church membership will continue to grow in America, but a dominant source of that growth will come from immigration.[11]

Asian families are growing at fourteen times the rate of the native population, and Hispanics are increasing at five times the rate. In our vacation Bible schools in the fifties these people might well have been the foreign missions project. Today they are living in the vicinity of our churches, and leaders must give serious consideration to how they will evangelize and integrate them into the church body. By far the most significant reason for the growth of the church, Barna says, is the aging of the baby boomers and the presence of their offspring. Churches will see many new households visiting and evaluating what they have to offer, and selecting the one body they believe will meet their needs most efficiently.[12] I find that people are more demanding in their expectations of the church's educational program than they were thirty years ago. A consumer mentality prevails among many. Today's church leaders are competing with television and educational technology that demand greater creativity and innovative approach.

One of the most dramatic changes that I have witnessed take place in recent years is the increase in the amount and complexity of social issues that are affecting families. Church leaders in the fifties and sixties did not have to deal with drug use, gangs, battered children, sexual activity and AIDS, and so many other destructive forces. Radio, TV, and the movies now promote a lifestyle that is basically anti-Christian. Time magazine asked the question, "Will the 90s be known

9. Schaller, *Reflections of a Contrarian*, p. 158.
10. Naisbitt and Aburdene, pp. 271, 275.
11. George Barna, "Seven Trends Facing the Church in 1988 and Beyond," *National & International Religion Report* (1988): 2-3.
12. Ibid., p. 3.

as the 'Filth Decade?' "[13] Jamie Buckingham says, "The task of church leaders is now more clearly defined than ever before: to teach believers how to live—not only to survive but to flourish—in a hostile environment."[14]

In the fifties and sixties the average church family consisted of a dad, a mom (who did not work outside the home), and two or three children. The church could expect support from the home, and there was little difficulty enlisting enough moms for two weeks of morning vacation Bible school. In 1950 only 12 percent of married women with children under the age of six were employed outside the home; by 1987 that figure had grown to more than 50 percent. Some experts predict that by 1995, 80 percent of women between the ages of twenty-five and forty-four will be in the work force, and the majority of them will be mothers.[15] So today's church leaders face a more challenging task of enlisting lay workers for the Christian education programs. For many years there was little problem enlisting enough men for a strong Saturday morning Christian Service Brigade program. But when asked how they spend their discretionary time, today's adults are far more likely to list self-help classes, jogging, recreation, shopping, traveling, and watching television than participation in the traditional clubs, organizations, and programs of yesteryear that were organized so that volunteers could help others in general, and a younger generation in particular.[16]

In the face of these new challenges, today's leaders must not neglect their primary enlistment tool—prayer. Prayer often receives little more than perfunctory attention at the opening and closing of our planning sessions, but it must become the foundation of all that we do in ministry. I recall one effective primary department group that met monthly for its planning meetings in the homes of the teachers and staff. But group members also invited the noninvolved spouses to join them for dinner. During dinner they would share various needs in the department that the spouses would note. Following dinner the spouses would meet in a separate room of the home and pray about those needs while the staff had their planning meeting. This staff stayed together for many years and was always a performance leader. It is true, "The department that prays together stays together." God has promised to meet the ministry needs we face "according to his glorious riches in Christ Jesus" (Phil. 4:19), but prayer makes us aware that without Christ we can do nothing (John 15:5).

MULTIPLE STAFF RELATIONSHIPS

To see a church grow to where it needs to expand its ministry staff is exciting. But that day can bring about a new set of tensions for the pastor who until this

13. Richard Corliss, "X Rated," *Time* (7 May 1990): 92.
14. Jamie Buckingham, "Buckle Up for the 90s," *Charisma and Christian Life* (January 1990): 71.
15. Kenneth O. Gangel, "Ten Forces Shaping Christian Education," *Bibliotheca Sacra* (July-September 1989): 322.
16. Schaller, *It's a Different World*, p. 127.

time was the only pastor on staff. Not every pastor has the gifts necessary, or even the desire, to lead a team. He should seriously ask himself questions such as: (1) *Would I find it easy to share my ministry with other staff?* One pastor with whom I served found it difficult to enjoy my success when other areas of the church's ministry did not show the same vitality and growth. (2) *Does it bother me who receives the credit?* Early in my ministry preparation a professor shared the wise counsel that "there is no limit to what can be accomplished if we don't care who gets the credit." (3) *Am I secure in my leadership role?* Adding staff could place a great strain on that security if new members possess strong leadership gifts of their own. (4) *Would I enjoy spending time in staff meetings?* Administration time grows with the addition of staff. Many pastors possess the gift of leadership but not the gift of administration. Leadership is evidenced more by what a person is, whereas administration is evidenced more by what a person does. He must see meeting time as pastoral work. (5) *Can I deal with the dynamics of change initiated by others?* Change will be expected by the congregation when new staff is added, and this requires a degree of flexibility on the part of the pastor. Kenneth R. Mitchell describes this new experience well:

> Ordained clergy often dream of having partners, colleagues with whom to share thoughts, feelings, and responsibilities. They dream of creating a working partnership that will be the microcosm of the church, a way of demonstrating to the congregation, by working and living together, what the church is about in the first place. But when such an opportunity finally comes, the reality is often disappointing. Sometimes the partnership fits beautifully, but too often the hoped-for partner turns out to be unreliable or a loner or a bully.[17]

According to George Barna, the clergy is the single most frustrated vocation in America,[18] and the addition of staff to a growing church can add considerably to a pastor's frustration.

Before a pastor and people move to add a professional to the staff, they need to consider seriously the purpose for such action. Herman J. Sweet, in his classic book The Multiple Staff in the Local Church, says that the basic question to be asked by a church considering adding staff is: "Is it our intention to deepen the ministry of the church or to extend the institution?"[19] His concern is that if the church does not have in clear perspective the purpose for which it exists, adding more staff may only perpetuate and compound its weaknesses. Adding a staff member will probably increase activity in church programming. But if that is the sole result, the church may yet fail to see its people growing into maturity in Christ and becoming Christlike, multiplying disciples.

17. Kenneth R. Mitchell, *Multiple Staff Ministries* (Philadelphia: Westminster, 1988), p. 11.
18. George Barna, from a message delivered February 4, 1990, at Lake Avenue Congregational Church, Pasadena, California.
19. Herman J. Sweet, *The Multiple Staff in the Local Church* (Philadelphia: Westminster, 1963), p. 116.

The decision is made at a church to add a staff member because of a growing congregation. How can this be made an enjoyable and mutually satisfying experience? The answer lies in good quality staff relationships, basing those relationships on a commitment to God as well as to each other. Anne Marie Neuchterlein suggests that what is needed is a covenant.[20] She says that when we commit ourselves to one another and to God in faith and trust, we view our staff relationships in a more sacred way. In making a covenant staff members agree to:

> believe in the hope and forgiveness of Christ,
> remember we are holy,
> listen to each other,
> discuss and set common goals,
> discuss individual and group expectations,
> interact intentionally with each other,
> promote honest and open communication.[21]

By putting the covenant in writing, staff members are able to be particularly clear about their mutual commitment and accountability to each other. In addition to staff members making a covenant together, it is important that the church develop a job description for the position. By presenting this to the candidate, the church indicates that it has carefully studied its needs and what its expectations are for the position. After the candidate shares his own philosophy of Christian education and how he would approach ministry in that church, the search committee might recommend some modifications to the job description. Rewriting or changing a job description, however, has no power to improve relationships in multiple ministries.[22]

I strongly recommend that individuals considering making Christian education their life-time vocation consider ordination or licensure to that specific ministry. In this way the church sanctions the call of God in an individual's life and recognizes this call to specialized ministry as legitimate and vital. Ordination is essentially a recognition of abilities already evidenced in the life of a person and the authorization of that person to express those gifts in the Body of Christ.[23]

An increasing number of women are becoming a part of some church staffs. It varies according to the scriptural interpretation of particular groups and denominations. But one interesting factor has been noted where women fill some ministry roles—they bring a helpful balance to staff relationships. Men tend to see multiple ministries in terms of power issues, whereas women tend to see multiple ministries in terms of relationship issues.[24] A basic reason for this is the different

20. Anne Marie Neuchterlein, *Improving Your Multiple Staff Ministry* (Minneapolis: Augsburg, 1989), p. 22.
21. Ibid., p. 24.
22. Mitchell, p. 20.
23. Michael Green, *Freed to Serve* (Waco, Tex.: Word, 1983), p. 36.

natural tendencies with which we are born. Gary Smalley shares this interesting comparison in his excellent film series, "Love Is a Decision":

MEN	WOMEN
Tend to deteriorate physically about 10 percent every ten years with the rate increasing after age forty.	Tend to deteriorate physically about 2 percent every ten years, and in our country, to live longer than men.
Have about 40 percent of their body weight as muscle.	Have about 20 percent of their body weight as muscle, making it easier for them to gain weight and harder to lose it.
Tend to have heavier bones and thicker skins and skulls.	Tend to have smoother skin and more insulation cells under the skin.
Tend to talk less than women.	Tend to be more sensitive to sight and sound.
Tend to be lateral in their thinking, which means they tend to use one side of the brain at a time.	Tend to be bilateral in their thinking, which means they tend to use both sides of the brain at the same time.
Tend to favor the left side of the brain, where language and logic operate, and to be conquer oriented.	Tend to favor the right side of the brain, where the feeling, nurturing, relational part of life operates, and to be relationship oriented.[25]

Women's natural orientation to strong relationships is a great benefit in ministry.

The fundamental differences between men and women are also brought out in a fascinating experiment in group dynamics reported in "The Pryor Report":

> A group of twenty-one men and women were given a project to complete in the space of one hour. They were divided into three groups: a mixed group of men and women, an all-female group, and an all-male group. Each group gathered in a different corner of the room to begin work. The group of all women focused on how they would make decisions and attempted to reach consensus in all their decisions. They concentrated on the task and their relationships with each other. The all-male group joked about the way the groups were composed and predicted that the women's group would come in third. They could not reach agreement. After twenty minutes they sent a spy to learn what was happening in the other groups. In the group consisting of both men and women a conflict emerged early among the male members, who quarreled about procedures, ignoring the females. Finally, a woman moved into the discussion and acted as moderator. The mixed group was the first to solve the problem. Then the tension mounted between the all-male and all-female groups. The men teased the women about the hopelessness of their design. Although the mixed group won the contest, the all-male group continued to point out throughout the week that their design was the best.[26]

24. Mitchell, p. 22.
25. Gary Smalley, *Love Is a Decision* (Zondervan Films).
26. Fred Pryor, *The Pryor Report* (Kansas City: April 1987), p. 5.

The incident illustrates common differences in conflict management styles between men and women. Women focus on the relationships among the people involved; men focus on who wins and will struggle for power.

Although this experiment took place in a secular setting, it is reminiscent of how men and women Christian leaders sometimes relate. But God has called Christian leaders, both men and women, to be servant leaders. Jesus said in Matthew 20:28 that He "did not come to be served, but to serve, and to give his life as a ransom for many." And He calls us to the same lifestyle. Servant leadership is sometimes in short supply in local church ministry. I had the privilege of serving more than nine years under the senior pastoral leadership of Paul Cedar, author of the book *Strength in Servant Leadership.*[27] The beautiful aspect of the relationship was that Paul Cedar modeled that about which he wrote. He says in his book that "love is central to servant leadership"[28]—and love was evident in all of his leadership relationships. As Christian leaders, we are to manifest the fruit of the Spirit (Gal. 5:22-23), and love is the fruit that binds all of the others together. It is interesting that when one examines the qualifications for elders and deacons in the local church set forth in 1 Timothy 3 and Titus 1, it says nothing about spiritual gifts. It speaks almost exclusively about the fruit of the Spirit. I believe the Bible teaches that it is more important for Christian leaders to be godly than to be gifted. Without godly character no amount of spiritual giftedness will be effective in the Body of Christ. Spiritual gifts are what a person has; spiritual fruit is what a person is.

The multiple staff in a local church should be characterized by a team spirit. But it is essential that teams play the game together. There may be some superstars on the team, but it takes the gifts, talents, and skills of every member to make a winning team. Each member of the team has four key needs that must be met by fellow team members. These needs are: (1) to use one's skills to assist the team's effort; (2) to be accepted as a part of the team; (3) to have personal goals compatible with the team's goals; (4) to represent people and groups outside the team.[29] The relationships the staff maintains within itself should be models for the relationships in the congregation. When I candidated at my present church, I asked members of the congregation their impressions of the pastoral staff. Consistently the responses were centered on the love and unity they saw being expressed on the staff. Our team believes in playing together as well. One of our goals for this current year is to have more fun. Unfortunately, clergy tend to have a high work addiction and a high pleasure anxiety.[30] Three times a year we go away for a two-night retreat of planning, prayer, and playing. We do a lot of laughing together, which is wonderful therapy. Once a year our spouses join us on the retreat. We also hold quarterly social events for the team. Two of them

27. Paul A. Cedar, *Strength in Servant Leadership* (Waco, Tex.: Word, 1987).
28. Ibid., p. 43.
29. Myron Rush, *Management: A Biblical Approach* (Wheaton, Ill.: Victor, 1983), p. 61.
30. Robert C. Kemper, *The New Shape Of Ministry* (Nashville: Abingdon, 1979), p. 99.

include the entire family of staff members, and they are all designed to help us know one another better.

ASSOCIATES IN MINISTRY

The demand for competent church staff people is still great, and today they will most likely be called associate pastor of education, or associate pastor of whatever the person's specialty might be. The term *assistant* has been mostly eliminated in favor of associate. Associates must keep in mind that one of their highest priorities is to be supportive of the senior pastor's ministry. Differences of opinion or differences in ways of looking at things are bound to surface. But associates must develop a mind-set of a positive relationship with the senior pastor, even if he does not always affirm the ministry of those around him. Associates must demonstrate loyalty to the senior pastor. Loyalty produces trust and respect, which are essential to a good working relationship. Some people in the congregation may come to an associate to complain about the senior pastor because "they don't want to hurt his feelings." Associates must be careful never to allow members of the congregation to come between them and another staff member, particularly the senior pastor. His leadership is extremely public, especially the pulpit. He will not be able to please everyone, and those he does not please often seek out an associate to express their displeasure. A good response in such situations is to ask if they have shared their concern with the senior pastor.

Here are some other guidelines that associates should keep in mind when working with a senior pastor.

1. *Represent him fairly*. Emphasize the things in which he excels. Do not discuss weaknesses. We all have weaknesses, and often they are more apparent than our abilities.

2. *Share his vision*. Leith Anderson says that his role as a senior pastor is increasingly to look ahead for the entire body, and that means he must give up many wonderful strokes from hands-on ministry.[31] Help him communicate his vision to the congregation. Communication is a major challenge in the church. No matter how hard we try, information does not seem to get to some members, or else it is misunderstood.

3. *Keep him informed*. Share with him what is happening in your area of ministry. I have heard associates complain about the lack of support they feel from the senior pastor for their ministry in the church. But a pastor cannot support what he is unaware of, so associates should share with him what God is doing in their area. One tool we use at Lake Avenue Congregational Church is a "Hi Team" report on which we share how we are feeling, what ministry we have been involved with that week, and how the team can enter into prayer support for us and our ministry. This is distributed to each pastor by Friday each week.

---

31. Anderson, p. 120.

4. *Be willing to work hard.* It may sound strange, but many pastors feel (rightly or wrongly) that staff associates do not work as hard as they do. The demands on our time often contribute to difficulties such as stress, feeling of inadequacy, fear of failure, loneliness, isolation, and spiritual dryness. Ministry requires a high degree of personal discipline. We do not punch a time clock. Many tasks are performed outside office hours. We are responsible to God for how we use our time. One of my college professors reminded us that we have time to do all that God wants us to do. So work hard, but be sure you are not attempting more than God has called you to do. My wife and I claimed 1 Thessalonians 5:24 when we began our ministry: "The one who calls you is faithful and he will do it." God has promised to enable us for the work to which He calls us. If we feel burned out or overworked in ministry, we must ask ourselves if we are attempting more than God expects.

5. *Learn how to accept criticism.* Unfortunately, associates can be built-in targets for problems that develop in a church. Churches are like baseball teams. When things are not going well, it is easier to fire the manager or the coaches than to shake up the team. That is hard to accept, especially if it is unfair. But who said life would be fair? We must learn to accept criticism, or we will always find ourselves in a defensive posture. Pastor Chuck Swindoll has said that the secret is to cultivate a tough hide and a sensitive heart. That takes time and often healing from some scars. Here are a few other suggestions:

1. *Pray.* Ask the Lord to guide you in responding to criticism, to give you the ability to hear what should be heard, the ability to control temper and anger.

2. *Attack the problem, not the person.* Our natural reaction is to fight back, but that sets up a defensive struggle that usually turns into an argument over who is to blame. But that never solves the conflict.

3. *Verbalize feelings, don't act them out.* Men are particularly poor at expressing feelings. When something upsets us, we need to learn how to express what we are feeling. It is never wrong to say, "This is how I feel." Avoid the danger of simply releasing emotional tension.

4. *Determine what the real problem is.* Is there a deeper issue than what has been expressed? Look for the hidden factors and develop good understanding.

5. *Forgive rather than judge.* Jesus says in Luke 6:37, "Do not judge, and you will not be judged. Do not condemn, and you will not be condemned. Forgive, and you will be forgiven." How easy it is to justify our own reactions and condemn those of others. But that never resolves conflict. I have even seen leaders withhold forgiveness on the basis that they have a right to feel as they do. Jay Kesler sums it up well: "To be a servant is to give over all rights to your life to God. Then there's nothing left for anybody to take away."[32]

6. *Let the criticism be a source of learning.* Criticism stings, especially when it comes from other Christians and from right within the body. But every crisis

32. Jay Kesler, "Why We Love and Hate Ministry," *Leadership* 11, no. 2 (Spring 1990): 88.

in life has within it the seeds of spiritual growth and maturity.

In two of my long-term local church associate ministries, the senior pastor resigned to move on to other ministries. What should be the response of the other pastoral staff in such situations? When this occurs, the lay leadership of the church will usually request the remaining pastoral staff to continue being committed to their ministries until a new pastor arrives. In fact, it generally means that some members of the team will have to assume some additional ministerial duties for the interim. Kenneth R. Mitchel gives this wise counsel to the search committee for a new senior pastor: "The single factor that helps teams work most creatively and smoothly together is a search process in which the present staff has the strongest possible voice in the selection of new people."[33] When the new senior pastor does arrive, it is customary for the associates to offer their resignations to him. This gives him the liberty to change staff structure or personnel in any way he desires. In practice, a new senior pastor will ask most of the staff to continue in their ministry roles while he becomes acquainted with the church.

When any staff pastor decides to leave, there is a great sense of loss and a grieving period, particularly for those in the congregation who worked most closely with that pastor. Therefore, it is wise to wait before too quickly calling a replacement. Waiting gives the church leadership time to evaluate the position and whether the current needs might dictate a different approach to that ministry position. Waiting also allows time to seek the Lord's direction in filling the position. Generally there are lay people or students who can fill in for an interim period.

Pastoral staff changes always create an element of stress, but we all determine our own response to change. Rosalind Newton Enright says that when faced with change, some people are Threat Personalities and some are Opportunity Personalities.[34] The Threat Personalities always see the losses in change, rarely the gains. They want life to stay the same and are always hoping things will settle down. They are comfortable doing ministry the way they have always done it. The Opportunity Personalities, on the other hand, are positive people who tend to move quickly through the emotional reactions to the losses and focus on the gains.[35] They are stress resistant individuals because they have chosen not to doubt God but to believe His promise that "he who began a good work in you will carry it on to completion until the day of Christ Jesus" (Phil. 1:6). Often the Threat Personality will continue to focus on his losses, or even potential losses, and refuse to turn them over to the Lord and experience the freedom and rest there is in releasing the situation to God. Psychologists tell us that a mood will not stay alive unless it is nourished. The Threat Personality seems to derive a certain comfort in nursing the hurt or change to which he refuses to adjust. How much we all need

---

33. Mitchell. p. 24.
34. Rosalind Newton Enright, "Managing Change with Less Stress," *Executive Excellence* (September 1987): 13.
35. Enright, p. 13.

the incarnational leadership style that Jesus Christ revealed and modeled.

A local assembly of believers is the primary agency Jesus chose to entrust with the spread of His gospel. When the professional staff of a local church sees its primary task as the equipping of the church to be the people of God, they find that it is a most rewarding way to invest their lives. As we look ahead to the twenty-first century, I urge you to pass on to others what God has given you so that generations to come will have the benefit of good church leadership in Christian education.[36]

FOR FURTHER READING

Borthwick, Paul. *Organizing Your Youth Ministry*. Grand Rapids: Zondervan, 1988.

Fagerstrom, Douglas L., ed. *Singles Ministry Handbook*. Wheaton, Ill.: Victor, 1988.

Gangel, Kenneth O. *Building Leaders for Church Education*. Chicago: Moody, 1981.

———. *Feeding & Leading*. Wheaton, Ill.: Victor, 1989.

Mead, Daniel L., and Darrel J. Allen. *Ministry by Objectives*. Wheaton, Ill.: Evangelical Training Association, 1978.

Richards, Lawrence O. *Children's Ministry: Nurturing Faith Within the Family of God*. Grand Rapids: Zondervan, 1988.

Sisemore, John T. *The Ministry of Religious Education*. Nashville: Broadman, 1978.

Tidwell, Charles A. *Church Administration: Effective Leadership for Ministry*. Nashville: Broadman, 1985.

———. *Educational Ministry of a Church*. Nashville: Broadman, 1982.

Westing, Harold J. *Multiple Church-Staff Handbook*. Grand Rapids: Kregel, 1985.

---

36. See Ted W. Engstrom, *The Fine Art of Mentoring* (Brentwood, Tenn.: Wolgemuth and Hyatt, 1989) for good suggestions on passing it on to others.

28

Dennis E. Williams

The Board of Christian Education

THE BOARD OF CHRISTIAN EDUCATION
- **The functions of administration and how they assist the board do its work**
- **The passages of Scripture that support a biblical basis for administration in the church**
- **The responsibilities of the board of Christian education**
- **How the board of Christian education is organized to do its work**
- **The purpose of policies and procedures for a Christian education board**
- **How the church can effectively implement change with minimal negative response**

DEVELOPING A CHRISTIAN EDUCATION BOARD

How can the church develop and coordinate a program of Christian education that will meet the needs of the congregation and assist the church in fulfilling its purpose and mission? To respond to this important task, churches usually have some kind of administrative group or educational organization called a board, com-

DENNIS E. WILLIAMS, Ed.D., is professor of Christian education at Denver Seminary, Denver, Colorado; executive director of the Mountain Area Sunday School Association; and executive administrator of the National Association of Professors of Christian Education.

mittee, council, or task force. Many churches use a Christian education board and give to it all this important responsibility. This board is concerned with administering the educational program of the church.[1] The educational program includes more than Sunday school and must represent all the different interests and elements of the total educational program of the church.[2]

Accomplishing this major task requires more than merely creating a Christian education board or some other group. The board must act with efficiency, giving careful attention to the functions of administration. These are outlined by Lewis Allen, and include planning, organizing, leading, and evaluating.[3] The word *administration* has in it the word *minister*, which means to serve. Administrators are managers who serve others and work together with people to accomplish the objectives of the church. There are those who criticize any ministry that involves large amounts of time in administration. Yes, it is possible to be overburdened with many administrative tasks, but in reality, good administrative procedures will facilitate the work of ministry so that it can be performed effectively by people. This is the important goal of administration.

FUNCTIONS OF ADMINISTRATION

Planning is the first step in good administration. Questions such as, Where are we now? How did we get here? Is this where we want to be? What can be done to help us reach our objective? are part of good planning. This function leads us to set objectives, develop programs, establish budgets, and develop necessary procedures and policies. Prayer and careful thought must go into these elements, but when they are fully developed, the ministry of the church will go forward with efficiency.

Organizing is the next function in good administration. Simply stated, this function refers to the way in which the work of the church can be established so that people can accomplish it most effectively. Kenneth Gangel states that organizing means to arrange, acquire, and allocate adequate resources in order to achieve clear objectives.[4] Often we hear the statement "We need to get organized." What people are really saying is that the work is piling up to such an extent that there must be a better way to get it done. Good organization comes to the rescue. We do not set up organizational structures in order to look impressive or feel important. Organization is developed from a definite need to help the church accomplish its tasks. It should focus on the importance of individuals with their input and participation. Clarifying the tasks to be done with good job descriptions will permit individuals to be fulfilled in their ministries.

1. Werner C. Graendorf, ed., *Introduction to Biblical Christian Education* (Chicago: Moody, 1981), p. 260.
2. J. Edward Hakes, ed., *An Introduction to Evangelical Christian Education* (Chicago, Moody, 1964), p. 234.
3. Lewis A. Allen, *The Management Profession* (New York: McGraw-Hill, 1964).
4. Kenneth O. Gangel, *Feeding and Leading* (Wheaton, Ill.: Victor, 1989), p. 65.

Organization should not call attention to itself. It should allow us to accomplish our work in the most efficient and effective way without demanding all of our time and attention. Much like a car that is running smoothly, we seldom think about all that goes on in the engine as we drive down the road. When the car misses or stalls, however, we spend time trying to find out what is wrong, and fail to reach our destination. If we focus all of our attention on organization, then we will not be able to accomplish our objectives.

A key part of organization is delegation—sharing the responsibility and authority for ministry with others. Some believe that they can do the job themselves and then be certain that it is done to their liking. Realistically this is impossible. No matter how hard we work in ministry, our responsibility is always greater than our capacity. The members of the Christian education board may be responsible for the entire educational ministry of the church, but they in themselves cannot teach every class, organize and implement all the activities, and train all the leaders. They must call on others to assist. Delegation is an important part of any successful educational ministry.

Organization also divides work and responsibility into manageable assignments. Supervision will be discussed later, but at this point it is important to note that the span of control for an effective supervisor is a maximum of five to seven people. Organization helps us break down the work so that people can realistically complete the tasks assigned to them. It also makes it possible for people to work together in developing significant relationships in ministry.

Leading is the next function of good administration. This deals with the way we work with people to accomplish the objectives of the church. A key concept taught in Ephesians 4:11-13 is that the leaders are to equip God's people for works of service. This preparation involves finding, recruiting, training, developing, and encouraging people. The concept of servant leadership is important here. Leaders are to serve and equip others so that people can be fulfilled in whatever ministry God has for them. The Christian education board has a major responsibility to focus in on leadership development.

Supervision is part of the leadership function. This is described as the strengthening of human resources with an emphasis on the development of individuals for more effective service.[5] Supervision is an educational process whereby one person assists another in doing the work assigned. Technically there is a difference between a boss and a supervisor. The boss controls the worker and sees that the work is done. The supervisor, on the other hand, seeks to assist the worker, offering suggestions and ideas. The purpose of the supervisor is to improve the quality of the work being done.

How does this distinction fit the role of the Christian education board? Though the board usually appoints the worker to the position—and in this sense can be looked upon as the boss—the major part of the board's role is that of doing every-

5. Robert E. Clark, Joanne Brubaker, and Roy Zuck, eds. *Childhood Education in the Church* (Chicago: Moody, 1986), p. 269.

thing possible to make the worker successful. Too often we have merely filled positions with no thought to helping the worker improve his skills. Implementing the concept of supervision will change this practice and make the workers more effective in their service to the Lord and to the church.

Evaluating is the fourth function of good administration. This is one area that the church seems to neglect the most. Some feel hesitant about evaluating, afraid that they will be evaluating the work of the Holy Spirit. Others fear that if we look at how people are doing, they will quit. The important principle here is that "anything worth doing is worth evaluating." The purpose of evaluation is improvement, not punishment.

Lowell Brown states that it is important that "standards" or ways to evaluate be set prior to the beginning of an activity.[6] This way the evaluation can be more objective. Developing standards after the activity is completed is like drawing the bull's eye around the arrow after the arrow is shot. This may guarantee a good report, but it does nothing to improve the activity. A major task of the board of Christian education is to improve the educational ministry of the church, and this requires a thorough effort in evaluation.

BIBLICAL BASIS FOR ADMINISTRATION

Some say that people are trying to bring management theory into the church, and that we should not use secular theories in our ministries. But where do these "secular" theories come from? They come from a study of the people God created. It is important to realize that God makes us all with certain capacities and abilities, and if a secular theorist discovers ways in which we can work together better, then it is part of God's creation. The management functions mentioned above are not just from the literature in the field; we find many examples of these concepts in the Scriptures.

The key text supporting the importance of delegation is found in Exodus 18. Jethro, the father-in-law of Moses, discovered Moses sitting from morning till evening judging the people and wearing himself out. He pointed out to Moses that the work was too heavy for him and that he could not handle it alone. His advice was to select capable men from the people and have them assist him in judging. Moses took his advice and delegated some of his responsibility to others.

A study of the book of Nehemiah will reveal many important elements of administration. Nehemiah set as his objective the rebuilding of the walls and gates of the city of Jerusalem. Knowing his purpose, he prepared thoroughly by requesting letters of passage through the land and securing permission to gather timbers from the king's forest. As a leader he was able to encourage the people to accept the challenge. Using organization, he assigned responsibility to the

6. Lowell E. Brown, *Sunday School Standards* (Ventura, Calif.: International Center for Learning, 1986), p. 5.

various families to rebuild sections of the wall. He planned a defense strategy with some working and others keeping watch. He kept his mind on the task at hand and was not distracted by those who opposed the work. The evaluation came when the task was completed. He met his objective. These elements, found in the book of Nehemiah, are also found in "secular" management texts. God's people used these elements in doing God's work prior to the publication of our present-day textbooks on management.

Division of work is also found in the New Testament, in Acts 6. Because of the rapid growth of the church, some people were being neglected. The apostles met and selected seven men to assist them in their work. This was done so that they could continue in the work God had called them to perform. The apostles had the responsibility, but did not have the time to fulfill it, so they called upon others to help.

Why Have a Christian Education Board?

What are the educational needs of the church? This question focuses on the need for the board of Christian education to determine what these needs are and how to meet them through the church ministries, strategies, and organization. It is important to communicate the importance of education to the entire church and to make the church aware of its responsibilities educationally.

The Christian education board needs to lead the church in developing a curriculum plan so that there is a unified program of Christian education for all ages.

Unfortunately, when professional staff members or lay workers resign from a ministry, often the program of education suffers. If the Christian education board is in place and doing its work, this problem can be corrected by providing proper direction and continuity to the educational ministry.

Finally, we need a Christian education board to evaluate the entire ministry of education in the church, giving recommendations for improvements and challenging those programs that are no longer contributing to the accomplishment of the church's objectives.

The Responsibilities of the Christian Education Board

When one sees all that a Christian education board can and should do, the need for good administration is self-evident.

1. *To lead the congregation to see the importance of the educational ministry of the church.* Teaching is a mandate from Scripture. Consider Deuteronomy 6 and Matthew 28:19-20. Other passages can be listed, but these two are especially significant. The work of education is not just another program for the church; it is a mandate from our Lord Himself and is indeed a priority for church ministry.

The Christian education board should keep this fact before the people and seek to enlist the entire congregation into some part of the educational ministry.

2. *To lead the church in establishing its objectives.* The leadership needs to state clearly what it is Scripture teaches about the purpose and objectives of the church. Many times this statement is found in a church's constitution or bylaws. If the church has such a statement, then it needs to be communicated to the entire congregation. If not, then a statement needs to be developed. From the church's statement of objectives, the Christian education board can develop a more specific statement of educational objective. For example:

> Our educational objective is to make individuals aware of God's eternal plan for mankind through His Word, and especially through the revelation of Jesus Christ and His redeeming work; to lead the individuals to accept the provision of salvation offered by God, and to enter a life of discipleship that will lead to spiritual growth and nurture in order that the learners will function within the body of Christ, the Church, as it fulfills its purpose of being a worshipping fellowship engaged in evangelism, education and ministry.[7]

A statement like this provides direction to the educational leadership and helps to set the necessary standards for effective evaluation.

3. *To lead the church in discovering the educational needs.* Assessment of what is happening throughout the church educationally will certainly reveal needs related to ministries, facilities, budget, leadership, and curriculum. Time must be set aside in order for the board to fulfill this task. Often the board is bogged down with immediate crises and is left with little or no time to give to important issues. Perhaps an all-day retreat or meeting with people representing the various groups and agencies of education reporting on their needs could be arranged. Needs can also be discovered by observation, interviews, surveys, and reports. This step is necessary so that the Christian education board can make plans to meet the various needs discovered. This is a major way in which the quality of the education program of the church can be enhanced.

4. *To develop strategies and ministries in relationship to the objectives and the needs discovered.* Strategies and ministries are to be based on the biblical objectives and the needs of people in relationship to the objectives. In recent years the word *program* has become unpopular in the church. Probably this has been caused because some programs no longer meet objectives and needs. If this is the case, then they need to be dropped. Actually the word *program* is used to describe a strategy or way in which we as a church can meet our biblical objectives in relationship to the needs of individuals. If a ministry is developed because of a biblical need, then it has legitimacy in the church.

5. *To coordinate the strategies and ministries.* In churches today there are usu-

7. Dennis E. Williams, "Curriculum Planning for Evangelical Churches" (Denver: Dennis E. Williams, 1990), p. 16.

ally many different educational ministries, strategies, and activities. It is important for churches to be aware of all that is offered to the people and to coordinate these activities so that a balanced program can be provided. For example, in a children's division it is possible to have several different ministries for the same children. Consider Sunday school, choirs, Bible studies, and perhaps clubs. Each has its own emphasis, but it is necessary to coordinate these different ministries that are all sponsored by the church so that the children will have positive educational experiences. Coordination between the various age groups is also important. How many trips to the church must a family make in order to have each member participate fully in the programs? Coordination should lead churches to consolidate meetings and be conscious of the needs of the individuals they serve.

6. *To develop a curriculum plan for the church.* Similar to the need to coordinate the educational programs, it is most important that churches develop a balanced curriculum plan that fulfills the objectives and meets the needs of the people (see chap. 32). Careful attention should be given to curriculum planning so that this can be accomplished. When people teach whatever content they want and no thought is given to what has been previously taught, serious omission of significant passages of Scripture and/or unnecessary duplication of content can result. Learners may develop isolated impressions of the Scriptures with no understanding of how the Bible fits together with a unified theme. They may not be able to use the Word, except for those isolated passages studied. The church needs to determine what should be taught as it fulfills its educational objectives and this determination is described as a curriculum plan. Yes, there must be provision for choice in curriculum planning by individuals, but this choice should come from a balanced selection of courses and programs, not from an open-ended, choose-anything approach. Curriculum planning is a major task for the Christian education board.

7. *To lead in the selection, recruitment, and training of educational leaders.* One of today's major challenges for educators is finding people to serve as teachers and leaders in the educational ministries of the church.[8] Though the board has this responsibility, the statement does not suggest that they are directly involved in the task. The board appoints key leaders, such as coordinators and superintendents, and they—under the board's guidance—fulfill this task. These leaders come to the board with suggestions of names and prospects for the various educational positions. For the board to spend all its time trying to think of names of people to serve is counter-productive. The board should set up a strategy for recruiting and training and see that it is done properly.

A weak area of Christian education is that of training and equipping. If indeed our purpose is to improve the educational ministry of the church, then significant time must be devoted to training and equipping. The board does not do the train-

---

8. Beth E. Brown and Dennis E. Williams, "Summary Report: Christian Education Field Survey" (Denver: Denver Seminary, 1988), p. 4.

ing or equipping but sees to it that it is done. (See chaps. 30 and 31 for specific suggestions.)

8. *To supervise the educational workers of the church.* Earlier it was stated that the purpose of supervision was to improve the quality of the educational ministry of the church. This can be done by meeting regularly with the workers and offering suggestions on how to improve the work. It will require training and an investment of time. For too long we have given people a position in which to serve and then left them to themselves with little or no leadership or guidance.

A key concept in supervision is "span of control." One person can supervise five to seven people adequately. When leaders have too many people reporting to them, they are not able to provide the supervision necessary to improve the quality of work. By dividing up responsibilities with selected leaders and board members, the Christian education board can supervise the educational workers effectively.

9. *To oversee the financial needs of the educational ministry.* The board—in consultation with the various ministries and programs—will establish the educational budget and oversee the expenditures. Proper funding of ministries is essential, and the board is to represent these ministries to the church for financial support. If there is a shortage of funds in the church, then the board will need to see what areas can be reduced in funding and which ones may need to be eliminated.

10. *To allocate space and provide equipment.* Who decides who gets which room in the church? How does the church know when to add more space or build a new building? How is space assigned for the educational ministry? These questions focus on the role of the board in determining room assignments and in providing the necessary space for the teaching ministry of the church. Policies should be developed so that this assignment can be performed with minimal difficulty. (See chap. 35.)

11. *To meet the needs of family life education.* Earlier we addressed focusing on the needs of people in designing strategies and ministries. Families are under attack and the church needs to provide as much assistance as possible. Perhaps someone on the board can be assigned this priority and when educational planning is done, this individual can be the spokesperson for families. Special social events, training sessions, worship experiences, and personal encouragement are some ways this can be accomplished. Provide literature and think of ways in which the families of the church can be strengthened. Perhaps other groups in the church can assist, such as deacons or elders. The board will be able to facilitate these actions. (See chaps. 37 and 38).

12. *To maintain a program of evaluation of the educational ministry.* Earlier it was mentioned that evaluation was one of the weakest areas of the church. Though there may be reasons for this, it is still important that we look at how we are doing and try to find ways in which we can do a better job of ministry. Evaluation cannot begin until we have established our objectives and developed

standards for performance. Then we can compare how we are doing with what we feel should be done. Since this is a new area for the church, it is probably wise to move slowly. Look over the chapter on evaluation in this book for some specific ideas on how this important task for the Christian education board can be fulfilled. (See chap. 29.)

ORGANIZING THE CHRISTIAN EDUCATION BOARD

Earlier it was stated that organization refers to the way in which the work of the church can be established so that people can accomplish it most effectively. We want to set up the board in such a way that it will be able to fulfill the responsibilities given to it.

Who serves on the board? Usually churches elect some people from the congregation at large and choose others who serve on the board because of their positions in the educational ministry. The Sunday school superintendent or director, the age group coordinators, club directors, youth group sponsors, and other ministry directors—including church staff members working in educational areas—usually serve because of their positions. Elected members should have an understanding of the educational ministry and be serving in some area. Board membership requires involvement in the ministry.

How does the board do its work? Each person on the board is given the responsibility of some area of the Christian education program. Age group coordinators will represent their areas. Ministries not represented on the board will be assigned to board members so that at each meeting there is an up-to-date report from each educational ministry. Some, no doubt, will represent more than one ministry. When new ministries and events are planned by the board, these people will be alert to how the ministries will affect their areas.

At each board meeting reports are given from each ministry with needs identified and requests presented. In this way every member of the board knows what is happening in the total educational program. It is important that each report include recommendations to the board when special requests are presented. These recommendations should come from the people involved and should represent a consensus. The chairperson of the board should have these reports prior to the meeting so that adequate time on the agenda can be scheduled for each report and request. Like most boards, motions are passed and assignments given to individuals to carry out the actions.

Special projects of the board, such as curriculum selection or an in-depth evaluation of the educational program, usually will be assigned to subcommittees or task force groups. The board will receive the reports of these committees and then make their recommendations and decisions. Records of the board actions are to be kept in the minutes. Reports to the entire church from time to time will assist in the assignment of keeping the church educationally conscious.

POLICIES AND PROCEDURES

Someone has said that policy is what we always do and what we never do.[9] Policies usually come from experiences that have been negative or problematic. When we read policy manuals, we can get an insight into the kinds of problems the organization has experienced.

Educational boards have policies such as "Only members of the church may teach in the Sunday school," or "Teachers must use the curriculum approved by the board." One can see the rationale behind these policies.

Policies help us make decisions on issues that come up from time to time. Procedures, on the other hand, usually outline the steps necessary to carry out specific actions. A policy may state that nothing can be charged to a church account without a signed purchase order. The procedure to purchase materials for the education ministry will outline how to get the signed purchase order and how to secure the materials. An efficient board requires that policies and procedures be developed so that the work can be performed promptly.

Churches should have these policies and procedures written out in a handbook, and they should be given to prospective workers. Also included should be the purpose statement for the ministry, the objectives to be accomplished, and a clearly written job description. With this information in hand, workers will have a much better understanding of the ministry opportunity and be motivated to do a better job.

IMPLEMENTING CHANGE

As educational leaders, the board will need to implement change in order to improve the educational ministry of the church. It is important to make a distinction between "means" and "ends" in church ministry. The "ends" are represented by the church objectives and the educational objectives. This is what we as a church feel that God wants us to be and do. The "ends" are drawn from the Scriptures and can be considered as God's direction for our church. The "means," however, are not so permanent. Conditions and circumstances change—and so do the "means." Methods change, but eternal principles remain. This distinction is important when we consider implementing change in the church.

We live in a changing society. Change is inevitable, whereas constructive reaction to change is not. We can reduce this resistance to change by following the principle of involving the people who will be affected by the change in the planning. When people have a part in the planning, they will be less likely to resist. It is important that accurate and complete information be given to people. Change should not be implemented on the basis of hearsay and hunches. When a change is proposed, give the workers a chance to respond with their questions, objections, and suggestions. Some of the responses will most likely improve the idea. Lastly,

9. Bobb Biehl and Ted W. Engstrom, *Increasing Your Boardroom Confidence* (Phoenix, Ariz.: Questar Publishers, 1988), p. 109.

make only changes that are essential. People can tolerate only so much change. In other words, select and make only the changes that really count.

Change is needed to improve the educational ministry of the church, and we must do it in a way that will help us reach our objectives and meet needs.

Whenever change is proposed, it is important to seek the guidance and direction of the Holy Spirit through prayer. We want to discover the mind of the Lord and fulfill His will. This is not something that can be done in our own strength.

Through it all we want to maintain unity in the Body. There will be those opposed to change, and we must be careful not to force change on people. This will bring serious resistance. We want to use the above ideas and suggestions to lead people to see how change can improve the ministry and to involve them in the process.

SUMMARY

The Christian education board is organized by the church to assist in fulfilling the scriptural command to teach the Word of God. After determining the biblical objectives, the board seeks to assess the educational needs of the congregation, set specific goals, and design strategies and ministries to meet those needs. Using the benefit of good administrative procedures, the board leads the church to fulfill its educational responsibility.

FOR FURTHER READING

Brown, Lowell E. *Sunday School Standards*. Revised edition. Ventura, Calif.: International Center for Learning, 1986.

Cionca, John R. *Solving Church Education's Ten Toughest Problems*. Wheaton, Ill.: Victor, 1990.

Cousins, Don; Leith Anderson; and Arthur DeKruyter. *Mastering Church Management*. Portland, Oreg.: Multnomah, 1990.

Gangel, Kenneth O. *Building Leaders for Church Education*. Chicago: Moody, 1982.

————. *Feeding & Leading*. Wheaton, Ill.: Victor, 1989.

McDonough, Reginald M. *Working with Volunteer Leaders in the Church*. Nashville: Broadman, 1976.

Mead, Daniel L., and Darrel J. Allen. *Ministry by Objectives*. Wheaton, Ill.: Evangelical Training Association, 1978.

Rush, Myron. *Management: A Biblical Approach*. Wheaton, Ill.: Victor, 1983.

Schaller, Lyle E. *The Change Agent*. Nashville: Abingdon, 1972.

Wilson, Marlene. *How to Mobilize Church Volunteers*. Minneapolis: Augsburg, 1983.

29

Harold J. Westing

Evaluation and Long-Range Planning

EVALUATION AND LONG-RANGE PLANNING
- **Evaluators are always being evaluated**
- **Evaluation is a biblical mandate**
- **A standard is essential to accurate evaluation**
- **Evaluation can aid in life enrichment**

Every week the scrutinizing eyes of the regular attenders—and especially the visitors—evaluate your church and its programs. The visitor's evaluation results in a vote either to become a regular attender or to go elsewhere. Of course the vote also is expressed in the offering plate. Once in a while the pastor gets a sample reading on people's feelings through some casual comment or probing question, but most of the data that could guide church ministries remains unrecorded.

To say that we are accountable to the Lord for the nature of our church program—not to visitors or even the congregation—is easy and persuasive. Why should we measure our ministry's success by what every person says about it?

Some leaders quote Isaiah 55:11 declaring that God's Word will produce fruit as long as we are giving it out: "So is my word that goes out from my mouth: it will not return to me empty, but will accomplish what I desire and achieve the purpose for which I sent it." God's implanted Word does generate life in receptive

Harold J. Westing, M. Div, D.D., is associate professor of pastoral ministry and dean of students at Denver Seminary, Denver, Colorado.

hearts, but we can do much to encourage openness to His seed-truth. If merely speaking God's Word were sufficient, we would do nothing but read Scripture in church services and on street corners, then depart till the next meeting. Some Christians are satisfied simply to be involved in God's greatest task without ever stopping to consider if they are making the greatest impact possible.

REASONS FOR EVALUATION

The evaluation process is a major biblical mandate. There are more than two hundred references in Scripture that directly or indirectly deal with the need for and process of evaluation. It deals with every phase of the Christian life and with every part of the church and its ministry. Not to evaluate constantly is in fact to commit the sin of disobeying Scripture. "It is a badge of honor to accept valid criticism ["helpacism"]. . . . Any enterprise is built by wise planning, becomes strong through common sense, and profits wonderfully by keeping abreast of the facts. . . . to learn, you must want to be taught. To refuse reproof is stupid" (Prov. 25:12; 24:3-4; 12:1, TLB*).

Another strong reason for evaluating is to check the results of our ministry. "God only requires faithfulness" may be a cover-up for laziness or for unwillingness to face the need for something more than good intentions. We can know if God's Word is being taught to more people this year than last year. We can find out if our students are living God's Word more vitally this year because of our teaching ministry. We can know if our teachers are more actively involved with their students this year than last year.

No wise business executive would make a major administrative decision without a thorough evaluation to determine the need. The same should be true of church leaders. Before we decide to change the organizational structure of the adult department, for example, we should thoroughly evaluate the effectiveness of the current structure and the desirability of a new one. Many tragedies occur in churches and simultaneously in the lives of churchgoers because changes are made without exploring all the facts in given situations.

There are numerous things leaders need to know about their ministries before proper supervision can be given: (1) We need to know what we do best so we can concentrate even more on that strength. (2) We need to know the demographics of our target area to help us be more effective in reaching people in that area. We must find out what is meant by "back door of the church" to discover why so many people leave the ministry unnecessarily but can be kept from doing so. (3) We need to be aware of attendance trends so that we can tell when we should change leaders, leadership structures, or begin new groups or departments.

Henry Drummond makes a strong argument for the fact that the law of degen-

---

* *The Living Bible*.

eration is the same law in the natural world as in the spiritual world.[1] When we leave a wooden post alone, it eventually degenerates in the same way that an organization or a person will turn into a weaker form. We never like to admit that our church's ministry may be degenerating into an ineffective work. The beautiful thing about that law is that we can discover the weakness and then correct it. If we are not constantly evaluating our work, we may wake up one day and find that decay has set in almost to the point of no return. A regular habit of evaluation should find the early stages of decay in time for it to be corrected.

A STANDARD AT WHICH TO AIM

Scripture gives us criteria by which to evaluate our effectiveness, but since each church is uniquely designed and exists in its own cultural setting, additional interpretations of the guidelines are needed. An agreed-upon job description or standard of competency is absolutely essential. If you are not ready to adopt a formulated definition of a competent school and teacher, your staff should do some serious planning.

In the development of a standard for a competent teacher, you may want to use *The Role of the Teacher in the Church*.[2] Seven areas are listed that can and ought to be evaluated: disciple maker, counselor, manager of instruction, catalyst in society, interpreter to the community, staff participant, and member of a ministry.

A standard is a written guide or measure to help maintain excellence in the operation of the Christian education program. It is the worker's target. The standard becomes a covenant when it is signed, because then it is the agreement between the church and the teacher specifying commitments in their joint effort to serve God. A covenant is a promise of performance to Christ and also to the local body of Christ's church.

A standard or a covenant should clarify what is expected of the workers in the school in regard to (1) life-changing teaching objectives, (2) regularity and longevity of teaching, (3) efficiency of work, (4) cooperation with leaders, (5) curriculum and program, (6) involvement with students, and (7) ongoing training. Since a church's covenant is generally developed autonomously, it is recommended that the workers' covenant be formed by the entire staff under the title "What God Expects of Me." The covenant's demands must be reasonable enough to be met by the signers, and there must be no discrepancy between the real objective and the test used to measure their achievement.

A standard needs to express exactly what is expected. For example, your standard may state that each teacher should make home visits to each student on the roll—and that is all that may happen, just a warm, friendly visit. Yet what you really intended is a deep, life-sharing, discipleship relationship with each student.

1. Henry Drummond, *Natural Law in the Spiritual World* (New York: International Book Company, n.d.).
2. *The Role of the Teacher in the Church* (Instroteach, Inc., P.O. Box 2314, Wichita, KS 67201).

A danger always exists that a standard or covenant might promote a legalistic attitude. The standards themselves never become legalistic, but the attitude of workers who lose sight of the spiritual objectives can become rigidly mechanical or critical of others. Nonetheless, the standard remains a worthy instrument in discipleship.

You may confront another major objection to the development and use of a covenant in the assertion that each Christian is a priest who is responsible to God alone. As far as our individual lives are concerned that is true, but in our service with and to the Body of Christ, we are also responsible to the members of the Body. A covenant covers our actions in the fulfillment of specific, regular tasks within the Body. (See the accompanying form, which I have devised for such purposes.) Its lofty goal inevitably heightens our performance.

TRACING YOUR PROFILE

Drawing an accurate profile of your church's educational program is the first step in determining its effectiveness. The Sunday school will be primarily emphasized in this section, because it tends to be the major setting of the church's educational program. This will give you an illustration of the things you would evaluate in other church programs.

You cannot draw an exact profile of what your church history has been, but by gathering sufficient data you will visualize the outlines of the Christian education ministries and perceive some of the major influences shaping their impact. Although you are not primarily interested in the number of people involved, a study of the attendance changes will give a clue to the spiritual vitality of the congregation. A church that has not kept accurate attendance records will be hampered in making projections for the future. A church should keep records of each class and department, plus its total attendance and enrollment.

With these records for reference, you can develop the following graphs: (1) a ten-year study of the monthly average attendance of each class, (2) a ten-year study of the monthly average attendance of each department, (3) a ten-year study showing the total average attendance of the Sunday school and/or other programs, (4) a graph showing comparisons between the yearly average enrollment and the yearly average attendance of the school, (5) a graph showing comparisons for the last ten yearly average attendance with the average morning worship service, and (6) graphs depicting the attendance of various clubs and youth programs conducted within the Christian education framework.

When the graphs are completed, you are ready to translate your findings. A difficult but meaningful step at this time is to interpret the rises and falls in your various graphs. You will want to determine the effect that various staff people have had on attendance trends. Note the effect, if any, of attendance contests and special days on enrollment. What part has disciplined or casual leadership played in attendance figures? Was a calling program vigorous or apathetic?

LETTER OF CALL FOR SERVICE

The Sunday school hereby extends to you _____
a call to serve your Lord and Savior Jesus Christ as _____
for the period of _____ 19 _____ to _____ 19 _____.

We believe that you are qualified both spiritually and intellectually for service in the church.

With the aid of the Holy Spirit and your faithful endeavor you will to the best of your ability seek to maintain faithfulness in the following areas:

I. MY RESPONSIBILITY TO CHRIST

  A. I will seek to maintain a daily relationship of worship with Christ in prayer and Bible study and live according to its teaching.

  B. I will seek to keep my life pure from the defilement of sin by a disciplined lifestyle and availing myself of Christ's forgiveness when I sin.

II. MY RESPONSIBILITY TO MY STUDENTS

  A. I will seek to lead each one to Christ as Lord and Savior and to encourage his or her growth in Christ.

  B. Recognizing that discipleship is greatly facilitated by my personal involvement with my students, I will seek to spend time with them personally outside the classroom session.

  C. I will faithfully pray for and prepare my lesson with each student's spiritual growth in mind.

  D. To aid my growth as an effective teacher, I will regularly attend all staff meetings and take at least one training course a year.

  E. I will seek to contact prospective class members that they might be discipled for Christ.

  F. I will constantly contact students who are absent to encourage their faithfulness.

III. MY RESPONSIBILITY TO MY CHURCH AND THE CHRISTIAN EDUCATION TEAM

  A. All workers must be church members who will seek to follow the church covenant and constitution.

  B. In order to maintain a uniform teaching philosophy, I will follow the prescribed curriculum.

  C. Recognizing that my example is a strong part of my training, I will seek to be faithful in my attendance at the major church services.

  D. I will seek to cooperate with those who are assigned as my leaders. (e.g., my department and general superintendents).

  E. I will strive to be faithful in being on time for each teaching or leadership responsibility.

On behalf of the Board of Christian Education

Date: _____

Pastor: _____

Sunday school superintendent: _____

Please consider carefully and prayerfully this call of service. If you choose to accept this responsibility please sign and return to one of the above signers no later than.

Having studied and prayerfully considered the above call, being conscious of my dependence on the Holy Spirit and my own weaknesses, I hereby accept the call to work as _____ for this coming year.

Date: _____   Signed: _____

You will be able to correlate various spiritual highs and lows with the attendance records. You will be able to link special evangelism efforts, the number of people brought to Christ, and how many joined the church. As you connect historical events with the graphs, you can estimate the effectiveness of some programs conducted in the past. Both attendance gains and slumps can help you focus on causes that are important to your ministry.

To help you draw a profile of your community, visit city hall, county courthouse, school board office, or the chamber of commerce office. The average age of people in the community is one factor. When you have ascertained the number in each age bracket, calculate the percentage of each group to the overall population, then compare the proportions with these age groups in your congregation. A large discrepancy may signal your need to shift efforts and programs in new directions. The same is true regarding other factors.

Each community has a distinctive personality, though embracing many diverse characteristics. An honest study of your community profile[3] will prevent you from confusing your church with other churches and will help you make keener decisions about your program emphasis for the future.

Gathering the data about spiritual growth in your ministry will be much more difficult than the demographic studies. Here you will look for information concerning the effectiveness of evangelism, nurture, and service in your educational program. All three of these must be evaluated specifically as they apply to the student. Make certain that this is done on the basis of *fact-finding* and not *fault-finding*. Be as objective as possible and draw conclusions that are clearly verified by facts.

A basic requirement for this part of the evaluation is to know specifically the objectives of your Sunday school. Keep in mind that the effectiveness of teachers is proportional to the degree they have made the goals of the school their own. There is a strong tendency to evaluate the school in relation to its events and activities rather than its purpose and goals. And there is a common impulse to hand down the goals formed by the leaders rather than letting the workers discuss and shape them. This time-consuming process, however, ensures much deeper commitment by the workers to the overall goals of the Sunday school.

You will try to identify in the ministry profile:
1. Intensity of workers' involvement with students
2. Spiritual vitality of the staff
3. Effectiveness of the curriculum
4. Effectiveness of curriculum use
5. Extensiveness of staff training
6. How grouping and grading are handled
7. Cooperation between the church and Sunday school

3. Church Instrument and Development Services, 3001 Redhill Ave., Suite 2-220, Costa Mesa, CA 97201.

8. Level of proficiency in the teaching/learning process used by the staff
9. Kind of disciplines used and how effectively it is practiced
10. Type of evangelistic outreach practiced
11. Effectiveness of communication among all staff members
12. Efficiency of staff members (such as following through with responsibilities)
13. Type of equipment used in the teaching ministry
14. Availability of visual aids and reading aids for teachers

You will want to add some items of special importance to your situation.

SHAPING YOUR TOOLS

The proper instrument for testing can be developed only when you have the exact objective you are checking in writing. The more precisely your objectives are defined, the more accurately you can measure accomplishments.

There is no end to the various types of instruments that are available for testing. Our plan is to help you develop your own and to include a couple of samples in the process so you can accurately test your self-chosen objectives. The completed evaluation should be tested on a small group of people to make sure it measures the qualities in question. You may need to alter and refine some points before printing the final copy.

The following guidelines give practical suggestions for developing your evaluation instrument. Careful design will avoid indefinite and perhaps even faulty results.

1. An adequate job description for various workers should specify what kind of spiritual growth ought to occur in students, thus the instruments you use must include the examination of students' growth to see if their lives are growing as a result of their involvement in each educational experience.
2. Give opportunity to report both healthy and unhealthy practices, or positive as well as negative results. Because workers should be complimented on areas of efficiency, these competencies must be known to be commended.
3. Where teachers may express negative feelings on a point, give occasion for expressing the reason.
4. Allow plenty of latitude for free, accurate responses. In some sections it is appropriate to include an open question to cover a significant aspect you cannot specify.
5. When you plan to tabulate the results, list objective choices that can be systematically counted. Subjective, individualistic answers are nearly impossible to tabulate.
6. If you are asking for such things as attendance or population lists, or percentages of times, it is wise to leave sufficient spaces for all separate numbers.
7. When you sense an important question may be misunderstood or the blunt truth may be hard to admit, try framing two questions on the same topic.

8. Place the logical answer in a multiple-choice series low in the list. People have a tendency to mark the earlier choices in a list if they are careless or are uncertain about the question.

9. Since leaders' responsibilities cover wide areas, it is important to get information about each area covered in the job descriptions.

It is important to do an evaluation just on the ministry of your teachers. It will be important to allow the teachers or workers to judge their own effectiveness. This will lessen the pressure on the person conducting the evaluation. One of the meaningful ways to accomplish this is to provide two different forms. The first would ask teachers to describe an ideal worker in a number of areas of work. The same question would be reworded on the second form, and workers would express their actual practices.

The workers thus judge themselves, and correction may come much quicker because they have discovered their own weaknesses rather than having someone else judge them.

Most students do not thoroughly understand what a genuine teaching/learning process involves, and consequently would find it difficult to judge the competency of their teachers. A student evaluation form can provide a great deal of insight, however, into whether or not students are growing in Christ as a result of involvement with the teacher and class.

When you ask students to tell how their lives are affected by their involvement in the various Christian education programs, there will be a variety of answers. A good way to systematize the problem is to have them mark their opinions on a numbered grid (1 2 3 4 5 6 7 8). This allows them to express their feelings in a range of degrees that can be tabulated. To avoid "dead-centered" answers the total should be even numbered rather than odd numbered.

INTERVIEWS THAT ENCOURAGE

People who work as volunteers in the educational ministry of the church may see the evaluation process as legalistic, cold, and impersonal. There is a significant relationship between evaluating and disciplining a child. In the same way, if evaluation is to be successful, then it must be done within the context of a warm, friendly relationship, and the persons being evaluated must perceive the process as enriching their lives. The workers do not seem to mind being observed and evaluated as long as the interviewer is given the freedom to share the observations and will provide constructive insights about improving the practice of ministry. It should be a supportive experience that will help the workers see their strengths and come to appreciate the great things that are being accomplished through their work. *Evaluate and Grow* states:

> Those who evaluate are cast in the role of a modern day Barnabas, a Paraclete/encourager who stands alongside a laborer and provides plenty of positive reinforcement, much like Barnabas behaved toward his cousin John Mark in Acts 15.

Though interviews are generally best done on a one-to-one basis, it is sometimes profitable to evaluate the entire department as a group. This helps each worker to better understand the significant role that he plays.[4]

It is important for the interviewer to keep the evaluation objective and positive. Lyle Schaller, author and executive director of Yokefellow Institute, believes that average church workers have a rather low view of the effectiveness of their ministry. They tend to think small and to see themselves as far less effective than they really are.[5] Consequently, a positive way to start the interview is to get the parties being evaluated to talk about their apparent strengths. Once people start talking about their strengths, it makes them feel more positive about themselves. They are more anxious to try new things and are excited to share the ministry of their church and their Lord with other people. Beginning on a positive note also will open workers up to talk about their weakness later in the interview.

Help your workers see that God has put a great deal of effort into making each individual a genuinely distinct person. Therefore, it is not your responsibility to make individuals alike. In the same fashion, each church is uniquely and distinctly different, and it should not be your goal to make your church a copy of another church. As you conduct an interview, encourage interviewees to be proud of the uniqueness and distinctiveness of their congregation and ministry.

Other introductory questions you could ask might include:

1. What are the departmental goals you are currently working to achieve?
2. How do you evaluate your effectiveness in reaching those goals?
3. What do you currently see as your greatest strengths and weaknesses?
4. What would you like to see happen to your department or class if you had no limitations on money or personnel?

Keep in mind that it is extremely unwise to make any recommendations until you have gathered all the information that pertains to a particular aspect of your ministry. For example, it would be foolish for you to suggest a certain style of recruiting or training when the church has just finished testing that method and found it wanting. Even after you feel you have gathered all the pertinent information, it is best to take an approach something like, "Have you ever considered trying this?"

Inasmuch as you have available the various forms that have been completed by the students, teachers, and workers in each department or program, attempt to clarify this data by asking yourself, Why did they try this? or, Why haven't they tried that? or, What was the reason behind that particular approach? While you are gathering the information about the workers and clarifying various items, you will also need to discuss with the workers problems you may have uncovered in the classroom observation.

4. Harold J. Westing, *Evaluate and Grow* (Denver: Accent, 1980), p. 43.
5. Lyle E. Schaller, *Growing Plans* (Nashville: Abingdon, 1983), p. 20.

After you think you have gathered sufficient information, summarize your findings both by affirming positive experiences that you observed and making recommendations for things that might enrich the worker individually as well as the group's ministry.

A good way to finish the interview process is to ask the workers what kind of improvements they see themselves making as a result of the evaluation. Keep in mind that workers who make a self-evaluation are far more apt to implement those findings than if someone else tells them what to do. As the workers mention various steps that they plan to take to become a more effective servant of Christ, it is important that you affirm their efforts and leave them with positive feelings about their ministry.

Once you have finished the interview, it is appropriate to return to the interviewees the findings and evaluation in writing. A page with two columns listing affirmations and recommendations can go a long way in helping teachers implement the findings of your work together.

SIGHTING YOUR GOALS

This point of the evaluation process compares with halftime of a football game. You may conclude you need to shift your goals, as well as adjust your "shooting stance," in order to achieve a higher score in effectiveness. Do not be like the man described in the book of James who looked in the mirror, and when he walked away he forgot what he saw (James 1:23-24). That man ignored the facts he discovered. Your evaluation project will be a waste of time and energy if you fail to do anything about your findings.

After you have set the goals, you will discover if the people on your team are satisfied with the status quo or if they want to be on the cutting edge. Are the workers genuinely interested in strengthening their ministries?

If they are content merely to be critics, they will stop at this point. But most workers will be happy for an evaluation that is conducted with spiritual growth in mind. Setting goals will give encouragement to them.

People are more likely to implement goals vigorously when they have had a voice in shaping them. Simply to announce at a staff meeting that you have established a goal of seeing that all teachers are more adequately trained during the next year may kill your plans. Because everyone cannot be involved personally in the development of the goals, you need to see that as many leaders as possible are involved in their formation. When only a small segment of the team has formulated the goals, those leaders will need to design and implement a plan to help the others enthusiastically adopt them as their own.

Dealing with needs, goals, and strategies step by step is important. If you jump the step of goals, for example, you might limit your creativity and effectiveness. The evaluation process may reveal that you have a need to give additional training to your staff. Write that down as a *need*. The *strategy* might be to start a training program on Sunday evening. Not to write down your *goal* at this point may blind you to the possibility that there are many other strategies for training your staff. For instance, training could be done by taking a correspondence course or through an outside organization.

The following points give some guidelines for accurately formulating your goals once you have read your statistics. You will need to read your forms in light of the questions you have designed. Because it would be frustrating to try to work on all of your goals at once, you should establish a list of priorities. The natural chronological sequence and the urgency of various goals will help establish their priority.

In order to establish goals, here are some of the things to look for as you study the statistics gathered from your tabulation:

1. The gap between the ideals established by teachers and the actual performance will clearly indicate some strong need. Three-fourths of the teachers may indicate they ought to make visits in the homes of all of their absentees, whereas in actuality their teacher evaluation form indicates that only one-fourth of them are actually making home visits. This directly points out that you must provide some sort of a program to stimulate making those contacts.

2. Compare job descriptions and reports of performance to discover additional areas of need. The job description of the departmental superintendent may call for departmental meetings each month, yet the report indicates they are meeting only a couple of times a year.

3. Contrast the attendance percentage of each department against the attendance of the whole school, then compare that figure with the percentage of that same age bracket in your community profile. A careful study here leads you to see whether or not some age group ought to receive more attention in your outreach, staffing, and programming.

4. A careful study of all the figures from your attendance charts should help you establish a projected growth figure. From those figures you should be able to determine how many additional staff people will be needed and how many additional rooms should be provided for the coming year.

5. Check to see if serious consideration is being given to the interplay of worker and student relationships. Plan to take steps to improve structures that facilitate those relationships. For instance, if the students feel the teachers are not deeply concerned about their spiritual well-being, some significant steps should be taken to improve those relationships.

6. Discuss with workers the findings from your various studies. They will be able to help interpret the data, which of course will reveal other needs and problems.

You may find helpful a short evaluation program published in *The Super Superintendent*.[6] This program allows all of the staff to evaluate their own min-

6. Harold J. Westing, *Super Superintendent* (Denver: Accent, 1980), pp. 65-72.

istry and then set the appropriate goals to improve those needs.

One way to look at your leadership task is to illustrate the job that needs to be done as a brick that must be moved from position A to position B. If you are ever going to get it there, it is going to take more than merely thinking about it. It may require hard work. There may be some detours around which you will have to work. Strategy is the key word at this point. It means simply finding a way to move the brick from position A to position B most rapidly and with the least amount of effort.

Here are five basic rules to keep in mind as you think about designing and implementing your strategy:

1. *"Good goals are my goals, and bad goals are your goals" is a psychological fact of life.* We feel most responsible for those things that we have had a part in generating. It is only logical that the first law of discipline is identical to the first law of implementing strategy: People must have a say in the policy that regulates them.

2. *Devise a strategy that will meet your needs and fulfill your goals as closely as possible.* Strategies must contain or allow for flexibility. They must also include constant review to see if the approach is suited to the goals.

Creative administrators will observe that many other churches' programs will not work in the same way in their situations, but they will adapt some devices that will help them accomplish their objectives. They remind themselves as well as their co-workers that these strategies are simply a means to accomplish vital ends. That means the strategies can be scrapped or modified whenever they are not helping to meet those objectives.

3. *Any ideas worth developing must be assigned to a specific person* with a time and place for initiation and termination, and the designation of a person to whom he will be accountable. Do not end a planning meeting without making these assignments.

4. *It is very valuable to work together with your ministry team in developing a planning calendar.* You will seldom find a growing, progressive church that does not have a complete planning calendar. Usually the calendars are developed six to twelve months in advance. A useful calendar may list not only the events to be held but the days when the preparations begin. You can plan into your year's calendar the programs that will help you meet your observable objectives.

The church must deal with the idea of planning differently from a secular institution. As Christians we expect to be led by the Holy Spirit. Some groups may believe that planning is evil because they may feel that they are usurping the role of the Holy Spirit by planning events when in fact He will do that at the appropriate time for us. Others' theology on planning suggest that the Holy Spirit will guide them in the planning stage as well as in the actual implementation stage of a ministry.

Many churches use PERT charts which are used by most major corporations and agencies for their production. A PERT chart is simply a timeline chart of Progress Expectations Regarding Time. This planning is very important especially if these churches are trying to mobilize and organize a large program and staff. Each department brings to the large planning chart the various events they will be directing during the next agreed-upon period of time. It is so important at that time for each department to make schedule and time adjustments to accommodate all events and peoples. This will allow all of the departments to plan far enough in advance to keep any last-minute crises from occurring. The quality of the ministry events tend to be operated on a much greater level of efficiency because they have been thoroughly planned in advance.

That kind of planning means writing down all of the various activities that will make the event effective. That includes recruiting staff, their training, setting all of the planning meetings, ordering the curriculum, scheduling the marketing, scheduling the various prayer sessions, and even the post evaluation and debriefing event. Then they are all put in order on a calendar that is placed on a long calendar line on the page. They are marked within the appropriate dates so that they will allow for those events to be carried out to their most effective conclusion. There may need to be some adjustments so that the people involved can all participate and so they will not clash with other events that are planned for the people in the congregation who are expected to participate.

5. *People seem to make better progress when they have voluntarily made themselves accountable to others.* The concept of discipleship is based on this principle, and it is strategically important in accomplishing our objectives in the church of Jesus Christ. In organizational activities it works not only when the leader invites co-workers to share in setting their own goals, but when the leader asks team members to hold them accountable for their own goals.

Voluntary accountability is potent because it strengthens the caring relationship between individuals. It demonstrates the importance of our efforts with one another. The lack of follow-through attention causes many workers to slacken their endeavors or quit altogether. We are bombarded by so many demands and tempting diversions that we have a subconscious way of measuring the importance of tasks by how much interest others show in them. Accountability is a great way to express our interest in others. The follow-up must not fail on the designated date; neither can appreciative interest be forgotten.

Creating a program or strategy that is brand new and spectacular is not necessary. It is important to find a means to move your "brick" from here to there. Seldom do you see a weak church that is striving to provide the basic spiritual essentials and is instituting new programs to meet new needs.

It is true that God's work does not depend only on us, but He does ask us to labor in partnership with Him and to rejoice in the fruit of service done according to His will and in the power of the Holy Spirit.

FOR FURTHER READING

Brown, Lowell E. *Sunday School Standards*. Revised edition. Ventura, Calif.: International Center for Learning, 1986.

Gangel, Kenneth O. *Feeding & Leading*. Wheaton, Ill.: Victor, 1989.

Johnson, Bob I. "How to Plan and Evaluate," in *Christian Education Handbook*. Edited by Bruce P. Powers. Nashville: Broadman, 1981.

Mead, Daniel L., and Darrel J. Allen. *Ministry by Objectives*. Wheaton, Ill.: Evangelical Training Association, 1978.

Schaller, Lyle E. *Effective Church Planning*. Nashville: Abingdon, 1979.

———. *Looking in the Mirror: Self-Appraisal in the Local Church*. Nashville: Abingdon, 1984.

Tidwell, Charles A. *Educational Ministry of a Church*. Nashville: Broadman, 1982.

Westing, Harold J. *The Super Superintendent*. Denver: Accent, 1980.

30

Mark H. Senter III

Principles of
Leadership Recruitment

LEADERSHIP RECRUITMENT
- **Start with expectant prayer**
- **Place authority in the hands of-a key person**
- **Keep ministries visible in church life**
- **Implement a system for personal contact with potential workers**
- **Interview each worker to insure wise placement in ministry**
- **Deploy volunteers to specific places of ministry**

As I listened to David, I realized he was right. His years in public school administration had taught him a simple lesson that had a profound bearing upon the church's discipleship ministries. "No matter how excellent are the curricular materials or how well constructed the facility is, despite how well the media center is supplied and how many books are in the library, when the classroom door closes," he paused for effect, *"the teacher is the curriculum."*

It doesn't get any simpler than that, I thought. *No matter how many other things I do well in my role as minister of Christian education, if I fail to obtain and develop capable teachers and leaders to do the work of discipleship throughout the educational ministries of the church, everything else is window dressing.*

MARK H. SENTER III, Ph.D., is associate professor and chairman of the Christian Education Department, Trinity Evangelical Divinity School, Deerfield, Illinois.

The principle applies to large churches and small. The church that recruits and develops good leadership will have a significant ministry no matter what the other circumstances are in the learning environment. Of course it helps to have a spacious, comfortable room with attractive curricular materials, but unless the teacher can effectively "deliver the goods," the classroom may produce as many negative results as positive ones.

Willow Creek Community Church outside Chicago found the issue of leadership recruitment so strategic to their ministry that a staff member was employed exclusively to assist people to discover their passions for ministry and where these motivated abilities could be used within the ministries of the church. The more moderately sized Pantego Bible Church in Arlington, Texas, came to a similar realization. Using personal inventory tests and a class for people interested in lay ministry similar to that of Willow Creek, the church is constantly discovering new leaders with a disposition to serve in the church.

Smaller churches seldom have the financial resources or professional personnel to approach the recruitment of lay leaders such as Willow Creek or Pantego Bible do, but the principle remains the same. Some person needs to make his primary ministry that of recruiting and developing leaders for the age-graded discipleship ministries of the church.

BIBLICAL BASIS OF LEADERSHIP RECRUITMENT

Many people resist accepting leadership positions in the children's ministries of the church because they fear the stigma associated with asking people to serve with them. They fear being treated like a leper within church circles as they constantly cry "Come serve!"

BIBLICAL PRINCIPLES

Most of these fears rest in poor theology. Four statements based on biblical passages will put the recruitment process in kingdom perspective.

1. *Church leaders are appointed supernaturally.* The Corinthian believers had a problem similar to that faced by church educators today. Many of them believed that only those who spoke in tongues had been selected to serve the church. Paul cleared up that misconception, and took it a step further when he proclaimed that spiritual gifts were not only given to each believer but they were given exactly as the Holy Spirit saw fit (1 Cor. 12:11).

This means that every believer has a place of service awaiting him. The recruiter is merely acting in harmony with God when he helps each Christian discover a place of service within the church.

2. *Church leaders are appointed relationally.* When Jesus called disciples to follow Him, the first aspect of the appointment was relational, for He selected them for the purpose of being with Him. Only then did our Lord send them out to

serve (Mark 3:14-15). Service in the church is not to be done in isolation. Teachers and club leaders and people doing evangelistic visitation or preaching are to spend time together with the person who selected them to serve. There is no reason to suggest that an incarnational relationship among those doing the work of God is less important today than when Jesus physically walked with His band of Christian workers.

3. *Church leaders are appointed selectively.* Not everyone who volunteered to follow Jesus in the paths of discipleship was automatically given a place among the twelve. Luke described three would-be workers to whom Jesus in effect said, "Thanks, but no thanks" (Luke 9:57-62). One example was of a person who was not ready for the positions to which he aspired, although maybe he would be ready some day. A second person was making himself available for the wrong reasons, and thus was not appropriate material for leadership. Still another wanted to serve, but his half-hearted commitment would have had a negative impact upon his service.

Unless a recruiter of leaders has the capacity and permission to say, "Thanks, but no thanks" to would-be volunteers, he does not have the capacity to recruit effectively. Just as Christ was selective while maintaining His passion for the world, so recruiters need to be discerning in their choice of leadership personnel.

4. *Church leaders are appointed developmentally.* The assignments that Jesus gave to His disciples became more complex as He saw the increased capacity of His followers to lead. It was not until midway through our Lord's ministry that He sent this hand-picked group of men out to heal the sick and declare the presence of the kingdom (Luke 10:1-20). They simply were not ready to accept so demanding a responsibility before that time and even then they did not do it entirely right. The Lord had to debrief them afterwards and correct their motivation.

People change. Like Christ, the recruiter of leaders needs to be aware of the person's capacity to serve at any given time. Over time responsibilities will need to be increased or decreased in keeping with developmental changes.

PROBLEMS IN RECRUITING PERSONNEL

UNDERSTANDING THE PROBLEMS

Great lists of problems could be given to describe the factors that make the recruitment of age level disciple-makers difficult in the church setting. But these can be generalized into three difficulties. The first deals with *attitudes held by church members* toward the positions for which leaders must recruit personnel. The second deals with *factors internal* to the would-be disciple-maker, whereas the last is present *within the mind of the recruiter* of leaders.

1. *Content-oriented versus need-responsive ministries.* When George Gallup asked, "Who Volunteers and Why?" he discovered that 45 percent of adults eigh-

teen years of age or older volunteered for service in 1987. The amount of time the average person worked was 4.7 hours per week.[1] Among these helpers were professional young adults who had begun contributing their time and energy. They found the selfishness of their self-centered lifestyles to be empty and as a result were "penciling compassion into their calendars."[2] "If these factors are true," church recruiters ask, "why are we still having so much difficulty staffing the preschool children's church?" The answer is in the type of positions for which people volunteer most willingly.

Frank Tillapaugh may have identified the heart of the recruitment problem in the church when he spoke of two types of ministries in which lay people become involved. The first he calls the six to eight core ministries of the church (including Sunday school, club programs, choirs, children's church, missionary groups, and the like), whereas the latter he describes as parachurch-like efforts (such as tutoring, drug rehabilitation, homes for unwed mothers, foster care, English as second language classes, shelters for the homeless, and more).[3]

The first type of ministry tends to be content-oriented. Teachers and leaders are asked to communicate information, values, and skills to students who may or may not be interested in being there. The second type is need responsive. Volunteers find immediate affirmation in crusading against evil or helping a person in need begin to bring order to the chaos of his life.

Today's volunteers gravitate toward the latter kind of ministries, while still expecting the church to provide the content-oriented ministries for their families. This has caused many churches to hire people, frequently from within their own churches, to concentrate on the recruitment and development of volunteers for the content-oriented ministries. Unfortunately, the current flow toward parachurch-style ministries within the church is leaving the church with a heart for ministry but not a knowledge about the Scriptures that provides the basis for both faith and service.

2. *Conflicting pressures.* The second general problem related to enlistment of leaders is found within the would-be disciple maker. It is the factor called conflicting pressures. Gone are the idyllic days of Norman Rockwell (if they ever existed). The American family of the late twentieth century is living in a pressure cooker. Many times both parents work outside the home just to keep up with the continual mounting pile of bills. Single-parent families feel the dual stress of limited incomes and the absence of consultation and support in family matters.

Adult and continuing education is big business. High schools, park districts, libraries, community colleges, YMCAs, and churches offer adults a bewildering assortment of educational opportunities. Job requirements for formal education or the desire for career change sends an increasing number of adults back to

1. "Who Volunteers and Why?" *Time*, July 10, 1989, p. 37.
2. "The New Volunteerism," *Newsweek*, February 8, 1988, p. 42-43.
3. Frank Tillapaugh, *Unleashing the Church* (Ventura, Calif.: Regal 1985).

school each year. During 1984, 23.3 million adults were enrolled in classes (the last year from which complete records are available),[4] and with this additional activity, pressure mounts.

Children experience their own kinds of pressures, which in turn increases stress within the family. It is entirely possible for a family to have a dozen or more athletic events, music lessons, and other activities within a single week. David Elkind refers to them as "hurried children."[5]

Conflicting pressures have a negative impact upon discovering leaders for church ministries. Even the 4.7 hours of weekly volunteer efforts done by a large portion of the population may have been split between two or more activities, creating additional pressures. Such pressures are causing people to volunteer more selectively, although not necessarily less.

3. *Rejection stress syndrome.* A third obstruction on the road to recruiting leaders for church ministries is in the mind of the recruiter. It could be called rejection stress syndrome. No healthy person enjoys being rejected for any reason, and so when the likelihood of rejection is increased by asking people to take on extra jobs without monetary pay, stress is created.

The tension created by rejection stress syndrome results more from poor recruitment methodologies than the attitudes of people toward serving in the church. Too frequently leadership recruitment has taken place in a panic mode: "We've got to have someone to this position today!" The result has been inappropriately chosen people doing tasks they can barely tolerate for an undetermined length of time.

Even where a more careful approach to obtaining volunteer workers has been employed, rejection and its accompanying stress may be present. It is most commonly found in situations where the senior pastor takes a hands-off approach to staffing the core ministries of the church. If his preaching style does not include illustrating the joys of service and his sermon themes do not include the theology of volunteer Christian ministry, the context is set for rejection stress syndrome.

EFFECTIVE RECRUITMENT

PROCEDURES AND METHODS

There are no fool-proof approaches to effective recruitment except to be everlastingly at it. Church polity and styles of leadership influence the approaches that may be employed, but six factors are essential for effective recruitment of appropriate personnel.

Expectant prayer is the first and most important component in the recruitment

4. *Digest of Educational Statistics, 1989*, 25th ed. (Washington: National Center for Education Statistics, 1989), p. 319.
5. David Elkind, *The Hurried Child: Growing Up Too Fast Too Soon* (Reading, Mass.: Addison-Wesley, 1989).

process. Though this should include public prayer, the type of intercession spoken of here is a quiet meditating before the Lord asking Him to send laborers into the harvest field, which includes the age level discipleship ministries of the church. One way to accomplish this type of prayer is to get a list of all the people in the church and systematically pray for each person that God will show him and you the place of service most appropriate at the current time.

A designated *key person* to oversee the discovery and placement of leaders is the second element in the process. Although everyone needs to help in the recruitment process, there should be one person whose mission in the church is to liberate the laity to do the work of the ministry. This person works throughout the year to staff the ministries and at the same time help believers discover and develop their ministry gifts.

Although people with the kind of abilities necessary to lead in recruiting leadership seldom are detected in the average church's nominating and election process, the procedure may be necessary to validate the person's position in the church. In such cases the Sunday school superintendent or Christian education committee chairperson would be the logical choice. In those cases the nominee must be given the freedom to delegate other responsibilities in order to fulfill the recruitment tasks properly.

In churches that employ a director of Christian education, the position could be redefined to serve as the minister of spiritual resource development. His focus will be people. Before anything else is accomplished, the assignment to build people and mold a ministry team must be accomplished.

Continued *visibility of the ministries* would be the third essential part of the recruitment process. People do not seek involvement in activities about which they are not familiar. The best method creating visibility is for people who are enthusiastic about what they are doing to tell others spontaneously about their ministries. There must be formal means of publicity as well. The senior pastor and the public services of the church are key elements. Everything from slide presentations of the ministry in action to illustrations used by the pastor in his sermon will put the congregation on notice that God is doing something worthwhile in the age-group discipleship ministries.

The most important step in the recruitment process in this high-tech era is the high-touch relationship that results from *personal contact*. Slick brochures and pulpit announcements set the stage for personal conversations about volunteer ministry but seldom generate more than a handful of new or renewed workers. People want to be asked personally. In larger congregations the key person in the recruitment process may need help asking the question to everyone.

A simple question takes much of the tension away from the process of personal contact. The question that should be asked of every adult in the church each year is: "Where do you feel the Lord wants you to serve in the church during the coming year?" The inquiry assumes that everyone will be involved somewhere but does not pressure anyone to accept a ministry opportunity on the spur of the moment just because the position is vacant.

The fifth step in recruiting leaders for age-group discipleship ministries is the *interview*. One of the reasons many Christian education workers avoid public announcements of recruitment needs is because they feel obliged to use everyone who responds to such appeals whether he is well suited for the ministry or not. If the key person in the recruitment process will sit down with each volunteer and discover his "cutting edge" for ministry, placement will be more satisfactory for everyone involved. Though the process takes time, the benefits are enormous.

The final step in the process is *rapid deployment*. If the ministry does not start until autumn, rapid deployment means telling the volunteer that he has been appointed to a position within a week of the interview. At that time he should also be told what materials will be used, with whom he will be working, and when the first planning meeting will be held. If the ministry is more immediately pressing, rapid deployment means taking the volunteer to the ministry team within a week and personally introducing him to the departmental leader. People tend to operate on a three-week cycle of emotional energy. Enthusiasm for a commitment tends to wane within eighteen to twenty-one days, so it becomes very important to respond promptly.

Training in Recruitment

Recruiting leaders for the local church is an imprecise process. Although there are some books written to train those who are doing it, the best way is a trial and error method that draws upon resource people who contribute ideas from their experiences.[6] Such resource people are seldom found within the church facing recruitment difficulties, so the recruiter must turn elsewhere. Usually it is best if the persons to whom one turns for help have successfully tackled recruitment situations in a church of a similar size and social composition. Frequent telephone conversation will be a necessity as a learner goes through this self-training process.

Magazines and journals that deal with volunteerism are the best source for discovering new ideas about the dynamics of recruitment. Three of the best periodicals currently available are *The Journal of Volunteer Administration, Nonprofit and Voluntary Sector Quarterly*, and *Voluntary Action Leadership* (see bibliography for addresses). Unfortunately, the field is changing so rapidly that these publications may have changed bibliographic information by the time this chapter is published.

Ineffective Personnel

One of the primary reasons that Christian educators must recruit new lead-

---

6. Mark H. Senter III, *Recruiting Volunteers in the Church* (Wheaton, Ill.: Victor, 1990); Marlene Wilson, *How to Mobilize Church Volunteers* (Minneapolis: Augsburg, 1983).

ership both in the middle of a ministry year or at the beginning of a new ministry year is not because someone moved away, got sick, or took a new job. All of these things happen, and the mature leader accepts that fact, for there is little he can do about it.

Ineffective volunteers are an entirely different kind of problem. Their inability to do a job effectively brings discouragement to people around them and frustration to themselves. With this combination of responses, it is not uncommon to have several people resign at the same time, creating even greater recruitment pressures.

Before getting too frustrated at volunteers who are not doing a good job in ministry, it is wise to pause and ask why the ineffective behavior has occurred. There are four primary reasons that are possibilities. The worker may simply *not understand* what the job entailed. A written job description for each volunteer position is extremely helpful in minimizing the possibility of such confusion.

The *volunteer may have changed* since accepting the assigned responsibility. This is especially true of people who have served in the same capacity over a number of years. The father who worked so well with preschoolers while his children were of that age may have lost his enthusiasm for the age group and may need to be moved into a ministry more in keeping with his current stage of life.

The *expectations of the job may have changed.* The amount of preparation time, the leadership style of the department superintendent, an increase in the number of outside preparation meetings, the change in meeting time or location, new resource or curricular materials all may negatively affect the volunteer.

But the most common reason for ineffectiveness is *poor placement* of volunteers in the first place. The recruiter simply did not take adequate care to discover the current ministry skills and desires of a person and match him with the opportunities available in the church. The person may have been a round peg in a square hole from the very beginning.

What can be done about ineffective personnel? Robert Mager, in his brilliant book *Analyzing Performance Problems*, suggests a simple set of questions that will enable the Christian educator to understand how to correct ineffective behavior on the part of volunteer leaders.[7] Before taking any steps to deal with ineffective leaders, the Christian educator needs to isolate and define the behavior that is ineffective. This keeps a spiritual leader from confusing leadership style from leadership effectiveness. Three questions follow, and each has further questions to help identify performance problems.

1. *Is it important?* Many discipleship activities may not be the wisest but still accomplish the intended task. Since the important criteria are found in the end product rather than in the process (unless the process is unethical or immoral), the leader may conclude that the issue really is not important and then let the matter rest. If the issue is important, the second question is asked.

---

7. Robert F. Mager and Peter Pipe, *Analyzing Performance Problems* (Belmont, Calif.: Fearon, 1970).

2. *Is there a skill deficiency?* In other words, is the person ineffective either because he never knew how to do the job or because he has forgotten how to do it correctly? This problem is often associated with hasty recruitment and placement in leadership positions. If there is such a weakness, the response of the supervisor should be to provide training or supervised practice in using the ministry skill that has been identified as ineffective.

If after opportunities for correcting the problem have been provided the person still can not do the assigned task satisfactorily, then it may be necessary to remove the person from the position and seek to discover an alternative ministry opportunity for him. Such confrontation should always be done in a loving, face-to-face manner, remembering that the person is a brother or sister in Christ.

3. *What is keeping the person from performing his job effectively?* Maybe there is a negative reward system that has given the person additional work "because he is so good." Or, perhaps his excellence has isolated him from friends because he is so competent, and he responds by performing poorly in order to retain his friends.

The opposite of a negative reward system is a nonrewarding system. No matter how well a person does the job, no one seems to notice, and so the disciple-maker who needs at least some kind of affirmation becomes discouraged and ceases to minister with even a nominal amount of effectiveness.

A third factor that may hinder the Christian leader from performing his job well is the perception that the outcome does not matter anyway. The job feels like busywork. The last influence that Mager identifies is that of obstacles to accomplishing the desired task. Obstacles are generally external to the person (a cold room, poor teaching conditions, absence of help) but make the assigned task extremely difficult.

If the negative factors are corrected and the person resumes responsible discipleship, no further action will be necessary. But if the person has lost motivation and will not do the job adequately, then like the person that cannot seem to learn how to do the job, the supervisor must suspend the volunteer worker and help him find a different ministry opportunity.

EVALUATION OF LEADERSHIP RECRUITMENT

How does a person evaluate the effectiveness of the church leadership recruitment program? Popular wisdom suggests that if all the positions are filled, then the recruitment process is productive. That may or may not be true. It is entirely possible for a recruiter to have a lousy system but be in a location filled with leadership potential and as a result have all the slots filled. By contrast, a person may have an effective system but always runs short of volunteers because of the context. How can the second person give herself permission to accept her work as effective even though it could never be as successful as the leader in the first church?

The following four questions, if answered affirmatively, would indicate an effective leadership recruitment system:

1. Have we chosen to recruit only for ministries that are important to the kingdom of God in our community?
2. Do we have an adequately trained staff doing 90 percent of the important age-group discipleship ministries 90 percent of the time?
3. Are we recruiting staff for projected growth and new age-group discipleship ministries in the church?
4. Are we giving every person in our church a personal invitation to serve in the age-group discipleship ministries of the church every year?

CONCLUSION

The challenge of leadership recruitment in the closing years of the twentieth century and beyond may be the most significant single factor in determining the direction of the age-group discipleship ministries of the church. Although people remain active in volunteer activities, the kinds of tasks to which they commit their time have changed. Lay leaders have become more focused in their vision for ministering.

The person charged with the responsibility of placing qualified people in ministry positions will find that much of his energy is channeled into shepherding activities. Because he is primarily concerned with the persons who serve, much of his time in leadership recruitment will be spent in discovering the gifts, abilities, and current passion of Christian people. Only then would his attention shift to the discipleship activities to which the church has committed itself.

The encouraging part of the challenge of recruiting leaders is that the effort is God's work. There is a partnership between supernatural guidance and natural processes in accomplishing the biblical mandate to disciple all nations.

FOR FURTHER READING

Christie, Les. *Unsung Heroes: How to Recruit and Train Volunteer Youth Workers.* Grand Rapids: Zondervan, 1987.

Hendee, John. *Recruiting, Training, and Developing Volunteer Adult Workers.* Cincinnati: Standard, 1988.

Johnson, Douglas W. *The Care and Feeding of Volunteers.* Nashville: Abingdon, 1978.

McDonough, Reginald M. *Working with Volunteer Leaders in the Church.* Nashville: Broadman, 1976.

Roadcup, David. *Recruiting, Training, and Developing Volunteer Youth Workers.* Cincinnati: Standard, 1987.

Senter III, Mark. *Recruiting Volunteers in the Church.* Wheaton, Ill.: Victor, 1990.

Schorr, Vernie. *Recruiting, Training, and Developing Volunteer Children's Workers*. Cincinnati: Standard, 1990.

Stone, J. David, and Rose Mary Miller. *Volunteer Youth Workers*. Loveland, Colo.: Group, 1985.

Wilson, Marlene. *How to Mobilize Church Volunteers*. Minneapolis: Augsburg, 1983.

Wortley, Judy. *The Recruiting Remedy*. Elgin, Ill.: David C. Cook, 1990.

31

Richard Patterson

Equipping the Educational Staff

Staff Development, Equipping, and Training
- **Recognize dramatic population and societal changes**
- **Develop a person-focused equipping mentality**
- **Utilize the biblical definition of equipping**
- **Employ good motivational principles**
- **Provide a planned and structured curriculum experience**
- **Embrace extra-church resources for best effectiveness**

The development of staff for church ministry as contrasted with the training of staff for church ministry is a fresh concept that deserves considerable attention from church leaders today. Viewing church members as image-bearers who need to be developed to their fullest potential is dramatically different from simply utilizing people to accomplish a leader's goals.

Though the training of church staff has been an operational concept for many years, there is significant resistance to these training program models of the past because today's congregation sees those efforts as manipulative and exploitive. Church members feel that much training of the past has been designed to fill a job in the church that the church member may no longer be committed to. And such training is designed to assist the leader in worker recruitment rather than

Richard Patterson, Ph.D., is president, Evangelical Training Association, Wheaton, Illinois.

the development of the person. Thus, the development of the church worker for personal ministry in the local church carries much greater scope than simply the training of workers to be able to complete a ministry task, such as a Sunday school teacher. To be motivated to shift from a worker training model to a person development model, however, requires that church leaders consider the dramatic challenge of our age.

THE CHALLENGE OF OUR AGE

THE ALARMING STATISTICS

Is it now commonly reported that attendance in Sunday school has declined 37 percent in the last decade or so. Coupled with that are reports that despite several billions of dollars spent on evangelism, ten thousand hours of evangelistic television, five thousand new Christian books, and one thousand Christian radio stations, the percentage of born-again believers has not increased since 1980. Some say that around sixty thousand churches do not report even one conversion annually.[1]

We are now seeing evidence that there is a significant increase of those claiming they have had no religious instruction whatsoever in their lives. Many observe that church spending in America commits six times more for church music than for church education.

When we consider that the world population is now five billion, and is expected to soar to eight billion by the year 2000 and twelve billion by 2012, a massive shift is required in the strategy of the church if it is to be effective in reaching these masses with the gospel. These huge population changes are joined by dramatic shifts in the age cohorts of the population. It is expected that by the year 2000 there will be an increase of 5 percent in those of the children cohort, a 1 percent drop in the young adult cohort, a 45 percent increase in the middle aged adult cohort, and a 25 percent increase in the senior adult cohort.[2]

Not only will the church need to develop significant numbers of new ministry workers to meet such population increases, but these workers must also be equipped to meet the contemporary and unique needs of these new cohorts. It is interesting to note that these massive shifts in population and age group will be directed back to the city from the suburbs. It is expected that America will have 92 percent of its population in cities, in contrast to 82 percent of Europeans in cities by that time. All of this change demands fresh church ministry strategizing and creative new staff development if the church is to penetrate and influence such a changing society effectively.[3]

1. George Barna, *Marketing the Church: What They Never Taught You About Church Growth* (Colorado Springs, Colo.: NavPress, 1988), p. 3.
2. *Journal of Adult Training* (Wheaton, Ill., Evangelical Training Assoc., Fall 1989), p. 4.

THE ASSESSMENT OF EVANGELICAL LEADERS

Thirty-two national leaders recently reported to Evangelical Training Association that their findings were that the training of church workers was perhaps at its lowest ebb in memory. They cited that much of the cause of this phenomenon was because of inadequate preparation in practical ministry by seminaries and Bible colleges in the training of pastors and pastoral staff. In order to compensate, the church as a congregation will have to generate its own enthusiasm, sense of mission, and member equipping and training regarding the development of its staff during these challenging times.

THE BASIC ARGUMENT FROM SCRIPTURE

Though the term *training* occurs several times in Scripture, it is the concept of equipping that better describes what the Lord intended for church workers. Three basic concepts emerge when we search Scripture regarding the equipping of church members. First, equipping is the plan of God for each believer, the primary purpose of Scripture, and the intent of the God-given gifts to believers. Equipping is the primary end of God's plan for each believer: "That the man of God may be complete, thoroughly equipped for every good work" (2 Tim. 3:17). The context of that passage is the previous verse, which declares the inspiration of Scripture and its profitability for doctrine, reproof, correction, and instruction in righteousness. Thus, the primary purpose of Scripture is the equipping of the believer.

Another classic passage highlighting the concept of equipping is Ephesians 4:11-12: "And He Himself gave some to be apostles, some prophets, some evangelists, and some pastors and teachers, for the equipping of the saints for the work of the ministry, for the edifying of the body of Christ." Not only is the plan of God for each believer and the primary purpose of Scripture to be that of equipping believers, but it is also the purpose of God in granting special gifts to church leaders for the ultimate goal of the building of the Body of Christ.

The Biblical Definition of Equipping

EQUIPPING IS GOD'S PLAN FOR EACH BELIEVER

Contrary to what is commonly thought in our churches, each believer is part of God's plan for the completion of ministry. Hebrews 13:20-21 teaches that God has a specific plan for each believer, and that plan includes considerable preparation and equipping. Note the following three biblical exhortations regarding personal development.

1. *Equipping requires personal commitment.* Second Timothy 2:21 demonstrates the volitional commitment necessary from each believer to become equipped: "If anyone cleans himself from the latter, he will be a vessel for honor,

3. Ibid., p. 5.

sanctified and useful for the Master, prepared for every good work."

2. *Equipping demands a pursuit of righteousness, godliness, faith, love, patience, and gentleness.* According to 1 Timothy 6:11, such equipping is far more than training classes or job preparation: "But you, O man of God, flee these things and pursue righteousness, godliness, faith, love, patience, gentleness."

3. *Equipping carries a need for personal struggle and suffering.* "May the God of all grace, who called us to His eternal glory by Christ Jesus, after you have suffered a while, perfect, establish, strengthen, and settle you." As declared in 1 Peter 5:10, true biblical equipping demands considerable servant spirit and experience for proper fulfillment.

EQUIPPING IS TO TAKE PLACE IN THE CHURCH

Though there are many parachurch organizations and supporting agencies whose goal is the resourcing of the church according to Colossians 1:25-28, it is the church's responsibility to equip believers:

> I became a minister according to the Stewardship from God which was given to me for you, to fulfill the word of God, the mystery which has been hidden from ages and from generations, but now has been revealed to His saints. To them God willed to make known what are the riches of the glory of this mystery among the Gentiles: which is Christ in you, the hope of glory. Him we preach; warning every man and teaching every man in all wisdom, that we may present every man perfect in Christ Jesus.

EQUIPPING HAS SEVERAL PREREQUISITES

Scripture teaches that there are at least four prerequisites that must occur before biblical equipping will occur.

1. *Believers must own the concept of being called of God.* The Bible teaches that not only do the missionary and the pastor experience a call of God for ministry, but so does each believer. "God . . . has saved us and called us with a holy calling, not according to our works, but according to His own purpose and grace which was given to us in Christ Jesus before time began" (2 Tim. 1:8-9).

2. *Believers must realize that they are sovereignly gifted by the Holy Spirit.* The apostle Paul teaches in 1 Corinthians 12:7 that each believer was given at least one of the spiritual gifts for the purpose of conducting and performing ministry for the Lord: "But the manifestation of the Spirit to each one for the profit of all."

3. *Believers must appreciate that they will be evaluated by God for their life ministries.* It is essential that believers consider the big picture as they consider their life work. As seen in 1 Corinthians 3:13, the Lord will assess our life work (notice that the passage is singular), and this assessment should be the motivation for service rather than the satisfying of church leaders: "Each one's work will

become clear; for the Day will declare it, because it will be revealed by fire; and the fire will test each one's work, of what sort it is" (see also Matt. 25:14-30).

4. *Church leaders must awaken to their true ministry task of equipping others for ministry as the primary task for which they will stand before God.* Ephesians 4:11-13 demonstrates that the priority ministry of those entrusted with the gifts of church leadership is that of equipping members for ministry:

> And He Himself gave some to be apostles, some prophets, some evangelists, and some pastors and teachers, for the quipping of the saints for the work of ministry, for the edifying of the body of Christ, till we all come to the unity of the faith and of the knowledge of the Son of God, to a perfect man, to the measure of the stature of the fullness of Christ.

CHARACTERISTICS OF BIBLICAL EQUIPPING AND TRAINING

A DISTINCTION BETWEEN EQUIPPING AND TRAINING

Before persons in church leadership can shift their focus from that of filling vacant jobs to that of developing the individual for personal ministry, they must consider the distinctions between equipping and training.

1. *Equipping concentrates on the person, whereas training concentrates on the task.* Equipping is far more concerned with the development of the person than what the person does. Therefore, equipping will assist the individual in discovering who he is, what his spiritual gifts are, and what God's planned design is for him.

2. *Equipping develops individual potential, whereas training develops proficiency.* Task proficiency is the goal of training, whereas equipping is far more concerned with what the individual's capacities and capabilities are in his ministry for Christ.

3. *Equipping teaches problem solving, whereas training teaches technique.* By stressing problem solving, the ministry of equipping is able to empower the believer to resolve issues, adapt techniques, and modify approaches that go far beyond the current experience and ministry task. Equipping encourages learning transfer.

4. *Equipping makes things happen, whereas training keeps things happening.* The believer who has been developed individually and creatively will be much more entrepreneurial in sensing ministry needs and then responding to them in personal ministry.

5. *Equipping initiates new ministry, whereas training generally maintains existing ministry.* The individually developed believer is more open and responsive to the Spirit's leading to the fresh new challenges in his world.

6. *Equipping assures ministry future, whereas training perpetuates current conditions.* The equipped believer is more qualified to meet the challenges of change in society and community. To the equipped believer change is not seen as a threat but as an opportunity.

This distinction between equipping and training is not intended to discredit training at the expense of equipping. It is to demonstrate that the church needs both equipping and training. However, the more common model in the past has been only that of training.

In the last decade there has been considerable research regarding motivation. The literature has significantly contributed to a much better understanding of what motivates people. This particularly is true of adult volunteers. Many pastoral staff members complain that though they feel that the training of workers is their highest priority, their congregations do not share their view. Careful investigation has shown, however, that the cause of low congregational enthusiasm for training is usually because of inadequate consideration and employment of good adult motivational principles by the church's leaders.

Five basic motivational principles must be considered when church leaders attempt to abandon their old models of worker preparation and decide to consider the equipping and training of its membership.

1. *Equipping and training experiences must be programmed to personal time schedules.* With hectic, busy daily schedules, adults struggle to fit those time demands that are of most priority to them in their lives. Thus when a church determines its training program based upon what is convenient to the church, it is setting itself up for low enthusiasm among its target audience. Church workers are not resistant to equipping and training experiences when they see the church attempting to fit them creatively into their time schedules. The short-term, module package is far more attractive to the adult of today than the drawn-out semester experience.

2. *Equipping and training experiences must be seen as meaningful ministry to the individual.* What may be meaningful to the church leader may not be seen as such to the individual believer. Therefore the question that must be addressed by the church leader is, What can I do to establish a positive learner attitude for this learning experience? We must remember that adults will have to exchange what they consider valuable—their time and energy—for something they perceive as being more valuable—the equipping/training experience. That is the basis of all behavioral action.

3. *Equipping and training experiences must build personal confidence.* It is not enough to know the facts or content of such experiences, the individual must also feel that he is competent to carry out such a ministry task. This will require that the individual have opportunity to explore his spiritual gifts in a ministry setting where he can fail without risk to his self-esteem. The equipping/training experience must allow for this personal exploration in the educational experience while providing a security and support group for this confidence building.

4. *Equipping and training experiences must nurture healthy self-recognition.* One of the basic motivational principles is of the effect an event has upon the person's self-esteem. we often hear that such self-recognition must be carnal and therefore must be studiously avoided in all church endeavors. Although selfishness, greed, and aggrandizement can become distortions of this human need, Scripture frequently demonstrates that personal recognition is a healthy and biblical motivator (1 Cor. 9:25; 2 Tim. 4:8; James 1:12; Heb. 12:2; Rev. 4:4).

5. *Equipping and training experiences must foster genuine personal achievement.* Equipping/training experiences in the church must carry with them some evidence of personal achievement if they are to be motivational. Often this takes the form of a certificate of completion or some tangible evidence that the person has accomplished a task of some renown and value.

A DEVELOPED AND PLANNED CURRICULUM

A church equipping/training curriculum has five features that merit further investigation.

1. *A well-developed and planned curriculum creates a basic worker resource pool.* Every believer needs a basic equipping/training program beyond the scope of the Sunday school. Though Sunday school is a valuable ministry for the church (it has traditionally been the outreach and fellowship arm of the church), Sunday school is limited to what it can produce for the complete equipping of the worker. In addition, because 20 to 30 percent of our population moves each year, the church will have a constant demand for worker replacement.[4] There is, therefore, a constant demand for educational and edifying experiences that go beyond the Sunday school program. In the past we have seen this effort often termed "The Pastor's Class," which the pastor used to qualify all his people to a basic level of local church competency.

Today, the concept is much broader than that. It usually covers an entire church year and involves all new converts and church transfers. When a church initiates such a program, it usually requires all of its existing workers to take the program as well. This approach is highly recommended, as it appears to be one of the most critical elements in those factors that identify the healthiest churches of our day.

The curriculum of this basic program should consist of four elements: (1) *Bible survey* studies to provide the needed continuity to the person's understanding of the themes and scope of the Bible; (2) studies on *how to grow spiritually* that include a general discovery of spiritual gifts and the means whereby personal growth can occur; (3) a study of *human development* taught from a biblical perspective of age group characteristics, human needs and drives, which deals with the resolution of these individual needs through Christ; and (4) a study of *faith sharing* to enable the individual to develop an evangelism style

---

4. Aslanian Brickell, *Americans in Transition* (New York: CEEB, 1980), p. 29.

that is comfortable and productive for him. Such basic programs should allow for the discovery of spiritual gifts and personal approaches and techniques to ministry that are meaningful to the individual. These experiences are exploratory; therefore, they should carry the security of the equipping/training group as a support group that is committed to mutual ministry discovery.

Successful basic programs like this produce graduates who become a viable worker resource pool for worker recruitment and for further specialized equipping/training experiences. Such a program can be a major benefit and resource to any pastor or church leader.

2. *A well-developed and planned curriculum is committed to age-level needs.* Once believers are beyond the basic equipping/training status, they can be recruited into ministries of the church. Entering the basic equipping/training program, however, should not obligate the person to a ministry task or further education upon completion. When recruitment to a subsequent task has occurred, however, the person should then be offered further equipping/training experiences aimed at the age group to which he will be ministering. This should include not only the physical, social, and spiritual characteristics of that age group, but also those ministry techniques for evangelism and edification that are most productive for that group. This instruction must include actual ministry exposure to that age group.

The person should be given the opportunity to minister to this chosen age group under the supervision of an experienced worker. This supervised instruction should be failure-safe, that is, the fledgling worker, though experiencing failure, error, or weakness in these early exploratory ministry attempts, must find a group setting of support and gentle correction. It is often best to have this supervised setting include both an individual supervisor who is able to demonstrate a good model of ministry for the fledgling worker, and a peer group of others being groomed for other personal ministries. Such a setting encourages the personal exploration of one's spiritual gifts and talents and provides minimal esteem risk should it become necessary for the fledgling worker to make ministry or approach changes. This age group orientation should characterize the staff person's development throughout all his equipping/training experiences throughout his ministry life.

3. *A well-developed and planned curriculum capitalizes upon personal Bible discovery techniques.* One of the serious weaknesses of the church today is its fascination with Bible content over a Bible content directed to individual needs. The old slogan, "We don't teach the Bible, we teach people the Bible" is appropriate here. Learning Bible facts simply because they are Bible facts is not motivational to people today. People want to know what the Bible says about their needs, their problems, their family, and their life. And it is not enough for the church to tell them what the Bible says about those personal issues. They need to discover for themselves what God says regarding their needs. To teach the Bible as simply content is to deny what the Bible is. Its entire purpose is the

application to life of that which the Lord has revealed.

This is not to discourage the expositional teaching of the Scriptures—just the contrary. But church workers need to be instructed, guided, and made competent in their guiding of others, regardless of age group, in the personal discovery of what God is saying to them from His Word. This requires careful and effective instruction, demonstration, and personal participation in creative involvement techniques of ministry.

4. *A well-developed and planned curriculum calls upon the support system of the church.* The curriculum of the church equipping/training program should provide the following four support features: (1) careful guidance to discover one's spiritual gifts and ministry skills; (2) ample opportunity to explore various personal ministry options; (3) a structured, continued equipping/training program that is both group and individual in design, both general and specific to the ministry task, both demanding yet rewarding, and both short and long term; and (4) an annual public commissioning by the church of the individual to a specific ministry task that includes a specified equipping/training commitment from the church and an identified vacation period.

5. *A well-developed and planned curriculum certifies the worker's competency to ministry.* Not only does the worker seek recognition for his efforts in being equipped and trained, but those he ministers to seek tangible evidence of the competency of the worker's training and skills. Thus, a certificate or diploma identifying that person's completion of the required courses and competencies of the church curriculum is essential. These certificates or diplomas become the prized possessions of workers and often are proudly displayed in the areas of the church where they minister.

A DEPENDENCE UPON EXTRA-CHURCH RESOURCES FOR GREATEST EFFECTIVENESS

Many excellent resources are available to the church today to assist it in its ministry of equipping and training of its volunteers. A partial list of these includes:

Regional Sunday school or Christian education conventions. Held annually in major regional cities, such conventions are good sources of additional training for workers, as well as exposure to fresh ideas, new ministry tools available from Christian education vendors, and the inspiration emerging from fellowship with other church volunteers seeking stimulus to their ministries.

Evangelical Training Association (ETA). This association of two hundred colleges and seminaries produces competent local church leaders and teachers through a certification program. The Association has for more than sixty years produced an extensive equipping and training curriculum from the faculty of the colleges and seminaries that is popular in the local church. This curriculum is more demanding than typical Sunday school literature, but it is not as rigorous as college level training and provides for a three-tiered competency level in three separate ministry areas, each with its own certificate of completion. ETA also provides its international staff for on-site church evaluations, equipping and training seminars, and regional pastoral staff revitalization seminars. Churches can also become members of this association and secure free ministry counsel and monthly audio cassettes to assist them in their own equipping and training programs.

The regional Bible institute. Churches often find that their equipping/training program is so successful in their church that they make it available to other churches in their regional area. Often meeting in the mother church (though some use more neutral locations such as community halls), these institutes recruit their faculty from the surrounding area. Generally meeting in the evening, these schools find the societal interest of adults in lifelong education a valuable motivator for an education experience beyond the Sunday school. Each year half of all adults in America take some kind of continuing education course, paying tuition and book costs and driving significant distances to secure such training. Some churches are harnessing this vast adult interest through the creation of regional Bible institutes.

Many of these Bible institutes become the only source of preparation for minority groups seeking to minister full time. Evangelical Training Association's Classroom Series courses are the curriculum mainstay of a great number of these small Bible institutes.

Christian education publishers and organizations provide extensive training resources in their Sunday school materials with teacher guides as well as student books in addition to separate training support materials. Frequently these publishers offer specialized training workshops, seminars, and field staff to assist the church in the development of its workers.

The development of staff for ministry in the church is perhaps the most challenging ministry the church must address. Effective societal penetration with the gospel of Christ demands equipped and trained volunteers. Though church platform emphasis upon entertainment surely produces large crowds, it also produces a spectatorism that robs the church of its future. Wise church leaders carefully develop, employ, and constantly modify a volunteer equipping/training process that involves every member of the Body of Christ and produces competent and enthusiastic volunteers performing ministry in their sphere of life.

To this point we have been emphasizing what the church should be doing for its membership toward staff development. And that is certainly proper, for the Bible teaches us that it is a function of the church to motivate, provide, and complete such staff competencies for ministry (Eph. 4:11-16). But we must place in parallel the personal development of the staff member as well. The greatest single factor in a successful staff development effort is a sense of high need for personal development by each staff person.

In this day of high technology, opportunities to satisfy this thirst for personal growth are indeed awesome. Books and training aids abound from the multitudes of Christian publishers. Some organizations, such as Evangelical Training Association, offer adult self-study courses utilizing print, audio, and video materials, each supervised by ETA faculty. Others, such as Moody Bible Institute, Philadelphia College of Bible, Washington Bible College, Emmaus Bible College, and Columbia Bible College, also offer correspondence courses taught by their faculties.

Many Bible colleges, and some Christian liberal arts colleges and seminaries, also offer extension courses designed to satisfy this hunger for personal development. The numerical growth of these endeavors attests to their importance to the adult church staff member today. One of the phenomenal facts of this growth, however, is that although about 60 million adults take such courses each year, only less than one percent take them through churches. Among several things that tells us is that most adults do not perceive that their church is the means for their personal development. They feel they must go beyond their church for such experiences.

We must be careful to stress that we are not encouraging an "every man doeth that which is right in his own eyes" philosophy. We are encouraging, however, that good staff development emphasizes both good church programs and ample opportunities for personal training and equipping for ministry.

Successful churches have pioneered many unique tactics to insure this development balance. Many have tuition support or rebate offers to stimulate individual enrollment in either correspondence or extension classes. Frequently pastoral staff use the pulpit and church newsletters or bulletins to stress and support such efforts. An openness toward small group development in which a church educational department invites outside expertise in to provide guidance in an aspect of the church's ministry and personal development is also a mark of the church that sees individuality in staff development to be an asset.

Several churches also are providing book and periodical financial grants to its worker staff encouraging them to select those books and periodicals that are most meaningful to them. In addition to such financial grants, some churches are purchasing self-study materials for their libraries in print, audio, or video form, and giving them high public exposure from the pulpit and/or bulletin in an effort to stimulate personal development.

Whether the aspiring or in-service church worker has such benefits provided to him or not, it is part of the recruiting and commissioning process of the church to select carefully those persons who show present or potential interest in personal growth and development. Such personnel will be consciously and subconsciously searching for ways in which they can develop themselves so as to please their Lord and be more effective in their ministry for Him.

We are suggesting that the church workers of the next decade who will make the greatest impact upon their world will be those who assume an active role in their own growth and development. Such workers will see personal change as beneficial, will want to be a part of the planning of any in-service activities, will seek individualized training programs tailored to their interests and needs, and will choose goals that are unique to them.

FOR FURTHER READING

Blankenbaker, Frances, ed. *Teacher Training Manual*. Ventura, Calif.: International Center for Learning, 1982.

Brown, Lowell E. *Sunday School Standards*. Revised edition. Ventura, Calif.: International Center for Learning, 1986.

Callahan, Kennon. *12 Keys to an Effective Church*. Leader's Guide. San Francisco: Harper & Row, 1987.

————. *12 Keys to an Effective Church: The Planning Workbook*. San Francisco: Harper & Row, 1988.

Cionca, John R. *Solving Church Education's Ten Toughest Problems*. Wheaton, Ill.: Victor, 1990.

Gangel, Kenneth O. *Feeding & Leading*. Wheaton, Ill.: Victor, 1989.

Hull, Bill. *Jesus Christ Disciple-Maker*. Old Tappan, N.J.: Revell, 1990.

Messner, Robert C. *Leadership Development Through S.E.R.V.I.C.E.* Cincinnati: Standard, 1989.

Steinbron, Melvin J. *Can the Pastor Do It Alone?* Ventura, Calif.: Regal, 1987.

Stevens, R. Paul. *Liberating the Laity: Equipping All the Saints for Ministry*. Downers Grove, Ill.: InterVarsity, 1985.

FOR FURTHER HELP

RESOURCES FOR TRAINING MATERIALS

Accent Books Box 15337 Denver, CO 80215	Books
David C. Cook Publishing Co. 850 N Grove Ave. Elgin, IL 60120	Books, training meeting plans, workshops, and seminars
Evangelical Training Association 110 Bridge St., Box 327 Wheaton, IL 60189	Books, training meeting plans, cassettes, videos, church evaluations, seminars, and workshops
Gospel Light Publications/ GL Training Products 2300 Knoll Dr. Ventura, CA 93003	Books, videos, filmstrips, seminars, and workshops
Group Publishing, Inc. Box 481 Loveland, CO 80539	Books, videos, training meeting plans, and seminars for youth workers

Moody Bible Institute Center for External Studies 820 N. LaSalle Dr. Chicago, IL 60610	Correspondence courses and extension studies
National Christian Education Association Box 28 Wheaton, IL 60189	Annual directory, *Christian Education Organizations' Conferences/ Conventions,* listing regional Sunday school, Christian education associations, and other groups with addresses, phone numbers, and information about their training conferences
Scripture Press Publications/ Victor Books 1825 College Ave. Wheaton, IL 60187	Books, filmstrips, workshops, and seminars
Standard Publishing Co. 8121 Hamilton Ave. Cincinnati, OH 45231	Books, workshops, seminars, and age-graded teacher leader conferences. Also sponsors the Fellowship of Christian educators, which conducts regional leadership events and a national vocational staff conference.
Walk Thru the Bible Ministries Box 80587 Atlanta, GA 30366	Seminars and books
Denominational publishing companies	Books, filmstrips, workshops, and seminars

Lin Johnson

32

Understanding and Using Curriculum

EFFECTIVE USE OF CURRICULUM
- **Facilitates Bible teaching, does not replace it**
- **Is a guide for teaching, not inspired words to follow slavishly**
- **Must always be adapted for your students**
- **Should be evaluated carefully**
- **Must be correlated between ministries**

"We don't need curriculum. We just teach the Bible." Whether or not it is articulated, this attitude sometimes exists in churches and Christian organizations. However, it usually results in inferior education.

Good curriculum is designed to facilitate Bible teaching, not replace it. Therefore, an understanding of what curriculum is and how to choose and use it effectively is essential for Christian education.

DEFINING CURRICULUM

Literally, the word *curriculum* means "running" or a "race course." Just as a runner in a marathon runs along a designated route toward a finish line, so cur-

Lin Johnson, M.S., is a free-lance writer living in Niles, Illinois; managing editor of curriculum, Lederer Messianic Ministries, Baltimore, Maryland; and coeditor of *Christian Education: Foundations for the Future.*

riculum includes a defined course of action leading toward a specific goal.

Within such a course of action, curriculum has been defined in broad terms. For example, "all life is the curriculum. There is no experience which does not have an influence on what people become."[1] On the other hand, it can be narrowed to "the written courses of study generally used for religious education."[2]

This chapter focuses on the printed lesson plans with accompanying resources rather than on the sum of experiences that contribute toward spiritual growth. D. Campbell Wyckoff's definition perhaps summarizes it best: "Curriculum materials consist of suggestions and resources to be used to guide, inform, and enrich the teaching-learning process as individuals and groups undertake that process."[3]

Understanding Curriculum Design

Effective curriculum is built on the following foundations, principles, and structure.

Foundations for Building Curriculum

Biblical base. As evangelicals, the Bible is our textbook. We look to God's Word for the content of our curriculum as well as insights for teaching it. As H. W. Byrne summarized:

> The Christian curriculum begins properly with the Bible, the Word of God. . . . The Word of God provides both content and principles by which all subject matter content is evaluated and used.
>
> While it is recognized that there are a number of channels through which the truth of God can reach the human heart, the primary process now is through the written revelation of God contained in the Holy Scriptures. The Bible, therefore, becomes the center in the subject matter curriculum. It contains the record of God's truth as inspired by God's Spirit and revealing God's Person, His Son, and His dealings with man. As such, it is also the basis by which all other channels of truth are judged, used, and evaluated. All other subjects and truth are to be related to the Bible. It becomes the integrating and correlating factor in the subject matter curriculum. Through the Bible the interrelatedness of all subjects and truth take their rise in Bible study, draw from the Bible their materials wherever possible, and return to the Bible with their contributions of fact, interpretation, and practical application.[4]

Christological center. Although the Bible provides the content for curriculum, it also focuses our attention on the Person of Jesus Christ.

1. Paul Vieth, *The Church and Christian Education* (St. Louis, Mo.: Bethany, 1947), p. 134.
2. Iris V. Cully, *Planning and Selecting Curriculum for Christian Education* (Valley Forge, Pa.: Judson, 1983), pp. 11-12.
3. D. Campbell Wyckoff, *Theory and Design of Christian Education Curriculum* (Philadelphia: Westminster, 1961), p. 185.
4. H. W. Byrne, *Christian Education for the Local Church* (Grand Rapids: Mich.: Zondervan, 1973), p. 230.

God means His words to be more than facts, even eternal facts. He means them to reveal Himself and His Son. He never meant us to separate the written Word from the Living Word. The Living Word is contacted only through the written record. Therefore Christians have a curriculum that is Word-centered rather than Bible-centered.

And, lo, what an amazing thing we have now! A curriculum that is centered not in sinful human life, but in divine Life Himself, eternal life, fullness of life, the Living Word revealed by the written Word! What center can compare with that for vitality and power![5]

Pupil relatedness. Although all Scripture is "profitable for teaching, for reproof, for correction, for training in righteousness" (2 Tim. 3:16), not all of it is relevant to every age group. Therefore, effective curriculum is age-graded. Appropriate truths and stories are selected for each age group's level of understanding and needs, thus facilitating the internalization and practice of God's Word by students.

Sound education. Effective curriculum incorporates what we know about how people learn at various age levels and how they are motivated to learn. It grows out of sound teaching/learning principles (see chap. 7).

Application orientation. Teaching Bible facts and doctrine is not sufficient for changing lives, which is the ultimate goal of Christian education. Therefore, effective curriculum helps the teacher guide students to respond to truths studied in order to become "doers of the word, and not merely hearers who delude themselves" (James 1:22; see chap. 11).

PRINCIPLES FOR DEVELOPING CURRICULUM

In his classic work on curriculum design, *Theory and Design of Christian Education Curriculum,* D. Campbell Wyckoff outlined four major principles that govern the development of curriculum. Awareness of these principles aids in selecting the best curriculum for a particular ministry.

Context. Students are not taught in a vacuum. Therefore, the curriculum needs to be appropriate for the setting in which it is used. Some factors to consider are: place of ministry (home, church, school), type of ministry (Sunday school, youth group, etc.), theological focus, lifestyle guidelines (for example, not drinking alcohol), culture, language, and locale (urban, suburban, rural).

Scope. Curriculum publishers have invested a great deal of time and money in determining comprehensive scopes of content. A scope is broken down into appropriate content for each age level in a specific order that builds on previous studies. Copies of these scopes of study may be obtained by writing to publishers (see list at the end of this chapter).

In a ministry such as Sunday school, a student who uses one publisher's curriculum from age two through thirty will have studied the Bible several times in

5. Lois E. LeBar, *Education That Is Christian,* ed. James E. Plueddemann (Wheaton, Ill.: Victor, 1989), p. 256.

various ways and depths. Consequently, using materials from several publishers or frequently switching publishers—except for adult classes—weakens or destroys this principle.

Purpose. Effective curriculum seeks to aid in accomplishing the same purpose or objective as Christian education in general: "The whole-person-in-life doing the will of God is the object of the Christian curriculum. The personal goal is Christlikeness."[6]

Process. Biblical content is communicated by means of teaching methods, or process. Effective curriculum suggests a variety of age-appropriate methods and resources to help teachers grab their students' attention, lead them in discovering what the Bible says and means, and guide them to respond to the truth of God's word.

STRUCTURE FOR DESIGNING CURRICULUM

At the heart of a curriculum product is the lesson plan structure that includes a teaching aim tied to a life need and response, a hook that grabs students' attention, Bible study, and application of Scripture truth to everyday life (see chap. 11 for a detailed explanation of these elements).

Some curriculum products are organized in—or can be adapted to—units of learning. Instead of moving from hook through application in one lesson, the structure is spread over two or more lessons to allow for in-depth interaction with the Bible truth.

> In effective unit planning, both subject matter and experience are essential. Emphasis is given to three kinds of objectives—knowing, feeling, and doing—with the ultimate goal being a change of behavior.
>
> A unit of learning has many advantages. It encourages long-range planning, emphasizes a central theme or focal problem, focuses on the learners and their needs, allows time for accomplishment of objectives and meeting of needs, provides variety in use of methods and materials, and gives opportunities for review and application. A unit provides opportunity for better introduction to a new study and culmination at the conclusion of a study with possible carryover into life.[7]

TYPES OF CURRICULUM

There are basically five types of commercial curriculum available: (1) departmentally or group graded—more than one grade or age group studies the same lesson; (2) closely graded—each grade or age studies a different lesson; (3) uniform—all ages study the same Scripture passage; (4) unified—all ages study the same Scripture theme; and (5) electives—a class chooses the topic or Scripture

---

6. Byrne, p. 225.

7. Robert E. Clark, "Supervising Children's Ministries" in *Childhood Education in the Church*, ed. Robert E. Clark, Joanne Brubaker, and Roy B. Zuck, rev. ed. (Chicago: Moody, 1986), p. 265.

passage to study, with the approval of the ministry director or Christian education committee.

SELECTING CURRICULUM

Christian education curricula that aid teachers in introducing people to God and guiding them to spiritual maturity incorporate the following characteristics. They provide a helpful standard for selecting curriculum materials.

1. *Biblical and theological soundness* are important to assure that what is taught in the curriculum is genuine Christianity.

2. *Relevance* has to do with suiting the teaching to the nature and needs of the learners in their current situation.

3. *Comprehensiveness* means that the curriculum will include all that is essential in the scope and all that is essential to the development of well-rounded Christian personality on the part of learners.

4. *Balance* means that the curriculum will have neither overemphasis nor underemphasis of the various parts that make it up.

5. *Sequence* is the presentation of portions of curriculum content in the best order for learning.

6. *Flexibility* is important if the curriculum is to be adaptable to the individual differences of the learners, adaptable to churches of different types, and adaptable to the varying abilities of leaders and teachers.

7. *Correlation* is the proper relation of part to part in the total curriculum plan.[8]

EVALUATING CURRICULUM

Churches and parachurch organizations have more curriculum resources from which to choose than ever before, but this variety complicates the selection process. Using a set of objective questions or statements streamlines the procedure and aids in choosing the most appropriate materials. Perry Downs has developed a comprehensive set of questions under specific categories to help education committees and teachers select the best curriculum for them.[9] Some questions may not be pertinent to all situations, however.

    I. Content: What Does It Say?

      A. Biblical Orientation

        1. Does the material exhibit a strong biblical orientation with a high view of Scripture inerrancy?

        2. Are proper hermeneutical principles evident in the interpretive process?

        3. Are the best translations used, and is current biblical scholarship employed?

8. Howard P. Colson and Raymond M. Rigdon, *Understanding Your Church's Curriculum* (Nashville: Broadman, 1981), p. 50.

9. Perry G. Downs, "Criteria for Evaluating Curriculum" (class notes, Trinity Evangelical Divinity School, Deerfield, Ill., 1976). Used by permission. Minor changes and additions made.

    B. Christian Values

       1. Does the material seek to communicate a value system that is distinctly Christian?

       2. Are value issues presented and clearly defined with the various alternatives evident when Scripture is not dogmatic?

       3. Does the material promote the internalization of the values by the student?

    C. Life Issues

       1. Does the material present and deal with vital issues related to the life of the learner?

       2. Are contemporary life problems examined with deep insight and sensitivity?

       3. Are both the human and divine perspectives evident?

       4. Are solutions commensurate with the problems?

    D. Age Group Orientation

       1. Does the material evidence a clear understanding of developmental task readiness?

       2. Is the material sufficiently challenging for the age group without being too advanced for their level of understanding?

       3. Does the material show sensitivity to current interests of the age group?

       4. Is current developmental scholarship evident?

II. Philosophy: How Is It Designed?

    A. Life Orientation

       1. Is the ultimate objective of the material related to behavior rather than knowledge?

       2. Does the material use Scripture as a means to the end of a changed life?

       3. Does the material include adequate application of content to daily life?

    B. Response Orientation

       1. Is the material designed to lead the student to an active, life-oriented response to the biblical content?

       2. Does the material allow and encourage individualized student response?

       3. Do response aims vary in their life orientation?

    C. Home or Family Orientation

       1. Is the material designed to emphasize home and family orientations?

       2. Does the material provide practical suggestions for strengthening the home?

       3. Is the material relevant to contemporary home situations?

    D. Organizing Principle (i.e., systematic Bible study, life issues)

       1. Is the organizing principle one that our group needs?

       2. Is the organizing principle successfully carried out in all materials?

III. Methodology: How Does It Help?

    A. Creative Techniques

       1. Does the material demonstrate a proper understanding of the teaching-learning process, involving students instead of telling them everything?

       2. Is the teacher encouraged to use a variety of contemporary teaching techniques?

    B. Teaching Aids

       1. Does the material provide sufficient aids for the teacher?

    2. Are the aids conducive for a variety of situations?

    3. Is sufficient instruction provided for the use of the aids?

  C. Study Aids

    1. Does the material provide additional preparation help for the teacher, as background information and teaching tips?

    2. Are suggestions made for additional study on each quarter's topics?

    3. Are aids provided for both research and teaching techniques?

  D. Flexibility

    1. Is the material sufficiently adaptable for a variety of local church or organization settings?

    2. Does the material provide for various levels of competency for both teachers and students with alternative suggestions?

  E. Supplementary Materials

    1. Are supplementary materials (i.e., take-home papers) that are designed for a variety of local needs available?

    2. Is the quality of supplementary materials equal to that of the curriculum materials?

IV. Mechanical Features: How Does It Look?

  A. Layout

    1. Is the material pleasing to look at and easy to read?

    2. Is the layout conducive to popular study techniques?

  B. Color

    1. Is the material colorful but not gaudy?

    2. Is color used to its best advantage?

  C. Pictures

    1. Are pictures illustrative and helpful?

    2. Are pictures sufficiently contemporary but not offensive?

    3. Are pictures related to the interests of the students?

  D. Quality

    1. Is the material printed on good quality paper stock?

    2. Will the material stand up under heavy use?

V. Price: What Does It Cost?

  A. Price

    1. Are the materials competitively priced?

    2. Are the materials overpriced for the quality?

  B. Affordability

    1. Are the materials reasonably priced?

    2. Are the materials affordable for us?

USING CURRICULUM

Today there is a wealth of quality curriculum materials available, written, and edited by experts who have already invested much time in research, creative teaching suggestions, and supplementary resources. However, no curriculum is perfect. Even the best materials need to be adapted for individual students. After all, curriculum writers do not know the members of your group. But it is a rare church or other group that has people with training in this specialized field and enough time available to write an individualized curriculum. Therefore, it is recommended that teachers learn to adapt printed materials rather than write their own. To do so, follow these steps.

SURVEY

Before preparing the first lesson plan, skim through the entire teacher's manual to get the big picture, and read all the introductory pages. Note the overall theme and unit aims.

STUDY

Before reading through the teacher's lesson plans, do your own study of the Scripture passage and related texts, using the inductive method described in chapter 10. If you start with the printed materials, you cheat yourself out of discovering truth firsthand. Also, the Lord may direct you to a focus different from the one in the curriculum.

After your own study, read the manual and consult other commentaries if necessary. Also read the student's book, and do the work required of your pupils.

DETERMINE NEEDS

What general or specific needs of your students does the Scripture passage address? Find at least one point of intersection between your pupils' lives and the biblical teaching without doing an injustice to the text. Students who do not see how the Bible relates to them will not be interested in studying it.

WRITE YOUR AIM

Good curriculum always includes an aim, or statement of what students will accomplish as a result of participating in the study. Read the printed aim, and determine if it is relevant for your students. If not, adapt or rewrite it, keeping in mind your personal Bible study and knowledge of the individuals in your group. See chapter 11 for specific information on writing aims.

The aim determines the content of the lesson plan. Therefore, if you revise or rewrite the aim, you probably will not be able to use the printed lesson plan exactly as written.

DEVELOP THE LESSON

Using your aim as a guide, read through the teacher's manual. Then analyze each section of the lesson plan: hook, book, look, and took (see chap. 11 for an explanation). Almost all commercial curriculum is structured like this, although the titles vary. Frequently the look and took are combined in one section. For example, Scripture Press Sunday school curriculum calls the sections Focus, Discover, and Respond.

As you analyze the lesson plan sections, ask yourself the following questions:

- Does the content accomplish the aim and meet the needs?
- Are the methods appropriate for my students and the size of my group?
- Are the methods appropriate for my facilities and resources?
- Is there a more interesting way to teach this content?
- How can I involve my students in discovering for themselves instead of telling them information?
- Are there too many—not enough—activities for the class time I have?
- What additional materials will I need?

Make whatever changes are necessary to tailor the lesson plan to your group. Remember, curriculum is a guide, not the inspired teaching plan.

CORRELATION OF CURRICULUM

Sunday school curriculum publishers design their products to give students a systematic, progressive, comprehensive study of Scripture from preschool through adults. Therefore, it is best to stick with one publisher, at least through high school. Otherwise, students who grow up through the Sunday school may repeat the same passages and topics every year and fail to study other important truths.

Most pupils will also be involved in other ministries, such as children's worship, youth groups, clubs, and summer programs. Each of these ministries uses different curricula. So to avoid repetitions and omissions, the Christian education committee needs to supervise the selection of curriculum materials, using the Sunday school as the base, since it is usually the largest ministry affecting all age groups. Charting the subjects from each ministry will reveal any overlapping or overlooking of Bible content.

SUMMARY

One of the most important resources in a Christian education ministry is curriculum. Therefore, it should be evaluated and selected with prayer and purpose to aid teachers in guiding their students to spiritual maturity. But even the best curriculum materials can never substitute for a trained teacher who has a heart for God and a love for his group members. H. W. Byrne aptly summed up the relationship in these words:

> Regardless of the type of curriculum adopted, one thing to remember is that 90 percent of curriculum is the teacher. Regardless of the excellence of the curriculum, a poor teacher will turn out a poor product in a poorly educated student. And, conversely, a good

teacher can be successful with a poor curriculum. However, a good teacher can be better, and a staff of good teachers can be excellent, if they are united by a good curriculum.[10]

MAJOR NONDENOMINATIONAL CURRICULUM PUBLISHERS

Publisher	*Type of curriculum*
Accent Publications P.O. Box 15337 Denver, CO 80215	Sunday school, children's church, club
Awana Clubs International 1 E. Bode Road Streamwood, IL 60107	Club
Christian Ed. Publishers P.O. Box 261129 San Diego, CA 92126	Club/youth group
Christian Service Brigade P.O. Box 150 Wheaton, IL 60189	Club
David C. Cook Publishing Co. 820 N. Grove Ave. Elgin, IL 60120	Sunday school, electives, children's church, youth group, vacation Bible school, club
Gospel Light/Regal Books P.O. Box 3875 Ventura, CA 93006	Sunday school, electives, children's church, vacation Bible school
Group Publishing P.O. Box 481 Loveland, CO 80539	Youth group
Pioneer Clubs P.O. Box 788 Wheaton, IL 60189	Club
Scripture Press/Victor Books 1835 College Ave. Wheaton, IL 60187	Sunday school, electives, children's church, youth group
Standard Publishing Company 8121 Hamilton Ave. Cincinnati, OH 45231	Sunday school, electives, children's church, vacation Bible school, youth group

10. Byrne, p. 239.

Urban Ministries, Inc. Sunday school, vacation Bible school
1439 W. 103d St.
Chicago, IL 60643

Word of Life Fellowship, Inc. Club
P.O. Box 600
Schroon Lake, NY 12870

Many denominations also publish curricula. A number of book publishers offer selected curriculum resources; see your local Christian bookstore for specific titles or lines of materials.

FOR FURTHER READING

Cionca, John R. *The Troubleshooting Guide to Christian Education*. Denver: Accent, 1986.

Clark, Robert E.; Joanne Brubaker; and Roy B. Zuck, eds. *Childhood Education in the Church*. Chicago: Moody, 1986.

Colson, Howard P., and Raymond M. Rigdon, *Understanding Your Church's Curriculum*. Revised edition. Nashville: Broadman, 1981.

Doll, Ronald C. *Curriculum Improvement: Decision Making and Process*, 7th ed. Boston: Allyn & Bacon, 1989.

Ford, LeRoy. *Design for Teaching and Training*. Nashville: Broadman, 1978.

LeBar, Lois E. *Education That Is Christian*. Edited by James E. Plueddeman. Wheaton, Ill.: Victor, 1989.

Tyler, Ralph W. *Basic Principles of Curriculum and Instruction*. Chicago: U. of Chicago, 1948.

Westing, Harold J. *The Super Superintendent*. Denver: Accent, 1980.

33

Julie A. Gorman

Dynamics of Small Group Ministries

DEVELOPING SMALL GROUP MINISTRIES
- **Select the kind of group that fulfills your purpose**
- **Choose leaders who function as empowering leaders**
- **Recognize your choices of organization**
- **Utilize good group-dynamics principles**
- **Evaluate and celebrate**

"And, after He rested, on the eighth day God created small groups." Not really—although there are some who would attribute the frustration of committee work to the Fall. But God *did* create community.

As Godhead He existed in community.

As Creator He operated in community: "Let us make man . . ." (Gen. 1:26).

As promise-maker He structured for community: "I now establish my covenant with you and with your descendants after you . . ." (Gen. 9:9).

As proclaimer of the establishment of a new kingdom perspective, He chose community to display this new paradigm to the world: "But you are a chosen people, . . . that you may declare the praises of him who called you . . ." (1 Pet. 2:9).

JULIE A. GORMAN, D.Min., is assistant professor and chair of the Department of Christian Formation and Discipleship, Fuller Seminary, Pasadena, California.

A small group can be a vital expression of God at work, fulfilling the need for community that He placed in the heart of His created beings.

GROWTH OF THE SMALL GROUP MOVEMENT

The growth of the small group phenomenon today is not surprising, considering God's design of placing within the human heart a desire for relationship and belonging. Neither is it surprising when we focus on the priesthood of every believer, wherein all believers are ministers, relating to Him and to one another in His family. The small group format becomes a means for experiencing that for which God designed us. Its persistent survival and expansion verify that being in community is a basic human need.

EARLY CENTURIES

Through the centuries, from the first century onward, whenever relationship to God became distorted or was restricted to a certain class of the privileged few, small groups of the people of God have arisen to purify the church. Among these have been the Waldensians, forerunners of the Reformation; the Anabaptists, who met in homes to practice their faith; the Pietists, small group units who encouraged renewal within a dogmatic and inflexible church; the Moravians, who gave vision to a worldwide witness to the power of Christ; and Wesley, who urged methodical accountability and support within organized units of class meetings.

MODERN SMALL GROUP MOVEMENT

The study of small groups—recognizing their value and their uniqueness for accomplishing purposes—is of recent origin. Kurt Lewin, a Prussian who came to the United States in the 1930s, is considered to be the father of what we today call "group dynamics." His founding of a Research Center for Group Dynamics as Massachusetts Institute of Technology in 1946 opened the way for new studies that provided important insights for those who saw small group process as a frontier for learning and personal response.[1]

Church awareness of the deliberate cultivation of this process occurred in the 1950s. The educational arm saw value in incorporating group dynamics as an acceptable science, and utilized methodological insights to increase the effectiveness of Bible study in groups. The element of the church most receptive to acceptance of these humanly observed patterns to teach divinely inspired content was the parachurch sphere. Enthusiastic embracing of small groups by such organizations as InterVarsity, Campus Crusade, Navigators, Faith at Work (Sam Shoemaker), Yokefellows (Elton Trueblood), and others did much

---

1. Joseph Luft, *Group Processes*, 3d ed. (Mountain View, Calif.: Mayfield Publishing, 1984), pp. 8-10.

to establish it as a credible movement.

The decade of the 1960s in this country was a time of acting out concern over social issues. Christendom felt this influence, and the small group focus shifted to questions of renewal and reality both in the inner person and in the world at large. Influencers who marked this period include Keith Miller and his *Taste of New Wine* (Waco, Tex.: Word, 1965); the transparency of Bruce Larson of Faith at Work organization in Columbia, Maryland; the model developed at Church of the Savior, Washington, D.C., influenced by Gordon Cosby and Elizabeth O'Connor's *Call to Commitment* (New York: Harper & Row, 1963); and the Pittsburgh Experiment. (The Pittsburgh Experiment was an attempt by laypersons to integrate their faith with the business and work world. See *The Experiment of Faith* by Samuel M. Shoemaker [Waco, Tex.: Word, 1957]).

When "cause" was exchanged for the inner focus of the "me" generation of the 1970s, small group focus became person oriented. Growth was seen as prompted by inner examination and awareness of personality traits. Secular writers such as Carl Rogers, Fritz Pearls, Eric Berne (*Games People Play* [New York: Group Press, 1964]), Thomas A. Harris (*I'm OK, You're OK* [New York: Harper & Row, 1969]), and Sid Simon on values clarification (see L. Rath, M. Harmin, and S. Simon, *Values and Teaching: Working with Values in the Classroom* [Columbus, Ohio: Charles Merrill, 1966]) helped to fuel this emphasis. The result was that small groups became primarily focused on "What is happening to me in this group?"[2]

Lyman Coleman, a pioneer in the development of materials for church small groups, sees the 1980s as a period of integration. The focus of groups moved to a balance incorporating all three of the previous focuses: Bible study, social action, and personal growth. This multifaceted approach matched the wholistic emphasis of the 1980s culture.[3]

Although the small groups of the 1960s and early 1970s existed primarily outside the institutional church structures—and often in reaction to it—in the late 1970s and 1980s small group ministry became a part of organized church structure—even at the center of that ministry.[4] Organizations and experts in the propagation and refining of church small groups flourished.

In addition to the widespread influence of Serendipity, the church growth movement became a strong promoter for development of small groups in the creation of a healthy church. (Serendipity is an organization begun by Lyman Coleman to foster and equip small group ministries. Located in Littleton, Colorado, this group has been the driving force behind thousands of seminars and has produced numerous curricular aids for small groups.) Both the Church Growth

---

2. Lyman Coleman, *Serendipity Training Manual for Groups* (Littleton, Colo.: Serendipity House, 1989), pp. 94-95.
3. Ibid.
4. Jim and Carol Plueddemann, *Pilgrims in Progress* (Wheaton, Ill.: Harold Shaw, 1990), p. 11.

Institute of Fuller Seminary and the American Institute of Church Growth became centers for influencing the use of this means for evangelizing and unleashing the laity.

Stephen Ministries promoted small groups as caring centers. Paul Yonggi Cho amazed the church world with the growth of the Korean church due in large measure to the principle of home churches serving as contact points for outreach and nurture. Roberta Hestenes of Fuller Seminary and Richard Peace of Gordon-Conwell Seminary began teaching organized structures and principles for the development of groups.[5]

WORLDWIDE GROWTH OF GROUPS

Neither is growth limited to this continent. The Base Communities, springing up within the Roman Catholic church in South America, now number more than eighty thousand in Brazil alone. With such eloquent spokespersons as Leonardo Boff (Ecclesiogenesis of the Church), these laity-centered groups—in the pattern of liberation theology—reflect a concern for the poor and issues of justice.[6]

China was driven to the house church amid persecution, and today reflects the vitality of this relationship as millions of Chinese continue to attend thousands of house churches.[7]

Already mentioned is the Full Gospel Central Church of Seoul, Korea, which reported fifty thousand home cell groups in 1987.[8]

In England and Scotland, development of the house church movement began toward the end of World War II. Central Africa and eastern Europe are other centers of small group strength.

CURRENT CONDITIONS FOR GROWTH

There are many causes for a general receptivity toward small groups today. In general there has been a loss of former networks of community. Primary among these losses has been the breakdown within the nuclear family and the increasing distance between members of extended families. Divorce and other family fractures have produced insecurity and instability, damaged self-esteem, and created mistrust and fear of relationships.

The neighborhood, a unit of relationship in the past, has become for most a community of strangers whose frequent mobility and security-conscious mentality have made community-building the exception rather than the rule. Much in the work climate undermines community. The perspective that work is just a job

5. Coleman, pp. 94-95.
6. Karen Hurston, "Home Groups: Channels for Growth," *Ministries Today* (May/June 1987): 67.
7. Anthony P. B. Lambert, "Counting Christians in China: Who's Right?" *News Network International* (April 14, 1989).
8. C. Kirk Hadaway, Stuart A. Wright, and Francis M. DuBose, *Home Cell Groups and House Churches* (Nashville: Broadman, 1987), p. 50.

with no other commitments attached leads not just to lower quality of product but to impersonalness in the workplace. Economic conditions drive persons to get as much as they can, and competition is keen, with relationships seen as utilitarian for those on the way up. Employees and colleagues are often viewed as things rather than people. The world itself is basically seen as an impersonal place over-crowded with more persons than relationships can sustain. Our own boasted American individuality drives us to value personal more than group achieve-ment. Commitment is viewed as obsolete and incongruent in a generation that wants to be self-fulfilled.

These cultural conditions foster a loneliness and an isolation that trouble the modern individual and drive him in search of community. Today's baby boomers with their busy and affluent lifestyles are nonetheless hungry for a place of rela-tionship, a community that is safe, a place where they can be known personally. Pollster George Barna comments on how technology, with its impersonalness, and other social issues affect loneliness.

> One lasting consequence has been that we, as a nation, have begun to lose our abil-ity to communicate effectively with each other. That, in turn, has led to a diminution of our ability to forge meaningful relationships with other people. . . . The longer average work week, the fragmentation of our free time, the increased proportion of working women, our infatuation with new household gadgetry . . . , the decreasing reliance upon sit-down restaurants, the upturn in the number of people working independently from their homes—have all pointed to a society in which interper-sonal encounters are fewer and farther between, and the remaining interaction tends to be more superficial and utilitarian.[9]

Individuals want to make a difference in a world that seems too big to allow the person to matter. Adult and continuing education are popular, so learning in small groups is attractive. Concern for personal development and for making a dent on a damaged, unjust world is real. Support groups are acceptable—even desir-able. The time is ripe for building community in small group ministry.

BENEFITS OF SMALL GROUPS

How, then, does the small group minister to people who face the conditions noted above? What benefits occur to the one who joins a group?

MEETING INDIVIDUAL NEEDS

"Will my concerns be heard? Will my individual needs be met?" Although the complete satisfaction of each person's agenda is impossible, the most prevalent need that drives an individual to bond with others is the satisfaction of some

9. George Barna, "Seven Trends Facing the Church in 1988 and Beyond," *National & International Religion Report*, special report (1988): 5.

personal need. This may be a desire for experiencing a supportive climate among equals. It may be stimulation or growth. For others there is simply the desire to make friends and to have a sense of belonging.

FINDING ACCEPTANCE AND CARE

Groups become structures of hope. In a sense the modern-day small group serves as a city of refuge for those drained by the stress and debilitating situations of life. While the church can declare itself a place of acceptance and care, it is often within the small group structure that that claim is realized. Of particular note today are support groups for those affected by a dysfunctional situation affecting their lives. Popular for not only their acceptance but also their practical help are groups on divorce recovery, abuse, terminal illness, chemical dependency, workaholism, and so on.

EVANGELISM AND DISCIPLING

A united, corporate witness can speak loudly to an unbeliever who joins and observes the congruence between the group's proclamation of the Truth and the way members care for one another. Seeing is believing. In Acts an impression was made on those who saw the interactions of first-century Christians. John Wesley "wisely discerned that the beginnings of faith in a man's [sic] heart could be incubated into saving faith more effectively in the warm Christian atmosphere of the society than in the chill of the world."[10]

INCORPORATION AND FORMATION

Persons are effectively assimilated and discipled in the faith through group structures that allow them to participate interactively. Declaring and discussing an understanding of the faith is a necessary experience for incorporating new aspects of that faith that enhance or alter previous convictions. Members gain insights from hearing others in the group declare what it means to them to understand and apply what is believed. The values described in the Scriptures must be learned in relationship.

> To learn to trust, and to become trustworthy—to learn to love, and to become loving—we must become deeply involved in the lives of others, to whom we commit ourselves in Christ. To develop this kind of relationship we need to share ourselves with others, and they need to share themselves with us. All of this demands time. More than this, it requires a face-to-face relationship. A relationship we can have only with a few others at one time. And thus a church is forced to move to a small group structure.[11]

10. Howard A. Snyder, *The Radical Wesley* (Downers Grove, Ill.: InterVarsity, 1980), p. 56.
11. Lawrence O. Richards, *A New Face for the Church* (Grand Rapids: Zondervan, 1970), p. 153.

TASK ACHIEVEMENT

Corporate units can often accomplish what individuals alone cannot. A major benefit of groups is the sustaining power and complementary contributions of many for the completion of a task—whether that task be learning information, feeding the homeless, or bringing to fruition a vision. Fidel Castro declared, "I began my revolution with 82 men. If I had to do it again, I would do it with 10 or 15 men and absolute faith. It does not matter how small you are, providing you have faith and a plan of action."[12]

EQUIPPING BELIEVERS

The personal attention and interaction possible within a small group setting make it an ideal equipping center. Sometimes the skill development is intentional, such as learning how to study the Bible, counsel other Christians, or to evangelize. Many times a member is equipped with skills in subtle ways, simply by being an observer or participant in the group situations. Small groups are laboratories for learning how to love others (where else do you learn this in the church?), how to listen and communicate interpersonally, and how to deal with conflict and disagree agreeably.

CHANGING PERSONS

Overall, good small groups raise a person's level of self-esteem and confidence as persons contribute to the group and feel a sense of belonging. This atmosphere provides a safe, intimate environment for change. Certain methods of group discussion and decision-making appear to be more effective than information giving in prompting change, because interactive participation adds attitude awareness and valuing to the information.

RECOGNIZING GIFTEDNESS

Accompanying such change is often the recognition or affirmation of giftedness in members who observe the ministry of persons to one another within the group. This awareness that they are God's gift to the Body of Christ enhances their sense of value and mission.

MINISTERING

This confidence in being gifted in turn fosters a sense of being the people of God called to minister to one another and to display to the world the magnificence of Jesus. Small groups give the ministry to the people, unleashing the church to be salt and light and to learn from and respond to one another. This significant

---

12. John Mallison, *Growing Christians in Small Groups* (Homebush West, New South Wales, Australia: Scripture Union Books/Anzea Publishers, 1989), p. 4.

involvement and sense of investment are two of the main motivators small groups have for church growth.

EXPERIENCING OBEDIENCE

Being in community not only expresses the corporate nature of Christ, but it also provides scope and opportunity to carry out the commands of Christ. Biblical principles have a practical outworking that requires the presence of others. Corporately group members learn to understand the varied dimensions of the Word of God. Togetherness provides the supportive and accountable climate needed to act on the Word. Groups generate courage to move into the world with a biblical lifestyle.

MODELING COMMUNITY LIVING

Another asset of small groups is that they provide models for how to live biblically with others in the family and in the church at large. Seeing concepts enfleshed makes them transferable.

Types of Groups

There is great variety in small groups today. All of them, regardless of their uniqueness, share three purposes in common: (1) to meet the needs of the persons in the group, (2) to accomplish a purpose or task, and (3) to maintain group relationships to such an extent that the members choose to act in cohesion rather than on their own. The fact that people's needs, purposes, and relationships are so different means that the groups produced will also reflect this wide scope of differences.

WAYS TO DISTINGUISH GROUPS

The differentiation of groups can be based on many criteria: the type of organization, the ingredients that make up a meeting, the target audience, the length of commitment, the requirements for membership, the place of meeting, the methodology, the size of the group, and the major emphasis. Thus we have groups that are leader-led or leadership-shared; formal and informal; open or closed; worship or sharing or prayer; youth groups, teachers groups, and single-parent groups; regular or irregular; high commitment and low commitment; home, neighborhood, and workplace; informational, experiential, and action; work groups and study groups; clusters and triads; evangelism and fellowship. And among these every type has numerous expressions, each with its own unique characteristics.

SEVEN MAJOR CATEGORIES

Identifying groups by their major emphasis suggests seven general categories that reflect a broad diversity in how each is carried out. Those seven general categories are contact groups, evangelism groups, nurture groups, growth groups, support groups, service groups, and satellites. Bearing a heading that reflects a major emphasis does not infer that the other emphases do not occur in that category. But it does reflect that persons in these general categories put most of their energies into the identified focus.

Contact groups. These bridge-building groups serve the purpose of making interpersonal contact with potential Christians. They are highly relational, with a desire to increase the quality of relationships, and in a low-key manner to informally share one's faith. They are often organized around a neighborhood locality, and may be on a regular or irregular schedule but with no requirements of commitment. The format is usually a relaxed, conversational style. The ratio of non-Christians to Christians is high, and spiritual clichés or any kind of formalized study in Christianity is off limits. The goal is to share the faith casually in a nonthreatening setting.

Evangelism groups. The intent of these occasions is more overt. They are designed for believers to share the gospel. Persons who come to these groups have been advised that there will be some conversation about the Bible or Jesus Christ. Sometimes the plan is for several to share their faith stories. Although there is a presentation, a major part of the group time is open for discussion. The agenda is often set by the non-Christians' questions or comments. The open stance to discuss this focused content of the gospel continues the emphasis on building relationships. Sometimes these groups are designed for particular people, such as businessmen or those in a particular profession. As with the contact groups, a key to the success of the evangelism group is not to overload it with Christians and to be sensitive to the needs of the attenders.

Nurture groups. Some would identify nurture groups as follow-up groups. They primarily seek to help those who have taken a step of commitment (new Christians or new church members) understand the steps they have taken and become acclimated in the new culture they have entered. Along with a desire to inform, these groups seek to cultivate a sense of belonging and of being a part of a larger group that shares the same understandings and commitments. Groups of this nature generally follow a formalized plan and are in existence for a limited period of time.

Growth groups. The maturing of believers brings the persons in these groups together. That maturing may mean learning to understand the Scriptures, processing personal faith, discovering how to cultivate fellowship within the Body of Christ, developing a sense of stewardship for gifts and possessions, helping one another make application of known principles. This group form bears many names: Bible study, discipleship group, fellowship, covenant group, study group, prayer and sharing, and so on. The element all have in common is the commitment of the members to grow in their insight and understanding, in their application of truth, and in their skills of study, caring, communicating, and trusting.

Another shared principle among these groups usually is high commitment on a regular basis to agree upon expectations and responsibilities.

Support groups. Sometimes described as affinity groups, persons in these groups share commonality in some way, which enhances their ability to identify with and to understand how to minister to one another. This common identity may be gender, age, profession, geography, or shared experience. The focus is usually on coping with some issue that grows out of that categorization. For example, "What is involved in my living for Christ in my profession as a public servant?" Or, "How can my experience of going through grief be influenced by the faith I embrace?" These people deal with many pragmatic questions and are interested in putting what they know into practice. The fact that others share a like problem or also seek to achieve the same goal creates a bond that strengthens and enables the individual to take steps not possible if he stood alone. In a stress-filled world where Christian commitment is often compromised, these groups have spawned prolifically as needs are identified. They may be found among such widespread concerns as the unemployed, the terminally ill, the chemically dependent, the single parent, senior citizens, singles, nurses, lawyers, politicians, entrepreneurs, parents of adolescents, divorcees, victims of abuse, bikers, athletes, artists, and so on. Although most of these groups are primarily relational and spend much time in sharing and discussion, praying for one another, and checking in, they may also incorporate scriptural study and content.

Service/mission groups. These groups' main purpose is the fulfillment of a task. They are drawn together because of commitment to a common cause—not just learning about something but actively doing something. To succeed, this type of group needs at least one person with a vision, as well as many people who are willing to get involved in research or ministry outside of group time. The work accomplished usually results in a product or event that capsulizes or fulfills their goal. A favorite target is social concerns—poverty relief, injustice recognized and righted, tutoring the untaught, making provision for refugees or unwed mothers, or creating advisory councils for senior citizen concerns. The focus need not be outside the local congregation, however. Some service groups care for church facilities, design and remodel the church nursery, produce an arts and crafts festival to display the giftedness of church members, operate a telephone counseling service, or make provision for missionaries home on furlough. The calling of these groups is to support one another but also to move outside their group in ministering to persons who are not a part of their group. Perhaps two best-known examples of churches enthusiastically endorsing this emphasis would be the Church of the Savior in Washington, D.C., where church membership requires commitment to a mission group, and Bear Valley Baptist Church in Denver, which became the model for Pastor Frank Tillapaugh's vision of the church portrayed in *Unleashing the Church* (Ventura, Calif.: Regal, 1982). Committees and accountability groups where members are held responsible for completing assignments outside of the group are another variation of this category.

The satellite. As a category, the satellite is especially unique. It is distinguished by being intergenerational (usually larger than the other above-mentioned categories), by fulfilling the role of a congregational experience, by almost always including worship, and by often being independent and self-contained with financial commitment from the members. (There are some groups that are organized as satellites of and closely aligned with a mother congregation. The group provides a more intimate gathering and pastoring of the congregation and is limited to the role and time slot assigned by the supporting institution.)

GROUP LEADERSHIP

LEADERS NEEDED

The ministry of small groups requires leadership skills in a variety of ways. Those who are primarily responsible for conducting a group session are the group facilitators. As groups multiply, there arises a need for a small groups coordinator, who is responsible for seeing the overall picture and for organizing, channeling, and promoting the ministry of small groups and for helping the small groups function efficiently. Continued expansion necessitates a person with vision and expertise who can serve as designer and equipper. This persons takes the lead in evaluating, laying out plans for enrichment and expansion, and in equipping others to serve as facilitators and coordinators. Usually when small group leadership is mentioned, facilitator is meant, and it is in this context that we shall discuss leadership.

LEADERSHIP STYLE

Considerable research has been done on what kind of leader is most effective in a small group setting. What leadership style works best for small groups?

Some have believed that the firm, take-charge style of the authoritarian leader was best for getting a task done through the group process. However, others have pointed out the benefits of a group led by a democratic style leader. There were even those who believed that the freedom of the laissez-faire style was called for if group members were to be allowed to develop and form the group. The problem was that each style had its strengths and weaknesses. Further insight led to the development of a theory based not on the one style fitting the personality of the leader, but on varied styles needed depending on the situation of the group. This "situational leadership" theory equipped leaders to assess the dynamics of a group and then to adapt a leadership style that maximized those dynamics. Thus, as groups move through various passages in their development, they are effectively led through four different styles. These styles as described by Ken Blanchard are directing, coaching, supporting, and delegating. Such designations suggest that when a group begins and has little direction and motivation, a directive style proves most effective. The leader adjusts his style as the group's needs change.[13]

This "situational leadership" theory fits well with what many describe as servant leadership. A more recent label, "empowerment leadership," focuses on the good of the one served. It equips and releases those to assume the leadership roles God intended in placing each in the Body of Christ.[14] Such emphasis blends both the beneficial development of the individual with the corporate reciprocal development of the group as "the whole body, joined and held together by every supporting ligament, grows and builds itself up in love, as each part does its work" (Eph. 4:16).

LEADERSHIP SYSTEMS

Groups operate under three basic systems: (1) one leader who consistently serves in that capacity, (2) a shared leadership where roles and responsibilities are divided between two or three, usually along the lines of catalyst discussion leader and relational host/hostess who helps persons feel "at home," and (3) rotation of leadership where several or all members take turns in leading. Each system has its advantages and disadvantages, and choice is usually determined by pragmatic factors such as time and persons available.

Again, an empowering leadership model suggests a leader who is alert to the interests and abilities of group members. That leader seeks to do whatever is necessary to empower each person to make his contribution to the building up of the Body.

LEADERSHIP FUNCTION

The functions of a small group leader vary according to the type of group, but they always include a concern for both the task and the people. Every small group leader has three realms in which to facilitate: (1) to help each member become involved and mature, (2) to enable the group to accomplish what it set out to be or do, and (3) to cause members to learn to work together as a cohesive unit, which both enriches their lives as individuals and allows them to reflect Christ in His church.

ORGANIZING SMALL GROUPS

When multiple groups exist, there must be some form of organization or plan. An overall plan suggests ways to expand and strengthen what is already in existence. There are numerous plans for organizing and building such a ministry. The two major philosophies that help to determine basic strategies may be

13. Ken Blanchard, Patricia Zigarmi, and Andrea Zigarmi, *Leadership and the One Minute Manager* (New York: William Morrow, 1985).
14. Walter Wright and Jack Balswick, "A Complementary-Empowering Model of Ministerial Leadership," *Pastoral Psychology* 37, no. 1 (Fall 1988): 6-8.

labeled central control and central motivation.

CENTRAL CONTROL

Most churches are organized with a central control system. A core committee or administrator determines and sets up (recruiting, organizing, supplying) the number and type of small groups within the church. All groups are under the supervision of this central system and operate with the blessing and enabling of such. The system may determine curriculum, set leadership standards, form new groups, and even place persons in groups. In very high control systems, each person in the church is assigned to a group, whereas in others persons are urged to join but have a choice.

CENTRAL MOTIVATION

The central motivation system sees itself responsible only to call persons in the congregation to respond to the biblical command to be in community and to carry out the principles of biblical truth. Persons in the congregation determine and set up their own groups to carry out this call. The responsibility is placed in the hands of the laity. They select their own emphases and are free to develop varied kinds of small group ministries. Often the central motivation system does not know how many small groups are in existence in this system. It is satisfied to leave the working out of specifics in the hands of the laity who do the ministry. New groups form spontaneously as the laity recognize a need and respond to it.

Each of these two systems has its strengths and weaknesses, and the theology of the church and its perspective on the role of leadership will often determine which of these a church chooses to embrace.

ORGANIZING AN INDIVIDUAL SMALL GROUP

There are numerous ways of organizing persons into a group and questions that need to be decided.

The choice. Small group experts agree that for a group to become a group, those involved must agree on a common purpose. How that purpose is determined is an organizational facet. Do the interested persons come together and determine the purpose, or is the purpose determined by the leaders, who then invite persons interested in that purpose to join together in a group?

The purpose determines the size of the group (smaller for accountability and larger for family groups). It also can affect the openness of the group to visitors and new members.

Will the group be an open group—where anyone can drop in or out at any time—or a closed group—where persons commit to the group for the time period suggested and new members cannot join during that period?

The covenant. Organizing a group may include summarizing commitments to certain disciplines or responsibilities in a covenant or agreement. These covenants may include commitment to regularity in attendance, a pledge to confidentiality, a mutual agreement on what roles leaders and members will play, shared expectations of time and format of the meetings. These covenants demonstrate the seriousness of intent to secure ownership of the group by all and erect boundaries so members have a sense of what is expected.

GROUP DYNAMICS

Group dynamics is the study of group behavior. Group response is more than the sum of the behavior of individuals, it is a living system that is never static but constantly fluid. This study of group process has revealed principles that govern group behavior.

There is a climate produced within groups that impacts learning and change. More than skill is required for effective communication, and this intangible atmosphere created by setting, nonverbal behavior, interactive styles, and personality mix is a major factor in the dynamics of the group.

SELF-DISCLOSURE AND COMMUNICATION

Too much too soon when it comes to self-disclosure can be a threat to persons in the group. But too little means the group will probably never develop cohesion, because trust that comes through knowing has not been built. The process of how to help persons self-disclose in a safe way and how to progress in this at different stages of the group is at the heart of group dynamics.

Communication, both verbal and nonverbal, is a rich field of study as members are taught skills of interpersonal interaction. Group dynamics reveal the impact of observing the process of who talks to whom and what is heard, of how information and attitudes are communicated, of what signals are given that reveal inner responses, of learning the balance between empathetic listening and challenging confrontation. Interpersonal conflict occurs when persons feel threatened with loss or when they feel they can become transparent with one another. This freedom to disagree can be healthy, and group dynamics seeks to help members know congruence and resolution of conflict in order to grow from it. Conflict agendas include how to recognize it, how to encourage differentiation among members, how to manage conflict so that relationships are sustained while differences are voiced, understood, and worked through.

NORMS AND ROLES

A norm is an unwritten rule by which everyone in the group abides. Usually norms are unexpressed and may remain invisible until transgressed. A deviant is one who persists in behaving in the group counter to the accepted norm. Examination of these "unspoken rules of the clan" reveals much about the participants and the group climate—what makes it safe and comfortable.

A role is a set of behavioral expectations placed upon a person or group. Roles may evolve as group members settle into their patterns of group process. There may be vying for certain roles. Being in a role in one group does not guarantee the same role in another. What happens when a person begins to change to a different role is a fascinating phenomenon that brings "tilt" to the whole group. Roles and norms reveal much about power, trust, humor, decision making, and how communication takes place in a group.

SIZE

Group size is a part of the dynamic that can influence all of the above-mentioned group dynamics. "Thomas and Fink . . . report that, for most kinds of tasks or problems where group discussion is desirable, a five-person group appears to be an optimal size."[15]

. A. Paul Hare in his research says, "as size increases, there is a tendency toward a more mechanical method of introducing information (by round robin procedure, for example), a less sensitive exploration of the point of view of the other, and a more direct attempt to control others and reach solutions whether or not all group members indicate agreement."[16]

The addition of a new person or disappearance of a member scrambles the dynamics of an existing group. A group of more than eight will probably contain silent members. Size can affect the forming of subgroups and divisions or can foster interaction on different levels of intimacy.

STAGES

Passages or life stages within a group can be identified and predicted. Each has telltale signs of the life of the group with its struggles and settled issues. Although groups progress at different speeds, all seem to go through these stages in an order and with similarity of concerns. Awareness of such stages can enable group leaders to adjust their leadership styles and can encourage group members that they are normal and growing. There are various ways of labeling these stages, and studies include anywhere from three to seven identifiable periods. The basic phases are marked by orientation along with a hesitant participation in the beginning, followed by a period of conflict where general dissatisfaction and testing become the setting for establishment of what the group will be and who will play which parts. The third general stage is one of happy cooperation and productivity, followed by a stage of change and differentiation to keep growing or to produce a restlessness that leads to termination. This pattern is natural and helps in the understanding of what is taking place as the group moves to maturity.[17]

15. Luft, p. 23.
16. A. Paul Hare, *Handbook of Small Group Research,* 2d ed. (New York: Free Press, 1976), p. 226.
17. Luft, p. 33.

There are many other aspects of group dynamics: variables of dependence, independence, and interdependence; levels of intimacy; development of cohesion and a sense of belonging; self-regard; feedback; and more. Studying the process and identifying patterns and principles has made the possibility of intentional change and growth in groups possible.

EVALUATION

Evaluation within groups constantly occurs through feedback, as members state their satisfaction or dissatisfaction with processes and persons. Healthy groups regularly "take their pulse" to assess what should be continued and what improved. This assessment is often done as part of the closure of a period of study and the initiation of a new phase. Such evaluation forms the basis for improved, new agreed-upon responsibilities and changes. Since groups are living and dynamic, continual change is to be expected and desirable.

This period of self-examination need not be threatening and should always be concluded by a form of celebration over any results produced in and by the community. Four areas in which evaluation can take place include: (1) purpose—Did the group achieve its purpose? (2) content—What did the group learn? (3) group process—How well did the group work together? and (4) personal growth—How did individuals change and grow?[18] Sharing these results with one another gives a feeling of accomplishment and closure. They become the springboard for continuation of healthy small groups and keep the movement on target as small groups continue to serve as effective instruments for experiencing community within the church.

FOR FURTHER READING

Dibbert, Michael T. and Frank B. Wichern. *Growth Groups: A Key to Christian Fellowship and Spiritual Maturity in the Church*. Grand Rapids: Zondervan, 1985.

Griffin, Em. *Getting Together: A Guide for Good Groups*. Downers Grove, Ill.: InterVarsity, 1982.

Hadaway, C. Kirk, Stuart A. Wright, and Francis M. DuBose. *Home Cell Groups and House Churches*. Nashville: Broadman, 1987.

Hestenes, Roberta. *Using the Bible in Groups*. Philadelphia: Westminster, 1985.

Hunt, Gladys. *You Can Start a Bible Study Group: Making Friends, Changing Lives*. Revised edition. Wheaton, Ill.: Harold Shaw, 1984.

Kunz, Marilyn, and Catherine Schell. *How to Start a Neighborhood Bible Study*. Wheaton, Ill.: Tyndale, 1970.

Lum, Ada. *How to Begin an Evangelistic Bible Study*. Downers Grove, Ill.:

18. Sara Little, *Learning Together in the Christian Fellowship* (Richmond, Va.: John Knox, 1956), p. 60.

InterVarsity, 1971.

McBride, Neal F. *How to Lead Small Groups*. Colorado Springs, Colo.: NavPress, 1990.

Nyquist, James F., and Jack Kuhatschek. *Leading Bible Discussions*. Revised edition. Downers Grove, Ill.: InterVarsity, 1985.

Plueddemann, James E., and Carol E. Plueddemann. *Pilgrims in Progress*. Wheaton, Ill.: Harold Shaw, 1990.

34

Lowell Brown and Wesley Haystead

Utilizing Computer Support

UTILIZING COMPUTER SUPPORT
- **Computer decisions are broad-based, receiving input from all areas of church ministry**
- **Software is chosen for its suitability to all areas, not for strength in just one**
- **The computer is used to speed up repetitive office functions**
- **The computer is used to organize information for decision makers**

COMPUTERS AND THE CHURCH

Just because the business and educational world have enthusiastically embraced the computer is no reason churches should automatically do the same. Then again, neither is there a reason for churches to shun computers out of fear we will become too businesslike and not spiritual enough. During the 1980s most churches began (often reluctantly) to use computers in ways ranging from members occasionally doing some task for the church on a computer at home or work all the way to placing a terminal on the desk of every staff member (including the pastor).

Most people tend to think of computers in terms of one or two specific functions in which they are interested. Whereas youth directors often think first of com-

LOWELL BROWN, M.R.E., is president of Lowell Brown Enterprises, Santa Paula, California.

WESLEY HAYSTEAD, M.S.Ed., is editorial director, Lowell Brown Enterprises, Santa Paula, California.

puter games, business administrators and bookkeepers focus on financial records and reports. Teachers may think of instructional programs, pastors of computerized Bibles and concordances, and secretaries of word processing (the computer-age term for typing).

Similarly, Christian education leaders tend to rivet their highest interest on certain computer applications: tracking attendance, discovering people with experience or interest in teaching, targeting mail to specific groups, or identifying people who are prospects for specific church ministries. Christian educators also keep looking for a long-anticipated breakthrough in the use of computers as instructional aids. Even though a wide variety of instructional programs have been released for Bible study and other topics of interest for Christians, the quest remains elusive for computer applications in the Sunday school classroom or other study groups. For this reason, we shall focus attention in this chapter on the use of the computer as an administrative tool, not only in Christian education but in the total life of the church.

It is vital that Christian education leaders not limit their awareness of what the computer will do in their ministries. The natural tendency to focus on departmentalized computer functions poses some significant problems for the long-term, healthy growth of Christian education efforts. If we have learned anything after consulting with hundreds of church leaders on the use of the computer in their ministries, it is that Christian educators need to gain a broad perspective of the computer's role in the total operation of the church. Otherwise decisions will be made in other areas that may negatively affect Christian education.

COMPUTER DECISIONS NEED TO BE BROAD-BASED

During the 1980s most churches first began using a computer because of the initiative of one area of operations, most commonly, the business/financial personnel. In a large percentage of churches, the computer was brought into the office specifically to handle financial records. Even when efforts were made to involve all leadership in the decision, one individual or group tended to dominate the selection process. Sometimes the preeminence of this individual or group was the result of personalities or the level of interest and vision. In even more cases, churches were willing to invest in a computer for the business office because people more easily understood how the computer would serve accounting functions than how it would aid church program functions. This pattern of selection frequently resulted in software programs being selected because it was strong in the particular area of concern to those heading the selection process (i.e., accounting), but no one really knew if it would do the job needed in other areas. It is not at all uncommon to hear Christian education staff members moaning that they are "stuck" with a system that works for the business office but not for them.

As a result of the initial way in which the computer entered the church office, the computer tended to become the tool of whichever person or group led the move to make the purchase. Except for very large churches, churches tended to buy (or receive as donations) one or two computers. These were usually placed on the desks of the staff members perceived as most needing to use them. Rarely was a Christian education person one of those people. As a result, many churches have had computers in their offices for a fairly long time without really learning how to put them to use in directly aiding the ministry programs the church conducts.

SHOULD A CHURCH DEVELOP ITS OWN SOFTWARE?

When churches first began using computers, it was fairly common for someone in the congregation, a person with programming skills, to volunteer to write a program to do exactly what the church wanted. The church would buy a commercial data base program, and the programmer would customize it to do the functions the staff said needed to be done. Some churches were pleased with the results, especially in light of the relatively high cost of church management software in the early 1980s. However, most churches had severe problems in continuing to use custom-designed software. No matter how skilled and well-intentioned the programmer may have been, five major types of problems tended to recur:

1. *Time.* It always takes longer than the programmer plans. This is true of any significant software project, but it is especially so when the church leaders decide they want every conceivable bell and whistle on their system, or they keep changing their minds during the development process. Even without such delays, the time spent waiting for the system to be written, debugged, and installed is time in which a church management system could be in operation already. Saving money at the cost of valuable time has rarely proved to be a wise economy.

2. *Documentation.* Many churches have been stung when they discovered their helpful programmer had to take a few shortcuts to get done somewhere close to the time promised. Not writing a clear, complete instruction manual is the most common shortcut. This is usually explained away with the promise that the programmer will demonstrate all the features, but the lack of a well-designed reference tool always hampers the staff for years to come.

3. *Training.* Most volunteer (and paid) programmers agree to train the staff when they install the system. But who will be available to continue working with staff members who do not remember every detail from the initial training session? And what will happen if the church secretary leaves? Will the programmer still be available for additional rounds of training as staff members change?

4. *Service.* What will happen when there is a problem? (And there always is.) Will the programmer be available to fix it quickly, or will he have to work it into his after-hours schedule? When will he start believing he has done enough already?

5. *Upgrades.* Will the programmer be willing to modify and add features after the church has used the package long enough to realize that improvements are needed? How often will the system be refined to take advantage of new developments in computer technology? Unfortunately, the vast majority of churches who began with customized software found themselves locked into an obsolete system because their program was not regularly updated.

This litany of problems does not assume that churches that bought a church management system avoided all these troubles. Many people started small businesses in the computer field, often with a package they had designed for their own church. They managed to sell a few software packages but soon went out of business. In most cases, the demise of most of these companies was linked to their inability to solve the problems mentioned above.

On the other hand, a number of companies have established solid reputations among churches based on their commitment to solve those problems on a continuing basis. In the volatile world of computer software, firms that have weathered a decade or more of operation are deserving of the confidence of church leaders.

USING THE COMPUTER TO SPEED UP CHURCH OFFICE FUNCTIONS

Many tasks being done in the typical church office can be done more efficiently (faster, neater, cheaper, and with fewer errors) with the aid of a computer. The kinds of tasks at which computers shine are those that involve repetitive actions, especially if they involve the finding, organizing, and printing of information.

The following summary of typical church office tasks includes a brief description of how the computer helps and identification of which of these seven types of computer programs to use for that task:

1. [WP] = Word processing, programs used to type and edit text.
2. [DTP] = Desktop publishing, programs that combine text and graphics in typeset designed pages. (Many word processors include some desktop publishing features—and vice versa—but desktop programs tend to be much more sophisticated than word processors.)
3. [MS] = Management software, programs that retain and use information about people, addresses, phone numbers, attendance, contributions, areas of service, skills, and programs.
4. [AS] = Accounting software, programs that handle the church's general ledger accounts, accounts payable, and payroll.
5. [RS] = Research/study software, programs that aid in Bible study and sermon preparation.
6. [LS] = Library, music, equipment software, programs that inventory and aid in quickly locating books, articles, songs, supplies, and so on.
7. [CS] = Calendar/scheduling software, programs that keep track of what rooms

are scheduled for use by which groups and when staff members are available.

Periodic publications [WP] [DTP]. "If it weren't for the panic over the bulletin every week," a church secretary lamented, "I'd love this job. Just when I think I've got it all laid out and ready to go, someone rushes to my desk with an *urgent* announcement that just *has* to be squeezed in somewhere. Have you ever tried 'squeezing' in the pastor's pet announcement after everything else is already in position?"

A computer may never get all the announcements turned in before the deadline, but it will certainly make it easier to make things fit. Margins can be adjusted, spacing changed, placement of copy switched—all with no laborious retyping. And sections that have a repetitive format from week to week (such as the order of service or weekly calendar) can be left in the computer so only new information needs to be changed each week.

Not only does the computer aid in the handling of text, it allows the creation of eye-catching headlines and the insertion of professional-looking graphics: borders, artwork, and shaded backgrounds.

As the cost of laser printers has dropped dramatically since their introduction, fine quality reproduction is now possible at a fraction of its cost a few years ago. The laser printer (which works like a copy machine except it copies from the computer rather than from a printed original) can produce a typeset or near-typeset quality master (depending on the printer) and the individual bulletins or newsletters can be run off on a copy or offset machine.

Special promotional and information materials [WP] [DTP]. Much of a person's response to a church program and message is derived from printed materials. A bulletin insert announcing a special event can arouse or diminish interest in the activity. Fliers and brochures are vital tools in attracting both new people as well as members to church events. A word processor (especially if enhanced with a desktop publishing program) enables any typist to lay out quickly and attractively any printed matter for promotional or information use.

Personalized letters [WP] [MS]. If there is one place in a modern society where a person's individual identity should not be lost, it is the church. But as a church grows, it becomes more and more difficult to deal with people as individuals. More and more efforts are aimed at groups. Even the printed materials sent out of the church office convey a sense of whether or not individuals are important.

For example, most churches try to send personal letters to new visitors. But typing each letter individually is time-consuming and becomes almost impossible as numbers increase. Typing or writing names at the top of pre-printed letters lacks appeal. The computer allows an efficient way of quickly addressing letters to individuals. The letter is typed in the word processing program. The church management software is used to select the name, address, and any other personal information to insert in the letter—and to select the specific people who are to receive the letter.

For example, it would be nice to send a letter to all the Sunday school teachers inviting them to consider teaching for another year. How will they feel receiving a mimeographed notice addressed to "Dear Miscellaneous"? But who has time to type all those letters personally? A merge function makes it possible to type the letter into the computer quickly, identify the specific people who should receive it, and select from their records the information that is to be neatly typed by your printer along with the letter text.

Sermon or workshop notes [WP] [RS]. Is there a pastor or Christian educator anywhere who does not regularly decide in the middle of preparing a sermon or workshop that what had started out to be point 1 should really be point 3, and the illustration that at first seemed to be a good introduction would really make a better conclusion—and as a result, the notes need to be extensively rewritten or retyped? Again, the word processor speeds up these mechanical tasks. In addition, some word processors—and all desktop publishing packages—allow text to be printed in various sizes and styles of type that can be handy for quick visual reference.

Computerized Bibles and concordances have proved highly popular study aids by quickly locating pertinent verses and passages.

Agendas, minutes, and reports [WP] [MS] [AS]. Everyone complains about committees, but little is done to help them function better. A computer may not make much difference in whether the meeting starts and ends on time or whether the members agree with each other, but a computer can make life much easier for the people responsible for putting together the paperwork that is the lifeblood of any committee.

While the word processor is the tool for typing up agendas and minutes (making corrections easier than ever), church management and accounting software will quickly produce most of the reports needed for any meeting. Besides the standard monthly financial report, it is now possible for the church board to quickly project next year's budget, for deacons to have a list of shut-ins, the stewardship committee can see those who have or have not pledged, the Sunday school officers can identify those who have been absent a specified number of Sundays in a row—or a certain number of Sundays over a designated time period. A well-designed management system makes it possible to have helpful information when it is needed—including all the masses of statistics required for those annual reports.

Member/visitor records [MS]. Every church staff member has been embarrassed to dial a church member's home and discover the number now belongs to an all-night pizza parlor or a neighborhood video store. But that is not the most embarrassing part. That occurs when you finally locate your parishioner and ask when the number was changed and the answer is, "I haven't had that number in ages!" It is a little difficult to explain that your book is only one of seventeen places in the church office where names and addresses are kept. A computer with an integrated church management software package makes it possible to make a change only once—and every place that the person appears in the system is now current. Note the term *integrated*; it means that all the parts connect with each other. Many churches have bought a variety of separate software components and have created multiple mailing lists on their computers. What they end up with is a computerized version of all the old individual address books. They still have to be changed one at a time. A well-designed system removes that problem while still allowing multiple mailing lists to exist—all referring back to one central location for personal information.

Mailing lists [MS] [WP]. As long as mailing lists are being discussed, everyone needs to be reminded that sending mail to wrong addresses is wasteful—and common. While churches that do a regular newsletter mailing to church families are usually able to keep that list current, it is the more specialized lists that are used less frequently that get out of date in a hurry. Who can remember to change the youth list and the choir list and the women's association list? And because most churches only send a mailing list to the men on rare occasions, that list has to be typed up manually every third year, which may be why no one wants to go to the work of mailing to the fellows.

An effective church management system will print labels or envelopes for just the people who fit the criteria to receive a particular piece of mail.

Attendance records [MS]. It really is part of God's plan that His people meet together for Bible study, prayer, fellowship, growth, and encouragement. Hebrews 10:25 says, "Let us not give up meeting together, as some are in the habit of doing, but let us encourage one another."

Obviously, an important part of a church's ministry is to care enough about individuals to show love and concern for them, follow them up, and encourage their attendance at church functions that contribute to their spiritual health. Unfortunately, as a church grows it becomes increasingly difficult to be aware of each individual's current attendance pattern.

An effective church management program will provide accurate, up-to-date records and reports that enable leaders quickly to identify people who should receive some kind of contact. Imagine the impact on the life of a church when concerned leaders are able to know who were the first-time visitors last Sunday, the recent visitors who have and have not attended again, and the people who have been absent.

Far too often church leaders do not become aware of personal and spiritual problems until it is too late—the person has not only been absent for an extended period but has had time to withdraw emotionally as well. Effective weekly and monthly reports identify potential danger signals in people's attendance patterns, including comparisons of their attendance in worship with their attendance in Sunday school or other nurturing ministries.

Stewardship and financial records [MS] [AS]. Faithful stewardship is a key ingredient in any effective ministry. Similarly, accurate stewardship records are an important key to planning and carrying out that ministry. The posting of weekly contributions is one of the most time-consuming jobs the church office staff—or volunteers—face. The stewardship module of a church management program should simplify this procedure and help to provide accurate, up-to-date giving records.

The amount and type of record-keeping required in a stewardship program varies greatly from church to church, depending on the needs and wishes of individual members and the congregation as a whole. For example, many churches want giving measured against pledges, whereas others do not use pledges at all. Most churches provide some record of people's giving; others instruct their people to use their canceled checks for that purpose. Stewardship software should be flexible enough to provide the individual giving reports, statistics, and other reports that a church requires.

The stewardship software is usually separate from the accounting modules that are used to manage the church's overall financial affairs. General ledger, accounts payable, and payroll functions are sometimes bundled into the church management system. This may result in a church's paying for more software than it needs. Another approach has been followed by many churches that have bought accounting packages as independent programs. This can end up complicating life in the office if the program's design and operation is significantly different from the church management software. Generally, the optimum arrangement is to have the accounting modules compatible with, but separate from, the church management software. Staff members find it easiest to use the software when the stewardship and accounting modules follow the same design and data can be automatically transferred from one to the other.

Library, music, equipment [LS]. Every church has valuable resources that have an uncanny ability to get mislaid. Most church staff members entered the ministry intending to work with people only to discover their time is absorbed with taking care of supplies and equipment and books and tapes and sheet music and audiovisuals and additional stuff. Effective library software is a truly practical aid to handling the management of a wide variety of resources so that staff can focus on people instead of paper.

Library software should enable staff to keep track of equipment, books, or other supplies easily and quickly; locate a hymn, song, book, or article to fit a topic or special occasion; print informative lists of resources available for use by teachers, leaders, and staff; print labels and cards to aid in identifying and locating specific resources. Some packages that fit this category are specialized for just one particular type of resource (i.e., music or books), whereas others are designed to be all-purpose tools with separate modules for specific resources.

Calendar/scheduling [CS]. As churches grow, maintaining the master calendar and keeping track of which room is available for what group at any given hour of the week can become extremely complicated. Churches with large staffs also struggle with keeping track of who is available when and for what purposes.

Because there is so much variety in the ways churches operate their schedules and facilities, and the sophistication and flexibility needed to make the software truly functional, this kind of program has lagged behind the others that have been discussed. There are fewer choices available here than in other areas, but this should change as developers continue working to improve their products.

COMPUTERS EFFECTIVELY ORGANIZE INFORMATION FOR DECISION-MAKING

Church leaders need many kinds of information on which to base decisions. Unfortunately, the necessary data is often unavailable: the person who used to do that job kept everything in his head; the report could not be compiled in time for the meeting, no records can be found of the last time something was done, and leaders are able to gain feedback from only a limited portion of the people affected (their spouses and close friends). The computer offers great help in providing accurate information to assist leaders in more efficient management.

A Caution: Computers can sometimes interfere with good decisions by producing impressive-looking tabulations of incorrect or inadequate information. Most people have had enough experience with computers to learn that just because the printout says something, that does not necessarily mean it is so. Church leaders still need to exercise discernment in evaluating the information that a computer produces.

Analyze attendance patterns. All churches keep attendance records. Often, however, that is all they do with them. They keep them. They keep them in file cabinets and desk drawers, in record books and annual reports. Occasionally they send them off to their denominational headquarters where they are kept along with the records of many other churches who have been keeping records. In most cases records are kept on attendance totals, but it is usually difficult—if not impossible—to get information such as:

- How does our worship attendance pattern for the past five years compare with our Sunday school attendance?
- What segments of our church family have grown the most? the least?
- Which people have been absent for the past three weeks?
- Which people attend both Sunday school and worship? Worship only? Sunday school only?
- Which classes and departments will need additional space during the coming year?
- Which classes and departments need special attention to avoid further attendance loss?

Without answers to these questions, most attendance records provide little help to leaders in identifying problems or focusing on opportunities. If all the leader knows is that total attendance is up (or down), there is not much he can do besides smile (or frown) and say, "That's nice" (or, "Too bad"). A computer offers leaders the means to know enough about the attendance patterns of the congregation, groups, and individuals in order to plan effective actions that will contribute to healthy growth.

Evaluate visitor contacts. Many churches go to great lengths to try to welcome visitors. Greeters shake their hands, packets of information are provided, friendly invitations to return are extended, and some kind of follow-up (letter, phone call, visit) is launched. But then the visitors often seem to disappear. No one seems to know:

• How many visitors come back?
• How many visitors have been personally contacted?
• Which visitors began to attend regularly?
• What drew visitors who returned?
• What caused visitors not to return?

A computer can provide information for evaluating how your church is doing in reaching these people. It can quickly identify those who did and did not return. It can monitor those who were contacted and preserve comments they made as to why they did or did not come back. It can tabulate these activities to help leaders discern any patterns that would form a basis for improving their approaches to guests.

Identify membership gains/losses. The head of a church membership committee described his responsibilities: "Each year when the annual report is being compiled, I'm supposed to contact members who have not attended during the past year. They are asked if they wish to be transferred or dropped from the roll. It usually takes several hours of poring through the records, and a number of people are always discovered. We send polite letters expressing our concern about their nonattendance.

"Over the years we've followed this process, not one person whose attendance had lapsed has been drawn back into active membership. But it does help to keep our rolls clean."

The situation just described is largely due to no one's having current membership information throughout the year so that attendance lapses can be tracked quickly, instead of not being noticed until many months have gone, along with the wayward member.

The other side of the same coin is the church that enrolls and instructs new members only to have them drop out in the first year because they never really found their "niche." An up-to-date information system is necessary for leaders to plan and oversee adequately an effective system of nurturing and assimilating new people.

Track involvement in church ministries. Every church leader faces the problem of most of the work being done by a few people. When there is a job to be done, the tendency is to ask someone who has already proved willing and capable. Many churches have attempted to combat this problem by taking a talent or gifts survey, seeking to identify which people are best suited to which tasks. However, these surveys have several problems: (1) it is often tedious to retrieve information, (2) keeping the information current is extremely difficult, and (3) correlating the surveys with present involvement in ministry is time consuming.

As a result of these problems, most surveys tend to gather more dust than viable prospects for ministry. In contrast, the church that enters survey information into a computer has a means of minimizing those problems, thereby having quick access to current information on people's skills, experience, and present involvement. With this information accessible, leaders can take positive steps to broaden the base of participation in the ministries of the congregation.

Encourage stewardship efforts. Churches that help people stay aware of how much (or little) they have given find that giving increases. Even though recording each person's gift is only slightly quicker with a computer, the computer cannot be beaten at producing period statements or personalized thank-you letters indicating the amount given.

In addition, the computer can quickly generate lists and statistical reports to which stewardship leaders can refer in making plans for further stewardship efforts.

Project giving and plan expenses. The speed and precision of computerized financial records and reports makes it possible for church leaders to improve efficiency in making decisions about anticipated income and expenses. The budget planning process is greatly simplified, the impact of specific increases and decreases can be quickly seen, and progress through the year (or over the course of a multiyear building campaign) can be monitored continually.

Recognize family/congregational needs. Although the computer is an impersonal machine, it can provide information that helps leaders identify and then plan ways to meet human needs. For example, a church contemplating a ministry to single adults should identify:

• Who are the single adults presently in the congregation?
• Which single adults are in which age groups?
• Which singles have children living at home?
• What is the present attendance/involvement patterns of singles?
• What is the geographical spread of these singles?

Without a computer, information such as this is often simply not available because there is no efficient means to store, organize, and retrieve it.

SELECTING AND OPERATING A CHURCH COMPUTER SYSTEM

It is vital that the full spectrum of the church's ministries be represented in the process of selecting a computer system. Those who lead church ministries should have a major voice along with those who will actually use the equipment. Even if they have never touched a computer in their lives, these people are the ones who must be satisfied with what the system will do. If staff members believe that a system has been imposed on them, its effective usage will be severely impeded.

Focus on software before selecting hardware. Software is the program (the instructions) that make a computer operate. Hardware is the equipment, the pieces you can touch and see—the computer terminal and keyboard, the printer, and so on. Because the software is hidden inside the hardware, it is often overlooked. But without the right software, the world's finest computer hardware cannot do what your church needs. Thus, select the software first. Then find the hardware that will allow the software to work most efficiently. Keep in mind that the speed and memory capacity of the computer will significantly affect the performance of the software (just as the quality of speakers will affect the sound from a cassette or compact disk). Every comprehensive church management system requires a computer with a hard disk. A very small church may get by using programs with limited features on floppy disks.

Ask for a demonstration and references. Most software vendors provide demonstration disks at little or no cost. As a general rule, smaller, limited packages will provide a "working disk," one which allows you to try out the functions. More comprehensive packages provide "slide show" demos that emulate the program's routines. Because these more powerful programs require multiple disks to load the actual program, the full works cannot be compressed onto a single diskette.

Even better than a demonstration disk (which does not show how the program will operate when it is handling all the data for your church) is to visit a church using the software and see the real thing at work. Ask the vendor for churches in your area, churches of about your size, and churches of your denomination that use the software.

Plan your beginning use of the system. Even though everyone in the office will probably become involved in working on the computer sooner or later, it is wise not to start with everyone trying to learn everything at the same time. Start with one or two people working on one or two functions. If problems occur—and they will—it is easier to pinpoint the cause when only one or two people have been using the system. Once one or two people have become familiar with the system, they can make it easier for others to get started.

Networks. In the early days of personal computers, each one was an entity to itself. But people quickly dreamed of being able to share programs and data. Many churches, when they buy a second or third terminal, either operate totally different functions on them ("You do accounting; I'll do word processing") or try to share programs and data by carrying diskettes back and forth. Either approach gets very old quickly, and the solution is to network.

Connecting two or more terminals to each other is more complicated than just stringing some cable. Networking software is required as well as network versions of most other software packages. Before proceeding with any network installation, it is essential to learn from your church management system vendor the networking systems (there are many) for which it is designed.

DOS or MAC? In the early days of the personal computers, most brands were incompatible with most other brands, as each company had its own operating system. Through the latter half of the 1980s, the industry settled on two major systems: MS-DOS (IBM and compatibles) and Macintosh (Apple). A few other systems keep attempting to gain mass acceptance (for example Unix), but DOS and the Mac dominate.[1]

As a general rule of thumb, DOS machines provide more speed, power, and memory more inexpensively, whereas Macs excel in applications involving graphics. The Mac provides a user-friendly interface that appeals to many people who do not like to face a blank screen and have to type in commands. Various firms have produced graphics interface programs to operate on DOS machines to provide similar screen menus when the system is turned on.

The major issue churches have faced in deciding between the two types of systems has been availability of software. Far more companies have produced church management software for DOS machines than for the Macintosh. Because the software choices for the Mac have been more limited than for DOS, and equipment costs have been higher on the Mac side of the street, significantly more churches have purchased DOS systems than Macs.

SUMMARY

Certainly the computer age is here. Churches will need to consider seriously the possibilities of computer and technological support. These tools can assist in accomplishing many of the tasks the church will be required to do in the latter part of the twentieth and first part of the twenty-first centuries. Each church will need to make its own decisions as to what is best for it in computer equipment and software for programming.

FOR FURTHER READING

Bedell, Kenneth. *Role of Computers in Religious Education*. Nashville: Abingdon, 1986.

Bedell, Kenneth, and Parker Rossman. *Computers: New Opportunities for Personalized Ministry*. Valley Forge, Pa.: Judson, 1984.

Capron, H. L. *Computers: Tools for an Information Age*. 2d ed. Redwood City, Calif.: Benjamin/Cummings, 1990.

Clemans, E. V. *Using Computers in Religious Education*. Nashville: Abingdon, 1986.

Cook, Stuart S. "Using Your Personal Computer in Teaching." In *The Christian Educator's Handbook on Teaching*. Edited by Kenneth O. Gangel and Howard

---

1. Mac and Macintosh are registered trademarks of Apple Computer, Inc. MS-DOS is a registered trademark of Microsoft Corporation.

G. Hendricks. Wheaton, Ill.: Victor, 1988.

Dilday, Jr., Russell H. *Personal Computer: A New Tool for Ministers*. Nashville: Broadman, 1989.

Sargent, Richard B., and John E. Benson. *Computers in the Church: Practical Assistance in Making the Computer Decision*. Minneapolis: Augsburg, 1986.

35 *Lowell Brown and Wesley Haystead*

Facilities and Equipment for Education

PLANNING FACILITIES THAT SUPPORT EDUCATIONAL MINISTRIES
- **Observe the cardinal rule for facilities: "The building should be determined by the program"**
- **Facilities must be planned in light of the clearly defined "mission" of each local church**
- **Educational space should be planned according to a clearly understood educational philosophy**
- **Standard-sized rooms can be adapted to fit any group**

> The Church is not a building,
> The Church is not a steeple,
> The Church is not a resting place,
> The Church is a people![1]

We entered the main doors of the stately old English cathedral and were greeted by an incongruous array of portable dividers and drapes hung from wires. It

---

1. From the song "We Are the Church," copyright 1972 by Richard K. Avery and Donald S. March, in *Sing to the Lord* (Ventura, Calif.: Regal, 1976). Used by permission.

seemed that every nook and cranny of the building had been partitioned to provide space for some group. "It's not pretty," the pastor told us, "but we're making it work."

We walked purposefully from the narthex to the chancel, trying our best to look like knowledgeable experts from across the ocean, ready to offer true pearls of wisdom on how to accommodate a thriving church, which had the building bursting at the seams, with a Sunday school and weeknight groups.

We turned to face the pastor, cleared our collective throats, and one of us offered our thoughtful American analysis: "We'd suggest you tear this place down and build a real church."

The pastor sighed and patiently explained, "The government has declared this building to be an historical treasure. We can occupy it, but we can't change it."

Faced with the reality of life in ancient cathedrals, we looked again at the hodgepodge of dividers, nodded sagely, and replied, "You're right. It's not pretty, but you seem to be making it work." Unfortunately, the building that had been erected to aid God's people in worship and service had become an elegant and expensive barrier to ministry.

Whether your congregation meets in a cathedral or a drive-in theater, a modern, spacious temple or a living room, a rented union hall or a junior high school, a modest chapel, a converted warehouse, a storefront, or any other structure that is available, you continually face the challenge of making your building serve the needs of your church.

Whereas some people bird watch and others collect coins and stamps, we have made a lifelong avocation out of poking around church buildings, collecting examples of buildings that have become ends in themselves. We have learned that it is not just the grand cathedrals that face that danger. In more than one modern North American education wing we have encountered prohibitions against putting anything on the walls, rearranging the furniture, eating or drinking, or using any potential messy materials such as paint, Play-doh, or glue. We almost expected to see signs prohibiting the presence of people.

CARDINAL RULE FOR FACILITIES: PROGRAM SHOULD DETERMINE THE BUILDING

This is one of the basic principles of church life to which everyone nods assent. It makes such good sense to affirm that the building should be a tool that assists the church in carrying out its mission in the community. Far too often, however, the program ends up being structured to fit the building. No one ever intends for the building to dictate what ministries a church may pursue. Still, sooner or later, unless careful steps are taken to avoid this pitfall, most facilities start to shape the ministries that operate in them.

A common procedure of church life often results in buildings that end up limiting the church's ministries. When facility decisions are faced, a committee tends to be assembled, consisting of a representative of each ministry that may use the building. Each committee member feels an obligation to defend his "territorial rights," and the resulting plan often tends to resemble a politician's pork barrel—a little of something for everyone. The problem with this procedure is not so much the negotiating that goes on in such a committee. The problem is that rarely does such a group share a common vision of what the mission of their church really is. Without a unifying perspective, committees tend to pursue ideas of the most persuasive members, the most prominent programs, or the latest fashions. As a result, it is not uncommon for brand-new buildings to restrict rather than enhance the effectiveness of a church's vital ministries.

To avoid the building and maintaining of a museum instead of a facility that aids your church's ministry, three major questions must be carefully answered for the total church and for each agency within the church:

1. *What is our purpose?* What is the reason we exist in this community? What are we here for?

2. *Who are the people to be helped through our purpose?* Who are we trying to reach in our community? What age levels of people must we include? Also, who are the people we have available to do this ministry?

3. *What are the programs that will accomplish our purpose for those people?* What must these programs do in order to help reach our purpose?

Only when the purpose, people, and program have been clearly defined can effective buildings be planned. For example, to fulfill the discipling task of the church, provision must be made for effective instructional ministries for all age groups. In response to this requirement, during the 1970s and 1980s, vast numbers of churches made major changes in their facilities for teaching youth and children. Earlier in this century, the dominant plan for these age groups was an assembly area with numerous small classrooms grouped around the sides. That pattern has given way to larger, open classrooms.

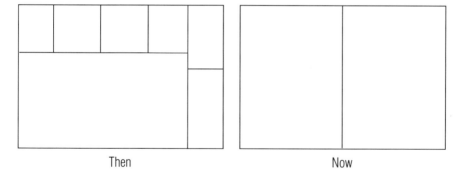

Then   Now

This change in building design was strongly promoted by curriculum publishers, teacher training organizations, and a great many Christian educators who wanted teachers to work as teams, supporting one another in a wide variety of instructional activities. As teachers and leaders adopted a teaching/learning philosophy that stressed student participation and choices, and encouraged teacher interaction, it became crucial to bring classes out of their isolated cubicles. However, many church leaders jumped on this design change because of its economic advantages and imposed open rooms on teaching staffs who were not prepared to adjust their teaching styles to the new environment. Although many churches with open rooms still operate as if the cubicles remain, gradually the more open environment tends to influence teachers toward greater cooperative efforts.

The move to larger classrooms has also provided great benefit in flexibility, allowing space to be used for other ministries during the week. As land and building costs have escalated, it has become increasingly vital that churches get as much use out of their buildings as possible.

Before looking at some specific recommendations for a building, we need to consider three different facility circumstances, one of which faces every congregation.

FACILITY CIRCUMSTANCES

EXISTING PERMANENT BUILDING

Congregations periodically face decisions about an existing building. When attendance grows, will the building need to be remodeled or enlarged? When attendance patterns shift, will space need to be reallocated? When new ministries are launched or existing ones change, will facilities need to be modified? As facilities begin to age, what kinds of maintenance, redecorating, and renovation should be pursued?

EXISTING TEMPORARY BUILDING

Vast numbers of congregations meet in facilities they hope to leave someday. Congregations meet in schools, warehouses, storefronts, buildings owned by other churches, private homes, community centers, and so on. Just a few years ago, these temporary facilities were used mainly by very poor or small, brand-new congregations. In many parts of the country where land and building costs have become very high, churches of all sizes remain in such quarters for five, ten, or more years.

Many vital, growing congregations find it less costly to relocate to larger, rented facilities than to enlarge or relocate to a building they own. However, as the congregation grows, the cost to move into a permanent facility grows proportionately, and may become impossible if the congregation has not been building equity through savings or property acquisition.

The education ministries often face the greatest difficulty in functioning in temporary space. Although most buildings suitable for meeting have at least the essentials necessary for an adult gathering, child-sized furnishings and educational supplies often must be moved in and out for every service. If the leaders and teachers are expected to be responsible for this effort, the church may burn out many of its best people after a period of time.

Also, adequate educational space may be difficult to secure in such facilities. The result may be a group of adults who feel comfortable in their meeting room while children and youth ministries suffer.

PROPOSED NEW BUILDING

One of the crucial times in the life of a church is when a new building is being planned. Among the many issues to consider is that it is often more difficult to raise funds for a building only one segment of the congregation will use (i.e., children), than for a building that everyone will use. Careful thought must be given to securing the support of the rest of the congregation, both by showing how members will benefit ("Moving the children will free up desirable space for adults and youth in the current building") and the long-term value of providing for the target group ("If our church is to have a future, we must reach young families with children").

PLANNING GUIDELINES

Whether a church is studying its existing building, using a temporary facility, or planning a new structure, building use must be decided in light of the purposes of the ministries. In other words, the ministry philosophy determines the facility priorities. For example, space that is used for instructional purposes should be planned according to a clearly understood educational philosophy. How students in a particular age group learn best determines how we teach, and how we teach determines how we design the room in which learning is to occur.

The following guidelines should be given careful consideration in planning a facility that will enable the church to operate its current ministries and aid growth and accommodate change in the future.

FLEXIBILITY/MULTIPLE USES

All educational space in a church should be planned to accommodate multiple uses, preferably among compatible age groups. Rooms for children and youth should be designed for Sunday school, youth groups, clubs, Christian school, day care, and so on. Rooms for adults should accommodate all types of classes and Bible study groups, fellowship activities, missions and service groups, committees, and so on.

Two special issues must be given careful handling in providing flexibility without sacrificing effectiveness.

Sunday school and day school. Although a well-run day school can be an effective ministry for a church, sometimes the sharing of facilities can turn into a war zone, or the school may be treated like an undesirable tenant, or the school may dominate and appear to have a church attached as a minor appendage. The following guidelines help the church's teaching ministry and the school to work in harmony, even when the church is renting space from a public school.

First, establish communication and common goals for leaders of both groups. This is vital to avoid making either program feel like a second-class citizen in its use of the building. Problems are much easier to resolve when the people involved have established a relationship and agree that the building is not "owned" by any one program—it is a shared resource that must be designed, organized, and operated for the benefit of each group. Even when a facility is being rented, the tenants have the right to expect a cooperative, mutually supportive arrangement with the owner.

Second, negotiate agreement on shared equipment and supplies and on items that are reserved for one group only. Adequate storage must be provided for the latter items so they are out of the way (see fifth point below).

Third, install reversible bulletin boards so each group can use them—or designate some boards for each group. If using a rented facility, provide portable display boards on which teachers can mount visual material and then store it safely away until their next session.

Fourth, use student tables that accommodate removable tote trays rather than individual desks. Student tables lend themselves to multiple room arrangements more easily than desks. Avoid having separate furniture for the two programs that require major custodial work every week. Also avoid forcing Christian education ministries to use a room that looks like a schoolroom—or making school students feel like intruders in Sunday school. Each program has a unique structure and purpose, and sharing a room should not force either one to try to operate like the other.

Fifth, provide ample storage for both programs. Wall-mounted cabinets with doors are desirable. Provide locks for those that contain supplies that are for the use of only one program. If a group's supplies must be removed from the room at the end of the session, provide sturdy, portable containers that teachers can easily carry in and out.

Finally, encourage shared events that involve both groups as a means of building understanding and a sense of common purpose. Although this suggestion has nothing directly to do with the facility, it can do a great deal to foster an environment in which facility issues can be successfully resolved.

Various age levels. It is most efficient to have the same age groups always use the same room. Although this is not always possible, the less shifting of furniture the better. Rooms other than early childhood (birth through five years) may be used for two or more ages if necessary, although furnishings may need to be moved back and forth.

In looking to the future—with the exception of early childhood rooms—space should be designed so that the room could be changed to accommodate any age group, children through adult. Reserve early childhood rooms for the early childhood age groups. Their need for restrooms, sinks, and in most cities, ground-floor access, make their rooms unique. Changing an early childhood room to fit another age group may require costly remodeling.

The following guidelines aid in making rooms meet the needs of any age group.

First, build standard sized rooms (at least 800-900 square feet, which can be easily divided in halves or thirds) that work well with optimum group sizes for any age level. This allows any room to be easily equipped for everyone from children through adults. (See section below, "Room Sizes," for further information on the dimensions of your rooms.)

Second, for small groups, divide large rooms into smaller ones. If your attendance does not warrant rooms that are 800 square feet or larger, build them that size anyway and divide them into smaller rooms by installing nonbearing walls that can be taken out when bigger rooms are needed.

Third, use movable walls between rooms when necessary to create even larger open space. The up-front investment is worth the savings gained by making your facility flexible enough so you can build fewer self-contained rooms. In the future, movable walls provide great flexibility for changes you may not be able to anticipate now, and the sound protection they provide is unmatched by any other kind of divider.

Fourth, provide ample storage for each group. Just as a house can never have too many closets, so a church that wants to get multiple use out of its facilities must provide plenty of convenient storage for the various age groups and programs that use any room. Wall-mounted cabinets work best for storing supplies between sessions. Low open shelves are helpful for placing materials to be used during the session in early childhood and children's rooms.

ROOM FEATURES

To make each room truly functional, care must be given to the following important features.

LIGHTING

Install ceiling lights that give adequate, even lighting. It is helpful if lights can be dimmed when only partial illumination is needed (i.e., when watching a video, using an overhead projector, during rest time, etc.). Also consider the impact of outside light. Are window coverings needed? Can the room be easily darkened for film or slide projection?

ELECTRICITY

It never ceases to amaze (and frustrate) church workers at how electrical outlets in classrooms are almost always placed on either the wrong wall, behind an unmovable piano, or directly in the path of traffic so that someone is bound to trip over the cord. Outlets sometimes seem to have been placed for the convenience of the electrician or in accord with some long-forgotten prior use of the room. The solution is to place several outlets on each wall.

Note that outlets in early childhood rooms should be placed at table or counter height so they (and any plugs and cords) are out of the reach of children. Plug guards should be placed over any unused outlets as a safety precaution.

FLOOR COVERING

Select a floor covering that is easy to clean, and secure the proper equipment for cleaning it. In most cases, it is best to use the same kind of floor covering throughout a building. If both carpet and linoleum or tile are used, one or the other may not get cleaned regularly because of the extra work required by the custodian. Carpet has the advantage of absorbing sound and of generally being more aesthetically pleasing.

HEATING/VENTILATION

Learning efficiency drops significantly if people are chilled or uncomfortably warm or stuffy. Separate controls should be provided for rooms in different zones to avoid the typical problem of rooms on the sunny side being too warm, those on the shady side being too cold, and only the hallway being comfortable, since that is where the thermostat is placed.

REST ROOMS

Early childhood rooms should be designed with direct access to child-sized restrooms. Follow your state or local guidelines that have been established for licensed preschools to determine the number of sinks and toilets needed for the number of children you intend to serve. A drinking fountain or a fountain attachment to child-sized sinks is a helpful addition.

Rest rooms for older children, youth, and adults should be located nearby their classrooms, providing enough facilities to handle between service congestion.

SAFETY/TRAFFIC FLOW

Look carefully at your classrooms and hallways in view of how they will accommodate an evacuation in case of a fire, earthquake, or other disaster. Also consider how the placement of various groups will impact hallway congestion before and after a session. For example:

- Early childhood classes where parents normally deliver and pick up their children tend to generate more hallway traffic than do other groups.
- Congestion throughout the building may be reduced by placing classes for young adults near to the early childhood rooms.

HANDICAPPED ACCESS

Of all public buildings, churches should lead the way in providing easy access for the handicapped.

ROOM SIZES

Earlier we mentioned building rooms of at least 800-900 square feet. This size room is recommended because it accommodates the maximum group numbers that are desirable for each of the age levels. The standard room size works out nicely because of a simple rule of thumb: the younger the age group, the smaller the group size and the larger the floor space per person. The following chart puts workable numbers to this rule of thumb:

EARLY CHILDHOOD	Maximum Attendance *	Floor Space Per Person	Square Footage
Ages 0 -1	12 - 15	30 - 35 sq. ft	900
Ages 2 - 3	16 - 20	30 - 35 sq. ft	900
Ages 4 - 5	20 - 24	30 - 35 sq. ft	900
CHILDREN			
Grades 1 - 6	25 - 30	25 - 30 sq. ft.	900
YOUTH			
Grades 6 - 12	30 - 40	20 - 25 sq. ft.	900
ADULTS			
Ages 18 +	30 - 40	10 - 15 sq. ft	450 - 900

* The Maximum Attendance numbers allow quality education and positive relationship building to occur only when adequate teacher/learner ratios are maintained:
Early Childhood needs one teacher per four to six children.
Children's classes need one teacher per six to eight children.
Youth classes need one teacher per eight to ten students.

Rooms that are built smaller than 800 square feet will require that the maximum attendance numbers be reduced proportionately. Smaller rooms will also reduce the options for certain learning activities. For example, in early childhood rooms, two valuable learning centers that require significant amounts of floor space are home living (where children can role-play typical family life experiences) and block building (where children learn to work together cooperatively).

Classrooms tend to be most efficient and flexible when the dimensions are slightly rectangular, A room that is 25 feet wide by 36 feet long works well for a variety of room arrangements.

FURNITURE AND EQUIPMENT

All age groups need chairs. Early childhood and children's rooms need tables—and youth/adult classes enjoy working around tables when possible.

GUIDELINES FOR SELECTING TABLES AND CHAIRS

1. Tables and chairs should fit the age group. No one learns well when they are uncomfortably seated.

2. It you anticipate significantly different numbers of people in a room for different programs (i.e., twenty teens during Sunday school, thirty at youth group, and ten for a midweek Bible study), it is helpful if the chairs are stackable (and they can be easily stored out of sight). Group dynamics suffer when participants are surrounded by empty chairs.

3. Tables should comfortably seat the number of learners who can effectively work together and interact. For example, there is no value in having a table that can accommodate twelve two-year-olds, since there are no activities that twelve two-year-olds can do together. Two or three smaller tables will be more efficient and flexible.

4. The shape of tables should reflect the activities that are most likely to be done on them. Rectangular tables work best for children who will be working on art projects, whereas round tables work best for youth and adult classes where fellowship and discussion are the dominant group activities.

APPROPRIATE SIZES FOR CHAIRS AND TABLES			
Age Group	Chair Height (seat above floor)	Table Height (10 inches above seat)	Table Top (approximate width and length)
Early Childhood	10-12 inches (1 per child)	20-22 inches (1 per every six children)	30 x 48 inches
Children	12-16 inches (1 per child)	22-26 inches (1 per every eight children)	36 x 60 inches
Youth/ Adult	18 inches (1 per person)	28 inches (1 per every eight persons*)	72" diameter (round) or 36 x 96 inches

* Some youth/adult groups prefer not to sit around tables. Also, if the room is crowded, tables may cease being beneficial.

Additional furniture and equipment contribute to creating a comfortable age level environment and conducting effective learning experiences. Although it is possible to get by without any of these items, group learning and fellowship are greatly enhanced when rooms are properly equipped. The following list is not complete but does present the most common items needed. Items marked "O" are optional—nice to have, but not essential, especially if space is limited.

APPROPRIATE AGE-LEVEL FURNISHINGS AND EQUIPMENT			
Early Childhood	*Babies*	*Toddlers*	*2-5 year olds*
Playpen	X		
Crib	X	O	
Changing table	X	X	
Sink	X	X	O
Baby swing	X		
Adult rocking chair	X		
Child rocking chair		X	X
Rocking boat/steps		X	O
Bookrack/shelf		X	X
Low, open shelves		X	X
Painting easels			X
Home living play equipment		O	X
Cassette player	X	X	X
Children	*Grades 1-6*		
Cassette player	X		
Sink	O		
Bookrack/shelf	X		
Low, open shelves	X		
Piano	O		
Chalkboard	X		
Projection screen	O		
Youth/Adult	*Grades 6 and Up*		
Cassette player	O		
Piano	O		
Sink	O		
Projection screen	X		
Overhead projector (available)	X		
All Ages			
Wall-mounted storage cabinets	X		
Bulletin boards	X		
Video monitor/player (available)	X		

Projection cart	X
Refreshment service	0
Secretary's desk/shelf	X
Waste basket	X

Room Arrangements

Furniture and equipment in any classroom should be arranged so that any session can easily provide both small group as well as large group involvement. Even in youth and adult classes, if the room is filled with chairs, people will find it difficult to participate in informal dialogue and fellowship. In contrast, leaving an open area in the back or to the side, makes the room an ally in encouraging group members to mingle and get acquainted before and after sessions.

In early childhood and children's classes, arrange tables, chairs, and other furniture so that a significant amount of open space remains. This space may be used during part of the session by one or more small groups working on the floor: listening to music, looking at books, solving puzzles, playing a Bible game, and so on. Open space between groups also acts as a buffer and helps children focus attention on what is going on in their particular group. Then, when it is time for all children to come together in one large group, children may either sit on the floor or bring chairs from around the tables.

Problem Solving

COMMON PROBLEMS

1. *We already have a building with small cubicles around an assembly area.* Take the doors off the cubicles and use them for small group activities. Better yet, tear out as many of the interior walls as possible. A few posts left in the middle of a large classroom are less of a problem than dividing walls.

2. *We are seriously overcrowded with no immediate way to gain more space.* First, evaluate every piece of furniture or equipment that is taking up space. Remove any rarely used pianos, desks, tables, chairs, counters, and so on. Replace any oversized tables with smaller ones. Replace any floor-level storage with wall-mounted cabinets that reach from around eye-level up to the ceiling.

Second, determine if any groups could be moved to alleviate some of the overcrowding. Avoid allowing any group to "own" a room, for the time may come when they should be moved to accommodate shifting attendance patterns.

Third, consider double sessions that allow the same room to be used by more than one group in a morning. Having two worship services and two Sunday schools has enabled many churches to significantly increase their usable space. Keep in mind that the early childhood rooms and any children's rooms that are used for a children's worship program usually cannot be put to extra use on

Sunday morning. These rooms tend to be fully used during both Sunday school and worship.

Fourth, explore the availability of nearby temporary facilities. Restaurants, schools, office buildings, private homes, buses, lodges, other churches can all provide temporary facilities. Be creative in thinking of potential locations and the groups in your church that could most easily utilize them. In most cases, youth and adult groups work best in off-campus locations.

Finally, start planning for expansion. People can put up with overcrowded conditions if they know that a plan is underway to improve the situation. However, if overcrowding continues too long, people will find it increasingly difficult to establish and maintain meaningful relationships within the group, and those on the fringes are likely to drop out. In other words, overcrowding will eventually stop being a problem when some of your people stop coming.

3. *Certain groups want to "personalize" their room by adding unique and sometimes costly features.* A certain degree of "personalizing" is beneficial, but be alert to some serious potential problems. Youth and adult groups can become extremely possessive of a room that they have decorated, especially if they contributed money and labor to the task. Possessiveness will pose problems if another group needs to use the room at other hours as well as if the "original" group needs to be moved to another room for better use of total space. Problems for multiple or future use also arise when specialized features are built into the room. For example, some adult and youth groups have added fireplaces, conversation wells, or coffee bars. The final result is often a room that has limited flexibility and may end up not even being used by the intended group should the originators of the idea move elsewhere.

As a general rule of thumb, it is wise to limit "personalizing" to selected bulletin boards or portable panels that can easily be reversed, removed, or covered when another group uses the room.

4. *Noise is a distracting problem in our open classrooms. Teachers and students are distracted by hearing what's going on in other groups.* There are two major ways in which noise is a distraction. The first involves very distinct sounds (clearly hearing what someone else is saying). This is most likely to occur in rooms where two groups are working. Each can hear voices in the other group. This kind of distraction tends to diminish when one or more additional groups are added. When three or more groups operate, a sound level is established in the room. Although each group hears the others, what is being said is no longer distinct and fades into the background. When only two groups meet, it is helpful for the leaders of each group to sit with their backs to each other so their voices are directed toward their own group and away from the other group. It can also help to play soft music in the background to help mask the background noise.

The second kind of distracting noise occurs when the background noise is so loud people feel they must talk louder in order to be heard. This tends to occur in a room filled with hard surfaces; sound reverberates instead of being absorbed.

Consider these ideas for turning down the volume:
- Carpet the floor.
- Mount absorbent materials on the walls: bulletin boards, fabric banners, decorative carpet strips, window drapes, and the like.
- Treat the ceiling—either spray it with acoustical materials or install a sound-absorbing drop ceiling.

CONCLUSION

Facilities are important in meeting the needs of people. Effective planning and use of facilities will be determined by the program the church has. Facilities should also be planned in light of the purpose for use. A clearly understood educational philosophy of how students learn and how we teach will enable those who design the facilities to do effective and efficient planning. From a practical point of view, standard-sized rooms can be adapted to fit any group of children, youth or adults.

FOR FURTHER READING

Brown, Lowell E. *Sunday School Standards*. Revised edition. Ventura, Calif.: International Center for Learning, 1986.

Cionca, John R. *Troubleshooting Guide to Christian Education*. Denver: Accent, 1986.

Daniel, Eleanor, John W. Wade, and Charles Gresham. *Introduction to Christian Education*. Cincinnati: Standard, 1987.

Smith, Roland A. *Before You Build Your Church*. Nashville: Broadman, 1979.

Part 5:

The Church's Allies for Christian Education

Biblical education has its foundation in the home, and the Christian education implications of Deuteronomy 6 and Ephesians 6 have a continuing validity. The family has always been the small group par excellence for the propagation of the faith. It is essential, therefore, for the evangelical church, as well as individual believers, to have a basic understanding of the need for building healthy families to assure a healthy, growing church family.

Three chapters in this closing section are devoted to the strengthening of the most important unit of our social order, the home and family. Chapter 36 provides a strong biblical perspective on marriage and family in contemporary culture. Honest and loving communication as fundamental to successful marriage and family relationships is a primary emphasis in chapter 37. Excellent principles for parenting in chapter 38 provide a basis for consistent spiritual formation in family life.

An examination of three major educational choices—public, private, and home schooling—is carefully given in chapter 39. The last chapter discusses growing opportunities for exciting, meaningful service in the field of Christian education through a variety of parachurch ministries.

36

James R. Slaughter

Biblical Perspective
for the Family

BIBLICAL PERSPECTIVE FOR THE FAMILY
- **Permanent commitment between husband and wife**
- **Viewing marriage partners' differences as assets, not liabilities**
- **Sacrificial loving by a husband and voluntary support by a wife**
- **Talking, feeling, and trusting in all family relationships**
- **Total openness and acceptance by all family members toward one another**

THE CONTEMPORARY VIEW OF MARRIAGE

Most of us feel like we are being catapulted into the twenty-first century. As we go flying into the new millennium, we hold on to our hats and watch the scenery of life race past, changing with breathtaking rapidity. Everything seems to be in a state of flux; new ideas abound, and new looks in fashion design, sports franchises, computer software, and communication media dot our landscape—even marriage looks different from a contemporary angle. If we are not careful we may fail to recognize it.

JAMES R. SLAUGHTER, Th.M., Th.D. candidate, is associate professor of Christian education, Dallas Theological Seminary, Dallas, Texas.

Society in the past has held marriage and the family in high esteem. Traditionally people have considered the family honorable and upright, an institution of integrity that reflected similar characteristics wherever it was found: an emphasis on high moral standards, especially in sexual matters; a great interest in children and concern for their proper education; the imprinting of values and attitudes that promote economic success and civic peace; at least the appearance of religious faith; a devotion to the "finer things" in life, especially the arts; and a sense of obligation to eradicate conditions perceived as morally offensive.[1] In the past we viewed marriage as relatively stable and permanent, for most a sacred trust with commitment and concern shared between husband and wife.

But marriage today has become a kaleidoscope of changing images and forms, a variety of shapes and configurations that dance through society in bedazzling and often confusing patterns. Shifting values change the face of the marital kaleidoscope so that a contemporary view of marriage is broad and eclectic indeed. More traditional roles often give way to egalitarianism and role interchangeability. Some who formerly held a conservative view of marriage now offer the viability of alternative marriage lifestyles including cohabitation, trial marriage, and homosexual marriage.[2] Even though 92 percent of the teenagers in America say they want to get married, the divorce rate for new marriages is a staggering 50 percent.[3] Two-thirds of all divorced people will be remarried within three years of their divorce. Modern culture pushes us to consider divorce as the acceptable solution to the problem of an unhappy marriage. Today's world seeks desperately to convince us to create the kind of marriage that best suits our own goals and interests without worrying about standards of morality. Ninety percent of American women say they want children someday, but over half of all college students say it is perfectly acceptable for an unmarried woman to have a child.[4]

The common denominator for the changes in marriage values appears to be a shift in focus from commitment of partners in marriage—or to the institution of marriage itself—to a concern for personal rights. Balswick and Balswick in their study of modern marriage conclude: "The focus has shifted to the individual's rights to personal happiness. This means that commitment to marriage . . . is rejected if it interferes with the individual's rights to happiness and fulfillment."[5] Cirner and Cirner agree that in contemporary secular society goals of self-fulfillment, personal happiness, personal convenience and pleasure, and individual satisfaction are the criteria that determine what marriage will be.[6]

1. Brigitte Berger and Peter L. Berger, *The War over the Family* (Garden City, N.Y.: Doubleday/Anchor, 1983), p. 7.
2. Letha D. Scanzoni and John Scanzoni, *Men, Women, and Change: A Sociology of Marriage and Family*, 3d ed. (New York: McGraw-Hill, 1988), pp. 156-203.
3. Anthony M. Casale, *Tracking Tomorrow's Trends* (Kansas City, Mo.: Andrews, McMeel & Parker, 1986), p. 106.
4. Ibid., p. 176.
5. Jack O. Balswick and Judith K. Balswick, *The Family: A Christian Perspective on the Contemporary Home* (Grand Rapids: Baker, 1989), p. 81.

Contemporary society invites us to please, pamper, and promote ourselves. It invites us to forsake absolutes in favor of a self-centered subjectivity that jeopardizes the very roots of our most sacred relationships—including marriage.

In the midst of our selfishness and instability, the Word of God provides the only reliable mooring for the drifting craft of marriage. The loving and sovereign God has given marriage to mankind as a gift, and with it a written revelation of what true marriage looks like. Only as marriage follows biblical designs and precepts can it fulfill our deepest longings. In that fulfillment we find that instead of receiving we have been giving; more than being served we have served because God is central. Only as we understand and observe biblical criteria and goals in marriage will that most sacred relationship be all it was meant to be.

THE ESTABLISHMENT OF MARRIAGE

God's plan for marriage leaps out at us from the opening pages of His revelation. Genesis 1 and 2 form a unit with a common theme—the theme of creation. In chapter 1 the revelation focuses on the creation of the universe. God creates heavenly bodies, stars, and planets—including the earth. He creates plants and animals, and finally the apex of His creation, man himself. Chapter 2 moves from the creation of the universe to the creation of two human beings and the details accompanying their beginning. The chapter's momentum builds to a climax when God joins the man and the woman in marriage. Here in chapter 2 God designs marriage and establishes it as the basic human alliance calling two people into covenant relationship with Himself and with one another. Marriage is not simply a social convenience contrived by men and women in an attempt at cooperative lifestyle. The sovereign and loving God ordains it, gives it His blessing, and sets forth specific principles for its effective operation.

THE BIBLICAL VIEW OF MARRIAGE AND ITS RELATIONSHIPS

Throughout the creation of the universe in chapter 1, God had declared the various aspects of His creation "good, . . . good, . . . very good." But in Genesis 2:18 God reveals something in that creation that He now considers not good: "It is not good for the man to be alone." The Hebrew text represents the words "not good" by an emphatic negative (*lo'tob*). The man's aloneness was more than "not good"; it was bad.[7] Adam had limitations that would hinder him in the fulfillment of God's design and purposes for his life, especially in his responsibility to populate and cultivate the earth. In order to remedy the evil of man's aloneness, God would create a companion for him. God would make for Adam a suitable helper

6. Randy Cirner and Theresa Cirner, "Is Christian Marriage Any Different?" in *Husbands & Wives*, ed. Howard Hendricks and Jeanne Hendricks, with LaVonne Neff (Wheaton, Ill.: Victor, 1988), pp. 19-20.
7. Umburto Cassuto, *Commentary on Genesis I* (Jerusalem: Magnes Press, 1978), pp. 126-27.

who would enable him to overcome his limitations and fulfill God's plan for his life. To help the man discover the reality and seriousness of his aloneness, God presented him with the task of naming animals that had been created:[8]

> And out of the ground the Lord God formed every beast of the field and every bird of the sky, and brought them to the man to see what he would call them; and whatever the man called the living creature, that was its name. And the man gave names to all the cattle, and to the birds of the sky, and to every beast of the field, but for Adam there was not found a helper suitable for him. (Gen 2:19-20)

As the animals paraded past Adam, the stark reality of his uniqueness (and deficiency) must have exploded into his consciousness. There was no one like him—no other creature who looked like him, who thought like him, who had an awareness of God like him. There was no one to talk to. No one to share with intimately. No one corresponding to him. Adam's observation and naming of the animals heightened his sense of isolation and prepared him for the woman God would bring as his companion and helper.

> So the Lord God caused a deep sleep to fall upon the man, and he slept; then he took one of his ribs, and closed up the flesh at that place. And the Lord God fashioned into a woman the rib which he had taken from the man. (Gen 2:21-22)

Adam was thrilled when God presented to him the beautifully designed creature who would be his wife. "The man said, 'This is now bone of my bones, and flesh of my flesh; she shall be called Woman, because she was taken out of man'" (v. 23). Adam responded with a ringing cry of exaltation, the spirit of which our English translations seldom capture. The cry is expletive in force and similar emotively to something like, "Wow! Where have you been all my life!"[9] Adam was overjoyed and nearly overcome by the wonder and the glory of this most superlative gift. The text calls her a suitable helper (*ezer kenegdo*) in verse 18. The description tells us much about this person God brought to Adam to be his companion. God made the man and woman alike in some ways, but different in others. The word *kenegdo* means "corresponding to," literally "according to what is in front of." It emphasizes that they are similar to one another. Adam was distinct from the animals, a unique creature. To this point there had been no other like him, but now another came given by God, to be like him spiritually, intellectually, and physically. Adam had someone he could fellowship with God with, someone to discuss with, someone to make love with. Adam's use of the words *woman* and *man* emphasize their similarity. The terms sound somewhat alike both in English and in Hebrew (*ishsha*, "woman" *ish*, "man"). This emphasizes the couple's uniqueness in dis-

8. C.F. Keil and F. Delitzsch, *Commentary on the Old Testament*. 10 vols. (repr.; Grand Rapids: Eerdmans, 1973), 1:87-88.

9. Howard Hendricks, *Don't Fake It, Say It with Love* (Wheaton, Ill.: Victor, 1972), p. 81.

tinction to the animals, and as Cassuto suggests, "aptly makes the affinity between the man and his spouse."[10] In their nature the man and the woman are the same—made in God's image and animated by His breath.

Though they are similar in important ways, differences also exist between the man and woman. The term *helper* (*ezer*) used in the text to describe the woman God gave to the man underscores the fact. Only a person with limitations needs a helper. The helper is someone who comes alongside to contribute what another person lacks in order to complete a task. The word implies a complementary relationship and shows God intends the two together to accomplish what the one could never do by himself. The woman in a sense completes the man. She will bring something to the marriage relationship he could never bring; he contributes something she could never contribute. But together as one unit—one flesh—they will fulfill that which God has for them in His plan. The man needs the woman to overcome his limitations. The woman will need the man to overcome hers. The term *helper* imparts no sense of inferiority. The Scriptures refer to God Himself as man's "helper," one who comes alongside to supply what is lacking (Ex. 18:4; Deut. 33:7; Ps. 115:9-11; etc.).

Paul Popenoe has noted the physiological differences between males and females, including such things as basal metabolism, skeletal structure, hormone production, and strength.[11] Others have noted psychosocial and emotional differences between men and women. Most agree that broadly speaking the same traits are found to one degree or another in both sexes, although observable differences do exist. Clark suggests men perceive and respond to situations in a compartmentalized fashion, whereas women do so in a more integrated way. For example, men tend to help by analyzing a situation or a person and thus isolating the particular sphere of need. By contrast, the female mode of care meets the whole person and cares for the whole person. The male tends to distance himself emotionally from a situation, whereas the female tends to identify or empathize with people in distress. Socially, men are more aggressive; women are more nurturing. Women experience their bodies as a firmly integrated part of their personality, whereas men experience their bodies more as tools to be cared for and used.[12]

God brings the husband and the wife together into a marriage relationship to enjoy being companions and to cultivate their likenesses and their differences. Rather than becoming frustrated with our partner's differences and trying to make them like we are, husbands and wives ought to appreciate and enjoy one another's differences. We should encourage one another's individuality. God has given us someone not only to be like us but also to be different from us to help us overcome our own limitations and add to our own special abilities. Together a husband and wife become stronger, more than they could be on their own.

10. Cassuto, p. 136.
11. Paul Popenoe, "Are Women Really Different?" *Family Life* 31 (February 1972): 1-2.
12. Stephen B. Clark, *Man and Woman in Christ* (Ann Arbor: Servant, 1988), pp. 371-93.

Companionship in marriage involves understanding and honoring our likeness as people made in God's image and being complements for one another, appreciating and taking advantage of our differences.

Having set forth foundational considerations for the institution of marriage (vv. 18-23), the author directs our attention to the basic components of the marriage relationship, God's divine plan for husband and wife: "For this cause a man shall leave his father and his mother, and shall cleave to his wife; and they shall become one flesh" (v. 24). For the sake of the wife and their new relationship, the man leaves his family of origin, joining with his wife in a separate and distinct unit. The term *leave* (*ya'azob*) is a strong word meaning "to abandon"—not in terms of responsibility and care but in terms of dependency. The husband and wife leave their families of origin both physically and emotionally. They move out from under their parents' roof to form a new family. Problems abound when a young husband and wife remain in the home of one of the parents—problems of administration, problems of responsibility. Leaving helps a couple avoid difficulties that arise because of unfilled expectations. Leaving also means severing lines of emotional dependency. Growing up as children in our parents' home we were dependent on them for our livelihood and for the decisions we made. In our early years our love and obedience were dedicated to our mothers and fathers. But when we marry, the primary object of human affection becomes our marriage partner. Our love for our partner transcends our love for parents. In marriage the husband and the wife together with the Lord Jesus Christ determine the direction for their life. These three in concert through the process of prayer and the revelation of Scripture make decisions as they think best. They may seek counsel from their parents but are no longer obligated to obey. This involves risk on the part of the new couple but becomes a key element in the process of leaving to establish a new home and family.

Cleaving to one another forms the second component of biblical marriage. Cleaving means bonding with one another for life. The word *cleave* in the Hebrew text (*dabag*) means "to weld tightly," "to join permanently." Job uses it of leviathan's scales whose shields are joined so tightly and permanently that not even air can come between them (Job 41:15). The word describes well the bonding between a husband and wife in marriage, which involves permanent commitment to one another.

Becoming one flesh constitutes a third component of biblical marriage. First Corinthians 6:15-17 relates becoming one flesh to sexual union between a man and a woman. We struggle to understand how two people can be "one flesh." Nevertheless when a husband and wife come together sexually, a bond forms just as real as the spiritual bond between Christ and the believer (Eph. 5:28-29). Kidner calls it a "God-sealed bond."[13] Keil and Delitzsch describe it simply as "a spiritual oneness, a vital communion of heart as well as body."[14] Christ and the believer become one by grace through faith, but we cannot exactly understand the mechanism. Man and woman become one through sexual union even though we may not understand the mechanism or how exactly we are one together. Perhaps Leupold takes it as far as we can when he says, "Becoming one flesh involves the complete identification of one personality with the other in a community of interest and pursuits, a union consummated in intercourse."[15]

The final verse of our passage, verse 25, serves as epilogue to the rest of the text: "And the man and his wife were both naked and were not ashamed." The man and the woman were comfortable in their sexuality, at ease with one another. A complete openness existed between them with mutual giving and receiving. Neither feared rejection or exploitation by the other but anticipated total acceptance, cooperation, and support. Nakedness represents that which was best about Eden. It reflects the true intimacy that comes from the vulnerability and transparency of one partner, met by the unconditional acceptance and love of the other.

The Song of Solomon reflects accurately the openness God intends for a husband and wife to enjoy in marriage. Interpreted in its normal sense (including both literal and figurative language) this book provides the reader with an understanding of God's view of married love. We observe Solomon and his bride throughout this love poem admiring the strength of each other's character and the beauty of each other's bodies (1:3; 2:1-3; 4:1-5; 4:10-16; 7:1-6). They spend time together (2:10-13), talk together (2:14-15; 8:5-7), and work through problems in their relationship (3:1-4; 5:2-6:13). Throughout the poem there exists the theme of sexual love in marriage, which God approves.

The Song of Solomon is innocently explicit in its declaration of the crucial place of emotional and physical intimacy in God's plan for marriage partners.[16] God means for a husband and wife to share vulnerability and acceptance in marriage—to be naked for one another physically but also emotionally; to share feelings as well as bodies, and both openly, freely, desiringly, without fear or shame. Committed to such a high standard of intimacy, Christian couples today can feel liberated to enjoy their sexuality to the fullest. They are free to revel in the intoxication of the experience (Prov. 5:19),[17] and at the same time help protect their partner from sexual temptation outside of marriage (1 Cor. 7:5).[18] Unfortunately, but unavoidable, the sin of Adam and Eve in Eden

13. Derek Kidner, *Genesis,* Tyndale Old Testament Commentaries (Downers Grove, Ill.: InterVarsity, 1967), p. 66.

14. Keil and Delitzsch, 1:90-91.

15. H.C. Leupold, *Exposition of Genesis,* 2 vols. (Grand Rapids: Baker, 1942), 1:137.

16. For an excellent treatment of Song of Solomon, including background, structure, and interpretation, see the following: G. Lloyd Carr, *The Song of Solomon,* Tyndale, Old Testament Commentaries (Downers Grove, Ill.: InterVarsity, 1984); Jack S. Deere, "Song of Songs," in *The Bible Knowledge Commentary Old Testament,* ed. John Walvoord and Roy Zuck (Wheaton, Ill.: Victor, 1985), pp. 1009-25; and Marvin H. Pope, *Song of Songs,* The Anchor Bible (Garden City, N.Y.: Doubleday, repr. ed., 1983).

17. The Hebrew *shagah,* translated "exhilarated" by the *New American Standard Bible,* "captivated" by the *New International Version,* carries the primary meaning "to err, stray." It can be used of the effects of drunkenness, which probably applies here metaphorically. "Be intoxicated" fits the context of Proverbs 5 and may refer to orgasm during sexual intercourse. There is little doubt that the word emphasizes the heightened pleasure of sexual love.

(Gen. 3) inflicted on their intimacy a nearly mortal wound. Fear, uncertainty, and suspicion uprooted former transparency as the man and the woman feebly attempted to protect (hide) themselves by covering their genitals. Only through a temporary sacrificial substitute, and the ultimate atonement of Christ on the cross, could the intimacy and integrity of the marriage relationship have been restored, and now only imperfectly. Nevertheless, oneness in Christ can produce oneness between husband and wife, replacing their fear, uncertainty, and suspicion with trust, assurance, and contentment.

The three basic components of biblical marriage—leaving parents, uniting with one another, and becoming one flesh—emphasize the permanence of the union between husband and wife. God desires one man and one woman to be together for life. Generations later Jesus Himself will quote this text adding His own commentary, "What therefore God has joined together, let no man separate" (Matt. 19:6).

THE BIBLICAL ROLES AND RESPONSIBILITIES IN MARRIAGE

A great deal of confusion reigns in households today—even Christian households—as marriage partners agonize over understanding and carrying out their part in the relationship. Husbands and wives struggle desperately to arrive at some orderly system that will alleviate tension, produce continuity, and allow the growth of healthy self-images. Our culture would have us believe it is every man for himself when it comes to marriage. Everyone seems to do what is right in his own eyes, often with little regard for the welfare of his partner. Once again the Scriptures become a compass to point us in the right direction. God's Word provides a model for marriage management that includes a description of husbands' and wives' roles and responsibilities.

The Bible teaches a fundamental truth that underlies any consideration of roles in marriage: between husbands and wives there is equality in essence but difference in duty. In other words, husbands and wives have indistinguishable worth but distinguishable roles. They share the same nature as human beings, but have been given different job titles in marriage.

Clearly God considers husbands and wives equal in value. First, they are both made in God's image and are each worthy of the same honor and consideration: "And God created man in His own image, in the image of God He created him; male and female He created them" (Gen. 1:27); "In the day when God created man, He made him in the likeness of God. He created them male and female, and He blessed them and named the Man . . ." (Gen. 5:1-2).

Second, they are justified by grace through faith and not by personal merit: "There is neither Jew nor Greek, there is neither slave nor free man, there is neither male nor female; for you are all one in Christ Jesus" (Gal. 3:28). This

---

18. Paul's point is that a person whose sexual needs are met by his marriage partner will be less likely to have those needs met through an extramarital affair.

clearly soteriological passage teaches that no Christian owns an advantage in his relationship to God because of his race, station in life, or sex. Although these passages do not address roles in marriage, they speak volumes about equality of the husband's and wife's value to God and their equal standing before Him as sinners saved by grace.

But just as clearly as the Scriptures teach equality in essence between husband and wife, they also reveal difference in duty between the two—indistinguishable worth, distinguishable roles. As Oberholtzer suggests, a person's role in marriage may be likened to a functional position or job title.[19] Both Old and New Testament passages help us identify the husband's role position as head of his wife and family. The wife is to be his corresponding helper. Genesis 2:18-25 helps us begin to understand the man's role in the marriage relationship. Both creation order (the male before the female) and the woman's purpose (to help her husband) suggest the husband's role as head or leader.[20]

In addition, authority to determine what his partner should be called reflects his headship.[21] The apostle Paul describes the husband's role more specifically in Ephesians 5:23: "For the husband is the head of the wife, as Christ also is the head of the church." Difference of opinion exists regarding the meaning of head (*kephalē*) in this passage. Some suggest it means "source," referring to Eve's creation from Adam.[22] But as House observes, the idea of source in *kephalē* seems to be absent in classical and early first-century literature. The same is true of the New Testament, where "source" as a meaning for the word is foreign throughout.[23] *Kephalē* in Ephesians 5 refers to the husband's role as leader of his wife, and in the context of the passage has the idea of authority attached to it analogous to the idea of Christ's headship over the church.

But the husband's biblical headship demands a function that is loving and Christlike, not arrogant, self-serving, or dictatorial. Biblical headship carries with it authority without authoritarianism. The husband functions as head of his wife by initiating committed sacrificial love for her. His primary responsibility as head is not decision-making or directing, but loving as Christ loved the church: "Husbands, love your wives, just as Christ also loved the church and gave Himself up for her" (v. 25). *Agapē* (Paul's word for love in Ephesians 5) is a unique love, which in the language of the New Testament carries the idea of unconditional acceptance, love that is permanent and sacrificial in nature. *Agapē* assures commitment and giving in a controlled, volitional sense. It often is used of God's love for man (John 3:16), man's love for God (1 John 2:5), and of man's unconditional commitment to his fellow man (Rom. 13:8). As the Lord Jesus

19. T. Ken Oberholtzer, "Building the Biblical Family," *Kindred Spirit* (Winter 1987): 10.
20. Ibid., p. 9.
21. Cassuto, p. 130.
22. Letha D. Scanzoni and Nancy Hardesty, *All We're Meant to Be: Biblical Feminism for Today* (Nashville: Abingdon, 1986), pp. 30-31.
23. H. Wayne House, "Should a Woman Prophesy or Preach Before Men?" *Bibliotheca Sacra* 145:578 (April-June 1988): 145-49.

has expressed perfect love through the sacrifice of Himself, so the husband sacrifices himself for his wife, expressing this love as the chief responsibility of his headship.

As Barthe concludes, Christ qualifies, interprets, and limits man's headship—not as one that has to be endured but one that should be anticipated with joy. When a husband understands his manhood and headship in this Christological sense, he will consider it both a privilege and a grave responsibility that requires him to love his wife by offering gladly whatever the sacrificial price may be.[24] Such sacrificial love means the husband must put his wife's needs above his own in importance, becoming her servant as Christ became servant of the church. He nourishes her (helps to edify her and enable her to reach her full potential), and cherishes her (cares for her deeply and specially as an extension of his own body).

Peter adds another dimension to husbands' love when he reminds them to live with their wives in an understanding way (even when they are hard to understand) and to honor them (give them respect) as coheirs of eternal life.

The husband carries out his chief function in marriage by loving his wife sacrificially the way Christ loved the church. He serves as facilitator, caregiver, protector, and lover—but never as dictator. Only in such loving service does headship take on a truly New Testament nuance.

The Bible identifies the wife's role position in marriage as suitable (corresponding) helper (Gen. 2:18), a term discussed previously. As helper she responds to her husband's loving leadership. "Helper" should not be interpreted as a derogatory term but one that affirms her important contribution as the husband's complement—to encourage, augment, and complete.

Whereas the wife's role or job title surfaces in Genesis 2, her responsibility (role function) finds definition through the apostle Paul's exposition in Ephesians 5:22-24:

> Wives, be subject to your own husbands, as to the Lord. For the husband is head of the wife, as Christ also is head of the church, He Himself being the Savior of the body. But as the church is subject to Christ, so also wives ought to be to their husbands in everything. (cf. Col. 3:18; 1 Pet. 3:1-6)

A wife fulfills her primary responsibility by placing herself voluntarily under her husband's leadership. The injunction "be subject" finds its root in the verb *hypotassomai*, which means "to subordinate oneself to another." Subordination (more than submission) contains an appeal to free and responsible agents that can only be heeded voluntarily, not by coercion.[25]

The wife's willing subordination is an example of the same mutual deference shown by the husband's sacrificial love. By subordinating herself to her hus-

---

24. Marcus Barthe, *Ephesians 4-6*, repr. ed. The Anchor Bible (Garden City, N.Y.: Doubleday, 1983), pp. 618-19.
25. Ibid., p. 609.

band, the wife actually renders service "to the Lord"[26] as she follows her husband's lead and responds to his love. It is one aspect of her obedience to Christ.[27] Part of the wife's response to her husband involves her sincere respect for him (v. 33). She honors him as her counterpart in marriage and her leader in the relationship. Her respect may take the form of trusting him to do the right thing in a difficult situation, thinking the best of him, or holding him in high esteem before others.

We must not be guilty of misinterpreting subordination. That the wife places herself under her husband's leadership (yields willingly to him) does not mean she becomes a doormat, something to be walked on and abused. Nothing justifies a husband's physical or verbal coercion of his wife to submit to his authority. He is to love her the way Christ loved the church. If the husband demands she do something immoral or otherwise disobedient to the Lord, she must refuse on the basis of the lordship of Christ. Neither does subordination force the wife to be a silent partner. It never calls for mindless dependence or voiceless participation. Instead, husband and wife form a team in the decision-making process. The husband invites his wife's encouragement, exhortation, and advice. Sell reminds us that Sarah complained to her husband about her servant Hagar and the son she had born to Abraham (Gen. 21:8-13). Yet Peter chooses her as his example of an obedient wife (1 Pet. 3:6). After Abraham had considered her grievance God warned him: "Whatever Sarah tells you, listen to her" (v. 12).[28]

The excellent wife in Proverbs 31:10-31 obviously has much responsibility for making decisions in the home. "She considers a field and buys it; from her earnings she plants a vineyard" (v. 16). Subordination never implies inferiority on the part of the wife who yields herself to her husband. Her subordination to him no more implies her inferiority than Jesus' subordination to God implies His inferiority to the heavenly Father. They are equals who carry out different functions. The wife functions as a helping partner for her husband, yielding to him voluntarily, respecting him genuinely, advising him knowledgeably. Together they work in tandem to achieve that unique purpose God plans for them as a couple.

THE BIBLICAL VIEW OF THE FAMILY

Few themes recur more consistently throughout the Bible than the theme of family. In the earliest portion of divine revelation, we observe the family instituted as the first and basic social unit. Family begins long before the church (even before Israel became a nation), with God's presentation of Eve to Adam in the Garden (Gen. 2:18-25). Children enter the family picture as early as Genesis 4. The

---

26. Harold Hoehner, "Ephesians," in *The Bible Knowledge Commentary New Testament*, ed. John Walvoord and Roy Zuck (Wheaton, Ill.: Victor, 1983), p. 640.
27. F. F. Bruce, *The Epistles to the Colossians, to Philemon, and to the Ephesians*, The New International Commentary on the New Testament (Grand Rapids: Eerdmans, 1984), p. 384.
28. Charles M. Sell, *Achieving the Impossible: Intimate Marriage* (Portland, Oreg.: Multnomah, 1982), p. 166.

abundance of genealogies in both the Old and New Testaments emphasizes the biblical importance of families, especially as they relate to the promise of Messiah's coming (e.g., Gen. 5; 9-10; 21 f.; 49; Matt. 1; Luke 3). We observe the crucial importance of families in the education of children (Deut. 6:4-9; Ex. 12:23-28; Josh. 4:4-7), in worship (Ex. 13:1-16; Deut. 16:10-11), in the concept of the kinsman-redeemer (Ruth 3-4), and in the many New Testament injunctions for marriage partners, parents, and children (Eph. 5:21–6:4; Col. 3:18-21; 1 Pet. 3:1-7; etc.). Ultimately families constitute the medium for bestowing blessings of the Abrahamic covenant (Gen. 12:3).

Another significant emphasis on the family is Exodus 20:1-17, which identifies the Ten Commandments. Certainly all Ten Commandments are applicable to families, but three of them relate directly and specifically to family members. In verse 12 the command to honor parents is given. The promise for prolonged days in the land is given in obedience to the command. Children are to have proper respect or reverence for authority. In verse 14 Moses emphasizes the command that we should not commit adultery. We are to keep ourselves sexually pure and not become involved with others sexually outside marriage. Verse 17 prohibits coveting anything that belongs to one's neighbor. As family members, we are not to be greedy and desire something we cannot or should not have.

The Scriptures unveil at least four purposes for family: (1) a theological purpose in which the family becomes God's useful medium for the advent and work of Messiah and for bestowing covenant blessing; (2) an educational purpose—the family acting as God's agency for the primary spiritual instruction of children; (3) a demonstrational purpose for which the family serves as an audiovisual aid to teach God's tender love for His people; and (4) a provisional purpose as the family provides a healthy environment for the nurturing of its members.

THE DISTINCTIVES AND GOALS OF THE CHRISTIAN FAMILY

We must never confuse the Christian home with a place of residence. The Christian home is not a dwelling place but a relating fellowship,dynamic and fulfilling. In it we love, serve, talk, feel, trust, and share our faith. A close look at God's Word surfaces a number of observable characteristics that dominate the horizon of the Christian family landscape. One such characteristic is spiritual training with consistency. Deuteronomy 6:4-9 commands parents to make the teaching of God's Word a regular part of daily life from the time they get up in the morning until they bed down at night. Casual instruction of children in the everyday experiences of family life keeps their understanding of the Lord and His work fresh and their love for Him vibrant. Ephesians 6:4 echoes this theme by reminding Christian parents to raise their children "in the discipline and instruction of the Lord."

Love with commitment emerges from the Scriptures as a characteristic of the godly family. Genesis 2:24 injects the element of commitment into marriage with its injunction to the husband to leave his parents, cleave (join permanently) to his wife, and become one flesh with her. Jesus makes clear that God plans for a marriage to last a lifetime (Matt. 19:1-6).

A third distinctive of the Christian family is discipline with dignity. Hebrews 12 reminds us that effective discipline never abuses but edifies so that we may share God's holiness. When we discipline children in the Christian home we do it fairly without anger, careful to choose an age-appropriate form. Such discipline protects the child's dignity as a human being.

A fourth distinctive is Holy Spirit guidance and control. The Holy Spirit indwells each family member who has personally received Christ as Savior (John 14:17). He is present to guide (John 16:13), teach, and remind (John 14:26), help and comfort (John 14:16), and will enable us to bear fruit and gain self-control (Gal. 5:22-23). As Christian families, we need the Holy Spirit's guidance and control.

Fifth, the Christian family will seek and follow God's will and values in daily living (James 4:13-17). They will not make plans and decisions without realizing they need God's direction in determining His will. Even in the small things in life, families need to depend on God for His wisdom in being in the center of His will (James 1:5).

A sixth distinctive is that prayer should be integrated into daily family living. Without Christ we can do nothing (John 15:5). Every part and phase of family living needs to be bathed with prayer. We need to talk about the Lord and center our conversations on Him. Prayer should be natural to invoke His blessing and seek His guidance in everything we do. Families should live in the attitude of prayer and be able to call on the Lord at any time (1 Thess. 5:17).

Finally, we discover the trait of mutual respect. The Christian house codes (Eph. 5:21–6:9; Col 3:18-25; 1 Pet. 2:18–3:7) demand deference one to another within the family—wives placing themselves voluntarily under their husband's leadership, husbands loving their wives sacrificially; children obeying their parents, parents treating their children justly and training them biblically; servants working faithfully for masters, masters treating servants kindly. Mutual respect for one another reflects the humble spirit of Jesus Himself, who considered the welfare of others more important than His own (Phil. 2:1-11).

The family knows no more noble goal than to be salt for our spiritually tasteless society. Jesus calls His disciples the "salt of the earth" (Matt. 5:13), a seasoning God wants to use to revitalize the bland, even foul-tasting menu served by our contemporary world. Society's love affair with selfishness and conceit, coupled with its blatant rejection of Christ and the principles He proclaimed, present a strong, intimidating force. But the resurrected, all-powerful Christ lives today in Christian families, softening hearts, influencing minds, and changing lives as His people maintain an impact on the world around them—in the public school, in the neighborhood, in the office. The Christian family, salt for society, becomes a vehicle for God to reach out to a misguided, oblivious world that so desperately needs His touch.

FOR FURTHER READING

Balswick, Jack O., and Judith K. Balswick. *The Family: A Christian Perspective on the Contemporary Home*. Grand Rapids: Baker, 1989.

Clark, Stephen B. *Man and Woman in Christ: An Examination of the Roles of Men and Women in Light of Scripture and the Social Sciences*. Ann Arbor, Mich.: Servant, 1980.

Hendricks, Howard and Jeanne, with LaVonne Neff, ed. *Husbands & Wives*. Wheaton, Ill.: Victor, 1988.

MacArthur, Jr., John, *The Family*. Chicago: Moody, 1982. Also available in video.

Scanzoni, Letha D., and Nancy Hardesty. *All We're Meant to Be: Biblical Feminism for Today*. Nashville: Abingdon, 1986.

Scanzoni, Letha D., and John Scanzoni. *Men, Women, and Change: A Sociology of Marriage and Family*. 3d ed. New York: McGraw-Hill, 1988.

Sell, Charles M. *Achieving the Impossible: Intimate Marriage*. Portland, Oreg.: Multnomah, 1982. Marriage study guide also available.

———. *Family Ministry: The Enrichment of Family Life Through the Church*. Grand Rapids: Zondervan, 1981.

37

Wayne Rickerson

Building Healthy Families

BUILDING A CHRISTIAN FAMILY
- **Key building blocks on which to build a family**
- **Communication as the lifeblood of family relationships**
- **Effective Christian families serving as a foundation and witness for the church, school, and the community**
- **Priorities in personal relationships with God, a spouse, and with children within the home**
- **An effective ministry to help build Christian homes within the larger church family**

Building Christian families in today's world is a difficult task. God's Word gives the blueprint for successful families, but satanic opposition and low societal standards and values hinder families from what God intended from the beginning. The psalmist says, "Unless the Lord builds the house, its builders labor in vain" (Ps. 127:1). Our task as Christian leaders is to equip parents in building Christ-centered homes.

The goal of this training should be, as the apostle Paul says, "love, which comes from a pure heart and a good conscience and a sincere faith" (1 Tim. 1:5). In order to equip people to build Christian families, we must give them solid biblical instructions and practical applications for developing loving relationships in the home.

WAYNE RICKERSON, M.R.E., is director of People Dynamics, Scottsdale, Arizona.

In this chapter practical tools are suggested that families can use to help themselves and others build Christian marriages and families.

BUILDING CHRISTIAN FAMILIES

LAYING FOUNDATIONS IN CHILDHOOD

Foundations for a strong Christian family are laid in infancy and early childhood. Clarence Benson, a pioneer Christian educator, had as a motto "Begin earlier." As children are born into the Christian family, parents must assume immediate responsibility for spiritual home training.

In the early years of childhood, children imitate the actions of their parents and others. The development of positive attitudes is extremely important. Also, children are pliable and plastic. Their personalities are easily molded even in the early months. For instance, they learn to trust or mistrust people by the time they are six months old.

We have the perfect model in the foundation that God laid for us. God, as our heavenly Father, is the perfect parent, and thus we have that model to follow in laying the foundation for our own families.

Four building blocks will enable parents to build a Christian family.[1]

1. *The need for uniqueness.* Every child needs to feel unique and accepted by his parents. The parent accepts the child's basic God-given personality, abilities, interests, looks, and intelligence. Psalm 139:13-18 shows how our heavenly Father has created and accepted us just the way we are.

2. *The need for unconditional love.* Every child needs to feel that he is unconditionally loved by his parents. He does not need to perform or achieve, or measure up to any standard to be loved. Romans 5:6-8 shows how our heavenly Father meets this need for unconditional love in our lives. God made a decision to love us apart from any merit of our own.

Every child not only needs to know that he is loved but also to feel loved. Parents need to demonstrate their love for the child through attitudes, actions, and words that the child interprets clearly. Each child has a "language of love," and the parent should learn and speak this language to the child. Time spent together, touch, words, and acceptance are all included in children's language of love.

3. *The need for honest, loving, and direct communication.* The entire Bible is an example of God's honest, loving, and direct communication with His children. Children need to have their parents say what they mean, mean what they say, and not say it in a mean way. The section on communication in the family will address this topic in more detail.

4. *The need for boundaries.* Boundaries are reasonable rights and limits

---

1. Wayne Rickerson, "Putting You Back Together" (Wayne Rickerson, 1990), pp. 1-2.

based on God's law of love (Matt. 22:34-40). Boundaries include such things as clearly defined limits of discipline that offer a healthy balance of limits and freedom. Boundaries also include a child's right to his own thoughts and feelings.

God can meet all four of these needs in our lives as we commit ourselves to Him. Although we can never meet these needs totally in our children's lives, we can make it a personal goal to do the best we can in each area.

PREPARING FOR MARRIAGE

The first phase in preparing for marriage begins in the home as children observe their parents' marriage relationship. Through parental modeling children learn basic attitudes and beliefs about commitment, conflict, and how to express love. Parents can teach about and practice biblical principles of marriage. Parents instill the concept that marriage is for life (Matt. 19:4-8), and that children are gifts from the Lord (Ps. 127:3). Parents can also teach biblical roles and relationships of males and females, and husbands, wives, and parents. Many of these concepts are "caught as well as taught." The natural setting provides opportunity for interaction through questions and answers in a loving environment.

The second phase in preparing for marriage is when children reach the dating age. Of course, foundations should be laid in early childhood to prepare them for dating relationships. They can learn proper male and female roles, respect, and proper social manners that will help them in dating. They can also learn how to feel more comfortable with the opposite sex. Parents can teach them how to select friends and build friendships.

One of the most popular topics for teens to discuss is dating. Through the youth group, churches can offer classes and seminars on dating relationships. In a book entitled *This Is The Thanks I Get?*, one chapter explores the subject of hormones, dating, and love.[2] The writer shows parents how to develop a dating covenant with their teens. Youth leaders can also use the content in group sessions.

The third phase in preparation for marriage is when couples have made a decision to be married. The church can provide premarital enrichment counseling. Some churches require couples who are planning to be married to have several sessions of premarital counseling. Some of these sessions can be in a group setting to provide interaction and also to lighten the load for those who do the counseling. Goals for premarital counseling include the following:

1. Provide a biblical foundation for marriage.
2. Motivate the couple to place a high priority on building a strong Christian marriage.
3. Build a close, ongoing relationship between the couple and the persons doing the counseling.

2. Wayne Rickerson, *This Is the Thanks I Get?* (Cincinnati: Standard, 1988).

4. Teach communication and conflict resolution skills.
5. Assess personality styles and how they fit together.
6. Help couples explore their expectations for one another and for their marriage.
7. Assist couples in developing a plan for spiritual growth—individually and together.
8. Provide information in such areas as sexual relationships, finances, family of origin issues, and in-laws.
9. Help couples make a final decision on whether or not to marry and when.
10. Work out the details of the marriage ceremony.

PREMARITAL COUNSELING RESOURCES

Prepare/Enrich. This is a very helpful inventory. The couple takes the Prepare inventory. The counselor sends the form to Prepare/Enrich, Inc., and receives in return a twelve-page printout that lists strengths and weaknesses in eleven areas of the couple's relationship.[3]

Christian Marriage Enrichment. The organization founded by H. Norman Wright has a wide range of premarital materials available. A free catalog will be sent if requested.[4]

COMMUNICATION IN THE FAMILY

One of the greatest needs in Christian families is for honest, loving, and direct communication. In the majority of dysfunctional families, communication appears to be a major problem. Three skills that every Christian family needs to develop are the following.

1. *Listening.* James 1:19 gives us a biblical foundation for developing good communication in the family: "My dear brothers, take note of this: Everyone should be quick to listen, slow to speak, and slow to become angry."

Listening is not something that one learns naturally. It is a difficult skill that must be developed. Parents need to learn the skill of reflective listening. This is simply acknowledging the feeling behind what a person is saying. "You seem to be upset with your teacher." "It looks to me like you're very angry with your brother right now." This skill improves communication and teaches children to become aware of feelings and express them appropriately.

2. *Expressing feelings.* Another skill that needs to be developed in many families is the ability to express feelings honestly with love. An excellent tool to teach families is "straight talk."[5] Straight talk is an honest and loving way to express feelings when a person is angry or upset. Straight talk uses the "I, When, Because" formula. For example, "I feel frustrated when you look away when I am talking to

---

3. Prepare/Enrich, Inc., Box 190, Minneapolis, MN 55458-0190.
4. Christian Marriage Enrichment, 17821 17th St., Suite 290, Tustin, CA 92680.
5. Shrod Miller, Daniel Achman, Elam Nannally, and Carol Saline, *Straight Talk* (New York: Rawson, Wade, 1981).

you, because it seems to me that you are not listening."

3. *Resolving conflict.* Many conflicts in families are left unresolved, only to resurface time and time again. Here are some rules for resolving family conflict:

1. Make a decision to resolve conflict.
2. Watch the timing (rest, cool off if very angry).
3. Do not hit below the belt (emotional beltliness).
4. Listen.
5. Express feelings with straight talk.
6. Negotiate and compromise.[6]

FAMILY RECREATION

One of the traits of a healthy family is to know how to play together. Unfortunately, in the last twenty years family recreation has been replaced increasingly by recreation for individuals within the family. For example, Dad plays golf, Mom plays tennis, sister plays on a softball team, and brother plays on a soccer team. The family ends up being involved in many recreation activities, but spends little time together.

Family Nights. One helpful idea is for families to have a once-a-week family night planned by the family members to have fun, learn biblical principles, and build family togetherness. Family night emphasizes how important the family is and how it serves as a tool in building relationships. Following are some guidelines that will help families make these times successful.

1. Make a commitment to regular family nights or times. (You will never find time. You will have to make time.)
2. Find ideas that will help make your times together enjoyable.
3. Let each family member participate.
4. Make the major focus to have fun.

Another possibility is to have a family night at the church. Families can be shown how to have a family night at home and can be provided with resources available to use at home. Integrate ideas from books or personal experience, and demonstrate and provide opportunities for practice under supervision.

Can of Fun. Another idea is to do the following after the evening meal. Find a small empty can and bring it to the table. Give each family member some small pieces of paper and a pencil. Family members are told they can write down ideas they believe would be fun to do as a family. The slips with the ideas are then folded and put into the can. Once a week the family is to draw out one of the slips and follow the idea written on it.

6. David Augsburger, *Caring Enough to Confront* (Scottdale, Pa.: Herald, 1973).

Family Time Coupons. An activity that will work well with families who have children (eleven years and younger) is to make coupons ahead of time. The family can take a sheet of the coupons and cut out the individual ones. Families should use the coupons on a regular basis, perhaps by having a different family member draw a coupon out of a container each week. Then the entire family can enjoy the activity written on the coupon.

FAMILY TIME COUPONS

Good for a trip to the ice cream store.	Invite the family of your choice over for a special treat.
Choose a table game—the entire family will play it tonight.	Have a Saturday Surprise. You and Dad or Mom may plan a surprise for the rest of the family for next Saturday (picnic, etc.).
Have "Pillow Fight Special." This coupon is good for one pillow fight.	Plan a "Crazy Night." You may ask the family to join you for a crazy activity of your choosing.
Plan a destination unknown—Dad plans an unknown destination to take the family.	Have a "Quiet Night." Each person must read a book in the same room. End your time together with the dessert of your choice.
Have a "Discussion Night." Each person writes something he would like to discuss on a slip of paper. Draw and discuss.	Schedule a "You are Special." Each family member, in turn, is told by other family members what makes him/her special.

THE FAMILY AND CHURCH, SCHOOL, AND COMMUNITY

The family and church. The church as the family of God comprises many family units. The church will only be as strong as its individual families. If we build strong families we will build a strong church. One of the major tasks of a church is to equip parents to build effective Christian families. Some suggestions on how the church can build strong families are:

- Create a Family Ministry Committee. This committee can plan and implement family and marriage enrichment opportunities for the church and the community.
- Offer classes, small groups, or seminars on parenting and marriage enrichment on a regular basis.
- Have a family camp through which families are given family projects and times together.

- Have a family weekend retreat for the sole purpose of helping families have fun and build relationships.
- Have a family emphasis week at your church.
- Suggest a series of sermons on the family.

The purpose of the family is not to serve itself but to serve Christ and His church. The final outcome—ideally—is to have loving, serving relationships within the home, and loving, serving relationships within the church.

The family and school. The family, equipped by the church in loving relationships and outreach, can have a significant impact on the school. The Christian family can be a model of marriage and family relationships to others. Many people today were reared in such dysfunctional homes that they have little idea what normal marriage and family relationships are like. Here is a suggestion for encouraging families to influence schools. Have an evening service to help families see the potential of their impact on schools. In this service:

- Have people (including children) give testimonies of how they have influenced someone for Christ or how they were affected by someone else as a result of school contacts.
- Have a brainstorming session on ideas for influencing schools.
- Encourage parents to be active in school organizations, such as PTA (Parent-Teacher Association).

The family and community. God expects all Christians to be lights unto the world (Matt. 5:16). The family, functioning as a small unit of the Body of Christ, can influence the community by its example. Whether the relationships are built in Little League, soccer, Boy Scouts, or in other ways, the family serves as Christ's ambassador to the community.

Building Christian Marriages

STAGES IN HUSBAND AND WIFE ADJUSTMENTS

The marriage relationship is like a kit we buy at the store. The carton says, "easy to assemble." We take the kit home and are eager to assemble our purchase. We dump the parts out. Then our hearts sink. It looks as if there are thousands of complicated pieces. The process is not going to be as easy as we were led to believe.

There are pieces of the marriage kit to assemble in six major stages of marriage. Within each of these stages there are major adjustments to be made. What are these stages in the life cycle?

Stage 1: Newly marrieds. Unfortunately, most couples go into marriage wearing rose-colored glasses. Through premarital counseling we do as much as we can to help couples face reality. In spite of our efforts, couples take many unrealistic expectations into marriage. Resolving these unrealistic expectations is the first task couples face in making husband/wife adjustments. Expectations that have to be resolved include areas such as husband/wife roles, shared responsibilities, sexual needs, emotional needs, spiritual growth, finances, leisure time, family and friends, careers, and planning for children.

Stage 2: First child. The second cycle of marriage that creates a need for adjustment is the birth of the first child. Although there are many other adjustments that occur during the twenties and thirties age span of this cycle, certainly one of the greatest tests of the marriage is the pressure brought about by bringing a third person into the family. Now time and attention must be divided three ways. There is an increased demand on physical, emotional, and financial resources. The role of parenthood brings with it differences and a need for adjustments. Young couples often feel a great strain in their marriage during this stage.

Stage 3: Teens. When the couple's children reach adolescence, there is often additional stress and the need for understanding and adjustment. Parents often feel anger, anxiety, and loss of control when their teens begin to seek independence and freedom. The husband and wife sometimes respond to the pressure of a rebellious teenager by taking out their feelings on one another. Differences on how to handle the teens surface at this stage.

Stage 4: Empty nest. Major adjustments are often needed when the children leave the nest, especially the last child. When the children are gone, the husband and wife often have to face the quality of their own relationship. Sometimes this means redefining and rebuilding the marriage relationship. If either the husband or wife has built his or her life around the children, this can be a time of intense feeling of loss and readjustment. Add to these factors the possibility of other mid-life crises and the growing sense of the aging process, and you can see the potential for enormous growth and adjustment during this stage.

Stage 5: Retirement. The retirement years bring more changes and needs for adjustment in the marriage relationship. There are many questions that need to be answered: Will our roles change with both having more discretionary time available? What will be our balance between time together and time alone? Will we work part time? How will we spend our money? How will we spend our time? How will we handle ill health? Of course, planning ahead for some of these things will help reduce the conflict between husband and wife.

Stage 6: Facing prolonged illness and death. Facing our own death or the death of an aging spouse calls for significant adjustments. During the seventies and eighties we are faced directly with the end of our lives here on earth. Often this will involve facing prolonged illness. Although we know of the joy of heaven, we are still human, and have to face the sorrow, losses, denial, and rebuilding of life without our lifelong mate. Besides the emotional adjustments, there are the practical issues of finances and care during the later years of our lives. What makes this time of adjustment more difficult is that there is often less energy available to make these decisions.

We can provide help to people by teaching them to identify these stages and prepare in advance for adjustments. Some excellent resources are listed in the bibliography.

HUSBAND/WIFE ROLES

The issue of husband/wife roles brings tension into many relationships. In Genesis 2:24 God declares that husband and wife are to become one. The problem is that many couples turn this into competition and ask the question, Which one? God intended for husband/wife roles to be those of completion—not competition. The wonderful uniqueness that God has given male and female make a completeness in the marriage that neither would have without the other. These different male/female gifts within the marriage are much like spiritual gifts within the church.

The primary question, then, is not who's in charge but "How can we use our differences to enrich our relationship?" Scripture is clear in Ephesians 5:23," where God pronounces man "the head of the wife as Christ is the head of the church." Although the position of head carries with it authority, the course is servanthood and love. "Husbands, love your wives, just as Christ loved the church and gave himself up for her" (Eph. 5:25). Jesus was not only head, but a servant. He had equality with God but chose to give it up. He chose servanthood as His leadership style (Phil. 2:5-8).

When a husband chooses a leadership style of servanthood, the marriage takes on a spirit of mutual submission and equality. Specific tasks within the marriage can then be negotiated based upon the individual gifts and needs. For example, the question of who will handle the financial details can be negotiated between the husband and wife according to which is more skilled or gifted in that area. Decisions on the distribution of household duties such as cleaning, laundry, and yard work can be resolved, not by command, but by sensitivity to one another's gifts and needs.

An excellent way to help couples work through this area of husband/wife roles is to present the biblical passage indicated above. Next have the couples list on a sheet of paper the specific husband/wife role issues they face in their marriage. Then, based on the biblical precept of mutual servanthood and submission, have them discuss with one another how these issues can best be resolved in their marriage.

IN-LAW RELATIONSHIPS

In-law relationships always rank among the top ten problems in marriages. Perhaps that is why early in Scripture God gives two vital principles for dealing with in-law tensions. In Genesis 2:24 God says that a man must "leave" his father and mother and "cleave" to his wife. The word *leave* means to abandon or sever one relationship before establishing another. The word *cleave* means to bond together permanently.

Often the problem with in-law relationships is that one or both spouses have failed to leave their families of origin. Although a person may leave his family physically, he sometimes fails to leave psychologically. The failure to leave a family psychologically is often because one or both parents tried to hold on to the child too long. This causes an unhealthy dependence on the family of origin. When there is an unhealthy dependence on parents, the couple cannot develop a healthy interdependence on one another.

One way to assist couples to come to grips with in-law problems is to show them God's priority system for the family. This system is simple. The first priority is one's own relationship with God. Nothing should stand between one's own personal relationship with God. The second priority is a person's relationship with his spouse. When this priority is in place, outside pressures such as work, children, and in-laws should not harm the marriage. The reason for this is obvious. When one's spouse is the number-one priority after the other spouse's relationship with God, parents and in-laws will not dominate the relationship. The spouse's first commitment is to meet the needs of the other spouse, not in-laws or parents. Often in marriages where there are serious in-law problems this second priority is not in place. The third priority is a person's relationship with his children.

H. Norman Wright gives the following list from his study of why some couples do not have in-law problems.[7] Here are some of the reasons:

1. They accept me. They are friendly, helpful, and close.
2. They do not meddle, interfere, or butt into my life.
3. We were determined to adjust. We respect each other's rights and work things out as they come up.
4. They are not demanding or possessive.
5. They love me. . . . They back me when I need it.

FAMILY FINANCES

Family finances is one of the most common marital problems couples face today. When there are financial pressures in the marriage, often other cracks appear in the relationship. Those in places of spiritual leadership have a great opportunity and duty to minister to couples in this area.

Many counselors discover couples face severe financial difficulties. The problems result from having a limited philosophy/theology of finances. There is little evidence of any careful planning. Some couples face the reality of a lack of planning in the early years of their marriage. The husband may handle the finances without any financial plan or budget. The husband makes the decisions on how the money is spent. His wife resents the control he has over the finances. As a result, there is continual tension over finances—not only because of the mismanagement, but because there is unequal sharing of financial input and responsibility.

The problem can be corrected by working out a budget together. It is a fairly simple procedure. Couples list fixed expenses such as tithe, rent, and utilities. The part of the income that is not committed to these areas is divided among the

7. H. Norman Wright, *How to Be a Better Than Average In-Law* (Wheaton, Ill.: Victor, 1981), pp. 46-47.

other living expenses such as savings, clothes, food, and transportation. The couple ends up with a list of items and the amount they have designated for each. The total must equal the net income. It is best to keep the accounting system simple. Checks are written for the fixed expenses, and the rest of the money—food, gas, general, and clothing is kept in envelopes. When the money in the envelope is gone, it is time to stop spending until the next pay day.

Here are some recommendations for the church in helping couples prevent or overcome financial problems:

1. *Have a financial seminar.* This should be very practical. Have someone qualified in your church or community who understands finances and budgeting conduct this seminar.

2. *Show a video series on finances.* Check with your Christian bookstore for availability.

3. *Have personal financial counseling available.* Ask someone in your church to develop some materials to help couples learn financial stewardship and budgeting.

4. *Make books available.* A number of excellent books on the subject are available through your Christian bookstore and can be made available for sale or loan.

SERIOUS MARITAL PROBLEMS

Serious marital problems are often the result of a breakdown in the priority system that was mentioned in the discussion of in-laws. When one or both spouses fail to put God first and one another second, the possibility of serious marital problems is likely.

When a couple fails to live out the God/spouse priorities, vital needs are often not resolved. For example, a spouse who is considered secondary to work or children in the mate's priorities often feels neglected. Needs such as quality time, affection, and communication are neglected. Bitterness and resentment often result in needs not being met in a marriage. Resentment may lead to an unhappy marriage, an extramarital affair, or a divorce. Affairs often occur in the following manner.

1. A basic need that affects self-esteem is not resolved, and the person becomes lonely and resentful.
2. An acquaintance is made with someone else.
3. There is interaction that in some way meets some aspects of the unresolved need.
4. The third person is seen as having qualities missing in the spouse (for example, is more caring and understanding).
5. Emotional distancing with the spouse increases.
6. The spouse having the affair feels guilty, depressed, and angry toward self and spouse and focuses on the weaknesses of his spouse.
7. The person having the affair loses love feelings toward his spouse and often

says he is no longer "in love."

8. Eventually the affair may lead to sexual relationships.
9. The spouse having the affair begins to rationalize the affair. "We should have never been married." "We have nothing in common."
10. A decision is made to divorce, separate, or continue the relationship.[8]

Not all serious marital problems lead to an affair, but the consequences of unresolved problems are always tragic. Marriage counseling is usually required. If Christian leaders do not engage in marriage counseling themselves, they should be able to recommend a competent Christian counselor. Many people do not seek help because they are to ashamed to ask.

DIVORCE

Divorce is the result of unresolved marital problems. No matter what the circumstances, divorce is always tragic. It is the ultimate breakdown of God's command that we love one another. Following are four responses that Christian leaders should have toward divorce:

1. *Stand firm in hating divorce.* In Malachi 2:16 God says, "I hate divorce." The reason? "Has not the Lord made them one?" (v. 15). As Christian leaders we must develop a passion for seeing Christian marriages stay healthy and have a godly hate for divorce.

2. *Stand firm in teaching biblical precepts on divorce.* We must not conform to the pressures of the world to change our theology because divorce is so prevalent among Christians. We have no right to condone divorce except for biblical reasons. Unfortunately, a number of Christians construct their theology of divorce on pragmatism.

3. *Extend grace to the divorced.* Divorce is not an unpardonable sin. Divorce is covered by God's grace and thus should be covered by our grace. The divorced should not feel that they are second-class citizens of the church because of a marriage that failed.

4. *Help the divorced work toward recovery.* Divorce is a terrible blow to a person's self-esteem. The loss of a spouse through divorce is much like that of losing a loved one to death, except the corpse is still alive. The divorced person must go through all the steps of grief if he or she is to recover from this experience. The church can help the divorced to recover. Love, acceptance, and being included in the family of God are foundational. The church can also help by offering divorce recovery groups. In the bibliography some sources are listed that will help in dealing with divorce.

CONCLUSION

Biblically, the church's responsibility is to equip parents to live out Christ's love

8. Wayne Rickerson, "Steps to an Extra-Marital Affair" (Wayne Rickerson, 1987), p. 1.

in their family relationships. We must not be deluded to think this happens automatically because of the teaching programs of the church. Every church needs a family life education ministry and ought to set specific goals in its ministry to families. Ask questions such as, How will we strengthen marriages this year? What will we do to help our people become godly parents? What can we do to help those reared in dysfunctional families recover and find God's fullness? Are our leaders living godly lives and modeling strong marriages and families?

As these questions are asked, the church can develop ministries to meet these needs. One of the greatest tasks for this decade will be for churches to strengthen marriages and families. God can use each of us in this significant ministry.

FOR FURTHER READING

PREPARING FOR MARRIAGE

Wright, H. Norman. *Premarital Counseling.* Revised edition. Chicago: Moody, 1981.
_____. *So You're Getting Married.* Ventura, Calif.: Regal, 1985.

HUSBAND/WIFE ROLES AND RELATIONSHIPS

Family Ministry Electives series. Elgin, Ill.: David C. Cook, 1985: *On My Own,* Tom Eisenman; *Newly Married,* Wayne Rickerson; *Now We Are Three,* Eldon E. Fry, Judson J. Swihart, and George A. Rekers; *Big People, Little People,* Tom Eisenman; *You and Your Teen,* Charles Bradshaw; *Just Me and the Kids,* Patricia Brandt with Dave Jackson; *Empty Nest,* Carl D. Wilson; *The Freedom Years,* Larry Ferguson with Dave Jackson.
Wright, H. Norman. *Communication: Key to Your Marriage.* Revised edition. Ventura, Calif.: Regal, 1979.

BUILDING CHRISTIAN FAMILIES*

Kesler, Jay, and Ronald A. Beers, eds. *Parents and Teenagers.* Wheaton, Ill.: Victor, 1984.
Kesler, Jay; Ron Beers; and LaVonne Neff, eds. *Parents and Children.* Wheaton, Ill.: Victor, 1986.
Money, Royce. *Building Stronger Families.* Wheaton, Ill.: Victor, 1984. Leader's guide also available.
Rickerson, Wayne. *Family Fun Times: Activities That Bind Marriages, Build Families, and Develop Christian Leaders.* Cincinnati: Standard, 1987.
_____. *Strengthening the Family.* Cincinnati: Standard, 1987.
_____. *This Is the Thanks I Get? A Guide to Raising Teenagers.* Cincinnati: Standard, 1988.
_____. *What Shall I Do Now? A Guide to Raising Children.* Cincinnati: Standard, 1988.

Smalley, Gary, and John Trent. *The Blessing: Giving and Gaining Family Approval.* Nashville: Thomas Nelson, 1986.

FINANCES

Blue, Ron. *The Debt Squeeze.* Pomona, Calif.: Focus on the Family, 1989.
Burkett, Larry. *Debt-Free Living.* Chicago: Moody, 1989.
_____. *The Financial Planning Workbook.* Chicago: Moody, 1982.

SERIOUS MARITAL PROBLEMS

Chapman, Gary D. *Hope for the Separated.* Chicago: Moody, 1982.
Harvey, Donald R. *The Drifting Marriage.* Old Tappan, N.J.: Revell, 1988.
Richmond, Gary. *The Divorce Decision.* Waco, Tex.: Word, 1988.

*See also the bibliography for chapter 38.

38

Spiritual Formation in the Home

SPIRITUAL FORMATION IN THE HOME
- **Parents must work in cooperation with God**
- **The goal of spiritual formation is a life-long process**
- **Spiritual formation should permeate the lives and the activities of the home**
- **The parenting style chosen can either facilitate or hinder the spiritual formation of their children**
- **Parents should form a cooperative effort with the church and with other parents**

After that whole generation had been gathered to their fathers, another generation grew up, who knew neither the Lord nor what he had done for Israel. Then the Israelites did evil in the eyes of the Lord and served the Baals. They forsook the Lord, the God of their fathers, who had brought them out of Egypt. (Judges 2:10-12)

What a startling and frightening statement. Within one generation, the children of Israel had forgotten that the God of Israel had delivered their parents and grandparents from the oppression and slavery of Egypt. The offspring of

CRAIG WILLIFORD, M.A., Ed.D. candidate, is minister of education at South Park Church, Park Ridge, Illinois.

those who personally witnessed the awesome display of God's nature, power, and love did not acknowledge or honor the God of Israel. He was now a stranger, a person of the past, talked about in fairy tales and folklore; He was only one of the gods, powerless and meaningless. The book of Judges is filled with this regular pattern of spiritual failure: a generation would call out to God, be delivered by God through a God-empowered judge, and then the following generation—while living in prosperity or peace—would forget the God of their parents and grandparents. How did this happen? Did the previous generations not explain who God was to their children? How could the children, who were eyewitnesses to the clear displays of God's nature and love, grow up not knowing God? What could the previous generation have done to help their children become adults who knew the God of Israel?

These questions are still asked by today's parents as they strive and struggle with the spiritual formation of their children. Many parents fear that their children might grow up and reject their faith, just as the children in the book of Judges did. The purpose of this chapter is to assist parents, future parents, and those ministering to parents to reexamine what spiritual formation in the home means. The chapter is also designed to encourage parents to establish spiritual formation as a key priority of their home and to give parents practical suggestions for spiritual home training.

Most people recognize that the family feels pressured from many different sources, and that no one has a perfect home. Spiritual formation of children does not require a perfect home, but it does require a home where family members are all working in cooperation with God to assist the growth of each member and the family as a whole. This chapter is written to assist those people who are willing to commit themselves to the challenges of spiritual formation.

BIBLICAL BASIS FOR SPIRITUAL FORMATION IN THE HOME

The Bible has much to say concerning the family. A number of principles, values, and attitudes emerge as one reads and studies the Scriptures. And in the field of family life, many modern writers have attempted to develop a theology for the family from these biblical principles and instructions.[1] This discussion shall not attempt to take an exhaustive look at the biblical principles or to explain a theology for the family; instead, Deuteronomy 6, which exemplifies the biblical principles of spiritual formation within the family, shall be explored and highlighted.

Deuteronomy 6 is one of the most important references in Scripture that describes the role and process of spiritual formation in the home. This vital book contains Moses' last instructions to his people, the nation Israel. Moses uses this time to reemphasize and stress the importance of the Ten Commandments, other aspects and requirements of the covenant and, most important, the God of the

---

1. Some current examples are Kenneth Gangel, Ray Anderson, Dennis Guernsey, and Stuart McLean.

covenant. This book is essentially Moses' last will and testament. Through Deuteronomy Moses shares his intimate and dynamic relationship with God so that others will remember to love and worship the covenant God, Jehovah. Moses is eager to ensure that the then current nation of Israel and the future nations of Israel would indeed fulfill the covenant of God and love God with all their hearts, souls, and strength.

In Deuteronomy 6 Moses gives a thorough explanation of how the people of Israel were to assist their children in remembering the covenant of God and the God of the covenant. The central truth of this chapter is the description of God in verses 4-6 and the instruction to the families on how they were to portray this God carefully and thoroughly to their children: "Hear, O Israel: The Lord our God, the Lord is one. Love the Lord your God with all your heart and with all your soul and with all your strength. These commandments that I give you today are to be upon your hearts."

These verses describe God as unique and special. He alone is God; there is no one else like Him. God is a jealous God and demands single-minded devotion and worship from His people. He and He alone should be the object of the nation Israel's worship. They should not have any alliances or allegiances that pose threats to this single devotion to God. Clearly, Moses is alluding to the first of the Ten Commandments and defining what that commandment means.

After describing God in this manner, Moses commands the nation of Israel to love God totally. He uses the phrases "with all your heart and with all your soul and with all your strength." These point out the way in which the love of God was to permeate all the lives of the Israelites. The heart refers to the mind, will, and emotions. The soul reminds one of the vitality, essence, or source of life. Strength suggests the disciplines of the body or the daily work or tasks. Moses' point is that the love of God must be consuming and permeate all that the Israelites were as humans and as the people of God. Loving God was not contained or compartmentalized; it was not something added as an afterthought. Loving God was the very purpose of their existence and meaning.

In the remainder of the chapter Moses encourages and requires the nation of Israel to pass this love on to future generations. Numerous principles for family spiritual formation are given by Moses. First, it is clearly the responsibility of the community of families that constituted the nation of Israel to impress these truths upon their children. Notice that Moses was not speaking just to the priests or prophets of that day; he was requiring the fathers, mothers, grandparents, aunts, and uncles to assume responsibility for the spiritual formation of the children.

The second principle is that spiritual instruction concerning the covenant, the Ten Commandments, and God was to be a continual part of the daily lives of God's people. Decrees, laws, commands, and the very Person and character of God were to be explained in the natural activities of the day by the parents and extended family. These abstract principles would be explained concretely as the families experienced the natural flow of life as the people of God. The rituals and festivals, stipulations, and the values and attitudes practiced in the regular routine of life served as catalysts for the child's natural inquisitiveness and were to be modeled and explained in detail. Worship and spiritual formation were to be the very fiber of life, and the families were commanded to take the role in this vital instruction. Also, note how informal and personal this instruction was. No one was designated teacher. Everyone was to take part in the spiritual formation, with the family assuming main responsibility. Notice, too, how the natural inquisitiveness of the child as he viewed the parents putting their faith into action set the agenda for the spiritual formation.

The final principle relates to the purpose of spiritual formation. While Moses' instructions emphasize the decrees, commands, and laws of God, these are not the main emphases or the purpose of spiritual formation. Instead, the core of spiritual formation is a relationship with the God of the covenant, the Deliverer of Israel. Moses is concerned that the future generations of Israel know and love God, not just the commandments of God. The decrees, laws, and commands were given to point people to the Person of God. The specific content of God's instruction to the nation Israel is important, but it is not an end or goal. Spiritual formation is not concerned with children knowing content for the sake of content; it is concerned with sharing content as one aspect of assisting children to know God and love Him totally.

Today, God still requires that families fulfill these principles of spiritual formation. Parents must assume the main responsibility for the spiritual formation of their children. The church of God is the community that should encourage and assist the parents in this role. The church cannot and should not assume this responsibility for the parents; also, parents must not expect the church to fulfill their responsibility. Lastly, the need for informal, natural, daily spiritual formation still exists. The mistake many families make is to view spiritual formation as an add-on instead of a core that permeates the entire life of the family. Clearly, Moses' instructions to the nation of Israel are true for the people of God today.

A DEFINITION OF SPIRITUAL FORMATION

From this look at Deuteronomy 6, the questions that might arise are: How do parents do this today? or, What exactly is spiritual formation? For sake of clarity, this definition for spiritual formation is suggested: "the intentional and systematic process of growing into the image of Christ through obedience to the Scriptures by the power of the Holy Spirit in our total personality."[2] The words *intentional* and *systematic* point to the deliberate and planned aspects of spiritual formation. Even though God is the author and main force in one's spiritual for-

---

2. Frank Bateman Stanger, *Spiritual Formation in the Local Church* (Grand Rapids: Zondervan, 1989), p. 17.

mation, parents must take an active role through intentional and systematic means in the lives of their children. This is not suggesting that parents can control or force the spiritual formation of their children, but parents must assume responsibilities in assisting the work of God in their children's lives. Also, "intentional and systematic" means do not eliminate the natural aspects of spiritual formation. Parents can and should understand the role that natural development plays in spiritual formation and use these cycles or stages as crucial times for spiritual formation. One example is the natural inquisitiveness that results from the cognitive development of the child. As the child begins to understand the world around him, he will naturally ask questions concerning the way the family practices and lives its faith.

The second part of the definition, "growing into the image of Christ," highlights the goal of spiritual formation. The purpose is to assist persons in the lifelong, dynamic process of becoming like Christ. Spiritual formation is relationship building between Jesus Christ and the individual. Although instruction, content, Scripture memory, and spiritual disciplines are all processes of spiritual formation, they are not the desired goal. Since spiritual formation is lifelong and continual, no one reaches the level of completion until he is fully united with Christ.

The third section of the definition, "through obedience to the Scriptures," emphasizes the importance of God's revelation. Spiritual formation is obedience to His Word and commands. This refers to the authority that God's Word must have in the life of a believer. Parents should help children understand and respond obediently to what God says is true and what He requires of them.

"By the power of the Holy Spirit" indicates the role of God in spiritual formation. It is His role that makes spiritual formation possible. All attempts to assist spiritual formation must recognize that the Holy Spirit is the motivating force. He is the Creator and One who brings His children to Himself. He empowers and enables spiritual formation in ways and workings beyond human understanding; He is not limited to human patterns or natural, empirical stages. No one working in spiritual formation can predict or reduce His activity to a formula that can be reproduced in everyone else's life. There are some apparent patterns and stages that seem common to many believers, but no guaranteed formula exists. Another vital aspect of this section on the definition of spiritual formation is that all parents working with their children will need to be aware of and sensitive to what the Holy Spirit is doing in the life of each child. The Holy Spirit's work will not be identical for all. Parents must prayerfully seek wisdom in understanding how they can see and assist the work that God is doing in the lives of each of their children.

The final phrase, "in our total personality," refers to the thoroughness of spiritual formation. The work and goal is not the elimination of one's humanness or the platonic denial of the body in order to elevate the spirit. Spiritual formation is concerned with assisting persons to become fully human in the sense that

Jesus Christ was fully human. This involves all that it means to be created in God's image and to be a human.

Spiritual formation does not call for compartmentalizing; instead, it encourages the believer to embrace and participate in all that it means to be in God's kingdom.

A final emphasis that is not highlighted by the definition but requires mention is the role of community. Spiritual formation does not take place in a vacuum; it is nurtured and assisted in community. Although this chapter is exploring the role of the family in spiritual formation, the church does take a vital role. Also, one cannot retreat from community or the world in order to mature spiritually. The family needs the assistance of other families and the church to complete its goals: parents and children with lifelong, dynamic, growing relationships with Jesus Christ who participate fully in what it means to be subjects of the King.

PRIORITIES OF SPIRITUAL FORMATION

With this definition in mind, two questions may still remain: How do parents assist in the spiritual formation of their children? and, What are the priorities of spiritual formation in the home? The most important aspect of spiritual formation in the home is the way the family lives its faith. Faith must permeate and be natural to all aspects of the family. Discussions of faith should be a normal part of everyday conversation. The family should have traditions that point to Christ and lead to conversations concerning meaning and application. Merely going to church, praying at mealtimes, and calling the family "Christian" does not constitute spiritual formation.

For spiritual formation to take place in the home, the *parents themselves must be living and striving for the goals of spiritual formation.* Children too easily penetrate facades and mere attempts at Christianity. Children will most likely reject what their parents only pretend to live and do not actually value. This does not require the parents to be perfect. It does, however, require that parents be actively seeking to mature spiritually and that they be honest with their children about their relationships with God. Appropriately sharing failures, mistakes, and exciting aspects of one's spiritual formation serve as models for children.

Time and relationship building are other priorities of family spiritual formation. There is no substitute for the family spending time together. At the pressurized pace that most families live, this is one of the most precious commodities. Time is scarce. Yet for spiritual formation to happen, parents and children must have time together. If parents are going to develop the kind of relationships with their children that will allow them to hear the key questions that their children ask—and then be able to answer them carefully—parents must make time. This could mean seeking new jobs, choosing not to climb the corporate ladder, deciding to work within the home, or giving up a career entirely while children are young. These decisions may demand a new approach to material possessions: settling for less. Parents must prayerfully seek answers from God and reestablish what their priorities are. Only then can they adjust lifestyles to match these biblical priorities.

PROCESSES IN SPIRITUAL FORMATION

In addition to these priorities, living the faith and dedicating time, many processes are important to spiritual formation in the home. Currently some writers and Christian educators suggest that family devotions are no longer valid for spiritual formation. This is not necessarily true. While the method of reading a daily devotional before breakfast or after dinner can be monotonous and boring for children, with correct planning and strategy family devotions can be vital to the family's spirituality. *Active and creative devotions geared toward developmental abilities* are keys to making the family worship meaningful and memorable. Preschool children love to read from the many excellent Bible storybooks and then act out these adventures. Children need this kind of commitment and fun time together with their parents as often as possible. Children also enjoy reviewing Sunday school lessons. Many times the Sunday school curriculum includes take-home papers for the unit that they are studying. These can be read and discussed by parents in order to reinforce understanding and application. If the child's Sunday school curriculum does not offer this, parents can go to the Sunday school teacher or department leader and request a list of Bible stories that the class will be using. Coordinating the reading of stories from a Bible storybook with reviewing the lessons from Sunday school can be effective for many parents and their children.

Finally, parents need to pray with their preschoolers and tell them about God's love for them. Spending time as a family doing these kinds of devotions will build childhood memories that will continue for a lifetime.

Once the children enter elementary school, parents should move to an active format for family devotions that involve the senses, making devotions enjoyable and fun. Acting out the stories and coordinating with the children's Sunday school are still appropriate. Active involvement by the children in as many aspects of the devotional as possible is the key element. Other devotional ideas may relate the developmental aspects of children to devotional topics from Scripture. One example would be to discuss the story of Elijah on Mount Carmel; the theme of the context there—that God can be trusted to keep His promises—can be compared to a child's fears of the night. Parents should, however, be careful to select stories with contexts that truly illustrate the developmental aspect that the child is facing. Inappropriate stretching of Scripture to make the context say what was not intended by the biblical author can be demonstrated in the use of Daniel 1 to teach children to eat good food (recently done by a writer in a printed curriculum). This application is obviously not what the biblical author had in mind when recording the story of Daniel. Some family devotion books on the market contain many different kinds of devotions that can be helpful.

Teenagers also require a different approach to family devotions. Instead of enforcing daily readings, parents and teens may benefit more from one night or breakfast time a week when important issues can be discussed in an open atmosphere. Reading quality books individually and then discussing them later as a family has also proved beneficial for many families with teenagers. The tasks and life adjustments (peer pressure) that many teenagers face also provide topics for quality discussion and application of biblical principles. Some devotional books for families with teenagers are available at local Christian bookstores.

Committing to family devotions is an essential element of home spiritual formation. With effort, the time spent with children can be helpful, fun, and extremely effective. As the children actually see and experience their parents making a commitment to their spiritual formation, this could communicate volumes about Christianity and how much their parents love and value them.

Bible memorization is another important facet of spiritual formation. Many different programs exist that families can use for this purpose. If one's local church has Awana, Pioneer Clubs, or another children's club, the parents may wish simply to reinforce these programs. Some churches also include Scripture memorization in the Sunday school program. Parents can play an important role in listening to children as they practice, congratulating them as they learn the verses, and by stressing the application of what they learn. Some families also include their own systems of rewards above the ones given by the church ministries. Two cautions need to be emphasized here. First, children can memorize far beyond what they truly learn or comprehend. Parents must work diligently to encourage their children in understanding what they memorize. Rewarding comprehension of meaning as well as rote memory is important. Second, children can become overburdened with Scripture memory work. Parents should watch carefully to ensure that their children do not get discouraged or stressed with overdemanding Scripture memory programs.

Teaching children to pray is also important for spiritual formation. Children have a tendency to pray more when they regularly observe their parents pray. As part of family devotions, regularly include times of meaningful prayer when everyone prays together. Encourage children to keep journals of their prayers. Parents may want to record the answers to prayer and share them with the family. Teaching children to pray involves regular parental participation and frequent prayer at times other than mealtimes. Before bed, before important events, during times of family difficulties or crises, and when children have major tasks are all times when prayer with parents will be meaningful for the children.

Another element of spiritual formation is *church attendance and involvement.* Normally Christians do not grow spiritually without the assistance of community and the opportunity to serve through that community. Families need other assistance because individual families do not possess all of the gifts of the Holy Spirit that are necessary for the ministry of spiritual formation. Church participation enables them to be served by the full expression of these gifts so that they can fully grow and mature. The church also provides opportunities for individual families and groups of families to serve each other and those outside of the church who are in need. Reaching out to the poor through clothing or food distribution, taking meals to the elderly, assisting the handicapped or widows, providing meals or help for those with family members in the hospital are all examples of service that can contribute to the spiritual growth of the participating family members. Parents should also talk with their children about why Christian service is so important: the motivation of love and sharing of the good news of Jesus Christ.

Currently many writers and researchers in the field of family spirituality are also stressing the importance of *training children concerning justice.* They argue that racism, stereotyping, violence, and oppression are all behaviors and values learned during these impressionable childhood years. Therefore, a necessary part of the spiritual formation of children is the teaching of Christian values that clearly stand in opposition to negative behaviors and values. Christian parents must teach and demonstrate correct biblical values and help their children develop these same values. One way to develop such values is by explaining the dignity of life (as created by God) and how believers are responsible for the stewardship of this creation and life. This is best demonstrated, not formally taught. And parents can achieve this only by constantly examining themselves and determining what values they are expressing to their children through their actions, words, and possessions.

Because values are also taught—and caught—from the child's school, church, television, and peers, *parents need to monitor these sources of values* and help the children sort through the many discrepancies that may occur. Parents should not take the approach of isolation—keeping children from all alternative value systems; instead, they must teach children to understand the values of others and how to think biblically with discernment. Some families watch television together and then critique the values that were expressed in that program. Others read together and then discuss the author's views. Family devotions should include a systematic look at biblical values (possibly by role-playing negative and positive values) and why God requests that Christians live these values.

All of these priorities, processes, and approaches to spiritual formation are crucial. Parents need to start slowly and work methodically, remembering that the work they are called to do is in cooperation with the Holy Spirit, the church, and other families. The result can be extremely rewarding and very satisfying.

EXPLAINING SALVATION TO CHILDREN

As children grow up in the environment of spiritual formation described previously, they will naturally be inquisitive about salvation. They will question, inquire, and gradually grow in understanding of their need for a personal relationship with Christ. In their zeal to ensure that their children receive Christ as Lord and Savior, some parents try to rush or overly influence their children's faith decisions. This only serves to push children from the gospel or to give a false security or false impression of personal salvation that may create future problems. Sensitivity to the Holy Spirit's leading and allowing children the opportunity to advance as they develop and are led by the Holy Spirit is important.

How will I know when my child is ready? or, What do I say? are some of the questions that parents ask when trying to explain Christ to their children. First, parents should answer the child's questions honestly and openly, attempting to use language they understand. Second, they should never use fear or coercion. Telling a child that unless he receives Christ separation from parents will result is damaging to that child's future relationship with Christ. Third, parents need to tell a child of God's love and that He wants His children to confess sins and receive Him as Lord and Savior. Fourth, asking the child open-ended questions that require an explanation in his own words is helpful to determine if the child understands and is actually ready for a personal commitment. Finally, if the child is indeed ready, the parent should ask him to pray to receive Christ. The parent may want to ask the child to pray first, to pray after the parent prays, or have the child repeat the parent's prayer. The parent will need to remember that as his child develops cognitively, he will revisit this issue and have additional questions; this is both normal and helpful.

PARENTING STYLES

> Speaking for a moment from our personal experience as parents rather than as experts, we would suggest that parents concentrate less on the technique of good parenting and more on the process of being a parent. Good parenting is a matter of interacting with our children day in and day out. It is these day-to-day experiences which build relationships with them. The best advice we can give to parents is to throw away their how-to-parent books and simply become real persons to their children.[3]

This quotation from the Balswicks illustrates that there is no one perfect form of parenting; parents need to spend less time worrying about making mistakes and more time just being parents to their children. In spiritual formation, parents need to heed this same advice. They do not need to be overly concerned with doing the wrong things; they need to be about the work of spiritual formation. With these cautions in mind, the following discussion centers on the role of parenting styles in spiritual formation of children. The relationship between parenting style and a child's development has been studied throughout the last four decades.

Early research examined the distinction of permissive from restrictive styles. Later researchers studied the variables of control and support in relation to the child's development. More recently, the instrumental and socioemotional styles of parenting have been given more attention. The instrumental research (which emphasizes tasks and content) looks at action—the parents exemplifying in their own actions the behavior required of children—and content—the parents attempt

---

3. Jack O. Balswick and Judith K. Balswick, *The Family: A Christian Perspective on the Contemporary Home* (Grand Rapids: Baker, 1989), p. 94.

to communicate and teach clearly the norms and values they desire. The combination of action and commitment produces four representative parenting styles: neglecting (low in action and content), discipling (high in action and content), teaching (high in content and low in action), and modeling (low in content and high in action).

Socioemotional research (which emphasizes emotional bonding) examines the two dimensions of support and control. The researchers define the word control in a proper sense of influence, not indoctrination. Again, four representative parenting styles result: authoritative (high in both control and support), neglectful (low in both control and support), permissive (high in support and low in control), and authoritarian (low in support and high in control).[4]

In their book *The Family: A Christian Perspective on the Contemporary Home,* the Balswicks look at (1) Myron Chartier's research on God's parenting style, which is demonstrated in Scripture,[5] and (2) Hersey and Blanchard's research in organizational behavior.[6] By combining and adapting these, the Balswicks form an empowering approach to parenting. The figure below illustrates the Balswicks' ideas.

Christian Parenting: Empowering to Maturity

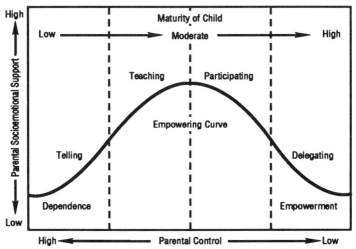

Adapted from Paul Hersey and Kenneth Blanchard, *Management of Organizational Behavior,* 4th ed. (Englewood Cliffs, N.J.: Prentice-Hall, 1988), p. 287. Reprinted from Jack O. Balswick and Judith K. Balswick, The Family: *A Christian Perspective on the Contemporary Home* (Grand Rapids: Baker, 1989), p. 105. Used by permission.

4. I am indebted to the work of the Balswicks in their excellent chapter on this area. Many concepts are adapted from this work.
5. Myron Chartier, "Parenting: A Theological Model," *Journal of Psychology and Theology* (Winter 1978) 6:54-61.
6. Paul Hersey and Kenneth Blanchard, *Management of Organizational Behavior,* 4th ed. (Englewood Cliffs, N.J.: Prentice-Hall, 1988), p. 287.

Their chart has four dimensions: socioemotional support, parental control, dependence/empowerment, and the maturity of the child. The four styles are telling (one-way communication), teaching (two-way communication), participating (modeling approach), and delegating (giving the child the responsibility). The four representative parenting styles combine the four dimensions in this way: telling (high in control and dependence and low in maturity and socioemotional support), teaching (moderate in all four dimensions), participating (moderate in all four dimensions), and delegating (high in maturity of child and low in other areas). The Balswicks want parents to use all four styles, but as the child matures, they need to move to a more participating or empowering approach.

Since spiritual formation is interested in reaching the goal of spiritual maturity and developing the relationship between God and individuals, the Balswicks' approach has a lot to offer parents. If too authoritarian or neglectful, parenting styles can limit or hinder the spiritual growth of their children. Parents who appropriately use all four styles as suggested by the Balswicks can help their children in both spiritual relationship building and spiritual maturity. The central issue appears to be that parents should use a balance of support and control in the process of helping their children to own and individualize their faith. Perhaps Bernard Spilka says it best:

> At the current time, the advice to parents is clear: be in agreement on the religious faith you wish to impart, sincerely model that faith in both word and deeds, and strive toward a relationship with your children that will encourage discussion of religion and its implications. But remember that it is also important that the child feel free to take his or her own position.[7]

SEX EDUCATION IN THE HOME

The role of the home, church, and school in the sex education of children is one of this past decade's most controversial issues. With many in the public sector actively arguing for a privatization of all religious values, the result is an individualistic value system that will result in further destruction of the moral fiber of America. Many public educators are trying to replace the parents as the primary sex educators: they intend to supplement what the parents are teaching in a supposedly values-free approach. With state-mandated AIDS education and school-based clinics that dispense free birth control devices, parents can no longer passively ignore this issue.

Although this chapter cannot discuss public sex education at length, the best counteraction to this dilemma is for families to take an active role in the public schools and in the teaching of sexuality to their children at home. The home must remain the primary place for teaching the biblical values that relate to sex-

---

7. Bernard Spilka, Ralph W. Hood, Jr., and Richard L. Gorsuch, *The Psychology of Religion: An Empirical Approach* (Englewood Cliffs, N.J.: Prentice-Hall, 1985), pp. 84-85.

uality. Children need to understand from their parents what sexuality is and how it is to be expressed according to God's instructions. Today's society and pressures force parents to address this in an intentional manner with their children. This section, then, will explore ways that parents can instill sexual values in their children.

Sexuality is not a topic to fear or hide. God has created humans as sexual beings and has provided proper guidelines for the expression of that sexuality. Parents should communicate to their children that sexuality is a natural part of human development and that it can be embraced in the Christian life. Telling children that God gave us this gift and that sexuality's proper use is wonderful and exciting is one aspect; modeling of proper sexuality by the parents is another vital part. Parents need to be affectionate and caring to each other so that the children can observe this.

As the child's interest and inquisitiveness grows, parents will need to answer the specific questions that the child asks. Offering more information than was requested or being afraid to discuss honestly with children the specifics of sexuality will send negative signals. Use of fake imagery or stories (the stork, for example) is improper and deters the child's development; instead, realism is important. Parents need not be overly graphic or concrete in their discussions. Helpful, educationally appropriate resources are available for parents to use in explaining sexuality to their children. See the bibliography for more information.

Teaching teenagers about sexuality is also important. Parents of teenagers must not assume that just because the teen uses correct anatomical language he understands sexuality from a biblical perspective. Again, resources such as videos and books are available to help the parents have honest, valuable discussions with their teens. These are very important times of sharing. One vital issue for teens is to develop dating standards. When done in advance by the teen—in cooperation with the parents—these standards can be helpful for the teen in his expression of sexuality. Parents must not develop the standards themselves; this kind of approach may actually encourage rebellion by the teen. Instead, having teens develop these standards involves them in the process of thinking through important issues. The key is to help teens view sexuality as a natural part of the Christian life and to encourage them to understand why God has instructed humans to express this sexuality in proper ways. Parents should help teenagers see that improperly expressed sexuality actually limits it and denies full expression of what God intended.

CONCLUSION

Parents take the primary role in the spiritual formation of their children. The purpose of this spiritual formation is to assist children in developing a lifelong, growing, dynamic relationship with Jesus Christ, a relationship that helps Christians conform to the image of Jesus Christ and expresses this conformity in a life of obedience and service. Parents must work with the Holy Spirit in encouraging their children to learn to live under the authority of the Lord Jesus Christ.

If parents are to accomplish this task, they must live their faith in a growing, active manner. They cannot suggest to children and teenagers that spirituality is important if their daily lives portray that it is not. Parents cannot be crippled by fear or neglect; instead, they must enter their children's lives and build open, honest relationships that can provide the catalyst for spiritual growth. Scripture teaches that parents must express their faith to their children as they walk, sit at home, lie down, and get up. May the next generation grow up to know God truly and to know all He has done for us.

FOR FURTHER READING

Balswick, Jack O., and Judith K. Balswick. *The Family: A Christian Perspective on the Contemporary Home*. Grand Rapids: Baker, 1989.

Concordia Sex Education series. St. Louis: Concordia, 1985: *How to Talk Confidently with Your Child About Sex: Parents' Guide,* Lenore Buth; *Why Boys and Girls Are Different* (ages 3-5), Carol Greene; *Where Do Babies Come From?* (ages 6-8), Ruth Hummel; *How You Are Changing* (ages 8-11), Jane Graver; *Sex and the New You* (ages 11-14), Richard Bimler; *Love, Sex, and God* (ages 14 +), Bill Ameiss and Jane Graver. Age-graded books also available in video.

Curran, Dolores. *Traits of a Healthy Family*. San Francisco: Harper & Row, 1984.

Dobson, James. *Dare to Discipline*. Wheaton, Ill.: Tyndale, 1973.

McDowell, Josh. *How to Help Your Child Say "No" to Sexual Pressure*. Waco, Tex.: Word, 1987. Also available in video.

McDowell, Josh, and Dick Day. *Why Wait? What You Need to Know About the Teen Sexuality Crisis*. San Bernardino, Calif.: Here's Life, 1987.

Merrill, Dean, and Grace Merrill. *Together at Home: One Hundred Proven Activities to Nurture Your Children's Faith*. Pomona, Calif.: Focus on the Family, 1988.

Sloat, Donald E. *The Dangers of Growing Up in a Christian Home*. Nashville: Thomas Nelson, 1986.

Spackman, Carl K. *Parents Passing on the Faith*. Wheaton, Ill.: Victor, 1989.

Strommen, Merton P., and A. Irene Strommen. *Five Cries of Parents*. San Francisco: Harper & Row, 1985.

Ward, Ted. *Values Begin at Home*. Revised edition. Wheaton, Ill.: Victor, 1989.

Williford, Carolyn. *Devotions for Families That Can't Sit Still*. Wheaton, Ill.: Victor, 1990.

Cliff Schimmels

39

Public, Christian, and Home Schooling

EDUCATING THROUGH SCHOOLS
- **What is the purpose of schools?**
- **With Christian schools, home schools, and public schools available, how do I make the appropriate choice for my family?**
- **Once the choice is made, what must I do to help my child get the most from the process?**
- **What are the limitations of the schooling experience in my child's development?**

When Moses gathered the children of Israel along the banks of the Jordan River to deliver his final speech before they were to cross over into the Promised Land, he began by giving instructions for the education of children. In Deuteronomy 6, Moses reminds us that this is the task of parents. Through the years, nothing has happened to change this mandate. Parents are still the chief educators of their children.

Along the way, however, parents picked up some helpers. That is the function of schools—to help parents fulfill their God-given responsibility in educating their children.

CLIFF SCHIMMELS, PH.D., is professor of education, Wheaton College, Wheaton, Illinois.

HISTORY OF SCHOOLS

The idea of schools is an old notion. In the Western world, we find types of schools in ancient Greece as early as six centuries before Christ. Fathers would bring their sons to a common spot where an educated slave would give lessons in such things as sports, music, and the writings of Homer.

When the Romans captured the Greeks, they also captured the concept of schools. They developed the program into a three-part system and made schooling a function of the government.

In our country, the idea of schools came with the earliest settlers. Although the schools were not highly developed in some areas of the New World during the colonial period, in other areas schooling became a high priority in establishing and maintaining the new life that the people had come to find.

For example, in 1647 the people in the Massachusetts colony passed a school law—sometimes called the Olde Deluder Satan act—that firmly established the concept of public education in this country.

In the first paragraph of the Olde Deluder Satan act, we find the purpose of education. If children do not learn to read and write, they can more easily be deceived by Satan. In the second paragraph, we find that the law requires that when a community reaches a population of fifty households, that local community must employ and provide for a schoolmaster to instruct the children.

The framers of the Constitution of the United States chose not to include schools anywhere in that document; thus, the task of developing and regulating our educational system has fallen to state control.

Since the forming of the republic, the history of schools in this country has—for the most part—been a story of growth and progress.

In addition to increasing the number of students and expanding the years they spend in schools, the educational system was also viewed as an instrument to deal with a variety of national crises. In fact, in the last two centuries, schools have not only dealt with a variety of crises, but frequently those crises became something of the purpose of education. For example, during the nineteenth century, the public schools in this country received the bulk of the task of putting together into one society and one culture the various ethnic groups that had migrated here.

During those times when the peace of the nation seemed to be at risk, schools were often seen as defense fortresses. For example, during the Cold War of the late fifties and early sixties, following the Soviet Union's launching of Sputnik I, the first man-made earth satellite, schools in this country became one of the focal points of national defense.

PRESENT PROBLEMS

This history of schools is valuable for us to understand what is happening to American schools as we near the end of the twentieth century. In recent years, in the midst of a rather lengthy period of national peace and prosperity, there is a growing dissatisfaction with the educational system in this country. Almost every day newspaper articles, television specials, and other forms of media draw attention to the inadequacies. We quote test scores. We compare ourselves to a system of the past. We compare ourselves to other systems in other countries. We search for our failures with such diligence that it would seem that we really do not want to believe in our educational system.

Proposed Purpose of Schools

Part of the problem is a confusion over the purpose of education. With no more students to be added to the system and no immediate national crisis to solve, what exactly is the purpose of education and—more specifically—the operational purpose of schools?

Many people are trying to answer the question, but that is part of the problem too. We have too many answers. Let's examine some of those proposals.

CULTURAL TRANSMISSION

Many people tell us that the chief purpose of schools is for the older generation to transmit to the younger generation the culture of this country. These people would define an educated person as the one who could locate France on a map of Europe or name several Shakespearian plays. They are shocked and discouraged when young people graduate from school and cannot do this.

Of course, as we begin to think of cultural transmission as an educational purpose, we do need to ask at least two basic questions: (1) Whose culture is worth knowing? and (2) Can we expect our young people to learn everything we learned when we were in school, plus everything the world has learned since we were in school? In other words, as a parent, would you prefer that your child study the causes of the French Revolution or the operations of a computer?

BUILD THE LABOR FORCE

Many people tell us that the purpose of schools is to build a labor force. We must compete with the Japanese and other countries for the world market. To do this, we must have young people coming out of the schools who can work effectively in American industry.

The labor force advocates tell us that it is not so important for our students to memorize the names of Shakespeare's plays as it is for them to learn to think critically and solve problems. Thus, the school curriculum and methodology ought to center on problem-solving activities.

SOCIETAL HEALER

Still others tell us that the schools should assume the role of healing the social diseases of our society. Schools must focus attention on such problems as drug abuse and AIDS. These advocates have been so successful that in many places, students now spend several hours a week learning how to deal with these social problems.

THE RELIGIOUS PURPOSE

On the other hand, there are those people who believe that education is still basically religious in nature—that the purpose of school is to study the work of God as creator, to see the hand of God at work in the human story, and to stand in awe of His presence.

OTHER VIEWS

Some people believe education should produce effective citizens in a democracy, or that it should produce moral beings. The list goes on, but we will stop here because this much of the listing does illustrate the point. We Americans are confused about what schools are supposed to be doing. If we asked one hundred people, we might get one hundred different ideas.

THE REAL ISSUE

Perhaps our impulsive response is to say that schools ought to be doing it all, but that's the problem. These purposes are not mutually inclusive, and some are contradictory. If we emphasize building a labor force, we will not have as much time to ask a student to remember the dates of the Civil War. If we require a student to spend five hours a week studying AIDS, he will not be able to read as many novels.

In this dilemma is the importance of the Moses mandate. Amid this rampant confusion about what schools are supposed to be doing, and this growing dissatisfaction with what they are doing, it is imperative that parents develop a clear understanding of what an education is, what they want their children to receive, and what is the best method to go about getting this. In the midst of all the confusion, it is imperative that parents synthesize the schooling experiences of their children.

In other words, the parent mandate is not easy. It has never been easy, but in recent years, as the schooling picture has grown increasingly complex, the mandate has become more difficult. And as the growing climate has grown increasingly precocious, the pressure on parents to know something about schools, their own children, and their expectations is not only necessary but imperative.

In the midst of this pressure, perhaps it would help for parents to identify their responsibility by asking three specific questions.

1. Which schooling opportunity is appropriate for a family?
2. What must parents do to help the child receive the best possible education from the school of their choice?
3. What are the limitations of the schooling experience in the child's development? Let's examine each of those questions.

WHICH SCHOOLING OPPORTUNITY IS APPROPRIATE FOR A FAMILY?

This question is based on the reality of choice. Although there is much talk about something called a public school monopoly, many parents do have some choice in picking an educational setting. We could wish that we had more choices or that the present alternatives to public schools did not come with built-in inconveniences and even sacrifices, but there are still some alternatives that could allow parents to make choices.

For simplicity, we will group those available choices into three general categories—public schools, Christian schools, and home schools.

It would make this matter of choice even simpler if we could just compile a list of advantages and disadvantages of each of those choices so that caring parents could study the list in light of their family situations and make an intelligent and easy decision.

But it is not just difficult, it is impossible to make such a list. There are two reasons for this. For one thing, every school is different. No two public schools are alike. No two Christian schools are alike. No two home schools are exactly alike. Every school has its own personality, its own strengths and weaknesses. There are simply no generalizations that can accurately describe every schooling situation in these categories.

The work of evaluating a particular schooling opportunity must go beyond generalization and must examine the specifics.

By the same reasoning, no two families are alike. Every family is different and has different needs. In some families, one school would be the right choice, but it may be completely wrong for the family next door. Thus, each set of parents must not only know the condition of the available schools but must analyze those schools in reference to the family situation.

Because we cannot compile a list of specific advantages and disadvantages, perhaps we can at least begin to simplify that significant decision by identifying four factors that parents will want to consider as they exercise their right of choice.

FACTOR 1: PHILOSOPHY

This factor is listed first because it is the most important. There are probably some protests to that claim. Many people would ask, What does a philosophy have to do with the education of children? But as we learn throughout the literature of education, a good philosophy is essential to the day-by-day activities of schools.

Although some schools do not know it, every school has a philosophy. In other words, every school has an underlying basic idea upon which it begins to make decisions about such important topics as what constitutes a curriculum, how teachers should teach, and how students should be treated. It is from this basic idea that schools can begin to achieve consistency in the decision-making process.

Conscientious parents will want to know what that underlying idea is. In good schools, that philosophy should not be too hard to find. According to educational researchers, one of the characteristics of an effective school is a working philosophy or mission statement that can be identified and expressed by administrators, teachers, students, and even parents.

Obviously, schools do not always thoroughly achieve these expressed philosophies with all students or with all parents. But the important idea is that all the people at the school at least know what the school is trying to accomplish. This gives the whole enterprise of the school direction and consistency.

For these reasons, it is essential that parents examine the philosophy of each alternative. Of course to do this, the parents need to understand their own philosophies of education.

It is at this point that Christian parents will want to ask, "Is there such a thing as a Christian philosophy of education? After all, isn't math math, history history, PE PE? How would a different philosophical approach make any difference in the way children are taught something like the multiplication tables?"

Although the difference may be subtle and difficult to ascertain, there is nevertheless a difference. One example would be the source of knowledge.

For our purpose, we will define knowledge as the recorded observations about the world and world events. For the purpose of teaching convenience, we divide those observations into categories such as science, math, and history, and we teach the children such things as the parts of the human body, $2+2=4$, and that the first-century Romans were self-sufficient and arrogant.

But underneath these specific observations is the idea that there is some reason behind these facts—somewhere all this knowledge started, in some form all these events took place. In other words, if we are going to study about the creation, we need to understand something about the Creator. We need to know there is a source for all knowledge.

Jesus gave Thomas an important lesson when He told him, "I am the way and the truth and the life" (John 14:6). But as the account continues, we realize that Thomas did not learn the lesson until he stood in the presence of Christ resurrected. It is at this moment that his learning was completed, and he could only say, "My Lord and my God!" (John 20:28).

When the teacher teaches $2+2=4$, he is attempting to give the students a necessary tool for surviving in the world. But beyond the tool is the idea of created coherence and beauty. In the mind and life of the student, the lesson is not complete until it reaches this insight. If the teaching philosophy of the school does not carry the lesson this far, parents themselves will need to know where the lesson ends and where their work as synthesizer and extrapolator begins.

This is how a philosophy works in the educational arena and why it is the most important aspect of a school choice.

The obvious question here is, "If this is how it works, don't Christian schools have a natural advantage over public schools in the area of philosophy?" It would seem on the surface that this would be true, but it is not always. Unfortunately, some Christian schools have not identified a clear philosophy of education, and some Christian schools may have an educational purpose that some parents would not accept. Again, this is a family concern.

The next obvious question about philosophy is how it relates to a home school. The answer is that a clear, identifiable philosophy of education is as vital to a successful home school as to any other educational setting. Before families move into a home school project, they must come to grips with the profound philosophical questions of how children learn, what is worth knowing, and what is the purpose of education. Without answering these questions first, the families simply cannot consistently answer the subsequent questions such as, Which curriculum to use? and, How much time is spent in study?

FACTOR 2: COMMUNITY

This factor is listed second because it is second in importance. Although learning is an extremely private and personal enterprise, in almost all formal educational settings it occurs in a community of people. Even in home schools where the community may consist only of family members, there is, nevertheless, a community.

At the same time that the learning is working in a community, we know that people learn more effectively when they feel comfortable, safe, and happy. Because of all this, the community plays a significant role in the quality of education that a student receives.

To analyze and choose the appropriate community, parents will want to consider three groups, or we might say three specific communities: the community of students, the community of teachers, and the community of other parents.

The community of students. Most parents live in constant fear of a rather unidentifiable generalization called peer pressure. In almost all the literature, we have been reminded or warned about the role of friendships in child and adolescent development.

Caring parents are concerned about their children's choice of friends and the kind of pressure applied by the community of peers. Although there is no research to attest to this, this is probably why many parents have chosen to send their children to Christian schools. There is obviously some thought that peer pressure in a Christian setting is different from peer pressure in a public school. This is also probably a significant factor in why some families opt for home schools. But in making this decision, parents need to consider two basic factors.

First, what is the role of socialization? Some educators and parents alike believe that socialization is one of the basic purposes of school experience. They maintain that students need to learn to associate with one another, to play together, and work together. In recent years, the demand for socialization has become so strong that one of the most popular new teaching techniques is something called cooperative learning—the practice of putting students together in small groups to let them learn in an actual community setting.

Parents in the process of making choices about schools must decide the value of socialization. They must also decide the value of diversity in the socialization process.

Is it valuable for children or adolescents to associate or to learn to work cooperatively with people from different ethnic backgrounds, different religious backgrounds, and different economic backgrounds? This question is one of the most significant questions parents must answer as they exercise choice.

Second, what is the role of the Christian testimony? Some parents, educators, and even students see the public schools as a great mission field, and they feel that Christian students can have a powerful witness in that setting. There is, in fact, some solid evidence in many communities to support this idea. There are several stories of the outreach success of school-based Bible studies, of the effectiveness of Christian students witnessing to their friends and even their teachers, and of the role of Christian youth organizations that work in public schools.

On the other hand, parents will still want to be conscious of two important questions: At what age is a person old enough to become a missionary? Is my child strong enough in his own basic convictions to combat the power of peer pressure?

The community of teachers. Despite the concern about programs, curricula, or school policies, the teacher is still the most significant feature of the educational system. Since this idea will be discussed later in this chapter, it is important here to remember that this is one of the basic factors of parent choice. The question parents need to ask is evident: Who teaches my child? From that are generated the other questions: What does this person believe? Does this person enjoy children? Is this person knowledgeable in the subject matter? Is this the kind of person I want influencing my child?

A school that puts more emphasis on curriculum or building programs than it does on the quality of its teaching staff is to be considered with caution.

The community of parents. In short, parents of a specific school must meet and mingle sometime. The questions parents will want to ask is simple: Are these the kinds of people I enjoy being around? Actually, this question is quite important because the more parents meet and mingle, the more the elements of the school turn into a community, and the more effective the educational program will be.

FACTOR 3: PROGRAMS

Just as people differ in their gifts and abilities and their educational needs, schools differ in their offerings and strengths. Parents need to be wise in helping to match their children's needs with what a school offers.

In some situations, this becomes a factor of common sense. For example, if a student has some sort of impairment such as a physical or learning disability, the family will want to search for the school with the best program to meet that special need.

By the same reasoning, if a child has a special ability to play a musical instrument, the family will probably want to consider the school that offers the opportunity. If the child is a talented long-distance runner, the family may want to consider a school that has a cross-country program.

Sometimes a student's special abilities become a factor in educational needs. For example, some people have a special ability to master words; so they read words, write words, and think words. Obviously, they need to attend a school that offers them the opportunity to develop the interest and ability. Not only will they then get the intensity they need, but they will be happier in the pursuit.

FACTOR 4: RESULTS

As families seek the appropriate educational setting, they will want to consider the results of a specific school. Schooling is, of course, a process, and it is important to examine the process; but it is more than that.

Schooling is also preparation, and the results of the process must be a significant factor in the choice.

Some of the results of a specific school are easy to identify. Scores on such tests as the ACT or the SAT or other standardized instruments provide some information about what is happening at a specific school. Other concrete pieces of information such as how many graduates attended college and what they majored in should also be available.

But there is more that goes on at a school and more results at the end than what is measured with test scores and concrete data. As the family makes a choice, it will want to consider some of that information as well. Such questions as how much the graduates enjoyed the school and the kind of loyalty they have toward the school will indicate the impact the education has had on their development as persons.

Such intangible information is more important than what is revealed in test scores.

What Must the Parents Do to Help the Child Receive the Best Possible Education from the School of Their Choice?

After the family has chosen the appropriate school to meet the family needs, it has only begun to fulfill the Moses mandate. It is important that people understand this. Too often parents say, "I've made the sacrifices to send my children to the right school. Now the rest of it is up to them."

But putting children in the right school is only the proper beginning. Regardless of what school the child is in, the parents still must be active in making sure education takes place.

To analyze what they should do, parents need to come to grips with three major educational principles.

PRINCIPLE 1

First, the public schools are designed to be local enterprises. Regardless of all our talk about bureaucracy, state laws, and federal decisions, public schools are still supposed to be at the hands of local control and input. In other words, if one does not like what is happening, he should be able to do something about it.

As individuals concerned about schools, we must come to some kind of terms with this concept. We often speak of a public school monopoly, but the idea of monopoly implies one board of directors, one C.E.O., and one corporate purpose.

The school system was never designed to be a monopoly. It was designed to be run by local people to meet local needs. That structure is still implicit in the system. If the school system is not working this way, then we need to examine our own efforts to be involved positively in making the local system work. By the nature of the structure of the system, we should have an opportunity for input.

Doing this really is not such a mystery. The most obvious technique, and one that is available to everybody, is to show up at school once in a while. Even if you are not a parent of school-age children, there are still ample invitations and opportunities. Attend open houses, parent conferences, extracurricular events, and forum discussions. This is not really just a nice suggestion; this is a must. Schools schedule these events for a definite purpose. The quality of the school depends on the parents' participation. When you take advantage of the opportunities to attend school functions, you not only help the students get a better education, but you also contribute to the quality of the whole school.

We do not have much right to complain about what is happening in our schools if we do not go when we are invited.

Other than that, there are other methods of becoming involved in school business at even deeper levels. Although many of the decisions about curriculum and policy do seem to come from state and even federal sources, there are still quite significant decisions made at the local level by school boards and various committees composed of people just like us, common citizens who are interested enough in their children's education to become involved in the process.

Because school board meetings are open to the public (except on some rare occasions), the first step is to call the school, find out when the next meeting is scheduled, and attend. Again, we do not have the right to complain until we have at least become familiar with the process of how decisions are made.

Another method of school participation is to volunteer services. If a parent or any other person is critically interested in the quality of education, he could spend a couple hours a week involved in the process. Most schools have some kind of volunteer program where they try to recruit people to work with special students, supervise playground or lunch room, work with reading groups, or whatever.

In order for schools to continue to function as local enterprises, they must have local participation.

PRINCIPLE 2

Second, for the student, the essence of the educational system is the classroom teacher.

We are critically interested in school policies, curriculum, textbooks, and facilities, and it is appropriate that we should be interested in those things.

But for the student, the major force of educational quality and opportunity is one classroom teacher. Regardless of what the policies dictate or the textbooks offer, if the teacher is courteous and organized, our children get a good education. On the other hand, if the teacher is burned out, tired, insecure, or arrogant, our children will struggle.

We do not want to underestimate the value of pleasant working conditions, adequate resources, and community interest in what teachers do. But the reality is that twenty years from now, the children will still remember the names of their teachers and their teachers' personalities long after they have forgotten the names and content of the textbooks.

Thus, if we want to evaluate schools, we evaluate teachers. If we want to make a contribution to education, we make a contribution to teachers.

This is actually a reassuring point for people who care about the way our children are educated. It gives direction to our interests and efforts.

Based on the reality of the role of the teacher in the process, there are some definite and rather simple techniques for a parent to know in order to have a positive impact on education.

Know the teachers. This is one of the simplest, more inexpensive, and most positive ways to interact with schools. There is a rule of thumb that merits attention. Teachers do a better job of teaching when they know the parents, know the parents' expectations, and know that parents care.

Take every opportunity you can to support teachers. I realize that all professions have inherent problems, but a teacher is unique in that the profession demands (of the good teacher, at least) so much emotional involvement, and the teacher rarely gets to see the finished product. Everything is always in process. One way that we can help teachers do their work better is to give them some encouragement along the way.

Again, the methods are not all that complex. If you ever catch a teacher doing something right, write that teacher a note. Support your church in having a teacher appreciation day.

Encourage Christian young people to enter the profession. Recent statistics tell us that we could be facing a rather severe teacher shortage within the next few years. Almost half the present teacher force is nearing retirement age, and fewer young people are showing interest in entering the profession. This is an excellent time to enter the educational picture in the most strategic spot—by becoming a teacher.

PRINCIPLE 3

Third, the American educational system is one of second chances. For all of our faults and for all of the ways our system does not seem to measure up to systems of other countries, the one factor that makes our system unique is that we never give up on anyone. Young people can goof up somewhere in the process and still have an opportunity to continue their education afterward.

Some may question this characteristic as one of the strengths. Could we not have a more efficient system if we would eliminate those who are not motivated?

But this characteristic serves as reassurance for so many parents. We do not have to shuffle our children around to try to get them into the right kindergarten. We do not have to give up on a child just because he happens to have lower marks in elementary school. We do not have to discard a child just because he has a learning disability. We do not have to discourage a child's ambitions just because he scores low on an intelligence test. Our educational opportunities are available to everyone who cares enough to take advantage of them.

WHAT ARE THE LIMITATIONS OF THE SCHOOLING EXPERIENCE IN THE CHILD'S DEVELOPMENT?

The parent has the primary responsibility for educating the child. Of course, this is a repetition of the opening point, but it needs to be repeated here as one of the strengths of our system. Because the parent is the primary educator, the school—whether it is a public school or a Christian school—is only a helper in the process. To ensure that our children get the most from the schooling experience, we must come to some understanding of what schools are designed to do and what they cannot do. In many areas, schools have failed to meet the expectations placed on them because the expectations have simply been too great.

WHAT SCHOOLS CANNOT DO

Let's consider some aspects of child rearing that schools are simply not designed to handle effectively.

Schools cannot give children a moral sense. Schools are designed to teach facts and ideas. Teachers prepare the lessons, make assignments, and give tests on facts and ideas. They function best when they teach facts and ideas. When schools reach into the topics of moral concern, such as drug abuse or human sexuality, they usually address these issues with facts and ideas. Information is valuable, but information is not a moral sense. If a child is going to learn proper respect for his body or the virtues of discipline, integrity, and righteousness, he probably will not learn them from the facts in a school course. There has to be something that takes this information and turns it into applied behavior. Most of us learn to apply the information by watching examples. And that is the role of parents, Sunday school teachers, and adults they meet. Most people will, as adults, have about the same moral codes as their own parents had, regardless of where they went to school.

Schools cannot give a child clear insight into his worth. This presents a rather interesting dilemma. The child's ability to function in school and to learn is largely dependent on his ability to think that he is capable of learning. In other words, he needs to have some sense of his own personal worth. But for most children, schools are not too good in producing this sense of worth. They often use some form of competition to accomplish the goal.

So this is another role for parents and churches, to help children come to a clear sense of how they were made and their unique role in creation and in the eyes of the Creator. This is the appropriate source of self-worth.

As concerned citizens. we are often concerned about defenses against such things as humanism and New Age, but the starting place is with self-worth. If our children are confident about who they are and about their relationships with God, they will not be so easily prone to fall into the traps of humanistic thinking.

Schools cannot give the child all the personal attention he needs for his educational development. This is a simple matter of arithmetic and logic. If the child is going to be a good reader, he must read somewhere other than at school. In the early stages, he needs to have someone to listen to him and encourage him. The teacher simply cannot give that child as much attention as he needs. Thus, the family becomes involved in the process of helping the child learn to read, to write, to work arithmetic, or to function as a student.

But this is a refreshing point as well. By asking parents to help their children with their studies, they should have just one more point of contact with them, one more reference point, one more place where parents touch the child's life, one more place where parents fulfill the mandate Moses spoke for us years ago.

FOR FURTHER READING

Adler, Mortimer J. *The Paideia Proposal: An Educational Manifesto.* New York: Macmillan, 1982.

Ballmann, Ray E. *The How and Why of Home Schooling.* Westchester, Ill.: Crossway, 1987.

Gaebelein, Frank E. *The Pattern of God's Truth.* Chicago: Moody, 1968.

Kienel, Paul A., ed. *The Philosophy of Christian School Education.* Whittier, Calif.: Association of Christian Schools International, 1978. Available from the publisher: P.O. Box 4097, Whittier, CA 90607.

Moore, Raymond and Dorothy. *Homespun Schools.* Waco, Tex.: Word, 1987.

National Commission on Excellence in Education. *A Nation at Risk: The Imperative for Educational Reform.* Washington, D.C.: United States Government, 1983.

Peterson, Michael L. *Philosophy of Education.* Downers Grove, Ill.: InterVarsity, 1986.

Schimmels, Cliff. *A Parent's Guide to the Elementary Years.* Elgin, Ill.: David C. Cook, 1989.

————. *A Parent's Guide to the First Three Years.* Elgin, Ill.: David C. Cook, 1989.

————. *Parents' Most Asked Questions About Kids and Schools.* Wheaton, Ill.: Victor, 1989.

40

Robert A. Barron

Parachurch Educational Organizations

PARACHURCH ORGANIZATIONS MINISTERING IN CHRISTIAN EDUCATION
- **Parachurch movements are born in the heart of men and women**
- **God has not left His world without a witness**
- **Parachurch organizations meet a need**
- **Parachurch organizations are an extension into fields where the church cannot go or has already gone**

Parachurch organizations are here to stay, although there is a debate as to their integral part in the local church. Such organizations as Awana Clubs International, Pioneer Clubs, and Youth For Christ have had a major impact upon the Christian education ministry of the local church and the church worldwide. Vic Glavach and Milford S. Sholund expressed it well:

> Parachurch youth movements are an evidence that God is no respecter of churches per se. These organizations are an effort of individuals and groups of individuals to express the will of God, to desire to witness and work in response to God's call and the needs of others. Some have often sensed a vacuum in the vitality and vision of churches. Others have recognized the limitations of the institutions and have sought to overcome these limitations. The parachurch youth movement is, in a sense, a phe-

ROBERT A. BARRON, M.A., is professor of Christian education, Moody Bible Institute, Chicago, Illinois.

nomenon among churches in a nation that has provided a congenial setting for religious freedom. It is not meant to rival the institution but to be an extension into fields where the institution cannot go or has not gone, much as the missionary is an extension of the domestic institutional church.[1]

The word *para* in Greek means "alongside." The term *parachurch* within the confines of this chapter will refer to organizations that are working "alongside the church" as not-for-profit organizations. As we will note later, these organizations serve in three distinct areas of ministry.

The development of parachurch organizations came about in response to need. Although the local church has sought to meet the needs of its constituents, it has not always done so. In some cases the church has militated against the establishment of new programs. One such case was that of the Sunday school, which was once the foremost parachurch movement.

Edwin Rice, noted authority on the Sunday school movement states:

> The churches not being ready for such a movement, it was practically necessary to establish it on a voluntary and union basis. Rooms were hired for holding its schools in rented halls. . . . Denominational organizations were jealous of their prerogatives. At first, therefore, this new scheme was rejected by the churches, though accepted by individuals. . . . It thus became a movement sustained by laymen.[2]

The Sunday school movement—like so many movements—was born in the hearts and minds of men and women who were distinct from the clergy.

"God has not left His church and His world without a witness. What the Lord could not get done through the formal, organized channels of the Protestant church organization He was pleased to do in a measure through parachurch movements."[3]

The major thrust of this chapter is to expose the Christian educator to the dynamics of various parachurch organizations and show how some minister directly within the confines of the local church, whereas others reach into areas that the church has not been able to penetrate. And then there are those who serve as a support ministry to the local church.

CHURCH-SPONSORED CHILDREN AND YOUTH ORGANIZATIONS

AWANA CLUBS INTERNATIONAL

Founded in 1950, Awana Clubs International is totally administered and operated by the local church leadership. Awana is a service organization that pro-

---

1. Vic Glavach and Milford S. Sholund, "Parachurch Youth Movements and Organizations," in *Youth Education in the Church*, ed. Roy B. Zuck and Warren S. Benson (Chicago: Moody, 1978), p. 374.
2. Ibid., p. 375.
3. Ibid., p. 377.

vides training materials, club supplies, and any assistance through its staff and missionaries. Awana Clubs is designed for three- and four-year-old preschoolers through high school teens.

The Awana objectives are twofold:

> To recruit as many young people (including children) as possible from the community so that they might hear the gospel of God's grace and come to know Christ as their personal Savior.

> Second, to prepare children and youth to accept the challenge of spreading the gospel through leadership, service, and witness.[4]

Although Awana has many things to interest the youth of our culture, such as games and special activities, the emphasis of the program is Bible memory. Clubber handbooks contain an average of ninety verses that have been carefully chosen in order to establish doctrinal truths. Properly taught by Awana leadership, these verses can be applied to the daily life experiences of the clubbers.

Unlike other club programs, Awana emphasizes competitive games that are a "vital nutrient in the child's physical and mental growth." Sportsmanship, fellowship, and friendship are emphasized in the Awana game period. Games provide a strong motivation toward achievement. "Psychologists tell us that our attitude and environment can directly affect our ability to learn and retain what we learn. In other words, things learned in an enjoyable experience will be more likely to 'stick.' Games provide this environment and can help to produce a favorable attitude."[5] Unique to Awana is the four-team competition and the Awana game floor plan, which is outlined in detail in the Basic Training Manual.

A strong emphasis is placed on the uniforms and awards, which are designed to motivate the memorization of Scripture. Uniforms have a unifying and disciplinary benefit to the clubs. The leader and clubber tend to develop a closer relationship through the wearing of a uniform.

A two-year Cubbies program is designed for three- and four-year-old preschoolers. It includes awards, Bible memorization, handbooks, and stimulating activities. Noncompetitive games are designed to develop motor skills appropriate for this age. Cubbies study basic Bible truths along with popular preschool concepts of colors, shapes, numbers, and letters. Material especially lends itself to parental guidance and involvement.

The five separate kindergarten through sixth grade clubs—Sparkies, boys and girls grades K-2; Pals and Chums, boys and girls grades 3-4; Pioneers and Guards, boys and girls grades 5-6—are organized on a three-part meeting plan: game time, handbook time, and council time. Each club uses its own handbooks, emblems, and achievement awards.

4. *Awana Overview* (Streamwood, Ill.: Awana Clubs International, 1984), p. 5.
5. Ibid., pp. 7-8.

Awana is more than a children's program. Emphasis is placed on a ministry to junior highers through the Junior Varsity program, which is designed especially for seventh and eighth graders. Although some of the elements of the younger clubs are evident, materials and methodology are geared to the spiritual and intellectual level of the junior high student. Junior highers wear a more casual sports-style uniform shirt, and work in loose-leaf manuals.

The Varsity program is designed for the senior high student. Lifeline, one aspect of the program, is the weekly activity that provides an enjoyable time of fun for both the saved and unsaved in a nonthreatening environment for the gospel.

Pathway is a self-study devotional booklet that is specifically designed for Christian growth and serves as a transition into the Alpha Kappa Chi (AKX) program. The AKX Bible study program is designed to provide leadership training for the spiritually mature teen.

Awana recommends that all leaders study the Training Manual. However, Awana missionaries are available to assist local churches with various training sessions. Leadership training conferences are also provided in various areas of the country.

Special programs such as area-wide Olympic competition between clubs, Bible quizzing, grand prix races, and scholarship camps are just a few of the many extracurricular activities provided by the Awana missionaries.

Awana missionary outreach around the world is supported by local churches and clubs which have become part of the Adopt-A-Club program. Awana clubbers are presented with a worldview and the necessity of foreign missions by giving financially through the Adopt-A-Club program and by praying for the salvation of children around the world.

CHRISTIAN SERVICE BRIGADE

The mission of Christian Service Brigade is to promote fathering among men by equipping them in their roles as parents, as active Christian influences to youth, and as Christlike examples to other men.

Since 1937, Christian Service Brigade has mobilized men to reach boys with the gospel message. It has trained men for leadership roles in Brigade programs and has created a network of committed men who are involved in ministry. These men have devoted themselves to evangelism and personal discipleship among boys of all ages. Brigade's goal is to assist fathers and all Christian men in fulfilling the biblical mandate of fatherhood.

To accomplish this goal, the Brigade ministry utilizes the following strategies: (1) challenging the church and Christian men to take fathering seriously, (2) developing programs for churches to get fathers involved with their children, (3) conducting special activities for fathers and their children, (4) establishing training seminars for men to improve their parenting skills, and (5) forming support groups for men.[6]

Local churches can choose from five programs for ministry with children and youth.

1. *Tadpoles* (ages 2-5). Tadpoles is a father-preschooler program that includes nature-related activities, physical fitness exercises, Bible stories, and father discussion topics.

2. *Tree Climbers* (grades 1-2/ages 6-7). Men and boys play games, enjoy a constructive project, focus on a Bible verse, and listen to a story with a biblical truth.

3. *Stockade* (grades 3-6/ages 8-11). Boys interact with Christian men who develop friendships in order to introduce them to Christ and encourage them toward Christian manhood.

4. *Battalion* (grades 6-12/ages 12-18). Every Battalion unit is directed by a leadership team made up of Christian men and teenagers. Often the men are fathers of the boys in the group and thus become a role model to them and other boys. The Word of God is integrated throughout the program and relates God's truth to all areas of a boy's life and interests.

5. *Man-to-Man* (18 years and over). This program is for men who wish to grow in Christ, develop close fellowship with other men, and reach out to others in Christ's name. Evangelism is an important goal of Man-to-Man as unchurched men are invited to discover how Christ can transform their lives.[7]

Christian Service Brigade sponsors regional Brigade Camps, which operate as an extension of the local church programs and are geared toward man-boy relationships.

The following resources are available for men involved in the above programs and other interested fathers and church leaders: *Brigade Leader*, a quarterly magazine for Christian men; *On the Father Front*, a quarterly newsletter on fathering issues; *Venture*, a bimonthly Christian magazine for boys; *Man-to-Man*, a quarterly newsletter for men in small groups; *Parenting Together*, a newsletter for single parents and church members with a concern for single-parent families.[8]

PIONEER CLUBS

Pioneer Clubs provides a ministry to children and youth of the local church ranging in age from two years old through senior high school. First founded in 1939 as a girls' club, in 1981 a change in outreach took place as a boys' ministry was added to the program, thus their name changed from Pioneer Girls to Pioneer Clubs. Pioneer Clubs has seven separate programs that cover a wide range of skill and interest areas from artistry and computer fun to camping. Weekly plan books are available for the leader that provide complete meeting plans, including Bible exploration, Bible memory, singing, games, and activity awards.

6. Correspondence from Paul H. Heidebrecht, vice-president of program development, Christian Service Brigade, Wheaton, Ill., June 21, 1990.
7. Fact Sheet (Wheaton, Ill.: Christian Service Brigade).
8. Correspondence from Paul H. Heidebrecht.

The junior high and senior high programs have some unique features. The Challenger program provides activity and awards with junior highers in mind. A special feature is numerous meaningful service opportunities.

The senior highers have the opportunity to be involved in an assistant Leader-in-Training course. While working directly with younger children in club and Sunday school, they develop valuable leadership skills.

Pioneer Clubs materials allow each church the option of having separate clubs for boys and girls or to run the programs as coed clubs. Another option is the use of uniforms and awards. Although uniforms and awards are suggested in the club supply catalog, little emphasis is placed upon their use.

The club program can be conducted anytime during the week. However, many clubs meet on a weeknight while adults participate in choir practice, prayer meeting, or Bible studies. If this time schedule is not the best option, clubs can be conducted after school, on Saturday morning, or on Sunday evening.

Weekly meeting plans provide enough materials for a one-and-a-half to two hour program. Materials can be easily expanded or condensed to meet the need of the local church. The curriculum is so designed that it can be conducted in the church or in the home.

An extension of the church program is conducted during the summer through the ministry of Camp Cherith (twenty-eight total camps) under the direction of Pioneer Clubs, with leadership from local churches.

The mission of Pioneer Clubs is to help children and youth put Christ in every phase of life, form healthy relationships, and develop positive feelings about themselves.[9]

The goals of Pioneer Clubs are fourfold:

1. To enable children to enter into a personal relationship with Christ and to know His Word.
2. To enable children to form healthy relationships.
3. To enable children to grow as whole persons.
4. To enable adults to understand children and help them develop.[10]

A biblically sound philosophy of Christian education is advocated by Pioneer Clubs, from believing in the uniqueness and dignity of each child to balancing a club curriculum that is child-centered and content-centered. A sound educational psychology of learning and an extensive statement of faith is presented in the Club Coordinator's Manual.

The best way to learn more about Pioneer Clubs is to write for the Let's Get Started Kit, which is complete with sample curriculum, audio-visual, and step-by-step guide.

9. *Club Coordinator's Manual* (Wheaton, Ill.: Pioneer Clubs, 1988).
10. Ibid., p. 4. Correspondence from Virginia Patterson, Ed.D., president, Pioneer Clubs, Wheaton, Ill.: June 20, 1990.

WORD OF LIFE CLUBS

Local church managed and administered, Word of Life Clubs offer a well balanced program of practical and meaningful Bible studies, fun-filled activities, evangelism of the unsaved, and Christian service.

Word of Life Clubs were founded in 1946 and minister to three age groups: Olympians (6-11), Teen Clubs for junior and senior highers, and Fellowship Ministries for young adults.

The philosophy of Word of Life Clubs is "to help gospel preaching churches build a strong and dynamic soul-winning youth ministry." After salvation, Word of Life curriculum seeks to establish "Godly ideals" in the minds of Olympians by teaching Bible character surveys on the life of Christ, David, Elijah, and Paul. Book surveys, daily Quiet Time Adventure, and Scripture memory are part of the six-year study cycle. Godly habits in minds of teens are established by dealing with such doctrinal studies as the "Greatness of God," "The Believer and God," "Future Events," and various topical studies.

Emphasis on a daily quiet time, reading of Christian books, evangelistic activities, and faithfulness to the local church are part of the Fellowship Ministries study cycle. "Godly goals" in the lives of the young adult are brought about through the study of various doctrinal subjects such as "Man, Sin, and Salvation," "Angels and Satan," and "Future Events." Book, topical, and character studies are also part of the study cycle.

Because young people need incentives to be motivated, Word of Life Clubs provides the "Discipleship in Action" program, which includes various scholarship programs. By establishing patterns of "Godly living," which include Bible study, quiet time, service, and so on, a financial scholarship can be earned toward a college education at a Christian school or a week at Word of Life Island in Schroon Lake, New York.

Joint evangelistic efforts between clubs from sponsoring churches are conducted. Such events, called "Round-ups," consist of the following activities: "Midnight Madness," "Basketball Marathon," "Volleyball Marathon," and "Super Bowls."

Leadership training consists of an orientation program that involves listening to training cassette tapes and working through a leader's manual, and personalized training from the local area's missionary. Youth leadership seminars, conferences, and periodic visitation by the Word of Life area missionary are all a part of the leadership training program. Throughout the club year a Word of Life missionary will teach such subjects as time management, goal setting, feeding yourself spiritually, and other areas of Christian living in special area leadership training conferences.[11]

---

11. Miscellaneous published promotional materials (Schroon Lake, N.Y.: Word of Life Clubs). Correspondence from Frank Roe, Area Representative, Word of Life Clubs, Winfield, Ill., June 25, 1990.

YOUTH ORGANIZATIONS THAT SERVE AS A SUPPORT
MINISTRY TO THE LOCAL CHURCH

SONLIFE

Founded in 1984, a distinctive of Sonlife is that it is not a program but a strategy that places discipleship and evangelism at the heart of all that is done in the local church youth ministry. Believing that some of Christ's initial disciples could have been teens, Sonlife seeks to model its ministry after that of Christ.

A second distinctive of Sonlife is that of "building discipling ministries." Sonlife's definition of discipling ministry is: "Ministering to all individuals at their level of spiritual interest."

A third distinctive is that of equipping leadership. Sonlife trains leadership in the local church to build discipling ministries. Resources are designed to equip student, volunteer, and pastoral/leadership teams.[12]

Sonlife sponsors seminars for youth pastors, lay leaders, and student leaders. The Sonlife Strategy Seminar consists of eleven hours of training at which time Sonlife's strategy of evangelism and discipleship for youth in the local church are presented. The strategy seminars are offered on various dates and at different locations across the country.

Advanced seminars provide the following: the opportunity for deeper discussions and planning of ministry, the opportunity for alumni to apply Sonlife principles to their unique situations, and the setting of long-range goals. Ministry assessments and the development of discipleship skills are discussed with Sonlife staff members.

Advanced Seminar II is expanded upon in the yearly Sonlife "Ongoing Ministry Team" conference. Graduates of this seminar are awarded a certificate and given the opportunity to become a Sonlife resource person in their local area of ministry.

Foundations is an eight-hour supplement to the Sonlife Strategy Seminar. This companion seminar helps the volunteer leader to interact with key students on beginning a discipling priority. The training is biblically based, principle oriented, and team applied. Foundations includes ideas and resource information for a strong ministry base.

Youth Discipleship Institutes (YDIs) are developed for personal training or group training in the local church setting. Each series of YDIs provides a variety of subjects along with teaching resources such as videos, cassette tapes, workbooks, action sheets, and discussion guides. Some of the subjects covered in the YDI format are: Principles of Ministry, Principles of Programming, Principles of Outreach, Principles of Ministry Teams, and Principles of Contacting and Relationships.[13]

---

12. *Overview of the SonLife Strategy* (Chicago: SonLife).
13. *SonLife Training Opportunities* (Chicago: SonLife).

Sonlife can be considered as a support group for a local church youth ministry as it seeks to implement a common strategy among youth and church leadership.

YOUTH SPECIALITIES MINISTRIES

> Things are changing so rapidly in youth culture—styles, languages, values, influences. It's hard to keep up, let alone prepare for what lies ahead. And teenagers of the 90's and beyond will be unlike any other generation. The pressures and obstacles they'll face are unique—and potentially deadly. Dysfunction. Family. Stress. Sex. Alcohol. Suicide. The statistics are alarming. The problems are real. More than ever, kids need the hope and love of Jesus Christ.[14]

Youth Specialities Ministries was founded in 1968 and considers itself to be a support ministry to help youth workers (both volunteers and professionals) be prepared to deal with the problems as mentioned above that are typical of the adolescent of today.

More than ninety Resource Seminars in as many cities are conducted each February through May across the country. The Resource Seminar for Youth Workers is a full day of "top-quality teaching and resources." In addition, Youth Specialties Ministries offers two five-day conventions in two key cities each fall. Nearly seventy elective seminars are packed into one day. Personal development and spiritual growth are addressed, as well as ministry development and teaching and programming. Such topics as "Reaching Unchurched Kids," "How Your Personality Affects Your Ministry," and "Teaching Sexuality to High-School Students" are discussed.[15]

As a support ministry, Youth Specialties publishes *Youthworker* journal, *The Door,* and *Youthworker Update.* Other resources consist of books, videos, cassette tapes, and the "Ideas Library," which provides hundreds of ideas for games, recreation, youth-group meetings, discussions, skits, and plays.

CHILDREN AND YOUTH ORGANIZATIONS
NOT UNDER LOCAL CHURCH SPONSORSHIP

CHILD EVANGELISM FELLOWSHIP, INC.

Child Evangelism Fellowship was founded in 1923 and is a service organization—an outreach of the local church. The purposes of Child Evangelism Fellowship are to reach children who are not being reached with the gospel message and to build up through a systematic teaching of God's Word those who have received Christ. The children are encouraged to attend church regular-

---

14. Miscellaneous published promotional material (El Cajon, Calif.: Youth Specialties Ministries, 1990).
15. National Youth Workers Convention brochure (El Cajon, Calif.: Youth Specialties Ministries, 1990).

ly and take an active interest in missions.

Child Evangelism Fellowship conducts Good News Clubs for children between the ages of four and twelve. These clubs meet in homes, community buildings, and occasionally in churches. They are conducted throughout the school year—once a week after school, in the evening, or on Saturday.

Born-again teachers who have a sincere concern and love for children and who are trained conduct the Good News Clubs. The program includes lively songs and choruses, Bible and missionary stories on the child's interest level, and Scripture memorization. Colorful visuals and review games make the club program appealing to today's child. The Child Evangelism Fellowship ministry stresses salvation by grace through faith in the Lord Jesus Christ. Many opportunities are given to receive Christ, grow spiritually, and serve Him.

Another ministry of Child Evangelism Fellowship, 5-Day Clubs, are conducted during the summer months. Children meet in backyards, vacant lots, and playgrounds for one hour each day for five consecutive days. A format similar to the Good News Clubs is followed.

Some of the teachers for 5-Day Clubs consist of senior high and college-age students, who, after successful completion of a ten- to fourteen-day training school, serve as summer missionaries in the United States and overseas.

Child Evangelism Fellowship also holds "released-time classes" in conjunction with public schools. In some school districts children are released early from classes, usually once a week for religious instruction (with permission from their parents) in a church or home setting. Hospital and fair ministries, day camps, and overnight camps along with 5-Day Clubs are conducted during the summer months.

Child Evangelism Fellowship is also a major force in world missions. More than 180 missionaries from the United States serve overseas along with 590 national workers and missionaries from other countries. More than two million children around the world have been reached with the gospel through this ministry.[16]

THE NAVIGATORS

Founded by Dawson Trotman, The Navigators began its ministry in the United States Navy in 1933. Bible study, prayer, and Scripture memorization were used to foster spiritual growth in order to fulfill the mission "To know Christ and to make Him known."

Throughout its ministry, The Navigators have been dispersed around the world as pastors, missionaries, businessmen, and teachers. Such organizations as Youth For Christ, Young Life, InterVarsity Christian Fellowship, and Campus Crusade for Christ were encouraged by Trotman to use the concepts of disci-

16. *Winning Children Around The World: Questions and Answers About Child Evangelism Fellowship* (Warrenton, Mo.: Child Evangelism Fellowship, Inc.).

pling to produce mature leadership. These concepts have also been taught in Bible institutes, seminaries, mission organizations, and local churches.[17]

Today, The Navigators is an international ministry. Serving in many countries around the world, The Navigators have been on the cutting edge of reaching traditionally difficult to reach cultures and peoples. A staff of almost three thousand is composed of forty-two nationalities, ministers in eighty-five languages, and serves in seventy-one countries. In order to minister to the many unreached people of the world, The Navigators have trained disciplemakers who use secular careers in foreign countries as a springboard to share their faith.

The Navigators sponsor special ministries in 112 cities across the United States. They reach out to business and professional men and women, pastors, church leaders, students, and military personnel to equip them to share their faith and disciple new believers. Ministry among ethnic groups is led by Hispanic, Asian, and Afro-American leadership.

Eagle Lake Camp in Colorado is the camping ministry of The Navigators. Adventure, fun, and spiritual direction through various programs is what reaches junior and senior young people. The Glen Eyrie Conference Center, also located in Colorado, hosts discipleship training conferences for church and parachurch groups, families, and single adults. The Development Institute trains men and women to be disciples in their spheres of influence. NavPress, whose motto is "Helping Christians Grow," publishes booklets, Bible studies, and books designed to equip Christians for personal ministry.[18]

The aim of The Navigators is to multiply leadership in every nation by evangelizing, establishing, and equipping.

CAMPUS CRUSADE FOR CHRIST INTERNATIONAL

Campus Crusade for Christ International is an interdenominational Christian ministry founded in 1951. The purpose of Campus Crusade for Christ is to help fulfill the Great Commission of Matthew 28:18-20 in this generation. In order to accomplish the above purpose five objectives are established:

> (1) To expose every person in the world to the gospel and make Jesus Christ an issue. (2) Win people to faith in Jesus Christ. (3) Build them in their faith. (4) Train them for ministry. (5) Send them to win and disciple others.[19]

> Campus Crusade has been and is primarily a one-to-one type ministry. It has, however, been the sponsor of a number of large scale, group-oriented Christian events such as "Here's Life," "I Found It," and "Explo '85." Presently, Campus Crusade is spear-

17. Correspondence from The Navigators, Colorado Springs, Colo., August 20, 1990.
18. *A Vision for the World, A Heart for the Individual* (Colorado Springs, Colo.: The Navigators, 1990).
19. Purpose, objectives, and emphases statement (San Bernardino, Calif.: Campus Crusade for Christ, 1989).

heading New Life 2000, a global strategy to help tell every person everywhere that there is "new life" available in Jesus.[20]

Campus Crusade for Christ works closely with pastors and churches throughout the United States and in many foreign countries where it ministers. Although staff members come from a variety of religious backgrounds, they are required to affiliate with a local church of their choice when on their field of service.

College ministry and the training of lay leadership in the local church has been the emphasis of Campus Crusade for Christ for many years. However, today there are more than forty subministries, including Athletes in Action, Family Ministry, Josh McDowell Ministry, Student Venture (high school ministry), Prison Ministry, and Executive Ministries.[21]

Affiliates of Campus Crusade for Christ are Here's Life Publishers, a publishing house which produces and distributes books, Bible study materials, and tools for evangelism and spiritual growth. The International School of Theology, with branch campuses in Asia and Africa, exists to integrate biblical principles with high academic standards. Its goal is to develop effective leaders who are Spirit-filled, biblical thinkers, apologists, effective communicators and competent managers.[22]

INTERVARSITY CHRISTIAN FELLOWSHIP

Founded in 1941, the vision of InterVarsity Christian Fellowship is to "build collegiate fellowships, develop disciples who embody Biblical values, and engage the campus in all its ethnic diversity with the gospel of Jesus Christ."[23]

In order to pursue its vision, InterVarsity is committed to biblical values such as evangelism (believing that everyone ought to have the opportunity to respond to the gospel), spiritual formation (that men and women can grow in their faith through the study of God's Word and prayer), the church (encouraging believers to worship and participate), human relationships (that we love one another in every aspect of life), righteousness (teaching the importance of integrity in an amoral society), stewardship (honoring God in the college community, home, and in the marketplace), and world evangelization (every believer is responsible to participate in reaching the world with the gospel of Jesus Christ).[24]

On-campus ministry is "the cornerstone of InterVarsity's ministry." Student chapters are led by students under the careful guidance of trained InterVarsity staff members. Activities include providing opportunities for witnessing to non-Christians, training of students to do likewise, and encouraging them to become involved in the local church.

20. General background material (San Bernardino, Calif.: Campus Crusade for Christ, August 1989).
21. Ibid.
22. Purpose, objectives and emphases statement (San Bernardino, Calif.: Campus Crusade for Christ, 1989).
23. Vision statement (Madison, Wis.: InterVarsity).
24. Ministry values (Madison, Wis.: InterVarsity).

Other activities conducted by InterVarsity staff members include weekend "Bible and Life" seminars, special summer camps, outreaches during spring break, and Nurses Christian Fellowship.[25]

InterVarsity's multiethnic ministry includes a ministry to more than 350,000 foreign college students studying in the United States, a ministry to graduate students to prepare them for future Christian ministry in their chosen profession, and finally, ministry to faculty members who have become Christians.[26]

Other ministries of InterVarsity include 2100 Productions, which seeks to communicate Jesus Christ through the media; InterVarsity Press, which publishes books and booklets used in student ministry on the college and university campus; Marketplace Ministry, which prepares students with the proper tools needed to become active lay leaders on the job and within the local church; and Urbana, which has been a key ministry of InterVarsity since 1946. Urbana is a student missions convention held in Urbana, Illinois, that has influenced more than a hundred thousand young people to serve Christ around the world. InterVarsity's concern for missions is evident through its Overseas Training Camps, InterVarsity Missions Fellowship, membership in the International Fellowship of Evangelical Students, and The China Project.[27]

YOUNG LIFE

Founded in 1941, Young Life clubs meet informally in homes and neighborhood centers on a weekly basis. The hour-long club meeting consists of lively singing, sometimes a humorous skit, and a talk by the leader about the Person of Jesus Christ. A casual and friendly atmosphere allows club members to invite their friends.

Well-trained staff members, who are educated for youth ministry, lead the neighborhood clubs. Volunteers who assist are supervised by Young Life's professional staff.

The purpose of Young Life is to introduce young people to Jesus Christ and to help them understand His relevancy for them in today's amoral and immoral society. Concepts are communicated to the youth in understandable terms and through meaningful relationships. Young Life's goal is to "never bore a kid with the gospel."

Young Life leadership seeks to develop friendships with young people by finding common interests. Leaders attend various athletic functions, plays, concerts, and other school activities.

Initiating contacts and conversation with teens in their environment tells them that adults have a genuine desire to know them and in turn to be known by them.[28]

25. On-campus ministry statement (Madison, Wis.: InterVarsity).
26. Multi-ethnic ministry statement (Madison, Wis.: InterVarsity).
27. 2100 Productions, InterVarsity Press, Marketplace, and Missions/Urbana statement (Madison, Wis.: InterVarsity).
28. Young Life's purpose statement (Colorado, Colo.: Young Life).

Young Life views itself as being "paraparochial," that is, coming alongside of the church. The result is that Young Life staffers encourage new believers to join a local church and to participate in its ministry.[29]

Young Life sponsors an urban club ministry to Afro-Americans, Hispanics, Asians, whites, and other ethnic cultures within the confines of the city. In addition to the clubs, Young Life maintains an active camp ministry—Holiday camps, long weekends, and summer camps, which provide opportunities for a leader to interact with his club kids.

YOUTH FOR CHRIST

Founded in 1944, Youth For Christ's mission is to "communicate the life-changing message of Jesus Christ to every young person."

Rising to the challenge of making "all the difference in the world," Youth For Christ's strategy is "to mobilize the Christian community to reach lost youth wherever they are and by all means possible."[30] With its committed and dedicated leadership, Youth For Christ is proclaiming more than just the message—it is moving into the streets, schools, neighborhoods, and wherever young people can be found. Chapters across the country are responding to the challenge to evangelize the city. Reaching beyond the student, Youth For Christ is reaching out to young people who have dropped out of school by sharing the message of Jesus Christ in a loving and caring manner.

Young people need alternatives to drugs, sex, suicide, and peer pressure. Youth For Christ programs, camps, Bible studies, discipleship groups, sports, and community events are providing the alternative. Youth For Christ also sponsors many "high adventure" experiences such as bike trips, repelling, shooting the rapids, and canoeing.

Ministries of tutoring, crisis counseling, and a chaplaincy program in juvenile institutions and group homes are additional outreach ministries of Youth For Christ. Foster homes and shelter care programs are also available.

The purpose of Youth For Christ is "to participate in the body of Christ in the responsible evangelism of youth, presenting them with the person, work and teaching of Jesus Christ, discipling them, and leading them into the local church."[31]

Working hand-in-hand with the local church, Youth For Christ offers ministry opportunities through the "Project Serve" program. Project Serve is a short-term mission trip that provides services to missionaries, pastors, and Youth For Christ national staff.

Staff and volunteers are kept on the cutting edge of youth evangelism through training conferences. An annual staff and board conference is designed for the veteran leadership, while Summer Institute meets the training needs of new staff members each year.

29. *Parents and Young Life* (Colorado, Colo.: Young Life).
30. *Youth For Christ: Our Mission* (Wheaton, Ill.: Youth For Christ/USA).
31. Ibid.

VOCATIONAL OPPORTUNITIES

Vocational opportunities are unlimited among the parachurch organizations that have been cited in this chapter. Staff personnel such as clerical workers, writers of curriculum and other published material editors, and various management positions are available. Most parachurch organizations are seeking field staff, representatives, missionaries, and campus workers, many of whom have to generate a personal support base.

Not all positions are considered skilled positions, but many of them are. They may require a bachelor's degree in specialized training from Bible colleges (some in the area of writing, Christian education or education, sociology, psychology, and camping). Some organizations require seminary training and possibly a master's degree. Several of the organizations provide additional training pertaining to their particular ministry.

A number of the organizations prefer that their staff have had some kind of experience as a volunteer or intern. Desired experience ranges from ability to teach the Bible, to relate to teens, or to have basic leadership skills. Some expected personal qualities are: maturity, personality, creativity, positive self-image, conservative view point, concern for others, spiritual alertness, ability to motivate, and a willingness to improve skills and knowledge through formal or informal study.[32]

According to Warren Benson, "the opportunities for serving Jesus Christ through parachurch ministries in the field of Christian education in our day have never been greater and more extensive."[33]

CONCLUSION

Twelve parachurch organizations have been presented, all of which in one way or another support the ministry of the local church. Working together and supporting these organizations will enhance the church's evangelistic and missionary outreach around the world. Furthermore, these organizations can become a means by which students of all ages can be funneled into the local church.

Opportunities are unlimited for a ministry vocation through parachurch organizations. It is suggested that writing to the organization of one's choice and asking for its doctrinal statement and other information may be the first step for finding God's will in this matter of a Christian vocation.

32. Warren S. Benson, "Parachurch Vocations in Christian Education," in *Introduction to Biblical Christian Education*, ed. Werner C. Graendorf (Chicago: Moody, 1981), pp. 350-54.
33. Ibid.

For More Information

CHURCH-SPONSORED CHILDREN AND YOUTH ORGANIZATIONS

Awana Clubs International
One East Bode Road
Streamwood, IL 60187

Christian Service Brigade
P.O. Box 150
Wheaton, IL 60189

Pioneer Clubs
27W 130 St. Charles Road
Wheaton, IL 60188

Word of Life Fellowship, Inc.
Schroon Lake, NY 12870

YOUTH ORGANIZATIONS THAT SERVE AS A SUPPORT MINISTRY TO THE LOCAL CHURCH

Sonlife
1119 Wheaton Oak Court
Wheaton, IL 60187

Youth Specialties Ministries
1224 Greenfield Dr.
El Cajon, CA 92021

ORGANIZATIONS NOT UNDER LOCAL CHURCH SPONSORSHIP

Campus Crusade for Christ International
Office of Communications 41-50
Arrowhead Springs
San Bernardino, CA 92414

Child Evangelism Fellowship, Inc.
Warrenton, MO 63383

InterVarsity Christian Fellowship
233 Langdon St.
Madison, WI 53703

The Navigators
P.O. Box 6000
Colorado Springs, CO 80934

Young Life
P.O. Box 520
Colorado Springs, CO 80901

Youth For Christ/USA
P.O. Box 228822
Denver, CO 80222

General Index

Moody Press, a ministry of the Moody Bible Institute, is designed for education, evangelization, and edification. If we may assist you in knowing more about Christ and the Christian life, please write us without obligation: Moody Press, c/o MLM, Chicago, Illinois 60610.